IN TRANSIT

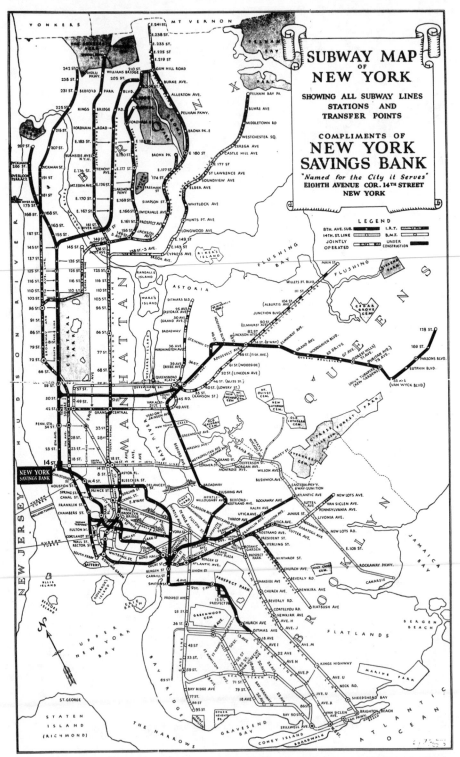

The New York City Subway System in 1936. Only those lines running partially or completely below ground are shown; several lines utilizing only elevated track also were in operation. As was common before World War II, this map was distributed by a commercial enterprise for advertising purposes.

In Transit

THE TRANSPORT WORKERS UNION
IN NEW YORK CITY, 1933–1966

JOSHUA B. FREEMAN

New York   Oxford
OXFORD UNIVERSITY PRESS

For Deborah Ellen Bell and
Julia Freeman Bell

Oxford University Press

Oxford New York Toronto
Delhi Bombay Calcutta Madras Karachi
Petaling Jaya Singapore Hong Kong Tokyo
Nairobi Dar es Salaam Cape Town
Melbourne Auckland

and associated companies in
Berlin Ibadan

Library of Congress Cataloging-in-Publication Data
Freeman, Joshua Benjamin.
In transit : the Transport Workers Union in New York City,
1983–1966 / Joshua B. Freeman.
p.   cm.   Includes index.
ISBN 0-19-504511-4
ISBN 0-19-507269-3 (pbk)
1. Transport Workers Union of America—History. 2. Trade-unions—
Transport workers—New York (N.Y.)—History. 3. Strikes and
lockouts—Transport workers—New York (N.Y.)—History. I. Title.
HD6515.T7F74 1989   88-22686
331.89′0413805′0—dc19

All photographs courtesy of the Transport Workers Union of America,
except for the bottom photograph on p. 133, which is courtesy of Maurice Forge.

9 8 7 6 5 4 3 2 1

Printed in the United States of America
on acid-free paper

PREFACE

Philip Murray, the second President of the Congress of Industrial Organizations (CIO), was once asked what a union means to working people. He replied "pictures on the wall, carpets on the floor and music in the home." To those of us who have pictures, carpets, and music, this may seem like a modest agenda. But for millions of American workers who lacked such comforts, material and spiritual, the wave of unionization that occurred during the 1930s and 40s, spearheaded by the CIO, represented a virtual revolution. The CIO helped cement the idea that all workers had certain rights and entitlements, both on and off the job, regardless of their ethnic origin, skill level, or income. Unionization meant higher pay, shorter hours, pensions, vacations, health insurance, grievance procedures, seniority systems, and greater job security. Such gains were part of a basic transformation in the social status of American workers. Until the 1930s, workers, especially those without valued craft skills, were virtual outcasts, on the margin of American social, political, and cultural life, with little say about conditions at their jobs or the shape of the society around them. By the 1950s, unionized workers had been largely integrated into the mainstream of American society. No longer was it easy to identify manual workers by the clothes they wore, the houses they lived in, or the things they owned. Equally important, through their unions many workers had won at least some voice in determining what their work lives, and to a more limited extent their nation, would be like.

With this change in workers' status came a redefinition of the very notion of what America was. Until the 1930s the accepted image of the United States was still as the land of the founding fathers, a white, Protestant, middle-class nation. By the end of World War II the dominant image had become "A House for All People," as immortalized in scores of movies and books in which the metaphor for the nation was the platoon consisting of soldiers from every class, regional, and ethnic background.

The labor movement, of course, was not alone responsible for these changes. The history of organized labor, and especially the CIO, was inextricably bound to the history of the political left and, more importantly, the New Deal. On the one hand the New Deal provided a favorable political, legal, and cultural environment for the growth of unionism. On the other hand organized labor provided a solid base of support for Roosevelt and the New Deal, acting as both an autonomous bloc and a component of the so-called modern Democratic party. Through both industrial and political action the industrial union movement contributed to a major recasting of the political economy. The economics of basic industry, daily work place relations, electoral politics, race relations, and the role of the state were all transformed by mass unionism. Although the most dramatic changes took place before and during World War II, the effects of those changes were most pronounced after the war. By raising the working-class standard of living and altering workers' consumptive patterns, expectations, and values, industrial unions contributed to the long postwar Keynesian prosperity. By accepting, after considerable turmoil, the basic assumptions of Cold War liberalism, the union movement also helped sustain a foreign policy that provided short-term benefits for many Americans but had terrible long-term costs for millions of people at home and abroad.

The CIO never completely lived up to what many saw as its promise. During the heady decade between 1937 and 1946, conservatives and radicals alike commonly believed that the CIO would bring about far more profound changes in the social structure than in fact occurred. The CIO failed to achieve many of its stated goals, not only in the area of labor relations but in regard to national economic planning, housing, welfare programs, race relations, and electoral politics. It also failed to make significant organizing inroads in huge sectors of the economy, such as service and clerical work, and in important regions of the country, most notably the South. By the end of the 1940s the CIO already had shed its most radical elements. CIO leaders, like Walter Reuther, who at the time loomed large on the national political landscape, within a decade carried little social weight outside the labor movement itself.

The failures of the CIO make it tempting to see the history of industrial unionism as anti-climactic. To do so is a serious mistake. The organization of the CIO was one of the central developments in modern American history. The rise of industrial unionism and the New Deal brought about the most profound metamorphosis in the lives of working people since the Civil War and Reconstruction. Together they helped reshape the very fabric of American society.

In a broad sense, the era of the New Deal lasted nearly four decades, from the 1930s well into the 1960s. During those years the United States underwent many changes, but the basic economic, political, and ideological structures around which it developed were largely the product of the 1930s and 40s, when the CIO was at high tide. For precisely that reason, until recently there were special obstacles to deciphering the historical significance of industrial unionism. What exists always tends to seem natural; the particularity—the newness—of past decisions, events, and assumptions is obscured by a seemingly inevitable outcome. Today, as the world the CIO helped create is crumbling, amidst economic stagnation, deindustrialization, and political reaction, industrial unionism can no longer be taken for granted. At least in that regard, conditions are better suited now than ever before for seeing the CIO for what it was as well as for what it was not.

This book is an effort to shed light on the history of the CIO through an examination of one particular group of workers, New York City transit workers, and the main union to which they belonged, the Transport Workers Union of America (TWU). It begins, in Part I, with a portrait of the New York transit industry in the years before the TWU was organized. It shows how the financial structure of the industry led to abysmal working conditions and an unusually violent pattern of labor relations. Part II is a detailed account of the successful unionization of the New York transit industry during the mid-1930s. Particular attention is paid to the role of the Communist Party and veterans of the Irish Republican Army in the intricate process of social construction that brought workers of varied skill levels, political views, and ethnic backgrounds together in the TWU. Part III examines what unionism meant, materially and symbolically, for transit workers and their families. It also discusses the internal politics of the TWU, focusing on the sharp contest between Communist and Catholic activists for control of the union. In Part IV the interrelated problems of transit politics and publicly operated transit are considered. Because the transit industry was highly politicized, the TWU was unusually active in the electoral arena. Nonetheless, the 1940 municipal takeover of most of the New York City mass transit system threw the union into crisis. Fiorello La Guardia's pro-labor reputation is reassessed in light of his role in transit labor relations. Part V discusses the war years, when the economic and ideological climate enabled the TWU to recapture much of the ground it lost as a result of the city takeover as well as to expand beyond New York City. Finally, Part VI traces the history of the TWU from the end of World War II through the 1966 New York transit strike. The Cold War led to a fierce battle within the TWU over its political direction, followed by a turbulent period when a new system of public-sector collective bargaining was developed.

Many of the questions this book grapples with are neither new nor simple to answer. How and why did industrial unionism make such great advances in the 1930s and 1940s after a long history of repeated failure? What was the relationship between the rank-and-file and the leadership in the new unionism of the CIO? How and why did the Communist Party achieve greater influence in the labor movement than in virtually any other sphere of American life? Why did the union movement, which in the 1930s and 40s seemed so combative and fraught with possibilities, by the mid-1950s fall into organizational and political stagnation? And most broadly, what was the relationship between industrial unionism and the changes in American social, economic, and political life that occurred before, during, and after World War II?

These questions are about institutions. Raising them by no means implies a rejection of the "new labor history," the social history of ordinary workers that has so enriched the study of labor in recent years. During the period this book covers the unionization rate in the United States was at its all-time high. It seems obvious that the history of American labor during these years to a large measure has to be a history of institutions. But unions—the central institutions of American labor—cannot be understood when looked at alone or even in interaction with other institutional forces, such as employers, political parties, and the state. To understand any union it is necessary to look at the workers who organized and belonged to it—at their lives at work and away from it, at their culture, history, and worldview, even at their character structure. Accordingly, at the price of lengthiness, what follows is something of a hybrid: in part an institutional history of the TWU, in part a study of transit labor relations and politics, and in part a social history of transit workers.

It is always dangerous to draw too broad conclusions from a case study. The TWU never was one of the largest unions in the CIO, though because of its strategic position in New York City and the flamboyance of its president, Michael J. Quill, it drew more than its fair share of publicity. Nor was the TWU a *typical* CIO union. There really was no such thing. In some ways the TWU was quite unusual. For one thing, nearly half the TWU's New York members were born in Ireland, a rare circumstance in the 1930s. For another, while most CIO members worked in private-sector manufacturing or mining, the TWU was centered in the transportation industry and eventually included a large number of publicly employed workers. Yet in many ways the TWU was *representative* of the new CIO unions: it grew out of the political and economic crisis of the early 1930s; its success entailed overcoming ethnic and occupational divisions within the work force; it brought workers previously shut out of public life into the structures of organized reform; and it transformed the economics and work culture of its industry. The bitter factional struggle within the TWU during the late 1940s was simply one of the most dramatic manifestations of the break-up of the center-left coalition that had nurtured the CIO and sustained the New Deal.

The TWU, then, is important because it was symptomatic of broad historical processes. But it is also important for its particularity. Throughout its history the TWU played a central role in New York City politics. The union was a mainstay of the American Labor party and later the Democratic party, developing complex relations with a series of local political leaders from La Guardia through Mayor Robert Wagner. Mike Quill was one of only a handful of labor leaders in the modern era to simultaneously head a union and hold a major elective office. The TWU was also a pioneer in public-sector unionism, the only major area of union growth during the past three decades. As one of the most prominent Communist-led unions during the 1930s and 40s, the TWU provided the left-wing of the union movement with an important base both in New York City and nationally. The TWU's unusual combination of a heavily Irish-Catholic membership and a leadership close to the Communist Party illuminates both the character of a particular immigrant group, the Irish, and the relationship of the Communist Party to the rank-and-file members of the organizations in which it was influential.

This study is meant to contribute to an understanding of important national historical developments. But the story of the men and women who operated the enormously complex transportation system that made life in New York City possible, if not easy, also deserves telling for its own sake. It is a story of tens of thousands of people who are normally socially invisible. Subways—like trains, postage stamps, and Civil War battles—attract a large number of buffs. But for some reason the intense interest that many people have in mass transit systems does not extend to the people who run them. Almost all the numerous popular books about the history of subways, trolleys, and other forms of mass transit, while lovingly dwelling on engineering problems, equipment, and even accidents, completely ignore the workers who brought those systems to life.

Most New Yorkers notice transit workers only when something goes wrong—when a subway is late, a bus overcrowded, a strike in progress. Too often the rage produced by a dreary, undercapitalized, badly managed transit system—and by all the other frustrations of metropolitan life—is directed at the nearest target, a transit worker with little control over the system he or she helps operate. This book takes a different point of view. It is written with sympathy and admiration for the transit workers of New York: for the difficulties of their lives, for their skill and fortitude in carrying out their jobs, and for their collective accomplishments. I hope it conveys some of the fullness of their lives.

The spark for this book came from a conversation in the summer of 1975 with Charles Monaghan, whose father had been an IRT ticket agent. Little did I suspect at the time how long it would be before this study would see the light of day. During the intervening years I received assistance and encouragement from many people.

First and foremost I would like to thank those who allowed me to interview them. In the course of my research I spoke with thirty-one people. Nineteen had been members or employees of the TWU, the rest in other positions to have special knowledge about the union or the transit industry. In most cases these were lengthy, tape-recorded interviews; in a few instances shorter, less formal discussions. These conversations proved invaluable. They gave me a rich picture of transit workers and their lives, enabled me to reconstruct the process by which the TWU emerged in much greater detail than otherwise would have been possible, helped in deciphering events obscure in the written record, and illuminated aspects of the TWU's history that were never committed to paper, particularly political relationships within the union and between unionists and outside groups. I owe a special debt to the participants in these interviews.

Two people I interviewed need to be singled out for the extraordinary assistance they provided. Gerald O'Reilly spoke to me on three separate occasions and helped me locate and arrange interviews with other former TWU members. In addition he lent me a number of important documents and gave me encouragement and inspiration at an early point in my labor. Then there is Maurice Forge. Over the course of several years I conducted six long, tape-recorded interviews with Forge. In addition we had numerous shorter or more informal discussions. Like O'Reilly, Forge lent me documentary material (which he has since deposited at the Robert F. Wagner Labor Archives, Tamiment Library, New York University) and put me in contact with other informants. Forge was centrally placed in the TWU during much of the period covered by this study and developed an intimate knowledge of the union. His memory is encyclopedic and proved uncannily accurate as I cross-checked his accounts with other oral and written sources. Forge never hesitated to provide information even when it was perhaps personally unflattering. Equally important, Forge himself had thought long and hard about the history of the TWU. His recollections were insightful and analytic. What began as a series of interviews turned into an ongoing discussion that became a form of collaboration. Forge's contributions appear throughout this book and greatly enrich it. In the course of our discussions of the TWU, a deep friendship developed that I continue to treasure.

I am very grateful to Debra Bernhardt and Brenda Parnes at the Robert F. Wagner Labor Archives, Robert Wechsler at the Transport Workers Union, and Philip Carey at the Xavier Institute of Industrial Relations for helping me gain access to TWU-related material. Robert Wechsler was extremely helpful as well in securing illustrations. Paul O'Dwyer kindly gave me permission to examine his oral history and that of his brother, William O'Dwyer, at the Oral History Collection of Columbia University. Peter Gottlieb at the Pennsylvania State University Libraries and Gary J. Arnold at the Ohio Historical Society aided me in my archival research. Shirley Quill, Max Gordon, Mark Naison, and the late Al Lutsky generously provided suggestions and assistance in arranging interviews. Sheldon Meyer, Rachel Toor, and Leona Capeless at Oxford University Press adeptly turned an unwieldy stack of papers into a book.

I met Steve Fraser the day I entered graduate school. Ever since he has been a close friend and colleague. Without his criticism, advice, and encouragement this study would be far poorer, while his own work on the labor movement has provided me with a standard to emulate. Nelson Lichtenstein also has been a cherished fellow traveler in the business of writing history. I have greatly benefited not only from his criticism of my work on the TWU, but from his outstanding scholarship on the history of the CIO. Norman Markowitz and David Oshinsky provided assistance above and beyond the call of duty during the first phase of this project. Both knew when to push and prod and when to step back. Judith Walkowitz, John Leggett, Paul Milkman, Rosalyn Fraad Baxandall, Steve Downs, Marian Swerdlow, David Paskin, and Robert Zieger read various versions of this manuscript; their criticism was much valued. Gina Fedele assisted in the preparation of the manuscript and, as always, was a firm friend. Mark Higbee helped tie up various loose ends as the finish line approached. My research on Catholic labor activism was made possible through the Hibernian Research Award of the Cushwa Center for the Study of American Catholicism. Additional financial assistance was provided by the Columbia University Council for Research in the Humanities. Finally, I would like to thank Deborah Bell for much more than words can say.

CONTENTS

Part VI: "Fortune's blows when most struck home . . ."

I

"History is a nightmare from which
I am trying to awake"

1

THE TRANSIT INDUSTRY

> "In most businesses, competition forces the own-
> ers to write off obsolescence as technology pro-
> gresses. But examination of a transit company will
> almost always reveal, as in a geological cross-
> section, the speculative abuses and vanished tech-
> niques of the past, capitalized for all eternity."
> I.F. Stone, *New Republic*, August 10, 1938

For over a century, New York City has been utterly dependent on mass transit. In New York, as elsewhere, rapid urban growth after the Civil War stimulated the development and expansion of public transportation, which in turn played a major role in the spatial, economic, and political evolution of the city. A succession of technologies—horse cars, elevated steam railroads (els), cable cars, trolleys, electri-fied els, subways, buses, and trolley-buses—were developed that permitted the daily movement of millions of people between home and work and around the city. By the early 1930s, New York City had by far the largest transit system in the country. In 1930, the last year before the Depression cut into passenger loads, 3.1 billion fare passengers were carried, an average of 452 rides a year for every man, woman, and child in the City of New York. By contrast, that year only one out of twelve New Yorkers owned an automobile.[1]

The New York City transit system of the 1930s was not the relatively integrated system of today, but rather a tangle of separate, overlapping route networks. The largest sector of the industry was rapid transit: subways, elevated lines, and a few grade-level lines. In 1933 there were 1.8 billion rapid transit fare passengers, two-thirds of all New York City mass transit users and several times the combined passenger load of the entire United States steam railroad industry. Three separate rapid transit systems were in operation, two large, privately run systems, the IRT (Interborough Rapid Transit) and BMT (Brooklyn-Manhattan Transit), and the smaller but expanding municipally run ISS (Independent Subway System).

Subways and els were particularly well-suited for relatively long rides through densely traveled corridors. Complementing them were numerous privately owned surface lines that used trolleys or buses. These were utilized mostly for shorter rides or in less dense and developed parts of the city, where they provided primary transportation and fed into the rapid transit systems. In 1933 there were 732 million trolley fare passengers and another 164 million carried on buses.[2]

Mass transit was big business. In 1918 *Forbes* magazine found that three of the nation's thirty largest fortunes had been made primarily in transit. In 1930 the IRT, the BMT, and the Third Avenue Railway (a Bronx, Manhattan, and Westchester surface company) were among the nation's 200 largest non-banking companies, with combined assets of over $850 million. Several of the most powerful financial interests in the world were heavily invested in New York transit.[3]

The corporate and financial structure of the industry was exceedingly complex. The New York transit companies of the 1930s were the end-product of numerous mergers, reorganizations, and divestitures. The greatest transit profits usually did not come from ongoing operations, but from the consolidation and restructuring of companies and the associated financial and stock market activity. In general, the strategy of transit financiers was to combine once separate lines and in doing so extract as much money as possible through watered stock, high dividends and debt, inter-company financial agreements, and other devices. Intricate arrangements of holding companies, leases, interlocking directorates, and subsidiary corporations were used to effect such maneuvers, making actual ownership and profit rates difficult to trace. High management salaries and large fees for banking, legal, and brokerage services further drained cash out of operations. With companies so milked, there was little money left for maintenance, rehabilitation, or moderniza-tion. Management could face both regulatory agencies and the work force with pleas of poverty. Such financial practices, however, left companies with high fixed costs and low cash reserves, susceptible to collapse whenever expenses unexpectedly rose or revenues dropped.[4]

The history of New York's largest transit company, the Interborough Rapid Tran-sit Company, or IRT, illustrates many of these patterns. In the nineteenth century, New York transit facilities had been built, owned, and operated by private compa-nies holding long-term or perpetual franchises. A different approach was taken in developing the subways. Under a plan approved in 1894, the city was to supply money to build a subway system which it would own, while private companies would lease, equip, and operate the lines.[5] In 1900 the city signed a contract for subway construction with J. B. McDonald, a leading railroad contractor backed by financier August Belmont. Both men were well connected with Tammany Hall, the local, ruling Democratic machine. Two years later Belmont formed the IRT to equip and run the new system and signed a second contract with the city to build and operate additional lines. The English House of Rothschild invested heavily in the new company.[6]

The planned IRT system posed a serious threat to the existing Manhattan trolleys and els. Four el lines, running up 2nd, 3rd, 6th, and 9th avenues, had been built in the nineteenth century and consolidated under the umbrella of the Manhattan Railway Co. George Gould (Jay's son), who controlled the company, had little interest in investing new capital to compete with Belmont. Accordingly, an agree-ment was reached in 1903 for the IRT to lease these els and absorb their work force.[7] A second consolidation came two years later when the IRT merged with the Metro-politan Street Railway Company, a holding corporation with a virtual monopoly over trolley transportation in Manhattan and the Bronx.[8]

The IRT was further enlarged by a third contract signed with the City of New

York in 1913. The IRT received the right to upgrade its leased el lines and to connect them with its subway system. The subways in turn were to be expanded using city and company funds. The end result was a physically integrated network of 117 miles of rapid transit reaching into every borough except Staten Island. After forty-nine years the entire system, except for the els, was to revert to city control, although the city could "recapture" the jointly constructed lines at any time after ten years by paying suitable compensation. A fixed fare of five cents was written into the agreement at the insistence of the IRT, which feared a popular clamor to lower the tariff.[9]

In theory, under this third contract IRT revenue was to be used to pay off both city and company investments and to provide profits for both. But the order of payment from established revenue pools was crucial. First to be taken out were the IRT's costs for its various leases; then its tax, operating, maintenance, and depreciation costs. After these came "preferentials," covering the IRT's debt payments and providing a fixed annual return on its investment. Only after all these payments had been made, including any accumulated deficits, was the city to receive money for the servicing and repaying of its transit debt and as return on its investment. Whatever money remained was to be split as "profit."

The IRT rapid transit system always produced a substantial operating surplus, but never any "profit" as contractually defined. Between 1909 and 1940 the city received, in addition to $80 million rent for the lines built under the first two IRT contracts, only $19 million, not enough even to cover the debt service on the $188 million it had invested in IRT construction. The company, on the other hand, made a real cumulative profit of over $90 million.[10]

In spite of these favorable terms, the IRT underwent a severe financial crisis after World War I, from which it never fully recovered. In taking over the els and trolleys, the IRT had greatly added to its already high fixed costs. Metropolitan Street Railway, overburdened by expensive leases, heavy debt, and highly watered stock, was a major drain on IRT revenue.[11] So was the Manhattan el lease; after 1917 el ridership unexpectedly failed to grow. Yet in spite of these problems, the IRT kept raising its dividends and failed to set aside adequate reserves. The company was thus unprepared for the inflation that came with World War I and the concurrent increase in labor costs, partially the result of strikes.

In 1919 the holding company that controlled the IRT and Metropolitan (by then renamed New York Railways) went into receivership and was ultimately dissolved. Under a reorganization plan worked out by the Morgan interests, who were heavy IRT investors, the two companies were separated, leaving the IRT as primarily a rapid transit company operating on leased lines. However, in spite of modifications in the Manhattan Railway lease and other financial adjustments, fixed costs remained high and prospects poor. Furthermore, a major influx of new capital was impossible; after World War I large investors shied away from the transit industry, unloading what securities they could on less sophisticated small investors (but retaining control through either voting trusts or sufficiently large minority positions).

Unable to reduce fixed costs or attract new capital, the IRT directors tried to cut operating expenses and increase revenue. However, a prolonged court battle to break the five-cent fare provision in the IRT's contract with the city failed. The company's lawyers, who had designed the clause, had done their work too well; in 1929 the Supreme Court dashed any hopes for a fare increase. The company then turned to an idea that was much-discussed throughout the 1920s; a government-sponsored unification of the New York transit system that would, among other things, bail out the IRT. But when unification finally came, in 1940, it was already too late; the Depression had caused a decline in IRT revenue and the company went into receivership in 1932. Thus when the TWU was founded, the IRT was under the ultimate jurisdiction of Federal Circuit Court Judge Julian W. Mack and under the immediate supervision of a receiver, Thomas E. Murray, Jr. [12]

The history of New York's second largest transit company, the Brooklyn-Manhattan Transit Corporation (BMT), was also complex. The BMT's immediate predecessor, the Brooklyn Rapid Transit Company (BRT), was a holding corporation that controlled a host of originally separate trolley, el, and private right-of-way surface lines, a sprawling empire that dominated Brooklyn and Queens transit. When the IRT signed its last contract with the City of New York, the BRT signed a similar agreement providing for the construction of a second subway system, to be interconnected with the BRT's existing rapid transit lines. Like the IRT contract, this agreement provided highly favorable terms to the company. By the 1930s a system of 101 route miles in Brooklyn, Manhattan, and Queens was in operation. (The IRT and BMT systems were physically and operationally distinct; free transfer between them was impossible). The BRT, and later the BMT, also operated the city's largest fleet of trolleys and buses; in the 1930s the BMT had the equivalent of 520 single track miles of surface lines, some of which dated back to the 1850s. [13]

The BRT engaged in many of the same financial practices and had many of the same problems as the IRT. It too was forced into receivership after World War I by a combination of high fixed costs, a fixed fare, and inflation. (It had problems with strikes and construction delays as well.) The company re-emerged in 1923 as the BMT. The new company had close ties to the Chase National Bank, the second largest national bank in the country. BMT Board Chairman Gerhard Dahl, an expert in financing, managing, and reorganizing transit and utility companies, had served as a vice president of Chase. Chase president Albert E. Wiggin headed the BMT Finance Committee.

Although the BMT was better-managed and more profitable than the IRT, its directors seemed more interested in insider stock trading and financial manipulations than actual operations. Like their IRT counterparts, they eventually came to see unification as the ultimate solution to their problems. In an effort to strengthen their hand in negotiations toward that end, during the 1920s a group of BMT investors bought a sizable block of IRT securities. By 1931 the group had obtained sufficient control to install Dahl as IRT board chairman and Wiggin as a director. Financially and operationally, though, the two companies remained separate. [14]

The third rapid transit system, the Independent Subway System (ISS), had a far shorter history. After World War I there was a public outcry over the terms of the IRT and BMT contracts and the financial practices and service deficiencies of the industry as a whole. Simultaneously, New York City was undergoing one of its periodic cycles of reform politics, electing a mayor opposed to Tammany Hall and its alliance with the transit industry. Accordingly, when the demand grew for more mass transit, a city agency, a three-member, mayoral-appointed Board of Transportation, was established in 1924 to plan, finance, and construct a new series of subway lines. The Board tried to find a private company to actually operate and maintain the system, but when no bids were received the city itself opened the ISS in September 1932. For this purpose, the Board of Transportation was converted into an operating organization.

In its first full year of service, the Independent had only 15 route miles and carried but 59 million passengers. Five years later there were almost 56 miles of line and 350 million riders. Newer, better planned, and more attractive than its private competitors, the ISS drew passengers away from the BMT and especially the IRT, whose routes in many places it paralleled.[15]

Like rapid transit, surface transit—bus and trolley travel—was under highly concentrated control. While the BMT dominated surface transit in Brooklyn and parts of Queens, the Third Avenue Railway Company played an equivalent role in the Bronx, where it was a potent political force. Its nineteen subsidiaries also operated lines in Manhattan and Westchester County. In the city, trolleys were primarily used; in Westchester both buses and trolleys.[16]

Most Manhattan surface lines not controlled by the Third Avenue were already converting to bus operation by the mid-1930s. The bulk of these routes were controlled by two interlocking companies, the Fifth Avenue Coach Company and New York City Omnibus, both descended from properties once controlled by the IRT. The former had always been a bus company, famous for its double-decker buses. The latter was set up by New York Railways to convert some of its trolley routes to bus operation. Control of both companies was obtained in the mid-1920s by the Omnibus Corporation, a Chicago-based holding company that also owned the Chicago Motor Coach Company.

The co-founder of Omnibus, and president of both its New York subsidiaries, was John A. Ritchie. As chairman of General Motors' bus division he was a key figure in a nation-wide effort to undermine passenger rail and trolley systems, substituting GM-manufactured buses and automobiles. New York was one of his great successes; by 1936 the conversion of New York Railways to buses was complete and the company was dissolved, with its assets and liabilities taken over by N.Y.C. Omnibus.[17]

In spite of the success of large financial interests in capturing the bulk of the rapidly growing bus industry, the introduction of this new, relatively low-cost technology did create the opportunity for some smaller companies to enter the field. The small companies were effectively shut out of the Bronx and Brooklyn, and were usually outbid for franchises in Manhattan by N.Y.C. Omnibus. In Queens, though, they were more successful. North Shore Bus, Triborough Coach Company, and Green Bus, for example, each developed modest route networks. Thus while in the main bus operations, particularly in the densest parts of the city, were controlled by a few major companies, a number of smaller concerns did manage to establish themselves.[18]

Though enormous profits had been made in New York mass transit, by the 1930s the industry was generally in poor shape. Companies lacked capital, fixed costs were high, and equipment deteriorating. Still, the interests with the greatest financial stakes in the industry were extremely powerful. Long accustomed to getting what they wanted, their reaction to hard times was to demand ever-greater concessions from the city, the public, and their workers.

To run a transit system as large as New York's, seven days a week, twenty-four hours a day, required a great many people, roughly 40,000 in 1933. The IRT had the largest work force, 16,403; the BMT was second with 13,427 on payroll, about equally divided between rapid transit and surface operations. The ISS had only 1,597 employees in 1933, but five years later it had 5,171. The Third Avenue, the largest surface company, employed 3,687, New York Railways 1,535, and Fifth Avenue Coach 1,447. The smaller trolley and bus companies each employed at most a few hundred workers. [19]

Although the major transit investors tended to be primarily concerned with finance and speculation, as the companies they controlled grew in size and complexity they realized the need for professional management. Copying from the railroads, they installed line and staff divisional structures and hired experienced managers. In 1907, for example, Belmont hired Theodore Shonts, a career railroad man, as IRT president, a job he held until his death twelve years later. He was succeeded first by Frank Hedley and then by George Keegan, both of whom had worked for the IRT from its very start. Even during the IRT's final receivership, Keegan remained in charge of day-to-day operations. Similarly, the president of the BMT, William S. Menden, was a professional manager, a Chicago transit executive who had joined the old BRT in 1905. [20]

The long tenures of Hedley, Keegan, and Menden were not unusual. Although outsiders were sometimes hired, foremen, superintendents, and other transit officials tended to be promoted from within, and extended careers with one company were common. In 1932, for example, the Third Avenue's ten divisional transportation superintendents had been with the company for an average of twenty-seven years. Well into the 1930s it was possible to find managers who had begun working in the transit industry during the previous century.

Promoting from the ranks meant that transit managers tended to be technically knowledgeable and often of the same ethnicity as the workers they supervised. In general, their style was decidedly old-fashioned and strictly hierarchical. Many foremen, supervisors, and even top company officials were Masons, which probably reinforced their tendency to maintain their distance from the ranks, even if they themselves had started there. Although during the Progressive era, as we will see, the transit companies experimented with various innovations in the labor relations, by the 1930s no new initiatives were being taken, and for the most part line supervisors were in charge of dealing with labor. [21]

Transit jobs varied greatly in function, work setting, and skill level. Most companies had four main departments: transportation, shops and car barns, maintenance-of-way, and power. The transportation departments were the largest, since they included both the operating crews and the station workers. About one-third of the industry work force was engaged in actually operating transit vehicles. Trolleys and buses had either two-man crews, a driver and a conductor, or a single operator who handled both functions. On the subways and els, crews included motormen, conductors, and guards (sometimes called trainmen). The motormen were the most skilled, working their way up through a series of other jobs, training programs, and examinations. Conductors were in charge of all aspects of a train except the actual locomotion, and along with the guards opened and closed the doors and supervised passenger flow. Switchmen, towermen, and yard men switched trains, made them up, and moved them into and out of yards and barns. [22]

Station employees included ticket agents, platform men, porters, and elevator-escalator operators. The largest group, ticket agents, had once actually sold tickets, which were then collected by "ticket choppers." By the 1930s, however, the name was largely anachronistic, since coin-operated turnstiles had been widely introduced and most agents were actually change makers. Platform men maintained order and safety during the loading and unloading of trains. During rush hours they would push aside those debarking and shove new passengers into the already crowded trains. Some platform men were guards or conductors with low seniority, and it was not uncommon to spend part of the day on the trains and part on the platforms. Generally speaking, the transportation promotional ladder was from platform man to guard to switchman to motorman, or platform man to agent. There were no promotional opportunities for the porters, who cleaned the stations. [23]

Maintaining the rolling stock and related equipment was a vast job. On the rapid transit lines it required almost a quarter of the work force. Trains and trolleys were regularly inspected at car barns, yards, or special inspection stations. The IRT, for example, had about 400 inspectors who checked each car every 1,000 or 1,200 miles, the equivalent of five or six days' use. During the inspections, while car cleaners swept and washed the equipment, minor repairs were performed. Each company also had at least one and usually several shops where major repairs and overhauls could be done. These were large, complex industrial establishments, employing hundreds of workers. Not only were parts replaced, they were often reconditioned or manufactured in the shops themselves. At one point the Third Avenue even constructed its own trolley cars, using new steel for the bodies and reconditioned motors and trucks. There were scores of different shop jobs, ranging from unskilled laborers to specialists, such as airbrake maintainers or armature oilers, to highly skilled craftsmen—machinists, mechanics, blacksmiths, tinsmiths, and the like. The bus companies performed equivalent work in their garages, where there were cleaners, mechanics, carpenters, blacksmiths, machinists, electricians, painters, oilers, tinners, and various sorts of helpers.

Much of the transit equipment, of course, had to be inspected, maintained, and repaired in place. This was the job of maintenance-of-way workers. They too encompassed a vast array of crafts and titles. Probably the largest group were the trackmen. On the combined trolley and train systems there were over 2,000 men engaged in maintaining and replacing track and several hundred trackwalkers, who literally walked the track looking for defective areas. Then there were men who maintained the tunnels and elevated structures, the pumping equipment, lighting and signal devices, the third rails, the turnstiles, the communications equipment, and so on. There were plumbers, painters, roofers, masons, electricians, laborers, carpenters, machinists, and blacksmiths assigned to maintenance-of-way. [24]

Finally, the power departments operated and maintained electrical distribution

Maintenance work at the shop of the Surface Transportation Company, a bus subsidiary of the Third Avenue Railway Co.

systems. The IRT and BMT generated their own electricity—the IRT at two plants in Manhattan and the BMT at one in Brooklyn—while the ISS and the trolley companies bought power. The transit powerhouses each employed several hundred men, ranging from highly skilled engineers to ashmen. The IRT had forty different basic power department titles. To train these men, the department ran its own school, complete with entrance examinations, grades, and graduations.[25]

The large transit work force, and the relatively few raw materials needed after initial construction (mostly coal for power generation), meant that transit was a labor intensive industry. Nationally, between 1907 and 1937 wages accounted for 48% of the industry's operating expenses (excluding buses and trolley-buses). On the New York rapid transit lines the figures were even higher: wages equaled 68% of operating expenses on the IRT (between 1909 and 1939), 59% on the BMT (between 1921 and 1939), and 64% on the ISS (between 1934 and 1940).[26] Given the relative inelasticity of consumer demand and the legal and political constraints on the fare, profits were highly dependent on the cost of labor. Thus one of the central tasks of transit management was to hold down labor costs.[27]

One way to do this was to reduce the size of the work force relative to the number of passengers carried. The companies had some success in this after World War I. The IRT transportation department, for example, went from 85 employees per million car-miles in 1918 to 45 in 1928. Two changes were largely responsible for this increased productivity. First, the introduction of turnstiles decreased the need for station employees. Second, smaller operating crews were used. On the subways and els there originally had been a conductor or guard stationed in every car or between every set of two cars. In 1920 the IRT introduced multiple-unit door controls, which enabled one person to operate the doors of several cars. By installing these devices the company was able to replace the six men who previously had been needed to operate a ten-car express with three men: a motorman, a conductor, and a guard. The BMT followed suit, and by the mid-30s was running trains with just a motorman and a conductor. As a result, the combined total of IRT and BMT guards declined from over 5,200 in 1921 to just over 2,000 in 1939. (The ISS never employed guards at all.)[28] Likewise, the trolley companies introduced one-man cars, eliminating conductors. In 1928, 27.5% of the Third Avenue Railway trolleys were run by a single operator; by 1932 they all were. In the process scores of men, some with high seniority, were fired.[29]

Work force reductions, however, were only a secondary means of keeping down labor costs. The main technique was the extreme prolongation of the working week, compensated at subsistence or low wage levels, and worked under harsh conditions and strict discipline. Transit workers were forced to devote a staggering number of hours to their jobs. Many worked seven days a week, with work days often scheduled for as long as twelve hours, and sometimes in practice lasting eighteen. Work weeks of seventy or eighty hours were not uncommon. Only after the impact of the Depression was felt, followed by unionization, was there any dramatic decline in the hours of labor.

As late as 1940, of 103 surveyed industries, transit ranked fourth in the average number of hours worked. In the early 1930s, the seven-day week was standard in the IRT, BMT, Fifth Avenue Coach, and Third Avenue Railway transportation departments and part of IRT power. On the IRT, for example, agents generally worked seventy-two hours a week, with eighty-four hour weeks not unheard of. Porters and platform men worked seven ten-hour days. Third Avenue operating personnel also worked an average of seventy hours a week. In the shops and barns hours were long, but not as long. IRT shop men generally worked around fifty hours and rarely more than six days a week; Third Avenue shop workers generally put in five nine-hour days and six hours on Saturday. Most transit workers received neither paid vacations nor holidays and many had no scheduled lunch or dinner breaks. The only major exception to this pattern was the ISS, which as of 1938 had a standard six-day, forty-eight hour work week which included a paid half-hour for lunch.[30]

These were the working hours seen from management's point of view, the number of hours for which their workers were paid. Seen from the workers' point of view, the situation looked different, and even worse. There are problems scheduling work assignments in any urban transit system because passenger loads fluctuate during the course of the day and special runs, called "trippers," are often needed during rush hours, at school release time, and for large public events. To avoid paying throughout the day a work force capable of handling the peak-load, transit companies made extensive use of swing (or split) runs and "extras."

In swing runs, employees worked the morning rush hour, then had an unpaid "swing," followed by a second stint in the evening. "Extras" were low seniority workers, without regular assignments, who on any given day might be sent out on a tripper or a short run, replace a sick worker for a full shift, or be sent home without work. The use of swings and extras meant that transportation department workers put in an enormous amount of unpaid time waiting for or between assignments.[31]

A few examples illustrate what this meant for workers' lives. In 1933 John Nolan, a guard on the IRT Third Avenue el, was still an extra, in spite of four years' seniority. He reported seven days a week for possible assignment, once at 6:45 a.m. and again at 1:00 p.m. Some weeks he worked only a single run, receiving a week's pay of $1.45. The next year he was transferred down to the subway. Although his hourly pay was reduced, he was given a regular platform assignment, three hours a day, five days a week. After his seniority built up a bit more, he received his first full-time job, on the Broadway line. He reported at 7:00 a.m. to the 96th Street station, where he worked on the platform for two hours before going home. Then, at 3:30 p.m., he went to 191st Street where he directed traffic at an elevator until 6:30. Finally, he traveled to 168th Street where he worked as an agent until 9:30. Nolan's work day extended over fourteen-and-a-half hours, but he was paid for only eight.[32]

At the Kingsbridge barn of the Third Avenue Railway, extras with low seniority had to appear daily for the "dog-watch report" at 4:45 a.m. and remain until 2:45 p.m., even if they got no work. If they were fortunate enough to be given a regular shift, they might not finish until midnight, only a few hours before they would have to leave home again to report to work. BMT agents with low seniority had to go to a dispatching center; their waiting time and time spent traveling to assigned booths were uncompensated.[33]

Swing shifts were the plague of the operating crews. In 1914 daily paid time for BMT motormen ranged from seven-and-a-half to ten-and-a-half hours, but it took these workers between nine and fourteen hours to actually complete their shifts. Not until 1921 could 50% of the BMT rapid transit swing runs be completed within twelve hours. In the late 1920s and early 1930s, swings were still standard throughout the industry, and for workers with low seniority they could be considerable. When Patrick Reilly started as a platform man on the Ninth Avenue el in 1929, he had a four-hour swing; his working day stretched from 7:00 a.m. to 7:00 p.m. for but eight hours' pay. John Gallagher's first regular run as a trolley conductor out of the Kingsbridge barn included a six-hour-and-ten-minute unpaid swing.[34]

The use of swings and extras, on top of long regular hours, meant that both full and part-time workers spent an inordinate percentage of their waking lives at the service of their employers. Here truly was an illustration of Marx's comment that "in its blind unrestrainable passion, its were-wolf hunger for surplus labor, capital oversteps not only the moral, but even the merely physical maximum bounds of the working day."[35]

For their lengthy toil, transit workers were not paid well. In 1933 full-time New York transit employees earned an average of $32.82 a week. If managerial, clerical, and miscellaneous support workers are excluded, the figure drops to $31.76; if those working part-time, usually involuntarily, are added in, the figure further decreases to $29.65.[36] Generally craft workers in shop, maintenance, and power department jobs received the highest hourly rates, and many shop workers were also eligible for piece-work bonuses. Prior to the onset of the Depression, for example, skilled shop workers employed by the Third Avenue Railway could make as much as $38 to $45 a week. However, unskilled shop workers made far less; in the rapid transit shops the least-paid workers earned only about half of what the best-paid took home.

Among transportation department workers, subway motormen were paid the most, between 72 and 86 cents an hour on the IRT and BMT. Although this was less than top shop rates, hours were longer and therefore weekly earnings, which averaged $43 in 1933, often exceeded what shop craftsmen made. Average weekly pay for full-time trolley operators in 1933 was $34; for rapid transit conductors, $33; and for guards $29. Fifth Avenue Coach bus drivers averaged $34 a week and bus conductors $28. In all companies, hourly rates for transportation workers increased with seniority, but it could take as long as ten years to reach the top of the scale.

At the bottom of the pay hierarchy were agents, porters, cleaners, and laborers. Citywide, in 1933 the average full-time agent received $26 a week, with hourly rates ranging from a top of 45 cents on the IRT down to 29 cents for starting female agents on the BMT. Some IRT porters received as little as 34 cents an hour, while porters on the ISS got 40 cents an hour for a weekly sum of $19.20. These figures are all for gross earnings; take-home pay was often less, since deductions were taken out for relief funds, company union dues, and pension payments. [37]

Nationally, transit workers on the average actually earned more than manufacturing production workers. To some extent this reflected their longer hours, but even when hourly rates are compared transit workers were better off. However, except for those at top rates, one could hardly call them well paid. Although efforts to define a national poverty line are notoriously difficult, if we accept the mean of several estimates that have been made for 1929 ($1,650 a year for a family of four), the average New York transit worker hovered just above the divide. [38] A TWU summary of a 1937 survey of ISS workers gives a stark picture of what this meant:

> The average wage for a 48 hour week per employee is $26.886. Eighty-seven percent live in quarters which cost an average of $27.94 per month and . . . [that] means that 87 percent of our employees are living in slums. Sixty-five percent were in debt to loan companies, banks, and loan sharks. Only ¼ of one percent were found to be free of debt. Eleven percent were advised by school authorities that their children suffer from malnutrition. Sixteen and one half percent had to refuse their children money requested by school authorities for items necessary to their proper education. As startling as it seems, *51 percent* had to make use of *free hospitalization and clinical services* for themselves or families because of inability to pay a private physician, dentist, etc. [39]

On top of everything else, transit working conditions were quite miserable, and quite dangerous. Between 1914 and 1934 there was an average of 18.1 accident-caused employee fatalities a year on the IRT and 6.4 on the BMT rapid transit lines for a twenty-one-year total of 490 deaths in rapid transit alone. That meant that roughly one out of a thousand rapid transit workers was killed annually on the job. There were also hundreds of serious injuries. [40]

Workers complained constantly about filthy, unsanitary conditions, especially where they were supposed to change, eat, or relieve themselves—if such facilities were provided at all. In fact, train schedules often left little or no time to go to the bathroom. In one 1935 incident, an IRT conductor was killed crossing the tracks in his rush to relieve himself without throwing his train off schedule. Agents were forbidden to leave their booths unless a relief worker was present. Although the IRT did provide some relief men, ISS and BMT agents were expected to work eight hours and up with no relief. Besides discomfort, this could have serious medical consequences. Among female agents urinary tract problems were common, as were swollen legs and other ailments stemming from extended periods of standing. Older trolley drivers also developed urinary problems and some had to resort to "the motorman's friend," a urine collection tube and bottle that was strapped to the leg. Even in the shops, conditions were abysmal. At the 98th Street IRT shop, toilets had old, splintered seats and the toilet paper was cut up from newspapers that had been left on trains.

Each job had its own problems. Guards and conductors on old el trains frequently suffered ruptures from working manual gates. Stomach ulcers were so common among bus drivers that they were called "driver's stomach." El and subway motormen had to worry about suicides jumping in front of their trains and foreign objects, especially steel rail dust, getting in their eyes. Overheated booths and shops, cold weather for outdoor workers, crowded platforms, and decaying facilities all contributed to the dreary, discomforting, and unhealthful conditions. When the TWU began a free medical plan in 1939, resulting in a dramatic increase in transit worker doctor visits, a large number of previously undiagnosed cases of tuberculosis and other diseases was discovered.[41]

Discipline throughout the industry was harsh and repressive, designed to instill subservience and fear. One historian aptly characterized the IRT management as "autocratic." The companies had extensive rules governing every aspect of job performance and general behavior, and even minor infractions were stiffly punished. On most lines, for example, operating crews were required to buy expensive uniforms from company-designated stores and pass regular inspections. Irregularities as small as a missing button could result in disciplinary action. Workers repeatedly charged that the transit companies were in collusion with the uniform supply stores, with managers receiving kick-backs.

In the shops and other fixed work locations, foremen and supervisors were in charge of general discipline and making sure work was properly completed. However, since many transit workers, for instance train crews and ticket agents, did not work under direct supervision, the companies hired plainclothes agents, known among the workers as "beakies," to watch and report on employees. By one estimate, the IRT and BMT together had about 120 such operatives. Reports by unnamed beakies were sufficient grounds to fire or otherwise discipline employees, who had no recourse to established procedures for hearings or appeals. Furthermore, surveillance was not restricted to the job itself. According to an internal IRT memorandum, it was "regular practice of the Secret Service Department to go to the homes of employees . . . because a great many of the matters requiring shadowing have to do with a man's conduct both on and off the job."[42]

Old-time transit workers have many stories of harsh punishments for relatively minor infractions. When John Nolan was caught reading a newspaper while on duty, he was suspended for two weeks and lost his pay for the run involved. When Gerald O'Reilly and four other IRT men took off St. Patrick's day to see the parade, they were suspended for a week. Eddie Cabral was once told to go home for punching in two minutes late at the IRT 98th Street shop. His repeated protests only brought a five-day suspension. On the BMT, under the so-called "jump system," trolley and bus drivers who were so little as a minute late to work on five occasions were dropped ten places on the seniority list. Nor did the companies hesitate to fire employees. During just nine months in 1934, the IRT fired 231 men, or about 1.5% of the work force, for disciplinary reasons.

While punishments were harsh, the means of administering them were particularly degrading. Men charged with infractions were sent to company offices where they had to wait for hours before being called in to see company officials. They were then scolded, insulted, and mocked, sometimes by top corporate officers, before being told their punishments. Third Avenue Railway divisional superintendents, in charge of discipline, sat behind high judges' benches as men were called in one by one to stand before them. The entire style of management was designed to terrify and belittle workers, to make them feel at the mercy of supervisors and the companies, to create and reinforce deferential and hierarchical relations. Degradation and dehumanization were basic management tools.[43]

In letters and articles written by transit workers in the 1920s and early 1930s, and in their later recollections of the pre-union era, one term of self-description appears over and over again, slaves:

> The trolley-car workers are actually slaves. Even the slaves in early civilization had a few hours for recreation, but for us it is work, sleep and a few hurried meals.

> Some of the foremen and subforemen seem to think we are nothing but slaves. They drive us, curse us—anything to get more work out of us.

> [O]ur bosses can pay us better if they want to. They prefer instead to work us more and more unmercifully. They prefer to oppress their slaves even more cruelly.[44]

Wherever this language came from—perhaps from union or radical organizers— it was widely adopted because it seemed to fit. Transit workers did not use it metaphorically; transit work, as far as they were concerned, *was* a kind of slavery. Most people, of course, would object to this usage if taken literally, for in the traditional sense transit work was certainly "free labor." Yet, by the measure of time alone, it was within the domain of the companies that transit workers lived out most of their conscious existence. And within that domain (and to some extent outside it), every aspect of their lives, from what they wore, to what they did, to when they relieved themselves, was under the control of their employers. In that sense, transit workers' lives were not their own, and their recurring assertion that transit work was a form of slavery becomes understandable.

2

TRANSIT WORKERS

"History is a nightmare from which I am
trying to awake."   *Ulysses*

If keeping men "slaving" was a key to transit profits, it was by no means an easy task. Transit workers were intensely displeased by the conditions they faced. Individually and collectively they sought change, through protests, organization, or simply leaving the industry. In response, management developed a whole series of practices to maintain control and ensure the availability of a work force willing to labor on terms it set. Management's upper hand was reinforced by a complex array of political, social, and cultural structures outside the work place. The whole social order served to perpetuate the status quo. Only with the Great Depression and the organization of the TWU did fundamental changes occur.

Between the Civil War and the New Deal, transit labor relations were characterized by periodic waves of worker organization but an overall failure of unionism. Various unions tried their hand at organizing transit workers, occasionally achieving unexpectedly rapid success. Invariably, though, this led to clashes with management notable for their size, intensity, and violence. The usual outcome was union defeat and a subsequent period of quiescence, only to be followed by another cycle of organization and confrontation. Out of this history came the company practices and worker attitudes that eventually the TWU confronted.

The first major effort to organize the New York transit industry was led by the Knights of Labor. A series of short strikes in the mid-1880s forced most New York-area street car companies to sign union contracts. Working hours were shortened and wages and conditions improved. In 1895, however, the Knights lost a bitter lockout and strike in Brooklyn. For weeks 5,000 strikers engaged in a running street battle with 7,500 armed police, company agents, and National Guardsmen—a scene glimpsed in *Sister Carrie*—before they were finally beaten. Not until the TWU was formed a half-century later would an equivalent level of unionization again be achieved.[1]

After 1895 transit organizing in New York was largely the province of the railroad brotherhoods and the Amalgamated Association of Street Railway Employees. The brotherhoods were involved because until the turn of the century the els used steam locomotives. Even after electrification, train crews continued to think of themselves as railroad men. The Amalgamated, founded in 1892, was an affiliate of the American Federation of Labor (AFL). Centered in the Midwest, it was headed from 1893 all the way up to 1946 by the rather conservative William D. Mahon. The Amalgamated was unusual among AFL unions in that it had broad jurisdiction over the transit industry, in effect an industrial charter. In practice, however, it concentrated on motormen and conductors. [2]

In 1905 the IRT easily defeated a strike called by a coalition of two brotherhoods and the Amalgamated, [3] but a decade later New York's transit industry was shaken by a series of massive, violent confrontations, part of a national upsurge in labor militance. Throughout the country, transit workers were at the forefront of the labor offensive, with particularly bloody strikes in San Francisco (1907), Cleveland (1908), and Philadelphia (1910). [4]

In New York, the renewed union challenge began with a two-week Yonkers trolley strike in 1913. The strike led to an agreement between the Amalgamated and the Third Avenue Railway to arbitrate outstanding disputes on the company's Westchester lines. Three years later, when the company ignored the agreement during a conflict over wages, the Amalgamated again struck. This time the walkout spread to the previously unorganized Third Avenue lines in the Bronx and Manhattan, then to New York Railways (at the time still an IRT subsidiary), and finally to a number of smaller companies. Within a short while, surface transit was paralyzed in every New York borough except Brooklyn.

After two weeks the companies temporarily gave in, agreeing to bargain with employee committees, rehire the strikers, and recognize their right to organize. The IRT, however, soon broke this truce, firing twenty-five workers who had been active in the strike. It also took steps to prevent the unionization of its subways and els: a company union was established, wages twice raised, and workers forced to sign individual, non-union contracts. The company then prepared to extend these "working agreements" to its surface lines. In response, the Amalgamated struck the entire IRT-New York Railways system on September 6. Three days later, Third Avenue workers walked out in sympathy.

Over 18,000 workers participated in this second phase of the 1916 strike, while the companies mobilized a virtual army of strikebreakers. The IRT successfully concentrated on keeping its rapid transit lines running, since less than half the subway and el workers had struck. The trolley lines were a different story; most street car workers had left their jobs, violence was widespread, and thousands of police were needed to protect the cars that did operate.

There was considerable sentiment in the New York labor movement for a general strike in support of the transit men. To that end, local AFL leaders established a "Board of Strategy." However, Samuel Gompers, the president of the AFL, successfully opposed a broader walkout. Without such support, the transit strike soon weakened, and in December the Amalgamated admitted defeat. The union had spent nearly $150,000 on strike benefits, 1,147 strikers had been arrested, and nine people had died. Those strikers who were rehired were placed at the bottom of company seniority lists. [5]

In spite of the strike's outcome, transit worker unrest continued. On the BRT, the Brotherhood of Locomotive Engineers (BLE) successfully organized rapid transit motormen and guards. When the company refused to abide by a National War Labor Board order to reinstate twenty-nine men fired for union activity, the union struck on November 1, 1918. In an attempt to keep its lines operating, the BRT enlisted untrained men as motormen. On the first day of the strike, a scab lost control of his train while descending a tricky S curve into the Malbone Street tunnel. The train crashed into the tunnel wall, instantly killing scores of passengers. More were killed when company officials, unaware of the crash, restored third rail power, assuming it had been interrupted by union saboteurs. By most counts, a total of ninety-two people died in the accident, the worst in New York mass transit history.

The next day the company reached an agreement with the union, ending the strike. Nonetheless, the public outcry and municipal pressure that followed the crash were so great that within two months the BRT was in receivership. Worried about widespread dissatisfaction among the company's skilled workers, a court-appointed receiver signed closed-shop contracts with both the BLE, covering rapid transit motormen, and the Brotherhood of Railroad Signalmen of America (BRSA), covering a few hundred tower and signal workers. In the years that followed, the BMT continued to sign closed-shop pacts with these groups.[6]

The less-skilled BRT workers did not fare as well. In 1919 the Amalgamated, having failed on the IRT, turned to the BRT, where it already had some members. A recognition drive culminated in a three-day strike, strongest on the surface lines. A compromise agreement was reached that eventually led to a wage increase and new work schedules. However, as usual, it was only a temporary victory. When the company's receiver refused to accept artibration of some outstanding issues, a second strike was called in late August 1920. Following the model of the IRT's 1916 triumph, the company refused to negotiate and hired strikebreakers from a half-dozen agencies. The strike slowly weakened and by November was over. The Amalgamated was through on the BRT.[7]

Although by the end of 1920 the transit companies had largely succeeded in excluding unions, the price of victory was high. During 1915 and 1916, the IRT raised wages three times in an effort to forestall unionization, and it gave another three increases in 1918 and 1919. BRT and Third Avenue wages also rose sharply during this period, in some cases doubling. Moreover, the direct costs of smashing strikes were immense. In 1916 the IRT spent over $2 million to defeat the Amalgamated, including about $1 million in double wages for non-striking employees, $204,000 to hire strikebreakers, $98,000 to feed those working, $78,000 for "recreation rooms," and $60,000 for detective services. The 1920 BRT strike cost about the same. Fighting unions helped drive both companies into receivership.[8]

Even aside from the threat of unionization and strikes, maintaining low wages, long hours, and poor working conditions had its costs. Labor turnover was extremely high, as men generally entered the industry only as a temporary expedient. One BMT veteran remembered that before the Depression "a job with the B.M.T. was only a hold-over until you had time to find a job with a more humane employer." Turnover was highest among street car conductors, in part because many were fired for supplementing their wages by pocketing fares, a practice known as "nickeling." One report indicated that the average annual turnover of New York trolley conductors in 1904 and 1905 was well over 100%, and in 1906 over 200%. On the IRT, total turnover in 1912 was equivalent to 100% every seventeen months.

High turnover actually had some advantages for the companies—fewer men reached top rates and worker self-organization was undermined by the transient nature of the work force—but the associated expenses were great. Inexperienced men meant high accident rates and liability costs, low quality work, constant training, and disgruntled patrons. As IRT President Shonts realized in 1912, "[employee] restlessness and discontent are incompatible with efficiency." The transit companies, in Shonts's words, recognized "the great need of improving social conditions as a means of heightening the degree of labor efficiency." Upgraded conditions, so the thinking went, would reduce turnover and discourage unionization.[9]

Concretely, this meant the development of elaborate corporate welfare systems, eventually tied into company unions. The Third Avenue organized a relief and benefit society in 1890, during the height of the Knights of Labor activity; the BRT and IRT started similar groups in 1901 and 1907. Gradually welfare activities were expanded to include group insurance, some free medical service, pension plans, subsidized restaurants and commissaries, recreation facilities, sports teams, summer camps for workers' children, company magazines, emergency loan funds, and a seemingly endless round of picnics, outings, and dances. The BMT even offered an employee stock purchase plan.[10]

At first these programs were run directly by the companies or through voluntary associations they sponsored, but when the threat of unionization became immediate company unions were set up and welfare activities transferred to their control. The most elaborate company union was the Brotherhood of Interborough Rapid Transit Company Employees, started in August 1916 in response to the successful first phase of the Amalgamated strike. Devised by public relations expert Ivy Lee, working with the IRT legal department, the Brotherhood initially was in theory a voluntary association of IRT workers, though in practice the company maintained close control.

The Brotherhood mimicked the forms of independent unionism. Divided into thirty-three separate locals, which corresponded to various occupational and divisional groups, the Brotherhood regularly went through the motions of negotiating working agreements between the employees and the company. However, these contracts were put into effect even when the Brotherhood membership rejected the proposed terms. The one Brotherhood-led work stoppage, a one-day strike in August 1919 that ended with a 25% wage increase, was a sham; it was held with the cooperation of the company and was actually part of the unsuccessful IRT campaign for a higher fare.

In 1920 the Brotherhood constitution was revised to make membership compulsory, and each IRT employee was forced to sign an individual yellow-dog contract. Expulsion from the Brotherhood or involvement with an outside union meant dismissal, thus establishing the organization as a powerful tool of labor control. The new constitution provided for locals to elect their own officers and send delegates to a General Committee, which in turn selected the top Brotherhood leadership. In practice, however, the constitution was frequently violated and company pressure used to influence elections. From 1919 until its demise in 1937, the Brotherhood was headed by Patrick J. Connolly, a veteran, Irish-born conductor.[11]

The B.M.T. Employee's Benefit Association had less pretense of being a bona fide union. Established as an employee representation plan in September 1916, during the IRT strike, it in effect became a company union when a yellow-dog clause was added to its constitution in 1920 following the collapse of the Amalgamated walkout. The Third Avenue Railway and Fifth Avenue Coach sponsored similar groups.[12]

Company unions and corporate welfare plans were an important management tactic after World War I, even though they were used by only a small minority of the nation's firms. At first company unions were most prevalent in the metal trades, but by the mid-1920s over half their members worked for either railroads or utilities, and transit employees constituted the fourth largest membership group. Some of the most elaborate and best-known company union plans were in the transit industry—for example, the so-called Mitten Co-Operative Plan used in Philadelphia and elsewhere.

Although for many years historians tended to dismiss company unions as a crude management ploy, recent essays by David Brody and Daniel Nelson have convincingly argued that at least for a while they helped maintain class stability. Company unionism, they contend, was an important transitional phase between the pre-union era and mature industrial unionism.[13]

Their point is well taken in relation to New York transit. Although in retrospect many workers portrayed the company unions as much-hated, unilateral management schemes, until the Depression they had at least some genuine employee support. Undoubtedly, they played a role in preventing a recurrence of the sort of labor turmoil that characterized the World War I era. As a left-wing critic of company unionism pointed out in 1927, for its first ten years "the [IRT] brotherhood maintained comparative peace on the lines."[14]

Since company union membership was compulsory, in itself it indicates nothing, but participation rates in related programs are at least suggestive of worker attitudes. By 1926 over half of the IRT employees had joined the company's voluntary relief fund; by 1931, some 64% were members. In 1924 when the BMT announced its employee stock purchase plan, 10,000 employees subscribed, and 2,900 took up a second offering two years later. Even if some coercion was involved, these figures remain impressive.[15]

The company unions attracted support for many reasons. Some workers used participation to secure cushy assignments or win promotions. Others liked the sports programs—for example, the gym the IRT Brotherhood had at its Bronx headquarters. Still others enjoyed the social activities the unions sponsored. Even one die-hard company union opponent later recalled fondly the family excursions sponsored by the BMT's union.

On occasion, and to a limited extent, the company unions also acted as workers' advocates. Individual problems could sometimes be resolved through the unions, especially if a worker was on good terms with the leadership. Once in a while, significant concessions were won. The IRT Brotherhood, for example, secured an agreement that all extras would normally be offered work at least three days a week.[16]

Seniority systems were also used to reinforce managerial control while simultaneously providing real employee benefits. Most of the transit companies had seniority systems which they had copied from the railroads. Generally, they were used only in the transportation departments. At periodic "picks," workers would select their assignments—shifts, runs, stations, and so forth—in the order of their seniority. Usually, seniority was not system-wide. The IRT was typical in having a combination of divisional and line seniority. Each of the IRT's three operating divisions (eastern els, western els, and subways) had a seniority list used for choosing assignments to particular lines within the division, and sometimes for determining the order of layoffs. Each line in turn had its own list for selecting specific assignments. BMT seniority was even more fragmented; the company had twenty seniority lists for its surface lines alone.

Transportation workers gained some measure of equity through seniority. But the companies gained as well. Workers were less likely to quit if they could look forward to more desirable assignments, and the local character of seniority encouraged parochialism. The system also gave the companies a disciplinary tool; workers could be punished by dropping their seniority rating. Since seniority generally had no contractual basis, it could be manipulated when necessary or in extreme cases simply ignored.[17]

Company unions, welfare plans, and seniority systems produced at least a small core of loyal workers. They also generated a reservoir of good will among a larger group and, for a while, helped maintain labor peace. Still, most workers resented the company unions and those who led them. Moreover, because they were the one legitimated channel for the discussion of work-related issues, company unions held the potential for becoming centers of worker militancy. In 1926, precisely this occurred on the IRT.

IRT Brotherhood Transportation Local 7 was made up of 700 subway motormen and switchmen, some of whom had once belonged to the BLE. In May 1926, shortly before a Brotherhood contract was due to expire, the IRT began requiring motormen, for no additional pay, to take their trains into the car barns after completing their runs, a job previously handled by switchmen. A Local 7 meeting responded by threatening to strike, whereupon the IRT backed down and withdrew the rule. The local also formulated a demand for higher wages which it forwarded to the Brotherhood officials who were negotiating a new contract.

IRT workers widely assumed that there would be some pay hike in the 1926 Brotherhood agreement. However, the Brotherhood's General Committee simply renewed the existing contract for another year, ignoring the protests of delegates from several locals, including Local 7. On July 1 the overwhelming majority of Local 7 members followed their officers' advice and voted to reject the Brotherhood contract, withdraw from the company union, and constitute themselves as a new, independent entity, the Consolidated Railroad Workers of Greater New York. The next day they asked the IRT for recognition and a 15% wage increase. The company refused to negotiate, claiming that withdrawal from the Brotherhood forfeited their employment.

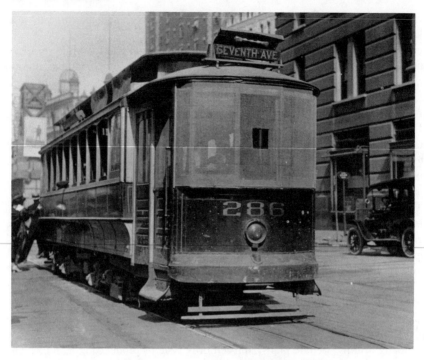

A trolley in service during the 1916 transit strike. Note the wire screen in front of the car, installed to prevent objects thrown by strikers from smashing the window and injuring the driver.

On July 5 about half the Local 7 membership struck. The company threatened the men with loss of seniority or discharge and mobilized scabs recruited from among previously fired employees and from out-of-town. Non-striking switchmen and conductors operated some trains as well. To prevent the strike from spreading, Brotherhood leaders suspended all membership meetings and called in the police to break up those that were attempted. Nevertheless, on July 8 and 9 three-quarters of the 6th Avenue and 9th Avenue el motormen and one-fifth of the powerhouse workers joined the walkout, and on July 17 there was a further walkout at the 74th Street powerhouse. The BMT, worried that the strike would be infectious, raised wages.

Impressive as it was, the walkout failed to shut down completely the IRT. The company had the advantage of money—it spent nearly $1 million hiring scabs—and cooperation from the police and the Brotherhood. On July 21, after the IRT rejected a plea for arbitration, the strikers offered to return to work en masse, but the company refused. A week later the walkout collapsed. Most of the strikers were rehired, but without their seniority. Their leaders were discharged.[18]

At that point, the Amalgamated, which had not been involved in the strike, decided to again try its hand on the IRT. It began a secret organizing campaign, absorbing the Consolidated Railroad Workers. In response, the IRT got an injunction against the defeated strike leaders and added a clause to its contract with the Brotherhood specifically forbidding Amalgamated membership, It also started firing union members, but reinstated them at the request of New York Mayor Jimmy Walker when another strike was threatened. The IRT then applied for a new restraining order, forbidding the Amalgamated or the AFL from organizing its workers. At issue was the validity of the Brotherhood contract and its yellow-dog clause.

In January 1928 the IRT's first injunction was overturned. A month later the New York State Supreme Court denied the IRT application for a second order, finding that its yellow-dog contract was legally unenforceable. Buoyed by this decision, the Amalgamated signed up some 3,000 new members. The court victory, however, was in practice meaningless. The IRT simply resumed firing union activists. When the Amalgamated again threatened to strike, this time to force the reinstatement of some ninety fired workers, the IRT seemed to welcome the opportunity to rid itself of the union once and for all. A thousand scabs were hired, training begun, and kitchens and a dormitory set up. Faced with this show of force, the Amalgamated

Scabs and strikebreakers inside the IRT 148th Street shop during the 1926 strike. Scabs were housed and fed in the shop during the confrontation.

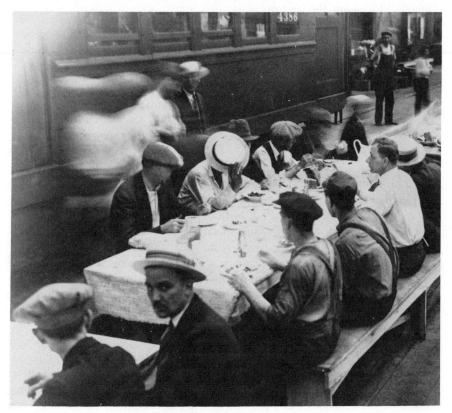

backed down from its strike threat, causing almost its entire membership to desert. As final indignities, the IRT fired twenty-one more workers and appointed Brotherhood President P. J. Connolly to the company board of directors.[19]

There were certain patterns common to all the New York transit strikes. Perhaps most important was the limited extent of worker unity. In 1926, for example, as in several previous strikes, the rapid transit motormen were the most union-minded and militant, but even they were divided. Furthermore, those motormen who did strike were largely isolated from the less skilled operating employees and the station, maintenance, and shop workers. This was partially the fruit of the motormen's own long-standing craft orientation; when militance had originated from outside their ranks, as in 1916, they had not been particularly strong strike supporters. (On the BMT, of course, the motormen had actually won craft recognition.) The failure to forge strong ties between the rapid transit and surface workers, and between the skilled operating and other employees, undercut the ability of any one group to lead a shutdown of the system.

Divisions within the work force were both a symptom and a cause of chronic organizational weakness. Union efforts were particularly weak among non-operating personnel. In the shops, jurisdictional disputes and the lack of sustained organizing led to minimal worker participation. Station workers were largely ignored by all unions. When strikes arose in one part of the system, local leaders thus found themselves thrust into the forefront of complex, system-wide struggles without previously established channels of communication or coordination.

Parent union bodies often provided little support. Sometimes—for instance, during the 1905 IRT walkout—they actually worked to break strikes. The Amalgamated in particular displayed continual incompetence, uncertainty, and reluctance to take militant action. Repeatedly, organizing drives would begin, only to be abandoned after failed strikes or anti-strike preparations, leaving behind a trail of fired workers, lost seniority, and disillusion. Top AFL leaders not only failed to mobilize support from non-transit unions, in some cases they undermined it.

The failure of transit unionism, of course, was also the result of determined and effective company action. In some industries, like garment, where workers succeeded in unionizing during the same period when transit workers failed, companies were typically small, underfinanced, and engaged in vicious market competition. Some employers were willing to make an accommodation with unions in order to rationalize the industry, achieve labor stability, and use wage parity to limit price competition. The transit industry, by contrast, was dominated by a few powerful corporations. Their monopoly status, combined with income flows limited by an all-but-fixed fare, focused their concern on keeping down wages. Transit managers believed that company unions, paternal benefit programs, and autocratic discipline enabled them to do this, and they were willing to marshal their considerable financial and political resources to stop unionization.

The companies fought with every available means. Union activists, fingered by company spies, were repeatedly fired during the early stages of organizing drives. When unions did establish a foothold, they were often eliminated through strikes the companies themselves provoked. Scabs, police, court orders, and mass dismissals were all used, tactics made possible by the cooperation of local political and governmental leaders. Given labor's weaknesses, the balance of power, except for brief moments, clearly rested with management, and in the early 1930s the industry remained overwhelmingly non-union.

Nonetheless, four decades of labor struggle left behind a legacy. In part it consisted of institutional arrangements: company unions, yellow-dog contracts, low wage scales, long hours. In part it consisted of memory. In the 1930s there were still men working in transit who had started on the horse car lines and had witnessed virtually every phase of the industry's labor strife. At least several hundred men who had worked in the industry during the 1916 to 1920 strike wave were still working in transit during the 1930s. Proportionately, there were even more veterans of the 1926 strike. Strike veterans were numerous in management as well. Menden of the BMT and Ritchie of Fifth Avenue Coach and N.Y.C. Omnibus had both played key roles in crushing World War I era strikes. Many IRT executives also had been in management then, and some had first come to the company as scabs. There were Brotherhood officials who had scabbed in 1916, and, of course, most of the leaders of the company union had opposed the 1926 strike.

Feelings remained bitter between strikers and non-strikers. When John Gallagher began working for the Third Avenue in 1930, he noticed "an awfully lot of friction" between men who had struck in 1916 and those who had not. He was warned by fellow workers never to mention unions, on the job or off. In the late-1920s, while Gerald O'Reilly was working as an IRT conductor, an el train preceding his crashed, killing the motorman. When he reached the wreck and saw the body, a motorman he was with commented that it was "no loss" since the dead man had been a scab in 1926.

The companies made the past difficult to forget. Into the 1930s the BMT continued to deny free passes to workers' families, a measure first taken in retaliation for the 1920 strike. More important, changed seniority lists resulting from various strikes were a constant reminder to each man of the role he had played and how he had been rewarded or punished. Even workers hired after 1926 were familiar with the earlier events. [20]

Perhaps the strongest effect of this collective memory was to increase the intense bitterness and fear commonly felt by transit workers toward the companies. This tended both to promote their desire to somehow get back at their employers and to inhibit them from taking concrete steps to do so. Men were particularly afraid that any contact with a union would lead to their dismissal. Deep divisions among the workers, both within job categories and between them, also persisted. Finally, the record of largely failed organizing efforts led to a distaste for the Amalgamated and a general skepticism that any legitimate union would ever triumph. [21]

One reason the companies could treat their workers so harshly, both during strikes and on a day-to-day basis, was the presence of a classic reserve army of labor, sometimes literally at the door. Immigration and high unemployment created a large pool of workers seeking jobs in those industries like transit which had entry-level positions with no skill requirements. In 1925 there were over 13,000 job applications to the IRT transportation department alone; by 1928, 21,268. The onset of the Depression so intensified the situation that by 1930, when John Gallagher applied for his Third Avenue job, job-seekers were lined up four deep around the block where the company was located. Even in the extreme case of mass firings following strikes, the companies were able to quickly replenish their work forces. The available labor surplus was an ever-present reminder to those with jobs of their expendability, a point the IRT none too subtly drove home by publishing application figures in its employee newspaper. [22]

The external reserve army enabled the companies to establish what were in effect internal reserve armies, the extras. In addition to providing an inexpensive solution to scheduling problems, the extras were a living reminder to those with steady jobs of the ease with which they could be replaced. Like the use of multiple seniority lists, the extra system fragmented the work force. Those who had already spent several poorly paid, disruptive years as extras had good reason to be reluctant to jeopardize their jobs by participating in union activity or otherwise deviating from expected behavior.

In their "bargaining-hunting in the labor market," as *Moody's Utilities* termed it, the transit companies found enough potential workers to allow considerable latitude in deciding just whom to hire. [23] A number of factors determined the social composition of the work force they selected, including specific manpower needs, ethnic patterns of occupational choice, changes in the labor market reflecting general economic trends, and racial and sexual prejudice. Some determinants were general to American industry, while others were specific to transit.

Like many industries, transit needed a large number of unskilled and low skilled workers and a smaller number of workers with a variety of specific craft skills. What was special to transit was that many jobs, essentially most transportation work, involved contact with the public and therefore required fluency in English and what were deemed acceptable manners and appearance. The public contact jobs were largely unskilled jobs or learned through on-the-job training, while most skilled jobs, except in the case of the motormen, involved no public contact. The combined pattern of skill and language requirements was the most important factor in determining company hiring practices. Within the limits so imposed and the limits of the labor market, the companies tried to assemble a work force that they felt would be reliable and controllable, even under conditions of intense exploitation. [24]

To do this, transit, like many industries before World War II, turned heavily to immigrant labor. No comprehensive figures are available, but of 14,052 residents of Brooklyn, Manhattan, and the Bronx classified in the 1930 census as street railway conductors, motormen, or laborers, 62% said that they were foreign-born whites. Other evidence suggests that a substantial majority of all New York transit employees were immigrants. [25]

What was particular to transit was that one immigrant group, the Irish, dominated the work force, partially as a result of the language requirement. It is difficult to say with any precision what percentage of the workers were Irish. Some estimates run as high as 75%, but these are almost certainly exaggerated. [26] Because the Irish were concentrated in public contact jobs and were a highly visible presence in the TWU once it was organized, observers frequently overestimated their number. Calculations from available evidence suggest that probably foreign-born Irish made up slightly less than half of the transit work force. Without question they were the largest single ethnic bloc; no other group even approached them in size.[27]

The percentage of Irish employees varied considerably from company to company and among occupational groups within each company. The large surface companies were the most Irish. In the 1930s and 40s, well over 90% of the Third Avenue Railway workers were Irish, almost all Irish-born. As one worker said, "you might call it a dumping ground for the Irish." (In general, Irish will be used to mean Irish-born; Irish-American to mean native-born Americans of Irish descent.) The non-Irish on the Third Avenue were mostly skilled shop workers, mainly German, less frequently Italian, Scottish, or English. Most of the company's managers and supervisors, although not the top officials, were Irish as well.[28] Similarly, the majority of employees and executives of the Fifth Avenue Coach Company were Irish.[29] By contrast, many if not most of the workers at the much smaller East Side and Comprehensive Bus Company were Italian.[30]

The IRT and BMT transportation departments were also heavily Irish. Most IRT agents, platform men, guards, conductors, and motormen were Irish-born. Among the non-Irish were a fair number of Italian conductors, motormen, and guards, mostly older immigrants with good seniority, and a scattering of Jews, Scots, English, Germans, and Poles. There were many Irish BMT transportation workers as well, although relative to the IRT they formed a smaller proportion of their department, which had a sizable number of native-born workers. (Census figures indicate that among "street railway" motormen and conductors *living* in Brooklyn, there were about equal numbers of native and foreign-born whites.) On both the BMT and IRT, the Depression led to a small decrease in the proportion of Irish, as both Irish-Americans and non-Irish unable to get work elsewhere, some with high school or even college degrees, took jobs which they would have previously spurned.[31]

Outside the transportation departments, the composition of the rapid transit work force was more varied. Although there were many Irish workers, they did not constitute a majority of those employed, and many other ethnic groups were present. The IRT shops, for example, had significant numbers of native Protestant and first and second-generation Irish, German, Italian, Slavic, English, and Hispanic workers. The company's powerhouses had a similar mix, but with a higher proportion of Slavs and Hispanics. The IRT barns tended to be heavily Irish and Italian.

In jobs requiring specific skills or general mechanical training, native Protestants and Europeans with industrial backgrounds were strongly represented. For example, a number of former English and Irish coachbuilders worked as IRT carpenters and car maintainers. Of course, there were also many unskilled and semi-skilled non-transportation jobs—car cleaner, inspector, maintainers' helper, and the like—which could be easily learned. Furthermore, through on-the-job training or attendance at vocational school, it was possible for inexperienced men to move into some skilled slots.[32]

On the BMT, the ethnic composition of the various shops and barns to some extent reflected the ethnicity of the areas in which they were located. Peter Mac-Lachlan, a BMT shop worker and later a TWU leader, recalled "Norwegians and Swedes, Italians, and then a few Englishmen, a few Scotsmen, a few Irishmen . . .

[and] a few [black] British West Indians." Some jobs were held largely by members of a particular ethnic group. For example, the BMT track workers—according to MacLachlan the "hardest working and poorest paid men in the whole damned railroad"—were primarily Italian. (IRT track workers came from various backgrounds but were organized into ethnically homogeneous gangs.) Peter Ezzo, who headed the BMT surface track section of the TWU, estimated in 1939 that 80% of his section's 300 members were Italians who could neither read nor write English and who understood it poorly. Scots, by contrast, worked mostly in the shops— usually in relatively skilled positions—or as signalmen. The men who did the heavy, dirty work of maintaining train trucks (which held in place wheels, brakes, and motors) were primarily Irish or West Indian.[33]

One TWU official described the ISS as "a little chapter all by itself." Because it was city-operated and completed after the onset of the Depression, the social composition of its work force differed significantly from the other lines. ISS workers were generally native-born whites, better educated and younger than their IRT and BMT counterparts. Although the ISS hired some veteran transit and railway men, particularly for operating jobs, the bulk of those hired were new to the industry. Many were out-of-towners, often from the South, who had come to New York looking for work.[34] Others went into transit as a result of the economic collapse. A large number of civil engineers, for instance, who had worked on the design and construction of the ISS, took permanent non-engineering jobs with the line when construction was completed and economic conditions worsened. Some Independent workers had passed civil service exams to be police or firemen but were still waiting for appointments. Quite a few others got their jobs through political connections. Before 1935 the Board of Transportation did not follow civil service procedures in hiring and promotion, and many men, often without relevant work experience, came in through Tammany clubs.[35]

As a result of severely discriminatory practices, the roughly 1,000 black New York transit workers were largely restricted to the bottom of the occupational hierarchy. Some companies, such as the Third Avenue, hired virtually no blacks. When blacks were hired by private companies, they were almost always assigned to cleaning jobs. The only black Fifth Avenue Coach employees were bus cleaners. On the IRT, essentially all blacks were porters and all the 300 or 400 porters were black. As one of their number, an ex-serviceman, put it, the IRT thought that "a colored man's fate is a gun in war time and a mop in peace time." Discrimination was so strong that the porters were not even permitted to have their own company union representative; they were served by a white station department delegate. On the BMT the situation was the same; except for a few men performing heavy shop work, blacks were restricted to porter positions and virtually all porters were black.[36]

When the ISS opened in 1932, it followed the pattern of the private companies, segregating most blacks in porter jobs. A few black men, however, were hired as agents to work in Harlem stations. The situation changed in 1934, when the New York City Board of Aldermen placed black ISS employees under normal seniority rules. The effect was to open up agent jobs in all stations to black workers. The following year, when civil service procedures were instituted, they were applied without regard to race, making the Independent one of the few railroads in the country that did not practice racial discrimination in hiring and promotions. The first black conductor was hired in 1935, and by the fall of 1939 there were 63 black conductors, 20 conductor-motormen, and a few black shop workers and clerks.[37]

Transit employment opportunities for women were even more limited. During World War I, New York Railways and the BRT had hired nearly 2,000 female conductors, guards, agents, and porters, but by the early 1930s only the BMT still employed women in non-office jobs. Most were ticket agents, either initially hired during the war or employed under a special program that gave jobs to women whose husbands had been killed or injured while working for the company. Mainly these women were Irish, and their average age was fairly high. (Although some men worked as BMT agents, women held most of the jobs.)[38]

Nationally, transit workers tended to be young, a by-product of high turnover. In New York, however, there was always a fair number of veteran employees. Of the 15,988 New York City resident conductors, motormen, and transit laborers identifiable by age in the 1930 census, 46% were under 35; 45% between 35 and 54; and 9% 55 or older. With the Depression, turnover decreased, and in the late 1930s improvements in wages, conditions, and pensions as a result of unionization furthered this trend. Thus after 1929 the transit work force was highly stable and aging. By 1941, 22% of the Fifth Avenue Coach drivers and 48% of the conductors were over fifty, and half of all the company's employees had been with the line for fifteen years or more. In 1945, only 4% of the potential beneficiaries of the IRT and BMT pension funds were under 35; 67% were between 35 and 54, and 29% 55 or older.[39]

To keep out unionists and select men who would be reliable and disciplined, the transit companies developed a number of special hiring practices. Trolley lines throughout the country exchanged blacklists of fired unionists, complete with detailed physical descriptions. (Some banned workers, however, were able to secure jobs by using false names.) Fifth Avenue Coach and the BMT gave preference to relatives of current employees; on the former line it was difficult to get a job without such a connection. The BMT also gave preference to men with letters from their parish priest. Many IRT men got hired by being "taken on" by someone already working for the company, who would sponsor them to the Brotherhood. If Brotherhood officials approved the man, they would recommend him to the company. Others got jobs through relatives or acquaintances either in management or in some other way connected to a transit firm. John Gallagher, for example, was hired by the Third Avenue because a policeman friend of his had witnessed a trolley accident and the company felt obligated to the friend for his cooperation in the incident.[40]

In spite of these practices, quite a few men were hired who had had union experience. Many of the European craftsmen had been unionists abroad. Most of the Scots, for example, came from industrial or mining regions and had joined unions at an early age. Other workers had belonged to unions in this country while holding previous jobs. A few even secretly kept up craft union membership while employed in transit. Most transit workers, however, never had been in a union, and many never had had any type of contact whatsoever with the trade union movement.[41]

Because transit workers came from such varied backgrounds, what they shared was often no more than work itself. If transit defined working life, other things—ethnicity, religion, family, neighborhood—were at least as central in defining non-working life. Ethnic ties were particularly important, for most transit workers were immigrants and many were deeply immersed in ethnic subcultures. Rather than identifying with other transit workers, or with the working class as a whole, many transit employees identified primarily with their particular ethnic group.[42]

Transit workers from different backgrounds did socialize with one another, both on and off the job. The companies and company unions actually encouraged this by sponsoring dances, outings, and other activities. There were even special transit branches of the American Legion and the Veterans of Foreign Wars.[43] Co-workers sometimes went out together after work, to bars or elsewhere, and strong friendships were formed. But such small groups of friends and work mates remained self-contained; they were not elements of a larger, self-conscious transit community. As one shop worker recalled, "in them days, you didn't talk to everybody . . . you had a group of your own" centered in a particular department or part of a facility.[44]

In some industries, ethnicity served to unite the work force. In transit, it was a two-edged sword: the demographic diversity of the industry meant that ethnic subcultures often kept workers apart, but one ethnic group, the Irish, was so large and pervasive that it became a source of cohesion. Irish community life and Irish culture permeated the industry. Even the non-Irish were affected. Thus to the extent that any one culture imparted its character to the industry, and later to the union that the workers in the industry formed, it was the culture of Irish immigrants.

Although Irish immigration is usually associated with the nineteenth century, the Irish continued to come to America in substantial, if diminished, numbers until 1930 (when the flow fell sharply). More than 700,000 Irish emigrated to the United States during the first three decades of the twentieth century, mostly from rural areas.[45] They came for much the same reasons as their predecessors. In part because of British domination, Ireland was economically stagnant. The countryside was overwhelmingly agricultural, the land poor, and holdings small. By custom farmers generally gave up their land only at a late age, and usually to but one son. Other male children and daughters without dowries were forced to compete for the few available rural jobs, head to the cities, or leave the country. In a land of few opportunities and little wealth, through the 1920s emigration—for generations an established part of Irish life—continued to hold great attraction for the young and energetic.[46]

The United States, and particularly New York, had long been a favored destination for Irish emigrants, and it continued to be so into the twentieth century. In 1930 there were 220,631 Irish immigrants living in New York City and another 392,375 second-generation Irish. Together they formed the fourth largest immigrant group in the city, after the Italians, the "Russians" (mostly Eastern European Jews), and the Germans.[47]

The Irish came for jobs, but those from rural areas had few skills of value in the urban labor market. Hence they were forced to seek work in industries with no entrance-level skill requirements and were willing to take jobs others rejected. Specific industries and even specific companies became centers of employment for recent Irish arrivals: construction, longshoring, teamstering, utilities, carpet factories, certain civil service jobs, and transit. By the 1920s and 1930s there were already large numbers of Irish working in these industries, and through them new immigrants would hear which companies were hiring and find aid in securing a job. With so many Irish concentrated in a few fields, it was common for workers to have many friends and relatives working for the same company, or at least in the same type of job. This was particularly true in transit, where many workers had relatives or acquaintances from Ireland in the industry, sometimes in managerial or supervisory positions. Such connections were helpful not only in obtaining a job, but in later advancement as well.[48]

Most of the Irish working in transit were "country people" from the poorer counties of southern and western Ireland: Cork, Kerry, and Galway. In many cases they were but a few years removed from the peasantry and retained social, political, and psychological traits there formed. By American standards, the countryside they had left was extremely backward. As late as 1946 there were only 4,500 tractors in all of Ireland, while 452,000 horses and ponies were still in use. Before 1948, less than 1,000 rural residents in the Irish Republic had electricity.

Although generally literate, many Irish transit workers had only a dim understanding of metropolitan life. Mike Quill, for example, who was to rise to the top of the TWU, first saw a telephone only upon his arrival in New York. Although Quill quickly developed a lifelong fascination with telephones, airplanes, and other technical marvels of the late industrial age, many of his fellow immigrants remained deeply suspicious. It was common, for instance, for Irish transit workers to send a neighbor or a child with a message, rather than use a phone. More important, in many cases Irish workers had had little if any experience with wage labor before their jobs in transit.

Quite different were the far fewer Irish transit workers who came from Dublin or other urban areas. Usually these "city people" had been skilled workers or received some industrial training in Ireland, and were thus able to secure jobs in the shops. While the rural Irish rarely had had any previous contact with unions, those from the cities generally had some knowledge of unionism, and in some cases had been union members.[49]

In New York, Irish immigrants found a large, complex ethnic community. Most Irish transit workers lived in heavily Irish neighborhoods: the South Bronx, particularly the area around 138th Street and Willis Avenue, which was sometimes called "Little Ireland"; the Fordham section, also of the Bronx; the West Side and Hell's Kitchen in Manhattan; and various parts of Brooklyn. Many transit workers were single. Although Irish immigrants generally married at a somewhat younger age than was the practice in Ireland, which was notorious for late marriage and high levels of celibacy, it took several years of work before most transit workers could afford a wife or children. Single men usually lived as boarders with Irish families or in rooming houses run by childless couples or widows. Married transit workers, in turn, usually had at least one boarder. One observer recollected that "there was hardly a transit worker whose family could afford an apartment all for itself. Almost every one of them had one room in which he kept other transit workers as roomers." Thus Irish transit workers were in continual contact with one another off the job as well as on.[50]

Irish New York was far from homogeneous. It included new immigrants, long-time residents, and the native-born, and was divided along various occupational, class, and ideological lines. Among blue-collar workers alone, sharp differences could be found. The typical Irish transit worker was far removed from the life of, say, a George Meany, the son of an Irish immigrant who grew up in a Bronx neighborhood of skilled, home-owning workers. As a union plumber, Meany could earn as much in two eight-hour days as an IRT ticket agent would make for a seventy-hour week.[51] Even farther removed were the old Irish families, well-established in business, politics, or the Church, the "lace-curtain" Irish.

Perhaps the Irish community is best understood as an arena, or series of interconnected arenas, in which various groups, customs, and ideas contested, all the while influencing one another. Certain institutions were central: fraternal organizations, the Roman Catholic Church, the Democratic party, and three newspapers, the *Irish World*, *Irish Echo*, and *Gaelic-American*, which supplied news from Ireland and of Irish activities in the United States. Most of these institutions had middle-class leaders, but to remain broadly inclusive they generally avoided class issues.

Fraternal organizations were numerous. Some were particularly favored by immigrants, for instance the county associations, such as the County Cork Men's Association or the Galway Men's S. and B. Association, in which men from the same part of Ireland joined together. The county groups were joined together under the umbrella of the United Irish Counties Association. Other organizations were more general, for example, the Ancient Order of Hibernians or the Gaelic School, which taught the language, traditional dancing, and choral singing.[52]

Nearly every Irish organization sponsored weekend dances. Admission was low, twenty-five or fifty cents or a dollar with beer. It was a cheap way to relax after a week's work and to meet those of the opposite sex. In addition, various groups used these dances to finance their other activities. The frequent dances sponsored by transit company unions and by enterprising transit workers in part reflected this tradition. Dances for workers from the IRT 148th Street Shop, for example, usually featured two bands, one playing Irish music and one American. This Irish sociability, the constant dances and affairs, provided "a very, very strong bond."[53]

Athletic events were also frequent. Not only did many Irish organizations sponsor teams and competitions, particularly in traditional Irish sports, but periodically teams from Ireland would tour the States. On one such occasion, a soccer team of IRT workers, the "I.R.T. Celtic," took on a team visiting from Dublin. When the World Gaelic Football Championship was held in New York, interest was so great that the games were played in Yankee Stadium, with Postmaster General James Farley throwing in the ball.[54]

The Catholic Church, of course, was at the heart of Irish New York. With its rites and rituals, it was the norm, the expected, the familiar. In both neighborhood life and city-wide politics, it wielded considerable power. Since Irish-Americans played a dominant role in the Catholic hierarchy, the Church also was a symbol of community accomplishment. Alongside the Church itself were a whole series of Church-sponsored organizations and institutions, from parochial schools to Holy Name societies. Loyalty to parish and priest, as Andrew Greeley has written, was "an important component of the cement that holds one's community together."[55]

The centrality of the Church in Irish life, however, did not mean that it was dominant in all spheres or universally accepted. Rather, a whole range of attitudes could be found, from devout acceptance of Church guidance in all matters to open anti-clericalism. Even the profoundly religious sometimes differed with their local priest or the Church as a whole in the political or social realm. Many felt that the priest's proper role was in the pulpit, and there alone. Furthermore, the stand of the Catholic hierarchy in Ireland, where it opposed the use of force by republican fighters and denied them the sacrament, led to widespread anti-clerical feelings among republican activists and sympathizers. This anti-clericalism was carried by some immigrants across the Atlantic, and it held sway with many transit workers. The Church itself, moreover, came to be deeply divided over social and political questions, particularly in its response to the New Deal and the rise of industrial unionism. Thus while Catholicism was a shared experience for most Irish, and the Church a pervasive presence, this did not guarantee a homogeneity of social, political, or even religous belief. [56]

Politics, too, was central to New York Irish life, both the politics of the new land and the politics of the old. The Irish had long been a crucial, often dominant, element in the New York Democratic party. As a result, until Mayor Fiorello La Guardia's election in 1933 the Irish had been able to secure a disproportionately large number of civil service and higher-level government jobs. The Democratic party, like the Church, was a major force in every Irish neighborhood. Immigrant Irish could neither vote nor run for office, at least legally, until they had acquired citizenship, which took a minimum of five years, and many transit workers were not yet citizens. But organizations which included recent arrivals, such as the Hibernians and the United Irish Counties, endorsed Democratic candidates, and it was not unusual for Irish immigrants to become active in Democratic politics before they could vote. [57]

For many, however, it was Irish nationalism and the ongoing struggles in Ireland that were their primary political passion. Irish New Yorkers, particularly those who were Irish-born, maintained an intense interest in Irish politics. As Lawrence McCaffrey pointed out, "emigration and the development of an Irish identity among American immigrants speeded the process of Irish nationalism on both sides of the Atlantic."[58] For nearly a century, a steady two-way flow of ideas and political leaders between Ireland and the United States influenced political developments among the Irish in both lands, a process that continued into the 1930s and beyond. [59]

Most Irish organizations in the United States were at least nominally anti-British and republican. Within that basic outlook, however, there were sharp political differences that roughly corresponded to the divisions in Ireland itself. Broadly speaking, there were three main tendencies. Some organizations and individuals supported Fine Gael, the party formed by supporters of the 1921 treaty giving southern Ireland its independence. (Fine Gael headed the first government of the Irish Free State.) Others supported Fianna Fail, the party Eamon De Valera formed in 1926 when he broke with the Irish Republican Army (IRA). (It took power in 1932.) Finally, there were orthodox republicans—mostly IRA supporters—who endorsed the use of both military and political means to create a united Ireland completely free of British ties. [60]

In this country, the IRA's strongest backing came from the Clan na Gael, a secret society with a long and venerable history. Founded in 1867 in an effort to reunite the fragmented American Fenians, at its height in the 1870s it had some 10,000 members. For eighty years the Clan supplied financial, political, and occasionally military support to the republicans in Ireland. During the "Black and Tan War" for Irish independence, the Clan sent money and guns to the Irish Volunteers and tried to pressure the American government to take a pro-Irish stand. The Clan then backed the IRA in its opposition to the treaty that ended the anti-British conflict by partitioning Ireland, leading to a civil war in the south. In fact, during this period American guns and money were critical to the IRA's survival. When De Valera formed Fianna Fail, the Clan remained loyal to IRA. By then, however, according to one historian, "the Clan as a mass movement was slowly decaying, membership slipped away, branches broke off and were not replaced, and second-generation Irishmen were attracted in fewer numbers."[61]

As the Clan shrank in size, its social character changed. Prior to 1923, when the civil war ended, the Clan had been predominantly an organization of native-born Irish-Americans. However, the cessation of fighting brought a large influx of republicans to the United States and into the Clan. In 1923 and 1924 the Irish Free State released thousands of IRA prisoners, many of whom found themselves without money or jobs and who chose to emigrate, primarily to the U.S. In the following few years, still more republicans, including many younger supporters of the movement, headed to America, as the prospects for renewed struggle dimmed and economic conditions remained poor. The flight of these "wild geese" to American shores transformed the Clan, particularly in New York, into primarily an immigrant organization, with ex-IRA men at its core.[62]

Although by the early 1930s the Clan was no longer the mass organization it had once been, it remained active and substantial. Its New York leadership met regularly at Tara Hall, near Broadway and 66th Street, and each of several local branches could on occasion fill a sizable meeting hall. Clan members followed events in Ireland, published a newspaper, and held weekly dances. Though they tried as best they could to raise money and arms to ship back to Ireland, Clan members were not well off, particularly once the Depression hit. Still, the Clan served as a center of republicanism in the United States, a meeting ground for ex-IRA men and republican-oriented immigrants, and was an influential group within the larger Irish community.[63]

Since the New York transit companies were among the largest employers of recent Irish immigrants, predictably quite a few ex-IRA men worked in transit. Some belonged to the Clan na Gael, while others were no longer politically active. Many of these men, particularly those in the Clan, were to become organizers and leaders of the TWU. The Clan, little known outside of Irish circles, was to play a crucial role in the creation of modern transit unionism.[64]

For the Irish, the very act of emigration was the beginning of a break with the past, an escape from the tightly structured world of the Irish countryside. In Ireland, parental authority was strong and usually continued until marriage at a late age. In New York, Irish workers were on their own, freed from the constant surveillance of family and village. If on the one hand this led to widespread loneliness, alcoholism, and neurosis, on the other hand it left men free of responsibilities and restraints.[65]

Nonetheless, the social order Irish transit workers found in New York had continuities with the world they had left behind. The transit companies in particular depended on traditional systems of authority: deference, obligation, and repression. Personal favor and kinship networks played an important role in transit, just as they did in Irish country life. The company unions, Tammany politics, and the Catholic Church—all Irish-dominated, top down, and highly hierarchical—were built around loyalty and obedience, traditional rural Irish virtues. As Robert Cross wrote, "it was the duty of the faithful to be faithful [to the clergy]—just as it was the duty of the precinct worker to follow the direction of the district leader." In return, the Church, the political club, and the company union could provide individuals, within given limits, with spiritual or temporal rewards. The dominant Irish political style, whether in clubhouse, church, or company, was personal and practical, not ideological or bureaucratic, and ultimately it depended on rank-and-file passivity.[66]

Beyond sharing certain structural traits, the Church, Tammany, and the transit industry had some explicit ties to one another. Many transit executives had considerable standing and influence in the Irish Catholic community and the local Democratic machine. Thomas Fortune Ryan had provided a model. A founder of the old Metropolitan Street Railway, before his death in 1928 he gave a reported $20 million to the Catholic Church and, like Belmont, wielded considerable power within the Democratic party. Nicholas Brady, a one-time president of the BRT, also active in Catholic charities, was appointed a Papal Duke. Other transit executives operated on a more modest scale, but they could be found in leading positions in various Irish and Catholic organizations: the Hibernians, the Knights of Columbus, and so on. Furthermore, if merely as a part of doing business, the transit companies always maintained strong ties to the local Democratic party.

These manifold connections generally ensured that the key institutions of Irish New York life would not be used to challenge the status quo. Of course, this alone did not guarantee that Irish transit workers would be docile; in fact, in virtually every major New York transit strike they played an important role. Nonetheless, the structure of Irish New York meant that under normal circumstances ethnic and religious identification were effectively harnessed to the cause of social stability.[67]

The recently rural Irish transit workers, then, faced a choice: they could accept a new way of life as they found it, or they could help to transform it. In this they were not unique. What made them special was sheer numbers. Any organization of transit workers could succeed only if it captured the support of Irish workers. And in doing so, it would have to unite the Irish not only with one another, but with the many others who worked alongside them, all those who together constituted the transit working class.

II

"Did you see the light?"

3

THE FOUNDING OF THE
TRANSPORT WORKERS UNION

A socialist republic is the application to agricul-
ture and industry . . . of the democratic principle
of the republican ideal.   James Connolly

The drive to organize New York City transit workers sprang from two sources: an
incipient, diffuse process of self-organization and activity initiated by the Communist Party of the United States. The integration and expansion of these two efforts
led to the formation of the Transport Workers Union and the successful unionization of the industry. In the interaction of the internal and the external, the most
advanced workers of a particular industry with a party that claimed to speak for
workers as a whole, lay not only the seed of the TWU, but the whole logic of its
development over the next fifteen years, within the confines of a given social,
political, and economic setting. For this reason, the reconstruction of the moment
of conception and infancy of the organization takes on an interest that transcends
the question of who deserves "credit" for founding the union and becomes a starting
point for understanding the social process that was the TWU.

The collapse of the national economy in 1929 led to a sharp deterioration in
conditions for transit workers. As annual city-wide ridership fell by 424 million paid
rides between 1930 and 1933, the transit companies introduced stiff cost-cutting
measures. In some cases these were more than sufficient to compensate for the
decline in revenue. Although spending on maintenance and depreciation was reduced, a large share of the cuts fell on labor.[1]

At first the companies lessened their payrolls primarily by shortening hours and
reducing or eliminating various types of bonus pay, rate differentials, and benefits.
The Fifth Avenue Coach Company, for example, eliminated paid vacations—it had
been the only company to provide them—and a profit-sharing plan. Soon, however, cuts were made in actual hourly rates. Both the IRT and BMT instituted
general 10% rate cuts in 1932 with the approval of their company unions, and other
employers took similar action.[2]

The companies also moved to decrease the size of their work forces. Total employment on the IRT, for example, fell from 17,430 in 1930 to 14,348 in 1937. In part

this was accomplished by the accelerated introduction of smaller operating crews. By installing additional multi-unit door controls, the IRT and BMT reduced their combined force of guards from 3,615 in 1929 to 2,176 in 1937. In surface transit, the BMT and Third Avenue increasingly replaced two-man trolleys with one-man cars. The conversion of trolley lines to buses, particularly in Manhattan, also led to manpower reductions.[3]

These operational changes resulted in the lay-off of hundreds of men and a worsening of conditions for many who remained. To the extent that seniority was followed in crew reductions, men with enough years to avoid being fired were often forced from steady jobs onto extra lists or into part-time runs. At one point, an extra list of IRT guards was headed by a man who had been with the company for twenty-seven years. Hundreds of shop men were also laid-off, occasionally to be later rehired at lower rates. Working-sharing programs forestalled still further lay-offs, but reduced the number of hours employees worked.[4]

The net effect was a sharp drop in transit workers' annual earnings. Gerald O'Reilly, an IRT conductor, was typical. In 1930 and 1931 he made slightly over $2,000 a year. This went down to $1,293 in 1932, to $1,642 in 1933, and $1,699 in 1934. Average annual earnings on the IRT fell from a peak of $1,861 in 1931 to $1,612 in 1934; on the BMT from a 1930 peak of $1,796 to $1,431 in 1935.[5] Although the decrease in ridership and some deferral of maintenance reduced the total work load, workers repeatedly charged that the lay-offs and shorter work weeks meant more work per person and additional safety problems. As one Third Avenue worker complained, "half the men fired and the other half doing two men's work at less than one man's pay."[6]

As conditions worsened, transit workers grew increasingly restless and discontent. Many immigrant workers, who only a few years earlier had been delighted simply to have a job, developed higher expectations just as their opportunities were diminishing. At the same time, the political climate was changing. The beginning of the New Deal, the election of Mayor La Guardia in 1933, the passage of the National Industrial Recovery Act, and various signs of labor movement revival all contributed to a growing sense that social change was possible. With reform administrations in the White House and City Hall, it was no longer certain that the transit companies could count on automatic government support.[7]

From the early 1930s through the triumph of the TWU in 1937, heightened worker unrest manifested itself in a number of ways. Most important, and underlying many other developments, was the appearance of a variety of small groups of workers actively seeking some solution to their deteriorating situation. These workers considered their situation not only as individuals, but as part of collectivities, no matter how primitive. Apparently there were dozens of such groups scattered throughout the industry. Understandably, they left behind very little documentation, so that any discussion of them must rely primarily on the memories of a few individuals.[8]

In almost all cases, these were informal groups, circles of workers who discussed among themselves the problems they faced and possible courses of action. Of the groups that can be even sketchily reconstructed, all but one were localized, that is restricted to one work site. Most were in either shops or powerhouses, rather than among transportation or maintenance-of-way workers. Generally they centered on some individual, who by personality, experience, or ability commanded the respect of his co-workers. Or at least that is how they were perceived by TWU organizers when they eventually began to encounter them. Thus the groups were known or remembered by the names of their leaders: Bill Zuidema's group, the Faber and Gahagan groups, the Joe English group. The one exception to this pattern was the largest and ultimately most important group, the network of Irish republican transit workers centered in the Clan na Gael. It consisted of men from a variety of locations and departments, primarily transportation and maintenance workers, and was not clearly identified with any one individual.

The appearance of these groups was a sign that the institutional, political, and psychological structures that had previously maintained stability in the transit industry were beginning to break down. Since no alternative structures had yet appeared, a period of uncertainty and exploration ensued. During this time, the various worker groups, along with scattered individuals, "began to look for a way out."

The first direction they turned was toward the known, toward those institutions that in the past had played a role in transit. On the IRT, for example, there was increased interest in the company union. In the early 1930s more workers began attending Brotherhood meetings and more raised questions, with some worker groups hoping to reform the organization. Similarly, BMT motormen began to revivify their somewhat dormant local of the Brotherhood of Locomotive Engineers (BLE), opposing the established leadership and demanding a more militant stand toward the company.[9] Other groups and individuals, particularly in surface transit, turned to the AFL Amalgamated Association, which once again began trying to organize in New York City,[10] while an ISS group operated within the Civil Service Forum, a public employees association. Still others hoped "to go to Tammany to get some political push." Finally, there was some sporadic agitation among transit workers by the IWW and various Socialist Party-affiliated groups.[11]

Mostly, however, workers in informal circles simply discussed their problems with one another and with their fellow employees, agitating against the companies and about the need for change. Even those groups that were exploring the possibility of working through or with established organizations generally maintained their autonomy and remained open to various possibilities. At least two groups, in fact, hoped to eventually form new, independent unions.

In spite of the fact that many worker groups were looking toward unionism of one sort or another to alleviate their woes, it would be an exaggeration to see in their development the beginning of union organization. Though ranging from the loosest of small cliques to more self-conscious networks, all but those few that joined the Amalgamated remained, in one observer's excellent formulation, "non-union discontent groups."[12] None of the groups by itself expanded beyond its initial base, nor did any assume the functions and forms of a union.

The "discontent groups" are best understood as fluid elements within the everyday structure of work place relations during a period of heightened stress and unrest. As such, they represented as much a continuity with the non-union era as a glimpse of the future. Though impossible to know, it seems unlikely that any, on its own, would have been the start of the unionization of the industry. The groups that took the clearest step toward unionism, by affiliating with the Amalgamated, were generally crushed within months.[13] The others remained as potential building blocks for a future organization, but alone were not the beginning of it.

In the end, it was from outside the industry, from the Communist Party, that the impetus and leadership for a new union, the TWU, originated. But it was only the Communists' ability to enlist the resources and leaders of the existing groups, especially the Irish republicans, that enabled them to succeed.[14]

For the Communist Party, the decision to organize New York transit workers was an outgrowth of a general political and strategic conception that led the Party to participate in a whole range of unionizing efforts during the late 1920s and early 1930s. In 1933, when the Communists began systematic work in New York transit, they were at the tail-end of their "third period." Along with Communists throughout the world they believed that it was a period of imminent revolutionary upsurge, and therefore a time for independent militant activity distinct from and opposed to liberal or social democratic efforts. In trade union work, this meant both organizing new "revolutionary" industrial unions and building caucuses within existing AFL affiliates.

Party organizers also tried to recruit workers directly into the CP. Where possible, Communist shop "nuclei" were established to conduct agitation about both work and Party issues and recruit new members. In New York transit, the CP initially sought to organize both a new industrial union and a network of Party shop groups. Although these objectives were seen as complementary, the balance between them was an occasional source of tension. The distinction between recruitment into the Party and recruitment into Party-led "revolutionary unions" was not always clear to either those doing the recruiting or those being recruited.[15]

The CP already had some experience in the New York transit industry, having actively supported the 1920 and 1926 strikes. It also had at least a few contacts and members in the industry. This was not the result of any particular strategic intention, but simply a by-product of the many Party activities in the New York area.[16] In early 1933, some agitational work was being carried out by an "IRT Workers Group" and a "BMT Workers Group" that reported on their activities in the *Daily Worker*. In leaflets and letters to the Communist paper they discussed proposed lay-offs, forced retirements, pensions, and pay reductions.[17] However, the decision to begin systematic organizing in the industry was not made until the Communist Party Extraordinary Conference in July 1933.

This important special national Communist gathering was intended to reorient the activities of the Party and overcome serious organizational and political shortcomings. In spite of the fact that by 1933 the CP had a dues-paying membership of 19,000, the Party leadership admitted that their organization had "not developed into a revolutionary mass party" of the working class and, in fact, remained "isolated from the most important sections of the American proletariat."[18]

The problem was two-fold. The older membership of the Party was very heavily dominated by first-generation immigrants who related primarily to foreign-language fraternal, social, and political activities, not to the programs that were in theory the main focus of the Party. Though heavily working class, these members commonly avoided politics at their places of work, often refusing to even join existing trade unions or CP shop groups. On the other hand, the younger, native-born Americans who began joining the Party in large numbers in the early 1930s were recruited mostly through unemployment activities and had little contact with factories. Thus four years into the Depression, the party of the working class found itself with very few members actually working in major industrial establishments, and only a small percentage of those so situated participating in on-the-job political activity.[19]

To break out of this isolation from employed workers, particularly in basic industry, the CP developed a strategy of "concentration." Instead of recruiting members and engaging in political work wherever the Party happened to be already established, key geographic regions, industries, and factories were chosen and organizational efforts focused on these "concentration points." The Extraordinary Conference and the "Open Letter" issued at its conclusion were designed to be dramatic and forceful measures to ensure that unlike in previous industrialization campaigns, a reorientation of activity would actually take place.[20]

In a speech at the Extraordinary Conference, New York District Organizer Charles Krumbein laid out the priorities for New York City:

> Marine *first and foremost* . . . . Next metal [and then] railroad . . . . Another point we should consider for concentration is city transport. Transport in all big cities plays a very important political role. I think it is a field that we must concentrate on. We have nothing yet. In addition . . . we can use the election campaign that we are now entering to put forward the proper issues, connecting the question of low fare, as it affects workers generally, with the conditions of transport workers.[21]

As Krumbein made clear, from the very start the Party concentrated on urban transit in part because the industry was both a major employer and a major service supplier to the working class as a whole. Furthermore, the terms of service—most importantly the fare—were regulated by local government agencies. The possibility therefore existed for linking transit trade union struggles with political struggles over the general working-class standard of living (the fare). Both in turn could be tied to Party electoral strategy. This linkage was an important factor throughout the history of the TWU, especially once the City took over the private subways and els. It also turned out to be a two-edged sword; fifteen years after Krumbein's speech it played a significant role in the Party's ouster from the leadership of the union it had helped to build.

Following the July 1933 Conference, several sections of the New York City CP began concentration work in transit. Louis Sass, Harlem Organization Secretary of the Party, later described the initial activity in his section:

> . . . we first carefully selected seven comrades, all new Party members, who are American workers, and formed them into a concentration unit. . . . We had a favorable start. A worker in the _____ shop of the transport system called up the *Daily Worker* and gave some information about conditions in the shop. We immediately contacted the worker, who was somewhat sympathetic to the Party. Through him we began to build a small group, to be the organizational committee for the union. We had a difficult time at first, for the men in the shop

> had been disappointed time and again by the A.F. of L. They had the company
> union, of course, and believed that all unions are detrimental rather than helpful
> to the workers. The first thing we had to convince them of was that our main
> interest is to protect their jobs by careful organizational methods. . . .[22]

Neither the head of the Harlem unit nor all of its members were, strictly speaking, "American workers," as Sass claimed. Its leader, Mike Walsh, was, in the words
of another Harlem Communist, a "synthetic Irishman." A Finnish CP functionary,
whose real name was Michael Wasdiller, Walsh "looked like a big, red-faced Irishman" and did nothing to discourage the impression. Nor did he discourage the idea
that he was a transit worker.[23] The other members of the unit were unpaid volunteers, including Maurice Forge, who was to play an important role in the TWU.

The Harlem group focused its activity on the two major IRT repair facilities, the
148th Street and 98th Street shops. The work was slow and required considerable
dedication. Leaflets and other literature would be distributed outside shop gates, and
workers would be approached during their lunch break. The main aim was to come
up with the names of men who might be interested in a union. These were followed
up with home visits. Forge remembers these visits as extremely difficult and unpleas-
ant. Meeting with workers in the kitchens of their cramped apartments, with the rest
of the family listening in, the question of a union would be discussed, but with a
careful, almost tortuous, vagueness. The enormous fear workers typically had was
frequently reinforced by glances of disapproval from their wives. Although over time
this approach was to yield key recruits, who then began to agitate and sign up
members inside the shops, it was tedious, depressing work.[24]

In the central Bronx, CP section 15 undertook a similar campaign, concentrating
on the IRT 180th Street repair shop, a smaller facility employing some 150 workers,
mostly Italian or Irish. At first, the concentration unit that was formed "failed
completely."[25] However, after it was thoroughly reorganized "a number of good
contacts" were made, and by late March 1934 a few IRT workers had been recruited
into the Party. John Santo, the Party organizer for section 15, was given the job of
coordinating the CP's transit work throughout the city, with other concentration
groups targeting a variety of facilities.[26]

The concentration approach took time to yield results. In the meantime, the
Party turned to existing contacts in the industry. The first group of transit workers
Santo met with to discuss forming a union were some two dozen men assembled by
IRT painters Joseph Sponza and Herbert Holmstrom. Sponza was an Italian immigrant who had been involved in radical activities in both his native land and the
United States. He was a member of the CP, attached to a Harlem unit that had no
particular transit orientation. Although his Italian background was somewhat unusual among Party members during this period, in many ways he was typical of what
had long been the mass base of the Party: an immigrant worker, deeply immersed in
a radical ethnic subculture, less confident and able in English than his native
tongue, prone to sectarianism and revolutionary jargon. Still, along with his co-
worker Holmstrom, a Swedish-American who had been with the IRT for over five
years, he provided the Party with a starting point.[27]

Similarly, the first meeting Santo held with BMT workers was arranged by William

Zuidema, a conductor of Dutch-Jewish descent. By his own account, Zuidema had been part of a small group of BMT workers, at first only three, who had been leafleting and agitating since early 1933. Apparently Zuidema had been involved with the CP for some time; his group was probably the "BMT Workers Group" written up in the *Daily Worker*.[28]

In November 1933 the Party reported that its organizers had developed "a group of about 40 workers [interested in a union] . . . four groups with some [CP] units concentrating on some of these shops."[29] Late that month ten workers met as The Committee for the Organization of a Transport Workers' Union and unanimously passed a motion that the Committee would become a union on February 1.[30] In December the first issue of the *Transport Workers Bulletin*, a small, four-page tabloid, was issued in the name of the Committee. Attacking the BMT and IRT company unions, and the AFL, the paper announced that a number of depot and shop committees had been established and called on workers to form more such groups. A five-point program was put forth:

1. Return of the 10% wage cut
2. Increased wage to meet the rising cost of living
3. Abolishment of speed-up system and lay-offs
4. Recognition of shop and depot committees
5. Recognition of the Transport Workers' Union[31]

Although the Party continued to pore over its membership lists and those of Party-oriented fraternal groups, such as the International Workers Order (IWO), in search of transit workers already in the Communist orbit, it was not depending on such contacts alone to form the core of the new union.[32] The whole point of the concentration approach was to throw out a broad net and bring into the drive sympathetic workers not previously known to the organizing groups. This was especially important since, based on the scant available evidence, it appears that the early Party contacts were not very representative of either the ethnic or occupational structure of the industry.

Communist organizers realized early on that if the union drive was to make significant progress, it would have to win support in the numerically dominant Irish sector of the work force. Special measures were taken for that purpose. The very choice of the proposed name for the new union, for example, was apparently made with an eye toward the Irish. The word "transport" is rarely used in the United States in connection with the transit industry, but it is the standard term in both Ireland and England. Furthermore, the chosen name was strikingly similar to that of Jim Larkin's and James Connolly's Dublin-based Irish Transport and General Workers Union.[33]

It was not the Party, however, that in the end directly recruited the mass of Irish workers into the TWU. Rather, it was a group of Irish transit men who independently of the CP had begun to explore forming a union, and who in early 1934 joined forces with the CP-led drive. These were the republican transit workers centered in the Clan na Gael. It was they who provided the nascent union drive with an established, competent Irish leadership, able to bridge the gap between the

Party and the Irish work force and to provide the union with an entrance into the world of Irish transit workers. The alliance between the CP and these republicans was one of the most important factors in the eventual success of the organizing drive, and it helped shaped the character of the union that finally emerged.

The transit workers in the Clan na Gael, like transit workers in general, were dissatisfied with their jobs. Most had been in America long enough to be no longer content with simply having work. As one Irish transit worker wrote to the *Daily Worker,* at first "we wouldn't admit we were fooled" by the promise of a better life in America. Now, he went on, Irish workers were beginning to admit to both themselves and to newer immigrants that the United States had many of the same problems that they thought they had left behind. "There are no more greenhorns here." Furthermore, many of the Clan men were at an age when they had just begun or were planning to begin families. In spite of the seniority they had begun to accumulate, they saw no hope for a decent standard of living.[34]

Two things distinguished the Clan men from most Irish transit workers. First, many of them had fought with the IRA against the Free State government, and in some cases before that against the British. They were tough men, men who had "gone through hell" together in Ireland. Having faced imprisonment, injury, or death, the beakies and the transit managers simply did not inspire the same fear in them that they did in others. Second, the Clan men reacted to their situation not as individuals, but as part of an organized movement.[35]

Sometime in 1933 a group of Clan transit men, mostly from the IRT, began discussing the possibility of forming a union. Among those involved in these discussions and later active in the TWU were Thomas O'Shea, Mike Quill, Gerald O'Reilly, Michael Lynch, Connie Lynch, Patrick Cunnane, Michael Clune, Patrick McCue, Jimmy Hughes, and Jack Teahan.[36] O'Shea, Quill, and O'Reilly were typical of the group. Born in rural areas of Ireland near the turn of the century, they served as young men with the IRA during the civil war years. Their work experience in Ireland had been extremely limited. In the United States they were employed only briefly elsewhere before settling down on the IRT, Quill as a ticket agent, O'Reilly as a conductor, and O'Shea as a turnstile mechanic.[37]

The Clan men soon began meeting regularly to explore the idea of a union and possible paths of action. They even approached some non-Clan workers with their thoughts and invited a few to join them.[38] These meetings may have been what Quill was referring to in his 1940 Congressional testimony when he said that he was first connected with the TWU in May 1933: "We formed a small group. It wasn't a union at the time. We didn't even name it."[39] In the minds of Quill, O'Reilly, and some others, this was the real origin of the TWU.

Past personal experience with labor organizations was not a primary factor in the Clan group's turn toward unionism. In fact, as far as can be ascertained, none of the Clan transit men had ever been a member of a trade union. A few non-transit Clan members had been in unions in Ireland, but even their experience had been quite limited.[40] Some transit workers in the Clan had had peripheral contact with unions in the United States. Quill, for example, at one point quit his job as a ticket agent— "It was a hell of a place to put a farmer's son—behind the bars of a cage," he later explained—and went off to sell religious pictures to steel and coal workers in western

Pennsylvania. "The miserable conditions there were the worst I have ever seen, and it was there I learned about unions.[41]

More important than such indirect interactions, however, were the ideas the Clan men had been exposed to in the republican movement. The Clan, like the IRA, included men with a range of social and political views. Members of both groups believed that the current Irish government was illegitimate and that true independence would be achieved only with the establishment of a thirty-two county Republic, completely free of British ties. For some, this was the full extent of their political agenda. Most republicans, like most Irish in general, were not radical in their social views and were anti-communist. The republican movement, however, had always had a progressive wing, in the 1930s represented in Ireland by men like Paedar O'Donnell, George Gilmore, and Frank Ryan. These left republicans saw themselves as the heirs of James Connolly and the combination of Irish nationalism, international socialism, and militant industrial unionism that he had preached and died for. Although this progressive tendency formed only a minority within the IRA, through the early 1930s it was tolerated by the organization as a whole. In fact, partially in response to the same world-wide Depression that led to the emergence of the TWU, left republicanism achieved its greatest influence in Ireland just as the New York transit organizing was beginning.[42]

In the New York Clan na Gael, the left variant of republicanism was proportionately stronger than in the IRA itself, a situation not uncommon among exile nationalist groups. Many of the transit workers in the Clan embraced this world view. Some had developed progressive views while still in Ireland. Gerald O'Reilly, for example, credits his reading of Connolly after joining the IRA and the impact of the Sacco and Vanzetti and Tom Mooney cases, which were widely publicized in Ireland, for his radicalization.[43] Others, like Quill, developed broadly progressive views only after they had come to America, probably in part as a result of their contact with left-wingers in the Clan.[44] In any case, through left republicanism, and particularly the writings of Connolly, the idea of unionism, and especially industrial unionism, was familiar and attractive to many of the republican transit workers, in spite of their own rural, non-union backgrounds.

Of course, the same forces that had given rise to the other transit "discontent groups" were also affecting the Clan men: harsh and deteriorating conditions, the beginning of the New Deal, and the growing national interest in unionism.[45] What distinguished this group from the others was its size, its representation in a variety of occupational sectors, particularly within the IRT, and its extensive contacts with other transit men. IRA veterans and Clan members had special status within the Irish community; they were an important and respected element, looked up to especially by the recent immigrants who were so heavily represented in transit. Furthermore, the Clan men collectively had a rich body of political and organizational, if not actual union, experience. Nonetheless, they too were but a relatively small group and lacked a clear sense of how to further their ambitions, how to turn their own discontent and the discontent they perceived around them into a coherent, effective movement.

Sometime in 1933 the Clan men began to look for help. To do so was a sober and realistic assessment of the difficulties ahead and their own limited resources.[46]

According to Gerald O'Reilly, they first approached two mainstream Irish fraternal groups, the Hibernians and the Friendly Sons of St. Patrick. Both organizations refused to get involved, and the latter, a businessmen-dominated group, "nearly hit the ceiling" since IRT General Manager George Keegan was at the time first vice president of the Sons. Turning to less familiar territory, the Clan men approached a civil liberties group which, although sympathetic, could not help. Finally, "it was recommended we go to the Communist Party."[47]

As O'Reilly recalls it, a delegation of Clan men, including himself and Quill, approached the Communist Party, which arranged several meetings for them with CP National Chairman William Z. Foster, New York State CP leaders Israel Amter and Rose Wortis, and other Party officials. The inclusion of Foster was probably dictated by the importance the Party attached to the meetings and the fact that he was one of the few Communist leaders from an Irish-American background.[48]

Foster and Amter questioned the Clan men at length about their plans, trying to make sure that they understood the difficulties and dangers involved. Amter pointed out the history of transit union failure and cautioned them that as non-citizens they faced not only the loss of jobs, but potentially immigration problems as well. After a couple of meetings, however, the CP leaders agreed to give full support to the Clan group's efforts.

Mike Quill once gave a slightly different, though not incompatible, account of how the first CP-Clan contact was established. According to his story, he had begun discussing the possibility of organizing a union with some men at the 148th Street shop when the CP sent an emissary to him in March 1934, inviting him to join forces with their effort.[49] Whatever the case, what is important is that the CP-Clan meetings almost certainly took place after both groups had independently begun organizing. It is therefore not surprising that they found one another. Moreover, there was already a channel for contact between the groups, the CP-sponsored Irish Workers Clubs (IWC).

In the years before 1933, the CP had had very little success in recruiting the so-called old immigrants, including the Irish. In an effort to build support among the latter group, in 1932 the Party began setting up a number of Irish Workers Clubs in New York and other cities. Although sponsored and led by Party members, the clubs were not themselves Party branches. However, their revolutionary character was quite open; invoking the name and language of Connolly they aimed to both organize the Irish in America around domestic social and political questions and to support the "struggle of the Irish people for complete liberation from the British empire, and the establishment of an Irish Workers' and Farmers' Republic." The clubs were small, and on several occasions there were complaints that the CP paid too little attention to Irish-American affairs, but they did succeed in conducting a variety of cultural, athletic, social, educational, and political activities.[50]

The establishment of the IWC coincided with and was linked to a revival of Communist activity in Ireland itself, part of a general left upsurge inside and outside of the IRA. In June 1933, after years of preparation, the Communist Party of Ireland (CPI) was founded, the last major European CP to be established.[51] In New York the IWC distributed the CPI newspaper, and in the spring of 1934 the secretary of the Irish Party, Sean Murray, toured the United States, helping to publicize the

IWC and complaining to his American counterparts that "work among the Irish masses is a weakest spot of the Communist Party," a criticism with which CP General Secretary Earl Browder agreed. [52] Jim Gralton, an Irish Communist who had lived in the U.S. in the 1920s, and who was deported back to the States by the Irish government in 1933, became a moving force behind the IWC and in the CP's Irish-oriented activities. [53] Thus at the very moment that the CP was beginning its transit work, it was also making its most serious effort yet to recruit Irish immigrants and Irish-Americans by linking the struggle in the United States to the struggle in Ireland, and the fight for an independent Irish Republic with the fight for a workers' state. With some justice, the CP could claim that it was fighting for "Connolly's Republic, the Republic of the Working Class of Ireland and America." [54]

In Ireland the IRA forbid its members from joining the CPI, but in New York some veteran IRA men joined the IWC, which quickly became a meeting ground for left republicans and radicals. [55] Thus when Clan transit worker Tom O'Shea ran into Charles McGinnity, whom he had known in Liverpool through the IRA, McGinnity told him about the IWC. When O'Shea mentioned his interest in forming a union of transit workers, McGinnity informed him that there already was a group organizing in the industry and arranged for members of the Bronx CP concentration group, led by Party-cadre Peter Starr, to visit O'Shea at his home. O'Shea, who later claimed that he did not realize at the time that this group was connected with the CP, then set up a meeting for it with five or six men from the IRT 179th Street elevated inspection barn who were interested in a union. [56]

According to O'Shea, this first meeting was a failure, since the concentration group consisted "mainly of Jewish fellows, and the union group . . . mainly of Irish. As you know, the Irish are extremely nationalistic." O'Shea raised this issue with Starr, who arranged for him to discuss it with Santo. Accompanied by two other transit workers, one a former CP member, O'Shea recommended to Santo that the unionizing effort use men from the IWC. Several weeks later, O'Shea and four or five others from the industry met with members of the Bronx concentration group and Santo. With Santo was Austin Hogan, an IWC leader whom O'Shea had known five or six years earlier, and who from this point on took an active role in leading the transit work.

By the early spring of 1934, through the Clan, the IWC, and perhaps other channels, the network of republican transit workers and the leaders of the Communist transit drive had come to know one another and join forces. With the addition of the republicans to the early CP contacts and the growing number of individuals recruited though the concentration work, the Party felt confident enough to actually establish a union. According to later official and semi-official accounts, the TWU was founded on April 12, 1934, in a Columbus Circle restaurant. Among the seven men present were Santo, Quill, O'Shea, Hogan, and Douglas MacMahon, a machinist's helper from the IRT lighting department. Santo was made general secretary of the union. At the time, according to O'Shea, the organizing group had about one hundred members. [57]

The attribution of the founding of the TWU to this meeting served several important functions both at the time and later. A mythology was needed for the union's worker-activists and for the industry rank and file which disguised the origin of the union in a decision made by the Communist Party and placed it in the hands of a more representative group; a mythology that accorded the prestige and legitimacy of union founder to the chosen leadership and linked together the insiders and outsiders as co-equal originators of the TWU. Furthermore, a story was needed that was more self-contained and easier to explain than the reality.[58]

Although it is possible, even probable, that such a meeting did take place, the process of "founding" the union in an historically meaningful sense was a more diffuse, more extended, less dramatic affair. By early 1934 Party-led groups of organizers and transit workers were simultaneously meeting in a variety of locations. For security reasons, the groups were kept separate. Although those involved knew of the existence of other groups and the names of some of the more important participants, at first probably only Santo was in touch with all of the activity. Then an informal organizing committee was formed, and later a formal group, a delegates council with representatives from the various companies and work sites. As Maurice Forge put it, "when we finally came together, each one of us was an old-timer. . . . What happened was that the outsiders began to meet the insiders, and willy-nilly an organization was formed."[59] The formal founding of the TWU was simply the declaration that the organizing network was now a union.

In April and May thousands of leaflets and copies of the *Transport Workers Bulletin* were distributed announcing the formation of the TWU.[60] The new union declared that it aimed:

> . . . to *safeguard, protect and improve* the working conditions and living standards of *all* transport workers regardless of race, color, nationality, or political views or affiliations—based firmly on the principle of industrial unionism and militant struggle and against company and craft unionism.[61]

In the third issue of the *Bulletin*, put out that May in a press run of 8,000, the new social amalgam that had been midwife to the union's birth, and now formed much of its core, was tacitly acknowledged when the IRT motormen demanded that "men not . . . be discriminated against when they take off special holidays such as May 1, St. Patrick's Day, etc."[62]

In the spring of 1934 the TWU was in its infancy, barely a thing at all. Yet, many of the features that were to long characterize the union were already present, including its top leadership. The four men who were to collectively lead the TWU from 1935 through 1948—Santo, Hogan, Quill, and MacMahon—had all been present at the "founding" restaurant meeting. Others who were to play key roles over a prolonged period were also already deeply involved with the union. These men, the union leadership, came to the TWU from two sources, the Communist Party and the industry itself.

In the early days, the dominant figure, without question, was John Santo. Born Desideriu Hammer in 1908 in Timisorara, an industrial city in the Banat district of Hungary (now part of Rumania), Santo began work at age twelve on the night shift of a shoe factory following his father's death from World War I wounds. Although Jewish, Santo attended a high school run by Benedictine Fathers, and he became active in the left-wing Hungarian student movement. In 1927 he came to America on a student visa, under the sponsorship of an uncle in Gary, Indiana, to study engineering at a Chicago technical institute. When his uncle lost his job, Santo quit school and moved to Gary, working first in an auto factory and then as a machinist's helper.[63]

In 1928 Santo was recruited into the Communist Party by Lajo (Louis) Bebrits, an editor of the Party's Hungarian-language newspaper, *Uj Elore*. After working on the Cleveland-based paper and in other Party activities in Ohio, Santo was assigned in 1933 as CP section organizer for the middle Bronx. Under his leadership the section, with close to 500 members, undertook a variety of neighborhood and trade union organizing projects.[64] From 1934 on, although he retained some internal Party responsibilities,[65] Santo's main job was organizing and leading the TWU.

Santo was very much an orthodox Communist. Once, when he found a book by Trotsky on Maurice Forge's bookshelves, he was genuinely appalled. Later, in moments of doubt, he would read and re-read his copy of Karl Radek's testimony at the Moscow trials, which became, in his own words, "my talisman, my defense against all evils of possible deviation from the party line."[66]

In the early years, Santo's central role in the TWU, although publicly acknowledged, may have been more obvious to key activists than to the rank and file. To some extent he remained in the background, concentrating on organizational work and small meetings, rather than public agitation. His lingering Hungarian accent and origins outside the industry served to demarcate him from the mass of workers. (Later on, Santo, like some other non-Irish associated with the TWU, developed something of an Irish brogue.) But initially it was Santo who was the clear leader of the union drive and for a short while even the formal head of the union. It was he who coordinated the various elements of the emerging union, who knew of the full range of activity, who pulled in key local leaders. And it was Santo who was the liaison between the CP and the union, and the main Party representative inside the TWU.[67] For all this, in later years some would publicly laud him as the father of the union.[68]

Although transport had been a concentration target of the CP since June 1933, the transit lines had not been given a high priority in the assignment of Party personnel. The Committee for the Organization of a Transport Workers' Union, and later the TWU itself, had ties to the Trade Union Unity Council, the central New York organization of the Communist-led Trade Union Unity League (TUUL). (This association was never made public in the belief that it would discourage workers, especially Irish ones, from joining the union.)[69] However, in early 1934 it was not transit but the taxi industry that was getting the attention of the TUUL and the CP. There were taxi strikes in New York in February and March of that year, and when the initials TWU appeared in the *Daily Worker* they referred not to the nascent transit group, but to the Party-led Taxi Workers Union.[70]

On May 1 a bitter article appeared in the *Daily Worker* by "the secretary of the B.M.T. section of the Transport Workers' Union." It complained that TUUC organizers were pulled out of transit to work on the taxi strikes or in less important light industries:

> In its relation with subway workers, the T.U.U.C., to be fair, has consistently acted the same policy. Organizers would be assigned and then when they became acquainted with the workers they would be withdrawn and replaced by new organizers, who in due time would also be withdrawn. . . . If this will be the method the comrades use to prove they are the vanguard of the working class, then there can be no serious disagreement with them, except they'll be the vanguard of the rear end.[71]

Apparently as a result of such complaints, the progress being made, and its contacts with the Irish republicans, the CP moved to establish a small, stable group to handle the transit drive. At its core were three Party members who worked full-time organizing the TWU: Santo, who remained in overall charge; Austin Hogan, who did general organizing and provided rapport with the Irish workers; and Maurice Forge, who assisted in organizing and took charge of the union's propaganda.[72]

Hogan, like Santo, had never worked in transit, but his background enabled him to fit more easily into the world of the Irish transit workers, to be less obviously an outsider. He was born Austin Dilloughery in Ennistymon, Ireland in 1906.[73] His family came from County Clare, but his father, a constable with the Royal Irish Constabulary (RIC), was stationed in Cork City, where most of Hogan's youth was spent. The RIC was the first centralized, national Irish police force, recruited from among the peasantry. Before World War I it was not particularly associated with pro-British sympathies, since most of its work consisted of enforcing minor regulations and taking care of drunks. A job with the RIC, however, put a man "a 'cut above' the farmers" and in a better position to educate his children. Hogan's family was able to send him to a Catholic Church-run monastery school, and then to a technical institute, where he studied civil engineering.

The outbreak of World War I and the growth of anti-British sentiment brought a change in the status of the RIC. The British assigned the constables to watch over what were deemed subversive elements and to use their familiarity with the local population to point out those who were likely to be involved in the independence movement. As a result, according to Paul O'Dwyer, "by and large, they were a hated group."[74] As the situation became increasingly polarized, some RIC members quit, but Hogan's father, with a large family and considerable seniority, remained. (According to one Irish transit worker, some TWU members later held this against Hogan.)[75]

With their untypically high levels of education, and in spite of, or perhaps because of, their fathers' role, it was not unusual for children of RIC members to become active in the republican cause. Two of Hogan's older brothers were in the IRA, while Hogan himself, too young to be a combatant, joined Fianna Eireann, the Republican Boy Scout movement organized in 1909 by Countess Markievicz, which served as the youth wing of the republicans.

In 1925 Hogan emigrated to New York, where for the next three years he studied engineering at Cooper Union. Of all those active in the TWU, Hogan had by far the most formal education. At the time the TWU was beginning, Hogan was working on the engineering plans for the Whitestone Bridge.

During a visit to Ireland in 1932, Hogan read for the first time the writings of James Connolly, which profoundly affected him. He later recalled that although even as a child he had hoped to fight against the conditions he saw around him, it was not until he read Connolly that he "was swept into a complete understanding of what all this oppression and suffering was caused by."[76] On returning to the United States he became active in the IWC, serving on occasion as its spokesman and even singing traditional Irish songs at a farewell party for Sean Murray.[77] He also joined the Communist Party and in 1934 was its candidate in a Bronx Congressional race.[78] It was during this period, when he was simultaneously working as an engineer and active in Communist politics, that Hogan changed his name.[79]

In convincing Hogan to give up his engineering career for the chancy enterprise of the TWU, Party leaders made a good choice. A competent organizer and good speaker, he had a familiarity with and access to the world of recent Irish immigrants that was extremely unusual in Party circles. Hogan became very popular among Irish transit workers. Many, particularly on the left, looked up to him as their leader and even as a father figure, although he was no older than the typical TWU activist. Hogan was also a loyal Party member, tending to closely follow Santo's lead on union and political issues.[80]

Maurice Forge was initially involved in the transit work as a volunteer in the Harlem concentration unit. Louis Sass had met Forge through the TUUL Food Workers Industrial Union, in which Forge was active. At the time he was working as a steward in a small private club, having lost his job with an advertising agency at the beginning of the Depression. When the transit drive began to make some progress, Santo asked Forge to join the union's informal organizing committee. Somewhat later a committee of leading TWU activists convinced Forge to work full-time for the union.

Forge participated in all phases of the TWU, but his main responsibility was propaganda. Competent and experienced as a writer, photographer, and graphic designer, he became the editor of the *Transport Workers Bulletin* and produced a virtual flood of leaflets, pamphlets, speeches, and picket signs. A short, energetic man, self-described as an "eager-beaver" and a "Jimmy Higgins," Forge took on many of the miscellaneous tasks that the top leaders had neither the time nor inclination to tackle. Although Polish-born (he was half Jewish), Forge was one of the most "Americanized" and cosmopolitan of the union's leaders, and after overcoming a speech impediment he became a forceful orator.[81]

The fact that Santo, Hogan, and Forge had not worked in the industry was not a serious disadvantage in their dealings with workers, with the possible exception of Santo, whose "extreme prominence . . . and marked foreignness" may have caused some resentment. Other Communists who were not transit workers were occasionally brought into the TWU as well. Also, during the first year of organizing, Mike Walsh, Peter Starr, and other members of the CP concentration groups continued to be active in the union drive. However, after 1937 few outsiders were given TWU jobs, and those who were were almost never assigned to posts in the New York region. Of the Communists from outside the industry, only Santo, Hogan, and Forge were truly central over an extended time period.[82]

The rest of the TWU leadership came from the ranks of the work force. Within months of the beginning of the organizing drive, many local leaders emerged. From among them a few were singled out for top roles. Presence at the "founding" meeting was one sign of this special status.

Douglas Lincoln MacMahon was a very early participant in the transit drive and was picked out almost from the start for the leadership. His background was not untypical of CIO leaders, but extremely unusual among transit workers; he was an aspiring petit bourgeois, forced into the working class by the Great Depression.[83] MacMahon was the only child of a real estate salesman. His family descended from early American settlers. They had lived in the Bay Ridge section of Brooklyn for generations and were devout Methodists; MacMahon's grandparents had been missionaries in India. Although raised in a household which stressed doing good, MacMahon's own aspirations were not spiritual; after finishing high school he took a job as a Wall Street board boy as the first step toward what he hoped would be a career as a stockbroker. With the 1929 crash, he lost his post and went to work in Brooklyn for the IRT in a variety of low-skilled maintenance jobs.[84]

According to Forge, MacMahon was extremely unhappy in this new, diminished status. "What drove him to the union, I think, was his personal unhappiness that he, the great Douglas MacMahon, would have to go around in a rat-hole there ten hours a day screwing [light] bulbs." What transformed this stymied personal ambition into a role and then a career as a labor leader was that MacMahon, like so many others who were to lead CIO unions, tried to understand his discontent, his fate and future, in terms that encompassed the fate and future of his fellow workers as well as of himself. He began reading anti-capitalist literature and, at some point, joined the Socialist Party. He also became active in the IRT Brotherhood. When the CP started its transit drive, MacMahon almost immediately joined the nascent union.

MacMahon was a natural leader, self-assured, able, intelligent, with the special status of "a white collar guy who came from Wall Street and talked much better and clearer than any of his fellow workers." However, his Socialist ties soon led to a falling out with key TWU organizers; after attending the "founding" meeting his role in the union diminished. Slowly, though, he drifted further left, finally joining the CP. At that point he was again given major union responsibilities. As Forge summed it up, "he was declassed into the subways and he emerged as one of the leaders."[85]

MacMahon was the most dramatic example in the TWU of the Depression-forged combination of acquisitive individualism and egalitarian ideology that appears repeatedly in the biographies of American industrial union leaders. In a broad sense Hogan, Forge, and even Santo embodied this same historical process. All four had been upwardly mobile, goal-oriented young men, with aspirations not limited to the status into which they had been born. Each had come to embrace a radical political vision as a result (except in the case of Santo) of the personal and general effects of the Depression.

The adoption by these four men of a commitment to the working class and its economic and political uplifting did not erase the character structures, world views, or latent possibilities that came before, a fact illustrated by their post-TWU careers.[86] Rather, their original orientation toward individual betterment, and the traits and abilities that made their success likely, were fused with a new ideological outlook. Simultaneously, the arena of their activity shifted, from private career-building to the TWU (and to a lesser extent the CP and the American Labor Party). While they genuinely had a deep concern for the condition and fate of the transit workers who joined them in creating the TWU, they nonetheless remained in no way typical of their co-unionists and followers.

Hogan, Forge, and MacMahon also represented types who were just beginning to enter the CP in significant numbers, but would soon play major roles within it. If Joseph Sponza symbolized the Party's past, Forge, Hogan, and especially MacMahon represented its future (and Santo its continuity). Ironically, in the early days of the TWU, MacMahon and Sponza were in the same small section of the union, IRT maintenance-of-way. Perhaps not surprisingly, they did not get along well; MacMahon found Sponza's revolutionary rhetoric and sectarian manner a constant irritant.[87]

MacMahon's leadership derived in part from his exceptionality. Mike Quill and Tom O'Shea, on the other hand, first became leaders largely because of what was typical about them, their origins and ease amidst the mass of unskilled and semi-skilled Irish.

Thomas Humphrey O'Shea was somewhat older than the other early leaders of the TWU, having been born in Cobh, Ireland in 1897. Between 1917 and 1924 he was active in the IRA, using his knowledge of explosives to help blow up police stations. He came to the United States in 1927 and, within a few years, took a job as a turnstile mechanic with the IRT.[88] O'Shea was one of the more prominent transit workers in the Clan na Gael, one of the first to discuss forming a union, and among the first to have contact with the CP organizers. A "great talker" and a well-known figure, he provided the union with an entrance to the Irish, among whom in its earliest phase the transit drive had made little headway. O'Shea moved rapidly into the TWU's forming leadership circle, solidifying his position by joining the Communist Party around May 1934.[89]

Michael J. Quill was the seventh of eight children of John and Margaret Quill. He was born on September 18, 1905, on a mountain farm, Gourtloughera, three miles from the town of Kilgarvan in County Kerry—an isolated area in a poor, undeveloped section of western Ireland. The Quills were Gaelic-speaking farmers. Their farm was a substantial 118 acres, but the land was extremely poor, so that while the Quills were not at the bottom of the Irish rural hierarchy, tenants or day laborers, they were also far from the top. In addition to farming, John Quill engaged in butter-making and farm marketing, buying milk and crops from other farmers and serving as a middleman in their resale, an activity that brought the family into a broader circle of contacts than a mountain farmer alone might usually encounter. Mike attended the local National School until the normal leaving age of fourteen. He had little interest in formal education, though like his father and sister, who was a schoolteacher, he was an avid reader.[90]

The Quill family, including various collateral branches, was deeply involved in the republican movement. Mike's father, who by World War I was already an older man, was a movement sympathizer and respected local figure with whom republican leaders often consulted. Mike's elder brothers were active combatants. Because the Quill farm was isolated and commanded a view of the surrounding region, it was used as the general headquarters of the local battalion of the Irish Volunteers during the anti-British struggle. In addition, important national republican leaders on the run would from time to time stay there. When the civil war broke out, the Quill family continued to aid the republican cause, as IRA members and by allowing the farm to be used as a republican center. As a result, the household was continually raided by the Free State forces; at various times John Quill and several of his children (not including Mike) were arrested and jailed. [91]

Later on there were many conflicting stories about Mike's role in the republican struggle, but there is no question that he was at least somewhat involved in the fight. Like Hogan, he was member of Fianna Eireann, the Republican Boy Scouts, and, according to Quill's 1940 Congressional testimony, in November 1920, at the age of fifteen, he transferred to active service in the IRA itself. He served until July 1921 and again during the civil war in 1922 and 1923. Quill occasionally embellished this record during his TWU years, and it was widely, though falsely, believed that his bad hip was the result of a Black and Tan bullet. [92]

Quill emigrated to America in 1926; there were few jobs and few prospects in his native area, and his family's well-known association with the republican cause further diminished the likelihood of employment. By then many of his relatives, including a brother, were already in New York. Some of them, including his father's cousin, Patrick Quill, an IRT conductor who had lost his seniority for striking in 1916, helped pay his way over. [93]

In New York, Quill worked a rapid succession of manual jobs: digging ditches for gas pipes, helping dig the 168th Street station of the ISS, working as an exterminator, and feeding a hotel boiler. Late in 1926 he got a job as a gate man with the IRT for 27 cents an hour, after signing a yellow dog contract and joining the Brotherhood as required. Within a year or so he became a ticket agent, but after a couple of months left to sell religious articles in western Pennsylvania. He came back to the IRT, again as an agent, in the spring of 1930. In 1932 he took a leave of absence to travel to Vienna for an operation on his hip, returning thereafter to his old job. [94]

Mike Quill was a remarkably energetic and sociable man, and in New York he plunged into the world of Irish fraternal and social activities. Eventually he began to emcee the dances of the County Kerry society to which he belonged. With his outgoing personality, extraordinary wit, and ability to put others to ease, he was so successful in making sure that everyone had a good time that all the Irish organizations were soon after him to run their affairs. As a result, he became widely known in the Irish community. Through his job and social activities, Quill came to know hundreds of Irish transit workers, which later proved an invaluable resource. Quill's social activities also brought him into contact with the Clan na Gael.

In Ireland, Quill had been a staunch supporter of the republicans, but on narrow, nationalist grounds. At that point he did not have broader social views, and in the U.S. he did not immediately get involved with groups such as the Clan or the IWC. But when Clan members were trying to ensure the success of their weekly Saturday night dances, they asked Quill to act as emcee, to which he agreed. Through this he came to join the Clan and develop a more generally progressive outlook. Unlike many night-shift ticket agents, who would sleep when things got quiet, Quill began to use the time to read, especially the writings of Connolly and Jim Larkin.

Quill was not a leader of the Clan na Gael. In fact, among transit workers alone, Tom O'Shea, Jack Teahan, and Connie Lynch all were more active and important in the organization. Quill rather was seen as a very useful, well-liked fellow, if perhaps somewhat less serious of purpose than the more political and involved core of the Clan. He was, however, part of the original Clan group that discussed forming a union, and he participated in the talks with the CP that led to a joining of forces.[95]

It was in the world of the TWU that Mike Quill came into his own. Like O'Shea, he provided the organizing drive with access to the crucial Irish bloc, particularly among the ticket agents. Soon Quill was devoting most of his time to the union, eventually sleeping nearly every night on a cot in the union hall. He quickly became part of the union's inner circle and moved into the Communist orbit, attending meetings of Party members, joining the IWC, and probably becoming a member of the Party itself.[96]

Quill's organizing and oratorical skills were considerable, his style intensely personal and highly theatric. According to Len De Caux, the chief CIO publicist, Quill was the "one other CIO leader who had much of [John L.] Lewis' crowd appeal."[97] Perhaps his most potent weapon was his ability to ridicule those in authority, using the gift of gab to shatter psychological and social structures of deference. He also had all the skills of a Tammany politician—remembering names, telling anecdotes, having a drink with the boys. As a result, Quill was better able to bridge the gap between the union and the mass of relatively apolitical and conservative Irish workers than those republicans more ascetic in manner, more acclimated to operating within small, semi-clandestine milieux, or more dogmatically devoted to Irish or Communist causes.

Mike Quill was a complex man, not the simple, humorous extrovert he at first appeared to be. At times he was prone to moodiness, and beneath the genial exterior was a master schemer. He was a committed left republican and a popular demagogue, deeply democratic and personally ambitious, a man of considerable moral vision but inordinately flexible and sometimes ruthless in his tactics. Perhaps it was these very contradictions that enabled Quill to thrive in, and eventually dominate, the complex social mix of the TWU.

In the spring of 1934, Quill, MacMahon, and O'Shea were still but three of the most active members of the TWU, holding no formal positions. However, by then it was already clear that they were unusually talented and effective. Over the next months, they emerged as the leading worker-members of the union and soon filled top union posts, O'Shea for but a brief period, MacMahon (with an important interruption) and Quill for the rest of their lives.

4

ORGANIZING:
THE IRT, 1933–1936

In mid-1937 the TWU achieved recognition, almost simultaneously, on all of the major New York City rapid transit, trolley, and bus lines (except the ISS). However, the union's growth had been far from uniform; it had varied in rate and form from company to company and occupation to occupation. In part, this reflected TWU strategy; in part, differences in the structure, history, and social composition of the various sectors of the industry.

Although the TWU always sought to organize the entire transit system—an early slogan was "One Industry—One Fight—One Union"—significant progress came first on the IRT.[1] As a result, IRT workers were disproportionately represented in the TWU leadership. The tactics and structures they helped develop became the models for the union elsewhere.

The IRT employees initially in contact with the TWU worked in a wide variety of jobs, but it was in the shops and powerhouses that the union first developed a solid base. The earliest and for decades most dependable TWU stronghold was the 148th Street shop, the largest transit maintenance facility in New York. This complex, covering two city blocks between Lenox and Seventh avenues, was responsible for maintaining equipment of all kinds. The bulk of the work, however, was devoted to keeping the IRT's fleet of subway cars in good working order. There were three levels of regularly scheduled maintenance: inspections and slight repairs; longer, more major repair jobs; and complete overhauls. Shop workers not only checked and replaced parts, but in most cases manufactured, repaired, or recycled them as well. Since each subway car was a complicated piece of machinery, and a variety of car models was in use, a great deal of versatility was required.

Like the other big transit shops, 148th Street was an extensive, diversified industrial establishment, utilizing a virtual catalogue of technologies and skills. The variety of work performed and crafts present was staggering. In addition to mechanics, to assemble and disassemble the cars, there was a blacksmith shop, an electric repair shop, a pipefitters department, a pit, gear, and case department, a truck shop, a wheel shop, and motor and armature departments. A machine shop, employing perhaps eighty machinists, undertook both recurring work, such as the manufacture of a modified part, and a daily variety of short jobs. Other men kept up compressed air equipment: brakes, compressors, and so forth. There were also tinsmiths, carpenters, and even workers to reweave the cane subway seats that many older New Yorkers remember fondly.

All told, some 1,400 men were employed, including a night shift of 250. About a quarter of the men were classified as skilled craft workers. Alongside them were a large number of "helpers" of varying skill levels, who had less responsibility. In many departments, helpers worked in teams supervised by a skilled man. Inspectors and car cleaners filled out the work force.[2]

The 148th Street workers came from diverse backgrounds, with no one group forming a majority. There were many Irish workers, mostly Irish-born though some Irish-American. Sizable groups of foreign and U.S.-born Germans, Englishmen, and Poles were present as well. The supervisory personnel tended to be English, though there were some Irish-Catholic foremen.[3]

The wage structure at the shop was chaotic; one worker called it a "mish-mash" of rates. Each trade had a separate wage scale, in which there might be three or four different hourly rates for skilled workers, often doing the same or similar work, and several rates for helpers. Altogether there were scores of different rates. Advancement from rate to rate was not based on regular, timed increments, but on promotions to new titles. In effect, every trade had a series of fixed slots, with each advance predicated on an opening developing from a death, retirement, or rare resignation. Since promotions were not determined strictly by seniority, some men could work for ten years without a raise, while others with less seniority moved rapidly up. Workers who had acquired considerable skill might long remain classified as helpers, an obvious economy for the company. Further complicating the situation, in the machine shop and some other departments there was a piecework bonus system, for which only some skilled men were eligible, applied to selected tasks.[4]

The pay structure at 148th Street was typical of the compensation schemes used for non-transportation work throughout the industry.[5] Like other transit labor policies, it served a dual function: it fragmented the work force and held forth the promise that faithful service would be rewarded. However, the multitude of rates, with little rational basis, ended up breeding considerable resentment. New hires with personal connections, for example, sometimes started off near the top of the scale.

Many factors in addition to seniority and ability guided promotions, lay-offs, and bonus piecework assignments. Relatives and friends of foremen or supervisors, and those who gave their superiors gifts—a case of liquor, for example—had the advantage. So did Masons; many of the supervisory personnel, especially the English, belonged to the Order and tended to favor their Masonic brothers. In fact, men from outside the shop, with no particular qualifications, were occasionally hired as foremen solely on the basis of ties to top shop officials through the Masons.

Favoritism in lay-offs was particularly galling because irregularity of work was a serious problem. When skilled craftsmen worked steadily, their earnings were good.

However, lay-offs were common. Furthermore, early in the Depression a round of firings was followed by the institution of short-time (forced reductions in the work week), first for machinists' helpers and then for almost the entire shop. By contrast, when a worker himself wanted time off, it was hard to get. One man recalled that when he asked for a day's leave to file his first naturalization papers, his foreman told him that if he couldn't hold a job he should resign. Those without highly valued skills faced constant intimidation and job insecurity.

Like other IRT workers, the men at 148th Street objected to the 10% pay cut in 1932. At least among the skilled workers, however, this was not the most serious gripe. The irregularity of work; favoritism in lay-offs, promotions, and piecework; the lack of meaningful seniority; and the foremen's arbitrary and degrading control were more immediate causes of discontent.[6]

The 148th Street shop was one of the first targets of the CP's transit concentration work. However, even before that campaign had progressed significantly, there was a dramatic demonstration of unrest at the shop. In March 1934 fourteen workers were fired, in apparent violation of a company pledge that as a result of the 10% pay cut there would be no more firings or lay-offs. In response, some 800 men, at a meeting of the shop's Brotherhood local, voted to demand an end to all lay-offs, the reinstatement of the fired men, and the reduction of the fifty-hour work week to forty-four hours with no loss of pay. Their resolution was distributed to all the other Brotherhood locals and presented to the IRT. Although the company rejected the demands, their mere presentation had been an unusual display of open protest.[7]

It is unclear what role, if any, those connected to the incipient TWU played in this incident. However, by the spring of 1934 the union was beginning to establish its presence. Through concentration activity a few contacts were made and a small organizing group was set up in the shop. While insiders began recruiting their fellow workers, outsiders continued to distribute literature in front of the shop.[8]

Among the first union activists at 148th Street were Jack Weiner, who became the first president of the TWU's 148th Street section, but later left the industry to go into business; Joe Dyack, an immigrant Polish blacksmith, probably of peasant background, who spoke English poorly; and Victor Bloswick, a Polish-American machinist. Other early recruits included Joseph Brumson; welder Patty Quinn; Scottish-born Alexander (Sandy) Scott; Frank Carberry, a veteran wireman in the armature department; John Plover, another machinist; Dan Savage, an American-born carpenter; Joe Carroll from the car shop, also native-born; and Alfred Hutt, a White Russian pipefitter with ten years' seniority.[9]

According to Maurice Forge, a few of these union pioneers had peripheral connections to the Communist world, in ways unrelated to their work: Brumson, for example, a Jew, belonged to the IWO, while Dyack probably belonged to a Polish workers' club. However, the group as a whole was not politically sophisticated. Rather they were "just meat and potatoes guys, who took their lives in their hands, plunked down a dollar . . . joined the union, and threw their fate to the wind." In Forge's eyes, it was the Party's ability to recruit to the union men like Hutt, "an absolute innocent . . . worth his weight in gold," that was the key to the TWU's first success.[10]

Most of these early activists were skilled workers. There were several reasons for this. First, experienced craftsmen were necessary for the shop to operate efficiently; accordingly, they were given more leeway and had less fear of losing their jobs than those less skilled. In a better position to be hired elsewhere if fired, they could more afford to be bold. Second, the union deliberately sought out skilled men, in the belief that they carried the most influence with their fellow workers, especially the helpers who worked under them. Third, skilled workers often shared craft traditions that predisposed them toward unions. Also, previous contact with unions was apparently more common among skilled men than among helpers or the unskilled.[11]

Victor Bloswick, for example, was a type who appears repeatedly in the story of the organization of American unions, a skilled worker with pride in his craft and union in his blood. Bloswick came from a family of Bethlehem, Pennsylvania, steelworkers. His uncle was a union activist and his wife, whom he had married shortly before the TWU began, came from a coal-mining family with a union tradition. Bloswick left high school after his father's death to help support the family. After completing a course in stationary engineering and holding a series of jobs in New York, he began working for the IRT at 148th Street in 1927, first in the blacksmith shop and later as a machinist on the night shift.

When Bloswick "got wind of some movement in the system" to start a union, he established contact with a group of TWU organizers that included some men from "outside" and others from the IRT transportation department. He was given pledge cards and he started signing up night-shift workers. At first he recruited fellow machinists; then he moved on to other groups, such as the electricians. Aware of his activities, the company first shifted him to days, where there was closer supervision and only a smattering of union members, and then began transferring him from job to job. The result was only to bring him into contact with men from a greater variety of jobs than he normally would interact with, facilitating his recruitment effort.[12]

Some of the shop's European immigrants had been familiar with or members of trade unions "on the other side," and they tended to come over to the TWU first. One activist remembered English, Scottish, and older Irish skilled workers with old-country trade union experience as among the early joiners. However, too strong a generalization is not possible, since the available evidence is scanty and there are plenty of counter-examples. John Plover, for instance, was from an Irish farming family and had no union experience prior to the TWU. His first and only job in the United States was as an IRT shop man. Like Bloswick, he attended vocational school, in his case at nights while already employed at 148th Street, which enabled him to move up to a skilled position. At least in retirement, Plover shared with Bloswick an interest in technical matters, pride in his skills, a self-image as a diligent, competent, hard-working man, and a conviction that his own attitude toward work was no longer being reproduced among transit workers. Thus, though their backgrounds differed greatly, Plover and Bloswick came to share certain fundamental attitudes toward their jobs and about themselves that were predicated on their status as skilled craftsmen. This was true in spite of their very different politics; though both became loyal union members, Bloswick was of the left, while Plover was a staunch anti-Communist.[13]

At first the secret TWU group at 148th Street had contact with the rest of the union only through outside organizers. After a while, though, a few activists began attending meetings with other union leaders, including Quill, MacMahon, and Hogan. The group also began making its presence publicly known at the shop. Around June 1934 the TWU started holding weekly lunch-time meetings outside the gates to the complex. Initially, the speakers were outsiders, such as Mike Walsh, who did not have jobs to lose, but some of the more audacious insiders soon joined them. Although at the time there were fewer than 100 unionists at the shop, the union claimed at the rallies to have signed up a majority of the workers.[14]

Simply to hold such meetings was a bold act—the most open display of unionism on the IRT in nearly a decade. The fact that shop workers were publicly proclaiming union membership, without serious reprisal, and the inflated membership claims helped open things up. Men previously afraid to join began to come over. The noontime meetings became a regular feature of the organizing drive. Eventually, when the union felt strong enough, on rainy days meetings were held inside the shop itself.

The company response to the discontent at 148th Street and to the TWU's activity was two-fold. In June management offered a small concession: additional lunch room facilities and an extension of the lunch period by ten minutes. At the same time, beakies were put to work gathering information on the new union, making organizing, inside or outside the shop, more difficult. Bloswick, for example, was followed by beakies wherever he went for over a year; he could not approach other men without exposing them. (He finally found a solution—sneaking out of his apartment building through the superintendent's back window.) Speakers at the noon-time rallies were threatened by thugs, presumably working for the company or the company union. However, though anti-union pressure was kept up through foremen, beakies, and the Brotherhood, the shop's management never undertook drastic measures, such as wholesale firings or the extensive use of violence. The company's tactics succeeded in retarding the growth of the union in the shop, but never in dealing it a serious setback.[15]

The TWU also won a toehold at the IRT's 98th Street shop, an elevated car maintenance facility that was essentially a smaller version of 148th Street.[16] Through the Harlem concentration group and perhaps other means, a small TWU group was established there by the late spring of 1934.[17] Worker unrest at this shop, however, primarily manifested itself within the Brotherhood.

In June 1934 a group of 98th Street workers, disgusted with the Brotherhood leadership, called a company union meeting without inviting the heads of their shop unit, Local 2. Instead of the usual small turnout, some 300 workers attended. Unsure of how to proceed, the men selected a committee of nine, including Patrick Clarke, who later was to head the TWU section in the shop, to pressure the Local 2 leadership into giving better representation. The results were negligible. After attending a few Brotherhood meetings, the committee, Clarke recalled, "came to the conclusion that the old delegates were not trying very hard and could not be of service to the men." It therefore decided to run a slate of candidates in the next Brotherhood election. It is unclear whether or not the TWU was represented on or cooperated with Clarke's committee. In its literature, the union, though not unsympathetic, pointed out the committee's limitations, and it continued organizing independently.[18]

In this, it was aided by a key recruit at 98th Street, William Grogan, who eventually became a top TWU official. Grogan was Irish-born, but unlike those in the Clan na Gael he came from Dublin and had not been involved in the IRA. A star athlete and skilled coachmaker, he had been a trade unionist while still in Ireland. After emigrating to New York he joined the IRT as a carpenter in 1928. An influential figure, he brought a clique of fellow workers with him into the TWU and rapidly became a leader of the 98th Street union group. Soon he was soap-boxing for the TWU at shop gate meetings. However, as he later recalled, 98th Street was a "tough place" for the union and "progress was slow."[19]

The union got an even slower start among the powerhouse workers; in June 1934 Santo reported that "very little headway has been made."[20] However, within six months the powerhouses, like the shops, had become centers of union strength. This was a particularly important development because the powerhouse workers occupied a key strategic position. Although far fewer in number than the shop men, in the event of a strike, they, like the motormen, were capable of crippling the system on their own. Conversely, over the years the failure of power workers to support various walkouts had contributed to their defeat.[21]

The larger of the two IRT powerhouses, which contained the headquarters of the company's motive power department, was located at 59th Street and the Hudson River. When built, as part of the original IRT system, it had been one of the largest generating plants in the world. In keeping with Belmont's grand vision, its exterior was designed by Stanford White. Inside, there were two great halls, one containing boilers and the other turbines and engines.[22]

Most of the plant's 300 non-supervisory workers were assigned to either the operating or maintenance crews, each of which in turn was divided between those working on the boiler side and those on the turbine and engine side.[23] Operating personnel in the boiler room included water stoker operators and their assistants, water tenders, coal passers, firemen, ashmen, and various types of oilers. The latter two jobs required little training and generally served as entrance positions. On the turbine and engine side, there were oilers and wipers, again relatively unskilled, pumpmen, generator tenders, and others controlling the actual production of electricity. The maintenance crew, which was at least as large as the operating group, was primarily made up of skilled craftsmen, including plumbers, boilermakers, steam fitters, masons, carpenters, electricians, and about twenty machinists. Since power was needed around the clock, the operating crew was divided into permanent "watches" which rotated between day and night shifts, working seven days a week for seven weeks straight, followed by one day off and a shift change. Maintenance men worked only the day shift, six days a week.[24]

The power men were ethnically and nationally heterogeneous, the result some workers felt of a deliberate company policy to divide the work force. Overall, the largest groups present were Spanish, English, German, and native-born Americans. There were smaller numbers of Scots, Poles, Irish, Puerto Ricans, Cubans, and even two or three Maltese, a Chilean, and a Turk. Social ties were generally along ethnic lines, a pattern reinforced as men got jobs for their friends at the facility.[25]

Each element of the work force had a somewhat different social composition. The engine and turbine operators included a sizable Spanish-speaking group, usually men who had acquired engine room experience while working as merchant seamen. Boiler room operators were mostly English, Scottish, or Irish, with a few Hispanics. A high percentage of the boiler maintenance men were native-born Americans, with some Germans mixed in, while those in engine and turbine maintenance, which generally required greater precision and skill, were mostly German. Supervisors, called engineers, were largely older men who had worked their way up from the ranks. Notable was their extreme deference toward top management. When the head of the plant, Chief Engineer Lawrence, walked by, engineers would actually tip their hats and often be afraid to speak.[26]

The complaints of the 59th Street men were both the general complaints of transit workers—long hours, lay-offs, low and inequitable pay rates—and problems specific to the plant—constant, often unbearable, heat and humidity, filthy conditions, coal dust permeating the air. The Brotherhood was largely ineffectual in dealing with these issues, although some men saw it as capable of helping them as individuals, a possible path of advancement and a way of getting soft assignments. Its greatest support came from the maintenance men, who in general already had the better jobs. In addition, quite a few machinists, who were among the best-paid men in the plant, maintained secret membership in the International Association of Machinists (IAM).

It is not clear how the TWU first established a foothold at 59th Street, but by mid-1934 there was considerable discussion in the plant about what was simply called "the outside union." A few men were trying to sign up members. Particularly effective was William Lychak. As the locker room janitor, each day he saw workers from every part of the plant. An older man, perhaps in his fifties, Lychak was a "yellow Ukrainian," part of an exile, anti-Communist, Ukrainian nationalist community, headquartered on a Connecticut estate, where he spent his days off. His support of the TWU may have stemmed from his bitter dislike of the Brotherhood.[27]

In the engine room, the key early union men were Anthony Seus, wiper Joe Rubertone, and oilers Robert Schneider and Joe Labash. Schneider was a German-American college engineering graduate, working at a job far below what his training would normally dictate. Politically, he was quite right-wing. Labash, who worked on a different watch, was a newly hired man from a staunchly pro-union Pennsylvania coal-mining family. His father was a long-time United Mine Workers loyalist and Labash himself had worked in the mines briefly. During the 1922 coal strike he had joined a group trying to organize non-union pits. As the strike dragged on, he left the area, eventually joining the Navy and then settling down in New York.[28] Other early TWU activists included Paul Muschalik, a Slavic-American furnace repairman, who while living on the West Coast had been a member of the IWW; George Swift, a machinist's helper in boiler room maintenance; and George Turnbull, a machinist and IAM member with eleven years' seniority.[29]

The first group to join the TWU in *sizable* numbers were the Spanish-speaking workers; Seus and one or two others who spoke better-than-average English joined the union at the very start and rapidly signed up most of their co-linguists. Although the Hispanics wanted to be in the union, they wanted to do so "on the quiet," keeping their membership secret. Perhaps due to language problems, they never played a major role in recruiting other workers. The first non-Hispanics to join were generally younger unskilled and semi-skilled men, often recruited over drinks at a nearby bar. "Stubbornest of all," recalled Labash, "were some of our American people," especially those close to the Brotherhood.

As Labash saw it, the plant was ripe for organization. Conditions were bad, the 10% cut deeply resented, and the mood profoundly affected by the election of Roosevelt. However, there was also great timidity and fear, and the widespread belief that it was impossible to fight the Brotherhood. Crucial to the union's growth, therefore, was its ability to undercut the workers' respect and fear of management and create an impression, first false and then real, of power shifting away from the company and Brotherhood and toward the union.

Shop-gate meetings helped in this. Workers from 148th Street would come down and claim that the bulk of men there had joined the TWU, giving an inaccurate but effective picture of the union as a solid, established organization. Simply having IRT employees publicly discussing the union helped to dissipate some of the fear. Top union leaders also spoke at these meetings, with Quill's bombastic style particularly effective.

Two incidents involving Labash illustrate how brash, irreverent action, even when not directly related to union issues, helped break the psychological hold of management. The first developed when Labash and some co-workers got drunk on the Fourth of July and skipped their scheduled night shift without notifying the company. After being sent home for a day, they were called into Chief Engineer Lawrence's office. When Lawrence suspended the men for three days, Labash "flabbergasted" him by asking for a week's suspension, saying that he hadn't taken a vacation in years and wanted some time off. Neither wanting to accede to Labash's cheeky request nor to make martyrs of the men, Lawrence reduced their suspensions to the day already missed and ordered them back to work. Within hours, the whole plant knew of the incident. Labash and the others were heroes, the union by association strengthened, and management's ability to command respect weakened.

In a second encounter with Lawrence, Labash, feeling sick one day, was sitting down on the job, a rule violation. As Lawrence approached, an engineer frantically told Labash to stand up or Lawrence would fire him. Labash refused. With others watching, Labash told Lawrence he was sick and wanted to go home. Although Lawrence would not allow him to leave, he never mentioned Labash's failure to stand. The engineer's deferential behavior was shown to be unnecessary and somewhat ridiculous. Again, awe of management was weakened and power relations were shifted, no matter how minutely, to the benefit of the union.

In spite of growing support, the TWU group made little headway in certain sectors of the work force, particularly among the more skilled, better-paid men.[30] The electricians, for example, remained aloof from both the Brotherhood and the TWU. The TWU also failed to win over the machinists, a tight-knit group dominated by the Germans and informally led by a German immigrant, Gustav Faber.

Faber had an extraordinary past. Already in his late forties or early fifties—twenty years older than most TWU activists—Faber came from Hamburg, where he had been a prominent figure in the trade union and socialist movements. During World War I he was affiliated with the Spartacus League and then was elected to a legislative post as a CP candidate. Sometime in the early 1920s, however, he was

Mike Quill addressing a lunchtime crowd of workers outside the IRT
59th Street powerhouse in 1935.

expelled from the German CP during a factional dispute. In disgust, he left Germany in 1924 for the United States. At the time the TWU started, Faber had been working at 59th Street for five or six years. He was universally respected, by managers and workers alike, and was the clear leader of the machinists and perhaps some of the other skilled maintenance workers as well.[31]

Although the TWU men in the plant repeatedly approached him, Faber refused to join their group. Labash had the impression that Faber thought that the TWU was a fly-by-night organization, which would not last long, and disliked the flippant anti-disciplinarianism of some of its young leaders. Also, Faber had secretly belonged to the IAM since coming to the U.S. and apparently preferred craft to industrial organization. In any case, as a result of his influence the machinists generally remained outside the TWU, with the important exception of George Turnbull—significantly of English extraction in a mostly German group—who helped keep the union informed of Faber's activities. What Faber's own plans were is unclear. The group around him remained independent of both the TWU and the Brotherhood, though, according to Labash, Faber would "hobnob with [William] Manning and other Brotherhood leaders, but not with TWU men." Faced with this situation, the TWU began to attack him.

The workers at 59th Street were thus divided three ways. The TWU had made rapid progress, particularly among unskilled and semi-skilled operating personnel, but had failed to enlist most of the better-paid men. The Brotherhood continued to have some worker support and the backing of the company. Finally, the machinists were mostly united around Faber's independent group. Meanwhile, with the help of men from 59th Street, the TWU established a beachhead at the other IRT power-house, at 74th Street and the East River, a smaller plant that resembled 59th Street in function, job structure, and social composition. [32]

In the shops, powerhouses, and car barns, large numbers of men worked in proximity; once a core group was established the union could grow through worker-led, on-site organizing. Continued outside leafleting, shop-gate meetings, and home visits abetted the process. Although organizing remained a slow and uneven business, it was under such circumstances that the union made the most rapid progress.

The majority of IRT workers, however, were in transportation, station, or maintenance-of-way jobs, where a quite different situation prevailed. As a rule, these men worked alone or in small groups. Their contacts with other workers were usually restricted in extent and often brief in duration. In the case of ticket agents, they were almost non-existent. One worker described an agent's job as "the most lonesome . . . anybody could have." During long hours of work, "all he [or she] sees is strangers, or a boss." [33]

In such jobs, unionism was not likely to arise as an extension of daily working relationships or to spread through on-the-job contact. Isolation accentuated workers' fears and made them more susceptible to company intimidation. [34] The camaraderie and mutual support among unionists, even when few in number, that was a day-to-day affair in large establishments was impossible in many sections of the system.

TWU activists developed a variety of tactics to reach isolated employees that took advantage of the inherent characteristics of the work process. Turnstile mechanics Tom O'Shea and Michael Clune, for instance, constantly visited different stations in the course of their work, enabling them to speak with numerous station depart-ment workers. Clune would carry leaflets to give out, and unionists on occasion would report broken turnstiles in particular stations he wanted to visit. Platform men would give out leaflets kept in trash cans to passing train crews. In addition, TWU members with low seniority were always being assigned to different stations, putting them in contact with otherwise isolated employees. Still, reaching men who worked in ones or twos always remained a problem. [35]

For this and other reasons, the TWU generally grew more slowly among dispersed workers than in the shops, powerhouses, and barns, and it developed through a somewhat different social dynamic. Rather than spreading primarily along the contours of the work process, the creation of the union among scattered workers was heavily dependent on off-the-job networks of acquaintance and activity. What facilitated this, and gave it its distinctive character, was the fact that a high percentage of the scattered workers were Irish, especially in the less skilled classifications. To a considerable extent, union organizing took place within the context of a shared community and culture, with Irish republicanism playing a central role.

The rate of unionization outside the large work sites depended on a number of factors, but heavily Irish sectors of the work force tended to organize first. Differing work conditions, craft traditions, and historical experiences also came into play. Roughly speaking, it was in the stations that the TWU men made the most rapid progress, while the going was slowest among motormen and certain unusually isolated employees, such as towermen and power sub-station workers. Falling in between were conductors, guards, and maintenance-of-way workers.[36]

The Clan na Gael group was scattered throughout the IRT transportation department, providing the TWU with a strong starting point among agents, platform men, guards, and conductors. In addition, Clan men working in other departments— Mike Lynch in track and Jack Teahan in structure, for example—helped form union groups and provided local leadership. The Clan men began their recruiting by approaching other ex-IRA members, for they viewed such men as tough, trustworthy, and able to keep secrets.[37]

John Nolan, for instance, an IRA veteran working as an IRT agent and platform man, knew Quill from the New York "Irish movement." As he recalls,

> [in] 1934 Mike Quill called me down to his booth on Christopher street [to discuss the union]. . . . I said god damn it, Mike . . . you won't be there a week and we're fired. So Mike says what the hell do we have to lose—[our] chains, you know. Well, I figured he was right. What the hell.

Similarly, two of the first men Gerald O'Reilly recruited, John Treanor and Joe Fleming, were IRA vets.[38]

As the union grew, the republicans next approached non-IRA men they knew well and trusted. Some they had known "on the other side." Others were neighbors or relatives or acquaintances from Irish groups or from bars where Irish transit men socialized. Quill in particular could call on a vast number of such associations. As it became known that the ex-IRA men were supporting the union, other Irish workers began to flock in. Nolan remembers that "they all wanted to know where the Clan na Gael were—they wanted to come in, you know. They were real hot under the collar. They were all a bunch of young fellows."[39]

Thus outside of the shops and powerhouses, the early TWU tended to be numerically dominated by young Irish workers, who also were the most likely to become active union cadre. Among the conductors, for example, O'Reilly recalls that the Italians did not oppose the TWU, but tended to be very fearful of possible reprisals. When the TWU eventually introduced union buttons, the Italians would take them but, unlike the young Irish, would not wear them on the job. Similarly, veterans of earlier strikes generally supported the TWU, but were very careful; they joined but did not take leadership roles. Older, with families, and victims of lost seniority, their caution was understandable.[40]

In fact, given the past history of broken unions and the atmosphere of fear, TWU leaders felt that they could attract members only if they could protect them by keeping their membership secret. As Forge remarked, "victims are expensive." A structure was therefore devised to maintain covert status for as long as possible, keep out company spies, and minimize the damage that any infiltrator could do. Most TWU workers interacted with the union only through a group of five to twenty fellow unionists with whom they regularly met. A leader of each group kept in contact with the central leadership and, in some cases, also sat on the delegates council. The average unionist knew the names of only a few other members, while the delegates knew each other only by first name. Any spy who managed to join the TWU could at most report a few workers.[41]

Unionists were repeatedly warned to avoid exposing themselves or acting like "Wild Bull Mikes." "We must carry on slow, systematic, level-headed organization. There is no quick cure-all. . . . We must be cautious and protect each other from exposure. Small groups, small meetings." To further minimize possible exposure, meetings were held in scattered and shifting locations—men's apartments, various Irish and union halls, and even Central Park.[42]

The Irish republicans saw the use of secret, small groups as an application of the tactics they had used in Ireland. "We organized it [the TWU] exactly along the lines of the IRA," said Gerald O'Reilly, whose own republican record included two escapes from Dublin's Mountjoy prison.[43] Although clandestine methods were employed primarily for security reasons, they served another purpose as well. According to Quill, many young Irish workers "liked the secrecy and intrigue." As other fraternal and labor organizations had long realized, mystery and ritual could elevate the import of routine organizational tasks and break up the boredom of everyday life.[44]

Of course, the Communist Party had also long used a secret, cellular structure.[45] This was one of several instances in which elements of the republican and Communist traditions converged, facilitating a smooth working relationship and enabling both groups to see TWU practice as an outgrowth of their past. But whatever the origin of the small group tactics, the ex-IRA men, with their wealth of organizational experience, were masters at this sort of semi-conspiratorial approach. Forge recalls that "we practically had a network of organization with their help without any visible surface iceberg."[46]

The union also tried to reach workers through street rallies in their neighborhoods. In the summer of 1934 at least three open-air meetings were held in Irish parts of the South Bronx. According to union and Communist reports, over a thousand people attended each of the first two gatherings. At one, rotten eggs and broken glass were thrown from a passing car, the work, TWU organizers felt, of company or Brotherhood thugs. Outdoor rallies were also tried in Hell's Kitchen, again heavily Irish and an area where many powerhouse workers lived, and in Bay Ridge, where many BMT employees resided.[47]

At the same time the TWU was being organized, a parallel campaign was being undertaken to recruit workers into the CP. Both efforts were directed by the same core of Communist cadre, for whom they were but complementary aspects of the same larger project. Both were directed toward the same pool of workers and both tended to be most successful in the same occupational and social milieux.

In general, Communist organizers, while enlisting members for the TWU, were careful not to disclose their political affiliation.[48] However, they did quietly approach "the most class-conscious and active workers" to join the CP, so that where the first TWU groups were forming a few workers also joined the Party. At 148th Street, for example, the CP signed up its first recruit sometime in the spring of 1934, when the union had about twenty-five members in the shop. By early the next year there were seven CP members at 148th Street. As the TWU spread, the number of Party members grew as well, particularly in the shops and powerhouses and among the Irish republicans.[49]

The primary Party work of these new recruits was to help build the TWU, and most of the other Communists they had contact with were transit workers or union organizers. At 148th Street, for example, as soon as there was a nucleus of three Party members in the shop, the leaders of the CP concentration unit "tried to place the leadership and responsibility [for the union drive] in the hands of the Party members on the inside."

Following the then-current CP practice, where there were enough members, shop units were established paralleling the organizational lines of the industry and the union. Isolated recruits were put into industrial units joining together CP members from different parts of the transit system. (Both types of groups had outside organizers assigned to them as well.) By early 1935, the CP's first transit unit, at 148th Street, had been formed. Other CP groups later set up on the IRT included a painters' unit and one of miscellaneous transportation and maintenance-of-way workers. The CP transit units were not integrated into the main Party structure—which was organized by geographic area—but were coordinated through separate industrial sections.[50]

In addition to union building, the CP transit groups undertook some distinctly Communist agitation and organization. Several produced openly Communist shop papers, including *Red Signal* (put out by the IRT painters), *Red Express* (coming out of 148th Street), *Red Dynamo*, and the *Times Square Shuttle*. These small, irregular, mimeographed newspapers discussed union and work issues and occasionally politics more generally.[51] Where possible, transit workers in the Party covertly distributed the shop papers and the *Daily Worker* on the job; otherwise non-transit Communists gave them away or sold them near work entrances. Both inside and outside Communists tried to recruit new Party members, drum up votes for Communist candidates at election time, and line up marchers for May Day.[52]

The Party's views on union strategy were talked over, at least in the early years, in a "leading fraction" that included the key Communists in the TWU, both those sent in from the outside and those recruited from the work force. On a few occasions, prominent CP figures discussed important union developments at larger gatherings of TWU Communists. Regular, small meetings were also held between top Party and union leaders. In one forum or another, all of the TWU's major strategic decisions were worked out in consultation with the CP leadership.[53]

Although a few transit workers exposed to the CP may have joined up simply out of agreement with its general principles, it was for the most part the Party's role in helping to found, organize, lead, and finance the TWU that was responsible for its growth in the New York transit industry. The one common characteristic of most of the early CP transit recruits was their early and active membership in the TWU; their decision to join the Party was usually an extension of their desire for a union.

John Murphy, for example, who by his own account was one of the first workers to join the CP as a result of its transit concentration campaign, later told the Dies Committee that "I suppose I would not have joined the Communist Party if the American Federation of Labor had been on the job."[54] Tom O'Shea told the same committee a similar story:

> Conditions in the industry at that time were anything but hot . . . and I felt . . . it was absolutely necessary to have a union. Now, I didn't see any activity on the part of the American Federation of Labor; and . . . [the CP] assured me that they were interested in building a union. . . . They were willing to spend money—to pay for a bulletin, pay for lawyers and give us as much protection as could be given. So I felt that really those people were interested in the working class."[55]

Although, given the context, such testimony was obviously self-serving, others who long stayed active in the Communist movement expressed similar sentiments. Gerald O'Reilly, for example, was impressed by the CP's provision of money, personnel, and sound advice, with no apparent strings attached. "They never asked us for anything. They didn't ask us to join. . . . They supported us fully."[56] Even workers who never joined the CP—including some deeply hostile to its views—repeatedly stressed their gratitude to the Party and various left-wing unions, such as the Furriers, for providing the TWU with money and assistance.[57]

While the TWU was still small, its members were in constant contact with the union's leading Communist organizers. Personal and political relationships were easily formed in the midst of the joint project of building a transit union. Santo, Hogan, Forge, and the other Communists active in the TWU were highly competent organizers and impressive figures; many neophyte unionists were in awe of their abilities, knowledge, and worldliness, traits that came to be associated with Party membership.[58] Their personal characters and organizational standing were major factors in the CP's ability to attract new recruits. Even after the TWU had grown in size, where Communists played important roles in key union developments, increased Party membership often followed. Where Communists played only a minor role in the union's growth, CP membership usually remained negligible.[59]

From the start, there was considerable overlap between the TWU hierarchy and the Party group within the union. Initially Santo, Hogan, and to a lesser extent Forge were at the center of both. As the earliest, most aggressive, and most able unionists began enlisting in the CP in disproportionately large numbers, they were soon joined by MacMahon, O'Shea, Quill, and a host of others. Once established, it was a self-perpetuating situation. Whatever credit Communists won in their positions as union leaders also cast a positive light on the Party, at least among those who knew that they belonged to the CP. Communist union leaders encouraged new Party members to take on leadership roles within the TWU and were in a position to aid them in doing so.

As it became obvious that the Communists in the union were, to a considerable extent, the de facto leadership, ambitious workers began to see Party membership as a step toward the center of the union and future positions of power and authority. Some workers charged that Communist officials tried to recruit them to the Party on this basis, offering the possibility of advancement within the TWU if they joined, while warning that their failure to do so would preclude their assumption of leadership within the union. Regardless of the truth of these accusations, it would not have required open offers for the more perceptive to realize that to the extent to which the TWU was developing into a going concern, the Communists within it held the keys to power, leadership, and staff positions. Thus a pattern quickly emerged that continued until the Party was forced out of the union's leadership in 1948: a disproportionately high percentage of all TWU officers and staffers were Communists and, conversely, a disproportionately high percentage of all Communists in the TWU were union officials. This overlap was so pronounced that there were never all that many Communist rank-and-file transit workers.[60]

In the first year or two of organizing, the union and the CP were so closely intertwined that a categorical confusion sometimes arose in workers' minds between the two. This was especially true among the newly arrived Irish, who often were unfamiliar with the idea of Communism, to the extent that some referred to it as "communionism." Edward Maguire, an Irish IRT ticket agent who joined the CP in early 1934, never fully understood the distinction between the Party and the union. This was evident in his 1938 Dies Committee testimony, when he tellingly referred to the meetings of his CP unit as "union meetings." With most Party transit recruits initially in cells composed strictly of other transit workers and organizers, led by union leaders, and whose immediate work was union-related, this confusion could go on for some time. When men like Maguire finally did realize that the CP had concerns transcending union organizing, their disillusionment could be sharp. According to Maguire,

> Sometime in the summer of 1935 I was addressing [CP] unit 19-S, and in doing so I digressed on union policy, whereupon I was interrupted by John Santo and reminded that "we are not building the Transport Workers' Union; we are out to build the Communist Party." This remark left me dumb-founded, as the agitation of these men standing before the workers was all for the union and for nothing else.

Maguire rather quickly left the CP and later became a bitter critic of its role within the TWU.[61]

If Maguire represented one type of Irish experience with the Party, a group of transit workers who joined the CP at roughly the same time represented another. By contrast, they developed deep ideological, organizational, and emotional ties to the Communist movement which survived years of red-baiting, government investigations, and shifts in the Party line.[62] Many in this latter group had developed left-wing views within the republican movement before they had had any direct contact with the CP. Their decision to join the Party was an extension of a pre-existing ideological orientation. Though few in number, these Irish transit Communists— and especially the active republicans among them—were a key nexus tying together the union, the Party, and the Irish community. They also conferred the legitimacy of the republican movement on both the TWU and the Party group within it.

The Irish workers who moved from the IRA to the TWU to the CP were but a special case of a general process. Both the IRA and the TWU were expressions of the demand by excluded groups for the full rights of bourgeois citizenship, including individual and collective dignity and opportunity, an end to paternalistic systems of social control, minimal standards of economic security, and participation in economic and political decision-making. It was an agenda that in theory was far from revolutionary, but that in practice many in both the Irish national and American union movements felt could be fulfilled only through the agency of radical political parties, in this case the CP. If in the abstract Communists were committed to ending the bourgeois epoch, their concrete demands and daily activities placed them on the leading edge of the struggle for equal rights, expanded democracy, and economic growth—the very promises of capitalist life.

For those transit workers who joined and stayed in the CP, the Party quickly became more than simply an instrument for unionization. If the Party provided them with the analytic tools, the organizational and material support, and the breadth of understanding needed to carry through the struggle for the parochial demands which had first engaged them, it simultaneously universalized their struggle. The effort by these workers to rectify specific interest group grievances led to a broader, more general vision of political and economic equality. The CP provided a way to concretize their self-definition as historical actors, as revolutionaries, as political men. Meanwhile, as the fight for their original, limited goals led to the creation of a new institutional structure, the TWU, the CP became a means of controlling that structure and finding places of personal importance within it.

The central role of Communists in organizing and leading the TWU almost immediately gave rise to anti-Communist attacks on the union. Officials of both the IRT and the Brotherhood quickly began to charge that the TWU was a Communist organization, led by "agitators" who threatened violence against the company and workers who refused to join the union. The Brotherhood even reprinted parts of a 1934 IWW pamphlet that portrayed the TWU as Communist-controlled, "an instrument to propagate the social theories of that particular organization to the exclusion of the immediate needs of transport workers."

As a result of such agitation, and pre-existing anti-Communist attitudes, TWU organizers found "a certain amount of antagonism . . . expressed by the I.R.T. men verbally and otherwise in regard to the 'redness' of the union." In fact, it was a serious enough situation that TWU organizers and activists felt that the union's ultimate success was predicated on its ability to overcome what they usually termed "the red scare."[63]

Initially there were differences of opinion over how best to do this. Some advocated "boldly" discussing the role of Communists in the union. One member of a concentration group, for instance, went against the advice of Party officials and told a shop worker contact that he was a Communist. He explained that "some members of the Union were Communists and some were not," but insisted that "we are not trying to force our political ideas 'down his throat'." The organizer was pleasantly surprised when as a result of this discussion the worker in question became much friendlier, providing valuable information about his shop and even agreeing to help distribute Communist literature.[64] Other workers and organizers agreed that the contributions of Communists to the union drive should be explained "at least to some of the more advanced individuals and groups."[65]

More typically, however, and after 1935 almost exclusively, transit organizers attacked the red scare as an anti-labor device, proclaimed the union's inclusive, democratic character, but avoided any mention of Communism or the role of Communists in organizing and leading the TWU.[66] From late 1934 on, ever greater care was taken to avoid any public association of TWU members, especially those in the leadership, with the CP. Austin Hogan, for example, was slated as a CP Congressional candidate in the 1934 election, but as he began to play a central role in the TWU systematic steps were taken to minimize the public record of his candidacy.[67] In fact, until 1948—and then under extraordinary and disastrous circumstances— no TWU member ever publicly acknowledged membership in the CP. Of course some union members, particularly potential CP recruits, were privately filled in on the Party's role, but the public record was carefully kept blank. Both anti-Communist critics and government investigators later had a hard time identifying and documenting which TWU members belonged to the CP.[68]

After 1934, explicitly Communist agitation was increasingly conducted only among those transit workers judged likely to be sympathetic, not among the work force as a whole. The change can be seen in the TWU and CP newspapers. In November 1934, the *Daily Worker* urged transit workers to vote Communist and join the Party, arguing that "communists are among the most active organizers of a rank and file Transport Workers Union." The next spring, letters appeared in the *Bulletin* urging TWU members to march in the May Day parade. Thereafter such statements and invitations became less common, eventually disappearing altogether, as both papers avoided anything that tied the TWU to the CP.[69]

Communist shop papers also began to disappear. Around 1935 a delegation of TWU members—it is unclear if they were Communists or not—complained to Party leaders that distribution of the *Red Express* was hurting organizing. Whether for this or other reasons, by the end of 1935 several of the transit shop papers had ceased publication. Apparently all were discontinued well before the 1939 Party decision to suspend such publications nationally.[70]

The TWU's rhetoric, too, was transformed. For example, a May 1934 draft union constitution stated that "the interests of the traction trusts who own and control the lines are directly opposed to the interests of the transport workers who possess nothing but their labor power." By 1937 the union constitution simply spoke of the need to unite workers, improve their conditions, and advance their "economic, political, social, and cultural interests." When that year a TWU activist from the ISS listed the paid holidays which he thought should be granted, he included Labor Day, not May Day as the IRT motormen had earlier done.[71] With the abandonment of left-wing phraseology, less and less was said about questions not directly related to transit. As early as November 1934 an official of the TUUL Marine Workers Industrial Union criticized the *Transport Workers Bulletin* for avoiding controversial political issues.[72]

Such changes in CP and TWU practice were part of a larger national and international reformulation of Communist policy. The TWU had been founded while the international Communist movement was, in Irving Howe's and Lewis Coser's phrase, "fidgeting towards a change in line" from the third period to the United and Popular Front policies. The union matured while the new strategy was undergoing concrete elaboration. For the TWU, this entailed no sharp or disruptive shift. The transit group had never been a "revolutionary" union in the same sense as some of the earlier Communist-sponsored TUUL unions. The 1933 "Open Letter" that had led to its start was in itself a long step toward a United Front policy, and between 1933 and 1935 there was considerable flexibility and experimentation within the American CP, leaving much room for the Communists in transit to feel their own way forward. Well before the Communist International formally adopted the Popular Front in August 1935, TWU practice was anticipating that direction.[73]

While the changes in the TWU certainly reflected the changing currents within the CP, they also reflected the dynamic of the union drive. Those Communists whose lives were almost totally consumed by the day-to-day problems of organizing a transit union increasingly became committed to that project in itself and to the institution to which it was giving rise. In seeking a response to the red scare and more general strategic questions, their tendency was to look for those approaches most instrumentally effective in building a union. Often that meant muting the public role of CP.[74] Apparently this policy paid off: by 1935 some Communists felt that the red scare on the IRT had been largely overcome.[75]

One of the major strategic issues the TWU faced was its relationship to company unionism, and in particular to the IRT Brotherhood. With its long history of company sponsorship and collaboration, the Brotherhood was ideologically anathema to the TWU group, which saw it primarily as an agent of management propaganda and control. However, the Brotherhood was the one organization to which all IRT workers at least nominally belonged, its meetings were the only approved and therefore safe arena for discussing work issues, and it had certain theoretically democratic features, including the election of local officers. In many locations, including the 148th Street and 98th Street shops, workers unconnected to the TWU were trying to transform the Brotherhood into a more active and militant workers' advocate. In fact, in mid-1934 probably more workers were taking this route than joining the TWU.

Some TWU members wanted to abandon the company unions immediately. A few, as individuals, had already done so by not paying their Brotherhood dues, risking dismissal. The CP position, however, was not to abstain from participation in the Brotherhood "until you either tried to save it or expose it." Correctly discerning that "there was still some illusions among the men as to the possibility of turning the company union into a fighting body," Party leaders convinced those unionists holding what they viewed as an adventurist position to accept a more moderate approach.[76]

After considerable discussion, the TWU settled on two-track strategy. On the one hand, Brotherhood leaders were attacked for repeatedly selling out the membership, and the need for an independent, rank-and-file organization was stressed. On the other hand, TWU activists began regularly attending Brotherhood meetings, where they raised questions, criticized the leadership, and proposed their own programs.[77] It was a policy designed, in the long run, "to break up the company union by fighting inside of it—by transforming the tool of the company into a battle-ground for the workers."[78]

This proved to be a highly successful approach. Most workers were not yet thoroughly convinced of the futility of working inside the Brotherhood, and only a few were prepared to join an organization like the TWU. Through participation in Brotherhood meetings, a continual education process was undertaken, slowly establishing the TWU as the most responsible and militant champion of the transit workers' cause. At the same time, those workers who were trying to change the Brotherhood, often informal leaders at their job sites, were not antagonized by a blanket condemnation. Through ongoing discussion and cooperative efforts, many were won over to the TWU. In effect, the still tiny TWU chose to operate within the larger current of discontent and activity taking place inside the company union, rather than to stand aside and demand an immediate choice of allegiance.

Fortuitously, a perfect issue arose for the union to use in hammering home its critique of the Brotherhood—a new pension plan. A previous pension system, introduced in 1916, had been wholly company-run and financed, providing benefits at age seventy or in cases of total disability to workers with at least twenty-five years seniority. In December 1932, the Brotherhood agreed to allow the IRT to develop a new plan, which was implemented eighteen months later. This plan shifted much of the financial burden from the company to its employees; participating workers were required to contribute 3% of their wages, but had no voice in administering these funds. Although the requirements for pension eligibility were eased, the TWU and others sharply questioned the actuarial soundness of the plan. Furthermore, a yellow-dog clause was introduced: workers who joined a union other than the Brotherhood would lose all their pension rights. In theory, the new plan was compulsory only for those hired after July 1, 1934; others could choose to join by signing individual enrollment forms. However, no new pensions would be offered under the old system and, according to the TWU, heavy company pressure was used to enroll workers. All but 2,500 signed up.

The new pension plan, with its de facto 3% pay cut, was deeply resented by IRT employees, especially once their take-home pay actually fell in July 1934. To capitalize on this discontent, the TWU launched a major campaign against the plan. Charging that the entire scheme was essentially fraudulent, the union demanded that the IRT replace it with a company-financed system providing half-pay after twenty-five years of service, regardless of age. In the meantime, the union insisted that individual workers be allowed to withdraw from the newly installed plan.[79]

The pension issue and the TWU's decision to work within the Brotherhood had the immediate effect of providing large, sympathetic audiences for union agitation. On July 27, for example, some 250 men attended a special meeting of the Livonia-Corona car barns' local of the Brotherhood, where they protested the pension plan and pay cut. A group of TWU activists demanded that a representative of their union be allowed to speak. When they were refused, leftist organizers Paul Green and Walter Case took over the platform and presented the TWU program, which included a demand for special Brotherhood meetings to consider the pension, restoration of the 10% pay cut, election of rank-and-file shop and depot committees, and recognition of the TWU.[80]

At 148th Street, a group including some TWU members circulated a "round robin petition" demanding the return of all the signed pension consent forms. One of the non-unionists involved was Mark Kavanaugh, a politically conservative, Dublin-born electrician, once jailed as an IRA member. Under pressure from Victor Bloswick, Kavanaugh agreed to meet with Santo to discuss the pension issue. About a month later he joined the union and became one of its leaders in the shop. Kavanaugh was just the type of worker the TWU leadership was increasingly eager to recruit. Although the TWU had already attracted men of remarkably diverse political views, its leaders were now consciously seeking out workers who disagreed with the CP's general world view but were willing to ally with it to build a union. Such men would quicken the spread of the organization, strengthen its base, and make anti-communist attacks more difficult. Kavanaugh was a perfect "united fronter"; well known for his conservatism, he was the last man one could accuse of being a Communist, yet he came to work closely with the left-dominated TWU leadership, in part because of Santo's sustained effort to form a close personal relationship.[81]

Responding to intense rank-and-file sentiment, the 148th Street Brotherhood local called a special meeting for August 3 to discuss the pension. The TWU asked workers from all IRT shops to attend and scheduled a nearby outdoor rally for the same time. At the meeting, company union leaders only admitted men from 148th Street, but they lost control anyway. When Jack Weiner from the TWU attacked Frank Moore, the head of the Brotherhood at 148th Street, for having accepted the 10% cut, and demands were made that he and other local leaders resign, the meeting was abruptly ended. Meanwhile, a string of TWU organizers were addressing the outdoor rally, which according to the *Daily Worker* attracted over 2,000 men. They were soon joined by some 500 workers leaving the Brotherhood meeting. One worker who was present recalled that for all practical purposes that day was the end of the company union at the IRT's largest shop.[82]

In the months that followed, TWU activists continued to use Brotherhood meetings as forums and for recruiting. Occasionally, they even snuck in outside leaders like Hogan or Forge. Once, when an IRT special officer tried to throw Hogan out of a meeting of ticket agents, the workers threw out the officer instead.[83]

During this same period, the TWU tried another tack as well, using the labor relations machinery created under the New Deal's National Industrial Recovery Act (NIRA). The union first turned to the government in June 1934 when John Murphy, an Irish-born ticket agent with eight years' seniority—and a union activist, delegates council member, and recent CP recruit—was fired. The charges were sleeping on the job (at 3:15 a.m.) and having a non-employee in his booth. The TWU appealed to the New York Regional Labor Board (RLB) to have Murphy reinstated. While admitting to the accusations, Murphy and the TWU claimed that these were minor infractions which would normally result in a one- or two-day suspension. A second case, involving Leon Cashman, a machinist's helper dismissed at 148th Street, was soon added.

The TWU never claimed to its members that Murphy and Cashman had been fired for union activity, nor did it publicize the RLB appeal. Probably union leaders did not want to frighten workers with the specter of company reprisals. The outcome of the appeal was also very uncertain, since the RLB felt that Murphy had a "palpably poor case." However, when the TWU filed a formal complaint, an investigation was begun. At first Thomas E. Murray, Jr., the IRT Receiver, refused to cooperate, but eventually he agreed to meet privately with RLB Director Elinore Herrick. Murray submitted beakie reports and other material justifying the firings. As it turned out, Murphy had been under secret surveillance for several days, during which time he had violated company rules on numerous occasions. Herrick found no cause to intercede. Murphy remained convinced that he was fired for union activity and continued organizing for the TWU until March 1935, when he was transferred by the CP to unemployment activities. He left the Party six months later and soon was bitterly criticizing the CP and the TWU leadership. (Cashman's case was never resolved; he could not be located for a hearing.)[84]

While the Murphy/Cashman cases were still pending, the TWU tried to enlist the RLB in its campaign against the IRT pension plan. Claiming that the scheme was "of yellow dog nature," and that workers had been coerced into enrolling with no idea of its provisions, Santo asked the Board in early August 1934 to "help us bring about [its] revocation." Although the Board declined to take get involved with the pension issue as such, it said that it would consider violations of NIRA section 7(A), which guaranteed workers the right to organize. In response, the TWU asked for an investigation of the yellow-dog clause in the Brotherhood contract. This was a straight-forward matter; the clause was specific in its wording and clearly illegal. In late September, Herrick wrote to Murray requesting that the IRT immediately void it. Murray promptly agreed to do so. After two decades, the yellow-dog contract was dead.[85]

Almost immediately, though, the IRT struck back, firing two more union members—Tom O'Shea and J. D. Garrison—on the basis of what the TWU charged were trumped-up beakie reports. Both men were vociferous union advocates and members of the delegates council. O'Shea, as previously mentioned, was among the most active Clan men. Garrison had been recruited to the union by MacMahon, with whom he worked in the lighting department. He had been with the IRT for over six years, was a skilled craftsman, and was making the company's top wage rate. Although not a leading figure in the union, as Maurice Forge recalls:

> the moment he saw the light you couldn't hold him down. . . . he was not used to being scared; he was a free spirit. . . . He came from Texas, it was his country and who the hell was going to tell him he couldn't do something, so he really was imprudent.

Forge speculates that because Garrison and O'Shea were so vocally pro-union, the company "must have thought they were great leaders of the union movement and they fired them."

The TWU quickly undertook a major campaign to get the two men rehired, its first all-out public mobilization. A complaint was filed with the RLB, charging a section 7(A) violation, and this time a strong case was presented. While the Board was scheduling and holding hearings, the union distributed tens of thousands of leaflets and held dozens of shop-gate meetings. Folders about the case were handed out to transit riders and the IRT offices were picketed. The result was a major victory; on December 12, before the RLB had reached a decision, Murray reinstated the two men.[86] For the first time, the TWU had shown that it could directly affect the actions of the IRT. At the same time, it had made good on its promise that men who joined the union would be protected.

There was an important by-product of this incident. Shortly after the two men were rehired, the TWU announced that O'Shea had been the secret president of the union, and Garrison secretly the secretary. Actually, this was not true; the only formal TWU officers were Santo and Hogan, and that was more or less by self-appointment. Forge contends that the retroactive designation of Shea and Garrison was done primarily to capitalize on the rehiring campaign. In any case, at first glance O'Shea was not an inappropriate choice for president. He was one of the first Irish republicans to join the union drive, he was well-known, outspoken, and committed to the TWU, and was in the spotlight first as a victim and then as a victor. By this time he was also a member of the Communist Party. O'Shea was selected president by the core group of organizers, which in effect meant the CP, without any sort of membership vote. It was a decision later deeply regretted.[87]

The November 1934 Brotherhood elections revived the internal TWU debate over company unionism. Again, some workers wanted to take an abstentionist stand, while the Party advocated participation. Not enough evidence is available to determine with certainty which unionists took which positions, but apparently some of the Clan group opposed involvement. Forge recalls that "O'Shea and that crowd . . . wrote off the company union," while O'Shea himself later testified that Quill had opposed taking part in the election and went along only after meeting with top officials of the state CP.[88]

The stand of these Irish republicans may have reflected the deep-rooted Irish tradition of boycotting institutions viewed as illegitimate. Irish republican politics were characterized by complex debates over what were and were not legitimate institutions, and under what circumstances participation was justified. It was over precisely this issue that De Valera broke with the IRA. Two factors were at work shaping this approach to politics: a long history of trying to maintain Irish identity in an environment of foreign-imposed structures, and the need to justify rebellion within the confines of Catholic dogma. The Church opposed the overthrow of national governments, but accepted efforts to expel foreign conquerors. The legitimacy of various national institutions thus became a central issue.[89]

As finally formulated, the TWU position was a compromise. The union opposed an election boycott, arguing that although the vote would probably not be fairly conducted, "all the terror resorted to by P. J. [Connolly] will only speed the awakening of the men." Non-participation, the union argued, would strengthen the Brotherhood. However, the TWU did not openly run its own candidates; those TWU members who ran did so without organizational identification. Publicly, the union only urged men to vote against the incumbent officers and delegates and to evaluate the candidates on the basis of their positions on the outstanding issues. At several locations, including 98th Street, independent slates ran on platforms that overlapped with the TWU program. Further reflecting the union's growing influence, even some incumbent officials put forth reform platforms that shared much with the TWU program.[90]

In the end, however, although some opposition candidates were elected, the top Brotherhood leadership remained intact. The Brotherhood then negotiated a new contract with the IRT in its usual manner, without rank and file participation or ratification. (Thomas Murray rejected a TWU request that he negotiate with it instead.) The Brotherhood pact, signed December 7, 1934, included some improvements. About 7,000 workers, including motormen, conductors, and powerhouse men, received 5% pay hikes, while another 7,000 trackmen, signalmen, and shop workers had their nine-hour days reduced by one hour without a loss of pay. A procedure for arbitrating grievances was also established. However, the bulk of the 10% cut remained in effect, as did the new pension plan, and other worker demands were unaddressed.[91]

The presentation of this agreement to the Brotherhood locals led to a new wave of protest and set the stage for the TWU to move to a higher level of organization. Several Brotherhood units voted disapproval of the pact. Additionally, the station department workers endorsed the TWU program. Opposition was strongest at 148th Street. At the shop's December Brotherhood meeting, workers voted to support the TWU program and send a delegate to the CP-sponsored National Congress for Unemployed and Social Insurance. Realizing their strength, TWU leaders made careful plans for the next month's meeting. There workers first complained about the contract, charging that through staggered hours and the introduction of "work checkers" the company was using a speed-up to compensate for the hour's reduction. Next a motion of no confidence in the delegates was unanimously passed. Finally, an unsuccessful effort was made to suspend the constitution for the remainder of the meeting, apparently with the intention of voting to affiliate the local with the TWU.[92]

The TWU leadership further built on the reaction to the Brotherhood pact by beginning to bring the union into the open. At 148th Street, where some 300 of the TWU's 560 members were located, 75 key union men were invited to attend the TWU's first mass meeting. Fifty showed up. Next came a meeting for all the unionists in the shop, which 200 workers attended. It in turn called a meting for everyone at 148th Street, whether or not they belonged to the TWU. As later reported at a CP conference, although this latter gathering "did not turn out so well because the company called a meeting for the same time . . . the majority of those present were new men and 58 joined the union."[93]

With these and similar developments elsewhere, locals were now formed at the strongest TWU locations to replace the system of secret, small groups. In January 1935, Local 1 was founded at 148th Street, Local 2 at the station department, Locals 3 and 4 at the Livonia and Corona barns, and Local 5 at the 59th Street powerhouse. Where the union was less firmly established, it retained a cellular structure and continued to agitate inside the Brotherhood.[94]

The TWU also began gathering signatures on a petition to the RLB asking for a recognition election. The company responded in kind, circulating pledge cards for the Brotherhood. In early March, 150 TWU members delivered the first batch of what were eventually over 1,600 signatures to the RLB. The IRT agreed to cooperate with the Board in validating the signatures, but stalled in doing so and indicated that it was neither acknowledging the Board's jurisdiction nor agreeing to abide by its decisions.

As the signature processing dragged on, the union grew increasingly impatient. One RLB official perceived "a mood which foreshadowed trouble brewing," including the possibility of a strike, if an election was not held soon. On May 27, however, the NIRA was declared unconstitutional. Santo immediately went to the RLB seeking clarification of the situation, but the best the Board could do was to ask Washington for permission to take up the election issue with Judge Mack, who supervised the IRT receivership. The request was apparently denied, for, on June 6, Elinore Herrick informed the TWU and the company that the case was closed. The possibility of an early union victory through a referendum was lost; the Wagner Act, which replaced the labor provisions of the NIRA, did not cover intrastate industries such as mass transit, and relevant state legislation was not passed until 1937.[95]

Even while the RLB was considering its petition, the TWU continued to make organizing advances. Particularly important was its growing success in recruiting key skilled craftsmen who had initially kept aloof, unsure of the TWU's staying power and not yet completely disenchanted with the possibility of working within the Brotherhood. Cautious, prudent, but not anti-union as such, these men, who Maurice Forge dubbed "solid citizens," formed a distinct subcategory of the relatively well-paid, more senior workers. Though they did not rush to join the TWU, in the end many became devoted members, stewards, and officers.[96]

The process of winning them over was most dramatic at 59th Street, where in spite of TWU gains the Faber group remained apart. In fact, at some point it had transformed itself into a formal organization, the "Independent Union of I.R.T. Workers," and begun issuing leaflets with what Forge remembers as a somewhat socialist slant. The TWU's central leadership, aware of their own union's growing strength in the powerhouse, suggested to the local TWU men that they seek a showdown with Faber in the form of an unofficial referendum. At a Brotherhood meeting this was proposed and accepted not only by Faber, but by local company union officials as well.

A storefront on 59th Street was rented and arrangements made for an April 9, 1935, vote. The Faber group stressed that it was "a real rank and file Union with no Boss-Rule from the inside or the outside," a veiled attack on the CP's role in the TWU. How actively the Brotherhood campaigned is unclear, since Chief Engineer Lawrence ordered powerhouse employees not to take part in the election. But in spite of his warnings, 127 men voted, and it was a near total triumph for the TWU; the Faber group and the Brotherhood each received but four votes.[97]

Once defeated, Faber quickly approached top TWU leaders about joining their union. They in turn were still eager for his participation, especially once they discovered that he had personally known Rosa Luxemburg and Ernst Thalmann, near-mythical heroes to American Communists. An understanding was swiftly arranged: Faber would bring the remainder of his group into the TWU and be given a position of importance as the officer in charge of finances. Eventually Faber also joined the CP, but that took some time since the Party first undertook a thorough investigation of his political past.[98]

With Faber now in the fold, the TWU was able to quickly consolidate its hold on 59th Street. The Brotherhood, in turn, began to collapse. By mid-1935 it stopped holding plant meetings; by October the TWU powerhouse unit was strong enough to pass a resolution forbidding its members from paying Brotherhood dues. The next spring the TWU was even able to force 59th Street Brotherhood official William Manning into resigning. By late 1936 the TWU had over 80% of the 59th Street plant organized and the local there became the first in the union to close its books on new applicants, giving them only until December 1 to join.[99]

A somewhat analogous situation developed at 148th Street with the "Gahaganites." Jimmy Gahagan was an Irish-American machinist and an extremely outgoing, happy-go-lucky, popular fellow. A World War I veteran and member of the American Legion, he was well known for his exuberant patriotism. When cutbacks hit the shop, Gahagan attempted to work within the Brotherhood, but when that proved a dead end he formed his own little circle, which Forge described as a "hip-hip hooray, I'm-an-American-day type of group." The TWU tried hard to coax Gahagan into the union, but he long resisted, until finally "he demanded to meet Quill eye-to-eye . . . and came over."[100]

At other locations, the TWU gained strength through the defection of Brotherhood officers. At 98th Street, for example, the rank-and-file committee's Brotherhood slate had been elected in November 1934, but the new chairman immediately allied himself with P. J. Connolly. The resulting fury was so great that the Brotherhood was forced to ban its critics from meetings. In the face of such steps, the local's financial secretary, Patrick Clarke, one of the original oppositionists, resigned his post and announced that he had joined the TWU. Also recruited at 98th Street was Maurice Ahern, a skilled worker, part-owner of a neighborhood bar, and a local leader of the Bronx Democratic machine. Politically ambitious, and disliked by some of the more radical shop workers for his Tammany ways, Ahern was nonetheless an important addition, and at his bar he made available a hall for union meetings. At the 74th Street powerhouse, six Brotherhood officials resigned in the fall of 1935. Some had probably been involved with the TWU even while holding company union posts.[101]

The Fabers, Gahagans, Aherns, and Clarkes not only brought the TWU a new respectability, but also a leadership capable of reaching men the union had previously failed to attract. Thus in spite of the fact that they were not true union pioneers, Faber and Gahagan quickly became the most important figures from their respective job sites in the union's central leadership. When the 148th Street local elected new officers in January 1936, it was not the old-guard that received the top posts, but Kavanaugh who became president and Gahagan vice-president, while at 98th Street both Clarke and Ahern were at various times elected shop chairman.[102]

Constant TWU agitation, the union's growing strength, and company hesitancy were changing the mood throughout the IRT. Both union and non-union workers were beginning to challenge company actions with aggressive responses, a sharp contrast with earlier patterns of fear and passivity. Most dramatic were a number of small but significant job actions centered in the car barns. Early in 1935 workers at the Livonia barn refused to do white-washing before starting their regular assignments, probably because it would have cut into their piecework pay. As a result, the company was forced to schedule a special Saturday afternoon white-washing shift. In May, 120 workers at the Corona barn went en masse to their foremen to protest new work loads, punitive transfers of union activists, and pay rates. After "some little excitement," a few grievances were adjusted.

On July 9 a more major clash took place at the Jerome barn. Six car cleaners refused orders to use a new type of squeegee to clean car windows, claiming that it would result in a speed-up. For this, they were fired. Other workers then stopped work and demanded to meet with the shop's general foremen. After being kept waiting for several hours, they were refused an audience and found their time cards removed. In response, sixty or seventy men walked out. Some belonged to the TWU, which took over the leadership of the struggle. The next day the barn and the IRT's headquarters were picketed, a formal strike authorization passed by the Jerome local of the TWU, and preparations begun for a mass meeting to consider striking the entire IRT.

Seeking to avert a wider walkout, Elinore Herrick stepped in and, after considerable discussion with the company and the union, arranged a settlement: the IRT was to consider the complaints of the Jerome men, who in turn were to return to work as a group. Although only minor adjustments resulted, this first TWU strike was considered a major victory. In spite of reported company efforts, no outside scabs were hired, all the strikers were taken back, including the six fired men, and the IRT was forced, in effect, to negotiate with the union. [103]

The strike had important, though very different, effects on the Jerome barn and the union as a whole. At the actual site of the walk-out, a sizable TWU group developed, but so did ill-feeling between strikers and non-strikers, as the latter had been given an extra day's pay and improved seniority. The local TWU leadership, a hard-drinking crew with little organizing ability, exacerbated the problem by alienating many potential recruits. It was well over a year before the rift was partially patched over, and even years later there remained a large group at Jerome opposed to the union. [104]

The effect on the rest of the union, however, was to bring a rapid increase in membership, perhaps as many as several hundred new members. Combined with a new dues structure, this gave the TWU a more solid financial base, enabling the delegates council to hire Quill and MacMahon in August 1935 as full-time organizers. (Hogan, Santo, Forge, and two others were already receiving $15 a week to work for the union.) Shortly thereafter the TWU moved its headquarters from near Union Square, the hub of the CP world, to a building on West 64th Street, an Irish neighborhood close to the main IRT powerhouse. As the union grew, it took over more and more of the building, which included an auditorium, until it occupied the entire structure, renaming it Transport Hall. [105]

The IRT responded to these developments by stepping up its anti-union activity. The results were, at best, mixed. The company, for example, began to suspend or fire more union cadre, but in each case the union took up the challenge. Letters were written to the IRT, its offices were surrounded by mass picket lines, and a defense fund was set up to aid fired men and their families. When Herbert Holmstrom, one of the first workers to meet with Santo almost two years earlier, was dismissed, he paraded in front of IRT headquarters with his wife and children, which drew considerable press attention. Perhaps growing out of the Irish tradition of shaming moral transgressors before their neighbors, the homes of individual IRT managers were picketed as well. In the end, most of the fired men were rehired and the union strengthened in the process. [106]

Physical clashes also began between company agents and unionists. On June 21, 1935, Tom O'Shea and two others were beaten up while preparing to speak at 148th Street. The attackers escaped in a car that belonged to a Brotherhood delegate who often served as P. J. Connolly's bodyguard. Then, following the "squeegee strike," the IRT retained the State Railway Police, a private firm prone to strong-arm tactics, to infiltrate the TWU and stop its growth. Almost immediately thereafter a full-scale brawl broke out at the Grand Central subway station between the Railway Police and some 150 unionists returning from a picket line at the IRT headquarters. The fighting began when company agents tried to arrest Quill, who was giving an impromptu speech. Although the TWU members, wielding sticks from their picket signs, at least held their own, five unionists, including Quill, O'Shea, and Holmstrom, were arrested. In a subsequent trial, those charged with assault were acquitted, and the TWU made considerable propaganda gains from the whole affair. [107]

Next came the exposure of a company spy, in itself a relatively minor incident, but interesting as an early example of Quill's talent and inclination for melodrama as a political and organizational tactic. Quill had come to suspect that a union ticket agent, Peter Engeheben, was working for the beakies. He took a number of steps, including having his future wife Mollie tail Engeheben, which seemed to confirm his suspicions. He and Forge then arranged an elaborate ruse. They invited Engeheben to a TWU staff meeting on a hot summer day, got him to take off his coat, and lured him out of the room. Quill rifled the coat's pockets and found a report by Engeheben that charged four TWU members with conspiring to sabotage the company's dynamos. While Forge kept Engeheben occupied, Quill had the report photographed. Quill then told Engeheben that at the next station department meeting he was going to be added to the local's executive committee.

When invited to address that meeting, Engeheben denounced the beakies. He was warmly applauded by the 150 men present, who were unaware of the real situation. Quill then sprung his trap, dramatically reading the intercepted report. Immediately, enraged unionists rushed the exposed informer. Quill and other TWU officers restrained them, but not surprisingly, given the temper of the meeting, Quill was able to get Engeheben to sign a confession admitting that his report was an attempted frame-up. Although Engeheben pleaded that he had become a spy only after being threatened with the loss of his job for union membership, he won little sympathy. After being forced to turn in his union book, and being told by Quill that he should jump in front of a train, he was finally allowed to leave. The IRT scoffed at the incident, but it received considerable press coverage. The *Irish Echo*, which previously had not been very sympathetic to the TWU, denounced the use of company spies. The net effort was to bolster the reputation of both the union and the hero of the day, Mike Quill. [108]

Although the IRT was clearly toughening its stance toward the TWU, its actions were still relatively mild by its own pre-Depression standards. The company, for example, never engaged in mass firings or made extensive use of physical force. By contrast, such tactics were being commonly employed by transit companies outside of New York and in various mass production industries.

Why was the IRT so restrained? Some of the reasons were political. New York's governor, Herbert Lehman, and the city's mayor, Fiorello La Guardia, had both been elected with labor support. Neither was sympathetic to corporate union-busting. With discussions already under way about a possible government-sponsored unification of the transit system, this was something management could not ignore. The possibility of unification also lessened the IRT's long-term stake in holding down labor costs.

The IRT's bankruptcy came into play as well. Thomas Murray, the company's receiver, was an Irish-American inventor, engineer, and businessman—a well-respected figure in the New York Irish community. Using physical force or mass firings to crush a heavily Irish union would have tarnished his community standing. Murray may also have had political aspirations he did not want to jeopardize; later in life he did seek public office.[109] In any case, he did not have a totally free hand; ultimately he was accountable to Judge Julian W. Mack, and Mack was a very unlikely union-buster.

Originally, Mack had not been in charge of the IRT receivership; the senior judge of the Federal Circuit Court of Appeals, Martin T. Manton, in a highly unusual move, had assigned the case to himself. Manton was a crook; he was eventually impeached and sent to jail for taking pay-offs. At his trial, there were hints of improprieties in his appointment of Murray to the lucrative IRT case. (In 1932 Murray invested over $20,000 in a Manton-controlled company that never paid dividends.) Apparently Manton was under suspicion for some time, which is probably why, in the fall of 1933, the Chief Justice of the United States, Charles Evans Hughes, ordered the IRT case transferred to Mack.

Julian Mack was a classic Progressive. The son of a German-Jewish tailor, and a Harvard Law School graduate, in Chicago he was heavily involved in Jewish philanthropy. Drawn into the Hull House circle, he became close to Jane Addams, succeeding her as president of the National Conference of Social Workers. In 1913 he was appointed a federal circuit judge, and during World War I additionally served as an umpire for the War Labor Board. Mack was one of Louis Brandeis's closest associates in the world Zionist movement and many other endeavors. Through Felix Frankfurter and Benjamin V. Cohen, his onetime law clerk, he was well-connected in the Roosevelt Administration. His liberal credentials were unassailable; he had helped raise money for Sacco and Vanzetti and, at the very time he was given the IRT case, served on the board of *Survey Magazine*, a major voice of Progressivism. Although it is unclear how actively Mack concerned himself with IRT labor policy, it is inconceivable that he would have allowed Murray to embark on a heavy-handed, union-busting crusade. His entire career had been devoted to the resolution of class conflict through negotiation and compromise.[110]

Mack's assignment to the IRT case was the result of a chain of complex circumstances—an unpredictable event. Yet his appointment was emblematic of the changing political tides. The arrangements and understandings which a judge like Manton depended on were beginning to unravel at the same time that a cadre of old judicial Progressives were achieving new influence with the coming of the New Deal. For the TWU, Mack's involvement was a stroke of luck; it meant a limit on the intensity of the opposition it would have to face.

By December 1935 the TWU was collecting dues from about 900 workers, mostly on the IRT. In addition, there were at least several hundred others who supported the union but were not paying dues.[111] Together, these groups represented only a very small minority of the IRT work force. Still, in the previous year the union had over doubled its membership and established formal units, now called sections, in many locations. To ensure further growth and stability, the TWU embarked on two organizational and political projects: establishing a structure and leadership corresponding to its increased strength, and entering the mainstream of the labor movement by affiliating with an AFL union.

The decision to enter the AFL came from outside the TWU, from developments within the CP. When the TWU was founded, the CP was already moving away from dual unionism. The TWU was one of the very last independent, CP-led unions to be established in the United States. In September 1934 the TUUL proposed unity to the AFL. When its offer was spurned, individual TUUL unions began seeking mergers or affiliations with individual Federation units. By the spring of 1935 in those industries where this tactic failed, TUUL unionists were simply joining AFL unions one-by-one. (TUUL itself was shortly laid to rest.)[112]

There was no evident internal TWU impulse toward AFL affiliation. The union, however, went along with the change in CP policy with little debate, even though it meant considering the previously unthinkable, affiliation with the hated and oft-attacked Amalgamated Association. In the spring of 1935 a TWU committee was established to explore just that possibility. Since the Amalgamated's organizing in New York was concentrated on the surface lines, the TWU apparently was willing to cede jurisdiction there in return for an industrial charter covering all three rapid transit lines.

After preliminary discussions with an Amalgamated representative, Hogan, Quill, Santo, and O'Shea traveled to Detroit to meet with the union's General Executive Board. Problems arose when the TWU leaders requested that their union be admitted as a separate district, without individual initiation fees or dues raised to the higher Amalgamated rate. The Amalgamated, in turn, was suspicious that in spite of their denials the TWU leaders were Communists. Although the Amalgamated sent a committee to New York to investigate the proposed affiliation, the TWU bid was ultimately rejected.[113]

With AFL affiliation for the moment blocked, the TWU moved to consolidate its own structure. In January 1936 elections were held for section officers and the union had its first convention.[114] The most important organizational step, however, had already been taken the previous month: the delegates council had elected Mike Quill as union president, replacing Tom O'Shea.[115]

O'Shea had turned out to be the TWU's Homer Martin.[116] Although a popular figure, a good speaker, and an enthusiastic unionist, he was a poor organizer and unable to operate well within the collective, CP-dominated leadership. Once given the title president, he tried to act like one, not at all what was planned or expected. Furthermore, he had personal problems; a heavy drinker, he had been disciplined for a second time by the IRT, this time apparently with legitimate cause, and generally he was unreliable.

Equally important, over the previous year it had become clear that O'Shea's whole approach to building the union significantly differed from that of the CP and most of the key union activists. While many of the ex-IRA men sought to draw on republican traditions, including some specific tactical measures, such as cellular organization, O'Shea saw the entire TWU project as essentially analogous to that of the latter-day IRA. Instead of careful mass organization, O'Shea wanted to apply IRA terrorist tactics to the problem of unionism. For example, if there was a problem with a dispatcher, O'Shea's first reaction was not to issue a leaflet, but to suggest "removing" him. In both private and public talks, he proposed winning union recognition by threatening the IRT with sabotage—derailing trains, bombs, and the like.[117] In this O'Shea was not unique; terrorism was one aspect of the republican tradition, and one or two other TWU members, including John Murphy, had also advocated its use. These men, however, formed only a tiny minority, even among the ex-IRA men.

Meanwhile, Quill had emerged as an increasingly important figure. His success at organizing, his skill on a soap-box, his popularity and network of acquaintances, and his willingness to defer to and learn from Communist organizers brought him an ever-greater role in the union. If in the Clan na Gael Quill was a relatively minor figure, in the TWU he soon became the leader of the Irish workers and then the key transit worker in the union as a whole. His growing stature was at various times officially acknowledged; he served as the TWU's legislative director, was referred to as a leading union spokesman, and finally was given the title vice president. When money was available to hire organizers, he and MacMahon got the jobs, not O'Shea. In fact, by the end of 1935 he was already the top worker-leader of the TWU in everything but name.

The removal of O'Shea and his replacement by Quill was apparently initiated by the TWU's Communist organizers, but it was not acted on unilaterally. The entire issue was discussed at a series of meetings with key union cadre. Some men objected to the move, feeling that even if O'Shea was a bit out of line, he was sincere about the union. More, however, even among the Irish republicans, felt that whether or not they liked O'Shea personally, or felt that he had played an important role in building the union, his personality and political world view were simply inappropriate to the tasks ahead. Furthermore, they were being asked to replace him with a person who had all of his strengths and few of his weaknesses.

In the end, a consensus was reached to make the change. The relative ease with which the inner core agreed on this step was a mark of its political maturity. O'Shea, realizing that he could not be elected by the delegates council, in whose hands the decision lay, acceded to Santo's request not to seek the union's top post, leaving Mike Quill free to be elected without opposition to the presidency of the TWU, a position he held for the next three decades.

While all this was happening, a second effort was begun to enter the AFL, this

time on the coat tails of the Federation of Metal and Allied Unions, an amalgama-
tion of the TUUL Metal Workers Industrial Union, led by James Matles, and a
number of independent electrical and radio industry groups. The Federation's component locals were later reunited in the United Electrical Workers Union (UE), but
at the time the metal working units were seeking affiliation with the AFL's International Association of Machinists (IAM). Negotiations started in the fall of 1935 and,
at Matles's suggestion, parallel meetings were held to consider a simultaneous TWU
affiliation.

At first glance, the IAM was an odd choice for the TWU. Traditionally, it had been
a craft union of skilled machinists; its ritual defined as eligible for membership only
whites working in the trade. But, by the mid-1930s, it had begun a transformation to
its present character, a union of both craft and industrial units, and it already represented some transit workers. The Machinists were seeking members however they
could get them and were willing to make concessions when necessary. In any case, the
TWU had no place else to go, and under Matles's lead there was the possibility that
the IAM could be converted into a progressive industrial organization.

The TWU link to the IAM was a subsidiary element in the larger metal workers
merger, and Matles played a key role in negotiating both agreements. The IAM was
to give the TWU a charter as a new lodge with jurisdiction over all New York transit
lines. All current TWU members, including blacks, were to be accepted without
initiation fees, as the IAM ritual was to be waived for the two entering groups. IAM
President A. O. Wharton further pledged to support eliminating the ritual at the
next International convention. The IAM agreed not to break up the TWU along
craft lines, although it could not guarantee that other AFL unions would not make
jurisdictional claims. Dues were to be on a sliding scale, with the highest rate 75
cents a month more than current in the TWU.

In affiliating with the IAM, the TWU was entering just the sort of old-line craft
union it had long criticized. The Brotherhood, in fact, responded to the merger by
reprinting earlier TWU attacks on the AFL. The IAM agreement, however, gave
the TWU virtually everything it wanted; it would be able to keep its membership,
leadership, and structure intact. In February 1936 the proposed affiliation was
approved by a TWU membership vote and by the IAM Executive Council. The
next month, with over a thousand transit workers present, IAM official George
Bowen gave the TWU a charter as Transport Workers Lodge No. 1547.[118]

There was an important postscript to both the AFL affiliation and O'Shea's
ouster. Under IAM rules, the TWU was entitled to elect, by secret membership
vote, two business agents to be paid by the International. (Other officers were paid
with local funds.) The union leadership decided on Santo and MacMahon for the
posts. The only problem was that O'Shea decided to use this opportunity to attempt
a comeback, declaring his candidacy against Santo for one of the jobs.

TWU elections were always two-stage affairs, with one voting period for day
workers and another the next morning for the night shift. In this case, after the day-
shift vote, Quill, who was living at the union hall, decided to check the ballots. He
discovered that O'Shea was leading Santo by a considerable margin, enough to
almost guarantee his victory. If the inner core of the union—the delegates
council—had been convinced of O'Shea's failings, the membership-at-large re-

mained loyal to the man the union itself had carefully built up. Voting was light and O'Shea had actively campaigned, while Santo was still keeping a low profile and was resented by some as an outsider and a suspected red.

Believing that O'Shea's election would be disastrous, Quill approached another left-wing TWU leader and the two men took the ballot box up to Quill's room. Without consulting others, they stuffed the box with enough ballots to ensure Santo's victory, returning it in time for the night-shift vote. When the ballots were counted, Santo was the victor. No one, including O'Shea, knew of the tampering, although some in the inner circle probably suspected something.[119] For a while O'Shea continued to try to get back into the TWU leadership, but he was soon out of the picture. Thus the first real challenge to the union leadership was eliminated, the process of AFL affiliation completed, and the stage set for the next phase of organizing.

5

ORGANIZING: 1936–1937

At the time of its affiliation with the IAM, the TWU was still basically an organization of IRT workers.[1] The union was also active on the ISS, where a number of significant developments were occurring, but since that situation was quite unique it will be discussed separately in a later chapter. In the fall of 1936 the TWU began sustained organizing on the BMT; shortly thereafter it took on the surface companies as well. Less than a year later, the TWU won a series of recognition elections at all the major New York transit firms and signed closed shop contracts covering 30,000 workers. Just before these votes, the union left the IAM, reconstituted itself as an international union, and affiliated with the Committee for Industrial Organization (CIO), the labor federation formed in late 1935 by several dissident AFL unions.

During the first half of 1936, it would have been audacious to have predicted the TWU's great victories, which were to come but a year later. On the IRT the union still faced two very basic tasks: winning the allegiance of more workers, especially in previously untouched sectors of the work force; and finding some way to force company recognition. Neither was going well. Although the union continued recruiting and agitation, and a few more Brotherhood leaders were won over, there was no dramatic surge in membership. A 2% wage hike in May 1936 undoubtedly retarded the union's growth. The TWU had reached several layers down into the work force, but seemingly could go no farther. Those most inclined to join had already done so; everyone else was holding out.[2] The TWU fight against the IRT pension plan was also having only limited success. In response to a TWU petition, Judge Mack ordered pension contributions segregated from other company funds, but in June he upheld the plan and the IRT's refusal to allow withdrawals.[3] All in all, the TWU was stalled.

In an effort to regain flagging momentum, a special June 1936 TWU membership meeting approved a plan for a fall campaign for union recognition. A committee headed by Austin Hogan was chosen to draft contract demands and a drive was begun to get both members and non-members to sign cards authorizing the TWU to represent them in negotiations. To kick off the campaign, a large, open-air rally was held in the South Bronx.[4] The union received an important boost on August 20 when the AFL's New York Central Trades and Labor Council voted to back the TWU drive to "organize all workers in the transit system of the City of New York," language that the TWU interpreted as an endorsement of its jurisdictional claim over all rapid transit employees.[5]

A ten-point program of demands was approved and a bargaining committee selected at a September 17 meeting of 500 workers. The program called for wages to be set at a level 10% over the pre-1933 scale, with a minimum of $25 a week; a reduction in hours without loss of pay; overtime pay and annual vacations; strict seniority and improved safety and sanitary conditions; the right to resign from the pension plan and its eventual replacement; no lay-offs from technological change or the unification of transit lines; rehiring of workers fired for union activities; and recognition of the TWU as the sole bargaining agent for the IRT work force.[6] When Thomas Murray rejected this program, claiming that the IRT's financial position was such that it could not meet any of the demands, Hogan announced that the TWU would hold a strike vote on October 16. Meanwhile, organizing was stepped up. The union also asked Judge Mack to hold an election to determine who should represent IRT workers in negotiations. (The IRT-Brotherhood contract was to expire December 31.)

A showdown never came. Just prior to the scheduled strike vote, discussions began between the TWU and IRT General Manager Keegan on a broad range of issues. The company, in effect, granted the TWU partial recognition. It agreed that the TWU had the right to organize without interference and that there would be no discrimination against unionists. The TWU was empowered to represent its members in grievances, for which purpose its representatives were to be given release time. Company foremen were forbidden from distributing Brotherhood literature, which was also banned from company bulletin boards, and the TWU was allowed bulletin boards of its own in shops and terminals.

Given this progress, the 1,000 workers who met on October 16 were told that a strike vote was unnecessary. During the following weeks, the union repeatedly claimed that at long last it had won recognition. Day-to-day relations with management underwent a dramatic improvement, as grievances, for the first time, were successfully pursued. The TWU's growing power brought a new wave of membership applications.

The union's discussions with the IRT on wages, hours, and working conditions, however, did not go well. At one point, in early December, the IRT offered the TWU contract and a counter-proposal was made, but in the end no agreement was reached. Instead, the IRT quietly extended the Brotherhood's contract for another year. For TWU members, the exhilaration of mid-October ended in December with the realization that although their union had won certain rights, it was still far from having established itself as the sole bargaining agent for IRT employees.[7]

Throughout the fall and winter IRT campaign, the TWU paid special attention to recruiting workers in those job categories where the union was weak or not at all established, particularly elevated transportation workers; subway switchmen, tower-men, and motormen; and power substation workers. These men worked alone or in small groups and, with the exception of the el conductors and guards, were among the best-paid in the system. To recruit these groups, special campaigns were launched using volunteer organizers from the shops, barns, and powerhouses.[8]

The most important and perhaps most difficult to organize of the above-mentioned workers were the motormen. In any confrontation with the company they would, by the very nature of their job, play a central role, but in spite of TWU efforts they remained largely under the sway of the company union. There were several reasons for this. To become a motorman took years of service and training, but thereafter there was little chance for further advancement; as one said, "when you made motorman, you died a motorman." As a result, train drivers tended to be clannish and to look down on other workers. Into the late 1940's it was the rule that all non-motormen, and sometimes even newly qualified men, were banned from the motormen's waiting rooms at the terminals.

Such elitism was part of a general craft outlook. In the words of a 1936 *New York Times* feature, the motorman's "highly skilled craft lends him confidence and dig-nity." With the responsibility for human life literally in their hands, motormen took great pride in their competence and station, even though their job was lonely and monotonous. Some of the older motormen, who had operated steam locomotives before the els were electrified, did not even think of themselves as transit workers; in their minds they were railroad men. In fact, a few were allowed by the company to maintain membership in the BLE so as to remain eligible for union death benefits.

Within the context of their craft orientation, the motormen historically had been among the most militant and union-minded transit workers. However, they had tasted failure many times, including in the 1926 strike, only ten years earlier. As a result, they were divided between former strikers and former scabs, left fearful of the power of the company and its Brotherhood allies, and resentful of other workers who had largely failed to support their last walkout. Many of the motormen who still hoped for a bona fide union continued to think along craft lines.

The fact that the motormen were considerably better-paid than other road employ-ees contributed to their lack of enthusiasm for industrial unionism. One platform man, an early TWU supporter, remembers with bitterness that motormen "were getting the onmipotent sum of 65 cents an hour. And they thought they were King Tut. . . . Oh no. No union for them." A high proportion of the motormen were married, with children and sometimes even suburban homes; like all transit workers they faced harsh conditions, but they had more to lose than most.[9]

The TWU did not have a ready-made network of contacts among the motor-men as it did among, say, the ticket agents through the Clan na Gael or the shop workers through the Communist concentration work. For two years it made very little headway. Even after a sustained, targeted campaign was begun in the fall of 1936, progress was slow. The TWU's success in winning concessions from the company late that year, along with the continual agitation, finally began to yield some results. Still, in December 1936, when the company union as a whole was well on its way to collapse, the majority of subway motormen were paying dues to Brotherhood Local 7.[10]

The TWU's situation somewhat improved when two able and dedicated leaders emerged among the motormen, Phil Bray and James Fitzsimon. The two, close friends, had both been motormen since the late 1920s, and before that had been among the few non-motormen to join the 1926 strike. Both were Irish-born, married, and parents. Bray was from Limerick and had fought with the IRA in the anti-British war and the civil war. While jailed during the latter struggle, he had participated in a month-long hunger strike. Upon release from prison he came to New York and got a job as an IRT guard. Disgusted with the turn of events in his native land, he avoided Irish cultural and political activities. He joined the TWU in early 1935.

Fitzsimon was born in County Kerry in 1907. Two of his brothers were Church officials, but Fitzsimon, like his father, an architect, was a non-believer. In fact, he was among the more independent and adventurous thinkers in the TWU. While working as a motormen he completed several years of college-level training in engineering, an unusual accomplishment for a transit worker. Like Bray, Fitzsimon was not active in Irish politics, but he was approached early on about joining the TWU by Gerald O'Reilly and Jimmy McCue of the Clan group. Although sympathetic, he became active only after a period of hesitation—his wife was dying of cancer and he had three small children to care for. Though Bray and Fitzsimon did not join the TWU right away, once they signed up they became key figures among the motormen. Eventually, both served as TWU staff organizers.[11]

In seeking to attract motormen, the TWU contrasted its growing strength to the financial and moral bankruptcy of the Brotherhood. Bray and Fitzsimon promised that the TWU would fight to restore seniority rights lost in the 1926 strike, but the union also let it be known that it "lets 'BYGONES BE BYGONES' and welcomes ANY motorman and switchman, no matter what his past labor record may have been." The union arranged to make available a sick and death benefit to counteract this attraction of the BLE and the Brotherhood.

The TWU was helped greatly by the national explosion of industrial unionism in the winter of 1936-37. In Bray's words, "Detroit," where auto worker sit-downs were taking place, "was beginning to teach [the motormen] a lesson about industrial organization."[12] By early 1937 the TWU was signing up more and more motormen and switchmen, with the Irish tending to join a bit earlier than others. The Brotherhood transportation locals were in clear trouble. But even at this late date, it remained a constant struggle.

The TWU faced similar problems, and adopted a similar targeted approach, in recruiting power substation workers and towermen. Again, progress was slow, craft and elite attitudes strong, and significant gains made only after the union was well-established elsewhere on the IRT. Partial recognition greatly aided the TWU among these hard-to-recruit workers. Union bulletin boards in substations, for example, helped lessen fears of company reprisals and were a tangible sign of the union's new legitimacy in the eyes of the company. Union conferences with divisional managers had the same effect. On occasion, the TWU threatened to institute high initiation fees for those who did not join before a given date, an effective device used again in later campaigns. In short, it was only as the union began to supplant managerial authority and was clearly becoming a permanent force, that the company and its employees alike would have to deal with, that many workers finally joined up.[13]

Union membership figures are extremely difficult to interpret in a pre-contract situation. On the one hand, they are usually inflated. On the other, for every dues-payer there are often several sympathizers. Estimates of TWU strength at the end of 1936 range from less than 5,000 to 8,000, with the bulk of these members concentrated on the IRT. Probably close to a third of all IRT workers were paying dues to the union, a impressive indication of strength. However, the failure to secure a contract and the renewal of the Brotherhood pact were significant setbacks, and the situation could well have again stagnated. But just as this possibility was developing, the entire picture was dramatically transformed by events elsewhere, on the BMT, the second largest transit company in the city.[14]

Considered in isolation, the BMT presented the TWU with a more difficult organizing target than the IRT. Though smaller, it was more physically spread out and included trolley and bus as well as rapid transit workers. Traditionally a better-managed company, it was being run by its own executives rather than by a court-appointed receiver. Also, it was more ethnically heterogeneous; the Irish republican network, which proved so important on the IRT, played little role on the BMT. Still another problem was the Catholic Church; its Brooklyn hierarchy very actively opposed left-wing unionism. Finally, although the BMT company union was not as formidable as the IRT Brotherhood, the TWU had to contend with legitimate union rivals: BMT motormen, signalmen, and towermen already were represented by craft unions, and the Amalgamated Association was trying to organize the company.[15]

The first phase of BMT organizing—between the late 1933 and the fall of 1936—resembled the TWU's early development on the IRT, but on a smaller scale, at a slower rate, extended over a longer period. Through the CP, TWU organizers had a few contacts with whom to work. In addition, CP concentration units were enlisted to leaflet selected locations with union and Communist literature. These efforts enabled the TWU to build a network of contacts that reached into many parts of the company, but was extremely thin.[16] As it became obvious that things were going better on the IRT, the TWU concentrated its resources there.[17]

The BMT employees first interested in unionism tended to be shop workers. The large Avenue X shop, part of a complex of BMT facilities in Coney Island, was, like 148th Street, its IRT equivalent, a center of worker unrest. During the first half of 1934 the Amalgamated Association succeeded in organizing a group of thirty-nine men in the shop. However, by promoting two members of the group in return for their cooperation, the BMT obtained an Amalgamated membership list and fired twenty unionists. The Amalgamated appealed to the RLB, but the BMT refused to recognize the federal agency's jurisdiction. Although some of the men were eventually rehired, the Amalgamated was effectively squashed. This left the field open to the TWU, which had been conducting agitation of its own. Still, TWU organizers succeeded only in developing scattered contacts; no actual TWU groups were functioning at Avenue X until 1937. The TWU also developed contacts at two smaller BMT repair facilities, a shop in East New York and the DeKalb Avenue shop, where the TWU men operated under the cover of a local Holy Name Society.[18]

Most of these shop contacts were low-skilled men. However, the TWU did have some success among skilled workers from the British Isles—usually from the Glasgow or Belfast regions—who had had previous trade union experience. At DeKalb, for example, a key recruit, although not one of the very earliest, was Peter Mac-Lachlan, a Scottish Protestant electrician who first joined a union as a sixteen-year-old apprentice in a Clydeside shipyard. MacLachlan eventually became one of the leading unionists on the BMT.[19]

The TWU also made some advances among rapid transit conductors and trolley operators working out of a number of different of depots.[20] The union largely stayed away from the BMT's 700 bus drivers, since the Amalgamated had recruited a substantial percentage of these men. Only later, in 1937, did the TWU win over the bus drivers. By then, the company had fired at least twenty Amalgamated members and in response the drivers had briefly struck. Although the walk-out was partially successful, the Amalgamated's support had been at best wavering. As a result, most of the drivers deserted the Amalgamated and joined the TWU.[21]

Similarly, at first the TWU made only a token effort to recruit BMT motormen, who had their own BLE local. Instead, it criticized the BLE leadership for turning their organization into a virtual company union and called for greater rank-and-file militancy. Given this stand, it is not surprising that the BLE ignored the TWU's repeated proposals for cooperative efforts. Not until the spring of 1937, when a recognition election was being discussed, did the TWU launch a serious drive to sign up the motormen.[22]

During the first phase of TWU's BMT activity, men joined up one by one, not in groups; according to MacLachlan, "it was like pulling teeth." Often there were setbacks, as new recruits grew afraid of losing their jobs and quit the union. When Douglas MacMahon was assigned to the BMT on a full-time basis in late summer or early fall of 1936, by his later estimate the union had but fifty or sixty members.[23]

MacMahon's assignment marked the beginning of a second, more concerted phase of BMT organizing.[24] With the campaign for IRT recognition under way, TWU leaders felt they could risk a major effort at expansion. Their confidence proved justified; in spite of all the difficulties the TWU faced, if, for the sake of argument, one looks only the second phase of BMT activity, it actually took far less time to organize and win recognition on the BMT than on the IRT. This was a measure of the fact that different social processes were involved on the two lines. On the IRT, outside organizers and inside activists created a new institution from scratch. On the BMT, an existing institution, with considerable resources, sizable membership, some concrete victories, and an experienced leadership, set out to extend its influence to a new arena. The BMT organizing drive—or at least its second phase—built upon the success already achieved on the IRT and occurred during the very height of a national union upsurge.

The big break on the BMT came in January 1937 and involved a group which had already proved on the IRT to be strongly pro-union, the powerhouse workers. At the time, thirty-five of the 350 or so men at the BMT powerhouse at Kent Avenue and the East River (in the Williamsburg section of Brooklyn) belonged to the TWU. A few were also members of the CP. Most of the TWU members were either licensed engineers or oilers born in Spain. The engineers were highly qualified men in semi-supervisory positions. One of their number, Ed Pollack, had leftish political views and had recruited some of his colleagues to the union. Apparently the engineers felt themselves underpaid for their qualifications and work. Many also sympathized with the plight of the lower-paid men in the plant. The Spanish oilers, low-skilled men, had been drawn to the left by the civil war under way in their native land, which in turn led some to join the TWU. [25]

On January 23, a Saturday, the BMT fired (or by some accounts suspended) two veteran engineers, with virtually no notice, for being absent from their posts. [26] The TWU charged that the real issue was their union activity, and it immediately swung into action. At an emergency meeting thirty-one Kent Avenue unionists voted by secret ballot to hold a sit-down strike the following Monday afternoon if the fired men had not by then been reinstated. The choice of the sit-down tactic undoubtedly was heavily influenced by the General Motors strike then in progress. Also, a dramatic move may have been seen as a way to revive morale on the IRT, where the TWU had become bogged down. On Monday morning MacMahon telegramed BMT President W. S. Menden demanding a conference to discuss reinstating the men. When no reply was received, the strike plan was put into action. [27]

At 3:00 p.m. when the 150-man first shift was due to leave work, two union officers entered the plant and joined in-plant unionists in urging workers not to leave until the two fired men were returned to their jobs. As the second shift took over operation of the plant, a large majority of first-shift workers remained in the building. TWU buttons began to be distributed throughout the plant. When the next shift change came at 11:00 p.m., once again most of the employees stopping work stayed in the building, so that while the plant continued to function it was filled with 250 strikers under the leadership of the TWU. New York City's first "stay-in" strike was under way.

As word of the strike spread, both sides began mobilizing their forces. Regular BMT beakies and plainclothesmen hired from detective agencies descended on the plant; by early the next morning 150 "guards" had been assembled. Half this force, uniformed and in some cases armed, was in the plant itself, where army cots and emergency lights had been brought in by the company. In an eerie evocation of the 1892 Homestead strike, an excursion steamer was chartered and docked next to the plant as a potential strikebreaking headquarters. BMT spokesmen let it be known that the company intended to begin evicting the strikers in the early morning hours using its own personnel.

On the union side, TWU members from throughout the city began arriving. Joined by members of the union's Ladies' Auxiliary, they formed a picket line in front of the plant. Members of the Retail Food Clerks Union brought food for the strikers, which was hoisted into the plant through open windows. On the street outside gathered the top TWU leadership, which was in touch with CP-leader Charles Krumbein. A hundred or so New York City policemen and a host of reporters and photographers also assembled.

As night settled in, the tense stand-off continued. Implicit in the occupation was the threat of shutting off the power, halting BMT trolley and rapid transit operations in the Borough of Brooklyn, which would affect two million daily riders. According to one newspaper account, around midnight Quill, from outside the plant, actually ordered the power shut down. However, either from a failure in relaying the message or a decision taken inside the plant, no action resulted. Quill quickly revised his order to say that as long as the company made no effort to seize the plant, power would continue. Grasping the opportunity created by the sit-down, the Amalgamated, which at the time was fighting for the reinstatement of its fired bus drivers, threatened a strike of its own. Meanwhile, the IRT, hoping to prevent a spread of the job action, posted copies of a standing injunction against interference with its operations.

The outcome of the stay-in was to a large extent determined by the New York City government, which through the police had a large say in who would control the plant. In the end, it was top police officials, apparently in touch with La Guardia, who negotiated a settlement. Discussions among the various parties began shortly after midnight and by early the next morning an agreement was reached and ratified by the men in the plant. All strikers and company guards were to leave the building, after which time a conference was to be held on the original issue of the suspended engineers. In addition to company officials and the two men in question, two unionists elected by the men in the plant, Pollack and fellow engineer Joseph Fody, were to attend. At 6:20 a.m. the plant was evacuated.

On January 27, following the agreed-to conference, W. S. Menden conceded that the suspension of the two men had been "possibly an error" and they were reinstated. In the following weeks, discussions were held between BMT officials, Fody and Pollack, and the plant's two company union representatives, Herbert Connors and Gus Eckroth, on the possibly of holding a recognition election at Kent Avenue. Connors and Eckroth, who were sympathetic to the TWU and possibly even members, claimed that a canvass of the powerhouse workers indicated that a majority wanted TWU representation. Although no election resulted from these talks, the strike had been, without question, a great success. As the *New York Times* said, the BMT, "hitherto impregnable in disputes with unions, yielded on the main point."[28]

The Kent Avenue sit-down, Santo later noted, "electrified the entire industry and changed the whole picture." On the BMT, the strike broke the pervasive fear of the company and, as far as MacLachlan was concerned, "was the beginning of the union. The union took hold after that." Membership increased rapidly and a union structure began to be built, though the TWU remained much weaker on the BMT than the IRT. The effect of the strike carried over to other lines as well. On the IRT, workers again began pouring into the union. On the Manhattan and Bronx surface lines, where the TWU had just begun organizing, the strike victory provided an important boost.[29]

The strike was also a boon for the CP, since the handful of Communists in the powerhouse had played leading roles. A subsequent Party recruiting effort quickly led to the formation of a Kent Avenue CP unit with fourteen members. By the end of 1937 at least two other CP groups had been set up on the BMT, one at Avenue X and one catch-all industrial unit.[30]

The BMT sit-down was a turning point in the history of the TWU. As was so often true in the organization of American industrial unions, it came when a relatively small number of workers, who had previously failed to win majority support, took direct action, in this case led by and over an issue involving engineers whose status as "workers" was not even clear. In the course of action, new union members were recruited. The victory they helped achieve shifted the balance of power away from management. This, in turn, led to a more major influx of previously passive, hesitant, or hostile workers. Maybe, though, as Forge contended, by this time "there really had to be no turning points, given the situation nationally, given the air, the whole Wagner Act movement, the whole awakening, and given the miserable conditions in the the transit lines."[31]

Even before the TWU was formed, some trolley and bus workers were trying to unionize. Generally these efforts took place under the aegis of the Amalgamated Association. The most dramatic developments occurred at the Fifth Avenue Coach Company. In August 1933 a group of Fifth Avenue workers, inspired by the recent passage of the National Industrial Recovery Act, organized Amalgamated Division 994. Apparently the group had ties to the Socialist Party. In mid-August the division held an openly-advertised meeting. Company officials used the occasion to identify the union's members, some of whom where subsequently shadowed. In October, nineteen unionists, including all of the division's officers, were fired. Later, eight more men were let go.

Among those fired was the division's secretary-treasurer, Nicholas Treanor, an Irish-born bus man with republican sympathies, who was one of those extraordinary examples of the living continuity of American labor history. In 1916, Treanor had been a trolley motorman in San Francisco and a supporter of Tom Mooney's effort to unionize that city's transit system; he was one of six men fired in an abortive strike called by Mooney. Treanor had met with Mooney on the morning of the bomb explosion that led to Mooney's long imprisonment. Blacklisted for his role in the strike and his refusal of a sizable monetary offer to testify against Mooney, Treanor eventually came to New York and, under a slightly different name, got a job with Fifth Avenue Coach.

Treanor and the other fired Fifth Avenue men fought a long, losing battle for reinstatement and union recognition. The Amalgamated filed charges on their behalf with the RLB, but the company refused to recognize that body's jurisdiction or in any way cooperate. In February 1934, during a city-wide taxi strike, some Division 994 members unsuccessfully tried to extend the walkout to the Fifth Avenue. Later that month, at the request of 150 employees, the RLB held a representation election on the line. The company again would not cooperate and so successfully intimidated its workers that only twelve out of 1,450 voted, forcing the Board to invalidate the referendum. Meanwhile, the national Amalgamated restricted its role to pursuing the RLB case. As the case dragged on, ultimately to fail, the fired men became increasingly estranged from their union. Their final effort, an attempted boycott in mid-1935, was futile.[35]

A similar situation developed on the Third Avenue Railway. In 1935 a group of workers, mostly from the line's Kingsbridge Division (in upper Manhattan and the Bronx), obtained an Amalgamated charter and signed up a considerable number of men. However, two leaders of the drive were soon fired and the Amalgamated abandoned the effort.[33] Simultaneously, a committee of workers at the company's main repair shop, in contact with the *Daily Worker*, agitated for a union, but nothing permanent came of this either.[34]

Early on, the TWU made a stab at organizing the surface lines, but it soon gave up (except on the BMT).[35] However, it did aid surface workers who were trying, on their own, to unionize. Most importantly, when the Amalgamated did little to support the fired Fifth Avenue workers, members of the still infant TWU picketed in their behalf. Through this cooperation, two of the fired men, Treanor and Matthias Kearns, a former member of the Hod Carriers, became close to the TWU and the CP. Both men later helped the TWU in its own surface organizing efforts, and Kearns eventually joined the union's staff.[36]

In December 1936, with drives already under way on all three New York rapid transit systems, the TWU again tried organizing surface workers. This time things went went extremely well, especially on the Third Avenue, where the union spread "like wildfire." Through Treanor, Santo and Quill arranged to meet with a group of Third Avenue workers, largely from the Kingsbridge division. Apparently some of the men had been discussing the possibility of unionizing; a few may have been involved in the abortive Amalgamated effort. Among those at the meeting were John Gallagher and Matthew Guinan, both of whom were to play important roles in the history of the TWU[37]

Gallagher was an Irish-born conductor, who had come to the United States in 1930 and almost immediately had gotten a job with the Third Avenue. He met Treanor when Treanor came to his depot to collect money for the fired Fifth Avenue men, and the two kept in contact. He also had a passing acquaintance with Quill through the Irish dance circuit. Articulate and self-possessed, Gallagher was picked by Santo to lead the group. Within a year he became the first chairman of the Kingsbridge section of the TWU and one of the union's main oppositionists.[38]

Matthew Guinan was to replace Austin Hogan as the head of the TWU's New York transit local in 1949, and later to succeed Quill as International President. In the early days, however, his role was modest. He was born in County Offaly, Ireland, in 1910, one of ten children of a carpenter and builder. With several of his brothers already working in his father's trade, Guinan's parents were able to send him to a Patrician Brothers School, where he received a far more extensive education than typical of New York Irish transit workers. After coming to America in 1929, he got a job as an automobile mechanic in a New York suburb.

Laid-off as a result of the Depression, in January 1933 he started as a Third Avenue motorman. For Guinan, this meant a sharp deterioration in pay and working conditions at the very moment he was getting married and starting a family, a shift from a situation in which "we were all gentlemen, we had a feeling of pride about our job," to the low-status, autocratic world of transit. Guinan bitterly resented this change, which was the root of his interest in unionism.

Although obviously bright and educated, Guinan was extremely cautious. In spite of his early involvement with TWU, he did not play a major part in organizing the union. But when the Kingsbridge section of the union chose its first officers, Guinan was made secretary, in part on Gallagher's recommendation and in part because of his ability to keep accurate records.[39]

At roughly the same time that the Kingsbridge men were recruited, TWU organizers also made contact with workers at a variety of other Third Avenue locations. To a large extent this was done through Irish IRT unionists, who had social and political ties to many men on the heavily Irish Third Avenue. The CP, by contrast, played little if any role in providing contacts.

Although the pattern of organization on the Third Avenue followed that elsewhere—secret meetings at first; leadership from younger men, usually unmarried; 1916 strike veterans joining early on but staying in the background—the union grew so quickly that it is difficult to discuss a detailed ontogeny. In mid-April 1937, immediately after the Supreme Court upheld the constitutionality of the Wagner Act, the Third Avenue unionists put on a show of force; they wore their TWU buttons to work. The company retaliated by suspending a few men, but by then it was already too late. TWU members took the company to court, kept wearing their buttons, and began holding open meetings. The Third Avenue backed down and "from then on the union grew by leaps and bounds."[40]

There are a number of reasons why the Third Avenue drive progressed with such ease and rapidity. Coming as one of the last of the original TWU organizing campaigns, it benefited from the success and renown the union had achieved elsewhere. Many Third Avenue men were hoping that the TWU would organize their company; these workers joined up quickly once the campaign began. The drive also benefited from the wealth of experience TWU leaders had acquired. The mood created by FDR's 1936 campaign, the auto sit-downs, and the TWU success at Kent Avenue helped as well. Finally, with so many Irish workers involved, some of whom had belonged to the IRA, the union could organize both on the job and through neighborhood, social, and political channels.[41] All these factors also came into play in the organizing drives the TWU soon launched on the Fifth Avenue Coach and New York City Omnibus lines. These campaigns also went swiftly and smoothly, though on the Fifth Avenue the lasting impact of the Amalgamated fiasco had a somewhat retarding effect.[42]

A comparison of the various TWU organizing campaigns shows that each successive drive occurred with greater rapidity than those previous, with the various stages of union development increasingly compressed and combined. Although the union was thus able to expand from its initial base with growing ease, the process of creating a new social institution, and the individual transformations associated therewith, was not fully repeated.

To join the TWU in 1934 or 1935 was a bold and risky break with the status quo. It often meant being seen and being treated as an oddball at work and in one's neighborhood. Sometimes this freed men to change their way of seeing the world around them. By contrast, to join the TWU in 1937 was to jump on a bandwagon. David Montgomery has written that:

> Culture patterns that had appeared ingrown and defensive over long periods of "normal" times, could provide the basis of powerful solidarities and apparently overnight changes in behavior, when workers smelled weakness in the authorities to whom they had previously been obedient.[43]

This was certainly true in New York transit. But when a whole culture was changing, less questioning of the culture itself was likely to take place. Accordingly, those involved in the last TWU drives, on the surface lines, were not as likely as the early IRT men to shift far to the left. Nor were they as easily integrated into the web of personal relationships at the union's core. As a result, considerable differences emerged in the political character of the union from company to company. These differences continued for many years and helped shape the TWU's internal political dynamic. However, at the time of the surface drives little attention was paid to this, for the more important fact was that the TWU at last seemed close to victory.[44]

In the spring of 1937 the TWU's central concern was shifting from signing up more members to winning recognition and contracts. The issue first came to a head on the IRT, still the union's strongest base. By March the TWU sections at the 148th Street shop, the 59th Street powerhouse, and four car barns had achieved close to 100% membership and had closed their books to new members. Two more car barns and the 74th Street powerhouse were close behind. The transportation and station department sections were growing stronger and new sections had been set up for power substation workers, towermen, signalmen, and the chief inspector's office.[45]

On March 19, a meeting of 4,000 IRT workers, the largest TWU gathering yet, demanded that Receiver Murray hold a representation election. Twelve days later he agreed. According to one account, Murray first sought and received assurances from City Hall that recognizing the TWU would not jeopardize the IRT's position in negotiations over unification.[46]

The IRT and TWU asked Elinore Herrick, who by this time was working for the National Labor Relations Board (NLRB), which had been set up by the Wagner Act, to supervise the election. In preliminary conferences the TWU dropped its demand for a single, system-wide election unit and agreed to twelve separate units organized along a combination of departmental and craft lines. When Herrick decided that the NLRB did not have jurisdiction, since no interstate commerce was involved, supervision of the referendum was handed over to a voluntary agency established by La Guardia to handle such situations, the City Industrial Relations Board (CIRB).[47]

With an election now a virtual certainty, other unions suddenly became interested in the IRT. The Brotherhood, already in an advanced state of disintegration, collapsed completely. Its president, P. J. Connolly, joined the BLE, which asked to be put on the ballot in the two motormen's units. The Brotherhood of Railroad Signalmen of America (BRSA) sought to represent the towermen and signalmen.[48] In early May, the Amalgamated entered the picture as well, both on the IRT and the Third Avenue, where the TWU had also asked for an election. The Amalgamated strategy was simple and bold; it hoped to win through jurisdictional claims and employer cooperation what it had failed to win through organizing. "We are not in favor of a poll on either line," announced Amalgamated spokesman John Sullivan. "The A.F. of L. has given the Amalgamated jurisdiction over the transit workers, and there is nothing to vote about.[49]

The Amalgamated had the backing of both the AFL and the president of the Third Avenue, S. W. Huff. Huff not only rejected the TWU demand for an election, but announced that he was prepared to recognize the Amalgamated as the sole bargaining agent on the line. According to Huff, when the TWU first began organizing, he had contacted national and state AFL leaders, who had informed him that the TWU had jurisdiction only over machinists and machinists' helpers.

Huff then "notified the Amalgamated Association that it was free to carry on such organizational activities . . . as it wished." Huff further claimed that the Amalgamated had signed up a majority of his company's workers, an outlandish contention.[50] On the IRT, the Amalgamated, with apparent AFL support, sought a postponement of the planned election, which it threatened to boycott.[51]

The TWU response to this attempted Amalgamated squeeze was swift and effective. On April 30 an emergency meeting of 2,000 Third Avenue workers authorized a strike if the company did not agree to an election within three days. Shortly before the deadline, the company gave in, accepting in principle a referendum, although it stalled working out specific procedures. A second strike vote and strike preparations finally led to the scheduling of a CIRB-run election, with the TWU, the Amalgamated, and a no-union option to appear on the ballot. The CIRB also accepted the TWU plea, strongly backed by Murray, not to postpone the IRT election, although at the company's request supervision of the vote was again transferred, this time to the Receivership Court, to ensure that the results would be binding. The Amalgamated, arguing that it could not leave issues involving jurisdiction "to the chance of a referendum," withdrew, threatening legal action.[52] In the meantime, the TWU was preparing for its most dramatic move, bolting the AFL and affiliating with the CIO.

The TWU decision to leave the AFL was not sudden, nor solely the result of its growing jurisdictional problems. Although its first year of IAM and AFL affiliation had been generally satisfactory, in early 1937 difficulties began to arise. For one thing, IAM officials had expressed reservations about the Kent Avenue sit-down. For another, the Amalgamated repeatedly protested to AFL President William Green that the TWU was invading its jurisdiction. Although the IAM continued to back its transit local, TWU leaders grew fearful that the AFL, IAM, and Amalgamated might formulate a nation-wide agreement on transit jurisdiction that would diminish their province. The issue became urgent in May when the Amalgamated made its move on the IRT and Third Avenue; when the TWU protested to Green, he upheld the Amalgamated's position that the TWU had jurisdiction only over transit machinists and machinists' helpers.[53]

At the same time, TWU leaders were increasingly attracted to the CIO; they liked both its industrial character and its militance. This paralleled the CP's growing support for the new labor federation once initial doubts about the wisdom of establishing a second union center were overcome. Furthermore, if the TWU stayed in the AFL, at most it would be one of many IAM locals, while in the CIO there was the possibility of becoming the core of a new international union. Apparently anticipating a possible change of affiliation, sometime in early 1937 the TWU began withholding per capita payments from the IAM.

In March, shortly after the CIO started issuing union charters in its own name, it began talks with the TWU. After some perfunctory internal discussion, the TWU leadership decided to go CIO. On May 7 this move was ratified, with almost no opposition, at a meeting of 7,000 TWU members. Three days later, CIO President John L. Lewis granted the TWU a charter as a new international union with jurisdiction over "all workers employed in or about passenger transport facilities, excluding steam railroad systems."

The move to the CIO was immensely popular. It was a time, Forge recalled, when "the CIO [was] in the air" and Lewis "was a god" to transit workers. As Quill wrote several months later, "the C.I.O. charter was a magic wand that worked miracles." With it came a cascade of victories.[54]

On May 15 the IRT workers had their long-awaited referendum, and even before the polls closed the TWU began its victory parade. The celebration turned out to be well justified; of 11,585 votes cast, the TWU received 10,638, an incredible 92%. The only significant opposition was in the el motormen's unit, where the BLE received 36% of the votes, and in the towermen's and signalmen's unit, where the BRSA polled 24% of the votes.[55]

Contract talks began immediately and on May 27, after a final negotiating session attended by Lewis, the TWU signed its first contract. The agreement, to run through the end of 1938, provided for a closed shop, a 10% wage hike, a minimum wage of $25 a week, some reductions in working hours, and paid vacations. (In a separate agreement two months later, the IRT agreed to end the much-hated pension plan, refund employee contributions, and set up a new, company-financed system—in effect another 3% wage hike.) It was a stunning victory and an enormous boost to TWU organizing efforts elsewhere. Overnight the TWU had achieved virtually its entire 1936 IRT bargaining program. Lewis announced that the IRT contract would be used as a model in all other New York transit negotiations.[56]

The message was not lost on the city's other transit workers. On June 4, Third Avenue employees elected the TWU as their bargaining agent, 2,373 votes to the Amalgamated's 362. Two weeks later, New York City Omnibus workers chose the TWU over a recently established independent union, 1,249 to 356, and on July 21 the TWU beat another independent union on the Fifth Avenue Coach Company, 832 votes to 222. The union quickly negotiated closed-shop contracts with all three companies.[57]

Things weren't so easy on the BMT. For one thing, its management put up stiff resistance. In the spring the company announced one-week paid vacations for all its workers in a belated effort to forestall unionization. Furthermore, although as early as May 10, BMT President Menden had indicated in vague terms that the company would hold a representation election, it took no steps to do so. Instead, company executives encouraged officers of the BMT company union to form a new group, the Independent Traction Workers Union, which embarked on an organizing campaign and opposed holding an election "at this time." According to the TWU, the BMT also began firing some of its members. Only after 6,000 BMT workers at a June 3 meeting authorized the TWU to strike, did the BMT become more cooperative, eventually asking the CIRB to supervise an election.

At that point, further difficulties arose. The BLE and BRSA, each of which had outstanding contracts with the BMT, vigorously opposed the inclusion of their units in any election. The BLE even made a thinly veiled threat to strike if that occurred. In response, TWU members again voted to authorize a strike of their own, charging that the BMT was reneging on its election agreement and encouraging the objections being raised by other labor groups.

After much deliberation, the CIRB decided to exclude the 1,200 BMT rapid transit motormen, switchmen, and towermen from the proposed referendum, since the railway brotherhoods held valid contracts and the TWU had failed to present prima facie evidence that a majority of the men in question sought to change unions. The TWU accepted this ruling, clearing the way for a July 31 vote, but stepped up its organizing of the excluded workers with a view toward a future election. Then, in a final election-eve maneuver, the BMT took out full-page ads stating that regardless of the outcome of the vote, it would continue to respect the contracts it had signed with its now-defunct company union until they expired in October 1938. [58]

Company intransigence and rival unions would not have presented the TWU with so serious a problem if they had not been combined with a type of opposition the union had not previously faced, anti-Communist attacks coming from within the Catholic Church. When, as on the IRT, the TWU had been red-baited by management and company unionists, it had been relatively easy to associate the attacks with anti-unionism and neutralize their impact. It was another story entirely, however, when the anti-Communist banner was raised by elements of the Catholic Church, since the Church commanded tremendous allegiance from the transit work force.

The majority of New York transit workers were at least nominally Catholic, and this alone tended to inhibit unionization. Gerald O'Reilly, for example, recalls that the early IRT unionists were generally less religious than the work force as a whole. Among the Irish, the Church tended to both reflect and reinforce the fatalism and deference to authority that formed one side of their culture. The Church, in this regard, was the spiritual analogue of Tammany Hall and company unionism. Furthermore, the Catholic hierarchy was deeply antagonistic to Communism, which furthered resistance to the TWU. It is not surprising, then, that those closest to the Church were slower to engage in the disturbing process of unionization than those more indifferent to religion or openly anti-clerical. [59]

The situation, however, was quite complex, for the Catholic Church itself was deeply divided in its reaction to the New Deal and the growth of industrial unionism. Most Catholic activists of the 1930s shared one thing, their use of the language and ideas of "Social Catholicism," a strain of thought derived from the writings of Thomas Aquinas and revived in the modern era by two papal encyclicals, Leo XII's 1891 *Rerum Novarum* and Pius XI's 1931 *Quadragesimo Anno*. In searching for a moral and structural response to the industrial revolution and working-class radicalism, both encyclicals stressed individual natural rights, including the right to own property. Both strongly attacked socialism. At the same time, however, they rejected the greed, individualism, exploitation, and class conflict that lay at the center of economic liberalism. Their solution was a call for a system of "social justice" that recognized the right of workers to a living wage and the obligation of capital to act in accordance with the dictates of the common good. Antagonistic relations of class were to be replaced by a harmonious partnership of labor and capital organized along vocational lines.

The ambiguity, vagueness, and contradictions of Social Catholicism—for in the end it was a sometimes noble quest for the impossible, capitalism without its logic, its morality, its necessity—enabled political perspectives ranging from Msgr. John A. Ryan's progressivism to the latter-day fascism of Charles E. Coughlin, the famed radio priest, to coexist within the same intellectual framework. Differences were particularly sharp over the question of industrial unionism. For some, the new unionism of the 1930s was a step toward vocational organization and a concrete means of achieving the living wage and the legitimate rights of labor. Others within the Church, however, profoundly disapproved of the CIO and its precursors. They viewed the sit-downs, militancy, and CP participation that characterized the new industrial unions as antithetical to the defense of private property, the anti-socialism, and the condemnation of class conflict clearly found in the papal writings.[60]

Eventually, advocates of almost every variety of Social Catholicism tried their hand at working with New York transit workers, sometimes to cross-purposes. All, however, were slow to see the significance of the TWU. It was only in late 1936 that Church-affiliated groups began sustained activity in transit. By then it was too late to have much impact on the IRT.[61] On the BMT, the situation was quite different. For one thing, the TWU coalesced later there. For another, some BMT workers had gotten their jobs through referrals from their parish priests, giving the Church unusually strong influence. Finally, the Brooklyn diocese was exceptionally conservative and deeply hostile to the CIO.[62]

The most direct Church challenge to the TWU was led by Father Edward Lodge Curran, an influential figure in the Brooklyn Church, a friend and supporter of Father Coughlin and chaplain of the Brooklyn branch of the Ancient Order of Hibernians. Curran helped organize the American Association Against Communism (AAAC), a group that worked against the TWU in the period leading up to the BMT recognition election, supporting instead the Independent Traction Workers Union. Father Curran was known to visit personally transit workers on the job in an effort to enlist their opposition to the TWU. Some parish priests, in Brooklyn and elsewhere, denounced the union from the pulpit. Apparently Holy Name Societies and the Knights of Columbus were also used to build opposition to the union.[63]

Just prior to the BMT election, the official newspaper of the Brooklyn diocese, the influential and widely circulated *Tablet*, printed a letter signed "American" attacking TWU leaders as Communists. The author urged transit workers to resign from the TWU and either join another union or establish a new organization. In the meantime, it exhorted, they should vote against the TWU as their bargaining agent. The letter, which provoked wide discussion, drew its information partially from an internal CP bulletin and partially from an affidavit by Tom O'Shea, who, apparently for the first time, publicly identified and criticized the TWU leadership as Communist.[64]

These attacks caused the TWU considerable difficulty. According Peter MacLachlan, among Catholics working on the BMT "the word Communist . . . was a disaster"; the Catholic anti-Communist agitation created a "very difficult" situation."[65] However, the effectiveness of the anti-TWU campaign was limited by two factors. First, it came late in the BMT organizing drive. Second, the split within the Church over the CIO meant that the TWU could find important Catholic supporters. Many liberal Catholics were more concerned with aiding the organization and recognition of the new industrial unions than with the possibility of Communist influence within them. In February 1936, for example, Dorothy Day of the *Catholic Worker* advised Catholics to join the TWU, pointing out that since the majority of the transit work force was Catholic, "they can bring into the union Catholic principles of Justice." Similarly, the TWU was able to quote attacks on red-baiting and company unionism that appeared in *Commonweal* and *America*, two Catholic journals. [66]

During the BMT election campaign, the TWU received the support of the newly formed Association of Catholic Trade Unionists (ACTU), an offshoot of the Catholic Worker movement. At the time ACTU was heavily Irish and Irish-American and primarily involved in supporting strikes and organizing drives, rather than the anti-Communist machinations of its later years. Acting in response to the *Tablet* attack, ACTU handed out 10,000 leaflets urging BMT workers to vote TWU. [67]

Anti-clerical attitudes among Irish workers also diminished the effectiveness of Church opposition to the TWU. As previously mentioned, the stand of the Catholic hierarchy in Ireland toward the republican movement had led to a certain amount of anti-clericalism on both sides of the Atlantic. One Jesuit priest who tried working with TWU members in the late 1930s noted that "very many of the men bitterly resent the action taken by the Irish Bishops and the Irish Clergy during the trouble with England." [68] Other workers simply felt that it was inappropriate for the clergy to become involved in a secular issue such as unionism. Furthermore, there was a certain amount of resentment among transit workers over the Church's lack of interest in their plight as workers until the TWU came along. One Irish-Catholic motorman was particularly blunt: "What the hell did the Church do for us? Not a god damn thing." [69]

TWU leaders, well aware of the potential impact of Church opposition, carefully avoided any direct confrontation. Many TWU leaders were themselves practicing Catholics and, as Mike Quill said, "Our going to Church did no harm either. Many a fellow who thought me a dangerous agitator found me more to his taste after meeting with me at the Paulist Fathers." With considerable caution, some unionists tried to build on existing doubts about Church interference by pointing out that it was the TWU, not the Catholic hierarchy, that was fighting for enough time off to attend church on Sunday and for enough money to make a contribution to the weekly collection. [70]

The competing poles of Church and union caused considerable strain for some Catholic workers, in spite of union efforts to keep the spheres separate. One worker, for example, who lived on Manhattan's West Side, switched parishes after his local priest denounced the TWU. Other workers chose not to inquire about the political beliefs or affiliations of union leaders, again to avoid being forced into an open choice between Church and union. Most, however, simply attended both church and union meetings and coped as best they could. [71]

If the BMT organizing campaign had occurred in isolation, the TWU might have been in very serious trouble. In retrospect MacLachlan believed that before the IRT referendum it was questionable whether or not the TWU could have won a vote on the BMT. After the IRT victory, however, fear of company reprisals diminished and the union gained momentum. According to the TWU newspaper, "workers by the hundreds joined the union" and "the new C.I.O. buttons appeared everywhere." [72]

The TWU did well in the BMT election, winning an overall majority of 6,269 votes to the Independent Traction Workers' 2,131. However, this was a proportionately smaller margin than on the other lines. Although the belated and divided Church response to the TWU failed to dissuade large numbers of workers from choosing the CIO union as their bargaining agent, it almost certainly had some effect. Furthermore, the TWU victory was not complete; the BLE and BRSA, of course, retained their units, since they were not involved in the vote, and in the ticket agents' unit the TWU was defeated by the Independent, 568 to 526.[73]

The agents had presented the TWU with special problems. They were the only large group of female workers in the transit system. Many were widowed and the sole support of their families. They were both deeply grateful to the BMT for having hired them and extremely fearful of the consequences of losing their jobs. The company played on these fears, telling the women that a TWU victory would lead to an equalization of their wages with male rates—women at the time received lower pay than men doing the same work—and, as a result, their eventual replacement by male workers.

In general, the Independent Traction Workers had failed to develop much rank-and-file support, but the group's vice president, Mary Murray, an agent, was an influential figure among female BMT workers. Prior to the formation of the Independent, she had been a company union representative and had spent her days going from booth to booth, handling grievances and talking to the agents. When she switched to the Independent, she brought many women with her. The TWU, by contrast, had no experience in organizing women workers. Furthermore, the female BMT employees were very heavily Catholic and generally more religious than their male co-workers. As a result, they were more influenced by attacks from within the Church on the TWU's leftism. The upshot of all this was the TWU's only election defeat on a major New York transit line.[74]

Following the vote, the TWU filed charges with the newly established New York State Labor Relations Board (SLRB) claiming that the Independent was an illegal company union. After much delay, the SLRB agreed, decertifying the group and scheduling a new agents' election for January 1939. This time the TWU was opposed by the Amalgamated, which, according to the TWU, "took over the discredited company union officials lock, stock, and barrel." The TWU had learned its lesson. It put agent Nora O'Grady on payroll as an organizer and assigned a top union staffer to the campaign. Working in its favor was the fact that the Independent had negotiated a weekly minimum pay of $16 for the agents, while the TWU rapid transit contracts had a $25 minimum. Also, Father Curran and the *Tablet* stayed out of the second contest, which the TWU won with 663 votes to the Amalgamated's 424.[75]

The TWU also continued its effort to win over the BMT motormen, but with less success. Like their IRT counterparts, the BMT motormen tended to think of themselves as an elite and, reinforced by their brotherhood membership, considered themselves railroad men. The BLE, if somewhat ossified, had a significant base of support. Also, there was also a strong current of anti-Communism among the motormen, making them particularly susceptible to the widespread red-baiting used against the TWU.

In late 1937 the TWU claimed to have signed up a slim majority of the motormen, but the SLRB ruled against granting an immediate representation election.

Although the TWU announced its intention to continue its drive, the BLE had a union shop clause in its contract, making further organizing extremely difficult. The effort was soon abandoned. Only seventeen years later, in June 1954, did the TWU finally displace the BLE as bargaining agent for the BMT motormen.[76]

Just as forcing and winning a recognition election had been more difficult on the BMT than elsewhere, so was securing a contract. Initially, the company tried to maintain its position that it already held valid contracts covering all of its workers. However, when John L. Lewis strongly backed the TWU rejection of this stand, negotiations began. The company at first seemed willing to provide some improvements in wages, but, on September 13, BMT Board Chairman Gerhard Dahl told the TWU that due to the company's financial condition it would be unable to grant a wage increase. The TWU immediately called mass meetings for its BMT membership, where, for a third time, a strike was authorized. A major campaign was begun to win public support that included open-air meetings in Brooklyn.[77]

The situation was complicated by the fact that the breakdown in talks came at a critical moment in the New York City mayoral election campaign; primaries were to be held on September 16 and La Guardia was seeking renomination by the Republicans to add to his American Labor Party (ALP) endorsement. A pre-election BMT strike would be a political nightmare. In fact, La Guardia later charged that Tammany had tried to provoke a walkout for just that reason. The TWU considered La Guardia an ally. For one thing, the TWU was affiliated with the ALP. (Quill was slated to be an ALP City Council candidate.) For another, it was looking to La Guardia for help in its struggle to win recognition on the city-operated ISS. Like the Mayor, the union therefore hoped to postpone a showdown until after the election. Nonetheless, it was determined to press for a contract and was prepared to walk out.

On September 15, the day before the primary, La Guardia appealed to the BMT to resume negotiations or accept mediation, and to the union not to strike. The next day he held an extended meeting with the TWU leadership and a group of key advisers and ALP leaders, including Vito Marcantonio, Civil Service Commissioner Paul Kern, and Sidney Hillman, the head of the Amalgamated Clothing Workers. After the gathering, which was apparently designed to pressure the TWU not to walk out, the union announced that it would withhold final strike action until the next day. That gave La Guardia time to appoint an impartial fact-finding and mediation panel. Both parties agreed to work with the group. The result was an October 11 contract, virtually identical to the IRT pact.[78]

The BMT contract marked the end of the TWU's 1937 sweep of the New York transit lines. Already, the union had begun to move on, organizing transit workers in other cities and taxi workers in New York. It had been a remarkable year. At its start, the TWU was an IAM local with less than 8,000 members, mostly on the IRT. By the fall, it was a CIO international with nearly 30,000 New York transit members under union shop contract, another 2,600 claimed members on the ISS, a large New York taxi division, and a scattering of small, out-of-town locals.[79] In the course of a few months, the half-century struggle to unionize the New York transit industry had ended in near total victory, laying the basis for a new national union.

"The New Men of Power": CIO leaders on the first annual TWU boat ride, Spring 1937. *Left to right*: Harry Bridges, president of the International Longshoremen's and Warehousemen's Union; Mike Quill; Allan Haywood, CIO regional director for New York City; Mervyn Rathbone, president of the American Communications Association; and Austin Hogan.

It was with a justifiable sense of triumph, then, that the TWU opened its first International Convention on October 4 with a parade from its headquarters to Madison Square Garden, where workers entered the hall to strains of "The Wearing of the Green." There they heard words of praise and victory from TWU and CIO leaders, culminating in an address by "Labor's savior . . . that great emancipator of the American Working People," John L. Lewis. In working sessions that followed, an International constitution was written, Quill was unanimously elected international president, MacMahon chosen as vice president, and Santo as secretary-treasurer. Later that year Hogan was elected president of the union's New York area unit, now known as Local 100, and Quill was elected to the City Council from the Bronx. John L. Lewis had good reason to say that "there may have been somewhere, sometime a better record of accomplishment than the record made by the Transport Workers Union during the last six months, but I do not know of any."[80]

III

"A revolution must come on the
dues installments plan"

6

THE FRUITS OF VICTORY

"A revolution must come on the dues
installments plan"   *Ulysses*

Between 1937, when the TWU won recognition, and the start of World War II,
New York transit workers began a long climb out of a state of special and intense
degradation toward the full rights, privileges, and bounty of the modern working
class. Slowly but steadily the TWU worked to eradicate the past, to create a future.
In part, this was done through contractual agreements that upgraded conditions and
pay, introduced new benefits, and ended some of the most resented company
practices. The TWU took over some of the power once exercised exclusively by
management. Other benefits were provided directly by the union, which, by offering various kinds of activities and services, partially displaced older ethnic, community, and religious structures.

Unionism, in short, was creating a new way of life. On the surface, this meant
greater collectivity among the membership. In subtle ways, however, unionization
also promoted individuation. The TWU meant different things to different people;
male workers were affected one way, female workers another, and their families still
differently. One thing, though, was certain; the new unionists were delighted that
their lives were changing, and they showed it in an outpouring of gratitude and
loyalty toward the TWU.

The first TWU contracts, signed in 1937, brought immediate economic gains.
The IRT and BMT contracts provided 10% across-the-board wage hikes and established a $25 minimum weekly salary for all male workers. The salary floor primarily
benefited the porters, in some cases raising their wages by over 30%. (The few
female agents the TWU represented at the time—those working for the BMT's bus
and trolley subsidiary—were not covered by the minimum.)[1] Agreements with the
major surface companies generally provided operators with 10-15% hourly increases, while reducing the number of years needed to reach top rates. Trolley and
bus shop and maintenance workers received slightly larger increases.[2]

The next round of rapid transit increases, negotiated in 1939, were more modest as a result of the national economic downturn, the prospect of impending transit unification, and improvements in non-monetary conditions. Instead of company-wide percentage hikes, a complex series of adjustments was made in the intricate rate structures. Although this served to mask how meager the union's gains were in comparison with two years earlier, more importantly it began a sustained TWU effort to rationalize the pay structure. Numerous inequities were eliminated, pay for equivalent jobs brought closer in line, and the number of different rates for given occupations decreased. On the IRT, for example, the six wireman rates at the 98th Street shop were reduced to three; the twelve cable hand rates to six. In selected cases, differential increases were also used to narrow the spread between top and bottom rates within given occupations. Thus IRT wage increases ranged from fractions of a penny to over eleven cents an hour. On the BMT, most raises were around two cents an hour, with a few groups getting more.[3]

The TWU's 1939 surface contracts varied considerably. The top rate for New York City Omnibus drivers jumped from 82 cents an hour to 90 cents, making it the highest in the city. The equivalent Third Avenue Railway rate was only 78 cents an hour, as the company agreed only to a modest payroll increase that averaged slightly over $100 per worker over the life of a seventeen-month pact. On the small Avenue B and East Broadway line, where the TWU was negotiating its first contract, a ten-week walkout—the union's first extended strike—won increases averaging $500 a man over two years.[4]

The 1937 and 1939 contracts called for a range of benefits previously unusual or unknown. In the summer of 1937 workers began receiving annual paid vacations, generally one or two weeks depending on seniority. Sick leave and overtime pay were introduced or improved and rapid transit pensions upgraded.[5] The IRT, of course, agreed in July 1937 to scrap its contributory pension plan and set up a new, non-contributory program to supplement the recently established social security system. The $1.8 million that workers had contributed to the IRT's old plan was refunded in two lump sum payments, averaging $150 to $200 a worker, and the 2,500 workers who had refused to join up had full pension rights restored. A year later the BMT replaced its pension plan with one modeled on the IRT's. (The TWU was unable to win adequate pensions from the surface companies until after World War II.)[6]

While the TWU was succeeding in improving pay and benefits, it made only very limited progress in reducing the hours of work. Before recognition the union had sought a 40- to 48-hour week with no loss of pay. Extended working weeks, however, were a long-established industry practice and the TWU soon discovered that both the employers and some employees had come to see the status quo as essential to the maintenance of their respective budgets. For the companies, long hours kept down labor costs and solved scheduling problems; for workers, they partially compensated for low hourly rates. The union thus found itself in the unfamiliar position of facing stiff resistance not only from management but from some of its own membership as well.

Although the transit companies agreed to reduce hours without reducing pay for a few selected occupational groups, they strongly resisted doing this across-the-board. In most cases they were willing to cut hours only if there were to be no compensating rate increases. Most workers, in effect, would have to give up part of their newly negotiated higher income, the product of upward rate adjustments, to get a shorter work week. TWU officials were willing to go along with this approach, but many workers were not; long accustomed to near-subsistence earnings, they viewed the negotiation of higher rates as an opportunity for maximizing income, not for reducing hours. The result was one of the first major debates between the TWU leadership and a sizable group of union members.

The issue first came up when, following recognition, union leaders proposed the complete elimination of the seven-day work week. Rallying under the slogan "you can't eat hours," groups of workers not only opposed the switch to a six-day week but in some cases even advocated lengthening hours, including the introduction of seven-day weeks where they were not the practice. The leadership responded by arguing that the union itself could not survive with a membership that worked every day, an echo of Ira Steward's argument seventy years earlier that reduced hours were a prerequisite to workers' economic and social progress. Resistance, however, was stiff and heated. When the IRT transportation section, for example, scheduled a union meeting to vote on the hours issue, attendance was so great that the meeting had to be transferred from the union auditorium to a ballroom across the street.

Faced with both a determined management stand and internal opposition, and recognizing in Santo's words that "you can't black jack people into accepting your views," the union leadership agreed to a compromise position. When possible, agreements were obtained to reduce hours without lowering earnings. Otherwise, when rates were increased the union leadership usually fought for a simultaneous, optional, uncompensated reduction in hours, which it then urged its membership to accept. Meanwhile, the union gingerly began to introduce contract clauses setting upper limits on the working week.[7]

The 1937 IRT contract and subsequent elaborating agreements, for example, reduced the work week in the power department to 48 hours with no loss of pay. In the station department, maximum work weeks were defined. Porters, for instance, could not work more than 56 hours; agents, not more than 52 hours over six days, with the option of working only 48 hours. In the transportation department, where there was the most worker resistance to hours' reduction, "a day's work" was defined as eight hours and "a working week" as six days, but a seventh day was permitted at overtime rates, and the option of working longer days with commensurate higher pay remained. Towermen were given the collective option of switching from a seven- to a six-day week, but with no provision for a compensating increase in hourly rates. In the 1939 contract this latter arrangement was made mandatory and agents were transferred to a 48-hour week with only minor pay loss.

The first contractual provision covering BMT hours, negotiated in 1939, roughly paralleled the IRT agreements. A few workers received reductions in working time without pay loss, while a much larger group, including most shop and power workers, continued on their existing schedules. Operating employees and agents had average or standard working days or weeks defined, after which time overtime was to be paid, but workers could still be required to work as much as twelve hours a day. The 1939 Fifth Avenue Coach pact established a 40-hour week for shop men and a six-day, 54-hour standard week for operators and conductors, although swings and overtime could extend the latter considerably.[8]

To reduce the working week, the TWU leadership had to drag both the companies and its own membership out of a degraded past toward standards the labor movement had been promoting for three-quarters of a century, and to which managers in other industries had already agreed. It proved to be a lengthy process, marked by continuing opposition from all sides. Although by the fall of 1939 the transit companies and all sections of the union had agreed to the elimination of the seven-day week, union leaders were sufficiently concerned about solidifying this position that they considered adding a clause opposing the seven-day week to the union's constitution, a measure they had declined to support two years earlier.[9] Furthermore, working hours remained long and the general issue of hours reduction very much alive. That year, for example, BMT porters still had a 60-hour week, not including unpaid lunch breaks or overtime; trolley crews employed by the major companies typically worked 50 to 60 hours a week. In mid-1941, 28.0% of BMT and 8.9% of IRT workers were scheduled for work weeks of over 48 hours. The 48-hour week was not solidly established as the regional industry norm until after the United States entered World War II and it took another decade to win the 40-hour week. In both instances, TWU leaders again had to overcome resistance from within the union's ranks as well as from management.[10]

By contrast, there was no union disagreement over the need to attack the associated problems of extras and swing shifts. Although the TWU was unable to eliminate either practice, through a variety of contractual provisions limits on both were established and the worst inequities ended. The 1937 IRT contract, for example, contained provisions ensuring the fair distribution of extra platform work and requiring the company to provide the union with copies of proposed crew schedules. The contract also called for a study of ways to reduce the number of swing runs without increasing costs. Contracts with the East Side and Comprehensive Omnibus Corporation limited extra waiting time to two hours, while Fifth Avenue Coach agreed to a minimum of five hours pay for all runs. In 1939 the latter company accepted a two-hour limit on swings and the Avenue B line restricted extras to 20% of the work force.

The 1939 BMT contract had the most extensive regulations covering swings and extras. Extras were to be paid for reporting time if they received no work or if specified waiting times were exceeded. To prevent favoritism, extra lists were to be posted and work assigned on a rotating basis according to seniority. In rapid transit, no more than one swing per man per day was permitted and swings had to be of at least one hour's duration. Furthermore, 75% of all conductor swing shifts had to be completed within twelve hours, and the rest within thirteen. Stricter limits were placed on swing shifts for trainmen and surface operators. Even with these provisions, low seniority workers still faced the twin miseries of unpaid waiting time and extended days, but the worst excesses were checked and the process of change begun.[11]

TWU contracts generally codified, and often improved, seniority, promotion, and work rules. Arbitrary disciplinary practices were checked by provisions providing for grievance machinery, union representation at disciplinary hearings, and, in some cases, impartial arbitration. The IRT's use of medical examinations by company doctors as an adjunct of its labor control system was ended by a provision allowing workers declared unfit to request a second examination by a doctor of their own choosing, with a third doctor to arbitrate in cases of disagreement. The BMT agreed to give other jobs to operating employees with at least five years' seniority who were declared medically unfit to continue in their present positions. Both companies agreed to pay for required medical exams. New safety and health regulations were instituted and provisions made for locker and washing-up facilities. Ticket agents on the IRT and BMT were guaranteed relief during their tours of duty, and BMT conductors and trainmen were given half-hour paid lunch breaks. [12]

Provisions were also made to protect workers' jobs. The BMT agreed not to contract out work if lay-offs would result; and, when trolley lines were motorized, to give operators the opportunity to retrain at half-pay as bus drivers. Similarly, the 1941 Third Avenue contract contained provisions to protect seniority and facilitate job transfers in the event of an anticipated conversion from trolley to bus operation. Contracts with the Fifth Avenue Coach Company in 1937 and 1939 forbade the line from converting its two-man buses to one-man operation without union consent, a change the company was eager to institute and the TWU determined to prevent. [13]

Step-by-step the union was forcing itself into areas once the exclusive domain of management. In the process, it was undoing the hated past. The issue of uniforms provides another example. In late 1938 the TWU won its long-standing demand to participate in the selection and buying of uniforms, ending the costly collusion between the employers and the uniform suppliers. The union insisted that all uniforms be manufactured in shops organized by the Amalgamated Clothing Workers and even arranged for the production of overalls incorporating the TWU insignia into their design. The IRT porters, according to the TWU newspaper, had their "drab, prison-like outfit . . . replaced by snappy, neat and durable clothes which are indicative of transit labor's liberation."[14]

The victory over uniforms came swiftly, but other changes required long and tenacious struggles. The TWU, for example, was committed to the elimination of the BMT's "jump" system of seniority penalties. In 1939 the union got the BMT to codify the "jump" regulations and initiate a study of their possible elimination. However, it was only in 1944, four years after the city took over the BMT, that an agreement was finally reached to end the half-century-old system. [15] Similarly, it took until 1941— and transit unification—for the TWU to bring pay rates for BMT agents up to the considerable higher IRT level, ending this de facto sexual discrimination. [16]

On occasion, the union was in such a headlong rush to eliminate all traces of past ways that it campaigned against practices that it later realized were actually beneficial. During its organizing drives, for instance, the TWU attacked company paternalism, and in particular payroll deductions used to finance company-run programs. The union won considerable worker support on the Omnibus for its opposition to deductions used to finance a group insurance plan and a free summer camp for workers' children. After recognition, however, a closer examination indicated that in fact the company was providing a sizable subsidy to the insurance plan. As a result, the union reversed its position and demanded the plan's retention. Likewise, union leaders realized that while the camp smacked of paternalism, it also was "one of the finest things that we can have." Rather than demanding an end to the small worker contributions that financed the program, the union itself took control of the camp's finances. [17]

Perhaps most poignant was the TWU effort to eradicate the lingering reminders of past union defeats. In January 1939, at the TWU's insistence, the IRT held a referendum of all current switchmen and motormen who had been employed prior to the 1926 strike, to determine whether or not their seniority should be returned to its pre-strike order. Some 405 of the 438 eligible workers participated, with 298 voting to restore the pre-strike order. Some forty men who would themselves lose seniority—former scabs—voted for the proposal, while others abstained. This gesture helped ease some of the tension over the events of thirteen years before. The next month a revised seniority list was posted, fulfilling the promise Bray and Fitzsimon had made while signing up the motormen and switchmen and, at least symbolically, reversing the verdict of history. The TWU went on, in 1941 and 1942, to win restoration of seniority lost in the 1916 strike by men working for the Third Avenue and New York Omnibus. [18]

Contractual agreements were only the most formal and visible aspect of the transformation of work relations. Through day-to-day union practice, greater changes occurred than written agreements alone would indicate. The union was a constant presence on the job. By union rule, all TWU members had to wear union buttons—distributed monthly to indicate dues payment—whenever at work. Union bulletin boards could be found in virtually every transit facility. In the shops, a steward system was established, while elsewhere staff organizers, section officers, and delegates to the Local 100 Executive Board took charge of grievances and related matters. [19]

In general, the union was able to resolve most work-related problems through grievance machinery or informal discussions. Men who previously would have been disciplined for minor rules infractions—running buses and trolleys ahead of schedule, reporting late for work, shouting at supervisors—were now protected by the union and often escaped with little if any punishment. Even when serious infractions were involved, the TWU frequently was able to intervene successfully. Peter MacLachlan, for example, who handled BMT grievances, saved the jobs of quite a few workers caught stealing fares—traditionally grounds for dismissal— by informally appealing to company supervisors. Through grievances, the union forced the companies to supply needed safety equipment. Eventually elected safety committees were established. [20]

Where workers labored in large groups, they were best able to assert their power (just as such locations had been the center of the union's early growth). At the 59th Street powerhouse, for example, the union all but took over the complex problem of scheduling work shifts. As in the pre-recognition period, militant individuals often played a key role in breaking old patterns. Eddie Cabral, for instance, a steward at the IRT 98th Street shop, ended a ban on having coffee in work areas by simply arriving one day with a coffee pot and giving out coffee, mocking the foreman who challenged him. [21]

Although job actions were infrequent, they did occur. Typically they took the form of slowdowns. However, in the shops there were also occasional short work-stoppages or walkouts. Some job actions were led by union officials seeking to resolve grievances on which the company was taking a hard line. According to one section officer, stoppages "got grievances settled quick." Other actions, particularly in the period immediately following recognition, were initiated by individuals or small groups of workers acting on their own. In these cases, union leaders almost always quickly stepped in, either to assume leadership or to convince the protesters to go back to work.

The constant guerrilla war of slowdowns and quickie strikes that characterized work-place relations in some newly organized CIO industries, however, did not occur in New York transit. By and large, other, less dramatic pressures were brought to bear. Why? For one thing, striking was not a common, shared experience. Strikes had played only a limited role in the organization of the TWU. Most transit workers had never taken part in one. For another thing, at least among older workers there was a strong ethos of service, which discouraged disrupting passenger travel. The union, too, generally opposed job actions, particularly if they would interfere with passenger operations. TWU leaders wanted a centralized, orderly system of labor relations and feared that any disruption of transit service would undermine public support for the union.

Still, the fact even some job actions occurred was an indication of how far things had come from the pre-union days. Prior to the TWU, workers correctly sensed that job actions would be met with swift and heavy measures; accordingly, they shied away from collective protest. With the union in place, this pervasive fear dissolved. In fact, the companies' autocratic rule had so broken down that those job actions that did occur rarely resulted in firings or other drastic discipline. [22]

It is difficult to determine how the rise of union power changed workers' attitudes toward their jobs or their actual work performance. Turnover was very low, one indication of satisfaction but also a measure of the continued difficulty of finding other employment. Some workers, especially those who had never liked their jobs, apparently did become more vocal in expressing their discontent. Among a segment of the public-contact workers, the feeling spread that it was no longer necessary to be deferential to rude or bothersome riders.

Officials of at least one company, Fifth Avenue Coach, complained that following recognition some workers—particularly young bus conductors—became increasingly inefficient and discourteous to passengers. According to the company, a minority of conductors began "to assume an attitude of disregarding authority," exhibiting "an outward display of false bravado." The company attributed this to "a misunderstanding of the functions, responsibilities and ultimate objectives of unionism itself."

Although undoubtedly TWU officials resented being told by management what true unionism was, they too were worried; they recognized that public support for mass transit and the TWU partially depended on the on-the-job conduct of the membership. Accordingly, in conjunction with the 1939 World's Fair, the union launched a safety and courtesy campaign that included discussions at union meetings, radio talks by Quill, and a union-sponsored safety-courtesy contest. [23] For all its verbal militancy and aggressive negotiating, the TWU always remained committed to the smooth, even rationalized, operation of the transit system.

The conductors' "false bravado" perhaps was a manifestation of a more general, though subtle, shift in workers' attitudes. Although the legal encoding, through contractual agreement, of pay rates, benefits, and seniority was a collective victory, at least some workers came to see their terms of employment, and their very jobs, as their individual entitlement. As we will see later, this could subject the union to

internal conflict, as groups of workers tried to defend their "rights"—seniority ratings, for example, or relative pay standing—from demands made by other groups of
workers. The very sense of possessing their jobs that led some members to stop
repressing their resentment toward customers and managers also led many to fear
anything that might threaten their newly achieved status, whether the threat came
from management, other workers, or the union itself.[24]

If some of the fruits of union victory were to be found in the changed relationship
between employer and employee, others came from programs sponsored by the
TWU itself. Even before recognition, the TWU had become a social center for its
members. Once its organizational and financial footing was assured by closed-shop
contracts, the union was able to expand its social and recreational activities and
initiate new services.

Some union programs—like some contractual provisions—were almost explicitly
efforts to undo the past. Many transit workers, for example, were heavily in debt.
Since banks were reluctant to lend them money, and they in turn did not like to take
time off from work to apply for and pick up loans, transit workers frequently resorted
to high-interest borrowing from loan sharks or personal loan companies. Loan-
sharking was widespread throughout the industry; at 148th Street, for instance, every
department had it usurious lender.

To break the hold of the loan sharks and make low-interest loans available at work
sites, in 1938 the TWU began establishing credit unions at various transit facilities.
In addition to lending money, the credit unions offered low-cost insurance to
workers with money on deposit. This was quite important. Transit workers, especially in high risk jobs, faced difficulties and high costs in obtaining insurance. One
reason why workers had supported the company unions and unions other than the
TWU had been their insurance and loan plans. Many rank-and-file members
wanted the TWU to provide insurance. TWU leaders, however, were reluctant to
take this step; they associated union insurance with the AFL and railway brotherhood traditions that they had repudiated and knew that many labor insurance
schemes in the past had failed. The credit unions, though, spoke to this problem at
least partially.[25]

By far the most important and innovative union benefit was the TWU medical
plan, begun in 1939. The plan was largely Santo's idea, and to help set up and
supervise it one of his friends, Frederick Bettleheim, a left-wing Hungarian doctor
with whom he had worked in Cleveland, was engaged. The plan's operation was
extremely simple. In each neighborhood where transit workers lived, a local general
practitioner was recruited. TWU members seeking medical help or yearly physicals
could use these doctors' services free of charge. All costs were paid by the union. In
addition, the plan had specialists, for more complicated problems, and paid for
hospitalization.

The medical plan brought about a revolution in transit worker health care. Prior
to its start, many transit workers rarely if ever saw doctors, while others were
victimized by charlatans and incompetents preying on immigrants unfamiliar with
modern medical practice. Both neglect and unnecessary treatment, including surgery, were common. Once the TWU made available capable, caring doctors, at no

charge, utilization of medical services dramatically rose. Transit workers, often for the first time in their lives, began to see doctors regularly.

In its first year alone, 11,835 union members used the plan. The were 31,269 office visits, 4,530 doctor home visits, and hundreds of specialist consultations. In addition to acute problems, an enormous backlog of chronic conditions was diagnosed and treated, including numerous cases of TB, ulcers, hernias, and piles—in part diseases of the poor, in part conditions particularly associated with transit work. This medical backlog included a great deal of needed surgery; in the first two years of the plan 588 operations were performed free of charge. The plan was so successful that in 1941 optional family coverage was made available at a small quarterly fee.

What made the medical plan possible was the very Depression that caused transit workers so much misery. Throughout the city, doctors were finding it difficult or impossible to establish and maintain practices, as potential patients were simply unable to afford medical service. As a result, in return for a steady stream of TWU patients, doctors were more than willing to accept extremely low, union-paid fees. Although some participating doctors were ideologically committed to the plan, others were simply eager for work. Given the large pool of available doctors, the union was able to assemble a highly competent medical panel and still keep costs so low that the entire plan could be financed by periodic contributions from general union funds and from the proceeds of two annual dances to which all union members were required to buy tickets. In addition, in some cases workmen's compensation awards were used, in part, to cover medical expenses. To help win such awards, which the transit companies traditionally had been effective in keeping to a minimum, the union arranged for a lawyer to be available at Transport Hall.

Although the medical plan was a model program and enormously popular with the membership, it was financially unsound except under Depression conditions. In October 1942 it was suspended for the duration of World War II because participating doctors were entering the armed services in large numbers. After the war, medical economics had so changed that the plan's resumption proved impractical. But during its three-and-a-half-year operation the plan had opened up the world of modern medicine to TWU members. Once the program ended, transit workers and their families often continued to see doctors regularly, many times ones they had first used under the TWU plan.[26]

In setting up credit unions and its medical plan, the TWU was adopting a strategy that had been most fully developed by the garment unions: having the union itself provided quasi-economic benefits unachieved in collective bargaining. It was a social democratic approach—although TWU leaders would never have called it that—that was particularly suited to well-organized unions in poorly paid industries. After World War II the TWU increasingly turned to bargained benefits, but other New York municipal unions adopted the service-providing model. Today, for example, the largest New York municipal union, District 37 of the American Federation of State, County and Municipal Employees, sponsors membership services ranging from union-run dental clinics to free legal help.

By providing varied services, the TWU was setting itself up as a rival to older, community-based, working-class institutions. Fraternal groups, the Democratic party, and even the Catholic Church won some of their support by providing insurance, access to medical care, and emergency assistance.[27] By the late 1930s, the TWU was taking over this role. In addition, workers with personal problems, who in the past probably would have sought advice or aid from their local political or ethnic leader, or their priest, began coming instead to the union. TWU leaders were besieged with requests for help with non-work related problems. Many members, for instance, came to the TWU with legal or immigration problems. Others needed help with personal finances. One black worker complained that he was being kept out of an all-white city housing project. Another worker, who had built an extraordinary model train system for his crippled daughter, asked a union leader to help him get it displayed. And on and on it went.[28]

Wages, benefits, and economic programs, then, were just the most obvious aspects of what the union meant to the membership. In 1937, for example, the TWU began an education program that within two years had 1,700 participants. Most of the courses offered, especially in the early days of the program, were designed to promulgate trade union ideology and teach relevant skills—public speaking, parliamentary procedure, and so forth. Such courses helped ensure orderly union operation and coopted and trained a secondary leadership. Their popularity indicated a genuine, widespread desire for what might be called union citizenship training. The TWU also provided technical courses, to help members working under civil service prepare for promotional exams, and general interest courses, including photography, dancing, singing, and creative writing. A drama group put on plays, including one subway worker's composition, "A Nickel Pusher's Delirium," and the union even sponsored an exhibit "Art for the Subway."[29]

Soon after recognition, an extensive sports program was also begun. Competitions were regularly held in baseball, soccer, basketball, softball, bowling, swimming, handball, and track, both between rival TWU teams and against other unions. Eventually three gyms and a game room were set up in Transport Hall. Beyond simply providing recreation, athletics were seen as a way of developing internal union cohesion and "breaking down the company union ideology" among men who had previously participated in the extensive company and company union sports programs.[30]

Even more important were the union's dances, the distinctive TWU social form. The first was held in 1934, when the TWU was still tiny. Thereafter the union's growth in membership was paralleled, in fact surpassed, by a growth in dancing. The highlight of the social season was the Local 100 Annual Ball. Every year more and more members attended, so that by the late 1930s thousands were dancing to the music of four different bands in two ballrooms, with an appropriate musical style for every taste. Individual union sections and the Ladies' Auxiliary also sponsored dances. New events, such as an annual boat ride and picnic, a spring dance, and a union field day, were constantly being added.

With an eventual Local 100 membership of over 30,000, social and athletic events were virtually the only occasions, outside of crises, when workers from every work location interacted with one another. As such, they played an important role in overcoming ethnic, racial, and occupational divisions. While the forms of activity were not new—dances and sports events had been regularly sponsored by Irish organizations, company unions, and enterprising workers—their adoption by the union turned them into agencies for creating a new social collectivity. Like company officials before them, TWU leaders realized that almost any popular activity, from dances to boat rides, could be used to solidify workers' identification with one another and with the sponsoring institution. As the union came to serve as a vehicle for workers' social impulses, the resulting activities strengthened the union and, as a side benefit, provided much-needed funds, first for organizing and later for social service programs.[31]

Although the numerical predominance of the Irish imparted something of an Irish air to all union activities—at dances, for example, there was always at least one Irish band—a common ground was found in a somewhat deracinated American culture of baseball, picnics, and swing bands. The TWU prided itself on the participation of all of its constituent groups in its social world. Some subgroups within the union, however, sponsored activities of their own, particularly the female agents and black porters, outsiders in the overwhelmingly white male world of transit. The BMT porters, for instance, had their own Welfare League, which supplied funds to needy members and ran dances and cultural events. In conjunction with the union educational department, the porters also sponsored courses such as "The Negro in the Trade Union Movement." Similarly, special courses on women's issues were set up for the BMT agents. Other worker groups, some of which pre-dated the TWU, operated outside of the union framework: Rosary and Holy Name Societies, American Legion Posts, a Gaelic Football team, and so forth.[32]

Social events gave the TWU a rare opportunity for at least peripheral contact with its members' families, an important consideration since many workers' relatives, especially their wives, were skeptical or opposed to the union, particularly in the early days. It was not uncommon for workers' wives to discourage their husbands from joining or becoming active in the TWU. In the mid-1930s many union cadre were single, but as time went on most married and started families, so in some ways the problem worsened even as the union grew more established.

For workers, the TWU was an organic outgrowth of their experiences, their creation, a means of revolt against personal and collective degradation. For their wives, tied to home and neighborhood, it was an alien, unfamiliar force, a potential threat to their husbands' jobs and their families' way of life. Among Catholic women, deep Church involvement often reinforced hesitancy or hostility toward unionism. Furthermore, while for its male members the union meant an opportunity for involvement in an exciting world of meetings, organizing, and secret cells, and a welcomed excuse to go out with the boys, for their wives it meant even less time when their husbands were at home.[33]

Sensitive to the dynamic at work, and at the suggestion of their Communist advisers, TWU leaders looked for opportunities to involve workers' families in union activities and impart to them a sense of participation in the labor movement. The union's most ambitious thrust in this direction, however, its Ladies' Auxiliary, was at best a limited success. Open to all female relatives of TWU members, the Auxiliary was formed in the winter of 1934-35 by a small group of BMT workers' wives. For a number of years Mary Santo, John Santo's common-law wife, closely controlled the organization, although she never formally headed it. (She also helped organize and lead the New York State CIO Council of Women's Auxiliaries.) Later

Miriam Murphy, the wife of a BMT motorman, an office worker at the TWU's Brooklyn headquarters, and a CP member, became the Auxiliary's leader in name and fact. [34]

At first the Auxiliary's primary focus was support for TWU organizing. Its members picketed company offices when workers were fired, sent delegations to see company officers, and, whenever possible, spoke to workers' wives about the union, sometimes visiting their homes for that purpose. At the Kent Avenue sit-down, some forty Auxiliary members marched in front of the powerhouse, made sandwiches and coffee, and explained the situation to the frightened and confused strikers' wives, many of whom, wondering why their husbands had failed to come home, began showing up at the plant. [35]

After the TWU won recognition, the Auxiliary continued to provide support in crises and serve as a channel of communication. During the TWU's 1941 bus strike, for instance, Auxiliary members joined picket lines, ran strike kitchens, and sponsored mass meetings—one attended by over 1,000 women—where strike news was transmitted and the necessity of the walkout explained. Women from the Auxiliary also served as volunteer organizers during the drive to enlist the BMT ticket agents, working in particular to counteract anti-union red-baiting and the common, if false, belief that the union was against women working for the BMT. [36]

Support work, however, was only one aspect of the Auxiliary's activities; the group also sought to end the enforced isolation of transit workers' wives and "change the drudgery which is now the lot of most of the women." To break up the pattern of "eat, sleep, work and worry [that] until now has been the typical routine of most of us," the group sponsored meetings, picnics, luncheons, raffles, an amateur theater group, and monthly social nights. For unionists' children, Saturday morning "Recreation Classes" were begun at the TWU headquarters, with teachers supplied by the WPA and 200 children in attendance. Children's parties and outings were also periodically arranged. [37]

Some Auxiliary leaders hoped that the group would become a vehicle for ideological and cultural transformation. Mary Santo was quite explicit about this:

> The Ladies' Auxiliary makes it its duty to teach these women and educate them so that they are informed . . . able to be competent parents in bringing up their children in true form, to be people who believe in trade unionism.

To teach progressive ways and union ideals, lectures were held on social and political issues and women were encouraged to enroll in TWU courses. The Auxiliary also undertook fund-raising and boycott drives for other striking unions. [38]

In spite of all these activities, the Ladies' Auxiliary failed to become a mass organization. Only a relatively few women ever joined, and those who did were disproportionately the wives or relatives of union leaders. The biggest problem was that the Auxiliary had to depend on union members to tell their wives or relatives about the group's existence and to encourage them to join. But the rank and file, and even much of the secondary leadership, was indifferent or hostile to the whole project. A delegate to the union's 1937 convention, for example, reported that "when some of the representatives of the Ladies' Auxiliary have visited the homes of members to try and ask their wives to join up they have actually been insulted." In

Children of TWU members singing the "Star-Spangled Banner" at the start of an Easter party, held by the Ladies' Auxiliary and Works Progress Administration Children's Classes, at Transport Hall, April 12, 1939.

those sections of the TWU where union leaders stressed the need for the Auxiliary, a somewhat larger membership resulted, but repeated exhortations to union members and section leaders to take the Auxiliary seriously usually came to naught. Although there was never any openly stated opposition to the group, as Bill Zuidema put it at the 1943 convention, "there are still too many of our people who feel their women-folk belong in the kitchen." The TWU, like the transit industry, was essentially a man's world, and most men wanted to keep it that way.[39]

Unionism, even of the progressive sort, could actually reinforce patriarchal attitudes. As David Montgomery has argued, male workers, particularly skilled crafts-men, long depended on a code of "manliness" to enforce standards and construct a collective, workplace culture. The bitterest complaint many workers made against autocratic management was that it made them feel emasculated. Incidents in which workers, individually or collectively, "stood up" to supervisors played a key role in organizing the TWU and other CIO unions. Strike victories and union recognition were often described by unionists as restoring their manhood.[40]

Manhood meant two things. It meant humanity, the humanity men reaffirmed most dramatically by stopping work, showing that they were the masters of machines, not vice versa, or expressed more generally by taking actions to assert control over their lives. But manhood also had a gender-related sense, unionism as an assertion of manliness. Having women involved was at best confusing. This may be one reason, for instance, why during the Flint auto sit-downs women were asked to leave struck plants, and why sit-down strikes that female workers themselves undertook received little publicity. It may also explain why TWU leaders paid too little attention to the BMT agents, until rudely awakened by an election defeat.[41]

Formally, women workers were welcome to participate in all TWU activities. A few even became second-level union leaders. However, the union's atmosphere was very male. Some female unionists felt more comfortable taking part in activities of the Auxiliary than those of the TWU itself. The Auxiliary was the TWU's women's sphere and, like most CIO Auxiliaries, a traditional one at that. The Auxiliary page of the TWU newspaper—for a while called the "Woman's Page"—included recipes, consumer news, and fashion photographs.[42]

Various approaches were periodically tried to strengthen the Auxiliary, but with little success. At one point, in late 1937, Mary Santo suggested that the group undertake campaigns for lower-priced food, electricity, and rent. "With such a practical and simple program [new members] . . . will clamor at our door." Her prognosis proved false.[43] Another tack was organizational; successive TWU conventions authorized a paid Ladies' Auxiliary organizer and a union Auxiliary committee, but these decisions were only sporadically followed up. A potentially more effective measure was introduced when the medical plan was extended to workers' families; the extended coverage was run through the Auxiliary and required Auxiliary membership. But the war soon ended the medical plan and, in any case, formal membership did not necessarily mean active participation. Extensive publicity in union periodicals, much of it contrived, was also tried, but it too had little impact.[44]

World War II created new problems as many Auxiliary leaders took jobs of their own, becoming union members in their own right instead of union supporters. A low point came in 1946, when delegates to a TWU convention broke into laughter when a list of those assigned to the committee on the Auxiliary was read. The Auxiliary leader who gave the committee's report was praised in patronizing tones and referred to as "the little girl . . . who just spoke." Although the Auxiliary kept going as a relatively small cadre organization, as time went on it became ever more ritualistic, more an ideological artifact than a significant social collectivity.[45]

The TWU operated only for a short time in the economic and legal context in which it had emerged. In June 1940 New York City took over operation of the IRT and BMT, and a year-and-a-half later World War II led to further changes in the bargaining environment. Yet during this brief period, the TWU won most of the demands around which it had been organized, and in some cases went considerably beyond them, while simultaneously establishing its own social and benefit programs. Although improvements in pay and hours were relatively modest, all told the TWU had brought about a profound change in transit work and the lives of transit workers. For that its members were deeply grateful.

In the summers of 1937 and 1938, many TWU members took the first paid vacation they had ever had, often their first vacation of any kind in decades. For some it was an opportunity for long-delayed honeymoons. Others extended their vacations with unpaid leaves to make return visits to European homelands. The *Bulletin* was flooded with letters thanking the union and its leaders for making these vacations possible. For months after the introduction of the medical plan, the union newspaper was likewise filled with letters of thanks. Workers repeatedly wrote in to contrast their pre- and post-union situations. When IRT employees received cash refunds from the old pension plan, many gave the equivalent of one day's pay to a special union fund.[46]

If the metaphor for transit work before the TWU had been slavery, the coming of the union was liberation. Buster Giordano, an Italian turnstile mechanic: "On account of this organization coming into existence, we are able to go to our bosses and talk to them like men, instead of . . . like slaves." William Novak, from the Third Avenue's 65th Street shop: "To us the Transport Workers Union came to free us from slavery." Alongside sweeping phrases about the end of slavery came concrete lists of what liberation entailed: better pay, vacations, holidays, sick leave, improved working conditions. Far from negating the associated imagery, these statements made it clear that in workers' eyes such specific measures were more than simply discrete contractual betterments, but rather in sum represented a transformation in their fundamental social status. With the union, workers now had a full claim on their bourgeois rights as workers and citizens. John Colgan, a NYC Omnibus driver:

> In the old days our property rights were our jobs as motormen or conductors, which was not secured beyond the payment of our wages by our employers. . . . [N]ow we have a free choice through the means of the TWU in the matters of our better welfare and progress, to develop in self-reliance and dignity and self-respect.[47]

The credit and thanks for this radical change went to the union, the workers' creation. But credit and thanks, too, went to the union's leaders, whom many came to see as the personalized agents of their deliverance. Novak again: "In 1937 and 1939 Mike Quill came to free us from our chains of slavery." John Gibbon: "Those men on the platform—Quill, Santo, Hogan and MacMahon—helped abolish the slavery act. . . . Once Lincoln abolished slavery and the second time Quill, Hogan, Santo and MacMahon came along and abolished it again." One worker went so far as to say: "I believe that there is a God in heaven that watched over us, and he picked out John Santo, and John Santo came in and freed those transit slaves." It was this gratitude for ending "slavery" that, above all else, gave the TWU and its leaders the political capital that enabled them to survive the growing challenges, internal and external, that were to arise in the late 1930s and beyond.[48]

7

CATHOLICS AND COMMUNISTS: UNION POLITICS, 1937–1941

Not all transit workers were equally involved or equally important in the internal political life of the TWU. For most workers, at most times, union politics meant looking over the TWU newspaper, sometimes voting in union elections, sporadically attending union meetings, and occasionally talking things over with friends or work mates. It was a much smaller group—those who spoke at meetings, ran for union office, wrote and distributed literature, joined political groups, agitated and schemed—who directly determined the policies of the TWU. Nevertheless, the great mass of normally inert workers set limits on what was politically possible and had the final say as to what their union was to be.

Two political poles structured internal TWU discourse and the activity of the engaged minority. The larger and more powerful was the CP, which had helped organize the TWU and whose members dominated its leadership. Their presence and position in turn led to the formation of a second pole, a series of anti-Communist opposition groups generally aligned with one wing or another of the Catholic Church. The development of these two tendencies, their reaction to external events and to one another, and their ability to mobilize or demobilize the rank and file defined the main lines of the union's internal political life. At stake was not only control over the TWU, but the whole institutional relationship of transit workers to reform politics and the general recasting of American life during the New Deal years.

The contest between the TWU's left leadership and Catholic anti-Communists for the allegiance of New York City transit workers, of course, predated the union's 1937 recognition election victories. Recognition, however, changed the terms of struggle, leading both sides to employ new strategies. Signed contracts gave TWU institutional stability; its financial standing and organizational hegemony were no longer immediately dependent on changeable attitudes and enthusiams, but were guaranteed with the force of law by the union shop and the state's labor relations apparatus. The previous contest over the status of the TWU was transformed into a dispute over who would control the union and what policies it would pursue.

Surprisingly, the organizational consolidation of the TWU led to little expansion of the Communist presence as such; although the CP continued to recruit transit workers, there was no dramatic increase in Party membership. As Nathan Glazer pointed out, in the TWU "the increase in [CP] membership that generally followed Communist control [of a union] did not occur, even with the availability of union jobs and posts of union power."[1] No firm statistics on TWU Party membership are available, but estimates from a variety of sources indicate that even at its height the number of CP members in the union was quite small, somewhere between 50 and 300 and probably closer to the lower figure.[2] Among those who did join in the post-recognition period, the decision was sometimes the culmination of an extended political evolution, but other times a perfunctory business, a gesture in imitation of the leadership and in quest of a leadership role.[3]

The failure of the CP to develop a mass membership within the TWU was partially a function of the industry's social composition and organizational structure. The lack of strong union and socialist traditions among the rural Irish, their common, deep-rooted conservatism, and their loyalty to the Church, made Communist organizing generally difficult among Irish immigrants, a situation that had unusually great impact on the TWU. Furthermore, the cultural gap between the typical Irish transit worker and the New York Communist milieu that Tom O'Shea had once noted made it hard to retain those Irish workers who did join the Party. Rose Wortis, in charge of transit for the New York CP, observed that Irish Communists "come to a meeting and after the meeting they go back to their Irish circles, to an atmosphere removed from our Party, and we remain among ourselves." The physical isolation on the job of so many transit workers also made Communist recruiting difficult; the Party always remained very weak among what Forge somewhat derisively called "the traveling circus," the guards, conductors, and motormen, while it was strongest in the shops.[4]

The problem, however, went beyond the question of industrial and ethno-cultural structure. After recognition, the Communist leadership within the TWU never made a sustained effort to recruit members for the CP. To do so, they felt, would rock the boat, jeopardizing their own union positions and the stability of the TWU. At first, outside Party leaders complained, pointing out that the growth of CP strength in the TWU was not commensurate with the role Communists played in organizing and leading the union.[5] Eventually, however, they acquiesced to the reluctance of TWU Communists to do recruiting and ceased pressuring them. Outside CP leaders wanted to avoid alienating the unacknowledged Party members through whom they had influence in the union, their "submarines." Equally important, they came to share the perception that in an industry with the social makeup of transit, the position of Communist leaders would always be fragile and had to be handled with great care. Recruiting drives and overt Communist propaganda coming from union leaders—and most Communists in the industry were union leaders on some level—might seriously threaten the carefully erected political structure of the TWU.

Communist leaders within and without the union might have been more concerned with the lack of mass CP membership if they had not come to the realization that a strong rank-and-file Communist organization was no longer needed to influence the political direction of transit workers and transit unionism, for the Party now had a far more powerful and effective structure for that purpose, the union itself. As long as the Party's main concerns were the direction of national and regional organized labor, and coalition and electoral politics, control of the TWU structure by Communists and their allies at least partially obviated the need for a large Communist following.[6]

What was going on in the TWU was far from unique. By the end of the 1930s the CP, in William Foster's words, was no longer simply "an opposition force" within the labor movement, but held "many official posts" and "shared the official responsibility of carrying on the movement." This meant that the Party had to be concerned with maintaining its hierarchical standing and network of alliances within the labor movement, especially after 1939 when the Communist left came under intense attack because of international questions. At the same time, Communist union leaders, particularly those whose ties to the Party were clandestine, were becoming increasingly loyal to the organizations they themselves led and fearful of any disruptions within them. In some cases, they began to see their unions as partial surrogates for the Party, adopting in effect a quasi-syndicalist outlook.

Under these circumstances, strong rank-and-file Communist groups within unions, and especially within those led by the left, were a mixed blessing. On the one hand, they gave the Party and left union leaders a core base of support. On the other hand, they held the potential for alienating non-Communist union leaders and rank-and-filers and could easily become rival centers of power to official union structures. The Party's 1939 decision to dissolve its trade union caucuses and generally eliminate CP shop newspapers and shop nuclei was partially a response to the problems of success and coalition. It also was an acknowledgment of what was already occurring without official sanction. The de-emphasis by TWU leaders of Communist recruiting and propaganda was an unusually pronounced variant of this general trend.[7]

Lacking a mass Communist base, the TWU leadership maintained its position through a combination of effective economic unionism, charismatic leadership, some internal political education, and a tailoring of style and policy to the culture and perspective of the membership. Bureaucratic measures were employed as well. In fact, the union's very structure helped the relatively small left group maintain dominance.

In 1937 the TWU leadership decided to establish one large local, Local 100, to cover the entire New York transit industry, a decision endorsed without debate at the union's Constitutional Convention in September of that year. Within the local, the basic organizational unit was the section, which usually consisted of all the workers at one job site, say 148th Street, or in one functional category, say the IRT station department. Each of the roughly 100 sections had its own elected officers and held regular meetings. Most workers had contact with the union primarily through section meetings, section officials, or shop stewards. For purposes of approving contracts, voting on strikes, and electing representatives to the Local 100 Executive Board, sections were united into branches corresponding to the various employing companies. The local as a whole was run by its executive board and four officers elected by membership referendum. The International, dominated by Local 100, was led by officers and an executive board elected at biennial conventions.[8]

Although formally democratic, the TWU structure served to bolster the power of incumbent leaders and make effective opposition difficult. The combination of a very large local and many small sections tended to breed cohesion in the leadership and disarray in the opposition. Only top officers and appointed organizers had continuing contact with all the various parts of Local 100 and its 30,000-odd members. Most rank and filers or aspiring activists were known only to the other workers in their sections. While information flowed regularly between the sections and the leadership, there was no established forum for discussion among members of different sections, except for occasional mass meetings, usually called in crisis situations.[9] The leadership also tightly controlled the union's publications, which virtually never printed dissenting articles or letters. Thus the TWU's structure, in Maurice Forge's retrospective view, "became a very oppressive instrument of control":

> An oppositionalist found himself hemmed in. . . . The publications were closed to them, and when it came to a meeting . . . all they could do was rant and rave in [their] own section, which was a small platform. . . . And if they occasionally had a meeting of the whole New York Omnibus, so what? . . . [I]t was them versus Quill, not them versus other local leaders.[10]

The TWU was so compartmentalized that the leadership itself regularized what had originally been an ad hoc instrument, the Joint Executive Committee. First called more accurately the Joint Council of Section Executive Committees, this body was composed of the officers, and in some cases additional delegates, from every section, as well as the Local 100 Executive Board. At an important meeting some 500 or 600 delegates would be present. Although it had little formal power, the Joint Executive Committee came to be a crucial institution, for it was the one way to call together all of the key union cadre—the activists, the organizers, the politically aware. In a sense, as Forge put it, "that was the union."

The Joint Executive Committee was used to mobilize the union, discuss problems, endorse new policies, and refine negotiating positions. Potentially it was also an arena for oppositionists to build support, but even there they were at a disadvantage. The leadership controlled the chair, formulated the agenda, and had the opportunity to work out its positions in advance. Meetings were carefully orchestrated, starting with a speech by Hogan, followed by reports from various parts of the local, addresses by Santo and TWU General Counsel Harry Sacher, a legislative report, and finally a speech by Quill, who "gave them the business." Against that, any dissident would have a hard time.[11]

While Communists made up at most 1 or 2 % of the union membership, they constituted a much larger percentage of the union's cadre, and a still larger percentage of its formal leadership. Their concentration increased the higher up one went: quite a few section officers were Party members, as were a large number of Local 100 Executive Board members and a majority of the International Executive Board (IEB). In general, however, especially at the lower levels, no special machinations were needed to win these posts. Communists in the TWU often had been union pioneers, they were among the most active members, and they tended to be highly competent trade unionists. Primarily on those bases they were repeatedly elected to union positions. Leftists, moreover, were helped by the fact that they generally ran on administration-backed slates, thus having the advantage of coordinated campaigns, open support from the generally popular top union leaders, and perhaps some assistance from the union bureaucracy.

The TWU's left-wing group was further strengthened by the existence of an informal decision-making structure parallel to the official union apparatus. Although after the early years there was no formal CP caucus in the TWU, there was an inner Party circle at the highest level of the union that usually met before any important decision was made. It was within this group that the union's course was to a large extent charted. The core of the group was the quadrumvirate who between the mid-30s and the late-40s constituted the union's top leadership: Quill, Santo, MacMahon, and Hogan. In addition, a somewhat changing group of five or six other leftists were generally included in their deliberations; at various times Forge, Jimmy Fitzsimon, Michael Clune, Gus Faber, and Harry Sacher were part of this penumbra.[12]

The inner circle meetings served several purposes. Sometimes they simply affirmed the special status of those who attended, a kind of cliquishness. Frequently, however, they served as a forum in which union policies could be frankly discussed and debated and unified positions arrived at. Discussion was freewheeling and disagreements common, though usually kept in hand. In general, TWU leaders, both those in the Party and those not, worked well together, giving the union an unusual degree of collectivity at the top. Nonetheless, even within the left-wing group there was not always harmony. Santo and Forge, for example, frequently clashed. On a number of occasions Santo even tried to maneuver Forge out of his elected position as the union's editor, hoping to replace him with an appointed left-wing journalist whom he could more easily control. However, even when disagreements were over fundamental issues, public unity was maintained. Hogan, for instance, opposed deep TWU involvement in the ALP, which he thought was social democratic and ill-suited for the TWU's constituency, but despite these views he supported the union's political program and even served as an ALP official.[13]

The inner circle meetings were also one of the main channels for coordination between the union and the CP. Sometimes a group member would solicit and report on the views of the CP leadership on a given issue. If a really critical problem was being discussed, or if the party wanted something from the TWU, a top Party official might personally attend a group meeting, usually someone from the state CP leadership—Rose Wortis, Max Steinberg, or Israel Amter, or later Robert Thompson. On occasion, meetings would even be held directly with "the ninth floor" (the national Party leadership). Heavy-handed pressure, however, at least in the prewar years, was almost never brought to bear. According to Forge, "give the devil his due . . . [the CP] gave TWU much more leeway than they gave some of their older things. Despite the theory of no exceptionalism, they certainly practiced [it]." For advice and assistance on particular trade union problems, TWU leaders often consulted other left-wing unionists, especially from the Furriers, believing that they had a far better feel for the dynamics of bargaining and union politics than had Party functionaries.

John Santo

Douglas MacMahon

Maurice Forge

Although in the early days Santo was in effect the Party's representative in the TWU, once he assumed an official union post his special role diminished, both because he himself began to identify his interests with the TWU as an autonomous institution and because other TWU leaders developed relationships with Party leaders. Of these, the most important was between Quill and CP General Secretary Earl Browder. The two men liked one another and got along well. Quill was flattered when Browder would occasionally stop by his house to talk things over or meet with small groups of TWU leaders. When Quill had a particularly difficult union situation or a problem with the Party, he could always go directly to Browder. According to Browder they "never had much difficulty to work it out because he [Quill] was usually right. On technical questions the party people were rather narrow."[14]

Just as recognition reinforced the shifting emphasis of the TWU left away from independent organization toward the use of the institutional structures of the union itself, so too did it change the nature and strategy of the anti-Communist opposition. With recognition an accomplished reality, opposition to the TWU as such largely dissipated.[15] It was replaced by anti-leadership opposition within the union. For a while the AAAC remained active, gaining adherents in section 2, which represented over two thousand IRT station workers. AAAC activists hoped to displace some of the section's left leaders, but not the TWU itself. Another AAAC group, which included some former Brotherhood leaders, formed at the IRT 98th Street shop. Until the summer of 1938, however, the AAAC maintained a low profile. Likewise, little was heard from outside groups opposed to the TWU.[16]

Instead, during the first year after recognition whatever opposition there was within Local 100 largely came from union cadre who had worked hard for the TWU's victories and had achieved official or unofficial positions of importance within their sections, but were ideologically anti-Communist. Among the more prominent such figures, who began developing ties to one another, were John Gallagher from the Third Avenue and James Flatley from New York City Omnibus, who headed their respective sections, and Robert Schneider from the 59th Street powerhouse. Their influence within the union, like that of their left counterparts, probably derived more from their personalities, their key roles in organizing the TWU at their work locations, and their aggressive unionism than from their political views, which were quite right-wing. (Gallagher and Flatley were supporters of Father Coughlin; Schneider apparently had pro-Nazi sympathies.)[17]

At the TWU's October 1937 convention there was sporadic opposition to positions taken by the leadership. Resolutions were introduced forbidding any "person who does not believe in the Democratic form of government" from holding union office and opposing "Communism, Fascism, Nazi-ism and any other 'ism' except Americanism." Schneider and Flatley opposed the procedure used to elect officers. By and large, however, there was a strong consensus on most issues. There was no spoken opposition, for instance, to a resolution supporting the ALP and calling for labor parties elsewhere. The "Americanism" resolution was easily defeated after a debate in which both sides were given time to air their views. Quill and MacMahon were elected to their posts unanimously, although there were apparently some votes against Santo and Forge. If anything, the convention was notable for the absence of clear political differentiation. In fact, the longest debate and closest votes came over the issue of officers' salaries, with the leadership working hard to defeat strong floor sentiment for raising the proposed pay levels.[18]

By December 1937, however, when the first Local 100 elections were held, the opposition had sufficiently coalesced to run a slate for the local-wide offices. Robert Schneider was the opposition's presidential candidate and Jerry McCarthy, an IRT ticket agent and AAAC member, the vice-presidential nominee. The administration ticket was led by Hogan and Michael Lynch and also included Gus Faber and Jimmy Fitzsimon. The campaign was dominated by the opposition's charge that the incumbent leadership was red and the countercharge that the anti-administration slate consisted of "union busters." The outgoing Executive Board, elected before the International had been established and therefore including Quill, Santo, MacMahon, and Forge, charged that former company unionists and their "stooges" were behind the opposition, which they associated with "the Economic Royalists, the Tories, the Chamber of Commerce, the Vigilantes, the reactionary press, and all other agencies and tools of the open shoppers."

The administration carried the election by a three-to-one margin, although less than 13,000 votes were cast, meaning that most union members did not participate. The left and its allies also won a large percentage—almost certainly a majority—of the local Executive Board seats, but some oppositionists, including Flatley, were elected. With many more key cadre and union pioneers seeking office than Board seats were available, several important activists lost out. On the Third Avenue, for instance, both Gallagher and left-wing staff organizer Matt Kearns were defeated. In the Board contests, like the section officer elections held the next month, personal popularity and skill at handling grievances and other problems generally counted more than ideology.[19]

The TWU leadership had been unfair and unfounded in charging its electoral opponents with being company unionists and open shoppers. However, it was true that the tide of opposition to the union leadership tended to follow the ebb and flow of the right nationally. Thus in the summer of 1938, with the country in a deep recession, the CIO and the New Deal stalled, and a general conservative reaction under way, opposition to the TWU leadership resurfaced after a quiet period following the union elections. This time, the opposition involved forces both inside and outside the union and represented a more sustained and substantial challenge than the earlier dissident activity.

In July 1938 the AAAC reappeared with leaflets and a meeting of some 150 present and former TWU members. Still led by Father Curran and still using the *Tablet* to publicize its views, the AAAC took the position that "The Union Must Stay—The Leadership Must Go." Since its last period of activity, the AAAC had joined forces with a number of former Communists who had been active in organizing the TWU. Its new secretary was Lawrence Barron, who had worked with Santo in the Bronx in the early days of the CP transit drive, and the speakers at its meetings included John Murphy and Tom O'Shea.

While praising the TWU's bargaining accomplishments, the AAAC made a series of charges and demands. Most prominent was the accusation that the TWU had "locked out" thirty pioneer unionists who had lost their jobs during organizing campaigns, while it kept "scabs" on its own payroll. The thirty included the men fired by Fifth Avenue Coach in 1934 for belonging to the Amalgamated and Murphy and Leon Cashman, who had been fired by the IRT. The AAAC's demand that the TWU reinstate the men was confusing, since the real issue was their lack of jobs, but presumably the union could have exerted more pressure to have them rehired. The AAAC called on TWU members to oust the union's leadership, which it charged was corrupt and Communist. The group also called for a union sick and death benefit, departmental working agreements (which were not established on the BMT until the following year), and shorter working hours.[20]

In response to the AAAC, the TWU leadership, which already had been running occasional articles in the TWU newspaper criticizing red-baiting and the interference of self-proclaimed Catholic activists in union affairs, stepped up its rhetorical attack.[21] It also moved swiftly to prevent O'Shea from becoming the focal point for an emerging opposition. The union previously had fined O'Shea $25 for violating a union rule forbidding unauthorized members from conferring with management on hours, wages, and working conditions. O'Shea had refused to pay the fine and went to court seeking an injunction preventing further action against him. When O'Shea's motion was denied on August 17, the TWU expelled him for not paying his fine. Under the terms of the IRT closed-shop contract, he simultaneously lost his job. O'Shea's further legal actions were unsuccessful. Sometime later he was forced to take a WPA job.[22]

The arena now shifted to Washington. In late August John P. Frey, a key leader of the AFL and head of its Metal Trades Department, testified before the House of Representatives' newly created Special Committee on Un-American Activities (commonly known as the Dies Committee after its chairman, Texas Democrat Martin Dies). Frey claimed that hundreds of CIO officials, including Quill, Santo, Hogan, and MacMahon, were Communists. Quill immediately retorted that Frey was "the Benedict Arnold of the American Labor Movement," denying that either he or any of the other TWU leaders Frey had named were members of the Communist Party. Nevertheless, he made it clear that he did not "choose to join the parade of red-baiters for whom all workers have nothing but contempt."[23]

The Frey testimony was only a prologue; on September 16 a subcommittee of the Dies panel held an extended hearing in New York on Communist activity in the TWU. Among those testifying were Michael J. McCarthy from the Fifth Avenue Amalgamated group; Murphy and Barron from the AAAC; and two other former Communists, IRT ticket agent Edward Maguire and William Harmon, a BMT motorman who had worked briefly as a TWU organizer. Somehow—perhaps through Curran—these local anti-Communist activists had linked up with the anti-CIO crusade getting under way in Congress.

The testimony given at the Dies hearing was a mixture of accurate information and wild, unsubstantiated charges. A host of TWU members were named as Communists, from top officers like Quill and Santo down to obscure rank-and-filers. Murphy and Maguire testified that Quill had been in their CP cell, and Maguire said that he had personally collected Quill's Party dues. At least a few of those named as Communists, however, were in fact not Party members.[24]

The Dies hearing was front-page news in the New York press and brought swift, sharp response from the union. Quill and other TWU members had attended the hearing and immediately afterward Quill charged that Murphy was "a stool pigeon and a liar" and implied that he was mentally unbalanced. Quill again denied that he was or ever had been in the CP or that the union was controlled by the Party.[25] The following day, at the first New York State Convention of the CIO, a resolution was passed asking Congress to "stop wasting public funds" on the Dies Committee. Quill charged that the hearings had been held at the behest of the transit companies, with whom the TWU was scheduled to begin contract negotiations the next month. Although the union was unable to prove this charge of collusion, there was one visible link between the committee and the transit industry, which the union made the most of. Among the members of the Dies Committee, although not the subcommittee that came to New York, was Rep. John J. Dempsey of New Mexico. Between 1917 and 1919 Dempsey had been a vice president and superintendent of operations of a subsidiary of the Brooklyn Rapid Transit Company. Dempsey had been deeply involved in the company's 1918 clash with the BLE. For his role in the Malbone Street disaster he had been tried, though acquitted, for manslaughter.[26]

A week later Quill again attacked the Dies Committee, this time before a convention of the United Rubber Workers. In probably the best-known statement of his career, at least until New York Mayor John Lindsay drove him to new heights just before his death, Quill declared that he "would rather be called a Red by the rats than a rat by the Reds." Denying that the TWU was controlled by any party, he went on to say that "if Dies is interested in routing 'isms,' he should go back to Texas where the people are menaced by a dangerous 'ism'—virtual nudism—because they don't have enough to eat and clothe themselves." Far from retreating before the Dies Committee, Quill called for greater labor involvement in electoral politics, laying forth a vision of a worker-controlled Congress which, if need be, would nationalize industries to raise wages and lower prices.[27]

Following the Dies Committee hearing, the AAAC disappeared from the transit scene. It was replaced by a new opposition network centered at the Xavier Labor School. Xavier was a Jesuit-sponsored adult education center on West 16th Street, attached to the Catholic high school of the same name. It had been founded in 1936 as the Xavier Institute of Social Justice in response to a call from Rome by the General of the Jesuits for more active steps to combat Communism and spread Catholic principles of social justice. Initially the Institute, which sponsored a library, courses, and forums, attracted largely lower-middle-class, white-collar students, many of whom hoped to use courses in public speaking and the like to advance in their jobs or otherwise aid their quest for upward mobility.

Xavier's orientation changed after Philip Dobson, a Jesuit scholastic teaching at Xavier High School, became the Institute's director in 1937. A staunch anti-Communist and an admirer of Father Coughlin and *Tablet* editor Patrick Scanlan, Dobson believed that "Catholics were doing too much talking about the social question" while "exercising no appreciable influence on the trend of the times." Dobson wanted to end the school's somewhat academic air and turn it into a tool for direct anti-Communist struggle.[28]

Perhaps influenced by Father William Smith's Crown Heights School for Catholic Workmen in Brooklyn and an ACTU-sponsored labor school at Fordham University in the Bronx—both started in 1937 as part of a growing Catholic labor school movement—Dobson renamed his own Institute the Xavier Labor School, revising the curriculum for the 1938-39 session. Two programs were organized: a lecture series for public-school teachers and a series of courses aimed at workers, especially union members. It was in the latter area that Dobson placed his greatest hope, for he believed "that the greatest good for the Church could be accomplished by focusing our energies on the most strategic points, and the unions seemed to answer that description." Like his Communist adversaries, Dobson was convinced that at the heart of the political universe and the fight over radical change lay organized labor. Accordingly, he set up evening courses in parliamentary procedure, public speaking, labor history, communism and union labor, and "unionism and sound organization."[29]

As part of his new program for Xavier, Dobson sought to become actively involved in the internal politics of a specific union, since "there is too much talk of labor unions in general, and too little action." The union he chose was the TWU, which "for many reasons . . . seemed to present a fine opportunity of furthering the cause of Christ in a tangible situation." According to Dobson:

> The enemies of the Church seemed to be directing most of their energies to capturing the T.W.U., and I thought it would be well worth the while to do some negative work, first of all, in stopping the Reds in the T.W.U. and secondly, some positive work, by educating leaders who would go in and make it a truly democratic Union.

Dobson believed that the TWU was of unusual importance because through it the CP had gained control of the New York transit facilities, which could be used in the event of a revolution "to cause chaos, confusion, anarchy, to prevent troop movements, and so forth."

Dobson was optimistic about his chances for success, since most of the TWU's Irish Catholic members, he thought, were "still practical Catholics" who "would listen to Catholic clergymen." By proving that the TWU leadership followed the CP line, Dobson hoped to show union members that their leaders were anti-Catholic. He believed that the union "tyrannized over the men in a fashion little different from that of Joseph Stalin" and failed to make a public account of its expenses, and that as a result "the men were thoroughly fed up with it."[30]

Dobson may have selected the TWU as his primary target knowing of the previous work of the AAAC; it is possible that the coincident cessation of the latter group's activities was agreed upon in discussions between Dobson and Brooklyn Church leaders. In any event, one of Dobson's first transit contacts, William Harmon, came through Father Curran and several leaders of the earlier anti-Communist campaigns, including John Murphy, Robert Schneider, Jerry McCarthy, and James Flatley, were soon either attending Xavier classes or meeting privately with Dobson.[31]

Dobson's plan was for "a combination of direct action and education." In October 1938 he began a special series of weekly classes at Xavier for TWU members, following the union's own pattern of a main session at night and a smaller morning session for night workers. To attract students, flyers were distributed near car barns announcing "A Program of Americanism," and calling for transport workers to "Drive Out the Communists; They are Enemies of Labor." One flyer specifically attacked Quill, calling on him to publicly state whether or not he was "A GOOD CATHOLIC" and asking "IF SO, DO YOU CONDEMN COMMUNISM UNRESERVEDLY, AS THE POPE DOES?" Dobson claimed that as a result of this recruiting drive about 300 TWU members registered for classes, but this is almost certainly an exaggeration; a list of transit worker students for 1938-39 in the Xavier files has only 125 names. [32]

It was Dobson's hope that those attending classes "would form the nucleus of a much larger movement which would be successful in cleaning up the Union." "For a time," he later reported, Xavier "made considerable headway in its efforts to teach these men that their union leaders were dishonest and communistic." To this end, "every week the men put out several thousand mimeographed sheets exposing the Union leadership and its communistic hook-up."[33] One week, for example, Xavier's "Rank and File Bulletin" attacked MacMahon's ALP activity and his alleged ties to the CP. In a rambling, crudely written denunciation of the union leadership, TWU policy was associated with labor practices in the Soviet Union, and the union was criticized for failing to fight speed-up and efficiency studies on the BMT, which were equated with Russian Stakhanovism. Although defending the need for the union—"*a great thing in itself*"—workers were called on to "throw off that yoke of fear caused by leaders who are neither American nor Democratic."[34] Dobson himself visited shops, powerhouses, and car barns "in an effort to prove that I was not a stuffed shirt, . . . an aloof creature that smelled of parlor plush."[35]

The Xavier effort had the greatest impact on the IRT, but it did not have equal appeal for all of the company's workers. Judging by the names on the student list from 1938-39, most of the TWU members studying at Xavier were Irish or Irish-American, with a few from Italian and other backgrounds. Listed job titles for 72 of the 125 men indicate that 34 were in transportation (27 trainmen, 1 conductor, and 6 motormen) and 31 were station workers (10 agents and 21 platform men.) Only four students had shop jobs, and only two of those in skilled titles. Thus it would appear that Xavier found the most support for its explicitly Catholic, anti-Communist but pro-union appeal among Irish workers in less-skilled, lower-paid IRT transportation and station jobs. Conversely, there was little support for Xavier in the shops and powerhouses, where the TWU itself and its left-wing were strongest, or in the higher skilled, better paid maintenance-of-way and operating titles. [36]

Xavier's success among the less-skilled Irish, limited as it was, reflected a more general phenomenon. Although the TWU's ability to attract precisely this group had been one key to its success, at least a significant number of these same workers remained open to ideological currents quite different from those adopted by the union leadership. In particular, many of these workers were influenced by Father Coughlin and his combination of Social Catholicism, inflationary monetary reform, isolationism, anti-Semitism, and proto-fascism. At the time Dobson undertook his campaign, Coughlin still had a large national following, especially among Catholics and Germans, even though his overall support was beginning to erode. According to a December 1938 public opinion survey, 50 % of all Catholics had listened to Coughlin's radio broadcast at least once during the previous month and 42 % indicated approval of "what he says." Coughlin's greatest Catholic support was among the unemployed, WPA workers, farmers, and of particular relevance here, unskilled blue-collar workers. As late as 1940, Coughlin's newspaper, *Social Justice*, had an audited weekly circulation of nearly a quarter-million copies. [37]

Most sources agree that Coughlin had a large following among New York transit workers, particularly among the less-skilled, non-shop Irish. These workers did not necessarily agree with everything Coughlin said, especially his increasing opposition to the CIO. Certainly some, and probably most, remained committed to the TWU in spite of the teachings of the Father. (Nationally, in fact, most of those who identified themselves as generally agreeing with Coughlin disagreed with him on at least some important issues, including his opposition to Roosevelt.) Nevertheless, Coughlin's followers constituted an important pool of potential recruits for those organizing against the TWU leadership, including the Xavier group. [38]

According to Joseph Fitzpatrick, a Jesuit scholastic who assisted Dobson in 1938–39 and then succeeded him, many of the men who came down to Xavier thought of themselves as Coughlinites. James Flatley, for example, who did not attend Xavier classes but kept in touch with Dobson, attacked bankers at the TWU's 1937 convention for controlling the money supply and called on "our President to petition Congress to grant the workers a living wage." Two years later he declared that "I will not hear any man knock the reverend Father [Coughlin] who walks in the footsteps of Christ." Dobson and Fitzpatrick themselves closely followed Coughlin's speeches, though the latter was soon to become disenchanted. The stress at Xavier during this period was decidedly on the dangers of Communism rather than social reform. Reinforcing this bent was an odd group of free-floating anti-Communist street intellectuals, led by a John Doherty, who congregated at Xavier, full of mysterious plans and apparently with some ties to the New York City police. Although Xavier's appeals were not explicitly Coughlinite, the school occupied the same political territory and undoubtedly benefited from transit worker support for the radio priest. [39]

Outwardly, TWU leaders ignored Xavier. According to Dobson and Fitzpatrick, however, as they became aware of the school's activities they encouraged union "scandal squads" to spread rumors that Xavier was being paid by the companies to break up the union. Quill even accused Dobson of being a false priest, an anti-unionist parading in priest's clothes. (As scholastics Dobson and Fitzpatrick wore clerical garb even though they were not yet ordained.) These counter-measures were apparently quite effective. Some workers who wrote to Dobson clearly believed that Xavier opposed the existence of the TWU and worked with fascists, and on at least one occasion when Dobson went to a transit shop he was personally threatened.

Dobson further accused the TWU of trying some men involved with Xavier on charges of violating the union's constitution, and with threatening to try others if they continued to attend Xavier classes. (Discussing union business with non-members was a violation of the TWU constitution.) Those tried, Dobson claimed, were usually fined or threatened with expulsion, which of course carried with it the threat of job loss. [40] When a member of the Xavier group was beaten up by unknown assailants, Dobson speculated that union-hired thugs might have been responsible. [41]

There is no independent evidence to confirm Dobson's charges and, at least at first, there was little real reason for a union campaign against Xavier. Although the school developed a small core of activists and a larger circle of followers, it failed to incite mass opposition to the union leadership. Early in 1939, however, the situation suddenly changed, as Xavier came upon an issue that briefly placed it at the center of TWU politics: the threatened loss of jobs resulting from the demolition of the 6th Avenue el. Here some background is necessary.

In the summer of 1938 Mayor La Guardia, deeply involved in complex, lengthy negotiations to unify the IRT, BMT, and ISS under city control, and anticipating the completion of the ISS 6th Avenue subway the next spring, set in motion plans to demolish the IRT-run 6th Avenue el. By late November the IRT and various government agencies had agreed that el operations would end on December 4. This created a serious problem for the TWU, since some 600 or 700 jobs would be lost. In shaping a response, union leaders had to consider two fundamental issues, the union's stance toward technological or organizational changes that would result in work force reductions and the application of seniority rules in cases of job loss. These issues would also have to be faced in relation to the motorization of the trolley lines, then under way, and, more importantly, in any unification of the rapid transit system.[42]

The TWU, in theory, was not against technological change or the restructuring of transit operations. In October 1936, Austin Hogan had argued that "no responsible organization could be opposed to improvements and innovations—to progress in general." The problem was what to do about the impact of such changes on the union's members. The union's preferred solution was to protect all jobs and job rights while accepting progressive change. However, it would, according to Hogan, "oppose such improvements to be made at a total disregard for the human welfare of the work men employed in the industry."[43]

In the case of the 6th Avenue el, the TWU initially proposed that demolition be postponed until the spring of 1939 when the new ISS subway would open, allowing the displaced workers to be transferred that line. As the date of the proposed demolition approached, the union pressed its position by establishing a citizens' committee for continued el service and holding picket lines and rallies. When it became clear, however, that the demolition plans would not be altered, the union, while continuing to call for a postponement, began pressuring the city for compensation or alternative employment for the 6th Avenue workers. To this end, on November 29 Quill introduced a City Council resolution calling for either city jobs or severance pay for the affected men. The TWU's position was thus confused. On the one hand, it formally opposed immediate demolition and any job loss whatsoever. On the other hand, by trying to get other jobs and some compensation for the displaced workers it seemed in practice to be accepting as inevitable the planned end of 6th Avenue operations. Furthermore—perhaps because they were preoccupied with contract negotiations and the enormous problems and dangers associated with impending unification—TWU leaders began stressing the el issue only on the very eve of the planned el closing.[44]

Meanwhile, the La Guardia administration was displaying a rather indifferent attitude toward the threatened workers. Two days before the planned shutdown a mayoral message to the Board of Estimate coolly noted that "in any undertaking of such magnitude . . . it is not at all unusual that some individuals are subjected to hardship." All that La Guardia offered the victims of progress was the possibility of places on a priority civil service list for ISS jobs and an agreement from officials of the World's Fair to give consideration to applicants from the closed line for ticket-taking "and like positions."[45]

The whole jobs situation was still unresolved when, in spite of continued TWU protests, on the night of December 4 the final el ran down 6th Avenue, ending sixty years of continuous service and putting the line's employees out of work. The TWU campaign, however, soon brought some results. On December 7, Quill was able to report to a meeting of 4,000 IRT workers that Manhattan Borough President Stanley Isaacs, working with La Guardia, had agreed to find jobs for all of the laid-off men. Some would be hired to help in the el demolitions, others would get city jobs, and efforts would be made to secure private employment for the rest. (The IRT itself planned to hire a few of the men for the 9th Avenue el to handle increased traffic resulting from the demolition.) Within a short period of time 160 men actually were given new jobs, but it was still an unsatisfactory situation. The el demolition work was temporary, most of the other promised jobs had yet to materialize, and none of the laid-off men had been assured that they would continue to receive their old wage rates.[46]

While all this was going on, officials of both the city's Board of Transportation and the IRT were suggesting another solution, allowing some of the laid-off workers with high seniority to displace low seniority workers on those IRT lines that were continuing to operate. This was an extremely problematic approach, for it both accepted the idea of some job loss and required a major breach in the existing seniority system. Accordingly, the union's initial reaction was extremely negative. "The issue here," Quill declared, "is not one of seniority but one of jobs." But as it became increasingly evident that the city was not going to find employment for all of the laid-off men, and certainly not equivalent employment, the union reconsidered its position.[47]

Strengthening seniority and eliminating favoritism in lay-offs, promotions, and job assignments had been one of the initial rallying cries of the TWU. After the TWU won recognition, the IRT transportation department seniority system, which went all the way back to the early days of the els, was given a contractual basis but left essentially unchanged: seniority applied only within particular IRT divisions, and for some purposes only on particular lines within divisions. There was no company-wide seniority.[48]

Winning a contractual basis for seniority rights was an important accomplishment and a source of strength for the TWU, but by the same token it situated disputes between different groups of workers over complex seniority issues within the union itself, raising the possibility of internal strife. What Ronald Schatz has written about the electrical industry is equally applicable to transit:

> Workers' attachment to their seniority rights . . . had both individualistic and collectivistic aspects. Workers believed that seniority rights were a collective achievement. . . . At the same time, workers thought of their seniority rights as their personal possessions.

Although TWU leaders leaned towards the creation of larger seniority units, any change initiated by the union would almost certainly alienate those workers whose particular situations would be worsened, even if in the cause of a more generally just arrangement. TWU leaders were therefore extremely cautious in dealing with proposals to modify the seniority structure. At one point, in anticipation of possible demolitions, Hogan had suggested combining the seniority lists for the two IRT el divisions, but long-established traditions and jealousies made even such a limited move difficult, and the idea was dropped. When the more radical step of introducing system-wide seniority for the whole IRT was proposed, Hogan made it clear that he had "no intention of turning this Union . . . upside down on this issue. Any such decision [for system-wide seniority] . . . would completely dislocate this organization."[49]

As long as there were no work force reductions, except by attrition, seniority disputes could generally be kept in hand. But the failure of the union to delay the 6th Avenue el demolition or secure new jobs for all of the laid-off workers left the union facing the inherited contractions of the seniority system. Senior 6th Avenue men, some with as many as thirty years' service, had lost their jobs and pension rights, while men with but a few months' seniority were continuing to work on other IRT lines. Under these circumstances it took but a few weeks for the union leadership to reverse its position, deciding that if the existing situation was allowed to continue "a great injustice would be done." The solution that the leadership proposed was to allow the transfer of divisional seniority for the purpose of lay-offs only, so as to permit senior 6th Avenue men to displace those with less seniority in other divisions. This plan was ratified at IRT section meetings, while an alternative suggestion put forth by Xavier supporters, to create new jobs by reducing working hours and limiting overtime, was rejected. Although the union leadership tried to deny that its plan represented a substantial change, it was an important modification of the decades-old seniority system.[50]

The whole lay-off situation was now reversed. As a result of the union's new policy, 380 6th Avenue men who had yet to find new jobs or choose retirement were scheduled to displace a like number of workers from other el and subway lines at the end of January. Those now threatened were men who generally had been working for the IRT for a year or less. For the most part, they had been hired as temporary employees or vacation relief men after the TWU had won recognition. To add insult to injury, the union, which was the immediate agency of these men's impending job loss, seemed indifferent to their plight. According to a TWU spokesman, the threatened men should have been thankful for the work they had had "because not until the Union fought for vacations . . . was there any vacation with pay, and therefore no vacation relief jobs."[51]

It was in these turbulent waters that the Xavier group thought it found an issue around which to mobilize mass opposition to the TWU leadership. After issuing a leaflet headed "Save Your Seniority," Xavier held morning and evening meetings on January 25, 1939, to discuss the layoff and seniority situation. Several hundred men attended the meetings, which were the largest Xavier had held to date. But as Dobson later admitted, most of those who showed up were there simply "because they thought that the School might do something to protect their ratings."[52]

Xavier's role in what followed is not completely clear, but probably as a result of the meetings at the school some of the threatened men sought an injunction in State Supreme Court to block their dismissal. Their leader was Thomas Stack, an IRT el trainman with less that a year's service and a follower of Coughlin. Stack had attended at least one Xavier meeting and his group was represented in court by a law firm that had ties to the Jesuit school. While the suit was pending and the dismissals temporarily postponed, Stack called a meeting at the Triboro Palace in the South Bronx. Although most of the 200 workers who attended were men whose jobs were threatened and whose main concern was the seniority issue, Stack announced that a transit unit of Father Coughlin's National Union for Social Justice was being formed. A police observer later reported that he had been told at the meeting that some of the men had decided to commit acts of sabotage if their jobs were lost.

On February 6, State Supreme Court Justice Samuel I. Rosenman, a longtime adviser and confidant to FDR, rejected the injunction application. That night a second meeting was held at Triboro Palace. Speakers this time denounced Quill as a Communist and the whole CIO for "communistic activities," and plans were made to picket City Hall. After the meeting adjourned, a small group, led by Stack, remained behind to make other kinds of plans for the next day.[53]

Shortly after 8 a.m. on February 7 the Triboro group went into action, as some twenty or so workers, mostly trainmen, threw the IRT into chaos. At scattered points throughout the system workers refused to move trains or stalled them by pulling emergency brake cords, removing fuses, or opening emergency valves. Other trains were returned to their barns. At 129th Street and 3rd Avenue empty cars were positioned at a switching point to block service in both directions. On one train in the Bronx a trainman, after pulling the emergency cord, gave a speech about the impending dismissals to the angered passengers, which led to his arrest. That afternoon, by which time the IRT was back to normal, some 100 workers picketed City Hall. When Quill emerged from a City Council meeting he was surrounded by protesters, who booed him and called him a red, making it necessary for the police to escort him to his car.

Although the February 7 stoppage lasted but briefly, it was the most serious labor-caused interruption of rapid transit service since the 1926 IRT strike. There was not to be an equally serious incident until the mid-1950s, when again it was not the TWU but its opponents who were responsible. Reaction to the stoppage was swift. On the company's part, ten men were summarily fired. On the union's, Quill quickly issued a statement denouncing the demonstration, which he blamed on "a small irresponsible group under the influence of outside forces." He added that the union was proud of its record of never having caused "a moment's interruption of transit service."[54]

On February 8 a meeting of some 7,500 TWU members passed a resolution condemning the "clique" who had carried out the previous day's protest and calling for union disciplinary proceedings against those involved. Speaking for the local Executive Board, James Fitzsimon blamed the whole affair on Coughlinite organizers, whom he also accused of trying to spread anti-Semitism among transit workers. The next morning a meeting of 3,000 night workers took similar action.[55]

On March 31, union trials of twenty-eight workers were begun in connection with the February events. Several of those involved, including Stack, admitted their parts and gave detailed statements. When rumors of a plan to disrupt a May 31 trial meeting surfaced, thousands of unionists assembled at Transport Hall, though only a few protesters appeared. Stack and several others were eventually convicted on various union charges, but the final disposition of their cases cannot be traced.[56]

In one sense, TWU leaders were correct in labeling the February 7 strike a Coughlinite affair. Stack was an open advocate of the radio preacher, leaflets for the Triboro meetings had been issued in the name of a Social Justice Club, and even Xavier was broadly speaking aligned with the Coughlin movement. Yet the specific situation that led to the protest was the result of the union's own failure to deal successfully with the lay-off/seniority issue. In recalling the Stack wildcat, Forge downplayed its political character:

> You know, when there is a grievance on the part of workers, they will do some-
> thing about it. . . . If we had taken leadership on that . . . we could have had a
> strike of the whole union. . . . But when the union takes an approach that it is
> inevitable, that you can't fight it . . . then those workers who don't trust you will
> turn to whoever will lead them. And who will lead them? An oppositionalist—a
> guy who's against you for some other reason.

That the oppositionalist in this case was a Coughlinite was not surprising. In the milieu of unskilled Irish workers, from which many of the wildcatters came, Coughlin was extremely influential, the starkest political alternative to the left-center New Deal-CIO coalition. Furthermore, the tactics the protestors chose reflected the weakness of their ties to the union and their lack of participation in the politically maturing process of forming it. If the TWU in part represented one outgrowth of Irish political culture, so too did the strike against it, for was not February 7 the tactical vision of Tom O'Shea actually brought to life?[57]

The IRT wildcat made clear to the TWU leadership the dangers of simultaneously having an articulate opposition and outstanding membership grievances. Accordingly, efforts to consolidate the union organizationally and politically were intensified. Dissidents were subjected to sharp attacks, intended to isolate them, and internal disciplinary procedures were used more liberally.[58] The main leadership reaction to the February events, however, was to try to ensure that no similar issue again arose around which opposition sentiment could be mobilized. Thus although Quill unfairly blamed the job loss resulting from the 6th Avenue el demolition on the late reaction of the threatened workers themselves, it was the union leadership that took the lead in avoiding any recurrence of the situation. When, for example, plans were announced in the fall of 1939 for the demolition of the 2nd Avenue and 9th Avenue els, threatening 2,800 jobs, the union pulled out all stops. Picket lines, mass meetings, testimony at public hearings, and political maneuvers were all used to win other transit jobs, at the same pay, for all of the affected workers.[59] Similarly, when the Third Avenue Railway planned the motorization of its trolley lines, and the Fifth Avenue Coach tried to drop conductors from its double-decker buses, the TWU fought extended and largely successful battles to prevent the loss of jobs.[60]

For Xavier, the February IRT strike effectively ended the school's ability to serve as a center of dissident TWU activity. Although Dobson denied any foreknowledge of the wildcat or direct Xavier involvement, TWU officials were quickly able to establish at least indirect ties. For the first time they publicly attacked the school and its director. Simultaneously, many of the men who had come to Xavier in the belief that the school could help them retain their jobs "melted away." By March 1939, Dobson came to believe that further agitation would be counterproductive, only providing union leaders with an opportunity to "slander" the school and its followers. Rather than ousting the TWU leadership, Dobson wrote, Xavier's "small efforts to expose the Communists have been used by those Communists to brand the Church and the clergy as union-busters, thus alienating the men from the Catholic Religion." Accordingly, the core of Xavier activists disbanded their group and the special classes for TWU men were ended. A few transit workers, in Dobson's words, "formed . . . outside groups and carried on in such a way that the Church would not be directly involved," but Xavier itself did not again become involved with the TWU until after the war when, under a different leadership and with a different political approach, it achieved somewhat greater success.[61]

Xavier's retreat did not end Catholic-led opposition to the TWU administration, which, if anything, grew during the rest of 1939. However, it did change the opposition's political complexion, as new leadership arose from groups to both the left and right of the Jesuit school. Initially, it was the extreme right—groups affiliated with the Christian Front—that tried to pick up the pieces after the Stack wildcat. Later, the ACTU also entered the fray.

The Christian Front was a loose network of activist groups, organized in May 1938 as a new vehicle for the Coughlinite movement when Coughlin's anti-Communism and anti-New Dealism took on an increasingly fascistic and anti-Semitic cast. In the summer of 1939, when the Front peaked in strength, it held as many as thirty New York rallies a week, sold *Social Justice*, and picketed Jewish-owned stores. Violent incidents involving Christian Fronters were common, especialy once anti-Coughlin groups began street-hawking literature of their own. The situation was exacerbated by the fact that many policemen were openly sympathetic to the Coughlinites.[62]

The Front was only the best-known of many anti-Semitic, anti-Communist groups active in New York in 1939. Others included the American Minutemen, the Knights of the White Camellia, the Christian Patriots, the Flying Squads on Americanism, and the Christian Mobilizers. (The term Christian Front was used to designate both that specific group and the whole constellation of organizations.)[63] This dramatic wave of right-wing activity was an extreme manifestation of the bitter disenchantment of part of the American Catholic community—particularly Irish Catholics— with the New Deal, as well as part of a world-wide surge of fascism. Most members and almost all the leaders of the Christian Front were Irish Catholic. Young, poor, unemployed Irish men were the movement's shock troops.

The Christian Front was not a large organization. In fact, throughout this period Coughlin's overall support was declining. However, his remaining followers were extremely active. Although the Catholic hierarchy was divided in its stance toward the Front, some priests openly supported it. When radio station WMCA refused to broadcast Coughlin's speeches without prior script approval, the Brooklyn *Tablet* began printing them each week, often on the paper's front page. Such backing helped the Coughlinite right maintain considerable influence among New York Catholics, and especially among the Irish.[64]

Although Christian Front leaders rarely addressed the question of labor, when the subject came up they generally indicated that they supported unions but felt that "Christian leadership" was needed to replace the Jews and Communists whom they charged were in command. In hundreds of police reports on Christian Front and Christian Mobilizer meetings held in 1939 and 1940, there are no specific references to the CIO, the AFL, or particular unions, with one exception, the TWU. Perhaps because of the transit union's social composition, perhaps because of the Stack wildcat, it was apparently the only New York labor organization that was a direct target for the "Christian" right.[65]

The Front began its anti-TWU campaign by picking up where Xavier had left off, with the els. On May 7, 1939, the group held a street meeting at 110th Street and 5th Avenue to protest the removal of the 6th Avenue and BMT Fulton street els and the resulting job loss. It is likely that Christian Fronters also organized the abortive protest at the TWU's May 31 trial of Stack and his associates.[66] The next month there was a direct clash between the Front and transit unionists at an open-air TWU meeting in the Bronx. The meeting, held to discuss legislation affecting transit workers and "to combat recent attacks made . . . by irresponsible elements concentrating on the T.W.U. in a drive to undermine the labor movement," was attended by over a thousand people, about half union members and their families. Also in the crowd were Christian Fronters, who had been directed to the meeting from a nearby rally of their own. After considerable disorder, bottles were thrown at the platform as Quill was speaking, missing their intended target but injuring three people and resulting in several arrests.[67]

TWU leaders were also attacked during this period by the Christian Labor Front, a recently organized group with loose ties to the Christian Front. Although small, whatever base this group had was centered among Irish Catholic transit workers. The TWU leadership was one of its main targets.[68] Christian Labor Front leaflets were marked by crude anti-Semitism. Sacher, Santo, Forge, and Faber, for example, were denounced as "JUDAEO COMMUNISTS," and Hogan and Quill as:

> Christian renegades . . . whose smeared hands are loaded with gold from ATHEISTIC JUDAEO interests to betray their CHRISTIAN BROTHERS pink while they prattle and peddle the false vicious line of TOLERANCE AND DEMOCRACY.

In the fall of 1939 even cruder leaflets of the same drift appeared, this time unsigned, including one denouncing "MOIKE QUILL," the central target of most of this propaganda.[69]

In September it was the Christian Mobilizers who took over the anti-TWU campaign. At one Bronx rally Quill was denounced as "a Irish stooge and a thief, who stole control of the TWU from Tom Shea [sic] . . . a Communist and . . . the type of man that the Irish killed in their last Black and Tan war." The Mobilizers also took up the favored issue of the right, the els, in this case the impending demolition of the 2nd Avenue and 9th Avenue lines, demanding that the Mayor guarantee jobs for the el workers. The group distributed leaflets at el stations, wrote letters to government officials, and held at least two demonstrations at City Hall.[70]

The Christian Front, Christian Labor Front, and Christian Mobilizers recruited only a few transit worker members, though they had a larger number of TWU sympathizers.[71] The groups lacked competent leaders and even accurate information. The issue on which they tried to make their stand, the els, was a loser, for they were too late to address meaningfully the 6th Avenue situation and the union itself successfully dealt with the later demolitions. Still, activity on the far right helped define the terms of debate within the union, pressing forward the issue of Communism and making it easier for others not associated with these groups to attack the leadership.

Ironically, the group that finally gave anti-leadership sentiment in the TWU concrete political form, ACTU, itself opposed the Christian Front. During the two years following the 1937 BMT election, when it had actively supported the TWU, ACTU played no significant role within the transit union, restricting its infrequent comments on transit to sympathetic publicity for various TWU efforts. In the fall of 1938, when the TWU was negotiating its second round of contracts and coming under attack from Xavier, an editorial in the ACTU newspaper, *Labor Leader*, came out squarely against the Jesuit school's campaign. Calling the TWU "one of the great new CIO unions" it argued that

> harping on the alleged Communist tendencies of TWU officials at the present time will only serve to weaken the union at a crucial moment and jeopardize the welfare of its thousands of members. Let the issue await its proper time and its proper forum—the 1939 convention.[72]

During this period, however, ACTU was changing. Although still aligned with the liberal wing of the Catholic Church, its emphasis shifted from helping in the organization of new unions to fighting communism within existing ones. Thus, as the September 1939 TWU convention approached, ACTU took its own injunction to heart with a call for the TWU rank and file "to crush the growing undemocratic control of the union's affairs by the present union officials." The issue was posed as one of internal democracy, not communism. "Opposition to the actions of the union administration, no matter how sincere or well meaning, " argued a *Labor Leader* editorial, "never fails to bring down a torrent of vituperation, and character assassination, quickly followed by star chamber procedures, fines, and expulsions." "The continued growth of the TWU is of vital importance to the progress of labor and labor can only progress when democracy is present in its ranks."[73]

Having made the decision to take on the TWU leadership, ACTU moved quickly on two front. First, it assigned John J. Sheehan, an attorney who headed its affiliated Catholic Labor Defense League, to defend suspended Local 100 Executive Board member Thomas McGuire in internal TWU disciplinary procedures. McGuire had been charged with misconduct and malfeasance for supporting transit legislation bitterly opposed by the union and for urging union members not to pay their dues. This was but the first of a number of TWU disciplinary cases in which Sheehan, a former teamster and brother of a Jesuit, became involved.[74] Second, ACTU worked to create a unified opposition in preparation for the upcoming TWU International convention.

Only a few transit workers belonged to ACTU, and they were not well-known figures in the TWU. To make any headway against the TWU leadership it was therefore imperative that ACTU join forces with other, more established opposition-ists. To this end ACTU hastily arranged a meeting just prior to the 1939 convention with John Gallagher, Robert Schneider, and James Flatley, who had been meeting for some time with a group led by Xavier stalwarts John Doherty and Bill Harmon.

As was usually the case among TWU dissidents, there were problems and dis-putes galore. Within the Harmon-Doherty group there was a sharp fight over accusations that one of their number was taking considerable sums of money for opposition activities from a source allied with the transit companies. The poor relations between the Coughlin wing of the Church and ACTU presented another, more basic obstacle. Fathers Coughlin and Curran had both attacked ACTU for its cooperation with the CIO. Xavier leaders also held ACTU in low esteem. ACTU's ties to the Catholic Worker and the Catholic Committee to Combat Anti-Semitism particularly disturbed Coughlinites like Harmon. Furthermore, for two years ACTU had in effect supported the TWU against charges made by the AAAC, Xavier, the Dies Committee, and the Christian Front. Still, some sort of agreement was reached, for when the TWU's second International convention opened in Atlantic City on September 20 there was a small group of opposition delegates operating under the ACTU banner, including Gallagher, Flatley, IRT conductor Daniel J. McCarthy, a member of ACTU's Executive Board, and pioneer BMT unionist Patrick J. Sheehan, also an ACTU member. John Sheehan was in the gallery providing tactical advice.[75]

The TWU leadership was well informed about these latest doings on the right and at the convention came out swinging. In his opening remarks Quill attacked critics of the TWU, singling out "a small group of stool-pigeons" within ACTU and their lawyer, "an ambulance chaser . . . now looking for a soft racket." When Gallagher protested, Quill called him a "rat." Such personal sniping continued for the dura-tion of the convention.[76]

Before things had gone very far, however, Quill played his trump, an appearance by Father Charles Owen Rice, perhaps the country's best-known "labor priest." In Pittsburgh, where he was based, Rice had founded the Catholic Radical Alliance and had helped set up an ACTU branch. A strong supporter of industrial unionism, Rice worked closely with top CIO leaders and a host of CIO unions.[77]

In his speech to the TWU delegates, Rice made it clear that he opposed Commu-nism. His main thrust, however, was to praise the accomplishments of the CIO and the TWU. He came out strongly against racial discrimination and anti-Semitism, calling for "you who wear the badge of Catholicism over your heart to have toler-ance and charity." At the same time he urged the union leadership to give its opponents the right to be fully heard. While saying that he had no idea if the TWU officers carried CP membership cards, Rice strongly implied that as a result of his discussions with Hogan and Quill he doubted that they were Communists. "I think I am much more radical than the two of them," he continued. "The only quarrel I have with the C.I.O. is that they have not gone far enough. The Pope's encyclicals are still far more radical than the C.I.O."[78]

Rice's appearance was a stunning coup; it was an implicit endorsement of the union's leaders, under whose sponsorship he spoke, and it denied the opposition the exclusive right to speak in the name of the Church. In fact, it even brought into question their right to speak for ACTU. It was also an example of Quill's growing political mastery. Quill and Rice had apparently first met at the founding convention of the American Communications Association in 1937 and had renewed their acquaintance at the first CIO convention a year later. Although Rice, in his own words, "knew that he [Quill] was a Communist by reputation," he "liked everything about him except his Stalinism." The two men shared an admiration for the IRA and Rice felt that Quill was "a good labor leader, better than the alternative." Quill carefully kept Rice informed about TWU developments, including the activities of Xavier. When Quill asked Rice to speak at Atlantic City, Rice agreed, even though he knew that would be helping to undermine the anti-Communist opposition. A personal appeal by an ACTU representative failed to dissuade him, for although he "hated to break ranks . . . to me Mike was a Trade Unionist First and a Red second."[79]

Even without the Rice appearance, the opposition stood little chance. They were hopelessly outnumbered and had virtually no support outside their own ranks. To make matters worse, McCarthy was obviously drunk at one session and was expelled from the hall, while Gallagher made reckless charges that were easily refuted. The opposition had no program for the key economic and political issues facing the union. Their few positive proposals concerned changes in the union's structure and procedure, most importantly combining Local 100 sections into larger units and setting up a separate taxi workers' local. These suggestions were not without merit—and both were eventually adopted—but the motive behind them was primarily political: the opposition would benefit if there were larger bases for dissident section leaders and if the left-dominated taxi unit was removed from Local 100. After extensive debate, both proposals received only a handful of votes. Constantly on the defensive, the opposition group spent most of its time trying to force Quill to withdraw his insults and have McCarthy readmitted to the proceedings. The failure of the opposition to challenge the administration's slate of International officers, which was unanimously elected, was an indication of just how weak it was.[80]

Within the context of the convention, the leadership's aggressive attack on the opposition was quite unnecessary, but the intended audience was really the Local 100 rank and file. TWU leaders were well aware that the opposition had greater support than the delegate count indicated. This was especially true on the surface lines, where in several sections oppositionists held key posts or had actual control. When Hogan, Quill, Faber, and Santo tried to follow up their convention success by attacking Gallagher at a meeting of his own section, their effort boomeranged; Quill was hooted down and Gallagher's leadership endorsed.[81]

A more accurate test of strength came in the December 1939 Local 100 elections. ACTU and the Gallagher-Flatley-Schneider group joined forces again to field a "rank and file ticket," with Gallagher running for president and a veteran ACTU member for vice president. Opposition candidates, including quite a few union pioneers, were put up for other local-wide offices and for the local Executive Board. A substantial campaign was organized, with ACTU lawyer John Sheehan playing a key role. (Someone gave Sheehan a thousand dollars to finance the campaign.) Once again the opposition platform stressed internal democracy, structural and procedural reform, and disassociation of the union from "pagan political theories such as Nazism, Fascism, and Communism," Except for a call for a sick and death benefit, no economic issues were addressed.

The incumbent leadership took this latest challenge quite seriously. A large campaign committee was established for the administration slate and at least two opposition Executive Board candidates withdrew, probably as a result of leadership pressure. Someone also printed cards falsely indicating that Flatley supported the administration candidates. On the day of the election, top International officers and their wives personally picketed the polling site with signs attacking Gallagher.[82]

When the results came in, it was a victory for the incumbents, but nonetheless an impressive showing for the opposition. Hogan defeated Gallagher with 13,231 votes to 7,622, and all of the elected Executive Board candidates, except for Flatley, were administration supporters. Hogan's slate easily carried all the local branches except for the Third Avenue, where the vote was very close. Gallagher and several ACTU members contended that there had been voting irregularities, especially in the taxi branch, where the opposition had neither a campaign organization nor poll watchers, but Sheehan advised against challenging the election.[83]

The 1939 Local 100 election marked the high point of organized internal opposition to the TWU leadership until the leadership itself divided almost a decade later. Attacks on the TWU administration did not cease—in fact, for the next few years they remained at a high level—but the opposition was increasingly fragmented. Furthermore, the forms of anti-leadership activity changed dramatically once the city took over the city took over the IRT and BMT in the spring of 1940. Transit unification presented TWU leaders with major new problems, but they faced them in firm control of their own organization.

One of the most explosive political issues the TWU faced during the 1930s barely appears in the public record of the union, racial discrimination in the transit industry. This matter was so sensitive that the TWU leadership generally avoided mentioning it in union publications or at conventions. For one thing, it threatened to divide the union's membership. For another, it brought the TWU considerable unwanted, often embarrassing, publicity and affected its relationships with crucial outside forces, including the city's black population, civil right groups, and the Communist Party. In indirect ways race was also a factor in the struggle between the TWU leadership and its anti-Communist critics.

In some respects the TWU's record on race was exemplary. From its founding, the TWU made it clear that it was open to all workers without regard to color. This was a marked departure from the policies of most railway brotherhoods and AFL affiliates, which either barred blacks entirely or gave them only second-class status. Not only had the TWU agreed to affiliate with the IAM only after receiving assurances that its white and black members would be treated equally, in spite of the IAM's normal whites-only policy, but at the one and only IAM convention at which the TWU was represented, in 1936, Quill and Santo joined James Matles and other left-wing delegates in an unsuccessful fight to eliminate the IAM's ritual, which was used by locals to keep out blacks.[84]

TWU leaders always made sure that the union's New York leadership was racially integrated. Black IRT porter Clarence King was on the first TWU Executive Board.

Later he was joined on the Local 100 Executive Board by black taxi worker Hislop Arkless and then by BMT porter Louis Manning. The union's clerical staff was racially integrated as were all of its dances, social events, sports activities, and its Ladies' Auxiliary.[85]

There was some white membership resistance to this policy of internal integration, especially in the early days. White opposition to black attendance at the union's very first dance, in March 1934, nearly caused a rift in the still tiny union. (Lingering interracial tension may have contributed to the decision by the BMT porters to sponsor their own Welfare League, dances, and classes in addition to participating in union-wide activities.) Top TWU leaders themselves were occasionally insensitive to the problems black members faced. The union, for example, held its 1939 convention at a hotel that barred blacks from eating or staying there. When a black delegate complained, Jimmy Gahagan and Quill dismissed the matter by assuring the delegates that blacks would be seated at the union's banquet, to be held in the hotel, as if that somehow solved the problem.

All in all, though, the TWU was quite successful in establishing and enforcing a policy of racial equality within its own structures. The union leadership also had little difficulty in committing the TWU to the general fight against racism. The TWU gave money and sent delegates to the National Negro Congress (NNC), supported federal anti-lynching legislation, and set up a committee to fight discrimination in the New York taxi industry.[86]

Non-discriminatory union practices, however, meant little if blacks could not get transit jobs or could get only the lowest-paying and most demeaning work. Since this was precisely the situation in New York when the TWU was founded, the most critical race-related issue the union faced was what role it should play in fighting discriminatory hiring, job assignment, and promotion practices. This question proved highly controversial within the union, the black community, and the Communist Party.

The first TWU constitution, written in 1934, pledged that the union would fight for "full equality" for black workers and for "their right to hold any job in the industry."[87] Before the TWU won recognition the issue of discrimination was occasionally raised in union publications. In 1937 the union tried but failed to get non-discrimination clauses in its first round of contracts. Between then and 1941, however, the union did not take the lead in struggling against transit industry racism. Rather, individual black workers, black organizations, and civil rights groups, sometimes but not always with union encouragement, led the attack. The union itself down-played the issue, taking action only when under strong outside pressure.[88]

Black transit workers made their earliest and greatest gains on the ISS, the result of a 1935 Board of Transportation decision to apply civil service regulations without regard to race. This policy was instituted in the aftermath of a riot in Harlem on March 19 of that year and after repeated appeals by black ISS workers and black civic groups. The TWU apparently played no role in forcing this decision. With the ISS continually expanding and hiring new workers, black made rapid gains on the line after 1935.

Because the TWU had not led the fight to desegregate the ISS, black municipal transit workers viewed the city, not the union, as their patron. Black ISS workers were largely unenthusiastic about the TWU and many distrusted it. With the open-shop ISS treating black workers more fairly than the union-shop private lines, many black New Yorkers, rightly or wrongly, came to view the TWU itself as an obstacle to integration. Only when the TWU intensified its activity on the ISS, at the time of unification, and began addressing the specific situation of black workers, for example by fighting for greater promotional opportunities for the mostly black porters, did the union's standing with the line's black employees somewhat improve. [89]

On the IRT agitation against racial discrimination began shortly after the TWU signed its first contract in 1937. The campaign was initiated by a few black employees who had been denied promotions to jobs traditionally reserved for whites. Although the TWU intervened with the company on their behalf, publicly supporting their effort to end racial bars, it did not aggressively pursue the matter. Frustrated, Rubert Bath, a black union activist who had been denied a power department job for which he was qualified, went to the NAACP and the Urban League. The two groups took up his case, pressuring both the IRT and the TWU to act. The company stood pat, while the TWU initially ignored the groups' entreaties. But when the NAACP began raising the race issue with Quill's supporters during his first City Council campaign, the TWU agreed to cooperate, pledging that if the black advancement groups pressured the companies to end their discriminatory practices it would work to counteract any resistance by white workers. [90]

Publicity over transit industry discrimination presented a tricky political problem for both the TWU and the CP. Throughout the 1930s job discrimination was one of the most discussed political issues among New York blacks. In Harlem various radical, reform, and nationalist groups competed with one another in organizing campaigns against racism in employment. Although the CP initially had won much black support by taking a strong stand in this area, by the late 1930s it was both under attack from the NAACP, with which it had a long history of hostility, and being challenged by the Harlem Labor Union (HLU), an anti-union, neo-Garveyite group that was pressuring uptown merchants to hire blacks. Continued racial discrimination in an industry organized by a union allied with the CP was a source of considerable embarrassment to the Party, undercutting its claim to be the leading advocate of black rights.

Because the Bath case touched on such sensitive political issues, the CP assigned Manning Johnson, a well-known black Communist, to help mediate the dispute between the TWU and the NAACP and the Urban League. Meanwhile, to regain the general initiative on the jobs issue from the NAACP and the HLU, the CP joined with the Reverend Adam Clayton Powell, Jr. and the Reverend William Lloyd Ames to form the Greater New York Coordinating Committee on Employment, which targeted employment discrimination by public utilities. In April 1938, however, Powell, a key Harlem leader who had often worked closely with the Communists, openly criticized the TWU; in dealing with the transit industry, he said, blacks would have to fight both "against the employer, and against the trade unions for admission, recognition, and advancement." Disgust with transit industry discrimination was also expressed in a more direct manner; in a series of incidents, seat covers were slashed on Harlem buses operated by companies that refused to hire black drivers.[91]

In the face of public criticism and possibly some quiet pressure from the CP, in mid-1938 the TWU again asked the IRT to upgrade black workers. With the NAACP and Urban League also applying pressure, the IRT finally began to concede: six black porters were given jobs as station agents or platform men. The problem now was to prevent white workers from blocking the move. In this the TWU leadership aggressively took charge. The Local 100 Executive Board and the Joint Executive Committee passed a resolution strongly opposing discrimination in hiring and promotions, which was circulated in a pamphlet entitled *Fair Play, Justice and Unity*. At a series of stormy, overcrowded membership meetings TWU leaders fought very strong rank-and-file opposition to the promotions. Things got so heated that after one meeting a brawl broke out between supporters and opponents of black rights. Some IRT motormen, upset by the upgradings, sent a protest delegation to the union's headquarters. The TWU administration responded to this white resistance by portraying the opponents of the promotions as opponents of the union. Quill in particular worked hard to isolate, ridicule, and eventually overcome the opposition. In the end the black workers took up their new positions without serious incident.[92]

Because turnover was low and the IRT was not expanding—with the el demolitions it actually shrank—black advancement was tenuous and slow. On occasion the TWU had to quietly circumvent seniority rules to prevent promoted black workers from being forced back into porter jobs. In 1939 there were still only a handful of blacks in once all-white jobs.[93] Not until the early 1940s were more major breakthroughs made. Again, the TWU was not primarily responsible. In 1940 the unification of the transit system extended non-discriminatory civil service rules to the IRT and BMT. This had great practical effect once labor turnover increased during World War II. Also, as we will see, in 1941 a major, successful attack was launched by Harlem-based groups against the discriminatory employment policies of the Manhattan bus companies.[94]

In the 1930s, then, the TWU never opposed desegregation of the transit industry but neither did it vigorously press the issue—for example, by threatening a job action unless the employers changed their racial policies. There were several reasons why the union behaved in this "reluctant," even "shame-faced" manner, as Maurice Forge later characterized it.[95]

First, although TWU leaders genuinely wanted to break down discriminatory practices in the transit industry, they did not consider it a high priority. They had other, more immediate goals and hoped to postpone the fight against discrimination until after they had solidified their position in the industry and with the work force. In their own minds, their inaction was justified by their belief, as Forge recalled, "that the problem [of racial discrimination] was so overwhelming that you couldn't win." The TWU leadership faced little internal pressure to act differently. Few white unionists brought up the issue of discrimination and those who did were easily dissuaded from pushing for a more militant policy. Black unionists did raise the issue, but were few in number—less than 3 % of the transit work force was black in the early 1930s, rising to roughly 10 % in the late 1940s. Also, out of loyalty to the union, black TWU members generally avoided creating a public controversy; the TWU insistence during the 1937 contract negotiations on a minimum weekly wage had brought disproportionately large economic gains for the union's black members, winning their deep gratitude. While some black workers were not satisfied with the union's go-slow approach, there was never an organized intra-union effort to change it. The specter of how an enlarged black work force after unification might view the TWU, more than pressure from current black members, eventually influenced union leaders to take a more active role in fighting discrimination.[96]

Second, the race issue illustrates how the views and culture of the rank-and-file could influence the course of the union without affecting its formal stand. Many white TWU members did not want to work with or compete for jobs with blacks. TWU leaders feared that if the union took a visible lead in fighting against discrimination a membership revolt would ensue. As the reaction to the IRT promotions indicates, this belief was not entirely unjustified. Furthermore, once a coherent opposition had formed the union administration had cause to worry that any racist rebellion would strengthen the dissident camp. By no means were all the opponents of the incumbent administration racist. ACTU supported the fight against discrimination and at least one AAAC leader publicly stated that he had no objections to black promotions. However, opposition to desegregation was especially strong in those sections of the union where Coughlinite influence was great, such as at the BMT's Flatbush surface barn. There is some evidence that the union's opposition caucus benefited from backlash against the modest TWU efforts to help black workers advance.[97]

Third, in the mid- and late 1930s the CP did not bring sustained pressure to bear on the TWU over the issue of discrimination. In fact, the controversy over transit employment practices reveals the considerable latitude the CP was willing to give the TWU. Although the Party placed a very high priority on winning black support—which continued discrimination in the transit industry was jeopardizing—Party leaders were reluctant to push the union hard. Although some black Communists became restive with TWU inaction, the top CP leadership accepted the union's assessment of its situation and generally insulated the TWU from internal Party criticism.[98]

In a memorandum prepared in March 1938 for Ben Davis, Jr., a leading black Communist, the TWU defended its record on race. "The union," it argued, "is fighting discrimination successfully but not miraculously." The memo blamed the shortcomings in what the TWU had achieved on the "hostility" of white workers, the distrust among blacks toward unions and whites, the tradition of racism in the railroad industry, the policies of the New York transit companies, and, finally, public indifference. It pledged that the next TWU contracts would attack discrimination through stricter seniority provisions and "the right of Union hiring." As for the 1937 negotiations, the memo asked "what real friend of the Negro people and of labor generally would advocate that the Union should have turned down the substantial gains won in the contract and entered into a wild gamble for the whole hog by striking . . . on the verge of reaching the first bona fide union agreement in the transit industry?"[99]

The TWU leadership was certainly accurate in portraying both transit management and its own membership as serious obstacles to ending racial discrimination. However, the way the TWU handled the race issue makes it clear that, even at this early date, institutional self-preservation had become a foremost consideration in the thinking of the union's leadership. In the short run, the TWU's cautious approach to racism helped ensure that the union's basic political orientation was preserved while its overall position was strengthened. In the long run, though, it meant that black transit workers would have no special loyalty to the union's left leaders either during the crisis that followed unification or during the Cold War fissure in the TWU.[100]

Virtually every aspect of the TWU's political life, including the issue of racial discrimination, was affected by the city takeover of the IRT and BMT in 1940. Before going on to look at those changed circumstances, however, it is appropriate to consider again the multiple structures of left-wing control of the TWU, for through them much can be learned about the union and its members.

The left-wing leaders of the TWU did not triumph over their conservative critics because the rank and file more closely shared their ideological views. If anything, the opposite was probably true. Yet because the style of leadership adopted by the left was so well suited to the character of the work force, the right was unable to capitalize on political differences between the rank and file and the union hierarchy. Along with the structural factors already discussed, it made for a one-sided contest.

The TWU leadership sold itself to the membership primarily on the basis of its ablilty to win economic and other contractual gains. One of Santo's favorite phrases was that the union "brought home the bacon." Older workers did not have to be reminded how much things had been changed by the TWU, while those hired after 1937 were constantly told in union pamphlets and articles.[101] TWU oppositionists never projected a trade union program that fundamentally differed from that of the established leadership, except on narrow issues like the 6th Avenue el jobs or sick and death benefits. They lacked the information, experience, and vision to formulate their own program and acknowledged that within the given limits the incumbent leaders were effective economic unionists. When debates took place over work-related issues, they were usually outside the factional alignment and brought little benefit to the organized right.[102]

Having in effect ceded that main terrain to the administration, the right focused on the issues of internal democracy and anti-Communism. Neither generated great rank and file interest. The tendency of TWU leaders to be heavy-handed and abusive toward their opponents, and to use unjustified and unwise disciplinary measures, may have alienated some members and benefited the opposition. In the main, however, the bureaucratic mechanisms of control employed by the leadership were subtle and the union formally democratic. If they bothered, workers *could* vote for sections officers, local leaders, and convention delegates and for or against contracts and strikes. Furthermore, if meetings on occasion were packed and voting procedures sometimes questionable, at least among the Irish there was a certain admiration for the shrewd political trick, the clever maneuver. A little fiddling had never hurt Tammany too badly and the same held true for Quill.[103]

Anti-Communism also failed as the main basis for an opposition movement. Most importantly, the TWU leadership was not trying to win transit workers over to Communism. They did not present themselves as Communists and did not attempt, except in limited and private ways, to promulgate Communist ideology within the union. Partially this was a conscious strategy, but it also reflected the outlook of some TWU Communists for whom Communism meant primarily effective unionism. Many Communists in the TWU—particularly secondary leaders— showed little interest in non-union-related CP activities. When they gathered together, what they often most wanted to discuss was how best to pursue grievances.[104]

After 1935 the politics of the TWU, as defined by the leadership and presented in union publications, convention resolutions, and the like, were by and large the politics of the CIO and the New Deal. Little could be found in the TWU *Bulletin* that could not be found in the newspapers of a half-a-dozen non-CP industrial unions. Scrupulous political self-censorship was normally practiced. No open discussion of socialism, no songs of praise for the Soviet Union, no open support for the CP were to be found in the TWU. On those rare occasions when their enthusiasm got the better of the them, union leaders generally did their best to cover their tracks. The printed proceedings of the union's 1937 convention provides a good illustration; in several places leftist rhetoric was edited out or toned down before the transcript of the gathering was sent to the printers. For example, during Quill's speech accepting the presidential nomination, he at one point replied in his inimitable manner to charges that he read the *Daily Worker*:

> Well, I read English very poorly, and Gaelic is the only language I read. The Daily Worker is not printed in Gaelic. If it was . . . I would read it because the Daily Worker is the only working class paper that I ever had the opportunity to read in this country, and the day that I don't get it I don't feel is a proper day.

In the printed version of the proceedings this became:

> Well, I read English very poorly, and it is about the only language I read. The Daily Worker is printed in English. If it was printed in Gaelic I would perhaps read it also because it is a working man's paper. . . . [T]he day that I don't get news of the labor movement I don't feel is a proper day.

Similarly, Quill's opposition to "all oppression of the working class, and that goes for the invasion of Spain today and the slaughter of our brothers in arms, the Spanish workers," became opposition to "all oppressors of the common people, whether it is Ireland, Spain, China, America, or elsewhere."[105]

Outside the union, TWU leaders were somewhat more open in identifying with CP-sponsored activities, but almost never with the CP itself. Quill in particular participated in many CP-led organizations, but he was the one TWU leader who could do so as an elected political figure as well as a unionist. Furthermore, the world of outside left-liberal politics was so distant from the world of most transit workers that the participation of their leaders in the League for the Protection of Minority Rights or the American Peace Mobilization meant little.[106]

The TWU left refused to cede either flag or church to its opponents. The union's newspaper reprinted the Declaration of Independence annually, praised Lincoln, and spoke of "The American Way." Likewise, some TWU leaders regularly made it known that they were good Catholics. In attacking Church-affiliated rightists, union leaders never attacked the Church itself.[107]

During the heyday of the Popular Front it was easy for CPers in the TWU to identify themselves with mainstream liberal politics, for the Party itself was doing much the same and a center-left alliance dominated the CIO. Between 1939 and 1941, when the CP's Popular Front policy was interrupted by the Hitler-Stalin pact, political alignments were, of course, quite different. However, the shift did not present serious problems within the TWU. The issue that most separated the leaders of the TWU from CIO centrists and the New Deal was foreign policy, but the isolationist stand the TWU leadership promoted was extremely popular among the TWU Irish, who generally opposed any aid to Britain. Also, John L. Lewis, and for that matter Coughlin, backed isolationism. The leftists in the TWU were thus far from isolated. Furthermore, the renewed Communist militancy of the period fit well with the changed conditions the TWU faced once the city took over the BMT and IRT.[108]

The difficult "flip-flop," as even Quill called it, was not in 1939 but in 1941, after Germany invaded the Soviet Union. At that year's September TWU convention the TWU leadership sought to win union support for Roosevelt's foreign policy and a stronger defense program. The result was the most extended convention debate in the TWU's history. Some delegates, like Mark Kavanaugh, who normally supported the administration, opposed the very suddenness of the turnabout. Others, including Flatley and Gallagher, saw the United States defense effort as primarily aiding either British imperialism or Soviet Communism or both. The leadership, however, with support from left-wing Irish republicans, other leftists, Italian and German anti-fascists, and a few delegates who were simply tired of constant deference to Irish interests, eventually carried the day by a large margin.[109]

Some issues did cause the union's left trouble, most notably the Spanish Civil War. Although American Catholics were not of one mind toward the conflict in Spain, they much more likely than non-Catholics to view Franco sympathetically. Furthermore, the Catholic hierarchy and press strongly backed the anti-government rebellion. The support Quill and other TWU officials expressed for the Spanish Republicans, though usually restrained in union forums, caused considerable membership unrest. Gerald O'Reilly, who helped transfer arms originally obtained for the IRA to the Loyalists, remembered this as one of the few non-union political issues raised by rank and filers at section meetings. To make matters worse, in July 1938 the *Daily Worker* reported that a taxi section of Local 100 had pledged money to bring back wounded Lincoln Brigade soldiers. When over a year later two backers of the rank-and-file opposition slate, Patrick Reilly and Michael Considine (a former IRA member), repeated this story at a section meeting, union leaders, claiming that the report had been untrue, expelled Reilly for spreading false rumors. The Spanish issue was so sensitive that some doctors who had served with the Loyalists in Spain were not allowed to work for the union's Medical Plan out of fear of antagonizing the membership.[110]

The Spanish Civil War also precipitated a break between a group of left republicans, including Quill and O'Reilly from the TWU, and the Clan na Gael. By the late 1930s the Clan, like the IRA, was drifting toward a more purely nationalist position and was increasingly wary of ties to the left. When the Quill-O'Reilly group refused to drop its public support for the Spanish Republicans, its supporters were expelled from the Clan. The rift was by no means total—in 1939 and 1940 Hogan and Quill were still addressing Clan-sponsored meeting—but just prior to the 1941 TWU convention Clan and IRA representatives lobbied among the delegates against the proposed foreign policy position. Thereafter relations between Quill and more orthodox republicans cooled.[111]

The whole pattern of political moderation by the TWU left helps make understandable a seeming oddity, the widespread acceptance by the TWU membership of their leaders' protestations that they were not Communists—protestations that at a distance seem so very transparent. Of course the source of many of the charges of Communist control—interests obviously opposed to the union—served to diminish their credibility, while the deep-bred Irish contempt for the informer undercut their impact. The very consistency of the leadership's stand also helped. The more TWU leaders were accused of being reds the more strongly they denied it. For example, after the Dies Committee held a second hearing on the TWU in April 1940, this time with Tom O'Shea as the star witness, Quill demanded an appearance of his own at which he challenged the government to come up with "one line of documentary evidence" that any TWU member was connected to the CP.[112] As one scholar put it, "all instances of red-baiting by newspapers, politicians, and clergymen alike were so quickly and soundly challenged that the members could readily believe, if they wanted to, that their leaders were God-fearing Catholic Irishmen."[113]

The key here, of course, was that many union members were deeply committed to believing precisely that. For the typical worker, who on the one hand subscribed to garden-variety anti-Communism and on the other hand had a great stake in supporting the union, the simplest solution was willful blindness, the avoidance of reality. If suspicions were common that at least some TWU leaders had links to the CP, there was considerable confusion as to just who fit where. Many workers liked to believe that their favorites, particularly good Irishmen like Hogan and Quill, certainly were not among the reds. The whole situation led to some strange contradictions. IRT shop worker John Plover, for instance, himself quite conservative, never asked Quill if he was a Communist and believed that he was not. He often got into fights, sometimes physical, with those who accused Quill of being a red, for which he himself in turn was red-baited. Thus an anti-Communist worker was accused of being a Communist for arguing that a pro-Communist union leader wasn't a Communist. If this seems odd, Plover's combination of anti-Communism, opposition to red-baiting, religiosity, and distaste for the Church-related opposition was, in fact, not unusual.[114]

Perhaps the best summary of what transit workers thought about their leaders comes from Maurice Forge, who described a spectrum:

> ranging from the extreme sympathizers, who not only knew they were reds, but were glad of it, to the other extreme, who would rather starve without these reds than get a crumb of bread from [them]. The mass inside was willing to settle for this formula: maybe they're reds, maybe they're not, but they're nice guys and they bring home the bacon, so I shrug my shoulders, I go home and I sleep well.

> This was the majority. . . . I'd say that there were ten to fifteen percent on
> either end, but the mass in between was complacent.[115]

What Forge called being complacent, Dobson termed being "terribly lethargic," a characteristic of transit workers ("a difficult class of men") that he felt, along with anti-clericalism, had contributed to Xavier's failure. The problem, he wrote, was "the selfishness of many who did not care about their religion or their Country as long as they received a few cents more in their pay envelopes."[116] Perhaps a better term for this perceived lethargy or complacency is passive allegiance—a powerful element in the edifice of left control, especially among the numerically dominant and therefore politically critical low-skilled Irish. In part, it was a question, as Forge and Dobson noted, of gratitude for changes brought about by the union overcoming ideological uneasiness. In part, it was the transfer of previous attitudes toward authority—deference, obedience, acceptance, and even fear—from one object, the companies, to another, the union.

The female BMT agents provide the sharpest example of this latter process. During the non-union years they had shown great loyalty and gratitude, mixed with fear, toward the BMT for providing them with jobs and security. Accordingly they were the last group of privately employed rapid transit workers to join the TWU. Once having made the change, however, they displayed the same deep loyalty toward the TWU that they had once shown the company, becoming among the staunchest unionists. Still, just as they had once seen the BMT in paternal terms, so too did they see the union. BMT agents, for example, were constantly coming to Peter MacLachlan, who handled their major grievances, not only with job-related problems but with personal ones as well, from unpaid installments on time purchases to medical difficulties that they felt union doctors had misunderstood. In appreciation of his help so many agents told MacLachlan, whom they called Mr. Mac, that they were saying novenae in his behalf that forty years later he joked that this was why he had lived to a ripe old age.[117]

If in organizing the TWU the core unionists had had to overcome fatalism, submissiveness, ignorance, and fear in the work force at large, these very traits certainly continued, if in weakened form, in the union era. Many a worker who freely criticized TWU leaders in his local saloon kept quiet on the job, a reflection of both deep characterological traits and the very practical fact that troublesome workers might find their grievances less vigorously pursued or, in extreme cases, their union memberships and jobs threatened.[118] Less dramatic, but more common, was the tendency to see the union as an outside agency, perhaps a beneficial one but still a thing apart. Only a small number of workers conceived of themselves as playing an active role in shaping the union's future. For all their great differences, CP and Xavier leaders were remarkably similar in the language they used to discuss the processes and strategies of politics, and both were far separated in this from most TWU members. Not surprisingly it was among the ranks of ex-Communists that the right found many of its key recruits.[119]

The complement to worker passivity was charismatic leadership. The top ten or fifteen TWU leaders were stars, larger-than-life figures on whom workers projected their hopes and pride. Quill was the star of stars, but beneath him lay a galaxy of lesser lights. When Santo, for example, got worked up while speaking, he had a habit of taking off his coat and rolling up his sleeves. This became like the favorite mannerism of a popular performer; whenever Santo took the podium shouts would ring out of "take off your coat, John." Even branch organizers shone when they showed up at this or that section meeting. [120]

TWU leaders did not necessarily promote membership passivity—at times, in fact, they worked for greater rank-and-file involvement—but nonetheless they came to master political rule under that circumstance, using backroom consensus, charismatic leadership, and the ridicule and isolation of opponents as integral elements in maintaining power. [121] And as long as they could continue to deliver contractual gains, as John Gallagher put it "the average guy figure[d] I have a vacation, I can tell the boss to go to hell. And thanks to the Communists, and if we have to use the Communists for that, well so be it." [122]

IV

"As . . . decent citizens of New York"

8
PUBLIC TRANSIT AND
TRANSIT POLITICS

As Communists, many TWU leaders were committed, at least in the abstract, to the public ownership and operation of industry, including mass transit. In practice, however, the New York employer with which the TWU had the greatest difficulty in the 1930s and 40s was the New York City Board of Transportation, the only public employer with which it dealt. At first the TWU's problems with the Board were merely annoying, since when the union was founded the only government-run transit line in New York City was the small ISS. But in the late 1930s, as it became obvious that the unification of the New York City rapid transit system under public control was inevitable, the issue of public transit drew ever more TWU attention. When the city actually took over the IRT and BMT in mid-1940, the TWU was plunged into a prolonged crisis. At the time there were few precedents for municipal unionism on a mass scale. By circumstance rather than choice the TWU was forced to become a pioneer in public sector unionism. As it discovered, that involved legal, political, and economic problems unlike those faced by the vast majority of American unions.

Starting in the late 1930s, the TWU became one of the most politically active unions in the New York region. While to some extent this was an outgrowth of the ideological outlook of the union's leadership, it was also linked to the drive for transit unification. Public operation of mass transit meant the further politicization of an already politicized industry. Accordingly, the TWU was drawn ever more deeply into the complex electoral politics of New York City and New York State.

Within months after the ISS began operations in September 1932, some of the line's 1,600 newly-assembled workers began seeking to improve working conditions, protect themselves from arbitrary action, and win greater security. To some extent what occurred paralleled developments on the private lines; small groups of workers, usually within given work locations or occupational categories, began to coalesce and explore various modes of action. The specific directions these informal groups took, however, were often quite different from those taken by their private-line counterparts, due to the unique legal and organizational setting of the ISS and the peculiar social composition of its work force.

For several years the exact legal status of ISS workers was unclear. The Board of Transportation, which ran the ISS with considerable autonomy, set the terms of employment and handled labor relations. For some purposes the Board was considered a state agency, for others a city agency. Not until 1935 was it legally determined that ISS workers were city employees. Even then it was unclear whether the city had the power to set transit pay rates or whether this was exclusively a power of the Board. Furthermore, prior to January 1935, ISS workers were not subject to civil service regulations; the Board was free to hire, fire, and treat its workers as it chose. Using this leeway the Board of Transportation adopted many of the practices of the private lines, leaving its workers, in the words of one of their number, "neither fish nor flesh," with most of the disadvantages and few of the benefits of both private and public sector employment.[1]

Given this confused situation and their varied backgrounds, there were considerable differences of opinion among municipal transit workers about how best to deal with their problems. Some advocated craft unionism. Many ISS workers, particularly in transportation jobs, had belonged to railroad brotherhoods while working for interurban railroads. A number continued to maintain their memberships. Some of these workers undertook to establish ISS brotherhood units. The BLE developed significant membership among ISS motormen, while at least a few motormen and conductors belonged to the BRT. Some former Amalgamated members, including a few fired by the IRT in 1928 for union activity, established a unit of their old organization. Several AFL craft unions also set up small ISS groups.[2]

In contrast to these union-oriented workers, other ISS men turned to religious, ethnic, fraternal, or patriotic groups for help, particularly in the informal grievance procedures established by the Board. On various occasions the American Legion, Knights of Columbus, Ancient Order of Hibernians, Sons of Italy, and even parish priests interceded on behalf of ISS workers. Black workers, at first restricted to jobs as porters or as agents in black areas of the city, sought assistance from the NAACP and civic groups such as the North Harlem Community Council in trying to break down discriminatory bars. Small, independent benevolent associations also began appearing. The Board of Transportation encouraged the involvement of groups organized along ethnic, religious, or craft lines, hoping in that way to divide the work force and prevent the emergence of a system-wide union.[3]

Nonetheless, the group that developed the greatest strength on the ISS was a system-wide organization, the Civil Service Forum, the New York City affiliate of the Civil Service Association of the State of New York. The Forum was typical of public employee associations in the era before public sector unionism became widely accepted. Although the Forum represented workers in grievance procedures, it did not engage in collective bargaining and was not a true union. Rather its main thrust was to try to use political pressure and legislation to improve and enforce civil service regulations and upgrade conditions. It opposed closed shops, check-offs, and strikes, and it included a large number of supervisory personnel, often in leadership roles.

Structurally it consisted of a series of semi-autonomous councils organized along craft and agency lines. The "Forum" itself was a representative body of council leaders.

From its founding in 1914 on, the Forum was dominated by Frank J. Prial. A one-time sewer claims inspector, Prial used his close ties to the Democratic party to build a civil service empire. Throughout the 1920s he not only ran the Forum but also served as New York City Deputy Comptroller, owned *The Chief*, a weekly paper that reported civil service news, and had close ties to the Delehanty Institute, a civil service training school. Prial's multiple positions gave him clout with top government and political leaders, influence over city salaries, and unparalleled access to the city's Civil Service Commission. Under his leadership the Forum was in effect a powerful, specialized political machine that acted in alliance with the Democratic party. Prial spent much of his time dealing with the individual problems of Forum members—appointments, promotions, transfers, and the like. In return he expected loyalty on election day.

Prial's empire began to crumble when, like many New York Democratic leaders, he failed to anticipate the shifting political tides of the 1930s. In 1933 Prial sought and won the Democratic nomination for Comptroller, defeating a candidate put up by the Democratic county leaders. But in the general election he lost to La Guardia's running mate on the City Fusion ticket. Four years later, to break Prial's monopoly over the dissemination of civil service news, the La Guardia administration encouraged the establishment of a rival civil service newspaper, *The Civil Service Leader*. Cut off from both the incumbent city administration and the Tammany wing of the Democratic party, Prial's influence waned and the Forum began a long, slow disintegration.[4]

In early 1933, however, when the Forum began organizing ISS workers, its woes were still ahead, and it quickly signed up members. Within a year newly organized Forum councils and several previously independent worker groups joined together to form an ISS Joint Council within the Forum. By mid-1936 the ten councils in the joint body claimed a combined membership of 2,500 of the roughly 3,000 ISS workers. Although this figure was probably inflated, the Forum was undoubtedly the largest workers' group on the ISS throughout this period.[5]

When the TWU was officially founded in the spring of 1934, it too indicated its intention of organizing the ISS. In fact, at first the new union made no distinction between the public and private sectors. Alongside material on the private lines, the *Transport Workers Bulletin* and the *Daily Worker* carried letters and articles on ISS conditions and calls for municipal transit workers to join the TWU. Just as they did on the private lines, early TWU activists contacted friends and friends of friends and old IRA compatriots in search of ISS recruits.

Until 1936, however, the ISS was a low priority for the TWU and progress was extremely slow. The TWU developed a significant following only among the shop and car barn workers, particularly the skilled mechanics and maintenance men at the main ISS shop at 207th Street in Manhattan. Because the ISS work force was dissimilar to those of the other transit systems, the social, political, and community ties of TWU members working elsewhere proved to be of only limited use in reaching ISS workers. Also, many ISS workers felt that because they were government employees a union was unnecessary or illegal. The Civil Service Forum was so well established among these workers that the TWU eventually was forced to permit dual memberships. Among the workers who were union-minded, many already belonged to craft units.[6]

ISS activists generally had two overlapping goals. First, like many if not most city subway workers, they wanted civil service procedures extended to the ISS. This was particularly true of workers who had taken ISS jobs while awaiting appointments to other civil service titles. It was also true of the numerous young, well-educated workers who had taken subway operating jobs after the Depression shattered other plans. Seeking the security, benefits, and pensions associated with civil service, what novelist Joe Flaherty dubbed the "economic holy Trinity," they hoped to use competitive tests to advance rapidly. Second, municipal transit activists widely sought to improve existing conditions by winning "prevailing" wages and benefits, either those prevailing in non-transit civil service titles or those in private-sector construction, maintenance, and interurban railroad jobs. What ISS workers did not want was to have their working conditions and pay levels pegged to those in private-sector transit, which to some extent already had been done. Although non-monetary ISS conditions were generally better than those on the IRT and BMT, the line's hourly rates had been modeled after those on the IRT. Since hours were shorter on the municipal system, weekly earnings were generally lower.[7]

The TWU, with its few ISS members, was slow to understand this mind-set. At first it mocked the pension plan and advancement possibilities on the ISS, features of public employment that even in their then-weak state held great allure for many workers. The union also apparently failed to take a formal stand on the extension of civil service to the ISS, though it sympathetically reported on efforts in that direction. In fact, it was quite some time until the TWU developed any comprehensive ISS program.[8]

Strategic as well as programmatic differences separated the various ISS worker groups. Most favored the Forum's approach, lobbying and legislation. When in July 1934 the Municipal Civil Service Commission held hearings on the possibility of granting ISS employees civil service status, prevailing wages, and vacations, several hundred transit workers attended. In part as a result of such pressure, on January 1, 1935, the Board of Transportation and the Civil Service Commission began transferring ISS workers into competitive civil service titles without requiring them to take exams, a process that took over three years to complete. Thereafter almost all hiring and promoting was done through competitive procedures. Although the Board initially had planned not to convert cleaning jobs, held mostly by blacks, into competitive titles, heavy lobbying by the workers involved led to their inclusion. Most ISS workers welcomed being blanketed into civil service, anticipating greater security and opportunity. Whatever sentiment there was toward unionism was probably for the moment diminished, as many workers developed at least temporarily a sense of gratitude and loyalty toward the Board.[9]

Some groups of ISS workers tried to improve their lot through lawsuits. Presumably under pressure from those affected, in December 1934 the New York City Board of Alderman voted to increase ISS station agents' pay to $6 a day. When the Board of Transportation refused to grant the increase 491 agents brought suit against the Board. Although the agents lost the case—this decision established the transit Board's exclusive right to set pay levels—it was an early example of a strategic approach other craft groups later employed, usually with no better results.[10]

The TWU and its backers were highly critical of the Forum's dependence on legal, legislative, and political initiatives rather than direct membership action. However, except for pursuing a grievance here and there, the TWU itself was in no position to do otherwise. When in the spring of 1935 the Forum urged the State Legislature to pass the so-called McGrath bill, which provided two weeks of paid vacation for ISS workers, the TWU tailed behind and endorsed the measure. Ever since the municipal subway had opened, its employees had sought the same vacation rights as non-transit city workers. Their campaign paid off when, with the help of lobbying by Forum subway leaders and State AFL President George Meany, the McGrath bill was passed and signed into law.[11]

Although the McGrath bill was to be the Civil Service Forum's only major accomplishment on the ISS, it was an impressive victory, since few private sector transit workers had vacations of any kind. Recognizing this, in early 1936 the TWU, which had yet to make much headway on its own, ended its public criticism of the Forum and began working with the ISS Joint Council to establish a unified legislative and lobbying effort.[12]

The key figure in this new alliance was the president of the Joint Council, Joseph B. English. English, a car repairman at the 207th Street shop, was a former railroad unionist. Born in South Carolina at the turn of the century, making him five to ten years older than most TWU leaders, by the age of nineteen he was the president of a Virginia local of the Brotherhood of Railway Clerks. Between 1926 and 1928 he attended Brookwood Labor College on scholarship, marrying the school's dietitian. Although not very politically active, over the years English maintained mildly socialist views similar to those promoted at Brookwood. Early on he became the leader of an informal workers group at 207th Street, which eventually joined the Forum. Thereafter he headed both the Forum's 207th Street council and its ISS Joint Council. English's union background, the dissatisfaction of many Joint Council leaders with the Forum's top leadership, and the TWU's growing strength on the IRT, all probably contributed to the Joint Council's decision to take part in a coordinated effort with the TWU.[13]

Several TWU-Forum bills were introduced in the 1936 session of the legislature. Douglas MacMahon, representing the TWU, and English and Joseph Morrison, representing the ISS Joint Council, were sent to Albany to lobby for their passage. One bill would have required private transit lines to bargain with representative unions, though it forbade check-offs, undoubtedly a concession to the Forum. A second would have established collective bargaining rights for ISS workers. Other bills would have placed private-line workers involved in any transit unification under civil service while protecting their bargaining, pension, and seniority rights. Over 40,000 postcards were sent to Albany in support of these proposals, but none passed. A measure opposed by both the TWU and the Forum, giving any transit system created by unification the right to fire or transfer workers deemed "unnecessary," was enacted.[14]

In spite of its immediate failure the TWU-Forum legislative campaign had important long-range effects. First of all, it exposed the anti-labor attitudes of the Board of Transportation. When English asked for two days' leave to go to Albany, his request was denied by Board chairman John H. Delaney, who told him that "the interests of the employees of the ISS will be adequately protected . . . without your interference." After English absented himself anyway he was suspended for eighteen days without pay. Later the Board, with the acquiescence of La Guardia, refused to promote English to an assistant foreman's post for which he was the top candidate, apparently in retaliation for his lobbying.[15]

The treatment of English reflected the general attitude of the Board toward its employees: it was paternal, patronizing, even somewhat contemptuous. In 1938, for instance, when some station agents asked Delaney for sick leave, he responded that "anyone who can get a better place . . . need not feel any obligation to stay here." The Board commissioners viewed the Forum with derision while steadfastly opposing the emergence of any bona fide union. Repeatedly they ignored requests for meetings with worker groups.[16] The Board members in effect adopted the labor policies of their private management counterparts, differing only in the greater effectiveness with which they carried them out. This did not reflect business domination of the Board, however, but the attitude of Tammany and craft union leaders toward a largely unskilled work force; two of the three commissioners had strong ties to the Democratic party and the AFL.

John Delaney, already in his sixties at the time the ISS opened, had been president of the Big Six local of the Typographical Union in the late 1890s and still carried his union card. His close relationship with Tammany leader Charles F. Murphy had led to his appointment from 1913 on to a series of city and state offices. In 1919 Delaney became the New York City Transit Construction Commissioner and five years later the chairman of the newly created Board of Transportation. Simultaneously he emerged as a major power in the inner circles of Tammany. During Al Smith's 1928 Presidential campaign he was an influential figure in the national Democratic party as well. Following La Guardia's election, Delaney largely withdrew from politics, though he maintained some ties to Tammany. Widely considered a brilliant administrator, Delaney was repeatedly reappointed to his transit post by La Guardia, who generally gave him much leeway and strong backing, at least in private, in the operation of the municipal subway. Delaney not only dominated the Board of Transportation but in general was the key figure in city transit policy throughout the 1920s, 30s, and 40s, something of a Robert Moses in his own more limited domain.[17]

Board member Francis X. Sullivan was specifically assigned to labor problems. Like Delaney, Sullivan had been active in Tammany. He also worked as a lawyer for a number of unions. In the mid-1930s, when ISS workers first attempted to organize themselves, Sullivan served as counsel to the State AFL, a connection that led to considerable conflict with the TWU once it bolted to the CIO. Sullivan's initial appointment to the Board in 1927 was probably the result of pressure from organized labor and a reward for his early support for Jimmy Walker's mayoralty campaign, but like Delaney he was retained by La Guardia.[18]

Particularly striking was the contrast between the way the Board and La Guardia treated permanent ISS workers and those engaged in contract transit construction.

In the latter case the city was extremely sympathetic to organized labor, on occasion even rejecting low bids from open-shop contractors to accept higher ones from unionized firms. La Guardia responded promptly and cooperatively whenever William Green, Meany, or local construction union officials approached him with problems, whereas requests from the Forum for meetings were always referred to the Board, where they were acknowledged and then ignored. As long as contract workers and the well-organized, politically connected construction unions were involved, the Board was more than willing to recognize the right to collective bargaining, but when it came to its own employees it was a very different story. [19]

A second effect of the joint TWU-Forum legislative campaign was to bring the TWU into closer contact with the leaders of the various ISS councils and the mass of municipal subway workers, for the first time giving the union a significant presence on the ISS. An April 1936 meeting co-sponsored by the TWU and the Joint Council to discuss pending legislation was attended by 2,000 to 3,000 workers, making it the largest transit worker gathering of any kind since the TWU had been founded. The TWU carefully courted Forum transit leaders, a few of whom joined the TWU while remaining members of the Forum. [20]

Probably in reaction to the Joint Council's cooperation with the TWU, in May 1936 the heads of the Forum ordered it to disband, which its leaders promptly refused to do. Seizing this opportunity the TWU proposed to the Joint Council that it merge with the TWU, a plan referred to the individual councils for membership votes. In the meantime the Forum expelled five councils that refused to abandon the Joint Council and began trying to set up new groups to replace them. [21]

Each council now went its own way in a period of considerable confusion that resulted in a sharp decline in the Forum's ISS strength and dramatic gains by the TWU. The TWU strongly urged the individual councils to affiliate with it, especially after the August 21 endorsement of its ISS jurisdiction by the AFL's New York Central Trades and Labor Council. At first it got no takers. At least one expelled council, the motormen and conductors, simply disbanded. For his part, English, acting in the name of the Joint Council, wrote to William Green seeking an AFL federal charter for a new union of ISS workers, but Green replied that the jurisdiction was already assigned to the Amalgamated and the IAM (with which the TWU at the time was affiliated), a ruling at variance with that just made by the New York AFL Council.

With the possibility of a separate AFL ISS union ruled out, some of the expelled councils came over to the TWU. During the last two months of 1936 the structure department, lighting department, and 207th Street shop groups all voted to join the TWU. The Forum still had the five councils that had left the Joint Council, most importantly the station agents and porters. But the TWU now had a considerable foothold on the ISS. In the fall it had formed an ISS organizing committee, it had the three ex-Forum councils and scattered individual members, and it had recruited Joe English to head its ISS drive. [22]

During the next year defections from the Forum continued. In fact, almost all of the early TWU ISS leaders were former Forum officials. Robert Franklin, for example, an ex-union bricklayer who had taken an ISS job while awaiting appointment to the police force, switched from the Forum to the TWU in 1936, replacing English as

Robert Franklin addressing a lunchtime meeting across the street from the ISS 207th Street shop, 1938.

the leader of the 207th Street group when English took on overall responsibility for the TWU's municipal subway organizing. William Burke, an Irish immigrant whose elder siblings had been active republicans, joined the TWU while still holding the presidency of the Forum agents' council. In June 1937 the entire Forum transit clerical council joined the TWU's newly established office workers division.[23]

The decision of various Forum transit activists and councils to switch their allegiance to the TWU foreshadowed the eventual widespread conversion of non-union municipal worker associations into bona fide unions. By the early 1950s many of the most aggressive Forum councils had bolted their parent organization and affiliated with national unions, contributing significantly to the growth of public sector unionism in New York City. Several key present-day New York municipal unions had their origins as Forum councils. Nationally, the affiliation of civil service associations with established unions became common after 1960, reaching landslide proportions in the 1970s and 80s. This process was one of the main factors retarding the decline of the labor movement during the latter period. Even what remained of the Forum eventually joined a national union.[24]

In January 1937 the Board of Transportation, under pressure from the competing labor groups, agreed to hold an election for representatives with whom it would discuss working conditions and pay. Originally the Board planned to hold separate elections in each of ten employee classifications, with signed ballots and compulsory voting. After vehement TWU protests to La Guardia, charging that the Board in effect was trying to set up a company union, the Mayor ordered the use of secret ballots, voluntary voting, and outside tellers, but the system of separate voting by classification was retained. [25]

At the insistence of the State Federation of Labor, the TWU agreed to nominate a joint "All-Union" slate with the Amalgamated. On January 27 a meeting of over 1,000 workers ratified the chosen AFL candidates, who were running for 62 of the 79 available delegate posts. The size of the meeting indicated growing pro-union sentiment on the municipal line. The election, held two days later, in which nearly 3,000 workers took part, provided confirmation. Fifty-one "All-Union" candidates, mostly members of the TWU, were elected, including all of the delegates chosen by the motormen, conductors, skilled shop men, shop helpers, maintenance-of-way workers, and trackmen. The TWU victory was so impressive that at least one election winner, station agent James J. Carroll, a former bank clerk, resigned from the Forum and joined the TWU, where he soon became a key ISS leader. [26]

The TWU treated the election as if it had been a vote for proportional union recognition. With a majority of the delegates and a clear strategy it was able temporarily to win over the other delegates to this position. A meeting of all 79 delegates not only chose an eleven-man bargaining committee dominated by the TWU, it also endorsed a TWU-proposed bargaining program that called for special pay increases for men making less than $1,800 annually (as provided by recent legislation for non-transit city workers); two week sick leave with pay; time-and-a-half for overtime; Board endorsement of proposed state legislation modeled after the federal Railway Labor Act, which provided for compulsory collective bargaining; improved safety and health conditions; and the establishment of working rules governing seniority and promotions. [27]

The Board of Transportation saw the election quite differently, insisting that it had been only to choose representatives to discuss separately the particular problems of the various classifications and in no way was a recognition vote. It therefore refused to meet with the bargaining committee as a whole or with any organizational spokespersons except for the elected delegates themselves. It also declined to consider the delegates' agreed-upon program.

On March 8 the delegates' bargaining committee met with La Guardia to protest the Board stance, but the Mayor refused to intervene. The TWU then held a large protest meeting, threatened a strike, and called on La Guardia to appoint a "referee" to help settle the issues of bargaining rights and working conditions on the ISS. The strike threat, however, was empty, since the TWU lacked the support needed for a job action, especially over a procedural question, and the Board went ahead with its plan for separate meetings with each classification group. [28]

When they finally met with the Board Commissioners, apparently only two of the delegate groups stuck to the program they had previously approved. It really made no difference. Each group presented its demands, but there was no bargaining. On

April 6, while the delegates were still waiting to receive minutes of the conferences, the Board and La Guardia announced a schedule of wage increases worth roughly $1.2 million a year. Individual increases ranged from $2.40 to $14.00 a week, which in some cases represented substantial boosts. The porters, for example, the lowest paid workers, went from $19.20 to $25.92 a week, giving them hourly rates generally above those on the private lines. (Since hours were shorter on the ISS, many municipal transit workers still had lower weekly earnings than their private-line counterparts.) Although La Guardia argued that the new rates had been "worked out . . . in keeping with modern trends of direct conferences between employers and the elected representatives of the employees," the TWU, after first claiming that it had played a major role in winning the wage increase, charged that the conferences had been a charade and the new rates unilaterally determined.[29]

Even before the increases had been announced, the TWU tried to circumvent the Board by adopting the Forum's strategy of going to the state legislature. Seven TWU-sponsored bills were introduced and passed by the State Senate. Four again were designed to establish a framework for transit industry collective bargaining and for the protection of private-line workers in the event of unification. The other bills would have given pay increases to workers making less than $1,800 annually, established paid sick leave, and mandated safe procedures for handling high-voltage electrical equipment. However, the union failed to win La Guardia's support for its legislative package, and in the face of Board opposition the TWU was unable to get it enacted.[30]

Equally disturbing to the TWU as the Board's refusal to accept bona fide collective bargaining was the Board's and La Guardia's apparent friendliness with rival unions. When A. F. Whitney, president of the BRT, indicated to La Guardia his union's intention to begin organizing ISS motormen and conductors, the Mayor reponded that "there is no objection on my part or that of [the] Board of Transportation." La Guardia met with BRT representatives and invited Whitney to visit him. It immediately became obvious that La Guardia had blundered. First, the Brotherhood of Locomotive Firemen and Enginemen was also contemplating an ISS organizing campaign and seeking sanction from the city administration. Second, as leaders of the NAACP and the Brotherhood of Sleeping Car Porters pointed out, the BRT was a whites-only union and there were a considerable number of black ISS conductors. La Guardia was thus forced to twice retreat. First he claimed that no special invitation or monopoly was being offered to the BRT. "It would seem," he said,

> that the logical crowd to organize the subways would be the Amalgamated
> Association of Street Railway and Motor Coach Employees, but if we favored
> any one, the others would raise the cry of company unionism.

Then, a few days later, he issued an order that in effect banned bargaining with discriminatory unions. Nonetheless, the whole sequence of events left the TWU questioning the Mayor's impartiality. In mid-May, shortly after its affiliation with the CIO, the union charged that the Board of Transportation was "playing ball" with AFL groups and the railway brotherhoods in an effort to stem the tide of TWU growth.[31]

CIO affiliation complicated the ISS situation. As long as the TWU was part of the

AFL, it could try to use the Federation's ties to Delaney and Sullivan and its Albany lobbying operation to further its cause. After mid-1937, however, these AFL assets were used against it, as the AFL-CIO rivalry spread to the ISS. Shortly after the TWU joined the CIO, twelve of its ISS members resigned and, led by elevator and escalator maintainer Bernard G. Brophy, formed the American Federation of Municipal Transit Workers (AFMTW). With the TWU gone, AFL leaders stopped worrying about jurisdictional niceties and gave the AFMTW a federal charter. Although the AFMTW failed to attract many members, the AFL hierarchy found it a useful tool in their battles with the CIO. At least later on it also received friendly treatment from the Board of Transportation. [32]

In spite of the activity of its rivals and its own failure to achieve even partial recognition, in mid-1937 the TWU's ISS group was growing. Undoubtedly it benefited from the TWU victories on the private lines and the national momentum of the CIO, as well as from the union's increased alertness in addressing day-to-day issues affecting ISS workers. When the ISS proposed creating a job title for men qualified as motormen but assignable to conductor's work, the TWU opposed the move before the Civil Service Commission. When the Board of Transportation sought permission to hire female agents at lower-than-usual rates, the TWU protested vehemently, objecting to unequal pay for equal work. When no time was provided to cash pay checks, the 207th Street workers walked out en masse to go to a local bank. [33]

One observer, who had the benefit of confidential interviews with both Forum and TWU officials, estimated that in 1937 the Forum had signed up something less than 20% of the ISS work force and the TWU around 10%. Maurice Forge concurred that at this stage the Forum was still larger than the TWU, but believed that between them the two groups represented a majority of the ISS work force. As always in such situations, undoubtedly the number of supporters of the two groups far exceeded the number of dues-payers. [34]

Even though it lacked majority membership, the TWU was confident that it could win a system-wide recognition election. Accordingly in May 1937 and again in July the TWU asked the Board of Transportation to hold an election to choose a sole bargaining agent for the ISS workers. The Board, however, ignored the TWU requests, and all approaches to La Guardia were referred back to it. In spite of these rebuffs it was not until October 1937 that the TWU took the next step, appealing to the State Labor Relations Board (SLRB). To understand this delay and subsequent developments, it is necessary to first look at the TWU's growing involvement in electoral politics, for the whole issue of municipal transit labor relations was becoming ever more politicized. [35]

During the TWU's first three years, while it was relatively small and lacked contractual recognition, the union avoided involvement in electoral politics. Although the CP urged transit workers to vote Communist in the 1934 election, the TWU itself announced that it would not endorse any candidates. During 1935 and 1936, however, occasional articles and editorials appeared in the *Transport Workers Bulletin* urging the creation of a labor party. In May 1936 TWU Vice President Jimmy Gahagan attended and reported favorably on a conference called by the

Trade Union Committee to Sponsor a Labor Party. When a labor party of sorts, New York's American Labor Party (ALP), was actually formed three months later, the TWU accepted an invitation to affiliate. The decision was made by the union's Joint Executive Committee, which after extensive debate voted 46 to 3 to accept a unanimous recommendation of the TWU Executive Board for affiliation.[36]

In its stance toward a labor party, the TWU followed the lead of the CP. Until 1934 the Communists opposed the formation of a national labor party; thereafter they pressed for one's creation if radically led and union-based. The ALP was not precisely what they had in mind. Its formation had been initiated by leaders of the needle trades unions and Roosevelt's Democratic lieutenants to give FDR a separate line in the 1936 election on which to attract liberal and left-wing voters. The party was also designed to provide Roosevelt with an alternate New York campaign structure to Tammany, which was notably unenthusiastic about the President, for what was incorrectly anticipated to be a close race. Although some of its backers hoped that the ALP would form the nucleus for a future national labor party, its only initial stated goal was to help re-elect Roosevelt and New York Governor Herbert H. Lehman. A broad spectrum of unionists, including George Meany and Joseph P. Ryan, the conservative Tammanyite head of the New York City Central Trades and Labor Council, co-operated with the new organization. Furthermore, under pressure from the old guard socialists of the Social Democratic Federation who joined the ALP in force, the party barred Communists from enrolling. Accordingly the CP remained officially aloof, running its own presidential candidate, but allowed Communist-led unions, including the TWU and the Furriers, to join up. The ALP in turn made no real effort to enforce its membership ban.[37]

During the 1936 campaign the TWU's ALP affiliation meant little. The union went on record in support of the ALP line and a few union cadre worked for Roosevelt, but the TWU's energies were still almost exclusively devoted to winning recognition. The ALP's remarkable success in its first election, however, changed the whole situation. State-wide the party won 274,925 votes for Roosevelt, 238,845 of which came from New York City, giving it 8.6% of the total city vote. ALP leaders almost immediately decided to make the party a permanent one. By the year's end it became clear that La Guardia, who had not participated in the formation of the ALP but had urged New Yorkers to vote for FDR on its line, would seek and receive ALP backing in his bid to become the first New York reform Mayor ever to win re-election. (At the time, La Guardia's renomination by the Republicans was by no means assured.) Simultaneously, the CP decided to back fully the ALP, and its members began enrolling in such large numbers that they soon represented a sizable bloc within the party. The ALP thus rapidly emerged as both a potent force in New York City politics and a potential organizational form for the Popular Front. On both counts deeper TWU involvement seemed natural; it would be consistent with the CP's strategic outlook, not so radical as to alienate a significant sector of the union's rank and file, and give the TWU greater leverage in upcoming political decisions affecting transit workers, including ISS bargaining rights and unification.[38]

In the early summer of 1937 Quill, Hogan, Gahagan, and Eugene Connolly, a TWU taxi organizer and onetime leader of a reform Democratic party club, attended the ALP's state convention. Quill was elected as one of the ALP's eight vice chairmen and given a seat on the committee that ran the party on an ongoing basis. This put him in a unique position; because of the formal ban on Communists there were few representatives from CP-led unions in ALP posts and none besides Quill at the highest level. [39]

Quill's political importance, however, was not in internal ALP affairs—although he regularly attended leadership meetings he played no outstanding role—but as a municipal candidate and officeholder. By August 1937 it was decided that Quill would be an ALP candidate for the New York City Council, running in the Bronx. This idea did not originate within the TWU. Rather several ALP backers, including Paul Kern, La Guardia, and Vito Marcantonio, urged Quill to seek office. The CP may have done so as well. After his initial reluctance to take on added responsibilities was overcome, Quill agreed to the race and his candidacy was approved by the TWU Executive Board. [40]

What made Quill's candidacy practical were recent changes in the structure of the New York City government. As an outgrowth of the scandals and investigations during the latter days of Mayor Jimmy Walker's administration and the reform momentum resulting from La Guardia's 1933 election, a new city charter was put into place in 1936. The old, Tammany-dominated Board of Alderman was replaced by a City Council to be elected by proportional representation (PR). The PR system was complex, but in essense it diminished the importance of major party sponsorship while facilitating the election of representatives from diverse interest groups. Each borough was treated as a separate district, with candidates nominated by petition. Voters listed on their ballots as many candidates as they wished in order of preference. Ballots were counted in a series of rounds. In each round as soon as a candidate received 75,000 first-choice votes he or she was declared elected. When a ballot had an already elected candidate listed first, the voter's second or if need be a lower choice was counted. After each round the lowest voter-getter was eliminated; thereafter the next highest choice on the ballots he or she headed was used. The whole process continued until one candidate for each 75,000 voters was elected. Under the old system, in each district only one candidate, usually a Democrat, was elected. The new procedure, though unwieldly, ensured that council members were elected in a ratio close to that of the number of voters supporting their respective parties. The 1937 election was the first held under the new charter, and therefore an ideal occasion for the ALP and Quill to make their entrances onto the municipal political stage. [41]

Quill's candidacy was extremely well suited to the needs of the CP, the ALP, La Guardia, and the TWU. For the CP, Quill's election would effectively give it a voice in the City Council even if all of the candidates on its own slate were defeated, which turned out to be the case. For the ALP, Quill raised the possibility of broadening the party's heavily Jewish base by bringing in some Irish voters. This would particularly help La Guardia, since his support among Irish-Catholics was extremely weak. For the TWU, Quill's election would give the union a spokesperson in the city government, which of course dealt with many transit issues, and any votes Quill brought to La Guardia and the ALP would be debts owed. Furthermore, Quill had a good chance of winning. Thousands of transit workers, especially Irish ones, lived in the Bronx; along with their families and friends they constituted a sizable base on which to build further support. The fact that Quill didn't live in the Bronx—at the time he was living in the union hall—didn't seem to be of much concern; he simply established a Bronx mailing address at a cousin's home.[42]

The political alignments in preparation for the 1937 election left the TWU in a complex relationship with the Mayor. On the one hand, Quill and La Guardia were running mates, La Guardia was the candidate of the TWU's party, and the CP was strongly backing the Mayor. Furthermore La Guardia was not without a certain popularity among transit workers. His support as a Congressman for Irish independence was not forgotten, and during the Kent Avenue sit-down the neutrality of his police department had greatly helped the TWU. On the other hand, most transit workers were traditionally Democrats, and La Guardia had generally backed the Board of Transportation's anti-union policies. For the latter reason at the TWU's 1937 convention E. H. Buford, an ISS motorman and former Forum activist, introduced a resolution condemning both the Board and the Mayor, arguing that it was best "to attack the enemy while he is vulnerable." Santo responded with a partial defense of the Mayor and a plea for a less hostile approach. Later Quill laid down what was in effect the official union line: "The Mayor is the first Labor Mayor the City ever had, and I say that he is not yet progressive enough." Further complicating the situation, the TWU found itself on the same side in the election as the very forces it was fighting on the ISS; the State AFL was backing La Guardia, and at the request of George Meany a labor committee in the Mayor's behalf was formed by Board of Transportation Commissioner Frank Sullivan.[43]

Throughout the summer of 1937, as the TWU pressed for ISS bargaining rights and La Guardia campaigned for the Republican nomination to add to his ALP line, the union and the Mayor carefully avoided direct confrontations. The TWU did not want to hurt La Guardia's chances for re-election and hoped that its backing for him would lead the Mayor to view more favorably its position on the ISS. For his part, La Guardia sought to sidestep any clash that would alienate the TWU, the AFL, or the public-at-large. The result was a shadow play in which the union bitterly attacked the Board of Transportation but ignored the fact that La Guardia was in practice supporting if not behind its stance, while the Mayor refused to discuss municipal transit labor relations, referring all questions to Delaney. Only after La Guardia won the Republican primary did the TWU, on October 21, ask the SLRB for certification as the sole ISS bargaining agent and for an investigation into the line's employee relations.[44]

In the meantime the TWU began organizing Quill's campaign. As was to be the pattern in future elections as well, where existing ALP clubs were cooperative Quill took advantage of their services, but primary responsibility for the race was assumed by TWU members, with some assistance from leftists from throughout the city. This was done for two reasons. First, the Bronx ALP was essentially controlled by the International Ladies' Garment Workers Union (ILGWU), which was quite hostile to the CP and its allies, including Quill. Second, by keeping the campaign mainly in-house the TWU was better able to mobilize its own resources. Internally the TWU sold Quill's political career by stressing loyalty to Quill and the practical advantages of having an advocate on the City Council, rather than portraying it as part of a left-wing crusade. In that way union members who admired Quill but were uncomfortable with abandoning the Democrats might be won over to voting and perhaps working for their union president.

To channel transit workers into the campaign a "Committee of One Thousand" was established for TWU members, a device to be used again in the future. Although the goal of a thousand TWU campaign workers was not achieved in this first race, several hundred unionists did take part. As Quill's campaign tactics became increasingly refined over the years, a division of labor developed corresponding to the main components of Quill's electoral base; ALPers and CP-sympathizers were put in charge of mobilizing votes from what was called "the progressive crowd," mostly Jews, while TWU members were in charge of getting out the vote from transit workers and "the reactionary crowd," the Irish. The corollary of this strategy was that Quill never tried to either take over the Bronx ALP or set up the kind of elaborate personal machine that Vito Marcantonio was so successful with. Although quite a few TWU officers and politically minded members became active in the ALP, and eventually several TWU-dominated Bronx ALP clubs were formed, Quill himself was content simply to maintain a political apparatus sufficient to ensure his own electoral success.[45]

And success it was in 1937, for both Quill and the ALP. Quill was the first Bronx Councilmanic candidate to be declared elected, going over the top when CP-candidate Isidore Begun was eliminated and 14,378 of his 20,946 first-choice ballots were transferred to Quill as the listed second choice. Five other ALP City Council candidates were elected, as were seven ALP State Assemblymen, and another Councilman soon joined the labor party. In the mayoralty race the ALP gave La Guardia 482,790 votes, over one fifth his total and more than his margin of victory.

Undoubtedly the TWU and Quill were at least partially responsible for the success of the ALP and La Guardia in the Bronx and among the Irish. The Bronx ALP vote increased 116% over the previous year (compared with 102% city-wide) and over half of La Guardia's votes in the borough were on the ALP line. Although the Democrats retained their hold on a majority of the city's Irish voters, their dominance had been much weakened; La Guardia won an estimated 41% of the Irish vote, including 10% on the ALP line. Thus not only was Quill elected, but the ALP was established as a key balance of power in New York City politics (to which La Guardia owed his re-election), while the Tammany forces failed to win back the power they had lost as a result of the post-Walker reform wave and the New Deal.[46]

With the election over and Quill on his way to Ireland to be married, the issue of ISS bargaining rights came to a head.[47] The Board of Transportation again made it clear that it would not grant union recognition. When the SLRB scheduled several informal conferences on the TWU's petition, Delaney refused to send a representative, arguing that the Board was a state agency and therefore not covered by New York's recently passed labor relations law, the "little Wagner act." TWU leaders continued to try to drive a wedge between La Guardia and the Board, proclaiming that they did not believe that the Mayor could possibly be supporting Delaney's position, but the best the TWU could get from La Guardia was his arrangement of a meeting between Delaney and the union, at which the Board chairman simply reiterated his opposition to the TWU's demands.

The TWU's appeal to the SLRB was based on several grounds. Most importantly, the TWU contended that in its operation of the ISS the City of New York was acting in a proprietary capacity, as a "railroad corporation," and therefore the exclusion of political and civil subdivisions of the state from SLRB jurisdiction did not apply. The TWU also argued that the January 1937 employee representation election, in which a majority of the representatives chosen had been from the TWU, should be treated as a de facto recognition election, and on that basis the TWU should be granted sole bargaining agent status. A second petition to the SLRB, filed by the TWU in January 1938, apparently in an unsuccessful effort to force some action from La Guardia, argued that by refusing to meet with TWU representatives the Board was engaging in an unfair labor practice.

The TWU appeals to the SLRB were opposed not only by the Board, but by the AFMTW, the BRT, and the Civil Service Forum Station Agents Council as well. The AFMTW's objections were the most significant. Supported by the AFL's New York representative, the AFMTW disputed the TWU's characterization of the ISS as a railroad corporation rather than a subdivision of the city or state, contending that such an interpretation would lead to the exclusion of ISS workers from civil service and the city's pension plan. Further, the AFL group argued, the results of the January 1937 election were misleading, since at the time the TWU was affiliated with the AFL; once it disaffiliated it could no longer rightly claim the fifty-one "All-Union" representatives as its own. [48]

On January 22, 1938, the SLRB ruled that it had no jurisdiction over the TWU petition for certification as sole ISS bargaining agent. Although the SLRB expressed the belief that government workers had the right to organize, it noted that the law clearly excluded them from the use of the SLRB machinery. Whether or not the operation of the ISS was a proprietary activity was irrelevant to the case at hand; there was no question that the Board of Transportation was a subdivision of the state, and therefore the SLRB was without jurisdiction. Two days later the SLRB rejected the second TWU petition on the same grounds.

The SLRB decision was a blow to the TWU—though not one for which it was totally unprepared—but it was a relief to many ISS workers. In ruling against the TWU the SLRB helped clear up lingering doubts as to whether or not ISS workers were really civil servants. Even many TWU supporters preferred losing their right to sole union representation to winning that right through a ruling that declared that ISS workers were not government employees in the usual sense. The desire for civil service protection was apparently stronger among municipal transit workers than the desire for union protection. If the TWU argument had been legally expedient, it had done nothing to reassure ISS workers that the union shared their committment to civil service. [49]

With the possibility under current law of compelling union recognition eliminated, the TWU again pressured La Guardia to force the Board of Transportation to voluntarily grant it. But the Mayor still referred all questions about ISS labor policy to Delaney. The TWU was left with three choices: put its ISS drive on the back burner, attempt to win recognition through direct action, such as a strike, or try to use the political clout it had demonstrated in the fall elections to circumvent the Board. In early January, Quill, back from Ireland, hinted at the possibility of a walkout, but it soon became clear that the TWU had decided to go the political route. Specifically, to push La Guardia out of his support for Delaney, or if need be to win bargaining rights without his approval, the TWU mapped out a campaign to win state legislation placing the ISS under SLRB jurisdiction.

In preparation for this effort the TWU first stepped up its ISS organizing. Municipal transit workers were asked to sign pledge cards indicating their desire to have the TWU act as their representative and were allowed to join the union by paying a one dollar initiation fee, with no further dues to be paid until recognition was achieved. By March 1938 the TWU claimed to represent 3,500 of the 5,200 ISS workers. The TWU also made sure it had the backing of the national CIO, since the issue of ISS bargaining rights involved the CIO's relationships with the AFL, La Guardia, and the ALP. In late February, Quill traveled to Washington, where he received the go-ahead from John L. Lewis for the TWU strategy.[50]

Even before then, a TWU-backed bill extending SLRB jurisdiction to the ISS was introduced in the state legislature by two Democrats, Assemblyman Edward S. Moran, Jr., and Senator Julius Bergin. Although the TWU was affiliated with the ALP, the labor party neither co-sponsored nor supported this measure, commonly known as the Moran bill. Instead ALP leaders maintained a careful silence on the issue of ISS labor, for it presented them with a serious dilemma. The CIO was the most important institutional component of the ALP and Quill a top vote-getter, strong reasons for supporting the TWU. However, the ALP had backed La Guardia, who remained key to the party's future, including it access to patronage and influence in the city government, and La Guardia apparently was against granting sole bargaining rights on the municipal subway. Furthermore, many AFL unions, at least on paper, were still affiliated with the ALP, and the AFL leadership had indicated its opposition to SLRB jurisdiction over the ISS. Faced with these conflicting considerations, ALP leaders avoided taking any stand on the "transit question."

With the ALP on the sidelines an alliance emerged between the TWU and a group of Democrats, who perhaps hoped to use the municipal transit issue to embarrass La Guardia and the ALP. Quill himself upped the pressure on the ALP by introducing a City Council resolution calling on the state legislature to pass the Moran bill. After efforts to get Quill to withdraw the measure failed, in early March the ALP council delegation joined with the Democrats to pass the resolution. Even then, however, the ALP as a whole took no position on ISS bargaining rights.[51]

In the meantime Democratic State Senator Thomas F. Burchill introduced a second bill to establish ISS bargaining procedures that had the blessing of the Board of Transportation. Unlike the Moran bill, Burchill's measure divided ISS workers along craft lines into eleven units. If the Board of Transportation introduced a new regulation on wages, hours, or working conditions that 30% of the affected workers objected to by signing a petition, the Board would be required to bargain with representatives of the unit or units involved. There would be, however, no exclusive representation even within units. If a dispute could not be resolved through negotiations, the city's Board of Estimate would be empowered to settle it unilaterally.

With two rival bills under consideration a heated battle broke out in Albany. Among labor groups only the TWU and the CIO backed the Moran bill, while the Burchill bill was supported by virtually all of the TWU's rivals, including the BLF, the AFMTW, the AFL, and various civil service organizations. George Meany personally led the AFL lobbying effort, working closely with Francis Sullivan, who was representing the Board. Although La Guardia took no public stand on the Burchill bill, when the Mayor had his own omnibus transit bill introduced, the so-called Desmond bill, it incorporated most of the Burchill bill's provisions. In spite of the TWU's furious efforts, the Burchill bill quickly passed the Democratic-controlled State Senate.

With the TWU's position looking increasingly grim, and La Guardia apparently having broken with the CIO for the first time, John L. Lewis intervened, sending CIO General Counsel Lee Pressman to New York. On March 11 thirty delegates from various CIO unions met with Pressman and CIO Regional Director Allan Haywood to pledge support for the effort to defeat the Burchill bill and the pass the Moran bill. Two days later Pressman and Haywood met with La Guardia, who held the key to the whole situation, since the leaders of the Republican-controlled State Assembly announced that they would not act on the Burchill bill unless specifically asked to do so by the Mayor. At the same time, probably under pressure from the CIO, the Legislative Committee of the ALP finally took a position on the pending transit legislation. Although it declined to comment on the Moran bill, the committee denounced both the Burchill and Desmond bills and called on La Guardia and organized labor to work out an agreement before any legislation was passed. At this point La Guardia retreated; on March 17 the Mayor, the ALP, and the Assembly leadership agreed to kill the Burchill bill. La Guardia promised to try to come to an understanding with the TWU before the next legislative session, and the Assembly quickly adjourned.[52]

The intervention of the national CIO saved the TWU from the Burchill bill, but the union's campaign in Albany had done little to advance its cause either politically or on the ISS itself. The TWU's entire legislative program was defeated, including not only the Moran bill but also bills to provide ISS workers with paid holidays and sick leave and to protect seniority and civil service status in case of unification. The TWU had plunged into electoral politics in part to advance immediate union interests, but the difficulties of operating through a labor party that was both a minority party and a coalition of distinct interests had become evident. At least in relation to the municipal subway system, the TWU's backing of La Guardia the previous fall had yielded nothing in return, while the ALP turned out to be at best a reluctant ally. Furthermore, even the ALP's belated support for the TWU had its costs. The fight over transit legislation embittered AFL-CIO relations and made their continued cooperation within the ALP impossible. Even before the Legislature adjourned the AFMTW attacked the ALP as "a stooge for the CIO," claiming that its opposition to the Burchill bill was a betrayal of the AFL voters who had supported the party. Meany later repeated this argument in a general attack on the labor party. Following his lead most of the AFL officials and affiliates still belonging to the ALP withdrew. In August the State AFL formally repudiated the party.[53]

Without any legal framework for achieving recognition—and none was established in the remaining years before transit unification—the TWU position on the ISS quickly deteriorated. Most ISS workers saw no point in belonging to a union which could neither bargain nor sign contracts, especially since civil service procedures were already in place. The TWU did not give up—it spent money on organizing drives, pressed for legislation establishing bargaining procedures, sent delegations to the Municipal Civil Service Commission—where they were sympathetically received by Commission Chairman Paul Kern—protested various Board of Transportation regulations, and ran training classes for promotion tests. But nonetheless the union's ISS strength sharply diminished after the spring of 1938. The best the TWU could do was to maintain a skeletal ISS organization—at the union's 1939 convention only two ISS sections were represented—and the sympathy of many of the line's workers. The situation was so discouraging that Quill began quipping that when he first came to America and had a job digging the ISS Eighth Avenue Subway he should have shoveled the dirt in instead of out. [54]

One can only speculate as to why the TWU did not attempt to win ISS recognition through a job action. There was at least some rank-and-file sentiment for so trying. Perhaps union leaders were simply overconfident about their ability to win a legal or legislative victory that would have paved the way for a recognition vote; by the time those possibilities were exhausted the union's backing was already crumbling. Perhaps at all times the union lacked the strength to shut down the system. Also, TWU leaders undoubtedly were worried about the implications of striking a government agency.

The TWU had never distinguished betwen union rights in the private and public sectors, but in the 1930s government worker strikes were rare. Any job action against the ISS would have entailed an unpredictable fight on political and legal grounds as well as the usual risks associated with a strike or slowdown. Even the CIO disapproved of public employee strikes; in July 1937, when granting a charter to the State, County and Municipal Workers, John L. Lewis said that strikes or picketing by that union would violate CIO policy. The chief methods of public sector unionism, he contended, should be "legislation and education." Just a few days earlier FDR had taken a similar stand, arguing that federal employees had the right to join unions and engage in limited, non-exclusive bargaining, but not the right to strike. The TWU was extremely careful, particularly in this period, to avoid any conflict with Lewis or the national CIO. Nonetheless, having declined to take direct action, and having lost the SLRB case and the fight for the Moran bill, the TWU could only hope that future developments would somehow reinvigorate its stalled ISS drive. [55]

Well before the full extent of its difficulties on the ISS had become clear, the TWU was already worried about an associated, much larger problem, the impact of any transit unification plan that put the IRT and BMT under city control. While the ISS had only a few thousand workers, the over 25,000 IRT and BMT employees constituted the bulk of the TWU's membership; unification could conceivably extend all of the problems encountered on the ISS to the latter group, threatening the very existence of the union. In the late 1930s, as a municipal takeover of the IRT and BMT grew imminent, the unification issue became a dominant factor shaping TWU policy, for it held the key to the union's future.

Transit unification was not a new idea; it first had been suggested right after World War I by various political figures including John Delaney and Al Smith. [56] By the early 1930s it had become the favorite plan of reformers, transit experts, politicians, and even some transit investors to solve a host of interrelated problems. For riders there were obvious disadvantages to having three interweaving rapid transit systems without easy or free transfer between them. Also, the IRT and BMT were badly rundown due to the failure of their operating companies to invest in maintenance or improvements. Transit planning, expansion, and modernization were difficult as long as three separate systems were involved.

From the city's point of view the most pressing problems were caused by the huge debt incurred in building the IRT and BMT and later building and equpping the ISS. By 1936 the total municipal transit debt had reached $739.7 million. Transit debt service that year alone cost $36.3 million, far more than the city received in net transit revenue. To make up the difference $28 million of general revenue had to be appropriated. In effect the city was both subsidizing the five-cent fare and paying a huge penalty for the incorrect assumptions behind its contracts with the IRT and BMT. This strained the city's budget and forced up real estate taxes, which were the main source of city revenue. To make matters worse the city's total debt was limited by the state Constitution to 10% of the assessed value of its taxable real estate. With so much debt tied up in the existing transit system, the city's ability to borrow for transit improvements or other capital projects was severely limited.

Unification seemed to be an omnibus solution to these problems. By unifying the three transit systems under public control overhead costs could be cut and the cost of debt service on outstanding IRT and BMT securities reduced through refunding with lower-interest, tax-free public bonds. With the resulting increase in available funds the combined system could be upgraded and improved, the five-cent fare preserved, and the need for city subsidies reduced or eliminated. For reformers, unification held a special allure, a chance to rationalize the irrational and demonstrate the efficacy of the public ownership and operation of utilities. The problem was to get all the interested parties—the city, state, private companies, and major investors—to agree on a unification plan, a terribly complex business given the labyrinthine legal, financial, and organizational structure of the industry.

The first step in this direction came in 1921 when the legislature charged the state's newly created Transit Commission with bringing about unification. In 1931, after years of discussion and study, the Commission presented its preliminary plan. The key to its proposal was the creation of a non-profit corporation, composed of representatives from the city and the private companies, which would issue bonds, purchase the leases and properties of the IRT and BMT (for a proposed $489 million), and operate the combined system. This approach was designed to win cooperation from the IRT and BMT and circumvent the city's debt limit, which prevented it from directly raising enough money to take over the private lines. But neither the city's Board of Estimate nor the private companies nor the transit bondholders embraced the plan.

Although La Guardia was a long-time supporter of unification, he also opposed the Transit Commission's plan.[57] In fact, shortly after his election he tried to have the legislature abolish the Commission and transfer its unification powers to the Board of Transportation. When that effort failed he appointed A. A. Berle, Jr., and Samuel Seabury to negotiate directly a deal between the city and the private transit companies.

In spite of their opposition to the Transit Commission's proposal, the companies were not adverse to unification. They knew that if the city government chose, under existing contracts it could unilaterally "recapture" the leases of the subway lines built with public money. Although the companies would be compensated, the heart of their systems would be gone and their continued operation impractical. Even if the city chose not to act on its own, the IRT was already in receivership, while the BMT, though still solvent, was unlikely to long remain so with the fare fixed at five cents. Unification was a possible means for transit stock and bondholders to unload their increasingly unprofitable enterprises, recouping part or all of their investments, rather than having future operating losses or unilateral city action further diminish the value of the holdings.[58]

By late 1935, Berle and Seabury had signed "memorandums of understanding" with the IRT and BMT for the purchase of their property. In June 1936 they presented a detailed unification plan to the Transit Commission, a modified version of the Commission's own earlier proposal. With these developments it was widely assumed that unification was close at hand. Understandably the attention of transit workers and the TWU was drawn to this prospect.

The TWU's basic position on unification was developed by the spring of 1935 and remained essentially unchanged until the unification process was consummated five years later. On the one hand, the union made clear its support for the concept of unification. "As all decent citizens of New York," went a TWU editorial, "the transit employees and their union stand for unifying the subway and elevated lines of the city." The TWU even proposed including the various privately owned trolley and bus lines in any merged, publicly run system. (Under existing unification plans only the BMT-owned trolleys and buses would be incorporated.) On the other hand, the union did not "wish to see a half a billion dollars go to the traction interests for property they never owned and equipment that is nearly useless." Rather the banks that held large amounts of transit securities should be paid "no more than their holdings are really worth." Furthermore, the continuation of the five-cent fare should be a formal condition for unification. In all this the TWU was in line with the CP position; in an October 1935 editorial, which took the whole unification issue rather lightly, the *Daily Worker* supported the notion of unification but objected to the proposed purchase price and the inclusion of a provision mandating a "self-sustaining" fare, a likely formula for continual fare hikes.[59]

Transit worker interest in unification was so high that when the TWU sponsored a meeting to discuss the issue in October 1935, 1,000 workers attended, hearing presentations from CP and SP representatives, Assemblyman Herbert Brownell, Jr. (later Eisenhower's Attorney General), Vito Marcantonio, and various union officials.[60] The most pressing concerns of most transit workers, and of the TWU, were the impact of unification on currently employed transit workers and the post-unification status of transit unionism, questions that the unification planners had barely addressed in all of their lengthy discussions, negotiations, and reports. What the TWU feared was that unification would lead to layoffs and the loss of seniority and pension rights, that private line workers would not be guaranteed jobs with the unified system, and that no provision would be made for collective bargaining. It was on these issues, and not unification as such, that the TWU concentrated.

The best defense of workers' interests in the event of unification, argued the TWU, would be complete unionization before the fact. Nonetheless the TWU sought protection both through legislation and provisions in the unification agreement itself. In every year from 1935 through 1938 the TWU promoted bills in the state legislature dealing with job guarantees, seniority and pension rights, civil service status, and collective bargaining in the event of unification. In every case the bills either failed to pass the legislature or were vetoed by the governor.[61]

The TWU's inability to win such protection, however, had no immediate consequences, for unexpectedly the movement toward unification virtually halted in May 1937 when the Transit Commission rejected the Berle-Seabury plan. The Commission criticized the plan for being too expensive and giving private interests too much say over future transit construction, but political factors were involved as well; the Transit Commission was a stronghold of Tammany, which hoped to use the unification issue against La Guardia in the upcoming election. A year-long stand-off then ensued, as the Transit Commission began its own negotiations with the private lines, while La Guardia resumed his effort to have the Commission abolished.

After he won re-election, La Guardia began to cooperate with the Commission, which had developed a new approach to unification. Instead of circumventing the city's debt limit by having a non-profit corporation buy the private lines, the Commission proposed that the city directly purchase the IRT and BMT. To make this possible a state Constitutional Convention, scheduled to meet for other purposes, was asked to give the city a one-time debt-limit exemption of $315 million to help cover the new, reduced, anticipated cost of unification. The necessary constitutional amendment was duly passed, and in the November 1938 general election it won ratification by the state's voters. With this financing mechanism in place, negotiations between the transit companies and a joint city-Transit Commission group progressed rapidly. Once more an early completion of the unification process was expected.[62]

For the TWU these latest developments made unification again a matter of utmost urgency, for the unification plans still failed to address the post-unification status of transit workers. The union's basic position remained unchanged; in September 1938 the TWU's International Executive Board came out in support of unification and the union campaigned for the passage of the debt exemption amendment, as did the CP. But even before then the TWU proclaimed that "neither unification nor demolition [of outmoded els], whatever noble purposes they may be designed to serve, can be allowed to come at the expense of transit jobs." Union spokesmen repeatedly demanded that the final unification agreement include provision for a closed shop and genuine collective bargaining and not impair any worker benefits already won. To back up its position the TWU sponsored a resolution that was passed at the first national CIO convention, held in November 1938, stating that in the event of unification the city should take over the existing private-line union contracts and accept the principle of collective bargaining.[63]

Since the TWU was unable to get its own proposals dealing with unification enacted, whatever influence it had over the transit merger came largely through its efforts to block undesirable legislation or unification provisions proposed by others. The 1939 session of the state legislature brought more of the same. On January 4,

Arthur H. Wicks, an upstate Republican who chaired the Senate Finance Committee, introduced a bill that required all employees of any municipal transit system in
the state—and therefore of any new, unified New York City system—to be appointed and promoted "pursuant to the provisions of the Civil Service Law." As the
TWU pointed out, this relatively simple provision, if passed, would have had
profound implications. In the event of unification, IRT and BMT employees would
not have automatically continued in their current positions, but rather would have
been forced to apply for civil service jobs with the new system. In doing so all of
their accumulated seniority and pension rights would have been lost, and there was
no guarantee that they all would have been hired. Some, in fact, almost certainly
would not. Under then-current civil service regulations, only citizens could be
given appointments, a bar to many IRT and BMT workers. Also, there already were
waiting lists, set up for the ISS, for city transit titles. Presumably applicants on these
lists would have been hired before those on lists subsequently established. And, of
course, even to get on the hiring lists IRT and BMT workers would had to have
passed civil service tests, and their places on those lists would have depended on how
well they performed in relation to one another and to other applicants not currently
employed in transit. Combined with the expected reduction in the transit work force
as a result of unification, if the Wicks bill passed thousands of TWU members
probably would have lost their jobs. There as another problem with the Wicks bill as
well; workers on the new unified system presumably would have been in the same
legal position as those working for the ISS—ineligible to use existing government
labor-relations machinery to win union recognition or genuine collective bargaining. Thus not only were workers' jobs in jeopardy, so was the very future of the
TWU as a major transit union.[64]

Wicks must have understood the implications of his bill; he was an experienced
political operator, both savvy and venal. Quill charged, without presenting any
evidence, that Wicks was acting on behalf of the IRT and BMT, seeking to raise the
purchase price for the companies by lowering future labor costs. Others suggested
that Wick's primary concern was to prevent tens of thousands of public transit jobs
from becoming a patronage tool in the hands of the normally Democratic New York
City government. Wicks apparently also wanted to prevent or roll back the growth of
the CIO; according to former *New York Times* reporter Warren Moscow, Wicks had
close ties to "the corrupt AFL unions."[65]

As far as the TWU was concerned, one thing was certain, the Wicks bill had to be
defeated. An editorial in the *Transport Workers Bulletin* argued that

> to the transit workers, the Wicks bill is the most serious threat to their jobs
> yet. . . . The man with 40 years seniority will have to compete in a physical test
> with the brawniest college athlete. The foreign-born worker will have to match
> his penmanship with the latest graduate from Columbia University. . . . [IRT
> and BMT employees] will have to undergo numerous tests to qualify for jobs
> which they have held for years and performed skillfully and safely. They will
> have to compete for jobs which they made decent through organization.[66]

Immediately after the Wicks bill was introduced the TWU launched an all-out,
desperate campaign to defeat it. In many respects the fight over the Wicks bill was a
more intense repetition of the struggle the previous year over the Burchill bill.

Supporting Wicks's measure were the AFMTW, the State AFL, the Forum, committees of IRT and BMT supervisory personnel, and some civil service reform groups. Opposing it were the TWU and its CIO allies. As in the previous year, the La Guardia administration avoided taking a public stand, while contradictory rumors circulated about its position on the bill and possible role in drafting it.[67]

The TWU's strategy in fighting the Wicks bill was somewhat different from that it had used earlier. In 1938 the union had banked heavily on its ties to the ALP and a group of Democratic legislators. In 1939, probably because the ALP's support for the TWU during the fight over the Burchill bill had been belated and lukewarm, the transit union paid scant attention to the labor party. As for the Democrats, they were of less importance because in the 1938 elections they had suffered a major setback; Governor Lehman had barely been re-elected, and the Republicans had won control of both houses of the legislature for the first time since 1932. Accordingly, in fighting the Wicks bill the TWU adopted a voluntarist strategy of lobbying and pressuring politicians of all parties around a narrowly defined issue, but supplemented this traditional AFL approach with a massive mobilization of its own membership, the CIO, and all the various organizations on which it had any influence.

To open its anti-Wicks campaign the TWU arranged for the New York State CIO Council to sponsor a late January 1939 conference of representatives of unions claiming a combined metropolitan-area membership of a half million. A resolution condemning the Wicks bill was passed and a committee to lead the fight against its enactment authorized. The TWU leadership then went to Washington to solicit John L. Lewis's personal support, which it received in the form of a telegram to La Guardia noting the seriousness of the situation and "the increasing anxiety among the Transport Workers Union because of the threat to their security." Lewis urged La Guardia to meet with TWU and top CIO representatives to discuss the post-unification status of transit workers. Finally, the TWU began a series of protest meetings of its members and a campaign to solicit support from outside groups.[68]

By mid-February, according to the TWU legislative department, some 400 CIO and AFL locals had gone on record opposing the Wicks bill, as had 200 church, fraternal, and civic groups. TWU members belonged to hundreds of voluntary associations of every conceivable type, and the union used their presence to press for organizational backing in its fight against the Wicks bill. For example, with an estimated 6,000 veterans among those who would be affected by the pending legislation, the TWU was able to win support from many American Legion and VFW posts. Similarly, it won backing from several Irish county associations, branches of the Hibernians, some Italian-American groups, and even a few Democratic and Republican clubs. The TWU circulated petitions asking La Guardia and the leaders of the legislature to work to defeat the Wicks bill; in the first four days alone 50,000 signatures were obtained. All stops were being pulled out.[69]

In the face of this extraordinary mobilization, first Wicks and then La Guardia began measured retreats from their respective positions. On February 16 Wicks announced a major modification in his proposed legislation; in the event of unification his bill would now allow the Municipal Civil Service Commission to declare civil service examinations for current IRT and BMT employees to be impracticable. Instead all workers on these lines who had been employed for over a year, were citizens, and were of good moral character could be taken into civil service without exams in the order of their private-line seniority. Then, on March 4, La Guardia broke his prolonged silence on the labor issues associated with unification. Although he avoided any direct comment on the Wicks bill, he announced that the Board of Transportation would not "countenance wholesale discharges" of former private-line workers, and that "all needed employees who are citizens and have good records will be continued in their employment."[70]

Although the new version of the Wicks bill and La Guardia's statement seemed to assure that most IRT and BMT workers would retain their jobs in the event of unification, the TWU was far from satisfied. There was still no guarantee of full job security and non-citizens apparently faced dismissal. Furthermore the crucial issues of pension and seniority rights and post-unification bargaining remained unaddressed. Accordingly the TWU continued its campaign to defeat the Wicks bill and force La Guardia to issue firmer assurances on the post-unification status of the transit work force. Members of the TWU and its Ladies' Auxiliary circulated more petitions, wrote more letters, and lobbied additional outside groups to take a stand against the Wicks bill.[71]

Both Wicks and La Guardia responded with further concessions. On March 24, Wicks introduced a third transit labor bill, this time allowing the city to operate an enlarged transit system through a non-profit corporation, which would have permitted greater latitude in labor relations and employment practices. A week later La Guardia announced his opposition to this or any similar measure, deeming it "premature" and an unnecessary intrusion on home rule. In a letter to Wicks, La Guardia argued that it would be best to wait until after unification was actually effected to consider how to grant "adequate security" to the workers involved. By merely introducing his legislation Wicks had "caused uncertainty in the minds of the [BMT and IRT] employees," undermining "the morale and spirit" that would be needed to complete the complex task of merging three separate transit systems. On the same day that the Mayor's letter was released, John Santo and Harry Sacher took a similar stand in testimony before Wicks's committee; there was no rush to settle the various labor issues associated with unification and the problem was one largely for the city and the transit workers to settle among themselves.

In all likelihood this new convergence of positions reflected some agreement between the TWU and La Guardia to cooperate to defeat the Wicks bill. Although the TWU had long been pressing for the resolution of labor-related issues *before* unification, it preferred having no prior agreement to the provisions of the Wicks bill. La Guardia, by contrast, was believed to support the basic principle of the Wicks bill—civil service status for all public transit workers. However, he was under intense pressure from the TWU and its allies, and in any case desired a free hand to determine the exact post-unification status of the transit work force by himself. By late April the La Guardia administration had begun work on its own plan for the labor problems associated with unification, and to that end city officials held several conferences with TWU representatives.[72]

In spite of the fact that both of the main interested parties were now opposed to any unification labor legislation, Wicks proceeded to introduce a fourth, and it turned out final, version of his bill, which made still further concessions to the

TWU. Once again the bill provided that in the event of unification IRT and BMT workers with at least one year of service were to be given civil service status while retaining their current or similar jobs, without having to take examinations. To be eligible the workers in question had to meet the usual civil service character require- ments and either be citizens or, in an important new provision, declare their intention to become citizens within six months of the bill's passage. Those in "unnecessary positions," however, could be laid off and placed on preferred hiring lists. Existing seniority was to be carried over to the unified system, but the private pension and benefit plans were to be continued rather than transferring workers to the city plans. Within a year after the private lines were acquired, the Municipal Civil Service Commission was to reclassify all existing job titles and determine which in the future would be filled by competitive exams. Pre-unification city hiring lists could be used only to fill jobs on the ISS; new lists would be established for all other openings. Finally, as in previous versions of the bill, no provision was made for collective bargaining and no mention made of employee organizations.[73]

On May 1 the State Senate passed the revised version of Wicks's bill, which the TWU still opposed, without discussion. Ten days later the Assembly followed suit. The battle, however, was not over; Governor Lehman had thirty days to sign or veto the measure, and it was not until the final hour that he made his decision.

Three days after the Wicks bill was passed the TWU asked Lehman to veto it, charging that its enactment had been the result of a "collusive plot by Republican party leaders and Tammany Hall to hamstring the La Guardia administration in expediting transit unification and to smash collective bargaining on the New York transit lines." Thousand of TWU members attended rallies protesting the bill, the union took out newspaper ads urging a veto and it succeeded in reversing the stand of some supervisory and clerical employees who had originally supported the mea- sure. In June, TWU leaders met with Lehman, as did representatives from the AFL, which still supported the bill.[74]

La Guardia also asked Lehman to veto the transit bill, citing the same grounds that he had used in his letter to Wicks. In response, Lehman told the Mayor that he did not "want to take any chance of jeopardizing the interests of the thousands of [affected] workers." Accordingly, he asked La Guardia to "give me your assurance that if I veto the bill . . . no steps will be taken that will endanger the continued employment, pensions and rights of the workers on the transit lines when they are taken over." La Guardia, of course, all along had been unwilling to give the TWU just such assurances, and he was no more willing to give them to the Governor. Instead, with less than two hours left before Lehman was legally obligated to either sign or veto the bill, La Guardia sent the Governor a telegram that in its key paragraph read:

> all employees who are needed and who can qualify will be protected, provided and if you can . . . give assurance that the courts will not interfere, disturb or otherwise prevent carrying out exactly what you and I have to have done in this matter.

Not surprisingly, Lehman found this response "not clear" and, as it obviously offered no meaningful assurances, he signed the Wicks bill into law, to the bitter disappointment of the TWU.[75]

9

UNIFICATION

For the TWU, the years following the signing of the Wicks Act were "a rough siege."[1] Just as union leaders had feared, unification took place without prior provision for union recognition or collective bargaining, enabling the La Guardia administration to move quickly to undermine the TWU's position. The transit union was unable to maintain its union shop and was forced into a bitter struggle to retain other provisions of the contracts it already held, let alone to establish any long-term bargaining arrangement.

Exacerbating the situation were political shifts that resulted from international developments. The Hitler-Stalin pact and the Roosevelt administration's move toward an interventionist foreign policy led to a temporary breakup of the Popular Front and various center-left alliances. The resultant factionalism within the CIO and the ALP isolated the TWU from onetime allies and further strained its relationship with La Guardia. Meanwhile workers dissatisfied with the TWU leadership saw in unification and the altered political landscape an opportunity to challenge the union's hegemony. Faced with threats from all sides, the TWU responded with a sharp attack on defectors, a drive for internal unity, and a massive campaign to win popular support. Only the spread of World War II, first to the Soviet Union and then to the United States, averted an all-out clash between the union and the city and somewhat eased the TWU's two-year crisis.

Although the TWU succeeded in eliminating the most troublesome provisions from the Wicks Act, the union considered the measure "insidious and vicious union-busting legislation." As far as TWU leaders were concerned, transit workers had suffered a sharp defeat in Albany. The prospect of an extension of ISS labor practices to the IRT and BMT left them deeply apprehensive.[2] Moreover, unification was no longer an ever-receding goal; on June 31, 1939, the City of New York signed a contract to buy the BMT for $175 million. Two months it contracted to purchase the IRT for $151 million. By early 1940, all that was necessary to complete unification was for the city to take formal title to the two transit systems.[3]

The TWU's response to the Wicks Act and the BMT puchase agreement was to hasten the negotiation of new contracts with the IRT and BMT while they were still in private hands. The TWU's original contracts with the companies had been scheduled to expire at the end of 1938. In part due to the uncertainty created by steps towards unification, these contracts were repeatedly extended for short periods rather than replaced by new pacts. In June 1939, however, with unification on the horizon and the Wicks Act in place, the TWU began pushing hard for longer-term arrangements, both to provide immediate improvements and strengthen the union's position with the city.

After a series of maneuvers, including a strike threat against the BMT, on July 12 the TWU signed new agreements with both companies. Although improvements were to be made in wages, benefits, and conditions, of special importance was the expiration date for the pacts, June 30, 1941, well beyond the anticipated date of the transit merger. TWU leaders immediately announced that they considered the IRT and BMT contracts binding on the city after unification occurred. Since the purchase agreement for the BMT called for the city to assume any outstanding BMT contracts, the union's stand was not without legal foundation, but the issues involved were complex and the city's precise obligations far from clear.[4]

The passage of the Wicks Act also led to a modification of the TWU's position on unification itself, although more in tone than substance. To a far greater extent than before, the TWU now stressed the inequities in the unification plan. The TWU International Executive Board noted that "ample provision has been made in this deal . . . to protect the rights of stock and bondholders . . . and conversely inadequate and inappropriate provision has been made for the rights of employees." Criticism of "the Wall Street transit-banking interests" and the benefits that were to accrue to them from unification now became a standard element in TWU rhetoric.[5]

The TWU's position was most fully developed in testimony on June 1, 1939, before the Transit Commission, which was examining the proposed contract for the purchase of the BMT. Although the TWU spokesmen, Austin Hogan and Harry Sacher, continued to support unification as ultimately beneficial to the public, they opposed the specific contract in question. In an insightful, prophetic analysis, Sacher argued that the high purchase price for the BMT, and the large debt that would be incurred as a result, would put a "straight jacket" on the financial future of the transit system. To meet operating costs and debt payments the city would be forced either to raise the fare, increase real estate taxes, or impose inhuman conditions on the transit work force. The danger for the TWU, Sacher pointed out in a later statement, was that the union, in seeking higher wages and benefits for its members, would be blamed by the public for higher taxes or fare increases, when the real fault would lie in the enormous cost of taking over run-down transit systems that the city itself had originally built.[6]

Sacher's testimony represented something of a change in position; only seven months earlier the TWU had supported the debt-limit exemption amendment which was predicated on purchase prices similar to those now being considered. Nonetheless, in spite of its new, more cogent analysis, the TWU still failed to take a clear stand on unification. At the union's September 1939 convention the TWU leadership successfully opposed a resolution calling for the cancellation of the unification plan because of its excessive cost. John Santo argued that the TWU should support unification as long as jobs, pensions, seniority, and collective bargaining were protected and the purchase price was not so high that in later years no raises would be possible. By the time Santo spoke, however, the Wicks Act and the IRT and BMT purchase contracts had already fixed the terms of the city takeover, and the very conditions he set for TWU support had not been met. Although the TWU continued to criticize bitterly many facets of the unification plan—so much so that the union often has been incorrectly characterized as having opposed unification—it was only a rearguard action. At no time did the TWU launch a campaign to halt or revise fundamentally the unification plan which it so accurately predicted would have disastrous consequences for the transit work force, the TWU, and the City of New York.[7]

The TWU was not alone in its failure to come to grips with unification; its allies on the left did no better. Although other left-wing unions and the CP generally shared the TWU's view of the transit merger, they did not treat it as an issue of great import, even though municipal politics and the transit fare were central concerns of the left throughout this period.[8] A number of factors, ideological, political, and organizational, contributed to the seemingly flat-footed TWU and CP approach toward unification.[9]

First, TWU leaders and other leftists were reluctant to oppose openly any municipal takeover of a public utility, since government ownership of utilities had been a rallying cry for socialists of all stripes for generations. Even believing, as many did, that in this case what was taking place was as much a bail-out of capital as a socialization of services, it was difficult for leftists to fight against the one plan with a chance for success to emerge from twenty years of unification discussion.

Second, broad questions of political strategy were involved for the CP-led left that undoubtedly influenced TWU policy. At least some Communist leaders believed that La Guardia's support for unification was in part an effort to make peace with the city's financial interests—a view for which there is considerable evidence. For precisely that reason they were reluctant to attack the unification plan. At least through the summer of 1939 the CP saw the ALP and its own somewhat shaky relationship with La Guardia as central to the Popular Front in New York. If La Guardia placed a high priority on shoring up his ties to capital through unification, to attack him on this point would have jeopardized its relationship with his administration and the unity of the ALP.[10] As had happened before and was to happen again, the acceptance by TWU leaders of the political needs and direction of the Communist-led left as a whole led them to avoid an open break with La Guardia, who in return made only the most limited concessions when it came to municipal labor relations.

Third, internal considerations may well have tempered the TWU's stand on unification. Many IRT and BMT employees welcomed unification; the prolonged economic depression made the security and benefits associated with government employment appear extremely attractive. Even in the Kent Avenue powerhouse, a TWU stronghold, a local union leader reported "a few . . . who were in ecstasy about going into Civil Service." Black IRT and BMT employees were especially enthusiastic about unification; they saw their ISS counterparts getting conductor and motorman jobs, while on the private lines those positions were still virtually all white. An all-out battle against the unification plan surely would have alienated some of the TWU's own members.[11]

Finally, and not to be underestimated, was the air of inevitability to unification. It had been in the works for years, everyone gave it at least lip service support, and some of the most powerful interests in the city were backing the specific plan in question. TWU leaders had a reasonably good sense of the limits of their union's power. Even if the TWU could have mobilized its left and union allies, success in making major changes in the financial basis of unification was extremely unlikely. Under such circumstances, it was easy for the TWU not to take its own predictions seriously. Rather than getting into a nearly hopeless battle against unification itself, the union chose to fight a guerrilla war, focusing on the labor aspects of the transit merger. The measure of success of this strategy were the modifications in the Wicks bill and the union's ultimate survival as the dominant employee organization on the unified transit system. The measure of failure in the short run were the problems the TWU faced in maintaining its status as a recognized bargaining agent, and in the long run the linkage of debt, taxes, fares, and wages that dogs both the union and the transit system to this day.

One of the ironies of unification was that the TWU muted its attack on the transit merger partially in deference to the Communist left's alliances with the Mayor and within the ALP, yet at the very moment when unification approached these same alliances were strained or shattered by events having nothing to do with transit. On August 23, 1939, the Soviet Union and Germany signed their non-aggression treaty. The differing reactions of American Communists, non-Communist leftists, and liberals all but destroyed the Popular Front and the broader center-left coalition. Although political conflicts and realignments occurred across the nation, they came first and most sharply in the ALP, with Mike Quill and the TWU at the center of the battle.

After the Hitler-Stalin pact Quill strongly supported the CP's advocacy of United States non-intervention in Europe. His September 30, 1939, remarks at a State, County, and Municipal Workers meeting received prominent news coverage and were often referred to during the ensuing debate within the ALP: "God knows Hitler is bad," Quill said:

> but Chamberlain is just as bad. . . . We say a plague on both their houses. We hope their reigns will end with the finish of the war and the workers of Europe will bring peace to the European people. But this time they are not going to have the manhood of America; they are not going to have the blood of America's workers.[12]

Quill's stand was both heartfelt and politically expedient; he had been active in the peace movement since at least 1937, and the CP's new position meshed well with his Irish nationalism and that of Irish transit workers. During the next two years Quill played a leading role in left-wing anti-war activites.[13]

The non-Communist leadership of the ALP reacted to the new international situation and the change in CP policy in the opposite fashion from Quill. At an October 4 meeting of delegates from ALP clubs and affiliates, the party's State Executive Committee introduced a resolution supporting FDR's recent move away from strict neutrality, condemning the Soviet-German treaty and the CP, and calling for the removal of Communists and Communist-sympathizers from the labor party. After a bitter debate the resolution was passed 605-94. ALP state secretary Alex Rose indicated that acceptance of the resolution would be a pre-condition for continued party membership.

The whole political architecture of the ALP was changing. All along the Social Democrats had fought CP participation in the party, but they made little headway without the backing of the garment union leaders who dominated the ALP's top-down bureaucracy. As long as the Communist left kept a low profile and supported Roosevelt, the latter were willing to accept its presence. However, when the CP and the Roosevelt administration began diverging on foreign policy, most ALP leaders wanted the party on record as backing the President. This was particularly important for the garment unionists because of the strongly negative reaction among their heavily Jewish memberships to the newest turn in Soviet and CP policy. Accordingly, the leaders of the Clothing Workers, ILGWU, and Hatters were now willing to join with the Social Democrats to create a forced consensus on foreign policy and, if need be, weaken or oust the CP-led wing of the party.[14]

As both sides quickly mobilized their forces—the left winning control of the Manhattan County organization and the center-right forces easily maintaining power in the other boroughs and on the state level—the issue that emerged as a key test of strength was Quill's City Council candidacy. Prior to the Nazi-Soviet pact, Quill had been slated for renomination for his Bronx Council seat, with his re-election all but assured. However, because Quill was the most prominent ALP officeholder close to the CP and vocally supported the new CP line, the right decided to make him a special target of their offensive. At the October 4 meeting a resolution was introduced from the floor and referred to the State Executive Committee calling for the ALP to withdraw its endorsement of Quill on the grounds that he was a Communist. Alex Rose telegraphed Quill, who was on the West Coast attending a CIO Convention, demanding that he accept the just-passed foreign policy resolution or lose his ALP nomination. When Quill responded by denying that he was a Communist but holding fast to his non-interventionist stand, both the State Executive Committee and the Bronx County Committee voted to deny him ALP backing.[15]

Immediately the TWU, the CP-led left, and the national CIO indicated that they had no intention of accepting the ALP decision. In a statement entitled "We Must, and Will Re-Elect Quill to the City Council" the Executive Board of Local 100 attacked "a certain clique" in the ALP for red-baiting and raising foreign-policy issues irrelevant to municipal affairs. Since the PR election process gave no formal role to party nominations, Quill could run as an independent. Within days union members had gathered thousands more signatures than necessary for a place on the ballot. Left-wing unions and organizations quickly came out for Quill, and the *Daily Worker* began sustained, featured coverage of his campaign, giving Quill much greater attention than he had ever previously received in the Communist press. Finally, Allan Haywood telegraphed ALP leaders to say that the New York delegates to the CIO convention unanimously requested that the labor party renominate Quill, almost surely a sign of support from Lewis. By the time Quill returned to New York so much momentum had been generated that a crowd estimated by the *Daily Worker* at 12,000 gathered to greet him.[16]

On October 17, Quill formally kicked off his campaign with a large South Bronx rally, the start of what turned out to be an extraordinary effort. Quill faced almost continuous red-baiting, including in Christian Front-type leaflets apparently written by or with the help of TWU members, and he lacked not only the support of the ALP but also of the Mayor, who agreed with labor party leaders not to endorse him. The TWU president, though, was supported by numerous CIO and AFL locals, such leading unionists as Haywood, CIO national secretary James Carey, and Elmer Brown of the Typographers, and some independent liberals like Heywood Broun. With the CP's own candidates knocked off the ballot for petition irregularities, the Party was free to focus its resources on Quill. The IWO, with its large Jewish Bronx membership, played an active role in the campaign, repeatedly praising Quill for fighting Irish anti-Semitism and the Christian Front, which partially offset the impact in Jewish areas of Quill's support for the Soviet-German treaty. Even within the ALP, Quill won considerable backing. Eventually about half of the Bronx ALP clubs endorsed Quill, only to have their charters revoked by the County Committee.

Over 3,000 volunteers—more than 1,000 from the TWU—took part in Quill's campaign. Sixteen Quill-for-Councilman headquarters were established, rallies and meetings were held virtually every day, hundreds of thousands of leaflets were distributed, and thousands of doorbells were rung. In the end it was almost, but not quite, enough for victory; Quill received 52,908 votes, only 2,000 short of the total needed that year for election. Almost certainly it was a decline in Jewish support, perhaps combined with a loss of some Coughlinite Irish votes, as much as the action of the ALP as such that cost Quill his Council seat.[17]

While the Quill campaign was a failure in the immediate sense, it was encouraging as a test of the TWU's ability to operate within a changed political configuration. The TWU had shown that it had growing political clout and sophistication even without its erstwhile ALP partners. Increasingly, TWU leaders, especially Quill, were coming to see the union's political and representational activities as a continuum. Politics was no longer seen as an adjunct to bargaining, but as an integral part of it, particularly given the municipalization of so much of the TWU's New York jurisdiction.[18]

The campaign had also shown that in its conflict with the center and right of the ALP, the TWU could count on strong support from the Lewis wing of the CIO, which controlled the labor federation's national and New York offices. The same issue which divided the ALP, neutrality, likewise was beginning to rend the CIO, with Lewis as opposed to American involvement in Europe as the CP. The result was a realignment of forces within the CIO, with an alliance of Lewis and the CP-left on one side and the right and Roosevelt supporters, led by Hillman, on the other.

Ever since the TWU had joined the CIO, Lewis had stepped in at key moments to aid the union. In return the TWU, the CIO's seventh largest affiliate, had closely adhered to national CIO policy and always kept Lewis informed of its doings. Unlike the leaders of some older and larger unions, TWU leaders viewed the CIO not so much as a conglomerate but as a parent organization. According to Maurice Forge, they tried to be "disciplined sons of the CIO." Quill in particular developed a deep admiration for Lewis; if in the early years he had looked to Santo for ideas and guidance, by 1939 Lewis was his model. Lewis in turn was appreciative of the TWU's deference, considering the union something of a pet project. After 1939, with political lines changing, the relationship between Lewis and the TWU grew closer than ever.[19]

The changed circumstances within the CIO made it possible for the CP-led wing of the New York labor movement to solidify its organizational position. In July 1940 the Greater New York Industrial Union Council was chartered as the city's central CIO body, with the left in control. Joe Curran of the National Maritime Union (NMU) served as council president, Hogan as vice president, and Santo as one of fourteen board members. Saul Mills of the Newspaper Guild, a leftist who had done occasional publicity work for the TWU, was put in charge of day-to-day operations. In August the council set up a political affairs committee, chaired by Quill. Left-wing control was so strong that the Amalgamated Clothing Workers refused to affiliate. The formation of the NYC CIO Council was both a sign of the CP-left's growing New York strength and the creation of an important institutional agency through which it could operate.[20]

The TWU willingly reciprocated the support it received from the CP-left and Lewis. In 1940, for example, the TWU recruited transit workers to help in the Congressional campaigns of Marcantonio and Joe Curran and joined the fight against the state legislature's Rapp-Coudert Committee, then on a crusade against left-wing teachers. The union vehemently backed Lewis within the CIO while attacking the Clothing Workers. Even though in the 1940 Presidential election the TWU supported neither candidate, its editorial on the subject was entitled "We Stand with Lewis," and it reprinted the CIO president's speech endorsing Wendell Willkie. According to one report, Lewis even got Quill to agree to distribute pro-Willkie literature, though when packets of campaign material arrived at TWU headquarters they were quietly sent to the incinerator. The TWU's backing of Lewis reflected broad areas of agreement, past gratitude, and personal affection, but it was also highly expedient. Without Lewis's support the TWU might well have faced catastrophe when unification finally occurred.[21]

On February 17, 1940, Mayor La Guardia announced that the city would take over the IRT and BMT on May 1. Almost immediately Quill wrote to La Guardia asking for a meeting to discuss whether or not the city would assume the existing transit contracts and in the future engage in collective bargaining. The Mayor failed to respond until the TWU began hinting at the possibility of a strike. Only then, on March 2, did La Guardia announce in a letter to Quill and BLE leader John J. Donnelly the city's post-unification labor policy.[22]

The Mayor's policy was not what the TWU wanted to hear. Although La Guardia stated that the wages and benefits provided for in the TWU contracts would not be reduced, he gave no assurance that at least temporary layoffs would not occur. On the crucial issue of union status, La Guardia indicated that workers could belong to unions, but a closed shop would not be in force, thereby making clear his intention to void at least parts of the existing labor agreements. Furthermore, while workers could individually or collectively "confer with" or "petition" management, there would be no exclusive or even preferential recognition. Finally, La Guardia noted that the right to strike against the city "is not and cannot be recognized."[23]

The TWU reacted with fury. In a letter to La Guardia, Quill charged the Mayor with being intent on "destroying the Transport Workers Union" and responding to its request for collective bargaining "in the manner of Girdler and Ford . . . with a yellow-dog company union formula." Quill, adopting the rhetorical style of his recent mentor Lewis, made it clear that the TWU's policy of not directly attacking the Mayor was dead. "We asked you for bread," Quill declared, "and you gave us a stone. Thus do you turn against labor—you who have always pretended to be a staunch friend of labor and who, under that pretense, have achieved high place and power."[24]

On March 5 a meeting of 6,000 BMT day workers voted unanimously to give the Local 100 Executive Board authority to call a strike whenever it saw fit. Over 8,000 IRT workers and 2,000 BMT night workers soon followed suit, while 3,500 private line workers pledged full support for any action taken. Ladies' Auxiliary meetings in Brooklyn and Manhattan were held in preparation for a showdown, and alliances with the rest of organized labor activated. Even when La Guardia traveled to Birmingham, Alabama, for a mayors' conference, he could not avoid the growing mobilization; a delegation of Southern labor leaders greeted him with a copy of a resolution passed by representatives of 300 New York union locals endorsing the TWU's stand in its conflict with the city. Increasingly the TWU was talking and acting as if a walkout was inevitable.[25]

La Guardia's first reaction to the TWU strike preparations was to appeal directly to the transit work force. In a March 13 open letter to IRT and BMT employees La Guardia repeated his stand of March 2 while singing praise to civil service. Nonetheless, his position changed just a bit. The Mayor now indicated that no workers eligible for civil service would lose their jobs as a result of unification and, in response to reporters' questions, seemed to imply that the city would continue to bargain with the TWU. He also portrayed his stand against public sector strikes as one of compliance with existing law, as opposed to policy of his own making, saying that if he was a transit worker he would personally retain union membership.[26]

That night Allan Haywood declared that "if the C.I.O. has to choose between Mayor La Guardia and the Transport Workers it will choose the Transport Workers Union," dashing whatever hopes the Mayor may have had that the national CIO would shy away from a transit strike. Accordingly, after an approach by Sidney Hillman, La Guardia finally agreed to meet with TWU leaders. On March 18, La Guardia and Delaney met with Quill, MacMahon, Santo, Hogan, Sacher and Hillman, Lewis, Lee Pressman, and Gustave Strebel from the CIO. Apparently no positions changed, but with La Guardia increasingly casting his position as one dictated by statute, it was agreed that counsel for both parties would confer and

Mike Quill and John L. Lewis leaving City Hall after meeting with Mayor Fiorello La Guardia to discuss IRT and BMT bargaining rights, March 18, 1940.

prepare reports on the relevant legal questions, with another meeting to be held in nine days. In the meanwhile, the TWU continued planning for a possible strike. At a March 25 Joint Executive Committee meeting there was a long discussion about how to handle scabs. In spite of Quill's public assurance that any strike would be peaceful, according to a police report Hogan ended the session by saying that any man who did not walk out would get his skull fractured. [27]

On March 27 the whole crisis was apparently resolved by the capitulation of La Guardia. After a stormy two-hour meeting between city officials and a TWU-CIO delegation that included Lewis and Hillman, at which the unionists made clear their intention of striking if necessary, the Mayor agreed to accept the key TWU demand, the continuation of the outstanding IRT and BMT contracts. The operative section of La Guardia's statement took the form of a recommendation to the Board of Transportation:

> that all the terms and conditions not inconsistent with constitutional or statutory provisions, of existing contracts between the B.M.T. and I.R.T. and the labor organizations be assumed by the city . . . the assumptions of the contracts and any issues arising from said contracts to be made subject to judicial review.

At least in relation to its most immediate concern, the TWU had seemingly gotten everything it could want from the Mayor short of a commitment to work with the union to change any relevant laws. As to the long-term status of collective bargaining on the unified system, that would have to be decided in the future. In full expectation that no serious problems remained both Lewis and La Guardia left the city. [28]

Things turned out not to be so simple. At conferences over the next two days between the Board and TWU officials it became clear that the transit agency was unwilling to accept the contracts in their entirety. In a strained interpretation of the Mayor's recommendation, the Board indicated that it would neither consider the terms of the outstanding agreements binding for their duration nor assume those contractual provisions that it itself decided were in conflict with the state Constitution or state law. By the time La Guardia returned to New York on March 30 things were back to where they had been before March 27.

Over the next three days, both sides made final preparations for the possibility of the first major New York transit strike in fourteen years. The TWU established strike headquarters throughout the city, printed up strike notices for an April 3 walkout, and held near-continuous meetings of its leaders and key cadre. The city dispatched police to the powerhouses; the IRT and BMT posted anti-strike injunctions; and La Guardia warned that in the event of a walkout, after unification the private-line contracts would be considered void and workers who had struck would not be given jobs with the unified system.

Even as all this was going on, however, the basis for a settlement was being laid in ongoing negotiations between CIO and city officials. It quickly became clear that the Board of Transportation would be forced by La Guardia to retreat and accept the IRT and BMT contracts in their entirety until such time as any provisions were actually ruled illegal in court. Nonetheless, the final resolution came only with the arrival of Lewis, who for the third time in two weeks stepped in to seek a settlement on terms favorable to the TWU.

On April 2, Lewis and La Guardia held a series of meetings, intermittently joined by Pressman, Haywood, Hillman, and Anna Rosenberg, then regional director of Social Security, who was acting as an informal mediator. Notably absent were both Delaney and the leaders of the TWU. At the conclusion of the meetings TWU officials were summoned to City Hall and a settlement to the controversy was announced, essentially the same one arrived at on March 27 as interpreted by the union. After ratification of the agreement the next day by the Board of Transportation and the Local 100 Joint Executive Committee the crisis was over; the TWU would have contracts covering the BMT and IRT divisions of the new, unified city transit system at least until June 31, 1941. The union had been saved. [29]

In early June 1940 the City of New York formally took over the BMT and IRT. By combining the two systems with the ISS, a unified New York City Transit

System (NYCTS) was created with 554 route miles (including 303 miles of BMT trolley and bus routes), 1,237 miles of track, and over 500 rapid transit stations. The new system had close to 35,000 employees, including over 26,000 transferred from the BMT and IRT, and an annual payroll of over $60 million. In its first full year of operation, the NYCTS carried 2.3 *billion* passengers, 1.8 billion on subways and els and the rest on buses and trolleys, making it both the largest mass transit system and the most heavily used passenger railroad in the world. According to an advertising agency survey, during a typical month 71 percent of all New York City residents used the system, making an average of 26.5 trips which took up about ten hours of their time. In short, the NYCTS was an immense operation, affecting virtually everyone in the city, without which the city simply could not function. [30]

For the TWU, unification created a vast set of new problems. The union had to monitor and when necessary intervene in the complex process of extending civil service to what were now the IRT and BMT divisions of the NYCTS (the ISS became the IND division). It also had to make sure that its contracts were actually enforced. Looking ahead, there was the problem of what would happen after the contracts expired. And most important, the union had to convince transit workers that unionism was both possible and necessary under conditions of government employment and civil service.

Well before unification actually took place, the TWU began partially reinventing itself as an organization geared to function in the public sector. In part this meant a greater orientation toward membership services; specifically aiding workers in coping with the Byzantine world of civil service. The first thrust in this direction began even before the Wicks Act was passed; anticipating that only those who had at least applied for citizenship would be accepted into civil service, the TWU set up a program to help non-citizens win naturalization. Pamphlets explaining how to become a citizen were distributed and an attorney retained to help members with immigration or naturalization problems. By the time unification occurred, 476 TWU members had been aided in filing for citizenship.

Even after unification the TWU pursued citizenship problems. A few workers had simply failed to apply for naturalization and were fired. More had filed preliminary citizenship applications but due to a nation-wide backlog of applications had been unable to file in time the formal declarations of intention required by the Wicks Act. They too were fired. The consequences, beyond job loss, could be tragic. In June 1941 an IRT trackwalker with seventeen years seniority and a wife and child received a termination notice for failure to meet the civil service citizenship requirement. Almost immediately afterward he fell or jumped to his death in front of a train, an incident the union directly attributed to the Wicks Act. Some relief came in April 1941 when the New York State Court of Appeals issued a liberal interpretation of what constituted an application for citizenship for civil service purposes. Then, a year later, the TWU succeeded in getting enacted a state law reinstating workers who had lost their jobs due to the Wicks Act citizenship provision but who had subsequently been naturalized. [31]

Citizenship was just one hurdle workers faced in qualifying for civil service; they also had to file notarized applications, be deemed of good character, and pass medical exams. In these regards, too, the TWU made itself useful. The union assisted workers in filling out the necessary forms and got permits for several of its officials to serve as notaries public, enabling workers to fully complete their applications at the union hall. It also interceded on the behalf of workers who had medical problems or criminal records. In the latter situation, considerable delicacy was required, since in many instances workers' families were unaware of their scrapes with the law. In later years, when the TWU lost its union shop, many workers remained loyal to the union partially as a result of the help they had received in qualifying for civil service. Most of the union's services were also made available to non-union white-collar workers, laying the basis for future support and organizing among the BMT and IRT clerical and administrative staffs.[32]

As soon as unification was actually effected, the TWU set up a Civil Service Department to deal with individual problems and advise the union's leadership on civil service matters. Simultaneously a *New York Weekly Transit Bulletin* was begun, to supplement the International's monthly paper, and devoted primarily to civil service news.[33] BMT and IRT workers had been suddenly submerged into the bewildering world of civil service, with its arcane language and peculiar classification, examination, promotion, and transfer procedures. NYCTS workers had to deal with two separate bureaucracies, the Board of Transportation and the Municipal Civil Service Commission, which shared and divided responsibility for hiring, promotion, and classification decisions. The TWU did its best to decipher this new reality for workers previously unexposed to its like and to position itself as an intermediary between the individual worker and the civil service structure, while maintaining its previous mediating role between line management and the rank and file.

Creating a civil service system for an operation on the scale of the NYCTS was an enormously complicated undertaking, even given the city's prior experience with the ISS. The initial phase alone, assigning classifications and grades to workers transferred from the BMT and IRT, took a full year to complete. Not only did every job and every worker have to be examined, but three different occupational structures and sets of operating procedures had to be merged into one. All the irrational labor practices of the IRT and BMT, developed over decades and only partially rationalized by unionization, were inherited by the NYCTS. At the time of unification, for example, there were seventeen different pay rates for IRT conductors, six for BMT conductors, and four for IND conductors. In the non-transportation jobs the situation was even more chaotic. The IRT alone had seventy-three rates for air brake maintainers, while the three systems together had more than 100 rates for fewer than 800 car cleaners. When the initial transition to civil service was completed the Board of Transportation found itself with over 1,600 different hourly rates in 76 classification schedules, as well as great variations in working hours and benefits for men doing essentially the same jobs in the three divisions of what was supposed to be one transit system.[34]

Through meetings with the Board of Transportation, appearances before the Civil Service Commission, appeals to La Guardia and the public, law suits, and threatened job actions, the TWU tried to protect and advance its members' interests during this transition process. This included making sure that no jobs, standards, or workers were downgraded as a result of unification; that contracts and civil service regulations were enforced; and that individual workers' problems, such as misclassification by examiners unfamiliar with transit work, were successfully resolved. Beyond that, the union sought to capitalize on unification by promoting the rationalization and upgrading of job titles, pay rates, working conditions, and benefits by standardizing each at the highest level to be found in any of the three merged systems. Since for any given job the pay rate might be highest in one division, the hours shortest in another, and benefits and conditions best in the third, what the TWU was lobbying for was a complex, potentially costly series of adjustments. In addition, the union wanted to expand promotional opportunities, especially for those in the lowest positions: porters, agents, and platform men.

The TWU's push for rationalization overlapped with the desire of the Board of Transportation and the Civil Service Commission for standardized, simplified titles, promotional paths, pay rates, and conditions. In the months following unification the Board made some changes along the lines urged by the TWU, though only halfway measures. In November 1940, for example, the top pay rate for IND agents was raised nearly three cents an hour to the IRT level of 65.2 cents, but the much lower rates for the mostly female BMT agents were left unchanged. After considerable TWU pressure, the minimum BMT agent rate was raised from 36 cents to 50 cents an hour, although the maximum remained at only 54 cents. Similarly, BMT porters were shifted from a seven- to a six-day week, but no new personnel were added, leading to considerable speed-up. Moreover, even these and other limited adjustments were untypical. For a full year after unification, while classification was proceeding, the Board resisted any wholesale upgrading or equalization, particularly on terms set by the TWU. Only in August 1941, after a full-scale confrontation between the city and the union, was a system-wide adjustment of wages, hours, and titles instituted.[35]

Although TWU officials were angered by their inability to win more substantial pay equalization, particularly, as in the case of the BMT agents, when gross inequities were involved, their sharpest protests came over what they perceived to be violations of civil service regulations, contracts, or promises from the Mayor. During the nine months after unification the TWU charged the Board of Transportation with failing to establish an effective grievance procedure; violating seniority rights; laying off transferred el workers or reducing their pay in disregard of earlier pledges; refusing to fill vacancies or grant promotions, leading to speed-up; and shifting vacations from the summer to the winter. By November 1940 there already had been at least one brief work stoppage, and when the Board of Transportation provisionally appointed six men without transit experience to jobs at the Kent Avenue powerhouse, passing over previously furloughed workers, TWU officials threatened a job action. That crisis was resolved only when the head of the Municipal Civil Service Commission backed the TWU contention that the Board had acted illegally. In February 1941 a short work stoppage occurred at the Corona car barn when a union notice was removed from a bulletin board.

It was not so much any one incident that angered the TWU as a whole pattern of non-cooperation by the Board, a pattern of "stalling, reneging, and obstruction" that amounted to a refusal to fully recognize the TWU and its contracts or to make good faith efforts to resolve differences. The Board commissioners seemingly were unreconciled to any loss of managerial prerogative. In the eyes of the TWU and its CIO backers, they were committed to an "anti-labor" course designed to undermine the union. Even after the Board agreed in December 1940 to hold weekly meetings with the TWU to discuss grievances, pay equalization, and other matters affecting the work force, the situation did not improve. By the early spring of 1941 a full-scale crisis was developing between the union and the Board.[36]

In spite of the TWU's efforts to ease the impact of unification, the transit merger led to a sharp decline in support for the union among IRT and BMT workers.[37] Broadly speaking, workers' reactions to unification fell into three categories. At one extreme were workers who had never particularly liked the TWU, whose opposition was emboldened by the city takeover. At the other extreme were those who saw unification as an occasion for redoubled union efforts. In the middle lay the largest group, workers who before unification had supported the TWU to one degree or another, but after it felt the union to be no longer as necessary nor as likely to be effective. Some in the latter group now rejected the union outright; others drifted away, though with little hostility; and still others continued to back the TWU, but with considerably less spirit—more as a matter of form or sentiment or as a hedge than out of the belief that it was still of central importance.

Although the TWU had at best been ambivalent about the extension of civil service to the IRT and BMT, many if not most workers involved warmly greeted their new status. Some shed their prior unionism simply as an affirmation of their new station in life. Job insecurity, resentment of favoritism, and the felt absence of rights had been among the deepest impulses originally leading workers to support the TWU. Civil service, in the eyes of many workers, provided even more assuredly the very things the TWU had brought—security, fairness in assignments and promotions, and protection from arbitrary management actions. In addition, many workers believed that the city was already providing better conditions and benefits than the union had won from the private companies. Accordingly, to many IRT and BMT workers the TWU now seemed superfluous.

Many workers also felt that even if needed, a union could not effectively operate in the public sector. Despite the TWU's propaganda and the city's assumption of its contracts, many workers accepted La Guardia's widely publicized view that civil servants could not strike or be forced to join a union. For some this reflected philosophic agreement. More commonly it reflected acquiescence to current realities and pessimism about the chances for change. Government worker strikes and closed shops were extremely rare and the daily press and government officials were virtually unanimous in opposing both. Furthermore, the TWU itself had failed in over half a decade of trying to win recognition, a contract, or a closed shop on the ISS. But if the TWU was unable to convince many of its members that La Guardia's assertions were just that, it had taught some of its lessons well; most BMT and IRT workers apparently believed that without a closed shop or the ability to strike a union could be of only limited effectiveness, if effective at all.

Probably only a minority of the workers who entered civil service as a result of unification were prepared to see the TWU disappear. Many were waiting to see what working for the NYCTS would be like and how much power the union would wield before reaching conclusions. Some even felt that unification increased the need for a union. The record of the Board of Transportation in dealing with its employees was poor, pay rates for many jobs were lower on the IND than on the formerly-private lines, and there was considerable concern over pensions and other outstanding issues. Furthermore, many workers believed that even with civil service the NYCTS was potentially subject to patronage abuse.

In summary, then, workers' attitudes toward the TWU were highly varied and fluid in the year following unification but, overall, support for the union declined. Apparently the drop was more precipitous among transportation workers than non-transportation workers. In this respect the pattern of union strength in the post-unification period replicated that during the initial organizing drives. Nonetheless, even in the shops and powerhouses there were sign of diminished union sentiment.

The TWU's flagging worker support might not have become obvious if its union shop had remained in force. However, in spite of the city's agreement to assume the IRT and BMT contracts in their entirety—at least until a court ruled any of their provisions illegal—the status of the TWU's union shop was soon called into question. In July 1940, IRT station agents Edward Maguire, John Cronin, Bernard Cunningham, and William Holloran, and IRT conductor Daniel J. McCarthy publicly resigned from the TWU. All five previously had been involved in oppositional activity. Probably under pressure from the TWU, McCarthy quickly repudiated his letter of resignation. The other men, however, with the aid of former AAAC leader John J. Murphy, who was no longer working in transit, proceeded with two moves designed to challenge the TWU's status as the sole representative of the workers within its jurisdiction. First, they formed a new organization, the United Transit Men's Association. Second, they asked the State Supreme Court for a declaratory judgement on the validity of the Board of Transportation's assumption of the TWU's closed shop. [38]

The TWU's response was in part predictable, a rhetorical and organizational offensive against the defectors. Maguire and his associates were denounced as "ambitious would-be Judases, tempted by visions of pieces of silver and soft berths." On August 7, while the newly formed group was holding its first rally, the TWU IRT station section held a rally of its own a block away. According to the TWU, the new group's meeting was attended only by its founders, while the TWU gathering attracted 2,500 unionists and their wives. What was less expected was that the TWU did not expel the men in question, or ask the Board of Transportation to invoke the union shop and fire them, or intervene in the pending court case.

What the resigning workers had failed to anticipate was that neither the Board of Transportation nor the TWU wanted an immediate legal test of the union shop. In effect they conspired to prevent such a ruling. The Board apparently was content to wait for the labor contracts it had inherited to expire before seeking a clarification of the legality of the union shop under civil service. When the TWU and the BLE and BRSA (which had contracts with the BMT) forwarded lists of non-dues-payers to the Board, the Board simply ignored them. In turn, the TWU and the brotherhoods never sought judicial relief from this lapse. Rather than chance an adverse court ruling, the unions preferred to leave the union shop in legal limbo. Since no one had taken any action against Maguire and his colleagues, in late September the State Supreme Court dismissed their request for a declaratory judgment. [39]

While Maguire and company failed legally to overturn the union shop or establish a viable organization of their own, they nevertheless accomplished much of their purpose. By the fall of 1940 it was obvious that the Board of Transportation was not going to penalize employees for not paying union dues nor was the TWU going to try to force it to do so. As a result, a growing number of TWU members stopped paying dues. If legally the status of the union shop remained unclear, practically it was dead.

The extent of the TWU membership drop was much disputed. At the time the union asserted that it had lost but a few thousand dues-payers, but TWU activists later estimated that as many as half, or even more, of the union's IRT and BMT members stopped paying dues in the year or so after unification. City officials claimed in June 1941 that the TWU had only between 5,000 and 8,000 paid-up NYCTS members, which would have represented a loss of roughly two-thirds to three-quarters of the TWU's former IRT and BMT dues-payers. The financial difficulties Local 100 began to face confirm the seriousness of the situation; substantial loans and gifts were required from the International over the next few years to maintain the local's operations. Available figures from somewhat later also point to a sharp membership drop; in April 1943 only 5,188 workers from the BMT and IRT paid TWU dues, while 7,883 had paid dues at some point during the previous ten months. Since in the powerhouses and at the 148th Street shop the TWU's paid-up membership apparently suffered only a modest decline, the fall-off in other sections must have been very large. Certainly in many and possibly most sections only a minority of onetime TWU members were still paying dues during the winter and spring of 1941.[40]

Neither the TWU's leadership nor its more militant members were prepared to sit idly by while the union's membership slipped away. On August 8, 1940, workers at the IRT's Livonia barn stopped working when lamp trimmer Frank Salvatore boasted that he was dropping out of the union. The stoppage ended only when Salvatore applied for union reinstatement and apologized for his actions. Three weeks later, when a foreman jacker at 148th Street with a reputation as a company stooge refused to pay back union dues, 1,000 men ceased work until he left the shop.[41]

Although the TWU newspaper was calling union drop-outs "degenerates" and "scum," it is not clear what role, if any, the central union leadership played in initiating these protests. In September Local 100 treasurer Gustav Faber appealed to the rank and file not to stop work to protest the presence of non-dues-payers without first getting union approval. Nevertheless, with or without such approval, the job actions, which were concentrated in the IRT shops, barns, and powerhouses, continued. The most serious incident involved John F. Connolly, the son of the former president of the defunct IRT Brotherhood and a worker at the IRT's 240th Street inspection barn. Connolly was refusing to pay his union dues, claiming mistreatment by the TWU in a seniority matter. On November 4, after Connolly failed to meet a deadline set for paying his dues, the 170 workers at 240th Street stopped work for two-and-a-half hours. The next morning they resumed their stoppage until Connolly finally went to Transport Hall to pay up. A third sit-down occurred when Connolly returned to work still defiant and it was learned that the strikers were to be docked for the time they had been idle.[42]

In docking the 240th Street men, the Board of Transportation was continuing what had become its established policy toward dues strikes: it refused to pay wages for lost time, but took no other disciplinary action. Shortly after the protests against Connolly, however, the Board notified its employees that thereafter they would be fired for stopping work without permission. The TWU then discontinued its dues strikes and introduced a new tactic, picketing the homes of non-dues-paying workers. [43]

On December 4, during lunch time, hundreds of workers from 98th Street, joined by members of the Ladies' Auxiliary, picketed the nearby home of shop worker Joseph McDonald. McDonald had announced that he planned to defy and if possible disrupt the TWU. [44] This was the first of what soon became frequent picket lines at workers' homes. Possibly as many as a hundred such demonstrations were held over the next few months. [45]

Besides avoiding a confrontation with the Board of Transportation, there were other reasons for adopting a new means of policing the union shop. Locally initiated job actions had been threatening to get out of hand. One worker, for instance, who was delinquent in his dues but had no intention of dropping out of the union, was physically blocked from going to work. There were charges that non-dues-payers were being threatened and assaulted. In October, William Holloran, one of the men who had brought the court case against the union shop, claimed that he was beaten by three men, implying that the TWU was responsible. (Shortly after this at least one of the founders of the United Transit Men's Association, probably Holloran himself, began providing information on the TWU to the FBI.) In another incident, a critic of the union found a dead rat hanging over his work bench. By organizing the picketing of non-dues-payers' homes, the TWU leadership was able to direct rank-and-file resentment against union drop-outs into an orderly channel, reasserting some control and preventing unseemly incidents. [46]

In picketing homes, the TWU was reviving a tactic it had used against management officials during its initial organizing drives. As had then been the case, the picket lines were an expression of the deep-rooted Irish tradition of publicly shaming those who were seen as violating community moral norms. Typically the signs carried in these demonstrations advertised to all passing by—neighbors, friends, family members, and strangers—the name of the offending worker, contrasting his or her behavior with that of "decent" workers who paid union dues. A placard displayed in front of the home of one IRT worker, for example, read:

> Lawrence McGlynn; 32-18 81 St. J.[ackson] H.[eights]; Won through T.W.U.;
> $200 Pension Refund; $250 Annual Raise; $92 Paid Vacation; $46 Paid Holi-
> day; Regained Seniority; Free Medical Plan; And Other Benefits; Chisels on His
> Fellow Motormen.

Leaflets calling the drop-outs scabs were even distributed to passengers on trains run by non-payers. Out of this same tradition came the silent treatment occasionally given on the job to non-dues-payers. [47]

At first, the home picket lines were initiated by individual sections and were few in number. In early February 1941, however, as the TWU began building toward a campaign for a new contract with the Board of Transportation, the Local 100 Executive Board ordered all sections with delinquents to begin picketing the home of at least one non-dues-payer, with sections without delinquents to help in these efforts. Accordingly both the number and size of the picket lines grew. By the first week in March, 66 homes were being picketed. Some demonstrations had as many as several hundred participants.[48]

Home picketing was not without problems. The very first demonstration, at Joseph McDonald's home, led to a fight between McDonald and two TWU members. Although the altercation took place off IRT property, when charges were preferred against McDonald he was defended by a Board of Transportation lawyer. Board officials also encouraged picketed workers to file disciplinary charges against unionists who demonstrated in their NYCTS uniforms. Then, on February 2, nine TWU members were arrested for picketing the home of a worker from the IRT's Jerome Avenue barn. Although the charges were later dropped, the arrests were a sign of the city's growing impatience with the picketing. Two weeks earlier La Guardia had written to Philip Murray, who had recently succeeded John L. Lewis as president of the CIO, asking him to persuade the TWU to call off its campaign, complaining of the "constant disorder" it was creating.[49]

Equally serious was the potential for internal dissension created by the picketing. Although many of the targeted workers were outspoken opponents of the union or former company union leaders, with thousands of transit workers not paying dues, personal resentments, past grievances, and inter-ethnic antagonism undoubtedly came into play in deciding just who would be picketed. There are indications, for example, that this was the case at the Jerome Avenue barn, which carried on a vastly disproportionate number of demonstrations. At one point more workers from the Jerome barn were being picketed than from the entire rest of the IRT and BMT. Significantly, most of the picketed workers from this ethnically heterogeneous work site were non-Irish. Apparently the tension first created by the 1935 walkout at the barn and the subsequent domination of the TWU there by a clique of Irish workers re-emerged with the collapse of the union shop.

Some TWU leaders recognized that dues picketing was generating unfavorable publicity and alienating wavering union members. However, the tactic was only dropped in April 1941 after a State Supreme Court justice issue a temporary restraining order against the picketing at the request of a group of Bronx workers, at least several of whom worked at the Jerome barn.[50]

Significant as it was, the Jerome situation was exceptional. In most sections, only a few workers who were believed to be die-hard anti-unionists were picketed. While some non-dues-payers were quite consciously and decisively rejecting the TWU, workers stopped paying dues for all sorts of reasons. Some simply forgot to make their monthly payments. Others were short of money or hoped to get a free ride for a while. Some had grievances with a particular union official or action and were expressing their dissatisfaction by withholding their money. Any union without a union shop faces such problems, which are not necessarily a good indication of the basic level of worker support. Union officials realized that to picket dues-delinquents whose attitude toward the TWU was still fluid would be counter-productive.

To win back these more typical non-dues-payers, the TWU tried a combination of more aggressive dues collection, peer pressure, and exhortation. Union activists were periodically taken off their jobs and put on union payroll to go from worker to worker collecting dues. Such cadre were urged by union officials not to be abusive to workers who had not openly rejected the union. Those who had, however, were denounced in ever more vehement terms, as "disrupters," "deserters," and "vermin." Union members were asked always to wear their union buttons while at work. Since the buttons were exchanged for new ones of a different design each month when dues were paid, delinquents and drop-outs could be identified easily. Additionally, the union began requiring workers to show paid-up membership books before using union services. Rallies, newspaper articles, and personal contacts were all used to try to convince workers to maintain their membership.[51]

Slowly the union was adapting to life without the union shop, a situation more similar to the pre-1937 period than to the previous few years. By the spring of 1941 it was clear that many IRT and BMT workers would have to be won over to the union again and again, and some would never pay dues unless forced to do so. For the indefinite future the union would have to function with fluctuating support, constantly launching membership drives and making gains for its members in order to maintain and expand its diminished following.

Unification presented different problems and produced different results on the IND than on the other lines. While on the BMT and IRT the TWU was forced to struggle to retain its membership in the face of its de facto loss of the union shop, on the IND it sought to build a mass following from what had become a very small base. At the time of unification, the TWU had only a skeletal organization on the ISS, having severely downgraded its efforts there after failing to obtain a recognition election in 1938. With the creation of the NYCTS, it became imperative that the union improve its standing with IND workers, for its failure to do so would undermine its position on the larger IRT and BMT divisions and make its goal of winning a contract with the Board of Transportation more difficult to achieve.[52] Accordingly, the TWU renewed its IND organizing, achieving at least limited success. While in the year after unification the TWU's membership on the IRT and BMT declined, on the IND there was modest but significant growth.

Unification looked quite different from the perspective of IND workers than from that of their IRT and BMT counterparts. If the latter were impressed by the city's assertion that union shops and strikes were incompatible with civil service, at least some of the former were impressed by just the opposite, the TWU's success in forcing the city to assume the outstanding IRT and BMT contracts. IND workers had had more time to learn the problems as well as the advantages of civil service and Board of Transportation employment. They were discovering that they were not going to be treated like policemen or firemen, as many had hoped when they first received civil service standing. Pay was low, management paternalistic, and favoritism and fear far from unknown.

While many IRT and BMT workers had been put off from the TWU when they discovered that some equivalent IND workers had better benefits, hours, promotional opportunities, and pay, some IND workers were shaken to discover superior conditions achieved by TWU-represented IRT and BMT workers. In many job categories IRT and BMT employees had higher weekly earnings, if not hourly rates, and in a few cases they worked fewer hours. Unlike IND workers, they had regular grievance procedures and in many cases their seniority rights were stronger. Since 1939, for example, when there had been a scandal involving thefts from turnstiles, IND agents had had only limited rights to pick their assignments on the basis of seniority.[53]

Capitalizing on its recent victory in retaining the IRT and BMT contracts, the TWU in April 1940 launched a major IND organizing drive by setting up a large committee of IND members who agreed to serve as volunteer organizers. A number of previously inactive members once again became active and some new members quickly joined up. Throughout the summer and fall of 1940 organizing committees or union sections were established or revived in various IND departments. By early 1941 the committee in charge of the IND campaign was reporting considerable progress.

The pattern of TWU growth on the IND was similar to that in past organizing drives. The strongest union sections were at the IND's two main repair shops, at 207th Street and in Jamaica, Queens, where a considerable number of workers had had previous union experience and conditions for organizing were optimal. By February 1941 the TWU was claiming 80 percent membership at 207th Street, and by May, 95 percent membership at Jamaica. Elsewhere the picture was spottier. There were active organizing groups at least among the agents, trackmen, road inspectors, and porters. The porter group was a significant breakthrough, since prior to unification the TWU had made little headway among black ISS workers. In February 1941 the TWU claimed that it had a majority of workers signed up in some non-shop departments. Even discounted for the usual inflation, the TWU membership reports clearly represented a significant advance.[54]

A particular problem the TWU faced on the IND was the burgeoning of rival organizations, often constituted as non-union benevolent associations. Several organizations formed well before unification continued to operate, including a few councils of the Civil Service Forum and the AFMTW. After unification both groups tried to expand to the formerly private lines and both succeeded in picking up a few BMT members. Once unification was consummated, new organizations proliferated. Many IND workers still looked toward law suit and lobbying to further their cause, and there was no shortage of lawyers, ambitious workers, and political operators to try to harness this impulse. The Board of Transportation encouraged the emergence of new groups to fragment the work force.

The United Transit Employees Association was typical of the post-unification groups. In December 1940 it held an organizational meeting, announcing its aims as including improved benefits, prevailing wages, grievance procedures, and full civil service rights. The meeting's featured speaker was former Mayor Jimmy Walker, who had recently made a minor comeback when La Guardia had appointed him impartial arbitrator for the dress industry. In spite of its prominent backer, the Association failed to attract significant membership. Another new group, founded in early 1941, the Independent Benevolent Association, eventually merged with the AFMTW.[55]

The new transit groups, though most active on the IND, were not restricted to that division. The New York Transit Employees' Association, for instance, founded in late 1940, was centered on the BMT. One of its early meetings featured as a speaker the assistant Board of Transportation counsel in charge of prosecuting disciplinary cases. Like the Forum, this group strongly supported civil service and saw lobbying as its main tactic. The Transportation Employees Industrial Union was also BMT-based. Militantly anti-Communist, it was supported by some one-time TWU activists, including a few section chairmen. Even the IRT had at least one new group, the Transportation Benevolent Association, which also eventually merged with the AFMTW. All told, according to Board of Transportation officials, by June 1941 there were, in adition to the TWU, BLE, and BRSA, thirteen groups claiming to represent NYCTS employees. [56]

It is difficult to gauge the relative strength of the TWU and its rivals. In June 1941 city officials claimed that, combined, the various non-TWU groups were about equal in size to the TWU. This seems unlikely. On the IRT, the new groups made virtually no headway. On the BMT, the BLE and BRSA were well established in their respective jurisdictions, and while a few newer groups may have briefly developed followings, the TWU remained dominant. Even on the IND, where the TWU was by far weakest, its rivals, with the possible exception of the Forum, were extremely small, weakened by their multiplicity and parochialism. Although in the spring of 1941 one observer believed that the TWU had only 1,000 IND members, less than a sixth of the work force, the TWU's own organizers were increasingly confident of their position. By June of that year, IND activists were pressing the Local 100 leadership to demand an IND representation election, convinced that they could easily win such a vote. Thus while rival organizations somewhat delegitimated the TWU's claim to represent the entire transit work force (except for those in the brotherhoods), they themselves failed to develop into significant organizational entities that seriously challenged the TWU for the allegiance of the work force. [57]

Throughout the second half of 1940 and early 1941, the TWU maintained a verbal barrage directed at the Board of Transportation. In newspaper editorials it charged that the Board commissioners were carrying out "Wall Street's program," developing "plots of destroying the Transport Workers Union" by causing "eruptions and frictions among the employees" so as "to wring from the sweat of the employees a regular flow of interest and gravy to millionaire bondholders and bankers." Such rhetorical onslaughts, along with IND organizing and dues picketing, were all part of the union's preparations for the all but certain clash with the city over whether or not a new contract would be signed to replace the IRT and BMT pacts, which were due to expire on June 31, 1941. [58]

In February 1941 the Local 100 Executive Board called on all NYCTS TWU sections to discuss possible contract demands to be presented to the city. As general, system-wide provisions, the Executive Board proposed a 33½ percent wage hike and full payment by the city of pension contributions. Other demands were to be worked out by individual sections. [59] This was the TWU's usual course of preparations for negotiations, in Maurice Forge's words "a semi- or pseudo-democratic procedure." Since each section met separately, union officials could edit the various "laundry lists" submitted without creating a general uproar. Demands were scaled down to what was deemed a realistic level, prioritized, and then re-inflated for bargaining purposes. Once an overall program was developed, it was sent back to local leadership bodies and section or mass meetings to be approved and popularized. The whole process was designed to provide genuine rank-and-file input, create a sense of widespread involvement, and mobilize the membership for upcoming battles.[60]

In this case, the TWU's preparations for confronting the city were interrupted by a crisis arising elsewhere; the union's contracts with the interlocking Fifth Avenue Coach Company and New York Omnibus Corporation expired on February 28, 1941, and negotiations were not going well. The union was seeking substantial pay increases, an eight-hour day for drivers, and improved benefits, including adequate pensions. Management not only rejected this program, but made demands of its own, including the elimination of sick benefit funds and either the introduction of one-man operation on some double-decker buses or pay reductions. Negotiations broke down when the TWU refused to extend its contract or accept mediation or arbitration unless the companies dropped their counter-proposals, which they declined to do. On March 10, some 3,500 TWU members at the two companies walked off their jobs, shutting down virtually all of Manhattan's bus lines and leaving 900,000 daily riders without their usual means of transportation.[61]

Both at the time and subsequently, some observers argued that the TWU called its 1941 bus strike primarily as a show of force to strengthen its hand with the city. There is little evidence to support this view. Neither the union nor the CP anticipated or desired a strike. Union members worked for nine days without a contract and did not take a strike vote until after the negotiations broke down. It was the companies' tough stand that precipitated the walkout. When TWU negotiators threatened a strike unless concessions were forthcoming—essentially a bluff, since they had made no strike plans—the president of the two companies, John A. Ritchie, refused to yield and told them to strike if they wished. Having already built up membership expectations, and unwilling to risk being forced through arbitration or mediation to accept any company demands, the union leadership decided that it would indeed have to call a strike. Only then were hasty preparations begun.[62]

Nevertheless, whatever the origins of the strike, the leading actors in the controversy over labor relations on the city-run transit system quickly turned the bus dispute into a test of strength for the larger, looming battle. La Guardia was particularly outspoken in criticizing the TWU. Before the strike began he announced that it "would not serve any useful purpose." When TWU leaders declined La Guardia's mediation offer, he called their attitude "bull-headed, obstinate, and stupid." Once the walkout started, he joined most of the city's daily press in denouncing the TWU. At one point La Guardia even ordered the police department to make preparations for protecting buses in the event that the companies chose to resume operations with scab workers. Other opponents of the TWU also joined the fray; the Dies Committee, for example, issued a report on purported Communist control of the TWU on the second day of the walkout.

The striking bus workers were not without allies. Thousands of non-striking TWU members, mostly from the NYCTS, attended mass meetings, joined picket lines, and distributed literature. The NYC CIO Council, local unions, and progressive organizations also provided support. Allan Haywood and Phil Murray met repeatedly with TWU leaders and La Guardia, spoke at union meetings, and played

Striking New York Omnibus and Fifth Avenue Coach workers marching in the St. Patrick's Day parade, March 17, 1941.

a major role in working out the eventual settlement. Even John L. Lewis got involved, giving TWU leaders advice and offering money and men if needed.[63]

One incident during the strike revealed the continuing divisions in Irish and Catholic circles over the TWU. The St. Patrick's Day parade was on March 17 and the head of the Knights of Columbus invited the TWU to march as a unit, wearing uniforms and union armbands, behind his delegation. Two thousand TWU members prepared to take up his offer, relishing the opportunity for publicity and to confront the Mayor, who was to be on the reviewing stand. The night before the parade, however, the head of the Parade Committee forbade the TWU to march as a group. Nevertheless, hundreds of TWU members wearing armbands marched with other organizations to which they belonged or informally joined the line of march. Special union leaflets, printed on green paper, were distributed along the parade route.[64]

After twelve days the bus strike was settled along lines first proposed by the union and later suggested in somewhat different form by a mayoral-appointed fact-finding board. The dispute was to be submitted for binding arbitration to William H. Davis, former chairman of the New York State Mediation Board. The new contracts were to be for one year, management demands for contract changes were not to be considered, and any improvements in wages, hours, and benefits were to be limited to a total cost of $1 million. The settlement was generally viewed by the strikers and outside observers as a union victory, though by no means a spectacular one.[65]

The bus strike—the TWU's first major transit strike—gave the union renewed confidence in its fight with the city. In the face of concerted opposition from the Mayor and the mass media, the union's members had displayed considerable solidarity, organizational ability, and esprit. At the meeting that ratified the strike settlement, Quill argued that the walkout had strengthened the TWU's position in its dispute with the city. According to some reports, he also threatened a strike of the NYCTS.[66]

La Guardia too apparently saw the bus strike as a possible portent, and he took steps accordingly. The Police Department was ordered to develop plans for keeping the municipal transit system in operation in case of a walkout, several hundred NYCTS police were hired, and surveillance of the TWU was stepped up.[67] At La Guardia's request, the state Legislature quietly passed the Wicks Anti-Sabotage and Anti-Violence bill, which made removing or damaging transit equipment, shutting off transit power, or leaving transit equipment in one's possession unattended felony offenses. Charging that the bill was an anti-strike measure, the TWU organized a campaign for a gubernatorial veto, putting considerable pressure on all wings of the CIO to come out against the proposed law. The AFL, however, argued that the bill would not prevent strikes, while the BLE, which had long operated under similar regulations, supported the measure. In the end, Lehman signed the bill, which he said did not limit the right to strike.[68]

On March 20, 1941, the TWU International Executive Board (IEB) formally opened the union's drive for a NYCTS contract, submitting a request for negotiations to La Guardia and the Board of Transportation. Copies of the IEB's "Declaration of Policy" were distributed to all of the union's New York City members and to several thousand organizations. The IEB also voted a $100,000 appropriation to aid Local 100 in the contract drive.[69]

A week later La Guardia responded by means of a letter to John Delaney, restating his long-held position that the city would not sign contracts with unions and that civil servants could not strike or be forced to pay union dues, though they could join organizations of their choice, including unions, and such groups could present their views and recommendations to appropriate officials. The Mayor went on to say that any municipal transit workers who struck would be fired and not rehired, and to ask the Board of Transportation to test in court the union shop clauses in the contracts it assumed at the time of unification.

As requested, on April 9 the Board declared that it would not enforce union shop agreements. The same day it initiated a court test of the city's right to observe, extend, or renew its transit labor contracts, including not only the union shop, but also clauses covering pay rates, terms and conditions of employment, and seniority and promotion rights. On April 10 every NYCTS employee received two copies of a pamphlet containing a letter from the Board of Transportation explaining its position, a reprint of La Guardia's letter to Delaney, and a copy of the Board's resolution on the union shop. Although there was little new in it, the pamphlet apparently had considerable impact on wavering TWU members, convincing some to drop out of the union.[70]

Before the Board even had time to distribute its pamphlet, the TWU responded with a letter from Phil Murray to La Guardia. Murray fully backed the TWU's position, arguing that there was no incompatibility between civil service and collective bargaining and no legal reason why the Board of Transportation could not sign union contracts. He also endorsed a view previously put forward by the TWU that transit was unique among city services in that it did not constitute "the performance of government function" but rather was "a business enterprise . . . a commercial venture in which money is made or lost" and therefore particularly suitable for private-sector style labor relations. The CIO president concluded by urging the Mayor to begin discussions with the TWU, which he offered to attend. The transit union distributed Murray's letter to all of its New York members and thousands of metropolitan-area organizations. [71]

Both sides were jockeying for position—making their cases to the public, lining up allies, and, most importantly, appealing to the transit work force. The TWU, deeply resentful of the coverage it received in the city's press (only the *Daily Worker* and the liberal *PM* were consistently sympathetic to the union), launched a massive campaign to reach the citizenry directly. On April 15 the union distributed a half million copies of Murray's letter to transit riders. Over the next six weeks it issued five more leaflets aimed at the general public, usually distributing over a million copies of each, mostly to transit patrons. Hundreds of union volunteers took part in this effort. Almost every week TWU or CIO spokespersons gave radio addresses, while open-air rallies, shop-gate meetings, and massive picket lines at the Board of Transportation became regular occurrences. On May 14 a TWU-sponsored conference of labor, civic, church, and fraternal groups backed the union's position, as did the NYC CIO Council. The Local 100 Joint Executive Committee, expanded to include shop stewards, met frequently, often with close to a thousand delegates in attendance. [72]

The TWU's campaign for public support culminated on May 21 with a rally at Madison Square Garden. To start the affair, over 5,000 members of the TWU and its Ladies' Auxiliary marched from Transport Hall to the Garden, where a crowd of 18,000 filled every seat and an overflow assembled outside to follow the meeting on a public address system. The program and audience reflected the strengths and limitations of the coalition backing the TWU in its struggle with the city. Other than TWU officials, the main speakers, led by Phil Murray, were all from the national CIO or the NYC CIO Council. Noticeably absent were representatives of the AFL, the ALP, or even the Hillman wing of the CIO. Not only was the CIO deeply divided over foreign policy and Roosevelt, but the Clothing Workers and the and ALP were looking toward supporting La Guardia for a third term. The CP and the TWU, while keeping their options open, were not behind the Mayor. The presence on the Garden platform of former Postmaster General James A. Farley, a leader of the anti-Roosevelt wing of the Democratic party, reflected the TWU's preliminary explorations of the possibility of supporting a Democrat against La Guardia. Listening to the speeches was a heavily left-wing crowd; according to an FBI informer, in addition to transit workers and their families there were large numbers of CP members and members of CP-led mass organizations present. Even the music reflected the political alignment; this time there were no Irish bands, but rather the left-wing Almanac Singers leading "Transit Tunes" written especially for the occasion.[73]

Though the TWU's backers were primarily from the left, the Garden rally once again showed that the union could count on strong support from Phil Murray and the national CIO office, despite growing tensions between Murray and leftists in other unions. In part, this may have simply reflected Murray's sense of his responsibility as CIO president. It also may have been part of Murray's tortured effort to fill Lewis's shoes; Lewis had always gone out of his way to help the TWU; at the Garden rally the introduction of five UMW representatives won some of the loudest applause of the evening. The TWU carefully extended to Murray the same deferential attitude it had displayed toward Lewis. Murray's stance, however, also grew out of his belief that the New York transit situation would establish crucial precedents as to the right of publicly employed workers to organize, bargain collectively, and strike.

In Murray's view—and apparently also Lewis's—the CIO's earlier position that public employees could unionize but not strike was no longer sufficient. Murray feared that civil service would be "altered into a weapon to be used against labor." His particular concern was not traditional government operations, but once-private functions taken over by government—housing, TVA-type projects, and the like. With the defense build-up making an expansion of such government activities likely, the CIO president wanted to establish definitively union rights in these situations. At the same time, he undoubtedly wanted to maintain some control over the TWU and the explosive situation in New York. Accordingly, he committed his personal prestige and the resources of the CIO to the complex, chancy effort to establish the TWU as the bargaining agent for NYCTS workers.[74]

Throughout April and May the city government was active as well. In mid-April the Board of Transportation announced a series of minor benefit improvements, denounced by Quill as "crumbs." In early May, La Guardia announced his intention to shorten transit work hours, blaming the TWU for the work schedules in the IRT and BMT contracts, which he deemed "cruel and completely out of line with the city's policy." Later that month the Mayor revealed that the Board of Transportation planned a series of improvements in pay and benefits, primarily aimed at IRT and BMT workers, worth an annual total of $1.8 million.[75] La Guardia also kept up his rhetorical assault on the TWU leadership, on one occasion saying, "I know the difference between a real labor leader and a dues collector"; and on another calling a short TWU strike of a small Queens bus company "just another typical example of irresponsible labor leadership." According to one report, La Guardia even asked Roosevelt in the event of a strike to use the subways to carry mail, thus qualifying them for federal protection, the ploy used a half-century earlier to break the Pullman railroad strike.[76]

La Guardia's hard-line toward the TWU seemed to belie his pro-labor reputation. Early in his career, La Guardia had served as an unpaid counsel to the garment unions. In Congress, he had led a long, ultimately successful fight to limit the use of anti-union injunctions. As Mayor he had restrained the use of police against strikers, ordered all government printing to have a union label, and repeatedly expressed his sympathy with organized labor. When it came to the city's own employees, however, La Guardia's attitude was quite different. At best, La Guardia was cool toward municipal unionism. Sometimes, as in the case of the TWU, he was outright antagonistic.[77]

La Guardia's attitude toward public employees reflected the Progressive reform tradition out of which he had politically emerged. Progressives believed that social opportunities should be distributed on the basis of individual merit, not social or political connections. They viewed patronage as both corrupt and inefficient. For most municipal reformers, including La Guardia, the antidote to patronage and machine politics was the civil service system, which they believed would distribute jobs on the basis of qualifications, undercut the power of political bosses, and introduce greater efficiency to government. When La Guardia took office 55% of the city's workers had obtained their jobs through competitive exams. Within six years he raised that figure to 74%.[78]

La Guardia's disdain for patronage sometimes spilled over into indifference or hostility toward municipal workers. Upon taking office, La Guardia laid off a large number of city employees and cut the often miserably-low salaries of those retained in an effort to balance the city's budget. Distrustful of the work force he inherited, he also contracted out much of the city's design and engineering work to private firms, resulting in massive lay-offs of civil service engineers.[79]

La Guardia believed that civil service provided municipal workers with "full and complete protection as to employment, rights, and privileges." Unions, in his view, were at best a secondary means of protection for city workers, since they had to operate within "the provisions of the Civil Service laws, which are most rigid." But the issue was not simply civil service. La Guardia wanted to be free to act as he saw fit, unrestrained by employee pressure. "The Chief Executive of a division of government," he wrote, "cannot be forced to do anything under threat of disorder, discontinuance of service or disregard of existing law." La Guardia's view of city workers was essentially paternal; they would be protected by civil service, but had to abide by decisions made by elected officeholders, who might consult with worker groups but in the end could and should act unilaterally.[80]

If city workers were to belong to unions, La Guardia wanted those unions to be as tame as possible, so that they would not limit his managerial prerogatives or create undo budgetary pressures. When city sanitation workers began joining a CIO organizing committee, set up in 1939 and partially funded by the TWU, La Guardia and his sanitation commissioner refused to recognize the group. Instead, they encouraged existing Civil Service Forum sanitation councils to affiliate with the AFL's American Federation of State, County, and Municipal Employees (AFSCME), then a weak, non-militant union. Thereafter the city dealt exclusively with the latter group.[81] In the TWU, La Guardia faced a large, well-organized, aggressive union, unlike the typical small, fledgling municipal worker unions of the time. If the TWU achieved exclusive recognition or signed a contract with the Board of Transportation, it would establish a precedent that might speed the unionization of the city work force, as eventually did happen.

The Communist issue also played a role in La Guardia's attitude toward the TWU. La Guardia was not prone to crude anti-Communism; he generally dealt with the CP and its allied organizations on a pragmatic basis. Many of his close advisors, however, including onetime Roosevelt brain-truster A. A. Berle, Jr., and

Parks Commissioner Robert Moses, were deeply anti-Communist. Berle in particular had long been hostile to Quill and the TWU. During the Hitler-Stalin pact period, when the CP was at odds with La Guardia over foreign policy, the Mayor was at least somewhat influenced by his advisors' fears about left-wing groups. In replying to one of Quill's attacks, La Guardia said that "I believe my contribution to American labor will be remembered when present trends of force and violence have been eliminated from the American labor movement," a thinly veiled reference to the CP. In explaining to Secretary of Labor Frances Perkins why he was at an impasse with the TWU, La Guardia cited the fact that the TWU was Communist-led. In addition, La Guardia found Quill personally infuriating, which colored his attitude toward the TWU. Normally quite cool and considered in dealing with labor, when it came to the TWU La Guardia was prone to emotional outbursts and rash action.[82]

As the TWU contracts neared expiration, La Guardia picked up important support for his position on the limits of public sector unionism. On April 21, Frances Perkins, when asked about the New York transit situation, indicated that while she felt agreements between public workers and their employers were desirable, there could not be collective bargaining in the usual sense, since decisions on wages and conditions were made by public bodies as part of the political process. ACTU also took the position that civil servants were in a special class; an early April editorial in the *Labor Leader* argued that although city workers had the right to unionize and bargain collectively, "the common good of the community makes it advisable if not mandatory for these workers to waive their right to strike." Two weeks later, ACTU called on Phil Murray to "supplant the present [TWU] leadership with a representative of his own choosing." Then, after a series of confrontations between TWU leaders and ACTU leafleters and an attack on the group by Quill, ACTU denounced "Mike Quill-Communist" and reversed its previous position that the transit workers should stay in the TWU despite its left leadership. By late June, ACTU was openly urging NYCTS workers not to strike, arguing that a defeat would mean the loss of their civil service status, while success would "only freeze the Communist Party in power, and give the workers a hollow victory."[83]

While charges and countercharges flew and lines of battle formed, little else happened. Murray and La Guardia met once in mid-May, but there were no direct discussions between the TWU and the city, in spite of repeated union requests. In late May the transit union resorted to a petition campaign in an effort to get La Guardia to begin talks, but the Mayor remained unmoved. In early June it became clear that the city's bid for a declaratory judgment on its right to sign contracts would not be resolved before the existing contracts expired; a State Supreme Court justice denied the city's request for a summary ruling, necessitating a full trial on the facts of the case.[84]

On June 19, with only twelve days remaining before the IRT and BMT contracts expired, La Guardia announced that the Board of Transportation would invite all employee groups on the NYCTS to present their views on wage and hour adjustments. This was in line with the Mayor's often-repeated view as to how labor relations on the NYCTS should operate: all interested representative groups could confer with the Board, but the final decisions were its alone, with no contracts to be signed. Since Delaney already had made it known that the Board had virtually completed a wage and hours equalization plan, it was unclear what the proposed conferences could accomplish.[85]

In the meantime, both sides made preparations for a possible strike. On June 10 La Guardia announced that in the event of a walkout the NYCTS would be kept in operation. Four days later the Board of Transportation put up posters warning against "reckless agitators," strike action, and sabotage, citing penalties in the Anti-Sabotage and Anti-Violence Act. For its part, the TWU continued to mobilize whatever support it could. On June 18 a meeting of the Irish Friends of Labor endorsed the TWU's demand for collective bargaining rights. Two days later the NYC CIO Council sponsored yet another mass picket line at the Board of Transportation. Then, on June 23, the TWU's Joint Executive Committee called a series of mass meetings for NYCTS workers to authorize a strike. The next day one hundred representatives from AFL, CIO, and independent unions met at Transport Hall to establish a joint strategy committee to facilitate cooperation with the TWU; the TWU wanted to make sure it had the backing of the rest of the labor movement in the event of a strike.[86]

On June 24 the TWU accepted the invitation to confer with the Board of Transportation on wages and working conditions, in itself a considerable concession since to do so under the circumstances was a de facto retreat from its claim to be the sole bargaining agent for the non-brotherhood BMT and IRT workers. The conference, held the next day, was a fiasco. After the TWU's counsel, Harry Sacher, proposed a pay increase of a dollar a day for all workers on top of pay equalizations, Board Commissioner Francis X. Sullivan responded that "you are not invited to negotiate a contract and . . . we will not sign a contract. You are invited here to express your view . . . on the question of wage equalization." When Quill asked directly if the Board was prepared to negotiate a contract, Delaney replied "a signed contract? No." At that point, thirty-two minutes after the meeting had begun, the TWU delegation walked out. Later in the day, at a meeting of 400 Ladies' Auxiliary members, Quill promised that "we will not work one hour in the month of July without a signed contract."[87]

In spite of the TWU's militant public posture and continuing preparations for a walkout, the union's leaders were desperately looking for a way to avoid a strike. Although ever since unification they themselves had intermittently encouraged strike sentiment, as the possibility of a walkout approached they grew increasingly hesitant. There were a number of reasons why.

First, although at least a large minority of the union's members were eager to strike, the TWU could not count on the complete loyalty of the transit work force. Since unification many BMT and IRT workers had dropped out of the union, while the TWU's position on the IND was tenuous. Even some union members in good standing might balk at a walkout. It is quite possible that the TWU could have shut down the NYCTS. The city had made no plans to recruit scabs. Furthermore, the union was solidly entrenched in the IRT and BMT shops and powerhouses. For technical reasons, the use of alternative power sources would have been extremely difficult. Also, without maintenance crews the system would have eventually ground to a halt. But even if effective, a strike without the full support of the work force would have been deeply divisive, leaving scars for years afterward. [88]

Second, the attitude of the public was uncertain. The TWU's public relations campaign had seemingly been successful in building public sympathy, and many unions told their members not to use the municipal transit system in the event of a strike. However, the city's press, particularly the conservative papers, were ruthlessly attacking the union. The *World-Telegram*, for example, in mid-June ran an extended series of articles attacking the TWU, harping on its ties to the CP. Anti-TWU editorials appeared virtually daily in one paper or another. [89]

Third, the inherent character of a New York transit strike, in the words of one TWU leader, left "both the union leadership and the [Communist] Party . . . scared stiff." An effective NYCTS strike would not only paralyze New York but, given the city's economic importance, if at all prolonged would affect the country as a whole. As a CP functionary assigned to transit put it, a transit strike was by nature a general strike and therefore a "touchy political strike." The very stakes involved, and the power that would necessarily be brought to bear by both sides, were so great that the TWU leadership and its Party advisers wanted if at all possible to avoid a showdown. [90]

Finally, added to these long-standing considerations, was an unexpected, last-minute development; on June 22, Germany invaded the Soviet Union, leading to a rapid change in the CP's view of the world situation and its own domestic tasks. The CP now sought maximum United States aid for Britain and the Soviet Union, which in turn meant renewing its support for Roosevelt, reviving the Popular Front, and at least partially subordinating domestic concerns to international ones. [91]

During the final week before the IRT and BMT contracts expired, developments occurred rapidly on two levels. Publicly both sides remained unyielding, continuing their preparations for a possible strike. At a series of mass meetings, NYCTS workers—14,000 altogether, according to the TWU—voted overwhelmingly to strike at midnight June 30 if no satisfactory agreement was reached with the Board of Transportation. City agencies and private businesses also finalized their plans for dealing with a walkout. [92] At the same time, however, out of public view, steps were being taken to avoid such an eventuality.

On June 25, Quill, Santo, and Allan Haywood secretly traveled to Washington to pursue a new tack for resolving the TWU's conflict with the city. Their strategy, quite possibly suggested by Murray, was to seek federal intervention, preferably by the National Defense Mediation Board (NDMB). The NDMB had been set up in March, as the country's military build-up accelerated, to prevent strikes or lockouts. The TWU delegation first met with William Davis, acting NDMB chairman and the arbitrator in the bus strike settlement. Davis had indicated his willingness to take up the case, but only if it was certified to the Board by Frances Perkins. [93]

Quill, Santo, Haywood, and Murray then visited the Secretary of Labor. Speaking for the TWU, Santo indicated a willingness to make major concessions in return for an extension of revised versions of the IRT and BMT contracts until such time as the city's court suit was resolved. Specifically, the TWU would drop its demand for a closed shop and any seniority provisions that violated civil service regulations.

Further acknowledging the special character of municipal transit, Santo proposed a no-strike agreement coupled with binding arbitration of any matters not settled through negotiations, either during the life of the contracts or in discussions for a new ones. According to Perkins, Santo said that the TWU "would like something very much like the Railway Labor Act written into our contract."[94]

Perkins suggested that Murray present this proposal directly to La Guardia. Murray, however, wanted Perkins to do this, and if the proposal was rejected to certify the dispute to the NDMB. Perkins replied that before she could take any action she would have to present the issue to the Cabinet and the President. What the labor group did not know was that Perkins had already determined (or assumed) that La Guardia would oppose NDMB certification, and on the previous day had asked Roosevelt for guidance. Sometime on June 25 Roosevelt replied with firm instructions: "Tell [Perkins]," he wrote,

> under no circumstances should a subway strike be certified to the Mediation Board, as the Federal Government has no jurisdiction whatsoever. Furthermore . . . in my judgement, the Board of Transportation in New York cannot enter into a contract with the subway workers.[95]

Shortly after meeting with the CIO and TWU leaders, Perkins wrote to La Guardia relaying Santo's proposals and suggesting NDMB arbitration of the "limited question of whether or not the Board of Transportation should . . . extend the life of the presently existing collective bargaining agreements" until a final court ruling was issued in the city's suit for a declaratory judgment on the legality of those contracts. Any contract extension would not include the closed shop or other clauses that conflicted with civil service regulations. Probably Perkins had not yet received Roosevelt's message when she wrote this letter. However, it is possible that she was using an empty threat of NDMB certification to pressure La Guardia to make concessions; not only did La Guardia not want third-party involvement, but when Davis had headed the New York State Mediation Board he and La Guardia had quarreled frequently.[96]

Whatever the case, on June 26 and 27, after Quill and Santo returned to New York, the outlines of a settlement were worked out in a series of meetings, letters, and conversations among Perkins, Murray, La Guardia, and Secretary of Interior Harold Ickes, all of whom were in Washington. The agreement was roughly along the lines discussed by Santo and Perkins and took the form of an exchange of telegrams between La Guardia and Murray.[97]

La Guardia's telegram, which he said along with Murray's acceptance would constitute a "memorandum of understanding," stated that pending final judicial determination of the Board of Transportations' contract-signing powers, the city would "continue the status quo under the assumed contracts," but with a series of provisos: the TWU could not strike; all hiring and promotions would be by civil service rules; and there would be no union shop. Employees could be represented by any organization of their choice, and all such organizations could confer with the Board of Transportation. Additionally, a Labor Grievance Board would be established within the Board of Transportation.

In his lengthy reply, Murray said that he would recommend TWU acceptance of the Mayor's proposal, but with a number of clarifications: to the extent possible under civil service law, contractual seniority provisions would be followed, and although the TWU would not strike until final court determination of the relevant legal issues, it was not conceding its right to do so. Murray also stated that he interpreted the Mayor's message to mean that since the city was continuing the contractual status quo, it would only negotiate with the TWU and the recognized brotherhoods, and that the Grievance Board would be given "power to make disposition of all matters affecting the ordinary labor relations between the Board of Transportation and the TWU." Finally, Murray asked that the city extend similar arrangements to the IND.

It was, to say the least, a peculiar agreement, in both form and content. If anything, it was an agreement to disagree. La Guardia simultaneously extended the conditions of the exclusive representation contracts, minus some provisons, and instituted his plan of non-preferential Board of Transportation consultations with any interested employee groups. Murray, in turn, interpreted the first half of this to negate the second half. Moreover, it was unclear what it meant to extend contractual conditions that specified in great detail pay rates, benefits, and conditions when both parties assumed that these would be improved in the near future and apparently even agreed to negotiations for that purpose. In short, each side seemed to have agreed to what it wanted all along, the CIO to a contract extension, La Guardia to no signed contract, no union shop, no strikes, and no exclusive representation. Only future events would determine what the agreement actually meant.

The exact role of the TWU in working out the final agreement was also unclear. The announcement of the exchanged telegrams was made by La Guardia, and some newspaper reports claimed the TWU leaders had learned of their contents only after the texts had been made public. Austin Hogan, however, told IND delegates to the Joint Executive Committee that TWU leaders had written Murray's message. It certainly seems likely that the TWU was involved in working out the agreement and gave its approval at every stage; Haywood was in New York acting as a CIO liaison to TWU and La Guardia; and Quill and Murray were in telephone contact. Still, the form of the agreement, an "understanding" between Murray and La Guardia rather than between the TWU and the Board of Transportation, served to emphasize its dissimilarity from a normal contract and encouraged the view, held by many, that the CIO had settled the dispute over the heads of the TWU leadership.[98]

Prior to the Murray-La Guardia agreement, the TWU had scheduled a meeting for June 29 to consider final plans for action in the event that no settlement with the city had been reached. Invited to join the union's Joint Executive Committee were representatives from the NYC CIO Council and other unions that had been cooperating with the TWU. It was to this somewhat irregular body, roughtly 400 TWU delegates and 600 non-TWU unionists, that the proposed settlement was presented.

Santo gave the main speech, reviewing the history of the dispute and explaining its resolution in as favorable light as possible. Haywood was next, dismissing rumors of differences between the TWU and the CIO. Then, before a wrap-up speech by Quill, a resolution was introduced by MacMahon to rescind the union's strike call, citing the exchanged telegrams and negotiations scheduled to begin the next day between the TWU and the Board of Transportation over wages, hours, and working conditions. The resolution was passed with but two dissenting votes.[99]

The June 29 vote, which effectively ended this round of the TWU's prolonged fight with the city, was somewhat deceptive. Although almost all of the union's cadre were willing to accept an agreement already announced and endorsed by TWU and CIO leaders, there was considerable dissatisfaction with the union's failure to strike. Many TWU activists, after nearly a full year of emotional and organizational buildup for a decisive battle, were unhappy that their leadership had settled for less than a signed contract, exclusive representation, and a closed shop. Some walked out of the Manhattan Center meeting in disgust. Maurice Ahern, who voted against the settlement, complained that "there was no provision to handle all the stooges who dropped out of the union." Once built up, strike sentiment was not easily dissipated. For years afterward the decision not to strike remained one of the union's most controversial, with many believing that a unique opportunity had been lost.[100]

The June 1941 settlement clearly failed to achieve the TWU's long-stated goal of full contractual recognition and union security. Nevertheless, even some of the TWU's harshest critics admitted that much had been won.[101] The city's claim that the TWU was an empty shell had been disproved; La Guardia had been forced to recognize, at least in practice, the TWU as the main representative of the NYCTS work force; the possibility of a contractual relationship between the TWU and the city had not been foreclosed; and steps had been taken toward improving work conditions. With its show of power and La Guardia's concessions, the TWU had positioned itself well to attract and re-attract members. In effect, the city and the union had agreed to an armed truce. As in most such cases, every prospect looked toward prolonged skirmishing and renewed conflict. The TWU's triumph was that it was still on the field of battle.

V

**"Events have abolished
all debates"**

10

WARTIME

Until the summer of 1941, the TWU steadfastly opposed the country's drift toward war. Participation in World War II, most transit workers and TWU leaders believed, would spill American blood only to strengthen the imperial powers, including Britain, Ireland's historic oppressor, while leading to a deterioration of labor's position at home. When war actually came, though, the TWU leadership and most of the rank and file strongly backed the American military effort. They did so primarily for ideological reasons, not out of narrow self-interest. Nonetheless, the war turned out to be a generally fruitful time for transit workers and the TWU.

This was not exceptional. For American workers, World War II was a time of sacrifice, but also well-being. Defense production ended the Great Depression. Weekly earnings (though not wage rates) soared, as steady work, extensive overtime, and promotional opportunities became widely available. Overcrowded cities, rationing, and consumer goods shortages made wartime living difficult. However, by the end of the war more civilian goods and services were available than in 1940. One sociologist's comment about the shipyard workers with whom she worked was applicable to the industrial work force as a whole:

> For the majority . . . the war was an experience of opportunity rather than limitation. Their wartime income was larger than ever before, and they ate more abundantly and lived more agreeably. The men of draft age were also aware that every day in the shipyard was a day not spend in a barracks or a foxhole.[1]

The war transformed labor relations. A severe labor shortage increased the bargaining power of unions. Unions, though, were forced to use that power within narrowed channels, as federal regulation of collective bargaining vastly expanded. Federal policy had two main goals, to prevent interruptions in production and hold down inflation. At the prompting of the government, both unions and businesses agreed to forgo strikes and lockouts for the duration of the war. Instead, a system of compulsory arbitration was established, administered by the National War Labor Board (NWLB), a tripartite agency with business, labor, and "public" members. NWLB guidelines, codified in the so-called Little Steel formula, limited most increases in wage rates to the rise in the cost of living since January 1941. To compensate for the internal political problems this would create for unions, the NWLB compelled employers to grant maintenance-of-membership—a modified form of the union shop—to unions that abided by the no-strike pledge.[2]

The ideological glue for this arrangement was patriotism. Unlike most American wars, World War II had broad public support. Most workers and union leaders rallied to the war effort, accepting the idea that sacrifices were necessary for victory. Although during the latter part of the war, strikes protesting speed-up, working conditions, disciplinary action, and the upgrading of black workers became common, the vast majority of workers continued to support the principle of the no-strike pledge. At least on the ideological level, the war brought an unusual degree of national consensus.[3]

Like many other industries, transit faced both a wartime labor shortage and an economic revival. As a result of gasoline and tire rationing, urban automobile travel fell nationally by 25% during the war. Combined with population influx to industrial centers and virtual full employment, this led to a 55% rise in public transportation use. On the NYCTS, between 1941 and 1945 ridership rose a smaller, but still considerable 8.3%, while the number of hourly employees fell by 5.2%.[4]

Wartime political conditions, like economic conditions, were favorable to the TWU. During the war, the TWU was able to rebuild old alliances and assume a position of greater power in New York City politics. Union leaders also felt less constrained in publicly expressing their left-wing views.

The war opened up opportunities for the TWU. The union proved remarkable adept at seizing them. By the time the war ended, the TWU had significantly improved earnings and working conditions for New York transit workers, while strengthening its own institutional position. In addition, as will be discussed in the next chapter, the TWU finally succeeded in expanding beyond the New York transit industry, truly becoming a national union.

Following the German invasion of the Soviet Union, the TWU moved away from its prior opposition to both United States involvement in the European war and federal intervention in labor relations to facilitate defense production. In mid-July 1941, the TWU International Executive Board endorsed a strengthened defense effort and aid to "subjected nations and the peoples defending their homelands," but stressed the need for preserving labor's rights and social priorities at home. At the September 1941 TWU convention, after extensive debate and more-than-usual opposition, Roosevelt's foreign policy and defense program were fully backed. In late October the TWU took part in a massive New York rally, addressed by AFL and CIO representatives, La Guardia, Marcantonio, and Quill, that called for the repeal of the Neutrality Act, aid to the Allies, and the opening of a Western Front. By November the union was attacking "isolationists" and "appeasers." That fall, with the cooperation of La Guardia's office, the union established a Civilian

Defense Council. Thus by December 1941 the TWU had already adopted an interventionist stand. Immediately after the attack on Pearl Harbor, it called on its members to unite behind the war effort, asserting that "events have abolished all debates. The hour for action is here."[5]

Over the next three years, most TWU members heeded this call, strongly supporting the war effort and willingly making sacrifices to speed the allied victory. Transit workers, like other workers, supported the war for a variety of reasons. Some saw it in Popular Front terms, as a war against fascism, in defense of democracy and the gains of the New Deal era, as a prelude to a new, more progressive world order. The TWU actively promoted this view; Hogan, for instance, called the conflict "a war of national liberation for the peoples of the earth, Ireland included." Similar interpretations were promoted by such national political figures as Vice President Henry Wallace and Wendell Willkie, though without the Hibernian twist. Others had more traditional, nationalist motives for supporting the war. The Japanese attack had changed the war from a battle to defend others into a defense of the homeland, mobilizing what historian Merle Curti called "the 'my-country-right-or-wrong' attitude." Racism also was a factor; Pearl Harbor led to a surge of anti-Japanese feelings. Beyond such abstract reasons, transit workers had personal motives for supporting the war. Throughout the 1930s the transit work force had been remarkably stable, so that by the early 40s it was an aging group; many TWU members had children in the armed forces. This undoubtedly contributed to the tremendous outpouring of patriotic sentiment. The once-strong anti-war sentiment among transit workers largely dissipated after Pearl Harbor. What remained of it became subterranean.[6]

Many transit workers themselves served in the armed services. By May 1945, some 5,380 Local 100 members had been or were in the military and seventy-six had been killed. Some were draftees, though many transit workers received deferments as vital war workers. The rest were volunteers, including quite a few older men. With their specialized skills, transit workers—especially shop and powerhouse workers—were of particular value to the military. Large numbers of TWU members served in the Army Engineers, the Engineer Aviation Battalions, and the Navy Seabees. Some TWU members with seagoing experience joined the merchant marine. Skills of other kinds were used as well; Patrick J. Reilly, an ALP activist from the IRT, was assigned to giving army orientation classes, which he turned into political education sessions promoting a Popular Front view of the war.[7]

The TWU worked hard to back the war effort and associate itself with the surge of wartime patriotism. The TWU helped sponsor pro-war rallies, adorned leaflets with the American flag, and even portrayed bargaining demands in patriotic terms, as "Victory" programs and efforts to get "In Step with the President!" During his 1943 City Council campaign, Quill often began street meetings with a recording of Kate Smith singing "God Bless America." The union was extremely active in sponsoring blood drives and war bond sales. At 148th Street, for instance, it fought local supervisors to win permission to sell bonds on the shop floor and hold war bond rallies on NYCTS property. Some TWU bond salesmen used their positions simultaneously to recruit workers into the union, helping to rebuild its strength. Great pains were taken to keep in touch with TWU members in the armed services, who were given free union membership and sent the union newspaper every month.

Letters from workers in the military were prominently featured in the paper, as were "Honor Roll" lists of men and women in the service. A number of bills to help transit workers in the service—for example, by protecting their seniority and promotion rights—were promoted by the union.[8]

The TWU cooperated, and sometimes even took the lead, in keeping the New York transit lines operating smoothly under difficult wartime conditions, as ridership rose and serious material and personnel shortages developed. The labor shortage was a sharp change from the prewar period; as late as mid-1940 the NYCTS had been swamped with job applications while already having a surplus of workers as a result of el demolitions. With the war, not only were thousands of transit workers lost to the armed services, but skilled craftsmen could easily find much higher paying jobs in war industries, and many did so.

To meet the growing crisis, the Board of Transportation began hiring a large number of provisional employees, but these workers lacked needed skills and often quit after only a short time. The NYCTS and some of the surface lines also hired women (including some black women) as bus and trolley drivers and ticket agents, again on a provisional basis. However, this effort was at best half-hearted. The Board of Transportation did not begin hiring women until 1943 and then declared that there were "about 16,500 [mechanical and operational] railroad jobs for which women are not fit or available." At the war's end the NYCTS alone had 3,000 vacancies.[9]

To facilitate operations under these circumstances, the TWU cooperated with employers in dealing with a variety of manpower, training, and scheduling problems. The union, for example, sometimes overlooked overtime regulations and allowed reductions in the number of workers required to perform given tasks. Transit workers voluntarily toiled for very long hours during the war. NYC Omnibus drivers, for instance, customarily worked weeks of seventy hours or more. On at least one occasion, the union even took upon itself the job of enforcing worker discipline. In July 1942 the officers of the TWU Third Avenue branch announced that trolley and bus drivers who departed from their schedules would be placed on internal union trial for undermining the defense effort. Because TWU activists believed the war to be just and necessary, the union did not have to be coerced into temporarily sacrificing prewar standards.[10]

The invasion of the Soviet Union led not only to a reversal of the TWU's stand on the war, but also a reorientation of its domestic political outlook. Following the lead of the CP, the TWU moved to rebuild alliances with liberal and centrist forces that had been broken during the Hitler-Stalin pact period. However, the union only reluctantly accepted the CP's implementation of this revived Popular Front policy in the arena of New York electoral politics.

Before June 1941, the ALP's left and right factions had been preparing for a September primary fight. The right was supporting La Guardia for reelection, the left searching for an alternative, possibly Marcantonio. Following the German attack on the Soviet Union, the CP forces within the ALP reversed course, endorsing La Guardia and offering to withdraw their primary candidates and create a joint slate with the right, an offer that was spurned. TWU leaders, however, like

BMT trolley operators relaxing in the Canarsie Depot in 1944.

Marcantonio, Joe Curran, and some other left-wingers, were slow to go along with the new line. They were particularly upset that they had not been consulted in the decision to back the Mayor.[11]

The union's relationship with the city administration had improved a bit after the June 1941 crisis. Negotiations—or discussions—were held between the union and the Board of Transportation, and in August the Board announced a series of wage increases worth over $5 million. Under the Board's plan, wages were standarized, with a maximum of six rates for any given occupational category. Also, working hours were significantly reduced, leaving only BMT trolley and bus operators with schedules of over 48 hours a week. Although the wage increases were three times those proposed by the Board before the negotiations had begun, the TWU still felt that they were too small and that there were other deficiencies in the package. Nevertheless, the union membership voted to accept the increases under protest and the TWU and the Board agreed to discuss the Board's proposed revisions of its rules and regulations, so as to bring them into conformity with the expired IRT and BMT contracts.[12]

These gains did not erase the TWU's bitter antagonism toward La Guardia for his handling of transit labor relations. Prior to July 1941, the TWU had been considering a number of plans to unseat the Mayor. One was proposed by Paul O'Dwyer, the younger, more liberal brother of the eventual Democratic nominee, Brooklyn District Attorney William O'Dwyer. Paul O'Dwyer wanted the Democrats to fund a challenge to La Guardia in the ALP primary, believing that without the labor line La Guardia would lose a three-way battle to William O'Dwyer in the general election. Although the plan fell through when William O'Dwyer and his Democratic backers balked, the TWU remained reluctant to endorse La Guardia, both because of labor relations issues and the still-considerable isolationist sentiment before Pearl Harbor among the union's Irish members. (La Guardia was strongly interventionist.)[13]

In mid-October the Local 100 Joint Executive Committee finally endorsed La Guardia by a 643 to 23 vote, a week after a similar move by the NYC CIO Council. The one-sided tally was more a testament to the body's loyalty to its leadership than to its enthusiasm for La Guardia; TWU leaders knew perfectly well that most transit workers would vote for O'Dwyer, who had a strong, pro-labor record. TWU leaders backed La Guardia because not to have done so would have meant a break with the CP and a further strain in the union's relationship with the Mayor if he was re-elected. In justifying their position to the membership, Quill and Hogan portrayed the election as a fight over the restoration of Tammany, avoiding praise for the Mayor or attacks on O'Dwyer. At the same time, they used the union's endorsement of La Guardia and O'Dwyer's active efforts to win the transit vote to pressure the Mayor into finally setting up a NYCTS Grievance Board, as promised in the June settlement. [14]

Given the mayoralty situation, the TWU concentrated its electoral activity on the concurrent City Council races, working through the "New York Trade Union Committee to Elect Labor's Candidates," a left-wing vehicle, rather than the ALP. The committee, chaired by Hogan, backed a number of independent and ALP candidates, including two TWU organizers, Eugene Connolly and William Grogan, and Adam Clayton Powell, Jr., who was making a bid to become the city's first black Councilman.[15]

It is impossible to tell how TWU members actually voted in November. La Guardia was re-elected in a close contest, with his margin of victory provided by a very large ALP turnout. His support among Irish voters, however, dropped significantly, to the lowest level in any of his three successful mayoral campaigns. The labor-backed Council candidates did well, with both Connolly and Powell elected. (Grogan lost.) In Brooklyn, the CP elected its first Councilman, Peter Cacchione.[16]

By this time, the TWU was beginning to be affected by the war build-up in another way, the loss of its own personnel. Over the next three years, three members of the TWU's IEB, eight past or present members of the Local 100 Executive Board, and numerous International Representatives, Local 100 organizers, and section officials were to serve in the armed services, leading to significant changes in the union hierarchy. Ironically, the net result was to strengthen the TWU bureaucracy and draw it closer to the rank and file.[17]

The first major departure, and the most significant, was John Santo's. At the TWU's September 1941 convention, Santo announced that he would not run for re-election and was leaving the union altogether for personal reasons. Although at the time he did not elaborate, what happened was this. Santo originally had entered the United States on a student visa, which eventually expired. According to Santo, over the years he had repeatedly applied for naturalization but was always turned down. In the meantime he simply stayed in the country illegally. When the draft was instituted in 1940, he claimed on his registration form that he was a citizen.

A federal investigation of Santo's immigration status was begun in mid-1941. Political motives were probably at work. During the Hitler-Stalin pact period the federal government stepped up its surveillance and harassment of organizations close to the CP. In December 1940 the FBI initiated an extensive investigation of the TWU that was to continue for years. Furthermore, the investigation of Santo was started at the time that the TWU was threatening to strike the NYCTS to force it to renew the IRT and BMT pacts. Learning that he soon would be arrested, Santo decided to leave the union and fight his possible deportation from the outside. [18]

The TWU did not abandon Santo. At the September convention, startled delegates heaped praise on Santo, many in deeply emotional terms. They also voted to pay him his salary for another year. After Santo was arrested on October 7 and deportation proceedings begun, Santo Defense Committees were formed on all levels of the union, from the International down to individual sections. [19]

Once the United States entered the war, the government dropped its active prosecution of Santo's case, again presumably for political reasons, and in June 1942 Santo volunteered for the army. While he was awaiting induction, the TWU's IEB hired Santo for the newly created post of National Director of Organization. Two months later Santo was sworn in as a private. It was a sign of the rapidly changing times that one of the speakers at the huge farewell party the TWU threw for Santo, so recently a marked man, was William O'Dwyer, on leave from his new post as an army major. Even the Lieutenant Governor sent his best wishes. For the next three years Santo was away, much of the time in Alaska. Although elected National Director of Organization at the TWU's 1943 convention, he played little role in the union's wartime affairs. [20]

Shortly before Santo left, Austin Hogan entered the army as well. Like Santo, for the next several years he was largely uninvolved with the TWU; while serving with an engineering unit in the Pacific he was seriously wounded and subsequently spent many months in a Hawaii hospital recuperating. [21] Thus the TWU lost two of its four top leaders, not insignificantly the two who had been the earliest leaders of the union and who had come from the CP rather than the industry.

While Santo and Hogan were away, their responsibilities were divided between two men. Both of their official positions were filled by MacMahon, who became the International's Secretary-Treasurer and Local 100's acting president. This was a major change for MacMahon. Prior to 1941, although he was the TWU's vice president, his main responsibility was for the BMT. Usually working out of the union's Brooklyn office, he was physically removed from the center of action. With the war, MacMahon's exile ended. He quickly proved more forceful than Hogan had ever been in running Local 100. He also became deeply involved in the union's out-of-town organizing and developed closer ties to "the ninth floor"—the national CP leadership. Increasingly, MacMahon saw himself, along with Quill, as *the* center of the union. [22]

It was not, however, MacMahon who primarily took over Santo's role as liaison between the CP and the union. That job was filled by Martin Young, an experienced, well-connected CP functionary who was put on the union's payroll at roughly the same time that Santo left. This was the only time after the TWU was founded that the CP sent in one of its own to act, in Forge's words, as "the guardian of the line."

Although Young did some trade union work, his main responsibilities were political, as an adviser, trouble-shooter, and contact with the CP. It was a potentially awkward situation. Quill for one at first resented Young's presence. Young, however, proved adept at his work. By deferring to Quill and making himself generally useful, he soon ingratiated himself with those who mattered. The TWU leadership was still remarkable parochial, even within the left-wing empire. Young opened up new worlds and made available untapped resources. Quill, for example, was amazed and delighted when Young arranged for novelist Howard Fast to ghost-write an important speech Quill was to deliver.

Most TWU activists had no idea who Young really was, though his conspiratorial manner raised more than one set of eyebrows. Furthermore, his political interventions sometimes raised objections among those who were in the know. Still, Young managed his job with a remarkable degree of success. Perhaps the best measure is that in later years, when the union was torn apart over the role of the CP, the resentment many felt toward the Party never spilt over into personal resentment toward Young.[23]

The absence of Hogan and Santo, combined with the TWU's wartime expansion outside of New York transit, opened up room for secondary leaders to assume greater responsibility. Some, like Forge, John Cassidy, and Matthew Kearns, became the heads of virtual fiefdoms, as the International expanded into new geographic regions and industries. Others, like Gus Faber, Peter MacLachlan, and Matthew Guinan, took on increasing responsibility for Local 100 affairs. To institutionalize this diffusion of power, in 1943 both the International and Local 100 executive boards were expanded and the number of Local 100 officers increased.

With so many union leaders away in the armed services, even on lower levels of the Local 100 hierarchy there was an opening of the ranks. Of the thirty-one members of the Local 100 Executive Board elected in 1943 only sixteen had served on previous boards. At the International convention that year, debate was not dominated by the same group which had played the leading roles at all the previous International gatherings. There were also quite a few new Local 100 staffers.

The net result of all this was to somewhat diminish the cliquish character of the TWU leadership. As unionists more recently working in actual transit jobs took on positions of responsibility, the staff became less sectarian and elitist. Also, more diverse viewpoints, especially within Local 100, were now institutionally represented. All in all, it made for a leadership more in touch with the views and concerns of the membership.[24]

The absence of Hogan and Santo also contributed to Quill's growing sense of confidence and self-importance. Whatever residues of dependence, insecurity, and deference he had retained in the prewar years dissipated with the temporary departures of his early mentors. During the war the TWU functioned as smoothly and effectively—perhaps even more so—as it had during the prewar period. Although MacMahon liked to think of Quill as a charismatic figurehead and himself as the nuts-and-bolts leader of the union, the fact of the matter was that Quill was gaining greater competence and experience in every aspect of the union's operation, includ-

ing organizing, bargaining, relations with government agencies, and internal administration, in addition to what had always been his strongest suit, rallying the rank and
file. Quill's realization that if need be both he himself and the TWU as a whole
could manage well without Santo and Hogan had no immediate effect, but in the
long run it was to be of profound importance.[25]

Quill's confidence and stature were bolstered by his activities and contacts outside
the union. During the war Quill improved his relations with both the liberal wing of
the Democratic party and elements of the Catholic hierarchy, including New York
Archbishop Francis Spellman. With the help of Gerald O'Reilly he also launched a
major effort to parlay his union position into a position of leadership in the New
York Irish community. In this, he had several interlocking goals: to win stronger
Irish support for the war effort; to unite the various Irish-American organizations
under progressive leadership; and to begin a campaign to place the issue of Irish
unification on the agenda for postwar peace talks. A conference to promote this
program was held in December 1943, attended by representatives of the United Irish
Counties Association and its affiliated groups. Half a million copies of Quill's
keynote address were later distributed. Near the end of the war, however, Quill fell
out of favor with many Irish activists when in a column in the *Transport Bulletin* he
bitterly attacked Irish Premier Eamon De Valera for visiting the German Embassy
in Dublin to pay his condolences after Hitler's suicide. As in his earlier speech,
Quill not only broke with the Irish government, but implicitly with the IRA as well,
making it clear he thought that Irish unity could not be achieved by military means
and pointedly paying homage to the fallen leaders of both sides of the Irish civil war.
However, it was not Quill's position on the IRA but his denunciation of the head of
the Irish state that led the United Irish Counties Association to condemn him and
the Gaelic Athletic Association to boycott a TWU field day.[26]

In 1943 Quill triumphantly re-entered electoral politics. In the late summer of
that year the Local 100 Joint Executive Committee, with but one dissenting vote,
endorsed a plan for Quill to run as an independent for a Bronx City Council seat.
Quill neither sought nor received ALP backing; the Bronx County ALP was still
controlled by the right wing of the party, and it was unlikely that he could have won
its endorsement. Nonetheless, Quill's campaign won broader backing than his
earlier efforts. In addition to the usual labor and left-wing groups, he was endorsed
by La Guardia, the United Irish Counties Association, the Police Benevolent Association, and a host of other organizations. His platform was a combination of win-
the-war and social reform programs, including staggered work hours, strictly enforced price and rent controls, day care, federal health insurance, pay increases and
collective bargaining for city workers, strengthened laws against religious and racial
discrimination, and post-war economic planning. In the course of the campaign, a
major registration drive was conducted, two and a half million pieces of literature
distributed, and 70 indoor meetings and 220 street rallies held. Quill was easily
elected, winning the most first-choice votes of any Bronx Council candidate.[27]

Because of the particularities of the Bronx situation, Quill had not run on the
ALP line, but in general during the war more TWU activists got involved with the
labor party, as opposed to simply aiding periodic Council races by Quill and
Grogan. Both Forge and MacMahon, for instance, became vice chairmen of the

ALP organizations in their home boroughs, Queens and Brooklyn respectively. TWU members also helped out in the campaigns of selected liberal candidates; in 1943, for example, Quill organized an Irish committee for Marcantonio after the Congressman's district was redrawn to include a significant number of Irish voters, and transit workers campaigned for Adam Clayton Powell, Jr. in his successful 1944 Congressional race.[28]

TWU members were also involved in the long-simmering ALP faction fight that came to a head in early 1944. The immediate issue was the ALP's relationship with the Democratic party. Sidney Hillman and the CP sought to tie the ALP more closely to Roosevelt and the Democrats, while their opponents wanted greater ALP independence. After the ALP right rejected Hillman's bid to turn the party into the New York arm of the newly established CIO Political Action Committee (CIO-PAC), which was working closely with the Democrats, Hillman joined forces with the CP-left in pushing for a showdown in a scheduled March 1944 primary. Although Quill and Joe Curran resigned from the ALP State Executive Committee to avoid riling those worried about CP influence in the party, the TWU took an active part in the "Committee for a United Labor Party," the Hillman-left vehicle. After a bitter campaign, the United Labor forces emerged victorious, winning control in sixty of the sixty-two New York City Assembly districts and finally defeating the right in the Bronx. The defeated Old Guard forces immediately left the ALP to form the Liberal party, opening the way for Hillman's control of the labor party and for greater involvement by all the CIO unions, including those with CP ties.[29]

The TWU's wartime politics can best be described as left-center. In the main, the union strongly backed Roosevelt and took its political cues from the national CIO. However, it stressed certain particular concerns of the Popular Front, such as the call for a second front, Henry Wallace's vision of a century of the common man, and postwar decolonization. The union also took a much stronger stand than ever before against anti-Semitism and racism, both within the union and in the society-at-large.[30]

In the wartime political atmosphere created by the United States-Soviet alliance, TWU leaders dropped some of their extreme caution in publicly identifying with the CP or the Soviet Union. At the union's 1941 convention, for example, Quill called for Earl Browder's release from prison; in April 1942 he addressed a "Free Browder" rally; and at the TWU's 1943 convention he spoke warmly of the Communist leader. At that convention, for the first time praise was heard for Soviet trade unions, though from invited speakers rather than TWU officers. Several times during the war the TWU newspaper ran articles on the Moscow subway. None of these were such bold steps, but they would not have occurred before June 1941. Still, there remained firm limits that neither the TWU nor the CP were about to breach; when three younger TWU leaders attending a CP national training school put up a fight to break with past practice and openly announce their Communist affiliations, they were convinced to abandon such designs.[31]

The TWU's wartime stance toward the Catholic Church was complex. On the one hand, ACTU and other Catholic critics of the union were denounced more vehemently than ever before. On the other hand, for the first time Quill began wrapping himself in a robe of Catholic piety. For every step toward more open leftism, Quill took a symmetrical step toward parading his Catholicism. Thus, for example, he concluded his praise for Browder at the 1943 convention by saying that "we believe in kneeling and praying and adoring our God as we please while others do it another way." Similarly, in the commemorative program for Local 100's tenth anniversary celebration a picture of Paul Robeson was balanced by a picture of Quill and Father Rice. Quill seemed to want to bathe in the glory of both Rome and Moscow. Several times, both publicly and privately, he expressed the hope that some understanding could be reached between the two.[32]

Quill's more open display of both leftism and religiosity was symptomatic of a more general phenomenon. At the same time that the TWU was somewhat more boldly identifying with the left, its leaders, especially Quill, were having a number of disagreements with the CP. The most important involved TWU out-of-town organizing drives: in a number of instances local CP officials discouraged TWU efforts, especially where jurisdictional disputes were involved, in the name of national unity. In most cases, the TWU simply ignored this advice. Other disputes arose as well. In 1942, for example, when the ALP nominated its own gubernatorial candidate, Hillman and the CP joined Roosevelt in backing a conservative Democrat. This was too much for the top TWU leaders, who refused to follow the lead of what they called among themselves the Rosie O'Grady family, Rose Wortis and her CP associates. The union sat out the election.

Later on, in 1948, for factional reasons Quill greatly exaggerated the importance of these disagreements. Most TWU leaders, including Quill, still respected the CP and generally accepted its views and advice. Quill remained personally close to Browder. When there were disagreements, both sides usually displayed considerable flexibility, and differences were patched over. Nonetheless, these wartime incidents indicated that neither the TWU nor Quill felt obligated to follow every CP directive or totally accept all of its views. If the TWU chose to go its own way on a particular issue, short of an open confrontation, there was little the CP could do.[33]

The TWU's patriotic stance enhanced rank-and-file support for the union's leadership. In general, the wartime period was one of internal union harmony, so much so that one Local 100 officer remembered "a certain let-down in the union at the time." In early 1942 the administration-backed slate of Hogan, Joe Fody, Faber, and William Grogan won the Local 100 officers election by a four-to-one margin over John Gallagher, James O'Keefe, Maurice Ahern, and James Flatley. Two years later the local's officers were re-elected unopposed. Most of the union's prewar critics kept quiet for the duration of the war.[34]

Nevertheless, there remained pockets of dissent. There were those who had always opposed the TWU leadership on anti-Communist grounds. There were those not fully reconciled to United States involvement in the war, mostly diehard Christian Fronters or pure Irish nationalists. And there were those dissatisfied with the economic gains and representation provided by the union. The one major wartime challenge to the TWU leadership tested the depth of such sentiment. It also pitted the policies of the CIO against those of its most potent critic, Mine Workers' president and former CIO leader John L. Lewis.[35]

The TWU's ardent support for the war, its renewed backing of the Roosevelt administration, its no-strike pledge, and its acceptance of massive federal intervention in labor relations brought it in line with the mainstream of the CIO. This was a dramatic change from the situation before July 1941, when both the CP and Lewis forces were becoming increasingly isolated within the CIO. However, while the CP wing of the CIO moved toward the political center, Lewis was charting his own, very different course.

In November 1940, Lewis had followed through on his pledge to resign from the CIO presidency if the rank and file of the federation did not follow his lead in backing Wendell Willkie's Presidential bid. By then, Lewis's alienation from Roosevelt was thoroughgoing; he believed the President had failed to reciprocate fully labor's support, he considered the New Deal an economic and social failure, and he opposed the administration's move away from isolationism. Following Pearl Harbor, Lewis ended his criticism of American foreign policy, backed the war effort, and offered a no-strike pledge. But unlike most CIO leaders, he opposed anything more than minimal government interference in wartime labor relations. Distressed by the increasingly close links between labor and the federal government, Lewis sought to push the union movement toward greater political independence. In effect, he reverted to the brand of militant business unionism he had practiced before the Great Depression. In 1942 Lewis even pulled the Mine Workers out of the CIO, which was becoming increasingly corporativist in its outlook.

The following year, by leading a series of national mine strikes, Lewis challenged the administration's entire wartime labor policy, including the no-strike pledge, the authority of the NWLB, and its "Little Steel formula." Lewis's course terrified the leaders of the CIO, who were attempting with only limited success to keep their own, increasingly restive members from striking. Although Lewis was vilified by the press and intensely disliked by much of the public for what was seen as undermining the war effort, he won the admiration of many CIO members. The threat Lewis posed to the CIO was brought home to TWU leaders when members of a small TWU local in Akron, Ohio, staged a wildcat strike. The TWU International representative on the scene, John Ryan, blamed the walkout on "a few 'garage lawyers' and admirers of Lewis." Ryan found it "very difficult to explain to [the Akron workers] why strike action is wrong at this time" or to "expose the Lewis gang as phonies." In addition to his influence on industrial workers, Lewis had a weapon for directly attacking the CIO, District 50 of the UMW, a catch-all unit that represented non-mining workers. Lewis's "private labor movement" not only organized unrepresented workers, it raided unions in which the rank and file was balking at CIO or AFL acceptance of wartime labor regulations.[36]

District 50 became involved in the New York transit industry as the result of a long-standing political situation within the TWU. Ever since the TWU had won recognition, opposition to the incumbent leadership had been strongest on the Manhattan and Bronx surface lines, where the union administration had failed to build a strong base, the work force was overwhelmingly Irish, there were few leftists, and articulate anti-Communists held office in several sections. As time went on, dissident bus and trolley leaders grew increasingly frustrated; though repeatedly re-elected to section posts, as the 1942 Local 100 elections once again showed, the union's structure made it unlikely that they would ever achieve positions of leadership above the local executive board level. Unification exacerbated existing tensions;

Local 100 continued to allocate its executive board seats as if the union shop was in effect on the IRT and BMT, but since in reality membership on those lines had significantly declined, the other members of the local, including the trolley and bus workers, were proportionately under-represented.[37]

In the early spring of 1942, a number of oppositionists, including James Flatley, John Gallagher, and Patrick Kennedy, decided that their only hope for getting out from under left-wing domination and achieving power on their own was to pull the bus and trolley workers out of the TWU. Accordingly, Kennedy arranged for a meeting with two District 50 organizers and a UMW executive board member to discuss chartering a new local and applying for a representation election. They chose District 50 primarily because of Lewis's enormous prestige among New York transit workers, though the union's prewar isolationism may have been a factor as well.

What neither UMW officials nor the TWU dissidents knew was that District 50's office secretary in New York was a leftist who was informing the TWU leadership of these developments, enabling Quill to set an elaborate trap. On the day of the scheduled meeting, Quill, MacMahon, Forge, and Walter Case hid in a van parked outside the District 50 offices, while up the block were assembled a large group of TWU members along with reporters and photographers from *PM* and the *Daily Worker*. Sometime after Kennedy, Gallagher, and Hugh McCann, an IRA veteran in Gallagher's section, were seen entering the building, the Quill group burst in. The second, larger group followed, running into Flatley and Joseph McGarr, president of the NYC Omnibus Holy Name Society, also on their way to the meeting.

Upstairs, things were not quite what the TWU leaders expected, since two of the UMW officials had to skip the meeting and the third, a black organizer named Henry Johnson, had not yet arrived. Undeterred, Quill ripped out the phone and then, in an act of symbolic patricide, took Lewis's picture off the wall and smashed it to the floor. When Johnson did arrive, ugly words were exchanged, including, according to Gallagher, racial epithets from Quill. If true, this was ironic indeed—District 50 had sent a black man to organize the TWU right, only to be denounced in racist terms by the TWU left.

In spite of the success of its raid, the TWU leadership found the affair troubling: Kennedy, Gallagher, and Flatley, after all, were elected section officers, and District 50 had just the combination that might seriously challenge the TWU—militant industrial unionism, an isolationist legacy, and Lewis. Quill argued that the issues involved were not trade union ones, but attitudes toward the war, virtually accusing District 50 of treason. He also denounced Lewis for trying to "rule or ruin," precisely the words he was to use six years later against the CP. The TWU participants in the aborted meeting were suspended from their union posts and put on union trial, but acquitted since the raiding party had arrived before any discussions with District 50 had taken place. In November 1942, the TWU got the Third Avenue Railway to agree to a four cents an hour wage increase, even though the existing contract was not due to expire for seven months.[38]

The TWU leadership made a special effort to undermine its opponents in John Gallagher's section, the Kingsbridge barn of the Third Avenue, perhaps the strongest dissident center within the TWU. The first step was the appointment of William Grogan as an administrator to run the section temporarily. A more permanent political solution, however, was needed. Quill soon found one in the person of Matthew Guinan. Guinan, who has been the Kingsbridge section's secretary since its founding, had worked closely with Gallagher, was personally conservative, and was part of a deeply relgious family (all three of his daughters became nuns, as did Gallagher's daughter). He was also extremely cautious, never openly committing himself to either the Gallagher group or the Local 100 leadership.

Unable to gain control of the Third Avenue membership, especially the Kingsbridge section, through inserted leftist organizers, in 1943 Quill offered Guinan a job as a staff organizer assigned to the Third Avenue. By that time Gallagher had been drafted, eliminating one possible obstacle. To overcome Guinan's reluctance to be associated with the left, Quill assured him that he would personally attest to the membership that Guinan was not a Communist. Quill also knew that Guinan's family was financially hard-pressed; accordingly he arranged for the union job to bring with it a substantial increase in pay and a union car. Guinan accepted, and in December 1943 he was placed on the administration's uncontested Local 100 officer slate as second vice president, a newly created post. It was thus in Quill's accommodation to the right that Guinan's rise in the TWU began, to culminate years later in the International presidency.[39]

In spite of these moves, and another round of contractual improvements, the Third Avenue remained an opposition center. In December 1943 the only successful anti-administration executive board candidates came from the line, Philip Davis, Thomas Keane, and Maurice Greaney. Keane and Greaney, both trolley drivers, had been union pioneers and long-time leaders of their sections. At the 1943 convention they were the most outspoken critical voices, opposing a resolution calling for a second front and pushing for the election rather than appointment of organizers. Nevertheless, along with Davis, they pledged their loyalty to the union and Quill. Quill was convinced that the Third Avenue situation was under control.[40]

He was wrong. In early July 1944, Greaney, Davis, Keane, and four other Third Avenue section officers joined with District 50 in a new effort to pull the line's workers out of the TWU. Within weeks they collected enough cards to file with the SLRB for a representation election. At the request of the TWU, the vote was scheduled for August 29, much earlier than District 50 had hoped for. Both sides threw considerable resources into the ensuing campaign.

Although the District 50 group had some criticisms of Third Avenue working conditions and internal TWU procedures, the main issues were political: CIO-PAC's support of the Democratic party; the UMW's wartime strike policy versus the CIO's no-strike pledge; Quill's political activity and allegedly insincere Catholicism; and, in Quill's words, "the 'Red' issue, the 'Black' issue, and the whole question of President Roosevelt and Irish neutrality." The TWU was helped by a timely War Labor Board decision approving an already negotiated, retroactive Third Avenue contract that provided substantial improvements in benefits and pay. Quill also pulled off a characteristic stunt right before the election; District 50 had scheduled a mass meeting for a Manhattan ballroom, but the TWU sent men to the nearby subway and trolley stops to tell those arriving that the gathering had been canceled. At the same time, so many TWU supporters went to the ballroom that they effectively took over the meeting.

When the votes were counted, the TWU won easily, 2,118 to 772. The Third Avenue Railway promptly fired Greaney, Davis, and Keane, apparently as a result of a TWU strike threat. With the help of another set of contractual improvements in 1945, the splits in the Third Avenue branch were largely overcome. When John Gallagher returned from the army at the war's end, he found his old section united and the union leadership "burning the bosses asses" as never before.[41]

The TWU's victory over District 50 was an important endorsement of the transit union leadership and the CIO. It was also a measure of the TWU's success at drawing the heavily Irish Third Avenue workers into the New Deal. Quill wrote Phil Murray that the election "to our minds, is an indication of how the Irish vote will go in relation to Roosevelt and I can say, it is very encouraging." Though Lewis's wartime reversion to voluntarism attracted a sizable bloc of disgruntled TWU members, most transit workers preferred the TWU's militant identification with the war effort, even with the limitations it entailed.[42]

Local 100's wartime bargaining involved two separate sets of problems. On the private surface lines, the union faced essentially the same problems as most unions throughout the country, winning the maximal contractual improvements possible without striking, and getting its contracts approved by the War Labor Board. On the NYCTS, the situation was different, for there the status of the TWU remained unclear and no regular bargaining framework was established. Thus the union had simultaneously to fight for immediate improvements and institutionalized collective bargaining.

Overall, the TWU did well in the private sector. Wage rates were increased, the number of years needed to reach top rates diminished, paid checking-in and swing time introduced, and overtime and vacations improved. Although the TWU failed to achieve certain objectives, most importantly the establishment of pension plans, its gains were sufficient to reverse a prewar situation: while formerly pay and conditions on the IRT and BMT were generally best in the city, during the war they were surpassed on the large private lines.

NYC Omnibus was representative; the top hourly rate for the company's bus drivers went from 94 cents in 1941 to $1.04 in 1945. In addition, workers at NYC Omnibus and several other companies received hourly bonuses under the "Vincent formula," a device the NWLB allowed to circumvent its own basic guidelines. With the bonuses, long hours, and improved overtime provisions, there were proportionately greater increases in weekly and yearly earnings than in basic hourly rates. By 1944, the average Omnibus wage employee was earning $57.55 a week, compared with a national average for street railway and bus employees of $49.71. (The average manufacturing production worker that year earned $45.70 a week, at an average hourly rate of $1.01.) On most of the private lines, TWU-negotiated wage increases considerably exceeded those permitted under the "Little Steel formula," a testament to the union's skill in designing compensation packages and marshaling them through federal labor agencies.[43] During the war years Local 100 also signed its first contracts with several small bus companies, including the Bee Lines on Long Island and Jamaica Bus in Queens.[44]

One reason the TWU was able to achieve these successes was that transit company profits increased substantially during the war. Ridership, and therefore revenues, went up significantly, while little new capital investment was possible, equipment utilization was high, and non-labor costs were held down by price controls. One brokerage house, in recommending the purchase of Third Avenue Railway securities, noted that "the War economy is proving of great benefit to [New York] transit companies." Under these circumstances, the companies were more willing than before to make concessions, especially since they knew that the NWLB would ultimately limit the increases in their labor costs no matter what the contracts they initially signed called for. This knowledge, combined with the union's acceptance of the no-strike pledge, led to increased use of arbitration. Before the war, Local 100 had rarely accepted arbitration; during it, it repeatedly accepted or itself proposed arbitration, generally with results it found satisfactory.[45]

The situation on the NYCTS was more complex. The July 1941 crisis had ended with the city agreeing that until its test of the legality of municipal union contracts was resolved, most of the basic provisions of the IRT and BMT contracts would be extended, but not the closed shop or exclusive recognition. In the interim, after consulting with all interested parties, including the TWU, the Board of Transportation would make periodic adjustments in wages and conditions.

In the months that followed, TWU leaders felt that at least limited progress was being made. The September 1941 pay increases, though far short of what the TWU wanted, represented a step forward. Over the course of the next year, the Board made additional adjustments to deal with inequities. Porters, for example, had swing shifts ended, and the lowest paid among them were given bonuses. Starting in October 1941 there was a series of conferences between the TWU and the Board to discuss what was to be a comprehensive new set of working rules. Also, in November, the Board, as promised by La Guardia, set up a Labor Grievance Board composed of three outside members.

Shortly after Pearl Harbor the city administration, with the assent of the TWU and other unions involved, postponed its court test of municipal union contracts for the duration for the war, prolonging indefinitely the existing limbo. Thereafter the TWU regularly consulted with the Board of Transportation, pursued grievances, obtained temporary leaves for workers so that they could act for the union, and in general maintained a strong presence throughout the municipal transit system. Although rival worker groups also met with the Board, the TWU, as one scholar put it, had "most favored union" status, a function of its aggressive actions, sizable membership, and political clout rather than any formal arrangement.[46]

In June 1942 the TWU launched a new campaign to improve work conditions and solidify its position. Inflation had begun to eat away at the earlier pay increase; the working rules, though apparently completed, had not been released; and the Grievance Board, which the Board of Transportation had given little authority, was failing to live up to union expectations. The TWU called for raising all "substandard" pay rates, eliminating pay inequities, a general wage increase to meet the rise in the cost of living, some system of "maintaining a maximum of union security," and the adoption of the drafted work rules. In addition, it asked for the formation of management-labor committees to help meet the demands of wartime operation. This was in line with Phil Murray's Industrial Council Plan, a proposal for management-labor-government committees to administer vital war industries.[47]

In July, August, and September, La Guardia and Delaney held a series of conferences with the TWU. According to the union, little progress resulted. Delaney rejected all of the TWU demands except for agreeing to expedite the issuance of the work rules and to consider some minor adjustments to eliminate pay inequities. As a result, in late October the union intensified its campaign, following a new, two-pronged strategy.[48]

TWU leaders still hoped to win concessions directly from the city. However, if that proved impossible they planned to appeal to the NWLB. Accordingly, they began a series of moves designed to both increase the pressure on the city and build a case for NWLB intervention. On October 20, at the request of the TWU, Phil Murray met with La Guardia and Delaney but got, according to Quill, only "the same run-around." Three days later the union held a staggered series of brief work stoppages at most NYCTS shops, barns, and powerhouses. Then came a barrage of mass meetings, delegations to City Hall, and petitions circulated by the NYC CIO Council. The union also gathered signatures from what it claimed to be 90% of the NYCTS operating employees authorizing it to represent them. When despite all this the city remained unmoved, on November 9 the TWU appealed to the NWLB.[49]

La Guardia and Delaney insisted that the NWLB had no jurisdiction in the dispute. They refused to even send representatives to so argue at a NWLB hearing, held on December 9. However, the Mayor privately conveyed his views to NWLB Chairman William Davis and FDR. He also joined seventy-eight other mayors in signing a statement denying the right of the NWLB to intervene in disputes between municipalities and their employees. Delaney went even farther; in early December he said that the TWU appeal had ended any obligations the city had under the extended IRT and BMT contracts, leading Quill to threaten a strike if the Board refused to continue discussions with the union.

La Guardia realized that policy as well as legal issues would be taken into account by the NWLB in its ruling on jurisdiction in the TWU case. Accordingly, he pushed Delaney to grant quickly a new series of wage adjustments, and on November 16 announced the city's intention to increase transit wages by $1 million in the coming year. The TWU dismissed this as totally inadequate and far below the increases allowed under the "Little Steel formula."[50]

On December 15 the NWLB ruled that it had no jurisdiction in the New York case or in two others involving municipal workers. What was especially bitter for the TWU leadership was that the decision was unanimous, with the AFL and CIO board members supporting it. However, the transit union was not without some consolation. At the December 9 hearing Davis and Board member Wayne Morse had been highly critical of the city for failing to send a representative. In the Board's full opinion, written by Morse, there was still more criticism of Delaney and La Guardia.

Morse argued that although municipal workers could not strike, they could "participate in a limited form of collective bargaining." In the TWU's case "adequate facilities for fair and impartial consideration and review of grievances and other objectives of a proper employee relationship policy" had not been provided. He termed Delaney's attitude toward the TWU "antagonistic" and, more generally, blamed much of the unrest and dissatisfaction among municipal workers on "those few administrative officials of government who . . . had taken a very uncompromising and unenlightened attitude."[51]

For a brief moment after the NWLB ruling, the TWU leadership seriously considered making good its threat to strike. Quill summarized the situation in a December 16 letter to Santo:

> Last night we had a Joint Executive [Committee meeting] . . . and there was a definite clamor for a strike. We issued a mild statement to the papers asking that the negotiations be resumed and at the same time we are actually going through with strike preparations. [Phil] Murray told us that since there was no court to go to, that the CIO would release us from our no-strike pledge and he would support us. Since there is a manpower shortage and since we have made tremendous gains in the ISS, we are confident that any strike we pull can be won. . . . We expect to call one large meeting . . . and right after that if things are not coming our way, it looks like strike. This time we can say the men are actually with us and I think our strike talk was badly needed or else we might have found it difficult to maintain leadership.

On December 23, MacMahon and Quill publicly implied that the union would strike if within two weeks the city had not resumed negotiations and agreed to impartial arbitration in the event of an impasse.[52]

The TWU leadership, however, quickly changed its position. After La Guardia announced that he would continue transit service in the event of a walkout, Quill and his colleagues accepted Santo's view—apparently sent by letter to Quill—that La Guardia would welcome a strike as an opportunity to be another Calvin Coolidge. (Coolidge had risen to national prominence by smashing a Boston police strike.) Extensive discussions were held with CP officials, and as Quill told Santo, "all members of the O'Grady family . . . at last worked out a plan of action without strike." Apparently it was Earl Browder who came up with the solution and sold it to La Guardia, an impartial panel to study the entire transit situation and relieve the Mayor of the embarrassment of reversing himself.[53]

While in public and private the Mayor and the union retreated from their extreme positions, top TWU leaders faced a new problem, the strong strike sentiment that they themselves had helped to create. Several union staffers and secondary leaders continued to press for a walkout. Quill believed that a majority of the union's members wanted to strike, with "some of the worst elements on the road . . . demanding action." Browder shared this assessment; he later recalled telling La Guardia that "if you let this situation continue as it is, you're going to have a strike anyway, and instead of it being led by the union, it will be led by Christian fronters." At a January 6 meeting of 5,000 transit workers there were repeated calls from the audience for a strike. Only strong appeals from Joe Curran and Quill finally turned the tide.[54]

On January 11, La Guardia announced the appointment of a committee headed by Fordham Law School Dean Ignatius Wilkinson with a broad mandate to investigate municipal transit labor relations and make recommendations. Wilkinson was in Quill's opinion "a Spellman man." Just prior to this Quill had met with the Archbishop, who had then called the Mayor to discuss the transit situation.[55] Although TWU leaders privately considered the committee an important victory, they continued their public campaign for the union's June 1942 program. With the help of other unions, the TWU distributed a million leaflets presenting its case. It also took out newspaper ads and bought radio time. On February 9, some 20,000 people attended a Madison Square Garden rally in support of the TWU.[56]

The TWU and the Board of Transportation continued to jockey for position. In mid-January the Board proceeded with its previously announced plan to increase wages by just over $1 million a year. This money was to eliminate inequities and therefore was distributed among only 13,000 of the system's 32,000 workers, primarily lower-paid employees. When the first pay checks after the hike were given out, the excluded workers were furious. A series of short work stoppages ensued. On the IRT, workers at eight shops and barns and at the 59th Street powerhouse briefly struck, with the largest action involving 1,100 men at 148th Street who extended their lunch break without permission. There were also stoppages by 800 workers at the BMT Avenue X shop, 600 workers at the IND 207th Street shop, and 150 workers at the IND Jamaica shop. There were two more stoppages—in this case sit-downs—at the last-named facility on January 28 and 29 after the Board of Transportation reversed an agreement between TWU and IND officials settling a dispute over seniority and job assignments. All these job actions lasted at most a few hours and ended when TWU officials appealed to the workers to return to work. It is unclear what role, if any, the union played in instigating them; the TWU leadership claimed that they were spontaneous, while Delaney charged that they were union-planned "acts of distinct sabotage."[57]

As so often happened, just as the situation seemed to be getting out of hand, both the city and the union backed off. In early February the Board of Transportation reversed its initial decision to dock the pay of the workers who had struck and reinstated the original agreement settling the Jamaica shop controversy. The strike wave ended, presumably as a result of union pressure. In March, LaGuardia announced the city's intention to grant another $3 million in wage increases after July 1, with the distribution of the money to be first discussed with the TWU.[58]

Meanwhile, testimony before the Wilkinson Committee began. The TWU proposed to the committee a general wage increase of 15%, the replacement of Delaney, maintenance-of-membership, "advisory arbitration," and the establishment of labor-management committees. Testimony and reports from two outside groups helped the TWU's cause. After the NWLB decision, the CIO had helped set up a "Citizen's Committee" of prominent liberals and labor relations experts to study the transit situation. Its report, although vague on the question of signed contracts and union security, was strongly critical of the Board of Transportation and generally supported the TWU's position. More damning, the Board of Transportation's own Grievance Board issued a report, leaked to the press by the TWU, highly critical of its parent body. The Wilkinson Committee was also undoubtedly influenced by the growing manpower crisis, especially among skilled workers, that the NYCTS faced in part as a result of its low wages.[59]

On April 28, 1943, the Wilkinson Committee issued its report. On the legal framework of municipal labor relations it supported most of La Guardia's views, arguing that under civil service signed contracts, strikes, collective bargaining as practiced in private industry, the union shop, and binding arbitration were all illegal. Nonetheless, it was highly critical of the procedures and attitudes of the Board of Transportation, "a large contributing factor" in the Committee's opinion to transit labor unrest. To solve the recurring crises, it proposed a major revamping of the Board's labor policies.

Most importantly, it suggested that the Impartial Grievance Board be replaced by a full-time Deputy Commissioner empowered to make final decisions on routine grievances and recommendations on wages and hours. For the latter purpose, it recommended periodic conferences with all employee organizations active in the system. It also suggested consultations with union representatives over the distribution of the already announced $3 million for wage inequities, further wage equalization beyond that, with non-binding arbitration in the event that an agreement could not be reached, and the institution of automatic seniority wage increases in those classifications without them. Finally, it urged the issuance of the uniform work rules after discussions with union representatives and endorsed in principle labor-management committees, which it suggested should be tried on an experimental basis.[60]

Although not all of the Wilkinson Committee recommendations were adopted, most were. Its report therefore marked a watershed in municipal transit labor relations and a significant victory for the TWU. Since unification, except for the temporary extension of the IRT and BMT contracts, all of the Board of Transportation's dealings with unions had been ad hoc. The Wilkinson Committee report established for the first time regular procedures that institutionalized union representation, with consultation on all matters of importance. This was a direct result of the TWU's campaign, and many of the union's specific proposals, if not its ultimate goal of a signed, union shop contract, were adopted by the Committee and subsequently by the city.

Shortly after the Wilkinson Committee completed its work, the Board of Transportation began a series of consultations with the TWU, the railway brotherhoods, and the AFMTW, which, according to the *New York Times*, was "substantially similar to collective bargaining procedure." The outcome was an agreement on a new round of wage increases to take effect on July 1, 1943, worth close to $4 million rather than the originally planned $3 million. Almost every worker received at least some additional money, with the largest increases generally going to the lower-paid workers. The starting rate for porters, for example, went for 57 cents an hour to 65.5 cents, while the top rate for the motormen went from $1.06 to $1.10. With these increases, every wage rate in the system was at least 15% higher than on September 1, 1941, so that overall the NYCTS increases exceeded those permitted under the "Little Steel formula." In addition, overtime provisions were extended and improved and automatic seniority increments established in every job classification. As the Wilkinson Committee suggested, a Labor Relations Department was established; Edward C. Maguire, a lawyer who proved generally sympathetic to the TWU on grievance cases, was appointed to head it. In late July, the long-overdue work rules were finally issued.[61]

The TWU's year-long campaign, beginning with the announcement of its June 1942 program and ending with the July 1943 pay increases, greatly enhanced its standing. To a considerable extent, the previous year's events had been the result of TWU initiatives. The TWU also had maintained a high level of agitational and organizational activity. To capitalize on its victories and push workers to join or rejoin the union, Local 100 threatened to limit its membership and end services and representation for non-members after August 1, 1943. Simultaneously, it began a drive for what it called the "voluntary closed shop," 100% membership. By early August a number of IRT sections had achieved that goal. Quill's election to the City Council in November further increased the union's prestige and membership, so that Quill by January 1944 could report that "we have outlived the stage in the IRT and BMT when men are debating whether it is worth or is not worth being a member of the TWU." Although the TWU's rivals continued to operate, the TWU was without question the dominant employee organization on the NYCTS and recognized as such by the city. Through its aggressive tactics, the TWU had won back much of the membership and status it had lost following unification.[62]

In the late spring of 1944, in preparation for another round of talks with the Board of Transportation, Local 100 developed a new, ten-point program. In addition to a general wage increase it called for shortening the time needed to reach top rates; special "quota rates" for the most skilled workers; paid lunch breaks for all workers; pay for swing time over an hour; overtime for supervisory personnel (some of whom belonged to the TWU); improvements in work rules and sick leave; the extension of collective bargaining procedures; and union security. To some extent the TWU was playing catch-up; in spite of federal price controls, the cost-of-living was continuing to rise. By mid-1944 an estimated 10% of the Board of Transportation employees were holding second jobs, a practice La Guardia tried to stop. Such moonlighting was especially prevalent among skilled shop men, who could easily find work at the Brooklyn Navy Yard or other defense production facilities.[63]

In the negotiations with the Board (in which the AFMTW and BRSA also took part), the TWU was able to win only a few of its demands. On June 27, 1944, the Board of Transportation approved a five-cents-an-hour pay increase for 13,000 employees. It also gave paid, half-hour lunch breaks to 11,000 shop and maintenance workers currently without them and put IRT shop and barn workers on a five-day week, already standard in the other divisions. After further talks with the TWU, the Board made a series of work rule changes.[64]

The TWU was not totally dissatisfied with these results, which helped the union in its drive to increase its IND membership, but nonetheless it pressed the Board of Transportation to accept arbitration of those elements of its program which remained unaddressed. The Board refused. Accordingly, as soon as the fall general election was over, the union launched a campaign to pressure La Guardia to intercede. To support its case for arbitration, it obtained the backing of a host of organizations, labor leaders, and politicians, including Senator Robert Wagner, Congressmen Charles Buckley and Adam Clayton Powell, Jr., Sidney Hillman, Phil Murray, the NAACP, and the County Derry Society. In November the City Council passed resolutions supported by the Civil Service Forum and the TWU calling for cost-of-living increases for transit workers and impartial arbitration. The TWU also launched a petition drive among NYCTS workers supporting the union's program and asking La Guardia to intervene. By January an impressive 26,000 signatures had been obtained.[65]

LaGuardia rejected arbitration but agreed to make some upward pay adjustments. The TWU was not placated, and Quill privately raised the possibility of a strike. At that point the CP intervened behind the scenes. Browder and New York State CP leader Gil Green convinced Marcantonio to intercede with the Mayor on behalf of the TWU, while Martin Young pressed Quill to be patient. Finally, after a meeting between La Guardia, Marcantonio, and TWU leaders, the Mayor announced a general five-cent-an-hour wage hike to go into effect on June 1, 1945, worth an annual total of $3.7 million. For about half of the work force the increase consisted of increment raises already scheduled to go into effect, but for the rest it was a genuine new gain.[66]

This was the last wage increase under La Guardia and Delaney, and it helped further solidify the union's position. When in May 1945 Local 100 scheduled a field day to raise money for its political action fund, 17,000 transit workers contributed 25 cents each to have their names listed in the program, an indication of how successfully the TWU had rebuilt itself by the time the war and the La Guardia era drew to a close.[67]

The TWU's wartime bargaining gains on the NYCTS were made possible by favorable economic conditions. With transit revenue rising and the city work force shrinking as men entered the armed services, La Guardia had funds available for wage increases. At the same time, the severe manpower shortage made it imperative that city transit jobs be made more attractive.[68] But political factors were important as well. Though relations between the TWU and La Guardia remained strained, the revival of the Popular Front enabled the transit union to enlist support from a broad spectrum of mass organizations, labor leaders, and liberals. By the end of the war the TWU had worked out a pattern of labor relations with New York City which, though short of full recognition, acknowledged the union's dominant position.

Across the board, the TWU's strong pro-war stance had aided the union. In contrast to the Hitler-Stalin pact period, transit workers no longer had to choose between the policies of the President and the policies of their union. Nor was the TWU any longer susceptible to charges that it was unpatriotic, "un-American," or undermining the defense effort. Some historians have correctly pointed out that during the war the CIO was somewhat domesticated, as it became ever more dependent on the federal government and the Democratic party.[69] The TWU illustrates the other side of the wartime labor experience; the war helped solidify the position of unions in the political economy. By the war's end, Local 100 once again clearly represented a majority of both the public- and private-sector transit workers in New York City. As we will see, the TWU also made gains elsewhere in the country. The TWU's increased membership, its new political and bargaining arrangements, and the internal union changes that occurred as a by-product of the war together left the union far stronger at the end of World War II than at its beginning. At the same time, they set the stage for dramatic changes that were to come in the postwar years.

11

Breaking Out of New York

As soon as the TWU received its charter from the CIO in the spring of 1937, giving it broad jurisdiction over urban passenger transportation workers throughout North America, it attempted to expand beyond the New York mass transit industry. This initial effort was a failure. However, the defense buildup that preceded World War II and then the war itself reversed the TWU's fortunes.

World War II was a good time for union organizing. The economy boomed, jobs were easy to get, workers were frustrated by having their wage rates limited by the government while corporate profits soared, the Popular Front was in full bloom, and unionism was often seen as a form of patriotism. Under these circumstances, organized labor overcame the stagnation that had set in during the "Roosevelt Recession" of the late 1930s and began to grow rapidly. During the war union membership rose from 10.5 to 14.7 million. Although some of this growth came from increased employment at already unionized firms, much of it stemmed from new organizing. By the end of the war, the so-called basic industries, like steel, auto, rubber, and meatpacking, were very heavily unionized.[1]

The TWU did not have the same economic imperative to expand as most industrial unions. Mass transit, by its nature, supplies a local market and cannot be relocated. Unionized transit workers in one region are not directly threatened by non-union conditions in another. It was therefore not labor market economics that pushed the TWU to grow but an ideological commitment to organizing the unorganized, as well as personal and institutional ambition.

The drive to expand was a measure of the same universalism that had been an important factor in the TWU's initial success in New York. Most of the TWU growth during and immediately after World War II was among transportation workers outside of New York City. However, the TWU also began signing up non-transit workers. In the latter case, the Irish nationalism that had been central to the union at its start was still influential; several groups of workers in non-transportation industries were signed up in part because they were heavily Irish.

249

The TWU's most important wartime organizing drive was in Philadelphia. That effort was a watershed in the TWU handling of the issue of race. Even before the war, the TWU moved, somewhat reluctantly, toward confronting racial discrimination more directly. During the war, pushed forward by developments in New York and Philadelphia, the TWU shed its prior hesitancy in acting against racial discrimination.

Although most New York transit workers were not directly involved in their union's expansion, they were affected by it. For one thing, New York transit workers financed the TWU's initial expansion, though later Local 100 was subsidized by the TWU International. For another thing, as the the union expanded, the influence of Local 100 on the International, though still dominant, diminished. By the late 1940s, the internal political dynamic of the TWU no longer derived solely from the New York transit industry.

Even before the TWU achieved recognition on the main New York City transit lines, it began exploring other organizing possibilities. Three main targets emerged, the New York taxi industry and the transit systems in Buffalo and Philadelphia. In the former case the TWU achieved at best an ephemeral success. In the latter two cases it failed completely.

From the winter of 1933–34 on, the New York City taxi industry, with its 40,000 licensed drivers and hundreds of mechanics and maintenance workers, was in a state of almost constant labor turmoil. Several major strikes occurred, a slew of unions were formed, and several political groups, including the CP, were very active in taxi organizing. In 1937 the TWU took over a taxi local affiliated with the United Automobile Workers (UAW) and used it as the core for a Local 100 taxi organizing committee. At first, it seemed as if the TWU would be as successful in taxi as transit. The union quickly won a series of representation elections at most of the city's major taxi fleets and signed union shop contracts that gave it a theoretical taxi membership of over 15,000. But this was just on paper; turnout in the elections had been low, and the real dues-paying membership was only a fraction of the stated total.

The New York taxi industry was far from the ripe fruit for organization that many thought it to be. It was plagued by a chronic oversupply of cabs and drivers, including thousands of part-timers and owner-operators; it was dominated by several large, financially powerful, virulently anti-union employers; and it was ridden by racketeering, loan-sharking, and corruption. Furthermore, taxi drivers were an exceedingly difficult group to organize. Quill called them "the limping proletariat." Some drivers were declassed intellectuals, others socially or psychologically marginal. For many, cab driving was a temporary or secondary occupation. The industry's commission system and the very nature of the work bred an intensely individualistic, competitive spirit.

Faced with these conditions, the TWU found itself unable to enforce its contracts or build a stable organization. The result was a long series of strikes and lockouts, marked by occasional violence, and repeated new recognition elections. Although the TWU was able to maintain support and contracts at some major fleets, its taxi membership constantly fluctuated and over time declined. What had looked like an easy arena for expansion was in fact a quagmire—a constant drain on resources and a source of endless difficulties. Furthermore, taxi organizing caused dissension within Local 100, as transit workers objected to the very substantial subsidies given to the local's taxi division.

By World War II, the Local 100 taxi organization had largely disintegrated. Wartime conditions hastened its demise. Toward the end of the war, the remaining taxi unionists were given their own local and a new organizing push was begun. The effort was not successful. Finally, in 1947, in the face of growing complaints by subway workers that to organize taxi drivers was "pouring money down a rat hole," the TWU abandoned the New York taxi industry once and for all.[2]

In Philadelphia and Buffalo the TWU faced different problems. Both the huge Philadelphia Rapid Transit Company and the International Railway Company in Buffalo had long used the Mitten Cooperative Plan for Labor Relations, a system of company unions, paternal benefits, and employee stock purchase plans. Both companies had strong ties to city administrations hostile to labor. With the coming of the New Deal and state "little Wagner" acts, the two firms were forced to dissolve their company unions. However, in 1937, as soon the TWU began signing up workers (in Philadelphia the BRT was active as well), independent employee associations were set up and recognized by the companies. In response, the TWU appealed to various administrative and judicial bodies seeking recognition elections. In June 1939 the Pennsylvania Labor Board ruled against the TWU's Philadelphia appeal. In Buffalo, where TWU activists were beaten, arrested, and fired, the TWU finally was able to force an election in August 1939, but by then its support had dissipated and it was badly defeated. Both drives were abandoned[3]

Before World War II, TWU locals of bus, trolley, or taxi drivers were established in some smaller cities and towns. Unlike in Philadelphia and Buffalo, the TWU took no initiative in the formation of these groups and devoted few resources to them. Most were independent, company, or AFL unions that voted to affiliate with the TWU. Generally they had been aided by local CIO officials and then steered to the TWU. During the prewar heyday of CIO organizing, workers did not primarily identify with a particular CIO affiliate but with the CIO itself. When a CIO union in one industry won a major battle, local workers in other industries flocked to the CIO. The first TWU out-of-town locals provided a virtual road map of CIO activity. There were TWU locals in Akron, Ohio, where the first major CIO strike (involving rubber workers) had occurred; Flint, Michigan, where the UAW had won its decisive battle against General Motors; Bessemer and Fairfield, Alabama, and Aliquippa, Pennsylvania, where the CIO Steel Workers Organizing Committee was active; and in ten towns in West Virginia, where the UMW was strong. Such locals gave the TWU at least the form of an International union, though the largest, in Akron, had only 309 members.[4]

In 1940 and '41, as the national economy picked up under the stimulus of defense production, the TWU began taking a more active role in out-of-town organizing. Because the TWU's International staff was small and concentrated in New York, the union was still dependent on others to provide leads and help run the resulting campaigns. Sometimes local CIO organizers or industrial union council officials played this role; at other times staffers for left-wing unions or CP functionaries. (In areas where the CIO was weak, these were often one and the same.) At some point, however, if an organizing drive involved a significant number of workers, the TWU would send in its own officers or staff to take charge. If a campaign was successful, an International representative, usually a left-wing TWU cadre from New York, would be assigned on a permanent basis.

In October 1941, for example, the TWU won a representation election at the main transit company in Omaha, Nebraska, which employed over 500 workers. Although the campaign had been locally initiated, shortly before the voting Douglas MacMahon and Warren Horie, an IEB member, arrived on the scene. After the election, John Cassidy, a former IRA member from the BMT and a leftist, was sent to Omaha to supervise the new local and serve as the TWU's midwestern representative. By the middle of the next year, a second Omaha local had won a contract with the city's Yellow Cab Company.[5] Late in 1941 the TWU also won an election to represent 500 transit workers in Columbus, Ohio.[6]

Not all the TWU organizing drives just before the war were successful. The largest, aimed at the 4,000 employees of the interlocking Los Angeles Railway and Los Angeles Motor Coach Companies, was a frustrating defeat. In January 1942, after a complex, year-long struggle involving the two companies, the TWU, a company union, the Amalgamated, and the BRT, the issue of representation rights was sent to the NWLB as its very first case. When the board ruled against the TWU (which of all the competing unions probably had the most worker support), the campaign was abandoned, since the only alternative was a strike in defiance of the CIO's recently announced no-strike policy.[7]

A wartime organizing campaign at the large Chicago Motor Coach Company also failed. First the TWU lost a close recognition election to an independent union; then, late in the war, the Amalgamated was granted recognition after it produced authorization cards signed by a majority of the workers. However, the TWU did establish a unit, Local 236, of 1,300 track workers employed by the Chicago Surface Lines. The track workers, many of whom were Yugoslavian (mostly Croatian), had been represented for many years by the AFL Hod Carriers. Early in the war, dissatisfied with the financial practices of their union, they ousted their leaders, disaffiliated, and began looking for a new parent body. In 1943 they approached the TWU. According to Quill's later account, Illinois CP State Secretary Morris Childs asked the TWU not to become involved, presumably because conflicts with the AFL might result. (The CP also had pressured the TWU to abandon its Los Angeles drive.) Nonetheless, Quill offered the group a charter and the new TWU local won a representation election by an overwhelming vote. Matthew Kearns, who had helped lead the TWU's Chicago efforts, stayed in the area as an International representative. According to the FBI, he also helped establish a small CP group within Local 236.[8]

The TWU's second organizing drive in Philadelphia dwarfed all its other wartime efforts. After the TWU abandoned its first Philadelphia drive, the independent Philadelphia Rapid Transit Employees Union (PRTEU)—which many felt was company-dominated—continued to represent the 11,000 Philadelphia Transit Company (PTC) workers. In early 1942, the BRT and a split-off from the PRTEU challenged the PRTEU for bargaining rights, but the PRTEU won a representation election. Nonetheless, there was considerable worker dissatisfaction, particularly after the PRTEU signed a poor two-year contract.

In early 1943 a group of PTC workers asked the TWU to launch a new effort to displace the PRTEU. Included in the group were Herbert Kaplan, a leader of the TWU's earlier Philadelphia drive, and the Daugherty brothers, Joseph B. and James J., whose father had been active in the violent 1910 PTC strike. After a trial TWU leaflet won a strong response, a full-scale organizing campaign was begun.

TWU leaders knew from experience that the PTC drive would be difficult. However, there was much to be gained, since the PTC was one of the largest transit systems in the country. Furthermore, there was a substantial left-wing movement in Philadelphia which could provide help and advice, while the proximity to New York meant that top TWU leaders could play a strong, personal role. Accordingly, the TWU made a major commitment of resources. In February 1943, Local 100 leader James Fitzsimon moved to Philadelphia to direct the campaign. He was aided by two veteran Local 100 organizers and several PTC workers who were put on staff. Forge, later joined by MacMahon, made weekly visits[9]

In contrast to many of the TWU organizing drives outside of New York, which were quick efforts to win over already existing groups, the Philadelphia drive was a carefully planned, well-executed campaign. Patiently a network of local leaders and supporters was built up. In effect, the TWU replicated the process that had led to its success in New York. Fitzsimon was particularly adept at attracting supporters from among the large number of Irish and Irish-American workers; it was from this group that most of the local TWU leaders came. (The largest ethno-cultural component of the work force, however, consisted of first- and second-generation migrants from the South, many from the Carolinas.) The local CP provided some help, though in the end it did not play a major role in the campaign. There were few if any Communist workers active in the drive.

In July 1943 the TWU filed for a representation election with the Pennsylvania State Labor Relations Board. By then it was claiming 4,000 paid applicants, had established a section structure, and was holding meetings attended by upwards of 1,500 workers. The situation, however, became complicated when the BRT and the Amalgamated petitioned to be included in the election along with the PRTEU and TWU. The BRT had been trying to organize the PTC for years; its local group was headed by veteran subway motorman James McMenamin. The Amalgamated backers were mostly defectors from the PRTEU, which was beginning to unravel in the face of the TWU challenge.[10]

As a result of various maneuvers by the PRTEU and the Amalgamated, the PTC election was not held until March 14, 1944, but by the fall of 1943 the campaign was already well under way. From the start, it was an ugly contest, and as time went on it got uglier. Both the PRTEU and the Amalgamated relied heavily on red-baiting in their efforts to defeat the TWU, which was generally seen as the front-runner. This line of attack was also promoted by Dennis J. Comey, the head of a local Jesuit labor school that was attended by, among others, McMenamin and Robert Lasher, the leader of a PRTEU faction that was considering jumping to one of the national unions. Comey was in touch with Philip Carey, the new director of the Xavier School in New York; together the two priests worked to convince Lasher not to go over to the TWU, feeding him information on the TWU's CP ties.[11]

More explosive than the "red" issue, however, was the "black" issue, the concurrent struggle going on to upgrade the status of black PTC workers. Although the union battle and the fight over black rights arose independently, they steadily converged, eventually leading to a massive crisis of national importance.

As was customary in most of the country, all of the PTC's 537 black workers were restricted to menial jobs. Even when a serious manpower shortage developed during the defense build-up, the company refused to hire more blacks or promote its black employees to motorman or conductor positions. In mid-1941 a committee of black workers protested this policy to PTC officials, but the company and PRTEU-head Frank P. Carney vehemently resisted any change, each putting the onus on the other. The black workers then went to the NAACP, which had no better luck in persuading the PTC to change its ways.

In November 1943, the federal Fair Employment Practices Committee (FEPC) ordered the PTC to end its discriminatory practices. The PTC, with PRTEU support, defied the order, claiming that it would violate its labor contract. Sometime later, over 1,700 workers signed a petition saying that they would refuse to work with black motormen, conductors, operators, or station trainmen. Meanwhile, the Action Committee on Philadelphia Transit Employment, which drew support from both the NAACP and the National Negro Congress, was mobilizing public sentiment against PTC discrimination.

Once the FEPC issued its order, the PRTEU and to a lesser extent the Amalgamated tried to make race the central issue of the representation battle. The PRTEU promised to keep blacks from being upgraded, while charging that "a vote for the CIO is a vote for Negroes to get your jobs." The TWU, by contrast, supported an end to the PTC's discriminatory practices. Nonetheless, it tried to soft-pedal its position, hoping to put off the issue until after it won recognition. Fitzsimon even unsuccessfully urged the Philadelphia CIO Council not to take a public stand on the FEPC order. As the TWU feared, the PRTEU succeeded in mobilizing workers' racism to its own benefit; by early 1944 it was gaining strength. As a result the BRT withdrew from the election and its supporters joined the PRTEU.[12]

The final weeks of the election campaign were very rough. The Amalgamated effort, which had been inept and ineffective, was completely taken over by national and local AFL officials. A huge staff of organizers was assembled and goon squads used to break up TWU meetings, decommission sound trucks, and in a few cases beat up CIO adherents. Meanwhile Comey and Carey arranged for Fifth Avenue Coach oppositionist Patrick Reilly to go to Philadelphia to red-bait the TWU. The TWU brought in more people from New York, and twenty-five PTC workers took leaves to work full-time for the CIO union. Martin Young arranged for help from the Electrical and Maritime unions, both of which had large Philadelphia memberships, and the CP pitched in. Belatedly, the CIO national office began vigorously supporting the TWU, with Phil Murray and James Carey addressing a large, pre-election rally.[13]

The long-awaited vote was a TWU triumph. The PRTEU carried only the clerical unit, which was uncontested. In both the maintenance and shop and the transportation units the TWU won well over half the votes, with the PRTEU and the Amalgamated dividing the remainder about equally. The TWU's PTC unit, Local 234, thus became the exclusive bargaining agent for 9,200 workers. By late June the company and the union had agreed on contract terms that included a substantial pay increase, pay equalizations, paid swing and reporting time, grievance arbitration, and maintenance-of-membership. On June 30th a mass meeting ratified the proposed contract, which had not yet been formally signed.[14]

The TWU's troubles, however, were far from over. Tensions over the "race" issue, rather than dissipating, soon exploded. The TWU response was shaped not only by developments in Philadelphia but also by earlier events in New York.

By the time the issue of racial discrimination arose in Philadelphia, the TWU attitude toward fighting racism had evolved significantly from the union's early days. The pivotal event in changing the TWU's stance was the 1941 boycott directed against the Fifth Avenue Coach Company and New York City Omnibus. These companies provided most of the surface transportation in Harlem, where they also had garage facilities, but employed blacks only as bus cleaners. As a result they were widely hated by black New Yorkers. In 1934 the CP-led League for Struggle for Negro Rights organized a campaign to force Fifth Avenue Coach to hire black drivers and conductors. The group tied its anti-discrimination demands to the demands of the Amalgamated members who had been fired by the company for attempting to unionize. With a few white members of the infant TWU participating, petitions were circulated, company facilities picketed, and a boycott organized, but the company held fast and after five months the campaign was quietly abandoned.

It was not until 1941, at the time of the TWU's bus strike, that a new campaign was launched against the Manhattan bus lines. The precise origins of this effort are unclear. Adam Clayton Powell, Jr., later claimed that he and Quill had discussed it before the TWU struck. Other accounts indicate that it was actually the neo-Garveyite Harlem Labor Union (HLU) that initiated the protest. Though the HLU was a nominal affiliate of Powell's Greater New York Coordinating Committee on Employment, it often acted independently and was politically at odds with both Powell and the CP. In any case, once the protest began, Powell's group dominated the United Bus Strike Committee, which it formed with the HLU, the National Negro Congress (NNC), and various black entertainers to lead the struggle. Through the NNC and Powell's group, black Communists played a key role in the movement.

As soon as the TWU bus strike ended, a highly effective Harlem boycott of Fifth Avenue Coach and New York Omnibus began. Picket lines were set up at Harlem bus stops and a series of mass rallies held. The protest lasted for nearly a month. The initial TWU reaction was somewhat disingenuous. During its own strike, the TWU had demanded that bus cleaners be given promotions in the shops on a strict seniority basis, like all other workers. TWU leaders also told the boycotters that they would fully support their struggle. However, at the same time the union distributed leaflets that portrayed the TWU as essentially neutral, asserting that the companies had the sole right to make hiring decisions and that the union had already proved itself to be non-discriminatory.

The TWU was under considerable pressure to take a more active role. At one point its headquarters was picketed, there were scattered incidents of violence against drivers operating buses in Harlem, and the CP was prodding the union. The TWU quickly yielded, proposing to the companies that in hiring new workers they pick blacks and whites in equal numbers until blacks were reasonably represented in the work force. The companies countered by offering to reserve the next 180 driver and maintenance jobs for blacks, but only if the TWU suspended the seniority of currently laid-off workers. Extended negotiations then began and on April 19 an extraordinary tripartite contract was signed by the TWU, the protest committee, and the companies. In essence it said that the next 70 mechanics hired and, after 91 laid-off drivers were rehired, the next 100 drivers would be black. Thereafter, whites and blacks would be alternatively taken on until blacks constituted 17% of the companies' work force, a figure equal to the percentage of the Manhattan population that was black.

As a result of this pact, black mechanics were soon at work. Because of low turnover, the first black bus drivers were not hired until January 1942. The TWU and black groups took great care in selecting and training the first black drivers, and the transition went smoothly. In February 1943 the Third Avenue Railway also began hiring black operators, primarily as a result of the wartime labor shortage.[15]

Prior to the bus boycott, the TWU record on race had been at best mixed. However, in signing the 1941 bus pact the TWU agreed to a program of preferential hiring with little precedent, a contract that probably few unions—including the TWU—would voluntarily sign today.[16] Once the agreement was signed, and with the concurrent spread of World War II, the TWU dropped its reticence on racial issues. The union began paying more attention to black workers in its newspaper and more persistently pressed for civil-rights legislation. Several TWU activists took part in the Harlem-based Negro Labor Victory Committee, which black Communist Ben Davis described as "the core of the Negro-labor-progressive coalition." The union leadership also made it clear that it would not tolerate racism in its own ranks. In August 1943, Quill wrote that if any TWU members heard others fomenting racial hatred, they should report them to government authorities and "at the same time, they should grab the nearest and most pliable weapon and let fly in the direction of our home-grown fascists." Symbolic actions were taken as well: Joe Louis was given an honorary union membership and Powell and Paul Robeson invited to address TWU conventions.[17]

During the recognition fight in Philadelphia, the TWU had downplayed the race issue. However, once recognition was achieved, TWU organizer James Fitzsimon began cooperating with the groups fighting the PTC's discriminatory practices. He also tried but failed to get the company to accept a non-discrimination clause in its contract with the TWU. Then, on July 1, 1944, just after the TWU had reached contract terms with the PTC, the federal War Manpower Commission ordered all future hiring of male workers in industries essential to the war effort be done through the United States Employment Service, which was non-discriminatory. With this, the PTC finally agreed to obey the FEPC's outstanding directive, an action endorsed by TWU Local 234 delegates in a 119 to 1 vote.

While the TWU was supporting the PTC's reluctant acquiescence to desegregation, others—most notably Frank Carney from the defeated PRTEU—were openly organizing workers to call in sick if black workers were upgraded. Meetings were held on company property, leaflets distributed, and notices posted on company bulletin boards. On August 1, the day eight black workers were to begin training as motormen, the defeated PRTEU group made good its threat, and a general strike of the system began. It was a well-organized movement. McMenamin, who along with Carney emerged as the leader of the walkout, organized a 150-member strike steering committee with representatives from every car barn. Over 3,500 workers rallied at a company depot. The PTC management made only token efforts to end the walkout, while officials of the city and state governments, both Republican-controlled, were nearly as lax.

The TWU quickly established the position that it maintained throughout the strike. First, without abandoning its support for black rights, it tried in every way it could to get the PTC workers to return to their jobs, cooperating with the CIO, the CP, and the federal government (including the FBI). Second, like the CP, it argued that although the race issue was a real one, the walkout was essentially a plot by the PTC, the defeated rival unions, and the city government to reverse the verdict of the representation election, undermine the war effort, and hurt Roosevelt's re-election bid. Third, it worked with the NAACP, the CP, the CIO, and other groups to prevent interracial violence.[18]

It soon became clear that the TWU could not end the strike, which was bringing one of the country's most important defense production centers to a virtual stand-still. Accordingly, on August 3 Roosevelt ordered the army to take control of the PTC. The next day, however, only limited transit service resumed, while Mc-Menamin made an open bid to displace the TWU as the bargaining agent for PTC workers. Losing patience, Major General Philip Hayes took drastic steps. Five thousand soldiers were brought into the city and it was announced that they would be used to guard, and if necessary operate, the system. Strikers were threatened with the loss of their draft deferments and stiff penalties under the Smith-Connolly War Disputes Act, which had been passed in response to the 1943 coal strikes. Carney, McMenamin, and two other strike leaders were arrested by federal agents and fired, and Hayes made it known that he considered the TWU the sole bargaining agent for the PTC workers. Through all of this, the TWU cooperated fully with the army. By August 8, normal transit service resumed. The next day the prospective black motormen began their training. On August 17 the last troops were withdrawn and the PTC was handed back to its management. The walkout had been the most costly "hate strike" of the war, with an estimated four million man-hours lost in defense plants alone.[19]

TWU leaders claimed that only a minority of the PTC workers had supported the strike, while the rest had been intimidated from working, but they acknowledged that the situation was "very dangerous ice to walk on" and that the TWU's "position among the men . . . will be very weak for months to come." The signing of the TWU's contract on August 9 began the rebuilding process, for it brought consider-able economic gains to the work force. Fewer than 10% of the covered workers took advantage of an escape period to choose not to belong to the union. In October,

U.S. Army troops guarding the mass transit system during the 1944 Philadelphia transit strike.

PTC workers voted 4,082 to 1,523 for a dues check-off, not the absolute majority needed under Pennsylvania law, but an indication of the union's strides in solidifying its position.

Nonetheless, problems remained. For almost a year after the strike, McMenamin kept trying to displace the TWU through overtly racist agitation. In October 1945, some 6,500 PTC workers signed a petition asking for the reinstatement of the fired strike leaders.[20] Ill-feelings over the desegregation issue even became a factor in the internal politics of Local 234. Once the local's first contract was signed, jockeying began over who should lead the union. Some International officers wanted Fitzsimon to run for local president. Fitzsimon, however, did not press his case vigorously. Moreover, many Local 234 activists wanted to get rid of Fitzsimon as quickly as possible, in part because they disliked his leftism, in part out of their desire for autonomy and personal power, and in part because they believed that hostility toward the union over the race issue was primarily focused on Fitzsimon, who had been the most outspoken union supporter of black rights. After much maneuvering, a compromise officers' slate was worked out. Fitzsimon was given no local post, though he remained in Philadelphia as the TWU's International representative. J. B. Daugherty was elected president, Joseph Marks, whom Fitzsimon had backed, was elected financial secretary-treasurer, and black activist Maxwell Windham was chosen as one of several vice presidents.

During the next year there was considerable tension between the International and Daugherty and his allies. Under International guidance, Local 234 began an impressive series of political education and trade union training classes, and a Detroit leftist, William Moody, was brought in to edit the local's newspaper. Nevertheless, by the spring of 1945 Fitzsimon had been effectively squeezed out. The following fall an officers' slate headed by Daugherty was elected by a comfortable margin over one promoted by the International. Moody was quickly fired and whatever influence the CP and the International had within the local was much diminished. Thereafter Quill took a personal hand in all of Local 234's contract negotiations—the only local outside of New York where he consistently did so—but otherwise the Philadelphia group remained largely autonomous, even while going though a further series of internal changes.[21]

The new locals in Chicago and Philadelphia represented a major TWU expansion in the transit industry. In the immediate postwar period, this expansion continued, as several new transit locals were organized. Two eventually had over a thousand members, Local 250, representing the carmen on San Francisco's Municipal Railway (Muni), and Local 176, representing the non-clerical employees of the Louisville (Kentucky) Street Railway. However, the opportunities for additional growth in the transit industry were modest. For one thing, relatively few major transit systems were still non-union. Some that were had already warded off TWU drives.[22] For another thing, the Amalgamated had grown increasingly aggressive in organizing and bargaining, partially as a result of competition from the TWU.[23] Accordingly, if the TWU was to continue to grow significantly, it would have to go outside the mass transit industry.

Even before the war, the TWU had begun looking beyond transit. To some extent, this was an effort to hedge the TWU's uncertain future on the NYCTS. Also, Quill wanted a large union, he wanted to increase the power of the union presidency, which he thought would be easier with a scattered, diverse membership, and he wanted new places to visit on official business, especially cities with warm climates. Quill was an opportunist, more adept at seizing chances that presented themselves than at planning strategies. Thus he pushed the TWU to mimic what eventually became it most hated rival, District 50, organizing workers wherever possible and worrying about jurisdictional issues afterward. From the 1940s on, this became an increasingly common practice throughout the CIO; once only the most recalcitrant employers (often in the South) remained unorganized in their original jurisdictions, many CIO unions looked to other fields for new members.[24]

In early 1941 a unit of about 600 New Orleans trucking workers, which had been directly affiliated with the CIO, joined the TWU as Local 206. This was the first fruit of a southern organizing campaign that the TWU kicked off the previous year.[25] Within the TWU, Local 206 was anomalous in several ways. First, it was the TWU's first non-transit unit. Second, its members were overwhelmingly black. And third, the local was more deeply entangled with the CP than any other TWU unit. Most of the leadership and staff of Local 206 and quite a few rank and filers belonged to the CP. The union openly sold the *Sunday Worker* in its offices. Since in 1942 the entire Louisiana CP, according to the FBI, had only 162 members (excluding a separate maritime workers branch), the twenty-five or so mostly black Communists in Local 206 represented a substantial proportion of the Party's state membership.[26]

Two years later the TWU took over a benevolent association of Columbia University maintenance workers. Here the connection was ethnicity; most of the Columbia workers were Irish maids and janitors, poorly paid and working under miserable conditions. It was on this occasion that Quill apparently first used what was to become one of his favorite lines. When asked how the Columbia workers fell into the TWU's jurisdiction, he replied, "they ride the subways, don't they?"[27]

While the TWU gains in trucking and education were fortuitous, its entrance into the utility industry was part of an ambitious plan. In early 1942 the members of an independent union representing 4,000 blue-collar and clerical workers at the Brooklyn Union Gas Company (BUG) voted to join the TWU. Anticipating this development, the TWU convention the previous fall had expanded the union's jurisdiction to include utility workers and even discussed a name change to the Transport and Utility Workers Union.

The TWU jumped into the utility industry without CIO approval. It was a field already crowded with competing unions, including the International Brotherhood of Electrical Workers (AFL), several independents, District 50, and the CIO's own Utility Workers Organizing Committee (UWOC), an inept outfit which had made little progress since being formed in 1938. This risky move was not as arbitrary as it might seem. Many utility companies owned transit systems, and the largest utility in New York, Consolidated Edison (Con Ed), sold electricity to the IND. The division of labor in the transit and utility industries was remarkably similar, a combination of large plants, maintenance gangs, and highly dispersed workers. There also was a cultural logic; at least in New York many utility workers were Irish immigrants. In addition, there was a question of timing. Having just parted ways with John L. Lewis over foreign policy, the TWU no longer had to worry about alienating Lewis's daughter and brother, both of whom were District 50 officials, while UWOC was looking more impotent than ever. Finally, in the case of BUG, politics were involved. Several key BUG activists, including John Lopez, who was elected as the first president of the TWU BUG unit, Local 101, were already in or soon to become members of the CP. Others, like Frank Sheehan, who had been the independent's secretary-treasurer, while not Communists, worked amicably with the left.[28]

Delighted as they were to take over the BUG union, the main prize TWU leaders were after was Con Ed. Local 1–2 of the independent Brotherhood of Consolidated Edison Employees alone had 12,000 members. Starting in late 1941, informal merger talks were held between Quill and the leaders of this local. UWOC, however, fervently objected to the TWU's move into its jurisdiction, lobbying furiously with the CIO national office to block the TWU. Furthermore, within the Con Ed union there was considerable sentiment for remaining independent.

For a while, in late 1943, the possibility that the Con Ed Brotherhood would merge with the TWU or take part in a three-way merger with the TWU and UWOC seemed strong. In the end, however, Phil Murray arranged for a merger of the Con

Ed group with UWOC alone. The resulting new International, the Utility Workers Union of America, was issued a CIO charter in August 1945 with clear jurisdiction over gas, power, heat, light, and affiliated industries.

While the jockeying over Con Ed was taking place, the TWU made several efforts to organize utility workers elsewhere, usually at companies which also owned transit systems. None of these drives proved successful, in part because of infighting with UWOC. At the end of the war the TWU's Utility Division consisted only of Local 101 and Local 102, the latter a unit of 600 workers at a Queens gas and electric company which the TWU soon lost as the result of a corporate merger. Thereafter, with CIO jurisdiction resolved, the TWU was effectively locked out of the utility industry except for its BUG unit, which it retained.[29]

While the TWU foray into the utility field proved essentially abortive, its push into the airline industry was more successful. Apparently the idea for this effort came from Charles Smolnikoff, an organizer for the Industrial Union of Marine and Shipbuilding Workers, the director of the Florida CIO, and, according to the FBI, a onetime head of the Florida CP. In early 1943 Smolnikoff got wind of grumbling among Pan American Airways workers in Miami. At his suggestion, in August Quill went to Miami, Pan Am's main base, where he met with a small group of airline workers and local CP officials. Upon his return, the TWU decided to begin organizing the airlines. TWU leaders believed that air transport would boom after the war. MacMahon told the TWU Executive Board that "if we can crack into the air transport field, we will have an opportunity to become one of the most powerful forces in the country."[30]

Smolnikoff, New York transit worker Richard Downes, and several locally hired organizers spearheaded the TWU's Miami effort, but wartime travel restrictions and staff shortages limited the International's role. In March 1944 the TWU won an election to represent a small unit of Pan Am maintenance workers. A year later, it defeated the IAM and an independent association in an election to represent a larger unit of Pan Am mechanics and mechanics' helpers. The two Miami groups, organized as Local 500 were the only airline units the TWU was formally certified to represent before the war ended. However, by V-J Day the TWU had already begun organizing Pan Am workers at New York's La Guardia Airport and American Airlines personnel in New York, Burbank, and San Francisco.[31]

As the TWU anticipated, after the war the airline industry underwent rapid, sustained growth. In 1936 certified air carriers employed 9,995 workers; in 1946 they had 97,191 workers, and in 1956, 143,514. Until 1946 the most commonly used commercial aircraft was the DC-3, with a range of less than 1,700 miles and a maximum capacity of 27 passengers. In 1946 came the DC-6, with a range of over 2,500 miles and a capacity of 58 passengers. Twelve years later came the first commercial jets.

Like transit, the airline industry was labor intensive. In 1947 labor costs accounted for half of all industry expenses. However, airline workers were generally quite different from transit workers. Above all, they were young. During the war airline jobs were draft exempt and many men went straight from high school into the industry to avoid the army. Relatively few were immigrants, though many had parents who were. Because of the desire to avoid the draft, and also the glamour associated with the industry, the airlines attracted quite a few workers from middle-class backgrounds. There were even some stewardesses from upper-class homes. However, there were also black porters and cleaners in Miami, Caribbean attendants on international flights, and Mexican-American maintenance workers in the Southwest. What most airline workers shared beyond their youth was their lack of previous union experience, their disinterest in politics, and—with the some exceptions—their "Americanness."

The economic and legal environment of the airline industry was also quite different from transit. Nationally, the industry was dominated by a few employers, flush with wartime profits. These companies were heavily regulated and subsidized by the federal government. As a result, they paid little attention to short-term costs, including for labor, since these could be passed on to the public through increased subsidies. Labor relations were conducted under the Railway Labor Act, which provided machinery for unit determination, recognition elections, mediation, cooling-off periods, and binding arbitration of grievances.[32]

Just before the war ended, Maurice Forge was put in charge of all TWU airline activities. A number of factors led to his assignment. First, Forge himself wanted to do more organizing. Second, although Forge, like almost all of the top TWU leaders except MacMahon, was an immigrant, he was the most assimilated of the group. As one unionist put, Forge, had a "finish" that enabled him to deal better with native-born workers. Third, Santo had long wanted Forge out of his position as editor of TWU publications, so that he himself could gain more control. Forge's assignment to the airlines accomplished this.

At the TWU's September 1946 convention, the elected post of editor was eliminated and Forge chosen as one of six vice presidents, assigned to head up a new Air Transport Division (ATD). Forge established separate ATD headquarters near La Guardia Airport and, in spite of occasional clashes with Santo, Martin Young, and Hogan, was able to maintain considerable autonomy for the ATD. Rather quickly, a number of capable airline workers were recruited as activists, local officers, and organizers, one of whom, William Lindner, years later became the TWU's third International president.[33]

Between 1945 and 1948, through a series of organizing drives, representation elections, and brief strikes, the TWU won a strong foothold in the airline industry. Doing so required not only convincing workers that they would benefit from a union, but outflanking rivals. Until the end of the war, most airline workers belonged to independent associations that were usually little more than company unions. (The pilots were an exception; they had their own union.) At roughly the same time that the TWU began signing up airline workers, the IAM and the UAW, the dominant unions in aircraft manufacturing, also entered the field. The TWU and the IAM generally avoided direct confrontations. Ironically, it was with its fellow CIO affiliate, the UAW, that the TWU clashed bitterly.

The bulk of the airline workers the TWU succeeded in organizing were located in Miami, New York, Tulsa, or San Francisco and worked for either Pan Am or American Airlines. The TWU represented all the mechanics and fleet service employees at both companies. In addition, it represented Pan Am flight navigators, engineers, radio operators, flight attendants, guards, and commissary workers. At

American Airlines it represented plant maintenance, ground service, and stores employees. The union also represented smaller units, most of navigators, at United, Northwest, Trans-Canada, and Trans-World Airlines, and the employees of a number of airline maintenance firms. All told, in 1948 TWU contracts covered about 12,000 airline workers, a few thousand fewer than the IAM. By contrast, the UAW had had little success. [34]

TWU members who entered the service early in the war returned to find their union transformed. Before the war, for all practical purposes Local 100 was the TWU. By the war's end, there were roughly 15,000 TWU members in other locals. Continued expansion in the immediate postwar period further changed the picture. As of September 1948, the TWU had a total paid-up membership of about 68,000. There were 35,000 members in Local 100; 10,700 in Local 234 in Philadelphia; and over 9,000 more in thirty-three other transit and miscellaneous locals. The airline locals had a combined membership of close to 9,000. Finally, Local 101 had 3,700 members. Thus from a union originally composed just of New York transit workers, the TWU had so expanded that its original jurisdiction now accounted for only slightly over half of its membership, and over a fifth of its members were not transit workers at all. Important as Local 100 was, in the postwar years other locals played an increasingly important role in the internal political life of the TWU. The TWU was no longer solely the creature of its originators. [35]

VI

"Fortune's blows when most
struck home . . . "

12

FROM THE GRAND ALLIANCE
TO THE COLD WAR

For the TWU, the first two years after World War II were something of an Indian summer—a last heyday before the political edifice of the Popular Front came crashing down. The Cold War was to have a profound impact on the TWU. For most of its history, the union had operated in an environment of national and local left-center coalitions. After World War II, international developments and political changes at home began to split apart the Popular Front, New Deal, and CIO alliances. But this did not occur instantaneously. In 1946 and 1947 the future still seemed very uncertain. Although Soviet-American relations were rapidly deteriorating, it was not until 1947 or even 1948 that it became clear that a permanent rupture was at hand. Domestically, while the Truman administration was moving to the right, both anti-Communist and Popular Front liberals remained hopeful about the possibility of reviving the New Deal. So were most labor leaders; with roughly a third of all workers belonging to unions, an historic high, they looked forward to exercising expanded social and political influence. During this brief interlude between World War II and the full onset of the Cold War, the TWU was able to solidify its wartime gains, especially on the NYCTS. At the same time, however, the political and legal context in which the union operated was becoming increasingly inhospitable.

TWU leaders were delighted when Mayor Fiorello La Guardia announced in the spring of 1945 that he would not seek re-election. The union's long-strained relationship with the Mayor was near the breaking point, and Quill had already begun discussions with William O'Dwyer's supporters about a possible endorsement.[1] CP and ALP leaders were likewise not displeased by La Guardia's withdrawal. New York City had always been anomalous in that the strongest supporters of the New Deal were outside of the Democratic party, while most of the local Democratic hierarchy was anti-Roosevelt. La Guardia's retirement opened the way for an ALP-Democratic coalition within the city, which would bolster the liberal wing of the Democratic party nationally and better position both groups to fight New York's Republican governor, Thomas E. Dewey.

With the civil service unions taking the lead, O'Dwyer was promoted as the ideal agent for such a realignment. To pressure the Democratic establishment to nominate the Brooklyn District Attorney, the ALP selected O'Dwyer as its own candidate before the Democrats made their choice. This strategy succeeded; O'Dwyer received the Democratic nomination and, except in the Bronx, the Democrats and the ALP generally endorsed each other's candidates.[2]

The TWU was particularly enthusiastic in its support for O'Dwyer. Quill, for one, got along well with the Irish-born candidate. Also, unlike in 1941, O'Dwyer's policy positions were written mostly by ALP members, not Brooklyn Democrats. Most importantly, however, union leaders believed that O'Dwyer would move toward institutionalizing collective bargaining in the NYCTS. In May 1945 Quill wrote to Santo that if O'Dwyer could be elected as a "unity candidate," "we would be on the main road towards union security."[3]

In July 1945 the Local 100 Joint Executive Committee endorsed O'Dwyer and established a "Transport Workers Committee of One Thousand for O'Dwyer and Quill." This was the only time that Quill's election machinery was directly used to aid another candidate. Because of the circumstances in the Bronx, this was more than a symbolic gesture. Bronx Democratic leader Edward Flynn opposed his party's alliance with the ALP, refused to run a joint City Council and Borough presidency slate, and did little to aid O'Dwyer. The TWU thus carried much of the burden of O'Dwyer's bid.[4] O'Dwyer was not unappreciative; on October 18, while addressing a large TWU election rally, he criticized past Board of Transportation labor practices and said that in the future labor-management differences should be dealt with through collective bargaining.[5]

The election results gave the TWU considerable political capital. Quill was easily re-elected, getting the highest number of first-choice votes in the city and the second highest in the city's history. Eugene Connolly was the only other ALP Councilman elected, though CP Councilmen Peter Cacchione and Benjamin Davis were returned to office. O'Dwyer won easily, receiving the largest plurality on record in a mayoralty election.[6]

The TWU moved quickly to take advantage of its political gains. Even before the election, a new mood of militancy began developing among the union's members and leaders. During the first six months after the war, there were at least three localized wildcat strikes on the NYCTS. By early 1946, Local 100 was stepping up its organizing on the municipal system and beginning to formulate demands, with an eye toward a spring offensive. However, because of unexpected developments, the union's first test of its new political alliance came earlier than planned.[7]

It had long been recognized that the powerhouses the city had taken over from the private lines were in serious need of modernization. In 1940, LaGuardia had proposed expanding the 59th and 74th street plants to supply power to all NYCTS divisions including the IND, which was buying its power from Con Ed. Although several engineering studies were carried out, the war prevented any construction. With the war over, in November 1945 a contract with a private engineering company was approved to develop plans for rehabilitating the 59th Street plant as the first step toward improving and tying together all the NYCTS power generating facilities.[8]

Immediately after this contract was signed, two members of the Board of Transportation, Delaney and George Keegan, retired, giving La Guardia the opportunity to make new appointments before his own departure. To replace Delaney as Board chairman, he chose Major General Charles P. Gross, a career officer who had headed the Army's transportation service. To replace Keegan, he appointed William Reid, the long-time City Collector.[9]

In spite of the fact that public power was a favorite cause of La Guardia's, Gross moved quickly to reverse the Board's power policy. On December 29 the Board canceled the recently let engineering contract and began talks with Con Ed about purchasing additional power from the company and possibly selling to it the NYCTS power plants. The TWU immediately protested. Although publicly the union stressed that such a move would be a blow to the principle of municipal operation of utilities and would lead to increased costs, its main concern was the effect on its members and its strategic position. The 1,500 workers at the three NYCTS power houses were solidly pro-TWU, and in a strike were well placed to shut down the system.[10]

What role, if any, O'Dwyer played in all this is uncertain. Reports circulated that city officials close to the incoming administration had tried to delay Delaney's original decision to sign the engineering contract. Once in office, O'Dwyer said that he would consider the advisability of buying power from Con Edison. However, he did not seem eager to confront the TWU. On January 1, 1946, his very first day in office, he appointed former Deputy Board of Transportation Commissioner Edward C. Maguire to head the Board's division of labor relations. Maguire in turn appointed former War Labor Board official Theodore W. Kheel to be his assistant. Both men were considered sympathetic to the TWU. O'Dwyer hoped that they would help forestall the constant labor turmoil that had characterized the La Guardia years.[11]

On January 18, Quill threatened a city-wide transit strike if the NYCTS power-houses were sold without a prior public referendum on the issue. Quill argued that the plants had been purchased as part of the unification plan, which had been preceded by a referendum on the needed bonding authority. Therefore, he reasoned, they should not be sold without a similar popular vote. Most observers felt that if a city-wide ballot was held, the sale would not be approved. Quill also announced that the TWU would soon demand recognition as the sole bargaining agent on the city's transit system, a flat two-dollar-a-day wage increase, a signed contract, and some form of union security. Quill warned that if the union was forced to strike to block the powerhouse sale, its members would not return to work until all of their demands had been met. While O'Dwyer avoided committing himself, and Gross criticized the TWU for interfering in the rightful province of management, the union began preparations for a walkout.[12]

On January 21, hours before the TWU was to announce the time of its strike, O'Dwyer capitulated, promising that no power plant sale would take place without a prior popular vote. This effectively killed Gross's plan. Beyond that, the Mayor said that the "other matters" raised by the TWU "must be resolved over the collective bargaining table between the union and the Board of Transportation." Quill was overjoyed; the outcome of the crisis, he told the press, "cemented the relationship between Mayor O'Dwyer and the American Labor Party."[13]

O'Dwyer did not share Quill's delight. He was widely criticized in the press for having given in to the TWU's threats and he resented Quill's adroit maneuvering. Accordingly, he moved quickly to distance himself from the TWU and Quill. On January 26 he pointedly met with a delegation from the Civil Service Forum, which was claiming that its members had been intimidated by violence and threats from the TWU. Two days later, when Quill sought a meeting to discuss outstanding transit labor issues, O'Dwyer referred him to Maguire.[14]

On January 29 the TWU formally requested that the Board of Transportation begin discussion on its other demands, including the two-dollar-a-day wage increase, sole recognition, a signed contract, union security, improved grievance procedures, wage equalizations, and upgraded working conditions. The Board's reply came on February 19 in the form of a letter from Gross to all the transit unions, inviting them to present their demands at hearings to be held by a specially appointed committee of transit officials. TWU leaders were furious; in effect, Gross was planning to continue the procedures used under La Guardia, rather than institute collective bargaining with the TWU, as promised by O'Dwyer. In response, Quill once again threatened a strike, and a series of mass union meetings authorized the TWU leadership to take whatever action it deemed necessary.[15]

The events of the following week were dramatic but familiar. The city's numerous TWU-induced transit crises had already developed a characteristic pattern; it was no longer a new art form. O'Dwyer, who upon taking office had discovered that the city had no plans to deal with a transit strike, had a high-level police committee draw up detailed emergency plans. He also let it be known that in the event of a TWU walkout he would maintain transit operations using other city workers. Both the Civil Service Forum and the AFMTW cooperated by announcing that their members would continue to work during a strike. For its part, the TWU set a strike deadline, February 26, and held a series of mass meetings and protest rallies. The union also mobilized support from the ALP, the NYC CIO Council, and various civic groups. The running debate over whether or not the city was empowered to grant exclusive union recognition resumed as well, with O'Dwyer adopting La Guardia's old position that to do so would be illegal.

O'Dwyer was so peeved at Quill that he refused to meet with him in person until the very end of the crisis. However, he did meet with Sacher and Santo, and a number of intermediaries, including Phil Murray, Joe Curran, State Mediation Board chairman Arthur S. Meyer, and RCA president David Sarnoff, joined city and union officials in a series of informal negotiating sessions. At a secret meeting at Sarnoff's house just before the TWU's strike deadline, O'Dwyer and Quill finally got together and an agreement was signed. The union withdrew its strike threat and demand for exclusive recognition, in return for which O'Dwyer appointed a Special Transit Committee headed by Meyer to study NYCTS working conditions, wages, and labor relations. In a last expression of his displeasure, O'Dwyer refused to allow Quill to attend the City Hall session at which he, Murray, and Sarnoff announced the settlement.[16]

The agreement ending this latest transit crisis was widely viewed as a setback to the TWU. The union had failed to convert its support for O'Dwyer into a position as the sole bargaining agent for the city's transit workers, its aim since O'Dwyer's candidacy had first been discussed. However, the outcome was also far from a total union defeat. O'Dwyer had again repudiated Gross's policies and had not even allowed the Board of Transportation to participate in the discussions resolving the dispute. Furthermore, the members of the Special Transit Committee were expected to be sympathetic to the TWU's demands. Finally, and perhaps most important, the TWU had again shown that it was the main force defining the issues and setting the pace of developments on the NYCTS.[17]

Many outside observers speculated that the TWU's push for sole bargaining rights was a response to the growing strength of its union rivals.[18] The AFMTW, and to a lesser extent the Civil Service Forum, had become increasingly active during the final stages of the war and the immediate postwar period. Louis Waldman, a well-connected Social Democrat, had become the AFMTW's lawyer and spokesman. The group continued to receive strong backing from the AFL. Stressing anti-Communism, it apparently made some gains in the BMT maintenance-of-way and bus shop departments. Meanwhile, in January 1946, after winning an election to represent the Long Island Rail Road trainmen, District 50 announced that it would next turn to the NYCTS. The UMW had just rejoined the AFL, and discussions soon began about a possible AFMTW-District 50 merger.[19]

The smaller NYCTS unions benefited from dissatisfaction among some higher-paid craft workers with the TWU's policy of seeking across-the-board wage increases, which had the effect of narrowing the wage gap between skilled and unskilled workers. Some better-paid workers who owned their own homes also disliked the TWU (and ALP) stand promoting increased real estate taxes as a way to subsidize transit deficits. Aware of these problems, the TWU tried to strengthen its position with the skilled workers by acknowledging their special situation. During the war the union won higher "quota rates" for a specified percentage of the most skilled shop workers and established a motormen's council with representatives from all three NYCTS divisions. In its 1946 program, the TWU pushed for raising the wages of skilled maintenance and construction workers to the levels prevailing in private industry and for shortening the time needed to reach top rates. Such steps helped to limit defections and win some new members, but the TWU's rivals undoubtedly continued to draw some support as a result of the tension between skilled and unskilled workers.[20]

Nevertheless, the importance of the TWU's rivals was exaggerated. Claims by the AFMTW and Civil Service Forum of some 5,000 and 6,000 members respectively were probably much inflated. Even if accurate, the TWU still had about twice their combined membership. Furthermore, the unions competing with the TWU fought one another as much as they fought the TWU. The AFMTW and the Forum were able to maintain their high profiles largely because they were convenient to O'Dwyer and the Board of Transportation. They provided a handy justification for not granting the TWU sole recognition and, in the case of the AFMTW, a way of maintaining good relations with the AFL. Both groups had little impact on eco-

nomic conditions, concentrating instead on denying the TWU sole or even proportional representation. By the time the AFMTW affiliated with District 50 in December 1946, it had lost whatever momentum it had once had. [21]

The TWU's postwar militancy increased its following, both absolutely and probably also relative to its rivals. In early 1946 the union made membership gains and
won over a few important converts from the Forum, the BLE, and the BRSA. The
proof of its dominant position on the NYCTS came in May 1946, when it submitted signatures from over 21,000 workers asking for a collective bargaining election.
In most job categories, including motorman and towerman, the TWU had signatures from over 75% of the workers. [22]

During the spring of 1946, seven transit unions made presentations to the Special
Transit—or Meyer—Committee. The TWU's was the most extensive, a reiteration
of its previously announced demands, except for the substitution of a call for a
representation-election for its earlier insistence on immediate sole recognition. On
September 9 the Committee issued its report, which was highly favorable to the
TWU. Although it did not accept the two-dollar-a-day wage increase, the Committee did recommend a not-much-smaller boost of twenty cents an hour, retroactive to
July 1. Many TWU proposals on wage standardization, reductions in increment
spreads, accumulation of sick leave, and swing, deadheading, overtime, and lunch
pay were accepted in part or full. On the issue of labor relations, the report substantially met the TWU's demands. It proposed that representation elections be held
and exclusive recognition ultimately be granted in units to be determined by the
SLRB. Until the legality of sole recognition could be established, it suggested the
use of weighted multiple representation in yearly negotiations on wages, hours, and
conditions and in grievance procedures. It also favored instituting voluntary check-
off of union dues. Treating the report as if it was a negotiated agreement, a meeting
of 6,000 TWU members "ratified" the proposals the day after they were formally
issued. [23]

The Board of Transportation and the O'Dwyer administration were deeply divided over the Meyer Committee report. On November 4 the Board approved the
recommended general wage increase, but withheld approval of any retroactive payments. Four days later, it rejected the Committee's labor relations proposals, choosing instead to continue the status quo. Dissenting from this decision was Board-
member William H. Davis, the former chairman of the NWLB. In June 1946, with
the strong approval of the TWU, O'Dwyer had appointed Davis to replace William
Reid, in hope that he could solve the perpetual transit labor problems.

TWU leaders were furious at the Board's failure to adopt most of the Meyer
Committee recommendations. Once again the union threatened to strike, this time
in demand of the retroactive pay increases and the proposed labor relations system.
After the usual developments—police preparations, strike votes, consultations with
Phil Murray, and so forth—in mid-November O'Dwyer arranged a compromise.
The Board of Transportation agreed to pay the back wage increases and O'Dwyer
commissioned Davis to develop yet another labor relations plan.

On December 17 the Board began distributing checks for retroactive pay ranging
from $172 to $400. This was the first time the city had ever given its transit workers

back pay. It was a tangible symbol of the TWU's success. The increased wages the TWU won through its sustained, year-long campaign helped win back more of the union members who had dropped out after unification. The TWU entered 1947 with more support than it had had in years.[24]

In mid-February Davis sent a draft of his labor relations plan to O'Dwyer, who endorsed it after minor modifications. As revised, the Davis-O'Dwyer proposal called for the Board of Transportation to determine the relative strength of the various unions within given units and then give their views proportionate weight in bargaining. If negotiating deadlocks developed, advisory arbitration was to be used. For all other purposes, including the voluntary checkoff of dues, all unions were to be treated equally.

The TWU was generally pleased with this plan. As Hogan pointed out, if the TWU could prove that it was the largest NYCTS union, it would have sole bargaining rights in everything but name. To this end, in April the union submitted cards from 23,105 workers authorizing it to represent them in negotiations with the Board of Transportation. Once again, however, the Board majority of Gross and Sullivan rejected any departure from the status quo. On April 25 they voted down the Davis-O'Dwyer plan. Shortly thereafter Davis resigned.[25]

By the time the Davis-O'Dwyer plan was rejected, it had been over a year since the Meyer Committee had been appointed and almost ten months since the last pay increase had gone into effect retroactively. Accordingly, the TWU had already begun formulating a new bargaining program, into which it incorporated a call for the adoption of the Davis-O'Dwyer plan. Other demands included a fifteen-cents-an-hour wage increase; improved pensions, sick leave, vacations, and holidays; revised working rules; reclassification of trackmen as higher-paid maintainers; and improvements for supervisory and clerical personnel.[26]

The TWU's fight for this program soon turned into a campaign for Gross's ouster. The TWU had always carefully distinguished between the Mayor's actions and the Board of Transportation's. Under La Guardia, this had been largely a tactical device; under O'Dwyer, it more accurately reflected reality. Gross and Sullivan were La Guardia holdovers and O'Dwyer was repeatedly frustrated by his inability to control the Board. Gross spent much of his adult life in the army; he was used to military discipline and military ways. He proved remarkably inept and insensitive in managing the NYCTS, a labor-intensive, unionized, civilian enterprise. Once, for example, he tried to cancel the free passes given to retired workers (sometimes illegally used by their relatives). Although a small savings would have resulted, transit workers were deeply insulted, viewing their passes as a "badge of honor." Gross was a great believer in increased efficiency and speed-up, which also brought him into conflict with the TWU. The rejection of the Davis-O'Dwyer plan was thus but one of many issues over which Gross and the TWU clashed in the spring and summer of 1947.[27]

In April the Board of Transportation unilaterally changed the schedule of IND job assignments from which the division's workers were to make their "picks." In protest, TWU members refused to choose new assignments. In May, IND transportation workers began a work-to-rule slowdown. By early June the slowdown had spread to the IRT and BMT and to the shops. At 148th Street, under the leadership of section chairman Adrian Cabral, known even within the union as a hot-head, there was a brief work stoppage. In retaliation, the Board fired Cabral and IND motorman James Kelly and suspended two others. Though aimed at the Board, these job actions were also a response to the Condon-Wadlin Act. This state law, recently passed by the Republican-controlled legislature after a series of upstate municipal worker strikes, outlawed public employee strikes and imposed drastic penalites on strikers, including automatic dismissal and a three-year pay freeze for those rehired.[28]

In mid-June the Board retreated, setting up a new IND pick and allowing TWU organizers to be present when assignments were chosen. Cabral and Kelly were eventually reinstated. Then, in early September, under pressure from the TWU and O'Dwyer, Gross quit. In his place the Mayor appointed William Reid, so that for the first time a majority of the Board members were O'Dwyer appointees. Pleased by these developments, the TWU once again began to press for its previously announced bargaining program, increasing its wage demand to 30 cents an hour in light of the changed circumstances and the time elapsed.[29]

While the TWU was fighting to solidify its position on the NYCTS, the international and political climate was rapidly changing. The first winds of the Cold War to affect the TWU were within the Communist movement. In 1944, under Earl Browder's leadership, the CP had carried its wartime Popular Front policy to an extreme. Browder interpreted the Tehran Conference as signaling the start of a prolonged period of cooperation between the U.S., Britain, and the U.S.S.R. that would extend well beyond the end of the war. He urged the CP to support this development by promoting a domestic alliance with progressive capitalists and by operating as a pressure group within the Democratic party and other mainstream institutions. At his suggestion, in May 1944 the CP dissolved itself, re-forming as the Communist Political Association (CPA).

The CPA proved short-lived. In the spring of 1945 French CP leader Jacques Duclos, with the aid and presumably encouragement of the Soviets, published a letter criticizing the dissolution of the American CP. CPA leaders, perhaps incorrectly, took this as a call for the complete repudiation of Browder. In short order, Browder was removed from power and the CP reconstituted. A new national leadership of William Z. Foster, Henry Winston, Eugene Dennis, John Williamson, and Robert Thompson was chosen, and Thompson replaced Gil Green as the head of the New York State CP. In early 1946, Browder was expelled from the Party.[30]

Quill had less reason than most to be surprised by these developments, for he was one of the few people who knew that there had been a sharp if lopsided struggle over Browder's policies within the upper echelon of the CP. In February 1944 Quill had attended an enlarged meeting of the CP's political committee—its top leadership body—which had discussed a letter from Foster objecting to Browder's program. Later, Duclos was to quote from this letter in his critique of Browder. Like most others at the meeting, Quill supported Browder, sharing his hopes for postwar international cooperation. In fact, in a private letter to Santo a month earlier Quill had been more concerned with the intentions of the U.S.S.R. than with those of the U.S. "If we can win the war in a short time," he wrote,

> I am sure that President Roosevelt, Churchill and Chang Kai-Sheck [sic] will be able to talk Premier Stalin into staying on his own side of the fence when the war is over. If this would only happen and if they would only make peace with the Catholic Church, all of us would thank God for the victory.[31]

Quill was not in complete agreement with Browder. In particular, he worried that Browder was downplaying the question of imperialism, which for Quill meant above all the question of Ireland. Still, Quill admired Browder personally, was flattered by his attentions, and broadly shared his views.[32]

The changes following the Duclos letter, according to Maurice Forge, caused "consternation and alarm" in the TWU. Most trade unionists close to the CP were reluctant to repudiate Browder, not so much because they were committed to his ideological position but because they felt comfortable with his leadership and disliked sudden reversals of policy. In the TWU, each Communist reacted differently—Quill at first took the whole affair rather lightly—but within a short time there was widespread unease with the CP's new direction and leadership.[33]

The TWU was particularly, and in some ways peculiarly, affected by the changes in the CP. Although all of the leaders of the Party renounced "Browderism," there were important policy differences among them. Most national leaders, led by Dennis, wanted to maintain the CP's alliances with New Dealers and liberal labor leaders even at the cost of considerable compromise. Foster, however, argued for a more thoroughgoing turn to the left. Although generally stymied on the national level, in New York State he usually prevailed through his close allies, Thompson and Ben Davis. On a whole range of issues, from the likelihood of war with the Soviet Union, to correct policy in "Negro work," to electoral strategy, the two camps disagreed. The result was a striking confusion in the CP's policies throughout this period. In New York, where the faction-fighting was most intense, the TWU was caught in the middle.[34]

The Spellman affair illustrated some of the consequences of this situation. In January 1946, Quill, on behalf of the TWU, had congratulated Archbishop Francis Spellman on his selection to be a cardinal. Since most TWU members were Catholic, this was not an unnatural courtesy. Although deeply conservative, Spellman had never publicly attacked the TWU. During the war, Quill had even enlisted his aid in the union's disputes with LaGuardia. Spellman had a great deal of clout in New York politics—his residence was known as "the powerhouse"—and his good graces could be valuable.

In early March a City Council resolution was introduced honoring Spellman. Davis and Cacchione opposed the measure, consistent with the CP's abandonment of its prior policy of holding an "outreached hand" toward practicing Catholics. Quill joined the rest of the Council in voting for the resolution. What was most significant was what followed. At a meeting of the state board of the CP, Thompson tried to have Quill censured for his vote. When Bella Dodd, a leader of the Teachers' Union, protested, Thompson replied that "communist leadership is superior to mass leadership. Anyone who opposes us must be eliminated from the labor movement."[35] Even before this, according to Quill's later account, CP leader Jack Stachel had opposed the TWU's threatened strike over the possible sale of the NYCTS powerhouses.[36] Perhaps as a result of these incidents, Quill chose not to march in the 1946 May Day parade, as had been his custom.[37]

In spite of these tensions, Quill and the TWU remained firmly within the liberal-left orbit. From late 1945 on, the TWU repeatedly denounced the Truman administration (though rarely Truman himself) for what were characterized as departures from FDR's domestic and international policies. Over and over, the union argued for a restoration of the wartime Big Three alliance and a battle at home against the "economic royalists." The TWU was very active in organizing delegations to Albany and Washington to lobby for CIO-supported legislation, such as the continuation of price controls and housing for veterans. Quill even put himself on the left side of the CP by calling, in May 1946, for a national labor party, a position rejected by his ALP-ally, Sidney Hillman, and handled gingerly by Dennis.[38]

The TWU also vigorously pressed the struggle for black rights. In Forth Worth, leaders of a TWU local supported the Texas Civil Rights Congress. In Tulsa, the TWU not only got rid of separate white and black facilities at an American Airlines repair base, but desegregated one of the local hotels. In Miami, the TWU won a non-discrimination clause in its contract with Pan Am and set up its own school to train black mechanics, who were not allowed to attend local vocational schools. And later, in 1948, Local 206 took part in a voter registration drive that more than doubled the number of blacks able to vote in New Orleans.[39]

The TWU leadership, including Quill, set a notably left tone at the union's September 1946 convention. Again, the Truman administration was attacked and Henry Wallace repeatedly praised for his criticism of the "get tough" policy toward the Soviet Union. Red-baiting, anti-Semitism, and racism were denounced in the strongest possible terms. Speakers included Marcantonio, who called for a new, national political party, Paul Robeson, and Irving Potash of the Furriers. There was even a visiting Soviet trade unionist, whom Quill introduced by saying that "the bankers and imperialists, are afraid of their very lives, of the people and the principles and policies represented by the next speaker." While all this went considerably beyond where TWU leaders had previously trod, it did not represent an extreme position. The views put forth by the TWU in 1946 were shared by many non-Communist, left-liberals. When Hyman Blumberg of the ACW, who after Hillman's death in July had become chairman of the ALP, spoke to the TWU convention, his perspective was virtually indistinguishable from Quill's or MacMahon's.[40]

Within the ALP, Hillman's death served temporarily to solidify the alliance between the ACW, the CP-led forces, and Marcantonio. MacMahon was chosen as the labor party's state secretary and the TWU plunged whole-heartedly into the 1946 election. Five TWU members ran for office on the ALP line, though none was elected. The ALP did well, capturing 9% of the vote state-wide and 14.5% in New York City, but the Republicans scored the major victory, sweeping the state-wide races in New York, and taking control of Congress.[41]

1946 ended with a tangible sign of the degree to which the changing political climate was affecting the balance of power within the CIO. At a November meeting of the CIO Executive Board prior to the annual CIO convention, Phil Murray asked for unanimous support for a resolution condemning communism. Quill was one of three leftists asked to serve on a six-person committee charged with drafting an appropriate measure. The upshot was the passage, with CP support, of a resolution stating that the CIO convention delegates "resent and reject efforts by the Communist Party or other political parties and their adherents to interfere in the affairs of the CIO."

The CP was trapped. Under pressure from the right, Murray, after much wavering, had decided to begin undermining the power of the CP within the CIO. He began secretly funding ACTU and won a sharp limitation on the policy-making powers of the CIO industrial councils, which, as in New York, were often left-controlled. The CP, a distinct minority within the CIO, had always depended on alliances with powerful centrists: Lewis and Hillman, then just Lewis, and later Hillman and Murray. If the CP had opposed Murray's limited measures, it would have courted an all-out battle with a center-right coalition, which it undoubtedly would have lost. The alternative, though, was to support a condemnation of itself, a position that undercut its moral standing, highlighted its weakness, and, above all, looked foolish. For Quill, so recently criticized for his own more modest compromise, the situation must have seemed ironic indeed. His comment after serving on the resolution-drafting committee, that he now realized for the first time "that no matter what side of the fence we are on, we are all CIO members," perhaps had greater meaning than was credited to it at the time.[42]

Almost immediately after World War II, a new opposition group developed within Local 100 that was shrewder, more sophisticated, and more effective than its predecessors. It was led by two clerical workers from NYC Omnibus, John Brooks and Raymond Westcott, who had first become unionists during World War II. In 1943 the TWU had begun exploring the possibility of organizing the Omnibus and Fifth Avenue clericals, who were mostly male and overwhelmingly Irish. Westcott, a convert to Catholicism, was worried about the TWU's reputation as Communist-dominated. He asked his local priest for advice and was referred to the Xavier Labor School.[43]

By this time, Xavier had undergone a leadership change. In 1940 Philip A. Carey, an ordained Jesuit priest, had replaced Fitzpatrick as the school's director. Carey was far better suited for the job than his predecessors. His father was a TWU member and a long-time employee of the Third Avenue Railway, first as a trolley motorman and then as a car starter. Carey's younger brother worked for the company in a management position. One of Carey's earliest memories was of helping his father post union broadsides during the 1916 transit strike. During his Jesuit training Carey had written an M.A. thesis "The Guilds and Modern Vocational Groupings" and later a dissertation entitled "Is the Right to a Family Living Wage Due in Commutative Justice?"

As the head of Xavier, Carey quickly developed a wide network of contacts in New York-area unions, transit management, and the national office of the AFL. Through CIO Secretary-Treasurer James Carey, and, on a more regular basis, Harry Read, James Carey's assistant and the former head of the Newspaper Guild and ACTU in Chicago, he also maintained contact with the CIO's national office and its anti-Communist factions. In addition, from 1946 on he kept in touch with former FBI agent Jack Keenan, who that year began co-editing *Counterattack*, an anti-Communist newsletter and blacklist sheet. Under Carey's leadership, student enrollment at Xavier sharply increased after the war (averaging 400 a year) and the range of the school's activities widened.[44]

Soon after Westcott met Carey, he, Brooks, and ten other Omnibus clerical workers began attending Xavier classes. Westcott later recalled that: "We weren't noble lads fighting red-fascism. We were men with wives and kids to take care of, and though it sounds funny to the intellectuals who're so sore at the commies, we just went to labor school to get ahead in the world." With Carey's advice, the Westcott-Brooks group formed an independent union and in 1944 filed for a recognition election among the Omnibus and Fifth Avenue clericals. They lost the vote in units of stenographers and statistical clerks, but won the largest group, the general clerks.[45]

As the war ended, the Omnibus management began taking an increasingly hard line toward the unionized clerks. Recognizing their isolation, in the fall of 1945 the members of the clerical union voted to amalgamate with the TWU. Except for the ties to Xavier, the story of the Omnibus and Fifth Avenue clericals was not unusual; in the late forties many white-collar transit workers were becoming union-minded. In November 1945 the Third Avenue clericals voted to join the TWU and in the years thereafter the TWU made inroads among the NYCTS administrative and clerical workers.[46]

Once in Local 100, Westcott and Brooks quickly decided that a thoroughgoing change in the political character of the TWU was needed. With the help of Carey and other advisers, they plotted a long-term campaign to oust the left from the TWU leadership. Westcott and Carey were pragmatic men, interested in victory rather than fighting the good fight. Their greatest strength was their keen strategic and tactical ability. Together they developed an approach to opposition politics markedly different from that of previous TWU dissidents.

Westcott and Brooks did not try to develop a mass base of their own. Instead they concentrated on winning over established or potential TWU leaders. Firmly believing that anti-Communist propaganda alone would fail as the basis for an effective opposition, they downplayed red-baiting while stressing economic issues, union democracy, and the need for strong union representation. Unlike other oppositionalists, they never dabbled in dual unionism. The Westcott group avoided close ties with past generations of TWU dissidents, whom they saw as tainted by failure. Similarly, they considered ACTU "the kiss of death" for its record of defeat, its loud rhetoric and weak base, and its strong identification with Catholicism. To avoid the latter problem, Westcott's group never operated out of Xavier, although it did encourage TWU members to take courses at the labor school, where Westcott and Brooks taught classes. Finally, Westcott and Carey stressed careful preparation, avoiding battles until they felt that they had at least a fair chance for success.[47]

Westcott and Brooks began their campaign by recruiting followers in other Omnibus sections. By the end of 1946, their supporters held most of the elected steward posts on the line. The Omnibus workers were generally younger than those employed on the other private lines and the TWU hierarchy was less firmly established there than elsewhere. In fact, for a long time the TWU leadership did not even realize that an organized opposition was at work.[48]

That changed at the 1946 TWU convention, which provided an opportunity for union dissidents to develop ties to one another and hand the leadership an unusual setback. Through most of the convention, little opposition was voiced. An alternative foreign policy resolution denouncing Yugoslavian and Soviet "red fascism" was introduced but apparently won little support. Trouble began, however, when elections were held for the International Executive Board (IEB).

The TWU procedure for electing International officers, though formally democratic, gave the leadership considerable power. At the start of each convention a nominations committee was appointed by the chairman (Quill) and ratified by the delegates. The committee, which usually had a top union leader on it, then chose a slate of candidates. By tradition, but not constitutional mandate, an effort was made to give each major component of the union IEB representation, with suggestions for candidates solicited from the locals, branches, and divisions. Then, toward the end of the convention, the proposed slate was voted on. There were no direct contests; for a substitute candidate to be considered one of the committee nominees first had to be voted down. All delegates voted for all IEB members, so that transit workers voted on candidates from the airlines, airline workers on utility candidates, and so forth.

The 1946 convention was the first at which the nominated IEB slate was challenged—not once but twice. First there was a fight over the candidate meant to represent the Local 100 private-line workers. Bill Novak from the Third Avenue had served on the outgoing IEB and, with only one slot reserved for the three major New York surface companies, the nominating committee had decided to rotate the seat by putting up Frank O'Connor from Fifth Avenue Coach. The Third Avenue delegates were furious. In an effort to heal old wounds, the line's former District 50 supporters and the TWU loyalists had united to suggest a candidate to replace Novak, and they now claimed that they had been betrayed by their own representatives on the nominating committee.

A second, more serious fight was over the ATD candidates. After caucusing, the airline delegates sent the names of six acceptable IEB candidates to the nominating committee. The committee chose three, including Charlie Smolnikoff. However, Daniel Gilmartin, a veteran TWU activist from the IND and a member of the nominating committee, submitted a minority report calling for the substitution of Richard Downes, another ATD-suggested candidate, for Smolnikoff. Westcott was one of the leaders, and possibly the instigator, of the effort to defeat Smolnikoff. It was an extremely clever maneuver. Smolnikoff, of all the TWU staffers and officers, was probably the most openly identified as a leftist. He had joined the TWU staff on a paid, full-time basis only six months earlier, after having been ousted from his post with the Marine and Shipbuilding Workers during a factional battle. A loss by Smolnikoff would be interpreted as a defeat for the left.

What made this ironic was that Downes was also a CP member, who was being used, apparently without his consent, as a weapon against Smolnikoff. Most delegates would have been surprised and bewildered to learn that Downes belonged to the CP. Unlike Smolnikoff, he had no ideological commitment to the left, rather seeing it as a means of personal advancement. Still, the TWU leaders were caught. They couldn't criticize Downes, their own staffer and ally, yet his victory would be seen as an administration defeat. The obvious solution, Downes's withdrawal, was impossible because he was in Boston working on an organizing drive. Furthermore, as a candidate Downes had important advantages over Smolnikoff. First, he was Irish. Second, although he had been heavily involved in airline organizing, he originally came from the IRT and retained strong ties there. Smolnikoff was well known only to the Miami airline workers, while Downes was known both in the airlines and Local 100.

The lengthy, heated debate over the contested IEB seats focused primarily on the candidates' qualifications, though charges of leadership domination were aired. Publicly, Quill, MacMahon, and Forge remained neutral. Santo, after praising Downes, backed Smolnikoff, arguing that airline workers, not subway workers, were needed to lead the ATD. This, however, backfired when it was pointed out that Smolnikoff had never been an airline worker. Allusion was also made to Santo's own non-transit background. Finally, MacMahon proposed a compromise; with the unanimous consent of the delegates, the committee on the constitution could be reconvened and two IEB seats added, so that Downes's backers and the Third Avenue workers could be accommodated without bumping O'Connor or Smolnikoff. Almost all of the delegates supported this solution, but eight objected, and it was therefore defeated. In the voting that followed, Smolnikoff was defeated, 62-82, and O'Connor elected, 110-34. Downes was then elected as a substitute for Smolnikoff.

Quill tried to put the best face on the IEB fight, arguing that it had been an exercise in democracy that developed leadership and was "the kind of stuff we should have back in the locals." Downes and Smolnikoff were already on payroll as International representatives and both remained so. Still, the TWU leadership had been shown, really for the first time, to be vulnerable. Westcott's strategy of carefully chosen, limited battles, attacking the left on non-ideological terrain, had been vindicated.

The convention ended on a disquieting note. Apparently questions had been raised, off the floor, about Quill's receipt of separate salaries from the TWU and the City Council. In the final moments of the convention, Quill felt obligated to defend himself, saying that his government salary was used to finance his constituency office. (Since 1945 the NYC CIO Council had been giving Quill a $12,000 annual subsidy for this purpose, but few knew that.) To clear his name, Quill appointed a committee that included Westcott to examine the books of his Bronx headquarters.[49]

Because Local 100 was so compartmentalized, the 1946 convention represented a rare oportunity for TWU dissidents to identify and establish ties to one another. With contacts made there, by the end of 1946 Westcott and Brooks organized a broader, more formally structured caucus, the Rank-and-File Committee of TWU members for Democratic Trade Unionism. Among those associated with them were Gilmartin; John O'Connell, a former seminarian and Third Avenue section officer; and Peter McCaffrey a one-time Quill supporter and a former member of the Local 100 Executive Board. The new caucus concentrated on solidifying its organizational standing by contesting section officer and steward elections. The TWU leadership fought back hard. Both sides were willing to steal elections if they could.

According to Westcott, his group's supporters were "a lot of guys fresh out of the Army, who didn't want to take this domination stuff from anybody, anytime." By contrast, the caucus had little success with more senior Irish workers, who by this time were generally loyal toward the TWU leadership and grateful for the benefits the union had brought them. On the private bus lines, the Westcott group's main base, the minority of Italian workers often responded more positively than did the Irish. Thus in its social composition as well as its strategy the Rank-and-File Committee differed from the prewar opposition. Rather than a parochial Irish backlash against the New Deal, it represented a revolt by more cosmopolitan, upwardly mobile, anti-Communist workers, seeking to break the monopoly on power held by the old guard leadership.[50]

In early 1947 Quill again got into a public squabble over Church-sponsored factionalism. During the question-and-answer period following a speech he gave in Boston urging greater Church-labor cooperation, Quill was asked about ACTU and the Crown Heights Labor School. He responded with a sharp attack on both organizations, which he reiterated in the TWU *Bulletin*. Quill charged that the two groups were "shot through with stool pigeons, and strikebreakers," consistently sided with employers, and issued "filth" and "lies."

An uproar followed. The *Tablet*, ACTU, and Father William Smith from the Crown Heights School all vehemently denounced Quill. TWU members at the Kingsbridge Third Avenue barn voted to censure him. So did a meeting of delegates from forty councils of the Knights of Columbus in the Bronx and Manhattan. Increasingly, Knights of Columbus groups and Holy Name Societies made up of transit workers were developing ties to the TWU opposition and mobilizing their memberships against Quill.[51]

Besides the Westcott group, there were other clusters of transit workers opposed to the TWU leadership scattered throughout the industry, particularly on the BMT. The TWU was also still fair game for raids by non-CIO unions. The AFMTW-District 50 merger had been a failure, but in 1947 those remaining with the group split in two, with each faction finding a new parent body. One group affiliated with the TWU's old international, the IAM, which had just left the AFL. It received support from ACTU. The other, led by long-time AFMTW president Bernard Brophy, hooked up with the American Federation of State, County and Municipal Employees (AFSCME). To help bolster his new affiliate, AFSCME International President Arnold Zander hired a young socialist, Jerry Wurf, to serve as an organizer, the inauspicious start of a career that ended with Wurf's AFSCME presidency. Both groups stressed anti-Communism.[52]

TWU leaders certainly could not ignore their opponents. However, in spite of the deepening Cold War, the union leadership faced no major immediate threat. In candid moments, those intimately involved in oppositional activities admitted as much. Wurf said that trying to "put Quill out of business . . . was a little like trying to melt an iceberg with a match." Carey, in November 1947, wrote to a fellow Jesuit that he was "working on an insurrection against Mike Quill, which I don't think will succeed." Significantly, both men saw Quill as their main object and obstacle.[53]

The full measure of the opposition weakness came in the December 1947 Local 100 elections. The Westcott group was able to mount a nearly full slate of candidates, most of whom were section officers. However, in spite of a vigorous campaign, support from ACTU, and tacit aid from the Hearst press, they were trounced. Hogan was re-elected with 10,736 votes to his opponent John McHugh's 3,340. The other local-wide administration candidates were also re-elected by very wide margins. The only branch that the opposition carried, and there by a narrow margin, was NYC Omnibus, Westcott's and Brook's home base. As a result, the Rank-and-File caucus ended up with only two of the thirty-three local executive board seats. Eight years earlier, John Gallagher had done far better.[54]

Westcott, Gilmartin, McCaffrey, and O'Connell were persistent, capable men. In spite of their setback, they gave no indication that they were planning to abandon their effort. Given the changing political climate in the nation and the CIO, their prospects were not totally bleak. Still, at the end of 1947 the leadership group which had led the initial organization of the TWU and thereafter had dominated it remained very much in control.

Throughout 1947, the deepening Cold War touched the TWU in a variety of ways. Center-left coalitions, created during the New Deal or World War II, strained or broke. Anti-Communist sentiment and activity grew in New York City and elsewhere. The demand for political conformity within the CIO increased. So did government repression of the left. Meanwhile, the CP vacillated, seeking compromises one moment, taking a hard line the next.[55]

Following the 1946 elections the ALP-Democratic alliance collapsed. More and more Democrats, including O'Dwyer, began following Ed Flynn's lead, refusing to work with the ALP. A number of considerations were involved. In response to international developments and Republican gains, the Truman administration was moving to the right. In New York, the growth of the Liberal party created a new potential coalition partner for the Democrats. At the same time, rising anti-Communism made ties to the ALP a possible liability. In 1947, for the first time in several years, the Democratic party and the ALP ran separate slates throughout the city.

O'Dwyer was particularly anxious to cut ties with, and eventually eliminate, Marcantonio. The East Harlem Congressman's 1946 re-election had been marred by the election-day murder of an opposition campaign worker, for which many held Marcantonio's supporters responsible. O'Dwyer viewed Marcantonio's dense web of relationships with Democratic leaders, mass organizations, city officials, and city employees as a threat to his own position. Accordingly, O'Dwyer initiated a purge of Democratic officials close to Marcantonio and began a reorganization of Tammany. To stop Macantonio's practice of running in and winning all of the major party primaries, the Wilson-Pakula Act was passed by the State Legislature, limiting such crossover bids.[56]

At the same time, a successful campaign was launched to end the use of proportional representation in City Council elections. Tammany had always opposed PR and had tried unsuccessfully in the past to have it repealed. With PR, a sizable Council opposition bloc was almost ensured, and there was always the possibility that an anti-Tammany coalition might achieve a majority, as had nearly happened in 1937. Without PR, the Democrats would totally dominate the Council.

In past years, mainstream opponents of Tammany, including the Republicans, liberal reformers, and good government leaders, had defended PR. However, by 1947 the presence of two Communists on the City Council had become profoundly disturbing to a broad range of conservatives, moderates, and liberals. Red-baiting thus provided a vehicle for a new anti-PR offensive. With the support of most of the city's Republican officials, the AFL Central Trades and Labor Council, the American Legion, the Veterans of Foreign Wars, the New York Board of Trade, most of the local newspapers, and much of the Catholic hierarchy, the Democrats led a furious campaign against PR, stressing the anti-Communist issue. In a light turnout, PR was repealed in a November 1947 referendum by a nearly two-to-one vote. Since during the war councilmanic terms had been extended to four years, starting in 1949 Council members would be elected by districts for terms coincident with the Mayor's. Under such circumstances there was little likelihood that ALP or CP candidates could continue to be elected. Quill's political career as a labor-backed independent was effectively over. [57]

Two days after PR was defeated, Peter Cacchione died. His funeral was the last great demonstration of the power the left had achieved in New York municipal politics. Twelve thousand people turned out to hear eulogies from Democrats, Republicans, ALPers, and Communists, with Quill delivering one of the main addresses. Already, though, the Popular Front climate that had made Cacchione's electoral career possible was over. When Quill and others compared Cacchione's death to the passing of Roosevelt, Hillman, and La Guardia, they were trading in nostalgia. The onetime followers of the four dead leaders were already or soon would be at each other's throats. In a break with past precedent and charter procedure, the City Council even refused to elect the Brooklyn CP's designee to fill Cacchione's seat until a special election could be held. [58]

Amidst all this, in September 1947 John Santo was re-arrested on the immigration charges outstanding against him since 1941. (A new charge, violating the Smith Act by advocating the overthrow of the government, was added to the indictment.) This time, the government moved promptly to deport the TWU leader. Hearings on his case began almost immediately. Testimony against Santo was given by Louis Budenz, Joseph Zack, and George Hewitt, ex-CP leaders who by then were virtually professional anti-Communist witnesses, and by former TWU members William Harmon and Tom O'Shea.

When the TWU leadership learned of Santo's impending arrest, Quill, Santo, and Sacher went to William Z. Foster for advice, but his only suggestion was that they get a good lawyer. That they did, but in the main they turned to the union's own resources to mount a massive defense campaign. The IEB formed a Santo Defense Committee and TWU locals were urged to establish similar groups. The International suggested that each union member contribute two dollars to the defense effort. Although there was some membership resistance—at least one Local 100 section voted against contributing—in general there was broad TWU support for Santo. The TWU was also able to enlist the support of the national CIO. At the October 1947 CIO Convention a resolution condemning the proceedings against Santo was unanimously passed. Phil Murray appointed a special CIO committee to take up the case and issued a statement defending Santo that was used as the introduction for a Defense Committee pamphlet, *John Santo, American,* 100,000 copies of which were distributed.

Sacher served as Santo's chief defense attorney, and Quill and other TWU members regularly attended his deportation hearings. A stream of union members testified on his belief, turning the proceedings into a recapitulation of the TWU's history and accomplishments. Many testified that Santo had made them better Americans. Anthony Alberto, from the BMT, went to far as to say that "if John did not come along . . . we might have all been in the Communist Party today. I think he kept us out of the Communist Party—because conditions were so rotten."[59]

TWU leaders charged that the Omnibus Corporation and its president, John A. Ritchie, were behind the government moves against Santo. This seems unlikely; Santo's arrest came amidst a broad federal effort to deport foreign-born CP and radical labor leaders. However, the TWU accusation gained some credibility because in the fall of 1947 the union was locked in a bitter dispute with the Omnibus Corporation over a pension arbitration award, and the company was using anti-Communism to strengthen its hand. Pamphlets were sent to the homes of the company's employees with titles such as "What Communism Means to You" and "Michael J. Quill; Is He . . . Communist? Labor Leader? or Politician?" Ritchie contributed financially to *Counterattack* and traded information on the TWU with the FBI.[60]

Because Santo was arrested when he was and not, say, six months later, the TWU was able to portray the proceedings against him as an attack on the labor movement. On this basis, CIO and TWU support could be mobilized. However, in spite of the impressive defense effort, in the spring of 1948 Santo's hearing officer recommended his deportation. Santo appealed, and throughout 1948 he remained free; but his chances for victory did not look good.[61]

Through all this, the TWU's public face remained at least as left, if not more so, as at any time since the early 1930s. Once Forge began working full-time on the airlines, the union's publications were reorganized and assumed a more political tone. Left-wing journalists Will Quaytman and Hal Poritz were hired to edit a new Local 100 newspaper, the *Transport Voice,* and eventually took over the *Bulletin* as well. Under Forge, the *Bulletin* had been rather staid; under Quaytman and Poritz, there was more coverage of international and national developments and bolder stands on racism, red-baiting, and national politics. Horse-racing columns and pictures of movie stars also appeared regularly.[62]

Throughout 1947 the TWU sharply attacked the Truman administration, both for its domestic and international policies, portraying Henry Wallace as a positive alternative. The union was particularly vehement in opposing the Taft-Hartley Act, a major revision of the National Labor Relations Act (NLRA) that was passed over Truman's veto. In addition to placing numerous restrictions on union activities, Taft-Hartley required union officers to swear that they were not members of the CP in order for their organizations to take advantage of the federal labor relations machinery. Although Taft-Hartley had little direct effect on the TWU—since few TWU units were covered by the NLRA—it, along with the Condon-Wadlin Act, made clear the price for labor of the recent wave of Democratic defeats. It also sparked a sharp debate within the labor movement over whether or not to comply with its anti-Communist provisions.

In the face of this increasingly anti-labor political climate, many TWU locals became more active in electoral politics. In Louisville and Miami, candidates from the TWU ran in the 1947 elections on labor-backed slates. In New York Local 100 activists began an intensive campaign to enroll transit workers in the ALP. While the TWU's political stance was still largely in line with national CIO policy, the whole tone of the union was growing more political and left-wing.[63]

At the same time, behind the scenes, Quill was becoming increasingly estranged from some of the CP leaders—"the men of the global minds," he liked to call them—with whom he had dealings. Part of the problem was Quill's continuing effort to assert his independence. Also, like many others, he found Foster and Thompson to be particularly difficult men. Both were arrogant and inflexible. It had been decades since Foster had worked directly with mass movements, and Thompson never had. In fact, much of Thompson's adult life had been spent in the military, first in Spain during the civil war and then, during World War II, in the Pacific. He had a hard time adjusting to civilian ways. Around other TWU leaders, Quill took to giving unflattering imitations of the two CP leaders, not trying to hide his contempt. To many close to or in the CP leadership, however, things looked very different. To them, Quill seemed the prima donna, unwilling to compromise or make the sacrifices demanded by difficult times. Still, on broad policy issues, through the fall of 1947 Quill, the other top leaders of the TWU, and the CP remained in basic agreement and the union itself remained strong.[64]

13

FRATRICIDE

During the first two years after World War II the political environment in which the TWU operated underwent rapid change. Internally, however, the TWU remained relatively untouched. That was soon to change. In early 1948, when a complex set of political and trade union issues arose, the nation-wide fissure in the left-liberal camp spread to the transit union. Some TWU leaders wanted the union to remain aligned with the CP, while others, led by Quill, sought to loosen or cut its ties. A year-long faction fight ensued, ending in the triumph of Quill and the expulsion of Communists from positions of power. Simultaneously, a new set of political and collective bargaining arrangements developed between the union, the New York City government, and the Democratic party. By the end of 1948, the first phase of the TWU's history was over.

Two issues precipitated a break in the long-standing unity within the TWU leadership and between the TWU and the CP. The first was the effort to raise the transit fare in New York. The second was Henry Wallace's third-party Presidential bid. Both require some background.

Starting right after World War I, there were repeated efforts to raise New York's transit fare. Given their massive debt loads, the five-cent fare made financially sound operation of both the private and public transit systems extremely difficult. However, by the 1920s the defense of the five-cent fare had become a virtual necessity for those active in electoral politics. Furthermore, the entire economic and social infrastructure of the city—including wage rates, residential patterns, and factory and office location—was predicated on cheap mass transit.

One argument for unification was that economies of scale would facilitate maintenance of the five-cent fare. For a while this proved true. Through the end of World War II the NYCTS generated significant operating surpluses. However, even then, there was never nearly enough money collected to cover the cost of servicing the city's transit debt. As a result, general city revenues, raised largely through real estate taxes, were used for that purpose.[1]

In 1942, a sustained, tenacious campaign was launched to raise the NYCTS fare. By then New York was the only major city still having a five-cent fare; elsewhere, the ten-cent fare had become standard. The fare hike effort was spearheaded by Paul Windels, the city's Corporation Counsel between 1934 and 1937. After leaving the La Guardia administration, Windels had become increasingly conservative, attacking the growth of big government and serving as counsel to the Rapp-Coudert Committee in its investigation of alleged Communist activities in public education. Windels sought to double the fare, place the NYCTS under an independent authority with the power to issue its own bonds, and convert the system to a financially self-liquidating basis. Substantial real estate, banking, insurance, and business interests supported Windels's plan, since it would indirectly lower property taxes by eliminating the need to subsidize the transit debt service. Furthermore, if the transit system was made financially self-sustaining, the city's transit debt would no longer be counted toward its constitutionally mandated debt limit. This would enable the city to borrow over $400 million for highways, schools, hospitals, and other capital projects. By putting the transit system under an authority, decisions on future wage and fare increases would be insulated from direct political pressure, which the TWU and opponents of an increased fare had proved adept at mobilizing.

At first, Windels made little progress, in spite of his impressive list of backers. Most politicians, especially Democrats and those on the left, opposed a fare increase. So did virtually the entire labor movement. To counter pressure for raising the fare, during the war a bill was gotten through the state legislature requiring the City Council to approve any Board of Estimate decision to change the transit tariff. If the Council failed to do so, any increase would be suspended until a referendum could be held on the issue. As long as this law remained in effect, a fare hike was virtually impossible. The City Council would undoubtedly vote against it—La Guardia noted that "there isn't a single, solitary elected official in this state who will take the increased fare side of the issue"—and in a referendum any proposed hike would certainly be defeated.[2]

Still, with the end of the war and the change in city administrations, pressure for a fare increase intensified. In the first year O'Dwyer held office, the NYCTS failed to generate any operating surplus to contribute to the $57 million cost of servicing the transit debt. Increased labor costs, largely the result of pressure from the TWU, were in part responsible. In 1940, NYCTS labor costs were equal to 54% of the passenger revenues collected; in 1945, 67%. At the same time, the need for rehabilitating and extending the transit system had grown urgent; years of deferred maintenance, first by the private companies and then, during the war, by the city, had taken their toll. Virtually everyone recognized that some new way of raising money for transit was needed. To this end, in his final year in office La Guardia tried but failed to win approval from the state legislature for a "transportation tax" plan, which included doubling the city's sales tax to 2%.[3]

When O'Dwyer took office, several of his advisers and a host of civic, business, and real estate groups urged him to raise the fare. O'Dwyer did not take their advice.

Without ruling out a later fare hike, in early 1946 the Mayor revived La Guardia's program and asked for authority to raise the sales tax. The Republican-controlled state legislature refused to grant this request or to make funds available from the state's large surplus. As a result, the financial condition of the transit system and the city government as a whole continued to deteriorate.

The fare issue was brought to a head in the fall of 1946 by the wage increases recommended by the Meyer Committee. For the first time, the city faced significant subsidization of the NYCTS *operating* budget. To cover the retroactive portion of the pay increase, special budget notes had to be floated, a legally questionable and financially unsound practice. Furthermore, the city's overall debt limit had been reached. Accordingly, at O'Dwyer's request, in February 1947 the Board of Estimate held public hearings on the possibility of a fare increase of five cents.[4]

The transit fare was a class issue, the modern equivalent of the bread assize. In 1942 Peter Cacchione calculated that for the average manufacturing worker a five-cent fare increase would have an effect equal to a 1.5% income tax. Since most New York workers lived in rent-controlled apartments, few would benefit from any accompanying decrease in real estate taxes. Nor would most benefit from highway construction financed from freed-up city funds; in 1945, two out of three New York City residents belonged to households that did not own a car. To raise the fare was to transfer wealth from the working class to large property owners. O'Dwyer himself recognized this; in rejecting a fare increase in January 1946 he cited the undue hardship on members of low-income groups that would result.[5]

Historically, the entire left, including the CP, SP, ALP, Liberal party, and NYC CIO Council, vehemently opposed raising the fare. The left argued that transit was, as Cacchione put it, an "essential social utility." Like other municipal services, it should be financed out of general revenues and not through a pay-as-you-go user's fee. Since the transit system increased real estate values, it was not unreasonable to subsidize the system through real estate taxes. A switch to a self-sustaining fare would unjustly make the working class almost exclusively responsible for paying off a transit debt held mostly by banks and large investors and incurred in the development of a city infrastructure benefiting all.[6]

For the TWU, things weren't so simple. The very nature of the union created a tension between the desire to unite with the left and the labor movement to oppose fare increases and the desire to capitalize on them through higher wages.[7] Ideologically and practically, the union was inclined to accept the left's arguments and fight to keep low fares. In its struggle for improved wages, benefits, and bargaining rights, the union depended on its ability to mobilize broad working-class support. However, well-funded transit systems, whether private or public, were more likely to make wage concessions than those starved of funds. The CP itself recognized this contradiction at the TWU's very start. In June 1934 the *Daily Worker* ran two articles, four days apart, about a proposed two-cent fare increase. One urged the TWU to prepare itself to demand higher wages as soon as the fare went up. The other urged it to help forge "mass militant resistance of the subway riders, the unemployed and the transport workers combined against the fare rise."[8]

Until 1947, the TWU never supported a fare increase in New York. At times it actively fought any change in the tariff; at other times it simply remained silent.

Above all, it tried to separate the fare and wage issues, so as to avoid being held responsible for any fare increase and, conversely, to avoid having tight transit finances used to justify poor wages and working conditions. "Transit wages do not determine the rate of fare," the TWU argued, "and . . . the fare has been a minor factor in determining how much or how little goes into the workers' envelopes."[9] Even while making such arguments, however, the TWU tacitly acknowledged that there *was* a connection between wages and an employer's ability to pay. It was for this reason that during the unification debate the TWU opposed the high purchase price and resulting high debt load. During the 1941 bus strike, TWU leaders explicitly argued that the union's demands had to take into account the financial status of the companies.[10]

In the face of contradictory pressures, the TWU position on transit fares was thus inconsistent. Generally, the union argued that regardless of fare levels or the financial standing of the employers, its members deserved decent wages and conditions. Sometimes the union went on the say that in New York this could and should be done while maintaining the five-cent fare. Other times, the union in effect said that the fare was none of its business. And finally, outside of New York there were times when as a last resort the TWU demanded fare increases to make wage increases possible.[11]

Under O'Dwyer, the TWU first declined to take a position on the fare, but by the fall of 1946 it came out against a fare increase. By contrast, ACTU and the BRSA were supporting higher fares. At the February 1947 Board of Estimate hearings, Harry Sacher, testifying for the TWU, argued that the transit system could not be adequately financed by fares alone even if raised to ten cents. Robert Thompson, speaking for the CP, Saul Mills, speaking for the NYC CIO Council, and Eugene Connolly, speaking for the ALP, all opposed a fare increase. Evidently the strength of opposition impressed O'Dwyer; on February 12, describing a fare increase as "a harsh and unbearable tax on the city's low-income families," he announced that an increased transit fare was unjustified "at this time."[12]

Within months, however, O'Dwyer reopened the whole question. Faced with gloomy budget projections and a pro-fare increase report from a study commission he had earlier established, in June 1947 he announced that he was leaning toward a higher fare. Any increase, though, would come only after a referendum, possibly to be held in November. Once again, fierce opposition developed, as the ALP and CIO made it clear that they would wage a full-scale battle against a fare hike. Speaking in the name of the TWU, Quill also came out strongly against a fare increase. Other TWU leaders, however, were less convinced of the wisdom of continuing the fight for the five-cent fare. In any case, there was no referendum; faced with the likelihood of a losing fight, the Board of Estimate sidestepped the issue.[13]

O'Dwyer did not give up; starting in September, he began searching for a way to raise the fare without a referendum. By this time, most TWU leaders, including Santo, MacMahon, and Hogan, were willing to go along. Whatever doubts they may have had were ended by an analysis of NYCTS finances undertaken by Sacher, which concluded that the system was really broke. Without a higher fare, wage increases would be very difficult to obtain.

Quill had always been the strongest TWU advocate of the five-cent fare and almost alone was reluctant to change positions. Over the previous months, he had become one of the city's most prominent defenders of the fare, and any change of line would be particularly embarrassing for him. Furthermore, this was before the repeal of PR; if Quill advocated a higher fare to facilitate wage increases, his political career would suffer greatly.

Whatever disagreements there were within the TWU were kept out of the public eye. From mid-October through mid-December the union indicated only that it was no longer unalterably opposed to a fare increase, having not yet taken a definitive position. In any case, Quill's hold-out was short-lived. Sometime after the repeal of PR in November, perhaps even earlier, Quill began leaning toward the higher fare position. It is possible that even at this stage he established some sort of quid pro quo with O'Dwyer; in late 1947 Quill held a series of private meetings with the Mayor and Board of Transportation Chairman William Reid, who was known as an advocate of both a higher fare and improved relations with the TWU.[14]

In early November, O'Dwyer came out publicly for a fare hike. His new plan was to seek state legislation enabling the Board of Transportation to raise the fare as necessary to meet operating costs without holding a referendum. To make his proposal more politically palatable and to eliminate the obvious class character of a fare increase, O'Dwyer embedded the needed revision of the state's Rapid Transit Law in an extensive legislative "package" that also included increased state aid, higher real estate taxes, changes in the city debt limit, and new automobile, taxi, truck, and liquor license taxes.[15]

As soon as O'Dwyer announced his proposal, the ALP and CP began campaigns against it. Almost every day the *Daily Worker* attacked O'Dwyer's "package," proposing instead its own program of increased state aid, "nuisance" taxes, higher real estate taxes, and a raised debt limit.[16] The TWU, by contrast, remained publicly noncommittal, and it was widely believed that the union leadership supported O'Dwyer's proposal. On November 11, the *Daily Worker* warned the TWU and the United Public Workers that if they supported higher fares "the whole structure of CIO reliance on public support may fall to the ground" and "without that support the ALP would be weakened." The CP newspaper contended that O'Dwyer was deliberately using "the bait of increased transit wages if and when the nickel ride was untracked" to "create some dissension on the [fare] issue among TWU leaders." A month later, the paper was more blunt. In editorials on December 16 and 18 the paper said that TWU support for O'Dwyer's "package" would be "a poor move," and that "it would be wiser, in the interest of all the wage-earners of New York City, for the TWU to help lead a united citizenry against the wealthy real estate crowd and the Dewey surplus."[17]

On December 20, the dispute between the TWU and the CP came out in the open, an event without precedent. The setting was ironic, a meeting of the NYC CIO Council scheduled to elect Quill as the body's new president. Joe Curran had recently resigned as president of the Council, realizing that because of his late 1946 break with the CP he could not be re-elected. Quill was designated to take his place as the titular head of the left-wing of the New York union movement. However, what ordinarily would have been the occasion for a show of unity turned into a stormy, bitter affair, for the CP also planned to pass a resolution opposing O'Dwyer's proposed fare hike.

Anticipating a fight, the CP mobilized all of its forces for the December 20 meeting. The TWU delegation was apparently taken by surprise and spent considerable time caucusing as the meeting began. Once Quill was elected—unanimously—a resolution was introduced supporting O'Dwyer's "package" with the exception of the bill related to the fare, which was opposed. At that point, a huge quarrel broke out. Quill asked that the resolution be tabled until the TWU could hold a membership referendum on O'Dwyer's plan. The CP group opposed this, and things quickly grew nasty. Quill called Irving Potash a "liar," while Ruth Young, from the UE, complained of "labor leaders who desert the people" for their own advantage. The only sizable bloc supporting the TWU was the Amalgamated Clothing Workers delegation. At one in the morning, the issue was put off until the next Council meeting.[18]

Two days after the Council debate the *Daily Worker* published a long article by Robert Thompson entitled "The Five Cent Fare and Trade Union Opportunism." Thompson criticized the TWU for its position on the fare and for linking its wage demands with the employer's ability to pay. "For opportunist reasons," he wrote,

> certain leaders of the TWU have chosen to tie together the essentially unrelated questions of municipal finances and the wage demands of transit workers. In doing so, they have found a convenient way of supporting the long-established banker-real estate program of solving the problem of municipal finances by making the poor pay via an increased subway fare.

The TWU's position, Thompson concluded, threatened "to become a strategy of political re-alignment, a bridge leading away from the labor-progressive movement and toward the forces of reaction."[19]

On January 5 the Local 100 Executive Board endorsed O'Dwyer's "package." Two days later an enlarged Joint Executive Committee meeting of over a thousand delegates did the same. Apparently, the TWU leadership was united in the decision to defy the CP; Quill, Hogan, and MacMahon all strongly endorsed O'Dwyer's proposals. Responding, without saying so, to Thompson's article, Hogan and Quill argued that O'Dwyer's plan was fundamentally different from those proposed by the bankers in that it did not call for a self-sustaining fare. Hogan also denied that the union was tying its wage demands to the city's ability to pay, saying that

> we are not putting all our eggs in one basket . . . transit workers are entitled to the 30 cents-an-hour increase, pension improvements and the whole TWU nine-point program, WHETHER THE HIGHER "PACKAGE" GOES THROUGH OR NOT.

On January 8 Local 100 began polling its membership on the O'Dwyer plan. There was no chance that the transit unionists would reject the "package" and in the end they overwhelmingly approved it. The five-cent fare had never been particularly popular with the rank and file; with virtually every union officer and activist, from the left to the right, now supporting a higher fare, the outcome was not in question. The real purpose of the referendum was to justify the union's change of line to the TWU leadership itself, the public, other unions, and the CP. However, on the very day that the TWU began its poll, the NYC CIO Council voted to oppose O'Dwyer's proposed fare increase. [21]

Simultaneous, and converging, with these developments was a simmering dispute between Quill and "the ninth floor" over Henry Wallace's Presidential candidacy. The issue was not Wallace himself but the potential effect of a third-party campaign on the CIO. Ever since Truman had forced Wallace out of the cabinet in September 1946, there had been considerable talk about the former Vice President running for President in 1948, either as a Democrat or as the head of a new political party. TWU leaders, especially Quill, were enthusiastic Wallace supporters and had long toyed with the idea of a national labor party. As the TWU president later put it, "I was for Wallace before Wallace was for Wallace himself."

Phil Murray and other CIO liberals had also often praised Wallace, but they were opposed to any third-party effort. Murray had always been skeptical of abandoning the Democratic party. Other CIO leaders were drawn closer to the Democrats by Truman's veto of the Taft-Hartley Act and the deepening Soviet-American conflict. Unsure of the prospects for a new party and fearful of the impact on the CIO, through the fall of 1947 Wallace, his liberal supporters, and the CP all wavered as to what course to take in the upcoming Presidential election. [22]

At the October 1947 CIO Convention, Murray tried to avoid an open break between the left and the center. After Secretary of State George Marshall personally appeared to defend the Truman administration's main foreign policy initiative, the European Recovery Program, Murray arranged for a compromise resolution endorsing the general aims of the program but not its specific features. On the issue of a third party, however, Murray stood firm. Quill, who came forth as the convention's strongest Wallace proponent, urged the delegates to take the ousted New Dealer "into the confidence of our organizations," but instead they passed a resolution calling for political action within the framework of the two major parties, which meant that if Wallace ran as an independent the CIO would oppose him. [23]

Between the CIO Convention and the year's end, the CP national leadership held a series of meetings with key left-wing unionists, including Quill, to discuss electoral strategy. According to Quill, at a climactic session, apparently held on December 15, Eugene Dennis, John Williamson, and Robert Thompson announced that the decision had been made to back a third-party Wallace campaign. Left-wing unions were to immediately begin pro-Wallace activities. Quill asked who had made this decision and was told by Thompson that the CP National Committee had done so. Quill then objected, both to being dictated to and to the decision itself; support for a third party, Quill argued, might split the CIO. Thompson replied that Communists in the labor movement had to support Wallace "even if it splits the CIO right down the middle." At that point Quill told Thompson "the hell with you and your Central Committee," instructing him to relay the message to "that crackpot" Foster. [24]

Quill was deeply torn. On the one hand, he thought that Wallace was the most attractive Presidential candidate. He also was in no rush to abandon fourteen years of loyalty to the CP. On the other hand, he resented CP leaders, whose political judgment he distrusted, telling his union what to do. Furthermore, if the left was important to Quill, the CIO was more so. Thompson's flip disregard for the implications of a Wallace campaign within the labor movement intensified Quill's doubts about the CP's leadership and direction. A January meeting with Foster, at which, according to Quill, the CP leader suggested the possibility of forming a third labor federation, deepened his concern. In desperation Quill went to Gerhart Eisler, a former Comintern representative, for advice. Also, by early 1948 he re-established contact with Browder. [25]

Quill was soon forced to commit himself publicly. Wallace announced his candidacy in late December and the CP moved quickly to round up labor support. In New York, it planned to have the CIO Council pass a resolution on January 8 endorsing Wallace. Murray, however, asked Quill to have the Council withhold any action until after the CIO Executive Board took up the Wallace issue. Hoping to avoid a clash with Murray, Quill told Saul Mills that the TWU delegation would not support an immediate Wallace endorsement.

Just before the January 8 NYC CIO Council meeting began, Quill and Thompson again argued over Wallace, and during the meeting frantic backstage discussions were held. When the TWU refused to accept an outright endorsement of Wallace, the CP's supporters proposed two weaker substitute resolutions. The final version did not actually endorse Wallace, but criticized the New York State CIO Executive Board for repudiating Wallace three days earlier, "a roundabout attempt to commit the State CIO to President Truman." Just as Quill feared the Wallace issue was splitting the CIO, especially in New York. On January 7, anticipating ALP backing for Wallace, the ACW, UAW, and Steel Workers representatives on the ALP State Executive Board had resigned. Quill was trying to do the impossible, support Wallace without antagonizing CIO centrists. Thus on January 7 he led the TWU in its decision to stay in the ALP, while the next day the transit union delegation abstained even on the weakened CIO Council resolution. [26]

The January 8 NYC CIO Council meeting was a watershed, for at it the TWU publicly opposed the CP on two crucial issues, the fare and Wallace. The two months that followed were an odd interlude, with the TWU leadership united in its estrangement from the CP. Over Wallace, the differences were not great. At a January 22 meeting of the CIO Executive Board, Quill joined the CP bloc in opposing a resolution that was passed declaring any third-party Presidential effort "unwise." Quill and MacMahon were among the first labor leaders to join the Wallace campaign committees that were being formed. Although the TWU had not yet formally taken a position on the upcoming election, its periodicals and locals gave Wallace considerable favorable publicity. Outside of New York, several TWU organizaers became key local figures in the Wallace effort. The TWU and Quill also actively supported Leo Isaacson's successful race on the ALP line in a mid-February special Congressional election in the Bronx, an election that was widely viewed as a preview of the Wallace campaign. [27] On the fare issue, however, the TWU and the CP went their separate ways.

Throughout February and early March the TWU mobilized all of its resources in support of O'Dwyer's higher fare "package." Hogan and Jimmy Gahagan led a massive lobbying effort in Albany and New York. Twice large delegations of Local 100 members traveled to the State Capitol to pressure for the passage of the Mayor's program. At the same time, the CP, ALP, Liberal party, leaders of the Wallace campaign, and the NYC CIO Council were all fighting to keep the five-cent fare. Legislators were confronted with the peculiar experience of one day being urged by TWU members to vote for the "package" and the next day being visited by representatives of the CIO Council, which in theory Quill headed, with the opposite message. The TWU's position, in the eyes of the *Daily Worker*, was leading the union "to isolation and defeat."[28]

While this complex political maneuvering over the fare was taking place, the TWU and Quill were in fact getting a taste of what isolation might mean—not isolation from the left but isolation from the mainstream of the CIO. Shortly after the January 22 CIO Executive Board meeting, which had also endorsed the Marshall Plan, Murray began moving against the left. Lee Pressman, the CIO's long-time, left-wing General Counsel, was forced to resign and Harry Bridges was removed as the northern California director of the CIO. Murray also informed all CIO regional directors and Industrial Union Councils (IUCs) that they "should be governed" by national CIO policy on Wallace and the Marshall Plan. Rumors circulated that a crackdown on the NYC CIO Council was being planned. In early March the NYS CIO Executive Board set up a state-wide Political Action Committee to replace the ALP as its political arm. To make sure that Murray kept up the pressure on the CP and its allies, in March Truman and Secretary of Defense James Forrestal each met with the CIO president. Meanwhile, O'Dwyer was pressuring Democratic county leaders not to let their candidates accept ALP endorsements, while the ALP was threatening not to endorse any legislators who voted for O'Dwyer's "package."[29]

A series of incidents in Miami, starting in mid-February, raised a particularly ominous specter—raiding of the TWU by anti-Communist CIO affiliates. The Miami events began with a visit to the city by Elizabeth Gurley Flynn, who was on a speaking tour to raise money for CP leaders facing deportation. Although the trip was meant to be low-key, the *Miami Daily News* gave her speech extensive, sensational coverage, listing the names of some of those who had helped organize her local appearance, including a secretary recently hired by the TWU. Because of this publicity, the woman in question offered to resign and TWU staffers Smolnikoff and Edwin Waller apparently agreed. Upset by this, Flynn and a local CP organizer asked to meet with Smolnikoff and Waller. A *Miami Daily News* photographer saw them together in a restaurant and the next day the paper ran photographs and a banner headline, "Communists and CIO Leaders Dine Here." In the days that followed, the newspaper kept hammering away at the story, and in particular at Smolnikoff's left-wing ties. The son of the paper's owner was on the board of directors of Eastern Airlines, which the TWU was trying to organize, which may have contributed to the fixation on the story. In any case, local conservatives soon jumped on the bandwagon; the Miami Chamber of Commerce, its newly formed Committee on American Security, and the Florida attorney general, who was running for governor, all denounced Smolnikoff. At one point Smolnikoff's home was even visited by fully robed members of the Ku Klux Klan—not the first time that the Klan had tried to intimidate Local 500 officials.

Local 500 was the most important CIO local in Florida and a significant base for the left. Its sister local, 257, had begun organizing non-airline workers with some success. The Miami establishment was therefore delighted to find a way to attack the TWU. The situation also played into the hands of a group of union dissidents, the TWU Committee for Democratic Action. Right after the *Miami Daily News* began its campaign, members of this group demanded an end to "communist domination" of Local 500 and Smolnikoff's removal. Even at this point the Committee was probably in contact with the UAW. It also had powerful backers; its cartoons were drawn by an artist from the *Miami Daily News*.

To try to settle things down, Local 500 president M. L. Edwards called a special membership meeting, but this backfired. Many of the local's members were genuinely disturbed by the charges against Smolnikoff, who was particularly vulnerable because of his outspoken leftism, his open and early support for Wallace, and perhaps, as Quill later suggested, because he was Jewish. Losing control of the meeting, Edwards, an ally of Smolnikoff, panicked and himself introduced a motion that was unanimously passed calling on Smolnikoff to remove himself from Local 500 affairs pending further discussions with the local membership and the International.

With the situation rapidly getting out of hand, Quill hurried to Miami. At another special membership meeting he strongly defended Smolnikoff and said that no matter what the local did Smolnikoff would remain as the TWU's International representative. Quill's visit helped win over the local's membership, but new outside assaults came almost daily. The House Committee on Un-American Activities showed up and Edwards and Waller were called to testify. Shortly thereafter Smolnikoff was arrested on charges (later dropped) of violating a voting technicality. Then, in early March, Walter Reuther announced that the UAW was planning to raid TWU locals throughout the Pan American system. The TWU Committee for Democratic Action swung over to the auto union and UAW organizers showed up in Brownsville, Texas, and San Francisco, where the TWU also had Pan Am locals. Although the TWU held its own (in the end keeping all of its Pan Am locals), there were disturbing aspects to all this. Because TWU officials had refused to sign Taft-Hartley oaths saying that they were not Communists, in any NLRB-supervised recognition elections the union would be ineligible to appear on the ballot, a problem that proved devastating to the UE. The UAW also seemed to have the support of the national CIO. Van A. Bittner, the director of the CIO Southern Organizing Committee, and Florida CIO Director Charles L. Cowl openly sided with the auto union. Cowl pointed specifically to the TWU's refusal to follow national CIO policy on Wallace and the Marshall Plan. Although Murray was publicly silent, he was fully informed about the Miami situation, which made his very silence ominous.[30]

At the same time that these events were occurring, trouble was also developing in Louisville. The TWU's International representative there, Walter Case, had endorsed Wallace without consulting the Local 176 membership. A rank-and-file revolt ensued. Quill was forced to go to Louisville to assure the local's members that the International would not force any Presidential candidate down their throats and that they would be given plenty of time to consider all of the contestants.[31]

The effect of the Miami and Louisville situations on Quill's thinking is unclear. Although he continued to defend Smolnikoff and Case, in Miami he had witnessed a nasty demonstration of what the combined forces of liberalism and reaction could do against a left-wing union, and in Louisville he saw the possibility that the TWU's membership might balk at the union's political course. Within days of returning from his trip to Florida and Kentucky, Quill broke openly and for good with the CP.

The immediate cause of Quill's repudiation of the CP, and the resulting split in the TWU leadership, was the same issues that were so vexing all along, the fare and Wallace. In early March, the Republican state legislators refused to grant the city increased state aid, an important part of O'Dwyer's "package." The Mayor then withdrew his program, sticking to his pledge that it was an all-or-nothing proposal. On March 12 the Republican majority proceeded to pass a bill giving the Board of Transportation the authority to set fare levels as it pleased but subject to the approval of the Mayor. The entire political onus for raising the fare was thus placed on O'Dwyer. Although O'Dwyer asked Dewey to veto the bill (Dewey refused), and said that he would not use the power it granted, there was widespread skepticism about the Mayor's revived commitment to the five-cent fare.[32]

As soon as O'Dwyer's package was abandoned, and with Quill still out of town, the TWU revived its campaign for a thirty-cents-an-hour pay increase and other improvements on both the public and private lines. The union was in a difficult position; anticipating that a higher NYCTS fare would be extended to the private lines, it had let all of its contracts with the major New York City transit employers lapse. Furthermore, O'Dwyer's aides were indicating that without a fare increase, wage increases would be impossible. Hogan quickly made it clear that the TWU no longer cared "where the money comes from"; regardless of the financial status of the transit systems, the TWU wanted immediate pay increases. Anyway, Hogan argued, following the line taken by the CP, the city had the money for increased wages even without a change in the transit tariff. In late March, Local 100 began preparing for a full-scale battle.[33]

Some observers felt that the TWU would still at least tacitly support a fare increase. The *Daily Worker*, however, interpreted the TWU's new stand as a repudiation of its higher fare position. With a sigh of relief, the paper welcomed the union back into the fold. CP leaders were taking no chances. Correctly anticipating that O'Dwyer would soon try again to raise the fare, in a series of private meetings they pressured TWU leaders to oppose such a move. One by one the left-wing group in the TWU—first Santo, then MacMahon, Sacher, and Hogan, and them most of the others—agreed to stop pressing for a higher fare.[34]

In the meantime, the Wallace issue once again came to a head. On March 8, John Brophy, who was in charge of the CIO IUCs, wrote to these groups to remind them that since 1946 they had been obligated to follow national CIO political policy. He ordered them to do so on Wallace and the Marshall Plan. On March 18, the NYC CIO Council voted to reject Brophy's letter. The Local 100 delegates sided with the majority. (Six other TWU locals, in New York and elsewhere, responded similarly to the Brophy letter.) Quill was in Florida at the time, communicating with Saul Mills through his secretary. He later claimed that he had advised against the Council's action, while Mills claimed that he had supported it.[35]

According to Quill, shortly after he returned from Florida, MacMahon asked him to attend a March 25 meeting in Sacher's office with members of the NYC CIO

Council to discuss the TWU's wage fight. To Quill's surprise, John Williamson, Eugene Dennis, and Robert Thompson were present, in addition to Hogan, Mac-Mahon, Sacher, Mills, and Irving Potash. Again according to Quill—and it should be said that Mills denied that this meeting ever took place—Dennis opened the gathering by saying that they would not discuss TWU wage policy until the TWU officers present condemned their actions in supporting O'Dwyer's "package," came out in full support for Wallace, and opposed any future fare increases. This was made in the form of a motion that was voted on and carried. Quill was furious; after some salty words, he walked out.[36]

The next day Quill resigned as president of the NYC CIO Council. On March 28 he urged Local 100 to quit the Council, explaining in newspaper interviews that he had resigned because he believed that the Council was "too ready" to split with the national CIO over political policy. Quill said that while he disagreed with Brophy's letter, he thought the Council should have quietly worked out its differences with its parent body. Quill told the *New York Times*, that he still personally favored Wallace but might support the Democratic party if it nominated "a man of the type of Eisenhower and revised its domestic and foreign policy." "I am for a peace policy," he went on, "but not peace at any price." Concluding, he said that

> the TWU will remain with the CIO at all costs and will follow the leadership of Philip Murray. So far as the 42,000 transit workers are concerned, I say wages before Wallace. Higher wages are the primary goal of our union, and we will allow nothing to stand in our way of achieving them.

In a telegram to Murray, Quill attributed his resignation to a "group of strange people within the CIO Council who were promoting disharmony."[37]

Those on the inside knew immediately what had happened—Quill had broken with the CP. Right-wing CIO leaders were delighted, speculating that Quill would soon follow Joe Curran and become an active leader of the fight against the CIO left. The *Daily Worker* expected the same. On March 29 and 30 the paper ran editorials accusing Quill of "going fast" toward "the bandwagon of the rich and reactionary forces." "It isn't the Marshall Planners in the real estate and banker crowd," the paper wrote, "who are going to back the TWU's wage demands." On April 4, George Morris, the paper's labor reporter, described Quill as cozying up to Democratic leaders. Implicitly threatening a fight within the TWU, he concluded "that it is Quill who has to be reminded that it is the interest of the members—not those of the Democratic Party—which should come first."[38]

In situations such as Quill's decision to end his long allegiance to the CP, it is often impossible to know just why a person acts as he or she does; even the person acting may not be sure. Usually there are many factors involved, large and small, obvious and obscure, no one of which alone forms a sufficient explanation. In this case, some reasons lay on the surface, the reasons Quill frankly put forward. Others were seated more deeply, in facets of Quill's personality, in the structure of the TWU, and in the changing political landscape of the nation.

The dispute over Wallace within the CIO was certainly central. Truman's veto of the Taft-Hartley Act completed the process that began with the Wagner Act and accelerated during World War II of trying the CIO to the Democratic party. Non-

Communist CIO leaders had come to see their success as predicated on federal support, which was not likely to be forthcoming under the Republicans. For this reason, Murray would not tolerate any threat to the Democrats. Hence the CIO split not over trade union issues per se, but Presidential endorsements and foreign policy. Murray's intention to act forcefully against the left was clear by early 1948 and it looked like an immediate crisis was brewing, with various CIO officials calling for sanctions against the NYC CIO Council. At best, the prospect for the CIO left was continual raiding by centrist and right-wing unions, administrative proscriptions, and marginalization. At worst, the prospect was expulsion from the CIO.[39]

The peculiar nature of the TWU—an industrial, predominantly public sector union, without a contract covering its most important unit—meant that it always needed allies to provide political support and rally public sympathy. In the past, it found backers in two places, the Communist left and the CIO. Now, Quill realized, it had to choose one or the other. To Quill, the national CIO and the Democratic party looked like a better bet than the CP, its allied unions, and the ALP. If Quill had to be dictated to by someone, he preferred Murray over Thompson. Furthermore, without the protection of the CIO, the TWU would probably come under increasing government attack. The deportation proceedings against Santo (as well as Potash, Williamson, Eisler, and others), the events in Miami, the Taft-Hartley Act, and the general, escalating federal campaign against the left were not unnoticed by Quill. Even if he admired Wallace, the price to be paid for supporting a man who was sure to lose was simply too high.[40]

Then there was the question of the fare. On this, many of those in the TWU who supported the five-cent fare in the spring of 1948 agreed in retrospect that Quill had been right. For the TWU to advocate keeping the transit tariff at five cents simply did not make much sense.

First of all, the very principle involved was not as clear as the low-fare supporters made out. Why should a particular union be responsible for fighting to control the price of the product or service its members produced? When Reuther had put forth this position during the 1946 General Motors strike, the CP had rejected it. Other left-wing unions—for example, the UE and the New York Hotel and Restaurant Workers—did not abide by it in their actual practice. While it is true that what Local 100 members produced, mass transit, was less discretionary than most other products and services, to single out one union and assign to it the enormous responsibility of stopping price inflation seemed arbitrary.[41]

Even the supporters of the five-cent fare realized the weakness of their argument and tried to recast it in broader terms. If the TWU took on as its responsibility the problem of employer finances, they argued, it would lead the union to limit its wage demands to the employers' claimed abilities to pay. This, however, was a contrived argument. No matter what ideological banner they fly, unions have to, and do, take into consideration the financial standing of employers. The CP itself had gone into intricate detail as to how the city could finance higher transit wages. In any case, no one, including Quill, was arguing for limiting wages to the ability to pay. The real question was should the union use its power to change that ability at the public's expense.[42]

Important as these issues were, it was a sterile debate, for no matter what the TWU did, the five-cent fare was already just about dead. Although for a brief moment O'Dwyer was again defending the fare, there was little question that he would soon revert to his previous higher-fare position. With the Republicans and Democrats now both in favor of a fare hike, the chances for keeping the five-cent fare were slim indeed. The CP had considerable political capital to gain by portraying itself as the leading defender of the fare, but a losing fight on the issue would yield little for the TWU.[43]

Quill also had to consider the effect of supporting the five-cent fare on his membership. Local 100 members had already made known their overwhelming support for a higher fare in the TWU's own poll. Furthermore, various union dissidents and TWU rivals, including the Westcott group and the Civil Service Forum, were vocally advocating a fare increase. If Quill once again reversed positions, against the wishes of his membership, it would seem to confirm all of the charges that he was a tool of the Communists, putting their interests above the transit workers'. Under those circumstances, there was a good chance that a membership revolt would ensue, perhaps even splitting the union.[44]

Finally, there was much to be gained by advocating a higher fare. Although O'Dwyer probably had the political standing to raise the fare over the objections of the TWU and the left, to do so would have been costly. The ALP, if increasingly isolated, was still formidable—in February, Leo Isaacson had defeated a Democrat supported by O'Dwyer, Eleanor Roosevelt, and the entire Democratic establishment—and in 1949 the Mayor would have to run for re-election. O'Dwyer was therefore willing to make heavy concessions to split the labor left. If he could win over the TWU, he could both portray the higher fare as a service to transit workers and make the TWU the scapegoat for the increase.[45]

In their private conversations in the winter and spring of 1948, O'Dwyer told Quill that without a fare hike there could be no wage increase. If, however, Quill agreed to support a higher fare, O'Dwyer would give the union a substantial wage increase and some form of union security. It is not clear if the details of this understanding were worked out before or after Quill resigned his CIO Council post, but almost certainly by then its general outline had been discussed.[46]

For most industrial unions, including the TWU, wages were a more central concern in the postwar period than before the war. This was due to inflation. During the 1930s the Consumer Price Index had fallen by 16%; during the 1940s it rose by 72%. In spite of all of the TWU's efforts, NYCTS employees were still very poorly paid, and the union itself was still fighting to solidify its status and legitimacy. Even on the private transit lines, wages lagged behind those in other heavily unionized sectors. In 1937 the top hourly wage for an NYC Omnibus driver was 119% of the average hourly earnings of U.S. manufacturing production workers; by early 1948 it had slipped to 95%. O'Dwyer was now offering Quill the opportunity to upgrade wages and secure the union's bargaining position. It was an offer Quill felt he could not refuse on ideological grounds alone.[47]

The fare and Wallace issues were only the most immediate factors in Quill's change of course. As Len De Caux put it, perhaps overstating the case, Quill's "decision to switch [political allegiances] was primary; timing and pretexts were secondary." The real underlying question was where Quill and the TWU would position themselves in a time of increasing political reaction.[48]

Quill's break with the CP was neither sudden nor rash. His relationship with the Party had been increasingly strained since the end of World War II. From the fall of 1947 on he had been feeling his way toward some redefinition. There are even indications that in the first months of 1948 Quill had begun making preparations for a break, quietly lining up allies inside and outside of the TWU.[49] The CP, as one historian characterized it, was demanding "militant political action in a period when the pressures for caution were immense." For Quill this was particularly unpalatable because he so distrusted the CP leadership. In his eyes, it was arrogant, and worse, unsuccessful. The Party's record since the end of the war was not a good one. Perhaps under the circumstances there was little else it could have done besides transforming itself into a mild, social democratic formation. But the fact was, it was being pushed, and pushing itself, farther and farther from the center of American political life. Month to month it careened from extremes of compromise to extremes of steadfastness.[50]

Until World War II, the CP had pretty much left the TWU alone. Now it seemed to be making ever greater and ever less rational demands. The Party was fast adopting a siege mentality, with all the associated paranoia and tests of loyalty. George Watt, who at the time was in charge of the CP's efforts among longshoremen, railroad workers, and teamsters, recalled that "what Thompson was doing, as Foster's front man in New York, was going after each union almost as if deliberately trying to isolate the Communists and force a confrontation." To disagree over the fare was one thing; to make it a test for membership in the left was another.[51]

For a man with as astute a political sense as Quill, the choices must have been clear. He could stick with the left and face increasing isolation, possible expulsion from the CIO, and a sustained effort by the O'Dwyer administration to crush his union. The fare probably would be raised without his support and his members would benefit little. Internal opposition would undoubtedly increase, especially if Murray encouraged it, and what had been mere annoyances, the raiding efforts by the IAM, AFSCME, and the UAW, might turn into serious trouble. Conceivably a united TWU leadership could have stuck with the left and survived; the experience of the Longshoremen's Union on the West Coast proved that it could be done, but it would have been a hard road indeed. The alternative was to steer toward the middle, pass a different loyalty test by abandoning Wallace, and construct a new set of alliances within the labor movement, the Democratic party, and mainstream liberalism. If perhaps less emotionally and ideologically satisfying, this was clearly the safer course.[52]

One could, of course, argue, as many did, that what should distinguish Communist unionists from their pure and simple brethren was their commitment to a larger political vision to which they were willing to subordinate parochial interests. It was precisely in the most difficult times that the greatest sacrifices were required. But the TWU and its leadership were ill-equipped to so act. For years, Quill and company had been essentially pragmatic unionists, expressing their leftism primarily on issues peripheral to the day-to-day business of their union. It was Santo, after all, who had promoted the idea that the membership should support its leaders because they "brought home the bacon." It was late in the day to suddenly call for sacrifices, sacrifices that might lead to institutional and political suicide.[53]

As American labor leaders go, Quill was not an exceptionally greedy or venal man. But he liked certain comforts of position and security. Often, he ruminated on the fate of his Irish heroes—in most cases disgrace, poverty, or the early grave. It was decidedly not a fate he wanted to share. Quill had not even a touch of a martyr's complex. He had started out in the United States as a common laborer and the fear that he could end up that way haunted him. He preferred the sins of the soul to the damnation of obscurity, powerlessness, and the mean struggle for survival.[54]

There was one final consideration: the effect of switching camps on the internal dynamic of the TWU. For fourteen years Quill had been part of a collective leadership. If at first he perhaps considered himself lucky to be in the group, as the years went by his view of himself and his colleagues changed. His own sense of self-worth increased, and being treated as the leader of the union made him feel like the leader of the union. During World War II he learned that the TWU could survive perfectly well without Hogan and Santo, half of the brain trust.

Now, Quill found himself faced with a unique opportunity. The TWU was poised between powerful, opposing forces. The TWU left was well entrenched and commanded the loyalty of the membership, but in spite of, not because of, its ideological outlook. The union had one set of allies on the left, but another was waiting, willing and able, to the right. Given Quill's prestige, hierarchical position, and broad network of contacts, his personal stand could well swing the union in either direction. By switching camps, Quill could greatly enhance his power within the union, and power was something Quill had grown increasingly fond of.

Not that Quill wanted, at least at first, actually to oust his long-time colleagues. In fact, he desperately argued with them to follow his course on the fare. But for their own reasons, most of the leftists in the TWU refused. Santo had little choice; with his future likely to be in Hungary, it was not a time to cross the CP. The others were either more committed to the CP than Quill, felt that the TWU needed the support of the left to survive, or thought that in an intra-union showdown Quill would lose. Still, for a while Quill refrained from attacking other TWU officers. Even after open factional warfare began, he continued to try to win over most of the TWU left, although increasingly on terms he alone set. Years later Quill still felt angry and betrayed that so many of his oldest and closest union associates had, in his eyes, deserted him.[55]

Quill also had not originally expected that his rupture with the CP would lead to a permanent estrangement from the organized left. His contradictory actions in the first months after his resignation from the NYC CIO Council indicated how tentative and unsure he was. On March 29, one day after he urged Local 100 to leave the CIO Council, Quill reversed himself after a long meeting with the TWU leadership and issued a joint statement with Hogan that repudiated his earlier remarks. Then he went off to Pittsburgh to see Murray. At an April 7 TWU meeting, however, attended by over 4,000 workers, Quill openly attacked the CP. The last of a string of speakers, Quill confessed that he had often met with Browder and Foster and had thought the CP "the only party who had the real idea of getting a living wage for the workers. Some say I am completely controlled by the CP," he went on, "but I have taken orders from Foster long enough." He concluded: "they say I have to read the *Daily Worker* editorials to make up my mind what to do. I will prove to you whether I am controlled by them," at which point he ripped up a copy of the Communist newspaper to the cheers of the crowd.[56]

In spite of his harsh remarks, Quill still had some hopes for a reconciliation with the CP, if the CP itself changed. On April 16 he put his name to an extraordinary letter, conceived of and written primarily by Browder, but with some unmistakable Quillisms. Addressed "Dear Friend," and delivered to Italian Communist leader Luigi Longo, its real intended audience was obviously the Soviet leadership. After introducing himself, Quill explained why he had resigned from the CIO Council, portraying himself as the victim of a *Daily Worker* "campaign of character assassination." He continued:

> I intend to resist and defeat the attempts of Mr. Foster and his clique to sever me from the labor movement. Mr. Foster will also learn that I will not join the camp of professional Communist haters, anti-Sovieteers and warmongers. This "crackpot" expects me to follow in the footsteps of Joseph Curran . . . who was driven to the camp of the enemy by Mr. Foster and his factionalists only a few months ago. . . . Foster has neither the power to drive me to the reactionary side, nor to destroy me directly. . . . I will maintain [the support of the overwhelming majority of TWU members] without serious difficulty, opposing both Mr. Foster and at the same time the reactionary camp, no matter to what extremes the Foster faction may go.

Next came the punch line:

> I was informed that it was intervention from abroad that placed this man Foster in control of the American Communist Party some time ago, and I am afraid that unless there is further intervention from abroad, there is little chance that Mr. Foster and his wrecking crew will be halted before it is very, very late.

After a detailed critique of CP trade union policy since 1946, the letter quoted Stalin's 1929 criticism of factionalism in the American CP as once again relevant. In ending, Quill wrote:

> as one who has played a small part in the fight for American-Soviet friendship, I am appealing to you to investigate the statements contained in this letter and use your own good judgment in dealing with the problems I have raised.

No reply was ever received.[57]

Quill's efforts to carve out a new, independent political position coincided with the renewal of the TWU's drive for higher wages. To a large extent, this campaign was secretly orchestrated by Quill, O'Dwyer, and Theodore Kheel, who had become O'Dwyer's key transit adviser. On April 6 the TWU struck the East Side and Comprehensive Omnibus Company. The immediate issue was a schedule change that would have resulted in layoffs and earnings reductions. However, the real motive for striking this small Manhattan bus company was probably to lay the basis for a renewed push for a city-wide fare increase by creating a crisis atmosphere without paralyzing the city. Reportedly, Hogan had opposed calling the strike, while Quill had been its main proponent.[58]

At the TWU's April 7 membership meeting, Quill, Santo, MacMahon, and Hogan were given a broad mandate to lead the wage fight. TWU leaders implied that the other private surface lines might soon be struck too. As if on cue, O'Dwyer hurried back from California, where he had been vacationing, and his aides told the press that a fare hike had become inevitable. While the TWU kept up the pressure by holding section and branch meetings, O'Dwyer announced on April 11 that he was re-examining the fare issue and would make a decision within two weeks.

On April 12 Saul Mills, speaking for the NYC CIO Council, and representatives of the ALP, SP, and CP testified against a fare hike at a Board of Estimate hearing. Hogan sidestepped the issue, while Quill called on the city to use "all its money-raising powers" to finance higher municipal wages. The next day, the three largest private transit companies announced that they would not meet the TWU's wage demands unless they were allowed to increase their fares. Quill immediately asked O'Dwyer to raise the transit tariff and "disregard the stupid double-talk of Saul Mills." The alternative, Quill implied, was a general transit strike. On April 14, at a City Hall demonstration called by the CIO Council, TWU members carrying signs reading "we are for Mike and a fare hike" jostled with those opposing a fare increase. [59]

Amidst all this, the TWU leadership gathered to consider the troublesome issues confronting the union and hear spelled out, for the first time, the differences among the top four officers. The Local 100 Executive Board debated the fare issue on April 15. Until then Gus Faber had been the only well-known TWU official publicly to join Quill in calling for a higher fare, although Guinan, Phil Bray, and Barney O'Leary also favored an increase. However, after a long discussion, Quill's position was overwhelmingly endorsed. That night, at a large membership meeting that authorized a private-line strike, Hogan was poorly received. A few days later, Mac-Mahon proposed to the IEB that it endorse Wallace, but after Quill threatened a union-wide fight a compromise was worked out; the Board voted unanimously to condemn "the bipartisan policies of the major political parties" and appointed a committee to "formulate an appropriate resolution on political action." When the committee was unable to come up with a statement acceptable to all sides, the issue was temporarily dropped. [60]

On April 15, O'Dwyer began the final phase of his fare-hike campaign by meeting separately with delegations from the AFL and of non-leftist CIO leaders (including Quill). Under considerable pressure from O'Dwyer, who red-baited the opponents of a higher fare, both groups agreed to support whatever fare decision the Mayor made. The next day O'Dwyer met with the TWU leadership and executives from the private lines, urging a suspension of the current bus strike and strike threats until after he announced his fare decision. Hogan and Santo, realizing that they had been outmaneuvered, told O'Dwyer that they would back a moratorium if he would guarantee that the private-line workers would receive the thirty-cents-an-hour increase they were seeking. O'Dwyer refused, and at a meeting of TWU section chairmen, Quill and Faber piously argued that the union should do its own bargaining. The left then backed down and joined in accepting O'Dwyer's proposal. [61]

On April 19, Quill appealed over the radio to the city's population to "ask our Mayor to raise the fare." Of course, by then O'Dwyer had already made his decision, which he announced on April 20: as of July 1 the fare on the NYCTS rapid transit lines would be ten cents, and on the municipal surface lines, seven cents. It was widely assumed that the state's Public Service Commission would follow suit and authorize the private surface lines to raise their fares to seven cents as well. That same day, Quill, who had been under constant fire from ALP leaders, resigned from the labor party, charging that it was "the prisoner of such crackpots as William Z. Foster, Robert Thompson, and a string of lesser job-holders." The Daily Worker, in turn, commenting on the fare increase, wrote that "Mike 'The Dime' Did It."[62]

The wage negotiations that followed were largely sham. O'Dwyer, keeping his end of their bargain, privately arranged with Quill to offer the TWU a twenty-cents-an-hour wage increase. When it became clear that this would face opposition within the union, including from Hogan and other leftists, O'Dwyer asked Quill what it would take to satisfy the rank and file and undercut the left. Told twenty-four cents an hour and a voluntary dues check-off, he agreed and got the private-line employers to accept a similar settlement if they too could raise their fares. On April 28, O'Dwyer called the TWU leadership, the large TWU negotiating committees, and the private-line executives to City Hall. When Quill demanded twenty-four cents and a check-off, O'Dwyer instantly acquiesced, to the amazement of Hogan, Mac-Mahon, Santo, and the other TWU members present, none of whom knew that an agreement had already been reached.

After that, it was just a matter of mopping up. The Board of Transportation officially approved the settlement on May 4 and agreed to consider pension adjustments, a health plan, and other issues in ongoing negotiations. The private lines held out for a while, trying to delay any wage increase until after they had actually received authorization to raise their fares, but under pressure from O'Dwyer and continuing TWU strike threats they soon capitulated.[63] Santo, Sacher, MacMahon, and Hogan, left out of the key wage discussions, briefly tried to recoup their position by arguing against accepting the twenty-four cents, urging the union to continue to fight for thirty cents and all of its other demands. But it was a ridiculous exercise. Even the Daily Worker had to admit that twenty-four cents was a major victory. It was the largest increase that the TWU had ever won and considerably more than most CIO settlements of the period. As recently as the fall of 1947 the TWU itself had only been asking for fifteen cents an hour. The left therefore retreated and joined in celebrating the settlement (later claiming partial credit, since it had opposed the earlier twenty-cent proposal).

Quill's strategy, at least in the short-run, had been enormously successful and the transit workers were jubilant. Over 5,000 attended mid-May victory meetings at which the settlements were ratified. In mid-June, in just six days, the TWU collected 18,013 dues check-off authorization cards. By September the total was near 23,000. If Quill's moves, starting with his CIO Council resignation, had terribly hurt the organized left and diminished the disposable income of the transit-riding public, they had paid off handsomely for the TWU membership. Accordingly, his standing in the union soared to its highest point ever.[64]

Despite their differences, throughout the fare and wage battles Quill and the other TWU officers had generally not criticized one another in public. Both sides had tried to portray the union as still united and shared credit with one another for the union's gains. Union publications avoided any mention of internal dissension. Once the fare raise was an accomplished fact, the most nettlesome issue within the union was removed. Although the ALP, CP, and NYC CIO Council launched a petition campaign to force a fall referendum to reverse the increase, the leftists in the TWU opposed and disassociated themselves from this effort. Of course differences remained—most importantly over Wallace and the union's relationship to the CP—but there were no significant disagreements over strictly trade union issues.[65]

Quill still hoped to avoid an internal union battle. To that end he proposed to MacMahon the formation of a united front within the TWU, with the CP as a junior partner. If, at the union convention scheduled for the fall, the followers of the CP supported Quill's re-election and the nomination of his supporters to a majority of the IEB seats, he would support their retention of the secretary-treasurer's post and a large minority on the IEB. The TWU left-wingers turned down this proposal, either on their own initiative or, more likely, at the insistence of the CP. Perhaps it was felt that the left could oust Quill and thus regain undisputed control of the union. Perhaps it was simply politically unpalatable to compromise with someone so repeatedly reviled in the CP press and by New York's leading leftists. In any case, once Quill's offer was rejected, a virtual civil war began.[66]

For the next six months the TWU was consumed by an extremely nasty faction fight. Since both sides were bureaucratically well entrenched, each could deliver and absorb repeated blows. Quill held the most powerful International post and could usually count on the support of about two-thirds of the Local 100 Executive Board. The left controlled the other top International positions and could generally carry the IEB by roughly a three-to-one margin. The Local 100 officers were evenly divided: Hogan, recording secretary Peter MacLachlan, and first vice-president James Gahagan allied with the left, while Faber and second and third vice-presidents Matthew Guinan and John Hamilton stuck with Quill. Both sides had their own newspaper: the left controlled the *Bulletin*; while starting in September, when Quaytman and Poritz were ousted as the editors of Local 100's *Transport Voice*, that paper became the organ of Quill's faction and was distributed throughout the International.[67]

Most TWU cadre chose sides early on, before the heaviest battling began, and thereafter remarkably few changed camps. In general, those in or long close to the CP—a high percentage of the oldest and most active union members—stuck with the left, although often it was an agonizing decision. Forge, for example, was personally close to Quill—Quill considered him almost part of his family—and privately disagreed with the CP's positions on the fare and the Marshall Plan. Quill had protected Forge during his repeated clashes with Santo. If Forge supported Quill and Quill emerged victorious, he could count on an expanded role in the International. But out of lingering loyalty to the CP and distaste for Quill's red-baiting, Forge stayed with the left. Similarly, some of those who went with Quill found the choice painful. Mark Kavanaugh, who had little sympathy for the CP's politics, was upset at the prospect of fighting Santo, whom he looked upon as his mentor. Bill Grogan, one of the few who wavered from side to side, was almost constantly distraught. Fratricide was not an easy business.[68]

Quill initially found himself with relatively few prominent and experienced backers, local-wide leaders in their own right, although he did have a large following among the second-level Local 100 cadre. Faber provided a well-known name and a useful sounding board, but otherwise Quill had almost no one within the union with whom he could map strategy and talk frankly. For that he had to go outside the union, to Murray and to Shirley Garry, his City Council secretary who became his closest confidante. For additional allies inside the union, particularly veteran factionalists, there was only one place to turn, the right.[69]

This was not an easy step. Although Quill's long-standing anti-Communist opponents had been pleased by his break with the CP, they remained skeptical. For his part, Quill had sworn that he would never turn to the right and he still detested most of the Church-tied dissidents. Nevertheless, the logic of the situation drove Quill in that direction. The shrewder rightists, especially in the Westcott group, which had recently won some followers on the IRT in addition to its surface line backers, realized that their moment had come.

As if to signal to Quill that they were willing to make an alliance, John O'Connell of the Westcott caucus in late May sponsored a resolution, unanimously passed by his Third Avenue section, condemning the *Daily Worker* for its attacks on Quill. Quill responded with a press release praising this action. On July 20, Quill met with Westcott and arranged for help from his group. Quill's rapprochement with other former opponents took longer; as late as September, Quill had to ask Father Rice to write to Catholic dissidents in out-of-town TWU locals to assure them that Quill's change of heart was sincere and to solicit their aid. Quill even tried, unsuccessfully, to recruit John Gallagher to his cause.[70]

In June preliminary factional skirmishes began. In Omaha, TWU International representative John Cassidy was forced by pressure from Quill and the local TWU membership to resign as chairman of the Nebraska Wallace campaign, a serious blow to the third-party movement there. Then, on June 22, the Local 100 Executive Board voted 22-12 to withdraw from the NYC CIO Council. However, it was at a series of Joint Executive Committee and mass membership meetings in July, August, and September that the crucial battles occurred.[71]

On July 12, at a meeting of some 1,000 track workers, Quill first brought the faction fight to the membership at large, announcing that "there is no unity among your officers." At the urging of Faber and Quill, and over the objection of Hogan, the meeting voted to condemn the "unholy Trinity" of the ALP, CP, and NYC CIO Council. Another mass meeting on July 20 passed a similar resolution. This time Westcott's supporters called for those on the platform to vote, forcing Hogan and James Fitzsimon to in effect put themselves on record in favor of the ALP, CP, and CIO Council. Next came a wild, six-hour meeting of BMT section officers. Quill's supporters, brought in from throughout the city, booed and interrupted Hogan and Santo, while Quill himself launched into bitter personal attacks on MacMahon, Santo, Hogan, and Local 101 president John Lopez. (Lopez had opposed the fare hike and the Local 101 Executive Board had voted unanimously to stay in the NYC CIO Council.) Quill was so disruptive that he was criticized by IEB member Robert Franklin, himself an opponent of the left.[72]

In the July 24 issue of the *Bulletin*, Quill presented his full bill of particulars against the CP, citing alleged acts of interference in the TWU going all the way back to the early 1930s. Six days later the Local 100 Executive Board condemned the CP, ALP, and NYC CIO Council and required local officers and staffers holding ALP leadership posts to resign from their positions in one organization or the other. The effect was to force nine officials of the local to quit their ALP posts. The Board also moved to limit Hogan's authority. Adopting a demand long put forward by the right, it ordered that organizers and staff members be elected by the membership rather than appointed by the local president, as had always been the practice. Hogan's right to represent the local within the State CIO was also restricted. The left counterattacked by calling on Quill to resign from the City Council, since he had been elected as an ALP candidate, but Quill called the bluff. At an August 10 Joint Executive Committee meeting he offered to quit his city job, but the delegates overwhelmingly rejected the move. [73]

At an overflowing meeting of the BMT membership on August 19—perhaps the most important gathering of the entire intra-union battle—Quill again displayed superior factional skills. The left tried to keep the focus of the meeting on the unfulfilled aspects of the TWU bargaining program. Quill, however, made Communism the central issue. As workers entered the meeting hall, they were handed leaflets asking MacMahon why he remained as state secretary of the ALP even while it was fighting to restore the five-cent fare and if it was true that at an April 15 TWU leadership meeting he had admitted to belonging to the CP for the last fourteen years. From the platform, Quill asked all those opposed to Communism to stand. By one estimate about 95% of those present did so. He then asked those who supported Communism to stand. Only BMT organizer Carl Mann and a few others rose. The leading leftists were caught, wanting neither to admit nor deny their Communist sympathies. But when Quill and his supporters kept hammering away at MacMahon, accusing him of taking orders from Thompson, the TWU International Secretary-Treasurer finally exploded. "That part about Bob Thompson was a lie," he announced. "I know it is a lie because I am a member of that party. . . . Now I have told you the answer." Pointing to Faber, Quill, Santo, and Hogan, he went on: "there are a lot of people on this platform who won't give you the answer now or at any other time. Mike won't make a statement like that." Workers from the floor shouted "How about you, Mike?," but the TWU president deftly avoided a confession of his own.

Quill pulled one more rabbit out of his hat before the meeting ended. When Hogan charged Quill with sabotaging the TWU's fight for higher NYCTS pensions, Quill announced that he had been privately told by city officials that within three weeks the Board of Transportation would improve its pensions and put into effect the long-dormant O'Dwyer-Davis labor relations plan. Even the left-wing faction had to join in the standing ovation for these victories. (The labor relations plan was not, in fact, put into effect.)[74]

MacMahon's admission of CP membership shocked the TWU membership; after all, for years TWU leaders had denied that they were Communists. It also appalled most of the left. MacMahon was the TWU's most formidable left-wing leader, with strong ties and great respect in both the International and Local 100. Now he had effectively eliminated himself as a rival to Quill. Few TWU members would follow an open Communist, no matter who he was. With Santo neutralized by his immigration status, only Hogan remained as a credible challenger to Quill. Realizing this, Quill increasingly directed his heaviest fire against the Local 100 president.[75]

As long as the Communist issue had been raised as an abstract ideological question by those without great standing in the union, most TWU members were willing to look the other way. However, once the charge of Communist domination came from the foremost leader of the union—himself the target of previous charges—and was directly tied to the issue of wages, it became a powerful weapon. Most of the Local 100 membership was surprised when the split in the leadership developed. Many were upset and saddened by it. Still, there was a widespread sense of relief that Quill had disassociated himself from the left. Some even interpreted this as a confirmation of their long-held belief that Quill was never a Communist but rather the victim of false charges or CP entrapment. Many were sorry to learn that MacMahon and most likely the other TWU leftists were indeed in the CP, but for most workers there was little question as to whom to support. In spite of lingering respect and affection for the left-wing old guard, most Local 100 members were relieved that they finally could back their union and its top leader and still be free of the red taint.[76]

Red-baiting was so effective that even the left occasionally dabbled in it. A few times members of the left faction pointed out or implied that Quill too had long been a Communist. But it was not a tactic they generally pursued. Instead, they repeatedly attacked Quill's red-baiting as a deliberate diversion. However, some of the rightists who were unreconciled to Quill gladly took up and turned around his now favorite weapon. At a September 2 mass meeting of IRT, IND, and private-line workers a list of thirteen questions about Quill's and Faber's past ties to the CP was distributed, forcing Quill to evade the very trap he himself had used.[77]

Quill undoubtedly had been sincere in his initial intention not to adopt the tactics of "the professional Communist haters," but as the battle wore on he took up all of their tricks and then some. Deep-seated resentments, repressed for years, were set free as Quill turned his mastery of mockery, ridicule, and invective—once reserved for the bosses—on his erstwhile colleagues. Sacher, who was well paid for his legal services to the left, became a "stinko pinko with Adler shoes" or a "pinko banker." Forge and Chicago TWU leader Angelo De Iulis were portrayed as ungrateful immigrants, men who had done well in the United States only to turn their backs on their adopted country. Other IEB members were "left wing puppets," "loafers," or "lackeys." Quill's supporters even picketed one IEB meeting with signs reading "Red Russians, go back to Russia." Quill played brilliantly on the cultural and psychological insecurities, class resentments, and fervent patriotism of the membership. Much of this was undoubtedly a carefully crafted act, but it also reflected Quill's greatest strength; more than any other top TWU leader, he was characterologically at one with the rank and file.[78]

By relentlessly pursuing the Communist issue, by repeatedly delivering proof that his policy of alignment with O'Dwyer was paying off, and by effectively mobilizing his supporters, Quill routed his opponents in Local 100. Quill won majority support in nearly every section of the local. Among the few exceptions were the BMT porters and agents, groups unusual in not being comprised largely of white men. Otherwise, Quill won the battle in just about every conceivable political, occupational, and demographic subgroup within the local, besides the left-wing group itself and perhaps the early union pioneers. (The ex-IRA men were another possible exception; they were to be found on both sides of the fight, but it is unclear who had a majority.) By September, Quill's victory was so complete that Santo, MacMahon, and Hogan were often unable to address large Local 100 meetings, finding themselves literally booed off the platform.[79]

Outside of Local 100, the situation was quite different. Members of non-transit TWU locals in the New York area were subway riders and had at least mixed feelings about the fare increase, one of the key issues of the whole fight. Elsewhere, TWU members knew little and cared less about New York City politics or the NYCTS fare. In fact, for most non-New York TWU members the International itself seemed far removed and of limited importance; the union, for them, meant primarily their own local and its particular concerns. Their contact with and information about the International came largely through International representatives, IEB members, visiting officers, and the *Bulletin*. Since most of the International hierarchy was aligned with the left, the arguments against Quill were widely disseminated and legitimated. To those removed from the scene, Quill's actions and accusations often appeared bizarre, and the left-wing charge that he was trying to institute one-man rule seemed credible. Wherever an International representative was with the left, as most were, the activists in his jurisdiction tended to go along with his views. However, in the few places were this was not the case, the situation was explosive. The worst incident of violence during the entire faction fight occurred in Omaha, where a group of Quill supporters led by Local 223 president R. A. Hayes badly beat up John Cassidy in the union hall. (A local seniority dispute was as much involved as the larger union civil war.)

In New York Quill used Local 100 job holders and sundry followers, including some from the Westcott group, to agitate in other locals. Elsewhere he had to depend on a ceaseless stream of written propaganda, local CIO officials who apparently were ordered to aid him, and flying visits by himself, Faber, and Downes (who had joined his faction from the start). Often visits by Quill were wild affairs in which he temporarily won over a local's membership only to see it reverse itself as soon as he left town. In the meanwhile, Forge, Lopez, Sheehan, Case, Cassidy, MacMahon, Smolnikoff, Edwards, and others worked steadily to shore up support for the left, although largely on non-ideological grounds. Philadelphia was the most important local other than Local 100, but the situation there was particularly unsettled. Both sides had their supporters and both tried hard to win over the rank and file. Through anti-Communist fusillades Quill made considerable headway, but the local leadership seemed most interested in using the split to increase its own power and autonomy. All told, then, the International (other than Local 100) was a fairly even battleground, with the left, if anything, having a slight edge.[80]

Throughout the late summer and fall of 1948, the factional maneuvering continued at an ever more furious pace. On August 31, Quill voted with the CIO Executive Board majority to endorse Truman. A week later the TWU IEB repudiated his vote, passing a resolution that rejected both major candidates without endorsing Wallace. Over Quill's objections, the IEB also empowered the International to set up an insurance plan financed out of dues—an idea long pushed by various dissidents—and issued a statement on wage policy critical of Quill. In addition, the left proposed that a referendum be held on switching the method of choosing the top International officers from a convention vote to a direct member-ship poll. Quill agreed to putting this question before the rank and file. Holding such a referendum necessitated postponing the convention, which the IEB sched-uled to begin on December 6 in Chicago. The location—an inconvenience and added expense for the largest TWU locals—was chosen to prevent Local 100 from dominating the convention atmosphere and to negate Quill's plan to hold a large, pre-convention rally featuring Murray and O'Dwyer. [81]

Even before the IEB met, the Local 100 Executive Board began taking steps to counter the left's strength in the International. On September 4 it barred Santo and MacMahon from attending or participating in any meetings or affairs of Local 100 (a ban soon extended to others) and urged the delegates to the next TWU conven-tion to oust them from their posts. On September 7 it fired Sacher. (He remained the International's lawyer.) At the same time, the board endorsed Truman, as did the Local 234 Executive Board shortly thereafter. In the weeks that followed, the *Bulletin* was kicked out of Transport Hall (which was owned by Local 100); the local's left-wing civil service director was dismissed; and following Quill's reversal of position the Local 100 Executive Board voted to oppose changing the system used to elect International officers. [82]

The referendum on how officers would be chosen turned into an extraordinarily contentious affair. Quill explained his about-face by saying that the proposed change would keep the incumbent International officers in their posts for too long. However, he probably also felt that he had a better chance of dominating a conven-tion than carrying a full officers' slate in a rank-and-file poll. In any case, Quill's faction launched a furious campaign for a no vote in the union-wide referendum.

In Local 100, Quill's supporters took no chances; they fixed the election. Some-one, probably Faber, ordered extra ballots, which were marked no and bulk mailed from various points in the city. The result was a 29,985 to 1,600 vote against the proposed change. This represented a participation rate of over 90%, unprecedented in the union's history and highly improbable.

MacMahon and Sacher quickly smelled out the fraud, which they reported to the U.S. Attorney's office. An IEB committee amply documented the irregularities, although it was unable to pinpoint who was responsible. The contested ballots were critical; excluding Local 100 the proposed change in the voting system was approved in a light turnout by nearly a two-to-one margin, but if the Local 100 votes were included the results were reversed. Eventually the IEB, unwilling to disenfranchise Local 100 or accept a fraudulent result, voided the whole election and left the issue up to the convention. In the meantime, on October 29, Hogan sued Faber and Local 100's printer, charging them with embezzling over $8,000. The implication was that the money had been used to finance Quill's factional activity. [83]

Which side, if either, gained the most from all this maneuvering and chicanery is unclear. Only the most active unionists could even follow all the multiplying developments. As the autumn went on there seemed to be growing rank-and-file disenchantment in Local 100 with the endless factionalism. The Quill side, in particular, was vulnerable; not only was it the frontrunner, but Quill had in effect told the membership that by allying with O'Dwyer the union could fulfill its entire bargaining program. As time went on, Quill found it difficult to produce all that he had promised.[84]

On the NYCTS, O'Dwyer and the Board of Transportation did make very significant concessions to the TWU and timed them to best aid Quill. At the same time, however, they sought to limit the TWU's growing power and introduce cost-cutting measures. It was a policy of two steps forward, one step back. Thus, for example, in July the Board ended the practice of paying TWU representatives to be present at picks. It also continued to refuse to institute the O'Dwyer-Davis plan, instead setting up a three-man Grievance Board that included a TWU representative. Workers pursuing grievances had to do so on their own time, another break with past practice. Finally, the Board tried to introduce new IRT and IND schedules that significantly increased the work load and required the motormen, rather than switchmen, to lay up trains in the yards, precisely the issue that had precipitated the 1926 IRT strike.

The left tried to make the most of these work-related issues, charging that Quill had gone soft on management. It seemingly picked up some new support. At an October 7 local Executive Board meeting the Quill forces had only a one-vote margin in tabling a resolution introduced by Gerald O'Reilly threatening a job action to protest the new schedules. On strictly intra-union questions, Quill's group in Local 100 was never this close to defeat. However, since O'Dwyer was acutely sensitive to developments within the TWU, the situation never got out of hand.[85]

On the private lines, where O'Dwyer had less influence, the situation was more serious, enabling the left to seize the initiative and come very close to reversing the whole tide of the internal union battle. The underlying problem was this: although in the spring the private companies had agreed to go along with O'Dwyer's twenty-four-cents-an-hour wage increase, the new rates were only to go into effect, retroactive to May 1, when the private surface fare was actually increased. Wrangling over how much and with what limitations the fare was to be raised delayed any action, so that all through the summer TWU members received only their old rates. Meanwhile, the companies threatened to rescind the pending wage increase, laid off workers, introduced new schedules, and refused to bargain over many issues that had to be resolved before new contracts could be signed.

Several times the TWU came close to striking, thereby winning various concessions, but on the main issue, the wage increase, there was no progress. Quill hoped to resolve the conflict peacefully through the use of his political influence but, on September 3, Santo and MacMahon called for an immediate private-line strike. It was this call that led to the ban on their participation in Local 100 affairs. Nonetheless, with Quill's support the local Executive Board did threaten to strike the Third Avenue, the most recalcitrant company.[86]

In late September the Public Service Commission (PSC) allowed the private lines to raise their fare on an interim basis from five to six cents, but not to eight cents, as they wanted. The companies then began paying their workers at the previously negotiated higher wage rates, and NYC Omnibus and Fifth Avenue Coach announced plans for lump sum retroactive wage payments. The Third Avenue, however, balked on the back pay, claiming that it was losing money on its city operations.

The issue came to a head when the Third Avenue asked the PSC for permission to transfer funds from one of its subsidiaries to the parent company to finance back wage payments. To pressure the regulatory agency to agree to this as well as to a permanent fare hike to a level adequate to cover the wage increase, Quill called on the private-line workers to quit work and rally at the PSC offices on October 26. The logic of Quill's wage strategy was such that he found himself forced to use a job action to impose a higher fare on the city's bus and trolley riders. Quill, however, made two tactical errors. First, he underestimated the frustration and militancy of the private-line workers. Second, he gave out mixed signals as to whether the shut-down was to be a short, symbolic stoppage, as he intended, or open-ended.

On the morning of October 26 over 8,000 workers gathered at the downtown offices of the PSC. After Quill and a string of his backers addressed the crowd, Hogan took the platform and urged the workers to turn the stoppage into "the real thing," a strike against the companies rather than the PSC. Mayor O'Dwyer, who appeared at Quill's invitation, told the strikers that they had effectively made their point and should return to work. Quill seconded this sentiment and called for a vote on ending the strike. Although all observers agreed that only between 25 and 40% of the crowd voted to terminate the walkout, Quill declared the strike over. For once Quill did not know what to do or say and simply walked off. The workers, stunned by his performance, stayed behind. In the confusion, members of the crowd took over the microphone and called for the strike to continue until new contracts were won. Finally, Hogan told those present to reassemble at Transport Hall to decide on a course of action.

At the TWU headquarters workers packed the main auditorium and overflowed into the streets. Quill, Guinan, and other members of their faction again urged the men to return to work but they were repeatedly booed down. Hogan argued for continuing the walkout and, after considerable chaos, called for another meeting that night at Manhatten Center. In the meantime, most of the city's privately owned buses were off the streets.

Quill and Faber realized that they had lost control of the private-line workers and desperately worked to prevent the left from moving into the breach. Faber canceled the reservation for Manhattan Center and notified Quill's supporters to gather at Transport Hall. When the strikers found Manhattan Center locked they too headed for the TWU headquarters. Inside the building, where Quill's backers were assembled, Quill took another quick vote and again declared the strike over. But when he tried to announce this to the larger crowd outside, he and Faber were booed down and unable to speak.

Later that night, with help from the left, a rank-and-file strike steering committee was formed and a mass meeting scheduled for the next day at St. Nicholas Arena. Quill's forces were also at work, using every means possible to break the strike. Workers from one line were told that workers at another had already returned to work and vice versa, while those calling the union were told that the walkout was over. By the next morning, most of the NYC Omnibus and Fifth Avenue Coach employees had resumed work, while a majority of the workers at the Third Avenue and some of the smaller bus companies remained on strike.

Given this situation, Hogan, his key lieutenants, and the strike committee decided that a continuation of the walkout would be counterproductive. The 1,200 workers who assembled at St. Nicholas Arena, however, were in a militant mood. Speaker after speaker denounced Quill for selling out the strike. Hogan, too, charged Quill with treachery, but nonetheless urged an orderly retreat. Quill tried red-baiting, declaring that "this is a communist plot," but it no longer worked and he was booed and jeered. But so was Hogan, for he had earlier sworn to support the strike no matter what happened. Quill and Hogan found themselves in the ironic position of being allied against a continuation of the walkout. In a hastily arranged secret ballot, the private-line membership voted 2,014 to 568 to return to work.[87]

The private-line crisis was partially defused in early November when the PSC authorized the Third Avenue to transfer funds internally and the company began paying the back wages it owed. In December the private surface fare was again raised, this time to seven cents, enabling the companies to reach settlements with the union.[88] Still, the wildcat had been a major setback for Quill, even if the left had failed to fully capitalize on the situation. Without question, the strike hastened an erosion of Quill's support within Local 100. The decline in Quill's standing, however, was too late to make much difference; many of the delegates to the upcoming convention already had been elected. Furthermore, disillusioned Quill supporters did not necessarily join the other side.[89]

The weeks following the bus strike saw a final flurry of factional blows. Enfuriated and perhaps frightened by Hogan's role in the strike and his suit against Faber, the leaders of the Quill group decided to take no more chances. On November 3, at a Local 100 Executive Board meeting, they exonerated Faber and launched an investigation into Hogan's recent activities. The next day a Joint Executive Committee meeting ended in a near riot when Quill called on his supporters physically to eject the leftists present. A week later Hogan, Gahagan, and MacLachlan were suspended from their local offices and union memberships by the Local 100 Executive Board. Quill's tactics had become so heavy-handed that even ACTU felt compelled to chastise him.[90]

The left countered with an investigation of its own; on November 5 the IEB appointed a special inquiry committee to be headed by Maurice Forge. Forge's selection was a modest move toward compromise; Forge had not been involved in the ugliest infighting and until recently had been close to Quill. True to this spirit, the committee report, although highly critical of Quill and his supporters, made only general recommendations designed to restore and protect orderly union procedures. It also proposed a bargaining, organizing, and legislative program for the International.[91]

On November 15 the IEB met to consider the report of its investigating committee and one on the disputed referendum. It was a long meeting, with rapidly shifting moods, bitter at one moment, oddly frank and even sentimental at others. The two factions were like weary fighters in the final rounds, alternately throwing wild punches and clinging to one another for dear life. The most poignant moment came when Santo gave what was in effect his farewell speech to his long-time colleagues and recent opponents.

The only significant action taken, besides voiding the referendum, came on the Forge committee report. After a long debate, a consensus was reached. The specific

Gus Faber and Mike Quill with their supporters just before the start of the 1948 TWU Convention.

charges the committee made were deleted from its report, which was then passed with the support of both sides. After the unanimous vote, Quill summed up the moment by saying, "Jesus, what has happened?" But it was too late for any real compromise, and both sides began final preparations for a showdown in Chicago.[92] In one last piece of business, the Local 100 Executive Board reinstated its suspended officers to avoid legal action initiated by the left and because only Hogan, as local president, could certify the credentials of the Local 100 convention delegates.[93]

The leaders of both factions went to the Chicago convention thinking that they had at least a chance for victory. Santo and MacMahon knew that the going would be rough, but they hoped that with the support of most of the non-Local 100 delegates and a minority from Local 100 they could piece together a slim overall majority. This turned out to be a wild misestimation.[94] Forge also overestimated the opposition to Quill, but nonetheless was convinced that the game was up for the left. Like some other ATD leaders, he initially wanted to pull the airline division of the TWU, believing that once Quill established complete domination over the International the ATD would be unable to function effectively. With this in mind, Forge scheduled a conference of ATD convention delegates for the day prior to the International gathering. The original purpose of this meeting was to show Quill the solidarity of the group and to lay the basis for a possible later withdrawal. CP leaders, however, vetoed any secession move in the belief that there was still a chance of defeating Quill and that, in any case, a split would be wrong on principle. Accordingly, Forge turned the ATD conference into a vehicle for creating a solid airline bloc at the convention and for developing plans for a more elaborate, autonomous ATD within the TWU. The ATD delegates also selected candidates for the International vice-presidential and IEB posts that were expected to be reserved for the airlines. Although there were a few Quill supporters in the group, there was little factionalism. All of the airline delegates, with the sole exception of Jules Harvell from Local 501 in New York, voted to support Forge for re-election as a TWU vice president and director of the ATD.[95]

Quill had more reason than his opponents to be confident about the outcome of the convention, but he too was anxious, wheeling and dealing until the very last moment. Quill sought not only his own re-election, but the complete elimination of CP influence in the International, a more difficult task. Furthermore, even if he captured formal control of the TWU apparatus, Quill had to make sure that he could effectively run the International and prevent secessions or a general disintegration of the union.

Quill knew that he had the support of almost all of the Local 100 delegates and at least a scattering of delegates from elsewhere, but he wanted a solid majority. Since the Philadelphia delegation was the second largest and as yet uncommitted, he paid special attention to that group, arranging for it to travel to Chicago on the same train as the Local 100 delegation. Although most Local 234 delegates were willing to back Quill, in return they wanted one of their own in MacMahon's secretary-treasurer's post. Quill balked, wanting Faber for the position. Finally, in Chicago, Quill had the Philadelphia leadership meet with Allan Haywood, Murray's man on the scene, who insisted that Murray personally wanted Faber in the number two slot. To placate the Philadelphia group, Quill agreed to add Local 234 president Andrew Kaelin to his vice-presidential slate. Similarly, to satisfy some other delegates who were still sitting on the fence, Quill reversed his original intention and pledged to support the re-election of Grogan, who had avoided strong identification with either camp, as an International vice president. Finally, Quill tried to win over the ATD by striking a deal with Forge. Through Grogan he offered to support Forge's continuation in his current posts and to grant the ATD a high degree of autonomy if Forge would publicly declare his factional neutrality. Although Forge did not reject the idea of a reconciliation out of hand, he was unwilling to accept Quill's terms. Indirect negotiations failed to come up with a mutually acceptable formula.[96]

With the assistance of Haywood and other advisers from the CIO, Quill devised a convention strategy that totally stymied the left and turned most of the convention into an anti-climax. Although an arrangements committee, on which both factions were equally represented, had developed a convention agenda, on the first day of the convention, December 6, Quill had the rules committee, which he appointed, propose holding the election of officers that very evening, rather than at the end of the convention as had always been the practice. The left got wind of Quill's plan, but there was little they could do besides protest what they called "steam roller" tactics. After an acrimonious debate, the agenda change was approved by a show of hands, with Quill ignoring cries for a roll call.

Next, Quill's backers introduced a constitutional amendment that settled the referendum dispute by continuing the practice of electing officers at the convention. It also eliminated the posts of executive vice president and national director of organization (held by Hogan and Santo respectively), increased the number of vice presidents from six to eight (to accommodate Quill's last-minute backing for Kaelin and Grogan), and enlarged the IEB. Once again, the proposal was approved without a roll call, but by this time it was obvious that Quill had the backing of a large majority of the convention delegates.[97]

With only two top International posts remaining, Santo and MacMahon took themselves out of the running, hoping in that way to minimize the Communist issue. In fact, they barely said a word throughout the convention, leaving it in the main to Forge, Lopez, Hogan, Smolnikoff, and Frank Sheehan to argue the left's case. Hogan was chosen as the group's presidential candidate, while against Faber the left backed Hugh O'Donnell from Local 234, probably part of a reciprocal support agreement with some of the Philadelphia delegates.[98]

The actual elections were perfunctory. Both sides forwent the usual nominating and seconding speeches and the convention proceeded directly to the presidential balloting. Each delegate had a weighted vote proportionate to the number of union members he or she represented. Outside of Local 100, Hogan actually won a majority, getting all 39 of the Local 101 votes, 24 votes to Quill's 83 from Local 234, 63 votes to Quill's 20 from the ATD locals, and 42 votes to Quill's 40 1/2 from the miscellaneous other units. Quill, however, carried Local 100 by a landslide, receiving 323 votes to Hogan's 18, enabling him to achieve his overall five-to-two victory. Faber was elected by nearly as large a margin.[99]

All of Quill's vice-presidential and IEB candidates, put forth by the convention's nominations committee, were also elected. His vice-presidential slate, in addition to Grogan and Kaelin, consisted of five supporters from Local 100 and Harvell from the airlines. His IEB slate was dominated by centrist and right-wing supporters from Locals 100 and 234 but included five men who voted for Hogan, one each from Akron and Louisville and three—including William Lindner—from the airlines. (The Louisville candidate declined the nomination.)

The ATD delegates were infuriated by the official nominations, since the recommendations of their caucus had been largely ignored. In particular, they protested the nomination of Harvell rather than Forge, their near-unanimous favorite, for vice president. Even some middle-of-the-road delegates from other locals were disturbed by this move, which so obviously flew in the face of the wishes of the workers most directly affected. However, there was little to be done. Although Forge was put up against Harvell, he was defeated.

The Local 101 delegates were even more upset. Their local was the third largest in the International and in effect had been subsidizing the rest of the union, since unlike most other locals it did not receive any services from the International staff. Lopez had long been a TWU vice president and Sheehan had served on the outgoing IEB. Quill, however, did not include any representative from the utility group on his officers' slates, apparently because the local had so solidly backed the left. Lopez, in protest, refused to even contest Quill's choices. Sheehan did agree to be part of a token IEB opposition slate, but with all of the delegates voting for all of the Board members, he didn't have a chance. The structural devices originally designed by the left had come back to haunt it.[100]

With the elections over, the main business of the convention had been completed. The remaining sessions, spread over three days, were kept short and did little. Even potentially controversial resolutions, for example, backing Truman and the Marshall Plan, were barely debated. The only important question remaining was would the left-led locals bolt the union, and that too was soon resolved. On the day after the elections, following a round of informal caucuses, the leaders of the various anti-Quill locals announced, to the cheers of the assembled delegates, that they were staying in the TWU. The anti-Quill forces were not reconciled to the new regime, but they had decided to fight from within. To coordinate the opposition, the presidents of twenty-nine locals, claiming to represent 40% of the TWU membership, formed a "National Committee for TWU Democracy."[101]

There was one final piece of significant business. In the last moments of the convention, Quill's supporters introduced an entirely new union constitution. Based on a United Steelworkers' constitution written by Arthur J. Goldberg, it drastically centralized power in the International leadership, especially the president. Quill, for example, was given the power to start proceedings against any officer or member he had "reason to believe" had violated the constitution. The IEB could suspend any local, branch, or section officer who refused to adhere to or carry out its decisions and directives. Furthermore, it could place an administrator in charge of any local whose officers it deemed were in violation of the constitution. Two more vice-presidential and three more IEB posts also were created, to be filled by the IEB, giving Quill cards to make later deals with. Finally, members or consistent supporters of the CP were banned from holding office at any level of the union. This constitution was so hastily drawn up that only a minority of the delegates were even given copies of it, but nonetheless it was passed without debate.[102]

Even as the convention was still meeting, Quill began the final stages of his purge. Virtually the entire International staff was fired, including Smolnikoff, Case, Kearns, and the editors of the *Bulletin*. Cassidy resigned when he was ordered to swear allegiance to the new TWU constitution before R. A. Hayes, the leader of the group that had beaten him up. Sacher was dismissed as the union's general counsel. Even most of the International's office workers were let go. A month after the convention, Hogan, Gahagan, and MacLachlan were removed from their Local 100 offices in a special membership vote and Matthew Guinan was elected by the Joint Executive Committee as the new president of Local 100. The old order was over and a new one had begun.[103]

14

THE NEW ORDER

Most Americans know nothing about transit workers in general, but they know a lot about one particular transit worker, Ralph Kramden, Jackie Gleason's Madison Avenue bus driver who reigned over network television for most of the 1950s. Gleason had first-hand knowledge of the transit worker's life; after Gleason's father deserted his family, Gleason's mother, Mae, got a job as a BMT ticket agent, which she held until her death in 1935. The Gleasons were so poor that only a collection taken up by Mae's co-workers made a proper burial possible. Later on, during the heyday of the *Honeymooners*, Gleason would occasionally drop by Brooklyn bus garages to gather material for the show. In many of the later *Honeymooners* sketches, Ralph can be seen wearing a TWU button on his bus driver's jacket.[1]

The poverty of the Kramdens—their austere Brooklyn apartment lacked a telephone, radio, television, or other modern appliances—was something of an exaggeration. Transit wages rose significantly during the immediate postwar years and probably few transit workers lived so bare an existence. But Gleason was not completely off the mark; during the early 1950s most New York transit workers could afford to live modestly at best. In the fall of 1950, when the first *Honeymooners* sketch was aired, starting pay for a Madison Avenue bus driver was $1.31 an hour, 162% more then in 1935 when the TWU was first being organized. But in the intervening years the consumer price index had gone up by 78%, significantly lessening the gain. In the early 1950s, New York bus drivers generally earned less on an hourly basis than unionized truck drivers, longshoremen, or manufacturing welders.[2]

By the time Gleason's show went off the air in 1957, the situation had changed significantly. During the two decades after World War II, New York transit wages rose more sharply than wages in most other local industries. On the city-run lines, between 1943 and 1965 real wages went up an average of 3.2% a year. Some transit workers took advantage of their increased income to move out of their inner-city apartments to houses in Queens or suburban Nassau or Westchester counties.

Some 5,000 TWU members demonstrate in 1951 for the 40-hour work week.

Given the historically low pay in the transit industry, however, even with substantial pay increases many New York transit workers in the mid-1960s still had to struggle to live decently. In 1965 the basic yearly earnings of hourly rated NYCTS workers averaged $6,229—5% below what the Bureau of Labor Statistics defined as an adequate budget for a family of four. Workers in the bottom third of the occupational hierarchy—ticket agents (by then renamed railroad clerks), porters, car cleaners, and platform men, made far less. The situation was not as bad as it seemed since with overtime and various allowances added in average annual earnings were $7,179. Still, the "adequate" budget was a spare one, and many transit workers, especially those with large families, had to scrape to get by.[3]

Wages, of course, were not the whole story. In 1950 NYCTS employees won a 40-hour work week, without loss of pay. Three years later, after a 29-day strike, private-line bus workers won the same. During the 1950s and early 1960s, pensions and other benefits were improved. The TWU also successfully fought to have social security coverage extended to municipal transit workers. And perhaps most importantly, transit workers no longer faced the insecurity and autocratic management that had long characterized the industry.[4]

Nonetheless, the greatest gains the TWU made in the 1950s were not economic but organizational. By closely allying the TWU with the Democratic party, which once again was in firm control of City Hall, Quill was able largely to win back the bargaining status the TWU had lost as a result of unification. By the late 1950s the

TWU again had exclusive bargaining rights for almost all New York transit workers and had institutionalized collective bargaining for municipal transit employees. In doing so, the TWU helped pave the way for the unionization of other government workers in New York and throughout the country. The price for these achievements was a moderation of wage demands and cooperation with a drive to increase transit worker productivity.

Quill's strategy for the TWU did not sit well with many transit workers. During the late 1940s and early 1950s the leftists ousted from the TWU administration led a substantial opposition movement. Then, from the mid-1950s through the mid-1960s, a generalized revolt against the TWU leadership took place in the form of dissident movements, dual unions, and wildcat strikes. The TWU hierarchy was able to maintain control only by enlisting the powers of the state on its behalf. Ironically, it was when the TWU's alliance with the city government was disrupted by the election of Mayor John Lindsay in 1965, leading the TWU to call its first general New York transit strike, that the union began to make more dramatic economic gains, while regaining at least temporarily a measure of internal unity.

It took Quill well over a year after the TWU's Chicago convention to consolidate his control of the union. With so many experienced cadre ousted for factional reasons, Quill had to build a new union apparatus. What emerged was a center-right alliance. A few right-wing dissidents assumed important positions. From the Westcott group, for example, John O'Connell was put on International staff and Danny Gilmartin and Robert Franklin on the new IEB. In the main, though, it was middle-of-the-road activists who moved into positions of power. In Local 100, the conservative but ever-cautious Guinan became the dominant figure, assisted by Mark Kavanaugh, Gilmartin, and Ellis Van Riper, an up-and-coming leader from the IRT power department. The new Quill team faced a host of problems: in addition to establishing a new political and organizational structure, it had to deal with serious financial difficulties, a new round of contract negotiations, and a formidable challenge from the left.[5]

Even before leaving Chicago, the defeated leaders of the old administration laid plans for a continuing anti-Quill effort, making two important decision. First, the fight would be conducted within the union, not through secessions or splits. Second, the ousted anti-Quill officers and staff would return to the rank and file to lead the struggle. Accordingly, O'Reilly, MacLachlan, Nora O'Grady, Gahagan, Fitzsimon, and a host of others went back to their old transit jobs. The most prominent leftists, however, had no jobs to return to. MacMahon had permanently resigned from the IRT in 1935; Santo, Hogan, and Forge had never worked in the industry.

Santo made no effort to remain active in transit. Instead, he abandoned his deportation appeal and voluntarily returned to Hungary in June 1949. Hogan also dropped out, resuming his former career as an engineer and maintaining only peripheral contact with the fight in the TWU. That left MacMahon and Forge as the de facto leaders of the anti-Quill forces. MacMahon supported himself by running a candy store in Brooklyn. Forge took a job as a mechanic's helper at a Long Island bus company that was under contract with TWU Local 252, a small unit he had helped to organize.[6]

The battle between Quill and the new, left-led opposition took place on three fronts: the non-airline locals still led by supporters of the left, the ATD, and Local 100. After the Chicago convention, Quill moved quickly to neutralize or eliminate the pockets of opposition control in the non-airline locals. In some cases he used the new International constitution to oust incumbent officers. Bob Franklin, for example, was sent to New Orleans to supervise a purge of Local 206. Local president Ernest Scott and International representative Raymond Tillman were expelled from the union and a new, pro-Quill leadership chosen. In other cases Quill used his powers of persuasion. Joseph Affrunti, the president of Chicago Local 236, had voted for Hogan at the 1948 convention. A month later, after a private meeting with Quill, he denounced the left and pledged support for Quill. Perhaps he simply saw which way the wind was blowing. Perhaps he was influenced by the ethno-politics of his local; some of the local's strongest left-wing supporters were Yugoslavians, who after Tito's break with Stalin moved away from the CP.[7]

In a few anti-Quill locals, incumbent leaders were so well entrenched that Quill did not attempt to oust them. Instead, he sought a reconciliation on neutral terms. The most important example of this was Local 101. Lopez, Sheehan, and the other utility leaders who had opposed Quill enjoyed strong rank-and-file support. Furthermore, their local always had the option of leaving the TWU and affiliating with another union in the utility field. Accordingly, Quill offered Lopez and Sheehan a permanent truce; if they would not oppose him in the International, he would not interfere in their local. Although some of Quill's own backers balked at this arrangement, in May 1949 the IEB once again made Lopez a TWU vice president and Sheehan an IEB member.[8]

Such measures did not completely eliminate dissent in the non-airline locals. There was considerable opposition to Quill from both leftists and non-leftists in Philadelphia, where Quill never really succeeded in asserting his control. In Louisville, Quill's continuing attacks on the leaders of Local 176 led the unit to disaffiliate from the TWU in the fall of 1949 and join the BRT. Still, by late 1949 Quill had won over, outsted, or arranged truces with enough opponents in the non-airline locals effectively to eliminate this sector of the International as a base for a left-wing resurgence.[9]

The airlines presented a more formidable challenge.[10] Most ATD leaders were genuinely dismayed by Quill's performance in Chicago, particularly his ouster of Forge and refusal to consider their plans for greater ATD autonomy. As soon as the convention ended, a large group of ATD leaders, with assistance from Forge, formed the Committee for Air Transport Autonomy (CATA) to press for structural changes in the TWU. Though few airline leaders were ideologically inclined to the left, most initially supported CATA.

Quill viewed CATA, with some justification, as an effort to establish a separate international within the International, and he set out to destroy it. Quill's agents— Grogan, Faber, Harvell, and O'Connell—worked to undercut support for the committee. A flurry of open letters, petitions, and pamphlets were issued by both sides. Then, in May 1949, the IEB declared CATA a Communist front. Through that summer, however, CATA continued to enjoy the support of many, and probably most, ATD activists.

Faced with the failure of his initial efforts, and under pressure from Phil Murray to rid Local 500 of leftists, Quill turned to stronger measures. In July 1949, Grogan was appointed administrator of the Miami local, and in September several of the unit's officers, including Phil Scheffsky, its president and an IEB member, were expelled from the TWU. Later, several leaders of Local 504 (Pan Am–N.Y.) were expelled as well.

Quill was aided by the May 1949 testimony of Paul Crouch at a Senate subcommittee hearing in Miami. Crouch, a long-time, well-connected member of the CP and a former ATD member, claimed that Forge and ATD leaders Fred Swick, Ed Bock, M. L. Edwards, and Armand Scala were Communists who had used the ATD to set up a CP courier network in Latin America. Although these charges, repeated by Crouch in a widely reprinted article in the *Miami Daily News*, were later proved false, they were an effective blow against CATA. [11]

In the face of these developments, the unity within CATA began to dissolve. Some CATA leaders gave up on the TWU and organized a new union, the Federated Airline Workers of America (FAWA). Others opposed FAWA but remained critical of the Quill administration. Finally, a few dissident ATD leaders decided that a Quill victory was inevitable and that it would be better to work with him than against him. James Horst, a local president who had been aligned with the left, became an ATD organizer and gradually took over responsibility for the airline division. Future TWU president William Lindner also abandoned CATA to back Quill.

All things considered, FAWA did remarkably well. It developed considerable rank-and-file support in several locations and successfully petitioned for a representation election in Miami. Crouch's testimony, however, proved very damaging, since Scala was a key FAWA leader, and the TWU narrowly won the Miami vote. After that, the anti-Quill movement in the airlines dissipated. By the end of 1950, Quill had effective control over the ATD.

In Local 100, the backers of the left were still a powerful force, even after the Chicago convention and the ouster of Hogan, MacLachlan, and Gahagan. They continued to control a minority bloc on the local's Executive Board and many section offices. Many left supporters commanded considerable respect as union pioneers, militant unionists, and long-time leaders. Right after the 1948 convention, the left-wing opposition formed the Local 100 Rank and File Committee for TWU Democracy to serve as its organizational vehicle. MacMahon was the informal leader of the group and Forge the editor of its newspaper. It was back to the old days.

The Rank and File caucus generally avoided ad hominem attacks on the Quill administration. Instead, it concentrated on putting forth a bargaining program, criticizing management, taking up grievances, and answering pension questions. When the group did attack the incumbent leadership, it was usually for failing to provide militant representation. The caucus urged transit workers to stay in the TWU, pay union dues, and attend union gatherings. It steadfastly avoided political stands and did not endorse a candidate in the 1949 Mayoral election. As a result of these policies, the caucus developed a broad base of support; although the caucus leadership came primarily from the left-dominated old guard, the group attracted many non-Communist and even anti-Communist backers, especially among the older and the better-paid workers.

While the opposition was organizing, the Quill-Guinan forces in Local 100 were having problems. With Quill and Faber devoting considerable time to the International, the Local 100 administration was thin on experience and competence. Many of Quill's new associates, in the words of one of his supporters, were men whose "chief ability was to defeat Communists." Some proved less adept at actually running a union. The new leadership could not produce all that it promised. In April 1949 it adopted an ambitious bargaining program, very similar to one already put forward by the opposition, but it was unable to make immediate progress toward its implementation. Meanwhile, the performance of the new officers and organizers was measured against that of their predecessors. The result was considerable rank-and-file disenchantment.[12]

A key test for the opposition came in the December 1949 Local 100 elections. The Rank and File Committee sponsored a full "Unity Slate" of officer and Executive Board candidates, headed by Phil Bray. Although Bray had vehemently opposed the CP position on the five-cent fare, his distaste for the new regime led him to line up with the opposition. Among the other "Unity" candidates were a host of pioneer IRT and BMT unionists, including Anthony Alberto, MacLachlan, Eddie Cabral, Clarence King, O'Reilly, Patrick Reilly, Peter Ezzo, O'Grady, and Nicholas Sacco. The "Unity Slate" campaign stressed these candidates' experience and the need for a more aggressive NYCTS bargaining drive, while suggesting structural reforms including a referendum on splitting Local 100 into several separate locals, a favorite proposal of the old right-wing opposition. The administration slate, headed by Guinan, consisted largely of incumbent officials. Quill was in London during the final stage of the campaign and made a strong anti-British speech there, hoping in that way to associate his supporters with the Irish republican cause.

The official results indicated that Guinan received 12,140 votes to Bray's 4,693. The "Unity Slate" was completely shut out; its strongest showing was on the BMT, but even there its Executive Board candidates lost by roughly two-to-one margins. The only non-administration candidates to be elected were some independent IND Executive Board contestants allied with Bob Franklin, who had fallen out with the Quill group.

The Rank and File leaders were thoroughly convinced that the election had been stolen and that Bray had actually won. This charge has some credibility since a few of Quill's backers later indicated that there had been massive tampering. However, there was no solid evidence of fraud and the caucus did not make any public accusations. Bray was secretly relieved that he had lost, having no real desire for the job. When a few caucus members suggested that they go see some Catholic lawyers they had heard about, Forge understandably discouraged them.

The election results disheartened the opposition, but it carried on and for a while remained influential. A proposed revision of the Local 100 by-laws, for example, which would have again made organizer positions appointive rather than elective, was defeated partially as a result of the caucus's agitation.[13]

Quill recognized that the Rank and File group was still a dangerous foe and began using cruder tactics against it. In March 1950 he personally brought Forge up on charges of violating the International constitution. Two weeks later the IEB voted unanimously to expel him from the union.[14] During the next months some opposition candidates were ruled off the ballot in organizer and convention delegate elections with contrived justifications. Quill also postponed the next International convention from its scheduled date in September 1950 to December.[15]

While all this was occurring, MacMahon dropped out of sight. Then, in October 1950, he wrote a letter to Quill that was published in the *TWU Express* and the *CIO News*. MacMahon told Quill that "I was wrong and you were right. I quit the Communist Party well over a year ago, having come to realize their policy was one of disrupting the labor movement." MacMahon went on to praise the TWU's post-1948 policies and denounce the leftists—Gerald O'Reilly by name—still active in the union. Shortly thereafter MacMahon got a job with the United Furniture Workers Union, eventually becoming its Eastern Regional Director.[16]

MacMahon's desertion and Forge's expulsion took much of the steam out of the opposition. At the 1950 TWU convention, Quill was in complete control. When Forge tried to appeal his loss of membership, he was physically ejected from the hall. Only a handful of dissidents were delegates, and Quill was so confident that when a TWU member called for the removal of one opposition delegate, Quill opposed him, arguing that "this would be a dull convention if we didn't have a few agents of the murder gang of Stalin and the North Koreans."[17]

The Rank and File Committee continued to function into the mid-1950s, putting out its paper, running and even electing some candidates for section offices, and pressuring the Quill administration toward greater militancy. However, it was an increasingly nostalgic exercise. The group took over the sponsorship of the Connolly Commemorations, held social affairs and retirement parties, and served as a meeting ground for old-timers. Although some new members continued to be recruited, by itself the caucus was no longer a serious threat to the established powers.[18]

For many of the leftists still working in transit, the 1950s were difficult years. The FBI repeatedly questioned and harassed members and former members of the Rank-and-File caucus. Various city agencies—the Board of Transportation and its successor the Transit Authority, the Department of Investigation, and the Civil Service Commission—conducted anti-Communist investigations of their own, engaging in wholesale dismissals of those with left-wing ties or who refused to answer questions about their political affiliations. Among those fired were Gabriel J. Skrokov, a TWU pioneer from the BMT, and Fitzsimon. (MacMahon helped Fitzsimon get a job with the Furniture Workers as an organizer in the South, where he remained until retiring.) Between January 1955 and February 1956 alone, seventeen municipal transit workers lost their jobs as a result of anti-Communist investigations. On Long Island, a former president of Local 252, Gordon Barrager, was deported to Canada while leading a prolonged bus strike.[19] Although in the mid-1950s a few individuals associated with the pre-1948 TWU left continued to be prominent in dissident activities, as a coherent political group the left-wing old guard was a spent force.

In June 1950 Local 100 signed a "Memorandum of Understanding" with the Board of Transportation. This agreement was the result of collective bargaining along the lines proposed in 1946 by the Meyer Committee and endorsed in the

O'Dwyer-Davis plan. The Board of Transportation negotiated with all the various transit worker groups, but weighted their views proportionately to their membership. Thus although nine unions were party to the "Memorandum," it was largely the product of talks between the Board and the TWU. In most respects the agreement was similar to a private-sector contract, but it did not provide for exclusive representation or a union shop and could be unilaterally terminated by the Board. In addition to reducing working hours, the agreement provided for an across-the-board wage hike, improved benefits, and a two-year no-strike pledge. It also set up a grievance procedure which culminated in impartial arbitration. Theodore Kheel was selected as the permanent arbitrator. [20]

Over the next two decades Kheel, who in 1949 had been named impartial arbitrator for the private bus lines, played a central role in transit labor relations. Like many other labor relations specialists who worked for the NWLB and then rose to prominence in the postwar years, Kheel believed that orderly labor relations required strong, centralized unions. Sympathetic to the TWU, Kheel worked to strengthen its position in relation to its rivals, while helping Quill to solidify his control over the rank and file. Kheel, for example, used a 1949 wildcat strike by New York Omnibus mechanics, which Quill turned into a full-fledged walkout, as an occasion to demand (successfully) that the TWU institute new rules giving top union officers greater control over job actions. [21]

In 1953, over the objections of the TWU and Mayor Vincent Impellitteri, who had succeeded O'Dwyer, Paul Windels's old plan for an autonomous, financially self-supporting Transit Authority (TA) was put into effect by the Republican-controlled state legislature. Simultaneously, the fare was raised to fifteen cents. Although the establishment of the TA lessened the formal control of the Mayor over the transit system and reopened the whole issue of the transit labor relations, the TWU was able to strengthen its position in the years that followed. To a considerable extent, this was a result of the union's close ties to the Democratic party. [22]

Following O'Dwyer's resignation in 1950, the TWU temporarily lost its access to City Hall; the TWU opposed Impellitteri in the special election to fill out O'Dwyer's term. But in the 1953 mayoral election the union recouped its position by early on backing the eventual winner, Robert F. Wagner, Jr. The TWU's support was significant because Wagner faced first a primary against Impellitteri, in which the Democratic county leaders were divided, and then a tough three-way battle against Republican and Liberal party candidates. [23]

The TWU's political influence peaked during the twelve years Wagner held office. Quill and International Brotherhood of Electrical Workers leader Harry Van Arsdale, Jr., who after the AFL-CIO merger headed the city's Central Labor Council, were Wagner's main labor contacts. Both men pushed the mayor to institute collective bargaining for municipal employees, as he had vaguely promised to do during the 1953 campaign. As a first step in that direction, in 1954 Wagner issued an "Interim Order" guaranteeing city workers "full freedom of association . . . to negotiate the terms and conditions of employment" and requiring city agencies to set up labor-management committees to discuss wages, hours, and working conditions. Two years later the city authorized dues check-off for municipal labor groups. [24]

In 1958 Wagner went a step farther by issuing Executive Order 49 (E.O. 49). Wagner's earlier actions had legitimated municipal unionism and committed the city to the principle of collective bargaining. E. O. 49 began the process of setting up the mechanism for such bargaining actually to occur. Among other things, it established the principle of exclusive representation and authorized the city to hold representation elections. Shortly after the order the city began certifying unions as bargaining agents and signing contracts. [25]

E. O. 49 is widely considered a major landmark in the development of public sector unionism. Along with John F. Kennedy's 1962 Executive Order 10988, which recognized the right of federal employees to join unions and bargain collectively, it helped reverse the trend in public sector labor law from proscribing collective bargaining to facilitating it. (Kennedy's order was drafted by Ida Klaus, a former New York City official who had helped write E. O. 49.) Many state and local governments soon began establishing regulations for public sector bargaining. This in turn helped accelerate the growth of public sector unions, to the point that today the percentage of government workers who belong to a union far exceeds that in the private sector, including in such traditional union strongholds as manufacturing, construction, and mining. [26]

Wagner's accommodation to municipal unionism was not solely the result of political factors; although the civil service unions were a significant element of his political base, they were not critical to either his initial election or first re-election. [27] However, municipal unions were growing in size and militancy throughout this period. This was especially evident after 1955, when 2,000 parks department employees held a one-day strike, forcing that agency to hold a representation election. Rather than attempting to stop the growth of municipal unionism, Wagner chose to control the process through administrative regulation. By granting to the city wide latitude in defining bargaining units and certifying bargaining agents, E. O. 49 enabled Wagner to influence the shape of the emerging municipal union movement. Until his last years in office, Wagner successfully maintained tight control over municipal labor relations. [28]

As the largest and best-established municipal union, the TWU was an important influence on Wagner's labor policies. Because after 1953 TWU members were not employed by the city but by the TA, they were not covered by Wagner's executive orders. Nevertheless, Wagner played a major role in transit labor relations. In fact, many of his labor policies were first tried in transit and then applied to the city work force. The TWU thus helped break the ground for other municipal unions.

The TWU's first round of negotiations with the TA in 1954 set the pattern for the next decade. The negotiations began with a threat by the TWU to strike on January 1 unless the TA signed a contract to supersede the union's expired "Understanding" with the Board of Transportation. The TA balked, but Wagner intervened, setting up a fact-finding panel. The panel's report, highly favorable to the TWU, was accepted by the union but rejected by the TA. However, under further pressure from the Mayor the TA agreed to hold a representation election and bargain with the chosen unions.

The TWU won all eight units it contested in the June 1954 vote by an overall margin of 17,643 to 4,039. (It did not contest units of Staten Island and Queens bus drivers already represented by the Amalgamated.) The only close vote was among the motormen, where the TWU defeated the BLE by 1,752 votes to 1,344, benefiting from the BLE's refusal to accept black members. (By then there were a large number of black motormen.) The next month the TWU signed its first contract with the TA, which provided for a wage increase, a grievance procedure topped by an Impartial Chairman, and a limited form of exclusive recognition; in the units in which the TWU was recognized, no other organization could represent workers in grievance procedures, though workers could represent themselves. In return, the TWU agreed to a no-strike clause and left open the door for a possible reduction of sick leave benefits.[29]

In the years that followed, TWU bargaining with the TA became highly stereotyped. Every two years, as the January 1 expiration date of the TWU contract approached, the union would make extravagant demands that would be vehemently rejected by the transit agency. Usually mediators or a fact-finding board would be appointed as a crisis atmosphere developed. But out of public sight, Quill and Wagner would quietly work out an agreement that would be announced just before the union's strike deadline. A retired TWU activist in Joe Flaherty's novel *Tin Wife* captured the biennial New Year's eve drama:

> by design Wagner would never settle it till the last moment. . . . All the major components were in place weeks before. He'd hold out on some pissant issue until Father Time was on his deathbed, then he'd grant the final demand and some small bonus so we wouldn't get feisty at the last minute. . . . The whole city was off acting madcap in their high heels and patent pumps without a thought in their heads except how to get their drunken carcasses home, and there was the Mayor with his shirt-sleeves rolled up at the bargaining table. Now, I admit it, it didn't look bad for our side either. Dedicated, tenacious union men fighting the clock. And as the ball was about to fall in Times Square, . . . out we would all come from the room like the College of Cardinals saving the city from chaos.

Many private-line contracts were settled in a similar manner, with Quill privately working out an agreement with top company officials, but creating a public crisis so that the companies could go to the city for fare hikes or indirect subsidies to cover increased labor costs.[30] Backroom negotiations to resolve transit crises, of course, were not new for the TWU. But during the 1930s and '40s the crises had been real. During the 1950s and '60s crises over contracts were largely artificial, created to justify to the work force and the public the deals Quill had already worked out.

In one respect, the bargaining strategy Quill pursued from 1948 through the mid-1960s paid off handsomely; by the late 1950s the TWU had largely regained its pre-unification status. Except for its lack of a union shop, the TWU practiced what were essentially private-sector style labor relations with the city. However, there was a price to be paid—moderate wage settlements and cooperation with the TA's drive for greater labor productivity.

The most important mandate given the TA when it was established was to eliminate NYCTS operating deficits. By law the TA had to finance operations out of fare revenue, giving it the choice of further raising the tariff—a politically difficult step—or cutting costs. Since the Board of Transportation estimated shortly before it was disbanded that 75% of its gross income went to labor, cutting costs meant primarily cutting labor costs. The TWU was seen as a major cause of low productivity. TA member Harris J. Klein believed that the TWU "flagrantly and continually encouraged and fostered waste, featherbedding, and inefficiency." Paul Windels counseled the TA that it had to gain control over operations "lost since 1946 to Michael J. Quill." From its inception, the TA pushed hard to decrease the size of its work force, chip away at worker benefits, and win unrestricted authority over run schedules and other operational procedures. [31]

Although rhetorically the TWU blasted the TA's drive for greater productivity, in practice it cooperated with the effort. The union quietly allowed the TA to reduce the NYCTS work force from 43,731 in 1953 to 34,334 in 1964, a drop of 21%. In these same years, rapid transit ridership decreased only 11%. The TWU did not fight schedule changes that increased the time conductors and motormen spent on trains and failed to stop the contracting-out of more and more maintenance work. The union did oppose the TA effort to sell the NYCTS power plants, but when the plants were finally sold to Consolidated Edison in 1959 it did not launch an all-out fight to block their sale as it had in 1946. Also, wage settlements during the TA's first decade were more modest than during the previous ten years, averaging between 1955 and 1965 only 2.7% a year after adjusting for inflation.

The least popular TWU concession involved sick pay. In 1955 the TWU allowed the TA to stop paying workers sick pay for their first day out unless their illnesses extended for at least nine days. This was a high priority for the TA, which claimed that a buddy system had evolved in which pairs of workers would alternate taking off sick days and working overtime to cover the absence, thereby appropriating for themselves both more leisure and higher pay. [32]

The TWU policy of trading off institutional stability for wage moderation and increased productivity—or speed-up as many workers saw it—precipitated a wave of worker opposition to the TWU leadership that dwarfed the dissent of the 1930s and '40s. This opposition took many forms, including internal union struggles, public demonstrations, wildcat strikes, withdrawals from the union, and the formation of dual-union splinter groups.

Even before the TA was formed, there were signs of significant worker dissatisfaction with the TWU, as evidenced by the initial success of the Rank and File caucus and the formation of another caucus which pressed for a special wage hike for motormen. However, it was the TWU's 1954 contract with the TA that sparked a surge of oppositional activity. The contract was ratified by a 17,643 to 4,089 vote, but those who opposed it militantly pressed their case, picketing TWU headquarters and City Hall and, according to the union, disrupting a Joint Executive Committee meeting. The union leadership responded by expelling seventeen dissidents, including John Nolan and Patrick Reilly, Rank and File activists who were among Quill's oldest associates from the IRT station department. In addition, seven local and section officers were removed from office for publishing "scurrilous and misleading leaflets" pertaining to the new contract. [33]

Such heavy-handed TWU action failed to quell the rebellion; worker opposition to the TWU increased the next year and continued to grow until the end of the decade. During the first six months of 1955, 1,700 TWU members took their names off of the NYCTS dues check-off list. The following year withdrawals occurred at an even greater rate. On several occasions when Quill appeared at transit facilities he was heckled or physicially attacked. There also was a rash of unauthorized job actions, including at least three in 1955 alone: a "sick-out" by IND Queens division motormen protesting new schedules, a refusal by Brooklyn bus drivers to work overtime after the TA announced the elimination of 219 bus runs, and another sick-out when the new sick leave rules went into effect.[34]

Quill believed that the limited form of exclusive recognition granted the TWU in its 1954 contract meant that "for the first time in 15 years [the TWU has] driven from the subways of New York the various splinter groups which served as the handymen of management." As it turned out, the contract had the opposite effect, leading to the formation of a host of new organizations seeking to challenge or displace the TWU. Estimates of the number of worker groups active on the NYCTS during the mid- and late 1950s range as high as five dozen.[35]

Although organizations of almost every kind could be found, most of the new groups were occupationally based benevolent associations, such as the Conductors Benevolent Association, the Signal Electricians Benevolent Association, the Towermen's Benevolent Association, the 207th St. Cars and Shop Association (repairers and inspectors), the Automotive and Associated Mechanics and Helpers' Benevolent Association, and the Building and Allied Trades Council (carpenters, masons, and the like). Even groups that described themselves as industrial organizations, like the American Transit Union (ATU), were largely craft based; the ATU drew most of its support from subway shop workers.

The most militant and probably the largest of the "splinter" groups was the Motormen's Benevolent Association (MBA). In June 1956 it led a one-day strike of some 400 to 500 motormen. The underlying issue was an effort to win a wage hike for the motormen, but the immediate spark for the walkout was a TA order that BMT motormen had to train dispatchers so that they could be used as scabs if a strike took place.[36]

Many observers felt that the impulse behind the benevolent groups was not the desire for craft recognition per se, but dissatisfaction with pay rates and the TA productivity drive. The occupational groups most active in anti-TWU activities, like the motormen, conductors, and shop workers, generally had been hard hit by TA rule changes and speed-up. However, occupational autonomy *was* an issue. The TWU always had made a special effort to upgrade pay and conditions for the worst-off workers. In its first round of rapid transit contracts, for example, the union insisted on a minimum wage as well as an across-the-board percentage wage increase. Similarly, over the years the TWU pushed to lessen the time it took workers to reach top rates. Such steps were not popular with higher-paid workers, which forced the union periodically to seek special raises on their behalf. Nevertheless, after World War II it became the general policy of the union to seek equal hourly wage increases for all workers, which had the effect of further compressing the wage scale. Many skilled transit workers saw their pay rates fall behind those of craft workers employed directly by the city whose remuneration was pegged to "prevailing rates" in private industry.

Feeling short-changed by the TWU wage policy, many higher-paid workers became increasingly parochial in their outlook. In 1954 even some Local 100 officials advocated separate bargaining programs for different NYCTS departments, what Quill called "misleading craft union babble." Supporters of the dual unions went a step farther, believing that they could achieve more on their own or in coalition with other occupational groups than through the TWU. Some groups specifically sought "prevailing rates." By contrast, lower-paid workers, like railroad clerks, car cleaners, and porters, were generally not involved in the splinter groups of the 1950s.[37]

The motormen, of course, had a tradition of craft identification and militancy that predated the TWU. Their sense of power stemming from their unilateral ability to shut down the transit system was reinforced by their 1956 strike. The walkout, coming without warning, had seriously disrupted commuter travel, while a one-day strike the same year by a similar number of shop workers had had no such effect. Furthermore, unlike other disaffected transit workers, many motormen had never belonged to the TWU, since until 1954 the BLE had represented the BMT drivers. Although the MBA first emerged on the IND, its greatest backing came from BMT workers. All these factors help explain why the motormen were the most militant transit workers during the 1950s and the most tenacious in their opposition to the TWU.[38]

The history of the CIO is usually rendered as a story of declining militancy; the CIO is portrayed as having been built through massive worker uprisings, but, it is argued, as it matured sharp class conflict was replaced by routinized collective bargaining. David Brody noted that the historiography of industrial unionism, particularly in its New Left variants, "turns on the theme of *containment*—of rank-and-file radical potential held in check and ultimately defeated."[39] In the case of New York transit workers, this model, at least in its crude form, is simply wrong. Transit workers did not become less militant over time, nor were rank-and-file dissidents necessarily more radical than union bureaucrats.

If militancy is measured by participation in job actions, demonstrations, and self-organized worker groups, New York transit workers were at least as militant in the 1950s as they had been in the 1930s and '40s. In the 1950s, though, militancy was as likely to be manifested in opposition to the TWU as through it. The New York transit experience was not unique. Nationally the late 1950s saw a high level of labor strife, both in the form of prolonged official strikes and a large number of wildcats. Furthermore, in the UAW, the quintessential new industrial union of the 1930s, a skilled trades revolt took place as craft workers sought either greater autonomy and power within the UAW or a new union of their own.[40]

Militancy in itself, of course, does not always have the same significance. While transit workers were highly combative in the postwar era, their struggles were narrower and had less lasting impact than their earlier collective activity. The industrial union movement of the 1930s was marked by a seeming open-endedness; New York transit workers, after all, were led by political activists who at least privately professed to be seeking a revolutionary reconstruction of society. While in practice the movement was less radical than it sometimes seemed, it was tied to sweeping ideological and political developments: the movement for the extension of broadly defined democratic rights to the previously excluded, the creation of a limited welfare state, and the extension of the rule of law to the work place. In the course of the largely successful fight for these goals, new institutional structures were created, ranging from the CIO itself to an expanded federal bureaucracy and the modern Democratic party.

Transit worker militancy in the 1950s was not tied to any larger reform effort and resulted in only modest institutional changes. In general, the leaders of the "splinter groups" of the 1950s lacked the broad social vision of the pre-1948 TWU leadership or its anti-Communist critics. Leaders of the dual unions tended to personalize their struggle into a fight against Quill. They themselves called their organizations "anti-Quill groups," and they revived all the old anti-Communist charges against the TWU president. In the political arena, the dual unionists concentrated on attacking Wagner for refusing to meet with them and tacitly backing the TWU.

The activists in the dual unions were generally unsophisticated. A few had had previous experience in labor politics. James Donegan, for example, the head of the ATU, had once been TWU section chairman at the 148th Street shop, elected on a dissident slate. Before forming the ATU he had repeatedly challenged the Guinan administration. Reportedly a number of leftists were active in his organization. But Theodore Loos, president of the MBA, was more typical of the dual union leaders; he joined the TWU in the late 1940s but was not active in union affairs until he became involved with the MBA. Perhaps if the splinter groups had pursued a different strategy they might have benefited from the experience of earlier TWU dissidents, but most veteran activists from both the right and the left viewed dual unionism as an anathema. At Quill's request, Phil Bray even returned temporarily to the TWU payroll to help fight the MBA, and was given free rein to hire whomever he chose to help him. [41]

In many respects the benevolent associations of the 1950s were a throwback to the early days of the ISS, when all sorts of small groups of workers formed their own organizations and sought special arrangements with management. The movement illustrates the fragility of industrial unionism; in industries like transit, with complex occupational structures that encompass both skilled and unskilled workers, many of whom have little if any contact with one another, circumstances can always arise that lead to a breakdown of worker solidarity and the re-emergence of parochial concerns. [42] In the case of the TWU, the pressure of postwar inflation and the TA's productivity drive were critical to this development. But so were the TWU's fragmented structure, its repression of dissidents, Quill's increasing reliance on back-room deals, and a general decline in the competence of the Local 100 hierarchy after the 1948 purge.

The TWU responded to the proliferation of rival groups by seeking to use the power of the state to destroy them, repeatedly pressing the TA to grant it a union shop. Guinan argued that "it is not possible for a union to demonstrate stability under an open shop contract." The TA was not willing to grant a union shop, but it did cooperate with the TWU in crushing its opponents. Whereas once the managers of the municipal transit system sought to encourage multiple worker organizations to weaken the TWU, now they sought to eliminate them so that centralized labor relations could be used to control worker unrest. Accordingly, the TA severely disciplined or fired participants in job actions and refused to hold discussions with the new worker groups, in effect giving the TWU more exclusive representation rights than called for in the 1954 contract. The TA even went so far as to bug electronically the MBA headquarters and hotel rooms its leaders used.[43]

In 1957 the TA held a new election to grant exclusive recognition. Although the vote was held as a result of pressure from the splinter groups, it was structured to ensure TWU hegemony. In all previous rapid transit representation elections, workers had been divided into occupational or functional units. In 1957 such a system probably would have resulted in at least some workers—most likely the motormen—choosing to oust the TWU. The TA prevented this by lumping virtually all NYCTS workers, except the bus drivers represented by the Amalgamated, into one unit.

Furious at how the election was to be conducted, and seeking a pay hike and recognition of their union, on December 9, 1957, members of the MBA went on strike. They were supported by six smaller craft unions. Altogether about 2,000 workers took part in the walkout, which caused the most serious disruption of the rapid transit system since the 1926 IRT motormen's strike, which in many ways it resembled. By the second day of the strike fewer than half the trains were running. Some strikers used tactics reminiscent of the 1939 Stack wildcat, pulling emergency cords, obstructing tracks, and calling in bomb threats. However, by using supervisory personnel and scabs to operate trains, the TA slowly broke the strike. On December 16 it was called off after a Republican leader of the state legislature promised to sponsor a bill taking away from the TA the power to define bargaining units. (Such a bill was eventually passed, but Democratic Governor Averell Harriman vetoed it.)

On the same day that the strike ended, the TA held its representation election. Most of the craft groups boycotted the vote, so that the TWU faced opposition only from a newly formed alliance led by James Donegan. The TWU easily won, but the turnout was extremely low; less than half the eligible voters participated.[44]

Following the 1957 strike and election, the TWU moved quickly to co-opt the craft rebellion. In its 1958 contract the TWU won a special $2.5 million fund to be distributed to skilled workers as well as improved vacations and restored sick leave rights for workers with high seniority. The same year, after intervention by Wagner and AFL-CIO President George Meany, the TWU reached an agreement with the MBA which led to its incorporation into Local 100 as a new United Motormen's Division with greater autonomy than the old motormen's sections. Similar divisions were set up for other occupational groups as well.[45]

The TWU's gestures toward the skilled workers, backed up by the strong support it received from the TA, undermined the dual unions, though without necessarily winning the TWU the loyalty of their members. In 1959 yet another recognition election was held, this time pitting the TWU against a coalition of craft groups that included a rump organization of MBA members who refused to join the TWU. Although the TWU was again victorious, four out of ten voters backed the craft coalition. But thereafter the craft groups largely faded away.[46]

Within a few years yet another generation of oppositionists arose. This time the dissidents were black and Hispanic workers protesting discrimination by the TA and the failure of the TWU leadership to reflect the changing ethnic composition of the work force. Throughout the country, the growing civil rights movement was inspiring non-white workers to demand full equality from employers and unions alike. By the mid-1960s a third or more of all New York transit workers were non-white, but the TWU leadership remained overwhelmingly white and heavily Irish. In 1963, Joe Carnegie, an IND conductor who in the early 1950s had been active in the Rank and File caucus, formed a "Minority Caucus" to fight for greater opportunities for non-white workers to enter skilled jobs. In the late 1960s, Carnegie's group, reorganized as the Rank-and-File Committee for a Democratic Union, a name nearly identical to that of the old left-wing opposition, unsuccessfully bid to displace the TWU as the bargaining agent for NYCTS workers.[47]

Although the TWU leadership faced repeated rank-and-file challenges during the 1950s and 60s, the very nature of those challenges revealed how much the attitudes of publicly employed transit workers had changed since the prewar years. Under La Guardia, municipal transit workers had debated whether or not they needed a union, could sign contracts, or go on strike. In the 1950s and '60s the issue was what kind of union to have and what policies it should pursue; with few exceptions, the groups opposing the TWU strongly supported collective bargaining and the right to strike. Local 100 emerged from the turbulent years between 1954 and 1965 with its legal and organizational standing strengthened. But its strategy for doing so had alienated thousands of the most militant transit workers. Having helped pave the way for public sector collective bargaining, the TWU had yet to resolidify its backing by the transit rank and file.

During the 1950s and '60s Quill maintained a high national profile. He did so in spite of the fact that the TWU was dwarfed in size by such unions as the Teamsters, Steelworkers, and Auto Workers. After 1948 the TWU continued to grow, organizing new transit and airline locals and in 1954 absorbing the CIO United Railway Workers Organizing Committee, but its growth was modest. In 1957 the union had a paid-up membership of only 77,337. Nevertheless, in an era when labor leaders were increasingly bland, the flamboyant Quill was a favorite guest on television interview shows and a continual source of headlines.[48]

True to his word, Quill turned out not to be another Joe Curran but rather America's Josip Tito. After a few years of paying his anti-Communist dues, often in ugly ways, Quill began drifting back toward the left. By the mid-1950s he was on the left edge of the narrowed political spectrum of the day. In 1954, for example, he criticized the CIO for tying itself too closely to the Democratic party, suggesting as an alternative the formation of a national labor party. The following year he was the only major opponent within the CIO of its merger with the AFL, citing as his reasons the latter organization's "three R's," racism, racketeering, and raiding. By the early 1960s Quill was again calling himself a socialist, arguing for the nationalization of major industry and a free NYCTS, to be financed by taxes on major real estate interests. Quill was an early supporter of the civil rights movement and a vocal and early opponent of the war in Vietnam.[49]

Quill's actions often seemed to belie his words. In New York he was intimately involved with the Democratic party, and even as Quill and other TWU leaders traveled South to march in civil rights demonstrations they did little to accommodate the aspirations of Local 100's non-white members. Quill's bold political stands perhaps were a way of deflecting criticism. But they also were heartfelt—an effort to use rhetorical flourishes to expand the horizons of the labor movement and reinvigorate political discourse.

During the 1950s, Quill slowly made peace with some of his former colleagues from the TWU left. At the 1952 TWU convention he threatened to resign when some delegates tried to unseat a duly-elected left-wing delegate. Two years later, on the twentieth anniversary of the founding of the TWU, Quill praised the roles played by Santo, MacMahon, Hogan, and Forge in building the union. Shortly thereafter he brought MacMahon back to the TWU as an International representative. After overcoming considerable resistance from the Local 100 hierarchy, in 1961 MacMahon became Quill's assistant and in 1965 was elected an International vice president. After Quill's death, MacMahon resumed his old number two spot as International secretary-treasurer. Frank Sheehan, from Local 101, by then had taken over Santo's old job as director of organization. O'Reilly, Bray, and a few other one-time Quill opponents also returned to the TWU payroll.[50]

Other original TWU leaders never came back. Hogan continued working as an engineer in New York and on the West Coast, setting up an apartment in Cork, Ireland, where he frequently spent time. When he was dying of cancer, it was to Ireland that he returned. Forge kept working in transit on Long Island. When the prospects for the left opposition dimmed, he accepted a promotion from bus driver to dispatcher, the first step into management. Within a short time he was running his company as its general manager. He later set up his own small bus company and bought out his old employer. After selling the combined company he went into semi-retirement, becoming increasingly active in social issues through the Unitarian Church. In 1984 his membership in the TWU was restored.[51]

Santo had the most extraordinary story of all. In Hungary he quickly assumed a position in the top managerial elite, eventually taking charge of the country's entire meat industry. However, in November 1956, during the latter days of the Hungarian uprising, he fled to Austria and immediately began seeking re-entry to the United States. Although Santo cooperated with Senate Internal Security Committee staff members who interviewed him in Vienna, he was denied admittance to the U. S. under an immigration law provision that required former Communists to actively oppose Communism for five years before re-entering the country. Finally, in January 1963, Santo returned to the United States. Shortly thereafter he testified before the House Committee on Un-American Activities about his experiences in Hungary. Although he never publicly gave testimony about the TWU, his private cooperation with the authorities made him persona non grata with both the old TWU leftists and Quill, who had aided him in 1957.[52]

Quill's final redemption and finest hour came with the monumental New York transit strike of 1966. After three decades of threatening but never calling a general transit strike, at 5:00 a.m. on January 1, 1966, the TWU completely shut down the NYCTS (which by then included most of the city's bus lines). Quill badly needed a militant fight and a huge victory to reunite the fragmented union, upgrade wages, and ensure his legacy, for by then he was a dying man. Under any circumstances, Quill probably could not have gotten a package of the size he wanted through backroom dealing, but even the possibility of that was precluded by the election in November 1965 of Republican-Liberal candidate John V. Lindsay as Wagner's successor, ending twenty years of Democratic rule. Quill was openly contemptuous of the incoming mayor; Lindsay, he said, was "strictly silk stocking and Yale. This nut even goes in for exercise. We don't like him." When, on the fourth day of the strike, Quill, Guinan, Sheehan, Gilmartin, Kavanaugh, and Van Riper were jailed for contempt of court, Quill told the judge to "drop dead in his black robes" and MacMahon took over the negotiations. Just after entering jail, Quill, who had a long history of heart disease, collapsed.

After twelve days, during which the TWU and Quill came in for extraordinary abuse and New York City was virtually paralyzed, the TWU won a settlement worth an estimated $43 to 70 million, far more than any previous NYCTS contract. Most of the money was devoted to a 15% wage hike spread over two years. In 1968, Lindsay, eager to avoid a repetition of the earlier disaster, agreed to an equally large package. During the eight years after 1965, the hourly wages for motormen increased at an average annual rate of 9%. The 1968 TWU contract also provided for retirement at half pay after twenty years service at age fifty or up, sparking a massive exodus of senior workers from the system, including nearly all those who remained from the generation that had organized and nurtured the TWU.[53]

On January 28, 1966, two weeks after the New York transit strike ended, Mike Quill died. His funeral was held at St. Patrick's Cathedral, his casket draped with an IRA flag. The cemetery workers, who happened to be on strike, dropped their picket lines so that he could be buried. Monsignor Charles Owen Rice conducted the final services, but perhaps the most appropriate epitaph for Quill came not from Rice's words that day but from a speech he had given at a TWU convention three months earlier: "Michael, you are a real prince; you are a prince of the working man. . . . You came from the peasantry of Ireland and you rose to the leadership of the industrial peasantry of the United States."[54] But by then, of course, transit workers were no longer industrial peasants; they were full-fledged members of the modern working class, with the relative bounty and relative powerlessness that has come to imply.

NOTES

**A Note on the Location
of TWU Records**

When I began this study, most TWU records were still in possession of the union and unavailable for research. However, a number of retired TWU activists graciously made available their personal collections of TWU-related documents, as cited below. A few holders of documents asked to remain anonymous; in those cases I photocopied the documents I used and cite the copies in my possession.

Midway through my research, the bulk of the historical records of the TWU were donated to the Robert F. Wagner Labor Archives at the Tamiment Library of New York University. This is a large and extremely valuable collection. The Wagner archivists generously allowed me to use the collection while it was still being processed. Documents that were already processed at the time that I examined them are cited by the name of the folder in which they permanently reside. Unprocessed documents generally are cited by either the number of the box in which they were conveyed to the Archives or by the name of the file series in which they were stored by the TWU (for example "Santo Files"). Some of these documents have since been transferred to new folders, while others remain in their original location. A finding guide to the TWU collection, available at the Archives, should make possible the location of all cited material.

Two additional TWU-related collections were donated to the Wagner Archives during the course of my research, the Shirley Quill Papers and the Maurice Forge Papers. These collections have not yet been processed. Both collections, though rich, are not voluminous; the documents from them cited below can be easily located.

Finally, a number of documents, including minutes of the TWU International Executive Board, the Local 100 Executive Board, and the Local 100 Joint Executive

Committee, remain in possession of the TWU, where I was kindly permitted to examine them.

Unless otherwise noted, all interviews were conducted by and are in the possession of the author.

List of Abbreviations

1. Document and Oral History Collections

CCOHP	City College Oral History Project, Tamiment Library, New York University.
FBI-FOIA	United States Department of Justice, Federal Bureau of Investigation, Files on Communist Infiltration of the Transport Workers Union of America-CIO, released to the author under the Freedom of Information Act.
JBF	In possession of the author.
LaGP	Fiorello H. La Guardia Papers, New York City Municipal Archives and Record Center, New York, N.Y.
MF-T	Maurice Forge Papers, Transport Workers Union of America Collection, Robert F. Wagner Labor Archives, Tamiment Library, New York University.
NYPL	New York Public Library, New York, N.Y.
OHCCU	Oral History Collection of Columbia University, Columbia University.
SQ-T	Shirley Quill Papers, Transport Workers Union of America Collection, Robert F. Wagner Labor Archives, Tamiment Library, New York University.
TWU of A	Holdings of the Transport Workers Union of America, New York, N.Y.
TWU-T	Transport Workers Union of America Collection, Robert F. Wagner Labor Archives, Tamiment Library, New York University.
XA	Archives of the Xavier Institute of Industrial Relations, Archives of the New York Province [Jesuit], Bronx, N.Y.

2. Publications

DW	*Daily Worker*
LL	*Labor Leader*
NYCTB	*New York City Transit Bulletin*
NYT	*The New York Times*
NYWTB	*New York Weekly Transport Bulletin*
R&FTN	*Rank and File Transit News*
TE	*TWU Express*
TV	*Transport Voice*
TWB	*Transport Workers Bulletin*

Chapter 1

1. State of New York, Department of Public Service, Metropolitan Division, Transit Commission, *17th Annual Report for Calender Year 1937* (Albany, 1938), 188–89 (hereafter referred to as Transit Commission, *1937 Report*), Mark S. Foster, *From Streetcar to Superhighway: American City Planners and Urban Transportation, 1900–1940* (Philadelphia, 1981), 59. For the purposes of this study, I have not included commuter railroads, such as the Long Island Rail Road or the Hudson and Manhattan Rail Road Co. (predecessor of today's PATH system) in the transit industry. I have also excluded facilities on Staten Island, which had their own, somewhat different, history. For a popular history of mass transit, see John A. Miller, *Fares Please!* (New York, 1941, reprinted 1960).

2. State of New York, Department of Public Service, Metropolitan Division, Transit Commission, *13th Annual Report for Calender Year 1933* (Albany, 1934), 111 (hereafter Transit Commission, *1933 Report*); James J. McGinley, *Labor Relations in the New York Rapid Transit Systems, 1904–1944* (New York, 1949), 5.

3. *Forbes*, vol. 132, no. 9 (Fall 1983), 48; Adolph Berle and Gardiner Means, *The Modern Corporation and Private Property* (New York, 1932), 24; Clifton Hood, "Underground Politics: A History of Mass Transit in New York City Since 1904," Ph.D. dissertation, Columbia University, 1986, p. 114; Cynthia Horan, "Agreeing with the Bankers: New York City's Depression Financial Crisis," in Paul Zarembka and Thomas Ferguson, *Research in Political Economy*, Vol. 8 (Greenwich, Conn., 1985), 205, 207; Robert Fitch, "The Family Subway: Space, Class and Power in New York City, 1927–1940," ibid., 183–84.

4. Most el and trolley franchises originally were granted to companies formed to run a single or a few lines. The franchises themselves were often the most valuable assets of these companies. When consolidations took place, the original companies were maintained as legal entities to preserve their franchise rights. See Harry J. Carman, *The Street Surface Railway Franchises of New York City* (New York, 1919). Transit industry financial practices are discussed in Delos F. Wilcox, *Analysis of the Electric Railway Problem* (New York, 1921); Harry A. Gordon, *Subway Nickels: A Survey of New York City's Transit Problem* (New York, 1925); Emerson Schmidt, *Industrial Relations in Urban Transportation* (Minneapolis, 1937); and Charles W. Cheape, *Moving the Masses: Urban Public Transit in New York, Boston, and Philadelphia, 1880–1912* (Cambridge, Mass., 1980). Also see *Moody's Manual of Investments: Public Utility Securities, 1931* (New York, 1931), 2287 (hereafter *Moody's Utilities*); McGinley, pp. 68–70, 191–197; Norman Thomas and Paul Blanchard, *What's the Matter with New York* (New York, 1932), 278; and *NYT*, Dec. 11, 1934, p. 6. The one serious effort to trace the profits of a New York transit company, Cynthia M. Latta's "The Return on the Investment in the Interborough Rapid Transit Company," Ph.D. Dissertation, Columbia University, 1974, is only partially successful.

5. The plan for city ownership was approved in a referendum in which many voters mistakenly believed that they were endorsing a municipally run system. In fact, city ownership was the result of the refusal of private companies to risk the large amount of capital needed to build a subway system. As a result, the plan was developed to use city credit to finance a privately run, for-profit system. See McGinley, p. 42; Cheape, pp. 77–81.

6. Interborough Rapid Transit Company, *The New York Subway: Its Construction and Equipment* (New York, 1904; reprinted in facsimile, New York: Arno Press, n.d.), 10, 16–17, 19–20; Board of Transportation of the City of New York, *Report Including Analysis of the Operations of the New York City Transit System for Five Years Ended June 30, 1945* (New York, 1945), 1–3 (hereafter Board of Transportation, *Five Year Report*); Latta, pp. 15–21, 32–41; Cheape, pp. 91–92; Hood, p. 114. Belmont took an intense personal interest in the

IRT, as evidenced in Boxes 4, 5, and 6 of the August Belmont Papers, NYPL. He even built a lavishly appointed private car, the "Mineola," to use in traveling around the system. See Stan Fischler, *Uptown, Downtown* (New York, 1976), 47.

7. Earlier investors in the els included Russell Sage, Cyrus Field, and Jay Gould. The Rockefeller family, originally minority shareholders in Manhattan Railway, eventually assumed control over the company. Robert Daley, *The World Beneath the City* (Philadelphia, 1959), pp. 85–89; McGinley, pp. 23–26, 29–30; Cheape, pp. 32–36, 40–42; Latta, pp. 41–44; Fitch, pp. 183–85.

8. Miller, pp. 107–8; Matthew Josephson, *The Robber Barrons* (New York, 1934), p. 385–86; McGinley, pp. 24–27; John Moody, *The Truth About Trusts* (New York, 1904), p 413–14, 423–24; Cheape, pp. 95–96; Latta, pp. 58–59, 71–80.

9. McGinley, pp. 48–50, 436; Board of Transportation, *Five Year Report*, pp. 3–4; Paul Windels Memoir, OHCCU, 113.

10. The investment figure is as of June 30, 1939. During this same period the IRT invested $232 million in construction, equipment, extensions, and improvements. McGinley, pp. 52–54, 62–65, 434–37; Charles Garrett, *The La Guardia Years* (New Brunswick, N.J., 1961), 210–12, 377fn; Transit Commission, *1937 Report*, 188.

11. Metropolitan Street Railway had been on the verge of collapse when it was merged with the IRT. Thomas Fortune Ryan, who controlled Metropolitan, very shrewdly had used the threat of competition—he proposed building his own subway system—to unload his failing empire. He then quickly got rid of most of his IRT stock. See Latta, pp. 71–81.

12. Even in receivership the IRT generated an operating surplus, but not one large enough to cover its fixed costs, particularly the Manhattan Railway lease. McGinley, pp. 24, 26–27, 191–96, 436–37, 524–25; Latta, pp. 246, 249; Foster, p. 53; Berle and Means, pp. 97, 112–13; Abraham Dollinger, "Father Knickerbocker, Transit Magnate: A Short History of Unification," mimeographed report dated May 31, 1940, copy in the Scudder Collection files on the IRT, Thomas Watson Library, Columbia University. During its post-World War I reorganization, the IRT retained control of one small trolley company, New York and Queens County Railway, which also went into receivership in the early 1930s, as did Manhattan Railway Co. See *Moody's Utilities, 1933* (New York, 1933), 2510, 2515. The Morgan involvement in the IRT can be traced in box 5 of the Belmont Papers, NYPL; the Scudder Collection files on the IRT; *Barron's*, Sept. 5, 1932, p. 6; and Harold Nicolson, *Dwight Morrow* (New York, 1935), 155–56. By the time of his death in 1924, even Belmont had sold most of his IRT stock. See Latta, p. 291.

13. The city fared even more poorly under the BMT contract than under its arrangement with the IRT. Although the city invested $208 million in partnership with the BMT, it received no return payments. The company, which invested $116 million, received, as of 1940, all of its operating costs plus a cumulative "preferential" of $94 million and $131 million toward servicing and repaying its debt. McGinley, pp. 30–40, 57–67; Transit Commission, *1933 Report*, 11; interview with Peter MacLachlan, Feb. 25, 1979.

14. While heading the BMT, Dahl worked for Hayden, Stone, & Co, a securities firm. McGinley, pp. 28, 32–38, 196–97; Memorandum of Julius M. Mayer, "In the Matter of the Receivership of Brooklyn Rapid Transit Company and of New York Railways Company and of the Bankruptcy of Interborough Consolidated Corporation," folder 293, Scudder Collection; Gordon, pp. 78–90; Moody, *Truth About Trusts*, pp. 408–10, 424; Gerhard M. Dahl, *Transit Truths* (New York, 1924), 15–18, 22–23; *The Chase National Bank of the City of New York, 1877–1922* (New York, n.d.), 3, 24; *Moody's Utilities, 1931*, 2280, 2287, 2289; *New Republic*, Aug. 22, 1934, pp. 35–39.

15. Construction of the ISS, of course, increased the city's total transit debt, which by

1936 reached $740 million. Annual debt service was $36 million, $28 million of which was paid out of tax revenue. McGinley, pp. 71–94, 441; Board of Transportation, *Five Year Report*, 4–6; Dollinger, pp. 6–7.

16. Third Avenue Railway Corporation, *Annual Report to the Stockholders for the Year Ended June 30th, 1933* (hereafter Third Avenue Railway, *Annual Report*); Third Avenue Railway, *Annual Reports for 1940, 1941, 1942*; Transit Commission, *1933 Report*, 250–51. According to Robert Caro, "it was considered an open secret in Bronx political circles that key borough politicians held large but carefully hidden interests in Third Avenue Transit." *The Power Broker: Robert Moses and the Fall of New York* (New York, 1974), 878. See also State of New York, Joint Legislative Committee to Investigate the Administration of Various Departments of the Government of the City of New York, *Second Intermediate Report* (New York, 1932), 57.

17. Miller, pp. 153, 163; Phoebe Sharfstein, "The Motor Bus Industry in New York," typescript, June 1946, pp. 5–6, N.Y.C. Municipal Reference Library; Leo Huberman, *The Great Bus Strike* (New York, 1941), 4–5, 8; *Moody's Utilities*, 1933, 1160; Fifth Avenue Coach Company, *Annual Report for Year Ended December 31, 1937*, 1, 4; The Omnibus Corporation, *Annual Report for the Year Ending December 31, 1949*, 4 (hereafter Omnibus Corporation, *Annual Report*); Box 5, Belmont Papers, NYPL. The role of General Motors in the decline of passenger rail and trolley transit is discussed in Bradford C. Snell, "American Ground Transport," in Joe R. Feagin, ed., *The Urban Scene: Myths and Realities*, 2nd ed. (New York, 1979), 241–65. A GM rebuttal can be found in Stanley I. Fischler, *Moving Millions: An Inside Look at Mass Transit* (New York, 1979), 266–86.

18. Interview with Maurice Forge, Jan. 7, 1979; Transit Commission, *1933 Report*, 111, 477, 480, 501, 518; Huberman, p. 15; Citizens Budget Commission, *Transit Handbook* (New York, 1934), 33–35.

19. Transit Commission, *1933 Report*, 250–251, 513; McGinley, p. 442; NYWTB, Sept. 7, 1940, p. 1. As conversion from trolleys to buses continued, these figures changed substantially. By 1937, New York Railways was out of existence, while N.Y.C. Omnibus was employing more than 1,600 workers in bus operations. *TWB*, July 1937, p. 4.

20. Cheape, pp. 57, 95–96; *Dictionary of American Biography* (New York, 1943), XVII, pp. 123–24; *The I.R.T. News*, Oct. 27, 1929, pp. 4–5; Dahl, p. 18.

21. Third Avenue Railway System, "Organization Chart: 1933," Third Avenue Railway file, Scudder Collection (seniority figure calculated from p. 4); interviews with John Gallagher, Apr. 20, 1979, and Joseph Labash, Aug. 3, 1979; letter from Mike Tierney to John Nolan, in possession of Nolan; Transport Workers Union, *Report of the Proceedings of the Convention, 1937* (hereafter *TWU 1937 Convention*), Oct. 7 morning session, pp. 57–58. On the role of Masons in the auto industry, see Peter Friedlander, *The Emergence of a UAW Local, 1936–1939: A Study in Class and Culture* (Pittsburgh, 1975), 129–31.

22. Transit Commission, *1933 Report*, 262–63, 513, 563; McGinley, pp. 131–35, 436–39, 450; interviews with Patrick J. Reilly, Sept. 7, 1978; Maurice Forge, Jan. 7, 1979; Philip Bray, Aug. 13, 1979.

23. The IRT also had "special officers" who patrolled the stations and trains, though they had no legal police powers. McGinley, pp. 127, 452, 492; Transit Commission, *1933 Report*, 262–63; interviews with Patrick J. Reilly, Sept. 7, 1978; John Nolan, June 1, 1978; Maurice Forge, Jan. 1, 1979; U. S. Department of Justice, Immigration and Naturalization Service, "In the Matter of Charges against DESIDERIU HAMMER, alias JOHN SANTO" (typescript of 1947 hearings, hereafter *Santo Deportation Hearings*), 745–46; DW, Jan. 4, 1935, p. 4.

24. Transit Commission, *1933 Report*, 250–51, 262–63, 513, 563; *Interborough Bulletin*,

May 1935, p. 15; interviews with Victor Bloswick, Jan. 23, 1979; Peter MacLachlan, Feb. 25, 1979; Third Avenue Railway, *Annual Report, 1935;* McGinley, pp. 454–55, 492–94; *The I.R.T. News,* May, 28, 1935, p. 2. The largest transit shop, the IRT's 148th street facility, is described in detail in Chapter 4.

25. IRT Co., *New York Subway,* 67–116; *The I.R.T. News,* Sept. 22, 1927, p. 12; *TWB,* Dec. 1938, p. 16; Transit Commission, *1933 Report,* 251–52, 262–63; McGinley, pp. 144, 452, 494–95. For a detailed description of a power plant, see Chapter 4.

26. Operating expenses do not include fixed charges, such as debt service or lease payments. McGinley, p. 448.

27. Wilcox, pp. 9–10; *Moody's Utilities, 1934* (New York, 1934), A87.

28. Even with these cuts, in the early 1930s guards remained the second largest group of transit workers, after trolley operators. McGinley, pp. 132–35, 434–40, 450; *TWB,* Nov. 1934, pp. 1, 2; July 1, 1936, p. 3; Nov. 1936, p. 6; Transit Commission, *1933 Report,* 262–63; Latta, p. 265.

29. Third Avenue Railway, *Annual Report, 1932; TWB,* Aug. 1934, p. 6; Nov. 1936, p. 6; *DW,* June 28, 1935, p. 4; *Tenth Annual Report of Brooklyn-Manhattan Transit Corporation for the Year Ended June 30, 1933* (New York, 1933), 5.

30. McGinley, pp. 150–64, 234–36, 461–69; *TWB,* Aug. 1934, p. 6; Jan. 1937, p. 4; Apr.–May 1935, p. 3; Oct. 1935, p. 4; July 1937, pp. 1, 5; *New York Post,* May 15, 1935; *DW,* Oct. 19, 1934, p. 4; June 7, 1935, 4; *Proceedings of the Third Biennial Convention, Transport Workers Union of America, Sept. 24–27, 1941* (hereafter *TWU 1941 Convention*), 42; Car Cleaners of Jerome and other IRT barns to Thomas E. Murray, Jr., and Murray to All Employees of the Interborough Rapid Transit Company, Aug. 8, 1935, in "Interborough Rapid Transit Co." case file, Regional Records, Region II, N.Y., National Labor Board, 1933–34 and Nation Labor Relations Board, 1934–35, RG 25, National Archives, Washington National Records Center, Suitland, Maryland (hereafter, NLB and NLRB records, 1933–35, WNRC); *Santo Deportation Hearings,* 848; John H. Delaney to Fiorello H. LaGuardia, Sept. 6, 1938, "Transportation, 1934–1939" folder, box 2642, LaGP; *Bronx Home News,* Jan. 1, 1947, p. 3; interviews with Philip J. Carey, Oct. 13, 1977; Patrick Walsh, June 1, 1978; *Proceedings of the Second Biennial Convention, Transport Workers Union of America, Sept. 20–23, 1939* (hereafter *TWU 1939 Convention*), 69–70; New York City Omnibus Corporation, *Annual Report for Year Ended December 31, 1940,* 11.

31. Schmidt, pp. 74–75; interview with Gerald O'Reilly, July 11, 1979. In 1933, of 31,844 New York transit workers (excluding office and managerial personnel), 6,555, or 22%, worked part-time, including 1,646 trolley operators and 1,239 rapid transit guards, most presumably extras. Some part-time work, particularly in the shops, was the result of Depression-era work-sharing programs. Transit Commission, *1933 Report,* 262–63.

32. Interviews with John Nolan, June 1, 1978; Gerald O'Reilly, May 15, 1978; Patrick J. Reilly, Sept. 7, 1978. Generally IRT extras were given work at least every third day. However, if they failed to report seven days a week they could receive a two-week suspension. On the BMT, extras also had to report daily, but were guaranteed a weekly minimum pay of $18. *DW,* June 22, 1934, p. 3.

33. Interview with John Gallagher, Apr. 20, 1979; *Santo Deportation Hearings,* 848.

34. McGinley, pp. 156–58, 468; interviews with Patrick Reilly, Sept. 7, 1978; John Gallagher, Apr. 20, 1979.

35. Karl Marx, *Capital,* Vol. I (New York, 1967), 264–65.

36. Calculated from Transit Commission, *1933 Report,* 262–63. Among the major companies, average system-wide earnings were highest on the IRT, followed in order by New York Railways, Fifth Avenue Coach, the BMT, and the Third Avenue Railway. The differen-

tial between IRT and BMT rapid transit earnings varied from about 5 to 15% in the early 1930s. Transit Commission, *1933 Report*, 260–61, 513; McGinley, pp. 526–27.

37. Transit Commission, *1933 Report*, 262–63, 513; McGinley, pp. 484–85, 492–95, 502–7; *TWB*, Oct. 1934, p. 3; Jan. 1937, p. 4; "Stenographic Report of Hearing in the Matter of Transport Workers Union vs. Interborough Rapid Transit Company," "Interborough Rapid Transit #806" file, NLB and NLRB records, 1933–35, WNRC; interviews with John Gallagher, Apr. 20, 1979; John Plover, Feb. 20, 1979; Patrick Walsh, June 1, 1978; *TWU 1941 Convention*, p. 42; *Santo Deportation Hearings*, p. 884; *DW*, June 8, 1934, p. 4; Oct. 19, 1934, p. 4; June 7, 1935, p. 4; May 5, 1935, p. 4; N.Y.C. Omnibus Corporation, *Annual Report, 1944*, p. 9.

38. McGinley, p. 460; U.S. Department of Commerce, *Historical Statistics of the United States, Part I* (Washington, D.C., 1975), 170. For a discussion of living standards in the 1920s, see Frank Stricker, "Affluence for Whom?-Another Look at Prosperity and the Working Classes in the 1920s," *Labor History*, 24, Winter 1983, pp. 5–33 (poverty line estimates on p. 23).

39. Michael J. Quill, "Memorandum on Bill Int. 679 Print 913," p. 3, in "Transportation, 1934–1939" folder, box 2643, LaGP. A similar survey of 400 IRT workers in 1935 found almost three-quarters in debt.

40. Calculated from McGinley, pp. 530–31.

41. *DW*, June 18, 1934, p. 4; July 6, 1934, p. 4; Jan. 4, 1935, p. 4; Mar. 19, 1935, p. 4; *TWB*, July 1, 1936, p. 3; Mar. 1940, p. 8; *Santo Deportation Hearings*, 848; Huberman, p. 20; interviews with Peter MacLachlan, Feb. 25, 1979; Adrian Cabral, Apr. 12, 1979; Maurice Forge, Jan. 7, 1979; Lewis Fraad, June 30, 1980. The last trains with hand-operated gates were not replaced until 1958. John Cunningham and Leonard Hart, *Rapid Transit in Brooklyn* (New York, 1977), 78.

42. Melvyn Dubofsky, *When Workers Organize! New York City in the Progressive Era* (Amherst, 1968), 129 ("autocratic"); McGinley, pp. 138–40, 240; *TWB*, Nov. 1934, p. 5; Jan.–Feb. 1944, p. 13; Third Avenue Railway, "Organization Chart," p. 4; George Keegan to Thomas E. Murray, Jr., Nov. 22, 1934, in "Interborough Rapid Transit #1100" file, NLB and NLRB records, 1933–35, WNRC; interview with John Gallagher, Apr. 20, 1979.

43. Interviews with John Nolan, June 1, 1978; Gerald O'Reilly, May 15, 1978; John Gallagher, Apr. 20, 1979; Adrian Cabral, Apr. 12, 1979; "Affidavit submitted by George Keegan to the National Labor Board," in "Interborough Rapid Transit #1100" file, NLB and NLRB records, 1933–35, WNRC; *NYCTB*, Sept. 1944, p. 1.

44. Examples of the use of the terminology of slavery are too numerous to list fully. The quoted passages come respectively from: *TWB*, Aug. 1934, p. 6; *DW*, June 8, 1934, p. 4; and *Traction Workers Bulletin of Greater New York*, Sept. 1, 1926, p. 1, as quoted in Samuel Estreicher, "Collective Bargaining in the New York City Transit System, 1937–1950: A Case Study in the Politics of Municipal Unionism," M.S. thesis, Cornell University, 1974, p. 25.

Chapter 2

1. Emerson Schmidt, *Industrial Relations in Urban Transportation* (Minneapolis, 1937), 106–9; Selig Perlman and Philip Taft, *History of Labor in the United States, 1896–1932* (New York, 1935), 124–25; U. S. Department of Labor, Bureau of Labor Statistics, *Street Railway Employment in the United States*, BLS Bulletin #204 (Washington, D.C., 1917), 264–65, 290–93; *Brooklyn Citizen*, Jan. 13–15, 1895; *The World*, Jan. 13–15, 1895; Sarah M. Henry, "The Strikers and Their Sympathizers: Brooklyn in the Trolley Strike of 1895," M.A. Essay, Columbia University, 1987.

2. In spite of its charter, the Amalgamated was often forced to cede jurisdiction over non-operating personnel to various AFL craft unions. James J. McGinley, *Labor Relations in the New York Rapid Transit Systems, 1904–1944* (New York, 1949), 258–60; Perlman and Taft, p. 125; Schmidt, pp. 230–31; Gary M. Fink, ed., *Biographical Dictionary of American Labor Leaders*, (Westport, Conn., 1974), 227.

3. Perlman and Taft, pp. 125–28; Philip S. Foner, *History of the Labor Movement in the United States*, Vol. 3 (New York, 1964), 102–5; McGinley, p. 266; Schmidt, pp. 184–85; Marguerite Green, *The National Civic Federation and the American Labor Movement, 1900–1925* (Washington, D.C., 1956), 62–64.

4. Bureau of Labor Statistics, *Street Railway Employment*, p. 290; Philip S. Foner, *History of the Labor Movement in the United States*, Vol. 5 (New York, 1980), 71–72, 143–63; Perlman and Taft, pp. 343–48; Michael Kazin, *Barons of Labor: The San Francisco Building Trades and Union Power in the Progressive Era* (Urbana, 1987), 134–35.

5. Of the nine strike fatalities, seven were killed in transit accidents caused by strikebreakers inexperienced in transit operations, one was a strikebreaker killed in a fight, and one an official of a company supplying scabs who was found dead on the el tracks. Even though the proposed general strike failed to materialize, some workers at companies supplying the transit lines with coal and other materials and 6,000 brewery workers did walk out. Perlman and Taft, pp. 348–51; Schmidt, pp. 185–86; Edward Levinson, *I Break Strikes! The Techniques of Pearl L. Bergoff* (New York, 1935), 172–81; McGinley, pp. 220–25; New York State, Public Service Commission, First District, *Report on the Surface Transit Strike in New York City* (New York, 1916), 364–70; Melvyn Dubofsky, *When Workers Organize! New York City in the Progressive Era* (Amherst, 1968), pp. 126–47; *TWB*, July 1942, p. 4; boxes 4 and 6, August Belmont Papers, NYPL.

6. McGinley, pp. 266–67, 269; Stan Fischler, *Uptown, Downtown* (New York, 1976), 75–83; Samuel Estreicher, "Collective Bargaining in the New York City Transit System, 1937–1950: A Case Study in the Politics of Municipal Unionism," M.S. thesis, Cornell University, 1974, p. 29; John Cunningham and Leonard Hart, *Rapid Transit in Brooklyn* (New York, 1977), 40. For an insightful discussion of labor activity during this period, see David Montgomery, *Workers' Control in America: Studies in the History of Work, Technology, and Labor Struggles* (Cambridge, Eng., 1979), 91–112.

7. McGinley, pp. 227–29; Levinson, pp. 216–19.

8. Perlman and Taft, p. 329; McGinley, pp. 167–69, 502–3; Levinson, pp. 214–20; Third Avenue Railway System, "Notice to Transportation Employees," July 15, 1920, in Third Avenue files, Scudder Collection, Thomas Watson Library, Columbia University.

9. Schmidt, pp. 83–84; BMT worker quoted in *TWB*, Aug. 1936, p. 3; Theodore P. Shonts to Frank Hedley, Oct. 10, 1912, box 4, Belmont Papers, NYPL.

10. Schmidt, pp. 96–97; New York Railways Association, *Annual Report, 1916*, 1–22; McGinley, pp. 209–15, 274–76; *B.M.T. Monthly*, Jan. 1933–May 1935, passim; *The I.R.T. News*, Aug. 26, 1927–May 2, 1932, passim; *TWU 1937 Convention*, Oct. 8 morning session, pp. 20–21.

11. McGinley, pp. 169–70, 220–27, 269–71; Perlman and Taft, pp. 351, 590; *Interborough Rapid Transit Company against William Green, et al., Brief for Defendants* (New York, 1928), 30–33 (hereafter *IRT vs. Green*); Brotherhood of Interborough Rapid Transit Employees, *Constitution* (New York, n.d.), 5; *The I.R.T. News*, Oct. 20, 1928, pp. 1, 4; Robert W. Dunn, *Company Unions: Employers' "Industrial Democracy"* (New York, 1927), 92–98.

12. McGinley, pp. 227–31, 274–76; *B.M.T. Monthly*, Jan. 1933, p. 3; Feb.–Mar. 1933, p. 7; June 1933, p. 2; interviews with Patrick Walsh, June 1, 1978; John Gallagher, Apr. 20, 1979; *DW*, Sept. 27, 1933, p. 3.

13. Dunn, pp. 9–11; David Brody, *Workers in Industrial America: Essays on the 20th Century Struggle* (New York, 1980), 48–81; Daniel Nelson, "The Company Union Movement, 1900–1937: A Reexamination," *Business History Review*, LVI (Autumn 1982), 335–57.

14. Dunn, p. 94.

15. IRT participation rates calculated from McGinley, pp. 437, 532; BMT figures come from *B.M.T. Monthly*, Mar. 1931, p. 2.

16. Interviews with Joseph Labash, Aug. 3, 1979; Peter MacLachlan, Feb. 25, 1979; *The I.R.T. News*, May 31, 1929, p. 1; *TWU 1939 Convention*, pp. 154–55; *DW*, June 22, 1934, p. 3.

17. *TWU 1939 Convention*, pp. 237–38; *TWB*, Nov.–Dec. 1946, p. 11.

18. Dunn, pp. 95–98; *IRT vs. Green*, p. 33; Perlman and Taft, pp. 590–91; McGinley, pp. 269–72; *The I.R.T. News*, Sept. 22, 1927, 2; *DW*, June 22, 1934, 3.

19. Taft and Perlman, pp. 591–93; McGinley, pp. 272–74; *New York Post*, Apr. 27, 1928; *The I.R.T. News*, Mar. 24, 1928, pp. 1–4, 8; Oct. 28, 1928, p. 1.

20. *TWB*, Mar. 1935, p. 6; May 1, 1936, p. 6; Feb. 1939, pp. 1, 14; July 1942, pp. 1, 4; Feb. 1945, p. 4; *NYWTB*, Oct. 12, 1940, p. 3; *The I.R.T. News*, Oct. 27, 1929, p. 12; *TWU 1941 Convention*, pp. 116–17; interviews with John Gallagher, Apr. 20, 1979; Gerald O'Reilly, May 15, 1978; Aug. 11, 1979; John Nolan, June 1, 1978; *DW*, May 24, 1935, p. 4; *B.M.T. Monthly*, Nov. 1934, p. 4.

21. Interviews with Patrick J. Reilly, Sept. 7, 1978; Philip J. Carey, Oct. 13, 1977; *DW*, June 22, 1934, p. 3; *TWB*, Dec. 1933, p. 1; Apr. 1934, p. 1; Mar. 1935, p. 5.

22. *The I.R.T. News*, July 19, 1928; Apr. 29, 1929; interview with John Gallagher, Apr. 20, 1979.

23. *Moody's Manual of Investments: Public Utility Securities, 1934* (New York, 1934), A87.

24. Interview with Maurice Forge, Jan. 7, 1979; Delos F. Wilcox, *Analysis of The Electric Railway Problem* (New York, 1921), 9.

25. The following discussion of the social composition of the work force is based primarily on oral sources, especially my interview with Maurice Forge on Jan. 7, 1979. Scattered written references were also used in determining the composition of particular segments of the work force. (Full citations appear in notes 28 through 41.) Figures taken from the U.S. Department of Commerce, Bureau of the Census, *Fifteenth Census of the United States: 1930*, IV (Washington, D.C., 1933), 1135, 1138, 1141 (hereafter *1930 Census*), in general confirm the picture derived from these sources, although indicate a slightly lower percentage of foreign-born. Unfortunately, the census is of limited value. The occupational categories used do not generally correspond with those commonly employed in mass transit, which was treated as a sub-section of the railroad industry. Just the three categories mentioned above clearly contain only transit workers. Foreign-born transit workers are under-represented in the census for two reasons. First, foreign and native-born blacks were combined into one category, a serious problem since many black transit workers were West Indian. Second, many transit workers were either illegal immigrants or unsure of their legal status; it is quite likely that some chose to evade census takers.

26. See, for example, interview with Patrick J. Reilly, Sept. 7, 1978, and Philip E. Dobson, "The Xavier Labor School, 1938–1939" (clipping of unidentified article), p. 269, in "History of Labor School" file, XA. Maurice Forge, a particularly astute observer, estimated that 50% of the total transit work force was Irish.

27. My figure was derived by first estimating the percentage of each component of the work force that was Irish, using the below-cited sources, and then multiplying those percentages by the total size of the components as taken from the Transit Commission, *1933 Report*, 250–51, 513. The margin of error is undoubtedly high.

28. Michael J. Quill to Philip Murray, Aug. 30, 1944, TWU file, box A7-34, CIO Papers, Catholic University; interviews with Patrick Walsh, June 1, 1978 ("dumping ground"); John Gallagher, Apr. 20, 1979; Maurice Forge, Sept. 15, 1979; James Sullivan (pseudonym), July 27, 1979; Third Avenue Railway, "Organization Chart," Third Avenue file, Scudder Collection.

29. Leo Huberman, *The Great Bus Strike* (New York, 1941), 8.

30. *TWU 1941 Convention*, 97–99, 112–13.

31. Interviews with Maurice Forge, Jan. 7, 1979; Gerald O'Reilly, May 15, 1978; Philip Bray, Aug. 13, 1979; *1930 Census*, IV, p. 1138. BMT officials were apparently dissatisfied with the demeanor of the Irish they hired, one reason why the company had proportionately fewer Irish transportation workers than the IRT.

32. Interviews with Maurice Forge, Jan. 7, 1979; James Sullivan, July 27, 1979; John Plover, Feb. 20, 1979; Adrian Cabral, Apr. 12, 1979; Victor Bloswick, Jan. 23, 1979; *DW*, Apr. 16, 1934, p. 4.

33. Interviews with Peter MacLachlan, Feb. 25, 1979; Maurice Forge, Feb. 25, 1979; Nat Cohen, Dec. 7, 1978; *TWU 1939 Convention*, 70.

34. On the other New York transit lines as well, a high proportion of the native-born workers were from out-of-town. In fact, in most American cities very few locally born workers went into transit.

35. Interviews with Maurice Forge, Jan. 7, 1979; Philip Bray, Aug. 13, 1979; James Sullivan, July 27, 1979; McGinley, pp. 81–83, 125; *TWB*, Oct. 1934, p. 3; Aug. 1936, p. 3; *DW*, June 22, 1934, p. 4; Rebecca Rankin., ed., *New York Advancing, 1934–1935* (New York, 1936), 289; Arthur W. MacMahon, "The New York Transit System: Public Ownership, Civil Service, and Collective Bargaining," *Political Science Quarterly*, LVI (June 1941), 174; John D. Delaney to Fiorello H. La Guardia, Mar. 3, 1934, and miscellaneous correspondence in "Transportation, Bd of" file, box 664, LaGP.

36. *1930 Census*, IV, pp. 1135, 1138, 1141; Huberman, p. 30; *DW*, Oct. 19, 1934, p. 4; *TWB*, Oct. 1934, p. 3; Nov. 1934, p. 5 (includes quote); Mar. 1935, p. 6; *Santo Deportation Hearings*, 745–46; interviews with Patrick Walsh, June 1, 1978; Patrick J. Reilly, Sept. 7, 1978; Maurice Forge, Jan. 7, 1979; Peter MacLachlan, Feb. 25, 1979.

37. Black ISS workers fell into three groups: Southerners, Northerners, and West Indians. Almost all had had previous railroad experience, many as Pullman car porters. McGinley, pp. 253–54; *TWB*, Oct. 1934, p. 7.

38. In addition, in one BMT shop there were a number of female armature winders, but following transit unification in 1940 they were eliminated through attrition. Schmidt, p. 165; interviews with Maurice Forge, Jan. 7, 1979; Peter MacLachlan, Feb. 25, 1979; McGinley, p. 241; *NYT*, Jan. 1, 1938, p. 30; Apr. 13, 1943, p. 22.

39. *TWB*, Aug. 1936, p. 3; interviews with John Gallagher, Apr. 20, 1979; Martin Young, Nov. 15, 1978; *1930 Census*, IV, p. 1131; Huberman, pp. 26–33; Board of Transportation of the City of New York, *Report including Analysis of the Operations of the New York City Transit System for Five Years Ended June 30, 1945* (New York, 1945), 117–18.

40. Interviews with John Gallagher, Apr. 20, 1979; Peter MacLachlan, Feb. 25, 1979; Carl Mann, Apr. 5, 1984; Gerald O'Reilly, May 15, 1978; Adrian Cabral, Apr. 12, 1979.

41. See, for example, *TWU 1937 Convention*, Oct. 7 afternoon session, pp. 10–11; *TWU 1939 Convention*, 224; *TWU 1941 Convention*, 91; *Report of the Proceedings of the 4th Biennial Convention of the Transport Workers Union of America, October 20–23, 1943* (hereafter *TWU 1943 Convention*), 91; *TWB*, Apr. 1, 1936, p. 1; Oct. 1937, p. 11; Nov. 1945, p. 1; interviews with Peter MacLachlan, Feb. 25, 1979; John Plover, Feb. 20, 1979.

42. Interview with John Plover, Feb. 20, 1979.

43. Interviews with Maurice Forge, Feb. 25, 1979; Joseph Labash, Aug. 3, 1979.

44. *The I.R.T. News,* Aug. 26, 1927; Sept. 22, 1927; Nov. 4, 1927, Mar. 3, 1928; Apr. 29, 1929; May 31, 1929; June 3, 1930; Nov. 26, 1930; Apr. 9, 1931; *B.M.T. Monthly,* Feb.–Mar. 1933; Sept. 1933; Oct.–Nov. 1933; Dec. 1933; Apr. 1934.

45. Richard B. Morris, ed., *Encyclopedia of American History* (New York, 1965), 772; U.S. Department of Commerce, *Historical Statistics of the United States, Part I* (Washington, D.C., 1975), 105.

46. Conrad Arensberg, *The Irish Countryman* (1937; reprint ed., Garden City, N.Y., 1968), 76–86, 97–98; Robert Kennedy, Jr., *The Irish: Emigration, Marriage, and Fertility* (Berkeley, 1973), 93, 102, 106, 163; Paul O'Dwyer Memoir, OHCCU; interview with Gerald O'Reilly, July 11, 1979.

47. In addition, there were 15,419 Irish immigrants living in adjoining Westchester County. Eighty-seven percent of the Irish immigrants living in New York City came from the 26 counties that made up the Irish Free State. *1930 Census,* III, pt. 2, pp. 298–99, 302; U. S. Works Progress Administration, *New York Panorama: The American Guide Series* (New York, 1938), 86–87, 101.

48. Kennedy, p. 76; Ronald H. Bayor, *Neighbors in Conflict: The Irish, Germans, Jews and Italians of New York City, 1929–1941* (Baltimore, 1978), 22–25; interviews with Gerald O'Reilly, May 15, 1978, and July 11, 1979; John Gallagher, Apr. 20, 1979; John Nolan, June 1, 1978; and Patrick Reilly, Sept. 7, 1978.

49. Kennedy, pp. 96, 102; interviews with Gerald O'Reilly, May 15, 1978, and July 11, 1979; James Sullivan, July 27, 1979; Maurice Forge, Jan. 7, 1979; Lewis Fraad, June 30, 1980; *New York Post,* July 2, 1937, p. 4; L. H. Whittemore, *The Man Who Ran the Subways: The Story of Mike Quill* (New York, 1968), 86.

50. Interviews with Gerald O'Reilly, July 11, 1979; Maurice Forge, Jan. 7, 1979 (includes quote); Paul O'Dwyer Memoir, OHCCU; Kennedy, pp. 139–45; *The I.R.T. News,* Nov. 26, 1930, p. 10; Dec. 24, 1930, p. 10.

51. Joseph C. Goulding, *Meany* (New York, 1972), 7–17, 20.

52. *Irish World,* Oct. 5, 1929; Oct. 19, 1929; Dec. 17, 1929; Jan. 4, 1930; Aug. 17, 1933; Bayor, pp. 95, 123, 127; Nathan Glazer and Daniel Patrick Moynihan, *Beyond the Melting Pot: The Negroes, Puerto Ricans, Jews, Italians, and Irish of New York City,* 2nd ed. (Cambridge, Mass., 1970), 239–40; *TWB,* Nov. 1934, p. 3; interview with Gerald O'Reilly, May 15, 1978.

53. Interviews with Gerald O'Reilly, Jan 11, 1979; Maurice Forge, Jan. 1979 (includes quote); Adrian E. Cabral, Apr. 12, 1979; *The I.R.T. News,* Nov. 29, 1929, p. 3; June 30, 1930 p. 4; Nov. 26, 1930, p. 4.

54. *The I.R.T. News,* Aug. 26, 1927, p. 7; *Irish World,* June 2, 1934, June 9, 1934.

55. Of course not all Irish transit workers were Catholic, but most were. Andrew M. Greeley, *That Most Distressful Nation: The Taming of the American Irish* (Chicago, 1972), 84–85; Bayor, p. 92; Simon W. Gerson, *Pete: The Story of Peter V. Cacchione, New York's First Communist Councilman* (New York, 1976), 178–78; interviews with Gerald O'Reilly, May 15, 1978; Maurice Forge, Jan. 7, 1979.

56. Greeley, pp. 84–85; interviews with Maurice Forge, Jan. 13, 1979; Gerald O'Reilly, May 15, 1978; Philip J. Carey, Oct. 13, 1977; Dobson, "The Xavier Labor School, 1938–1939," pp. 269, 270–72, 274; Philip E. Dobson to Philip J. Carey, Sept. 9, 1941, "41–42" file, XA.

57. Bayor, pp. 25, 40, 127, 130; *Irish World,* Oct. 19, 1929; Oct. 26, 1929; interview with Gerald O'Reilly, May 15, 1978; Paul O'Dwyer Memoir, OHCCU.

58. Lawrence J. McCaffrey, *The Irish Diaspora in America* (Bloomington, 1976), 109.

59. On Irish-American nationalism and trans-Atlantic political flow, see, in addition to McCaffrey: Charles Callan Tansill, *America and the Fight for Irish Freedom, 1866–1922*

(New York, 1957); Glazer and Moynihan; Eric Foner, "Class, Ethnicity, and Radicalism in the Gilded Age: The Land League and Irish-America," *Marxist Perspectives* 1, no. 2 (Summer 1978), pp. 6–55; Sean Cronin, *The McGarrity Papers* (Tralee, County Kerry, Ireland, 1972); Carl Reeve and Ann Barton Reeve, *James Connolly and the United States* (Atlantic Highlands, N.J., 1978); and Karl Marx and Frederick Engels, *Ireland and the Irish Question* (Moscow, 1971), esp. pp. 120–26. Also valuable was my interview with Gerald O'Reilly on July 11, 1979.

60. *Irish World*, Oct. 5, 1929; Oct. 19, 1929; Nov. 2, 1929; Jan. 4, 1930; Nov. 11, 1933.

61. Eric Foner, "Land League," pp. 9–10; Tansill, pp. 38, 53–56, 76–79, 157, 175–78, 191–93; Glazer and Moynihan, p. 243; McCaffrey, p. 126; J. Bowyer Bell, *The Secret Army: A History of the IRA* (Cambridge, Mass., 1970), 5, 26, 56–57, 74 (quote on p. 57); Cronin, pp. 93–101, 115, 137.

62. Bell, pp. 50, 57; Cronin, pp. 138–39; telephone interview with Sean Cronin, Apr. 9, 1979; interview with Gerald O'Reilly, Jan. 11, 1979.

63. Bell, pp. 57, 78; Cronin, p. 161; interviews with Gerald O'Reilly, May 15, 1978; Jan. 11, 1979; Sean Cronin, Apr. 9, 1979.

64. Interviews with Gerald O'Reilly, May 15, 1979; John Nolan, June 1, 1978.

65. Conrad Arensberg and Solon Kimball, *Family and Community in Ireland* (Cambridge, Mass., 1940), 151; interviews with Maurice Forge, Jan. 7, 1979; Philip Bray, June 13, 1979; Lewis Fraad, June 30, 1980; and Gerald O'Reilly, May 15, 1978.

66. Robert D. Cross, "The Irish," in John Higham, ed., *Ethnic Leadership in America* (Baltimore, 1978), 183; Glazer and Moynihan, p. 224.

67. *Forbes*, vol. 132, no. 9 (Fall 1983), pp. 48, 62–63; interview with Jerry O'Brien, Sept. 12, 1979; *TWU 1937 Convention*, Oct. 7, afternoon session, pp. 57–58; David Doyle, "The Irish and American Labour, 1880–1920" *Saothar*, 1 (May 1975), pp. 50–52.

Chapter 3

1. State of New York, Department of Public Service, Metropolitan Division, Transit Commission, *13th Annual Report for Calender Year 1933* (Albany, 1934), 188–89, 219; Third Avenue Railway, *Annual Report*, 1932–36; Brooklyn-Manhattan Transit Corporation, *Tenth Annual Report of Brooklyn-Manhattan Transit Corporation for the Year Ended June 30, 1933* (New York, 1933), 4–5, 10 (hereafter *BMT Annual Report*, 1933).

2. *BMT Annual Report*, 1933, p. 5; *The I.R.T. News*, Dec. 23, 1931, pp. 1–2; Fifth Avenue Coach Company, *Annual Report for Year Ended December 31, 1937* (New York, 1938), 4; *NYT*, Dec. 10, 1934, p. 1; *DW*, June 22, 1934, p. 3; June 7, 1935, p. 4; June 18, 1935, 4; James J. McGinley, *Labor Relations in the New York Rapid Transit Systems, 1904–1944* (New York, 1949), 171, 175; *TWB*, Aug. 1934, p. 5; interview with Patrick Walsh, June 1, 1978. The IRT cut exempted those making less than $22 a week.

3. McGinley, pp. 436–37, 450; *TWB*, Aug. 1934, p. 6; July 1, 1936, p. 8; Nov. 1936, p. 6; Third Avenue Railway, *Annual Report*, 1932; *BMT Annual Report*, 1933, p. 5.

4. *TWB*, Aug. 1934, p. 6; Nov. 1934, pp. 1–5; Nov. 1936, p. 6; *DW*, July 6, 1934, p. 4; Leo Huberman, *The Great Bus Strike* (New York, 1941), pp. 20–21; McGinley, p. 449; interviews with John Plover, Feb. 20, 1979; Patrick Walsh, June 1, 1978. The ISS was just starting up during this period and, unlike the other lines, its work force grew steadily.

5. Yearly pay receipts, 1929–36, in possession of Gerald O'Reilly; McGinley, pp. 526–27.

6. See, for example, *TWB*, Apr. 1934, p. 4; Aug. 1934, p. 6 (includes quote); *DW*, June 22, 1934, p. 3; June 7, 1935, p. 4.

7. Interviews with Maurice Forge, Jan. 7, 1979; Gerald O'Reilly, July 11, 1979; Joseph Labash, Aug. 3, 1979.

8. Maurice Forge provided an overview of these groups (interview on Jan. 7, 1979), while others provided additional information about particular groups. See citations below.

9. Interview with Maurice Forge, Jan. 7, 1979 (includes quotes); DW, trade union supplement, July 17, 1934, p. 2.

10. NYT, Sept, 21, 1933, pp. 1, 6; Oct. 2, 1933, p. 4; Jan. 16, 1934, p. 5; Feb. 6, 1934, p. 1; Dec. 21, 1935, pp. 1, 8; Dec. 22, 1935, p. 29; New York Herald Tribune, Nov. 10, 1934; Dec. 21, 1936; The Motorman, Conductor and Motor Coach Operator, Feb. 1937, p. 23; interviews with John Gallagher, Apr. 20, 1979; Peter MacLachlan, Feb. 25, 1979.

11. Interview with Maurice Forge, Jan. 7, 1979.

12. Interview with Maurice Forge, Jan. 7, 1979.

13. See note 10.

14. This is not to argue that only the Communist Party could have organized the transit industry but that it probably would have taken the intervention of some outside agency for successful unionization to have occurred.

15. However, as early as 1933 there was considerable debate within the Communist Party over Comintern policy, and many positions and practices that prefigured the Popular Front were already beginning to emerge. On CP policy during this period, see: David J. Saposs, Communism in American Unions (New York, 1959), 11, 15; Nathan Glazer, The Social Basis of American Communism (New York, 1961), 102; John Williamson, Dangerous Scot: The Life and Work of an American "Undesirable" (New York, 1969), 74; Bert Cochran, Labor and Communism: The Conflict that Shaped American Unions (Princeton, 1977), 71–75; Max Gordon, "The Communist Party of the Nineteen-Thirties and the New Left," Socialist Revolution 27 (Jan.–Mar. 1976), pp. 23–25; interview with Nat Cohen, Dec. 7, 1978, and Chapter 4.

16. Cochran, p. 21; Benjamin Gitlow to Jay [Lovestone], Sept. 29, 1926, box 6, Benjamin Gitlow Papers, Hoover Institute, Stanford University; Memorandum for Mr. L. M. C. Smith, Chief, Special Defense Unit, Apr. 20, 1942 (file #100-7319-36), p. 15, FBI-FOIA; interviews with Maurice Forge, Jan. 7 and Feb. 25, 1979. Of 1,730 new members recruited by the CP in its New York district between Dec. 1, 1931, and Mar. 18, 1932, twenty-seven were in "transport." Most likely at least a few of these recruits were employed by the major New York transit companies. Party Builder (District 2), 1, no. 4 (April 1932).

17. DW, Mar. 15, 1933, p. 3; Apr. 10, 1933, p. 2.

18. "Facts and Material on Organizational Status, Problems, and Organizational Tasks of the Party," Party Organizer, 7, no. 5–6 (May-June 1934), p. 6; "Why the Open Letter?" Party Organizer, 6, no. 8–9 (Aug.-Sept. 1933), pp. 1–2 (includes quoted passages).

19. Glazer, pp. 46–60, 100. As late as December 1933, of the over 4,000 dues-paying Party members in the New York District, only about half were employed, and of those only 350 belonged to Communist shop nuclei. Party Organizer, 6, no. 12 (Dec. 1933), pp. 5–6.

20. "Why the Open Letter?," pp. 1–4.

21. Charles Krumbein, "How and Where to Concentrate," Party Organizer, 6, no. 8–9 (Aug.–Sept. 1933), pp. 24–25. With the exception of railroad, the Party was remarkably successful in carrying out Krumbein's program.

22. Louis Sass, "Harlem Concentration on Transport," Party Organizer, 7, no. 3 (Mar. 1933), pp. 23–24.

23. Interview with Abner Berry, Dec. 5, 1978. Berry worked with Walsh for a full year before he realized that he was not Irish. The spelling of Wasdiller may be incorrect.

24. Interviews with Abner Berry, Dec. 5, 1978; Maurice Forge, Jan. 7 and Feb. 25, 1979.

25. Alex Schaffer, "Transport Concentration on the New York District," unlabeled clipping [late Feb. 1934], JBF.

26. Report of Convention Section 15, District 2 CPUSA/Middle Bronx./," in Earl Browder Papers, Syracuse University, microfilm edition, series 2–44, reel 3; DW, Apr. 16, 1934, p. 4; interview with Abner Berry, Dec. 5, 1978; U.S. House of Representatives, *Hearings Before Special Committee to Investigate Un-American Activities*, 75th Congress, 2nd Session, vol. 2 (Washington, D.C., 1938), p. 1074 (hereafter *Dies Committee*, vol. 2).

27. *TWU 1941 Convention*, 194; interviews with Maurice Forge, Feb. 25 and Aug. 9, 1979; Herbert C. Holmstrom to Thomas E. Murray, Jr., copy in case file "Interborough Rapid Transit #1100," Regional Records, Region II, N.Y., National Labor Board, 1933–34 and National Labor Relations Board, 1934–35, RG 25, National Archives, Washington National Records Center, Suitland, Maryland. Holmstrom was apparently not a member of the CP. David Holmstrom kindly provided me with information about his Uncle Herbert.

28. *TWU 1941 Convention*, 194–95, 201; *TWU 1939 Convention*, 77–78; interviews with Maurice Forge, Jan. 7 and Feb. 25, 1979; Peter MacLachlan, Feb. 25, 1979; DW, Mar. 15, 1933, p. 3; *Dies Committee*, vol. 2, pp. 1045, 1066–68; U.S. House of Representatives, *Hearings Before a Special Committee on Un-American Activities*, 76th Congress, 3rd Session, vol. 13 (Washington, D.C., 1940), pp. 7914–15 (hereafter *Dies Committee*, vol. 13).

29. "Small Progress in N.Y. District," *Party Organizer*, 6, no. 11 (Nov. 1933), p. 18.

30. Among those attending were Sponza, Holmstrom, and fellow IRT painter F. Svec; Zuidema; and at least three other BMT workers, possibly members of Zuidema's group. "How TWU Really Came to Be," *R&FTN*, Mar. 1950, p. 3; interviews with Maurice Forge, Jan. 7 and Feb. 25, 1979; Gerald O'Reilly, Jan. 11, 1979.

31. *TWB*, Dec. 1933, pp. 1–2.

32. Interview with Maurice Forge, Jan. 7. 1979

33. Both Forge (Jan. 7, 1979) and O'Reilly (Jan. 15, 1978) believe that the TWU name was chosen for this reason. However, it should be pointed out that Communists had used the term "transport" well before the TWU was founded. See, for example, Krumbein, pp. 24–25, or *Party Builder* (District 2), 1, no. 4 (Apr. 1932).

34. Interviews with Gerald O'Reilly, May 15, 1978 and July 11, 1979; DW, Mar. 5, 1935, p. 4.

35. The first of these factors, of course, also applied to former IRA men working in transit who were not members of the Clan na Gael, of whom there were quite a few. Interview with John Nolan, June 1, 1978 (includes quote); telephone interview with Sean Cronin, Apr. 9, 1979.

36. Interviews with Gerald O'Reilly, May 15, 1978 and Jan. 11, 1979.

37. *Dies Committee*, vol. 13, pp. 7879, 7892, 8094, 8099; McGinley, p. 315; A.H. Raskin, "Presenting the Phenomenon called Quill," *The New York Times Magazine*, Mar. 3, 1950, pp. 11+; interviews with Gerald O'Reilly, May 15, 1978 and July 11, 1979; *TWB*, Sept. 1937, p. 7; *R&TFN*, Apr. 1950, p. 3; *TWU 1937 Convention*, Oct. 5 morning session, p. 1A; *TWU 1943 Convention*, 114–15.

38. Interview with Gerald O'Reilly, May 15, 1978.

39. *Dies Committee*, vol. 13, p. 8098.

40. Interviews with Gerald O'Reilly, May 15, 1978 and July 11, 1979.

41. *Champion*, Dec. 1937, pp. 6–7, reprinted in U.S. House of Representatives, *Hearings before a Special Committee on Un-American Activities*, 77th Congress, 1st Session, appendix V (Washington, D.C., 1941), 1650–51 (hereafter *Dies Committee*, appendix V).

42. J. Bowyer Bell, *The Secret Army: A History of the IRA* (Cambridge, Mass., 1970), 52, 73, 77–88, 101, 104, 106–7, 111, 117; Communist Party of Ireland, *Outline History* (Dublin, 197?), 11–12, 22–24; interview with Sean Cronin, Apr. 9, 1979.

43. Interviews with Gerald O'Reilly, Jan. 11, 1979; Sean Cronin, Apr. 9, 1979; Bell, p. 81.

44. Interviews with Gerald O'Reilly, Jan. 11, 1979; James Sullivan, July 27, 1979. Sullivan is a pseudonym for someone who was active in the TWU and very personally close to Quill, who requested anonymity.

45. Interview with Gerald O'Reilly, July 11, 1979.

46. The following account is based primarily on an interview on May 15, 1978, with Gerald O'Reilly, the only surviving member of the original Clan group who could be located. O'Reilly said that the group was fully aware of the difficulties that a union drive would entail, having heard and read about the 1926 IRT strike.

47. O'Reilly believes, but is not sure, that some members of the group also approached the AFL Amalgamated Association, which, without outright rejecting the idea, implied that organizing IRT workers was a hopeless endeavor (interview on July 11, 1979). On Keegan, see *Yearbook of the Society of the Friendly Sons of Saint Patrick in the City of New York, 1975* (New York, 1975), 113–15.

48. Unpublished memoir by Gerald O'Reilly, JBF. Foster himself had briefly worked in 1901 as a trolley motorman for the Third Avenue Railway. He was dismissed when he tried to organize his co-workers into the Amalgamated Association. See William Z. Foster, *Pages from a Worker's Life* (New York, 1939), 27–28.

49. Raskin, "Quill," p. 67. Quill's story is plausible, but impossible to confirm or refute. Quite possibly the initial CP-Clan contact took place along several parallel paths.

50. To avoid alienating potential supporters, IWC leaders stressed the writings of Connolly and other Irish leftists, and avoided discussing Marx and other non-Irish Communists, a stand that upset some of the younger, Irish-American club members. Glazer, pp. 87–89; IWC leaflet, Jan. 19, 1936, JBF; *Dies Committee*, vol. 13, pp. 7893–94; DW, Nov. 8, 1933, p. 4; May 14, 1934, 4; May 19, 1934, 4; interviews with Gerald O'Reilly, May 15, 1978, and July 11, 1979; Sean Murray, *Ireland's Fight for Freedom and the Irish in the U.S.A.* (New York, 1934), 14–16 (quoted passage on p. 15).

51. Communist Party of Ireland, *Outline History*, 8–20; DW, May 19, 1934, p. 4.

52. DW, Apr. 6, 1934, p. 1; May 14, 1934, p. 4; May 19, 1934, p. 4 (includes quote from Murray); May 29, 1934, pp. 1, 6; June 1, 1934, p. 6.

53. Dw, Jan. 5, 1934, p. 5; Communist Party of Ireland, *Outline History*, 48–50; interview with Gerald O'Reilly, July 11, 1979.

54. Murray, p. 15.

55. Bell, p. 246. According to Bell, the IRA ban was issued more to avoid red-baiting than as a matter of principle.

56. This and the following paragraph are based on O'Shea's April 1940 Congressional testimony, in *Dies Committee*, vol. 13, pp. 7893–94, 7901, 7911.

57. Huberman, pp. 10–12; Gustav Faber, *And Then Came TWU!* (New York, 1950), 22; TWB, Apr. 1934, pp. 1, 3; *Dies Committee*, vol. 13, p. 7906; TE, May 1959, p. 3; May 1964, p. 6. Patrick N. Lynch, in "Transport Workers Union—Dublin, New York and Chicago—An Analysis of Organization and Collective Bargaining" (unpublished paper, 1968, in possession of John Nolan), lists Maurice Forge and Michael Clune as the others present at the meeting. In an interview on Feb. 25, 1979, however, Forge denied being present and questioned the existence of such a meeting.

58. Interview with Maurice Forge, Jan. 7, 1979. The published lists (see n. 57) of who attended this meeting varied over the years with the political needs of the moment. Leo Huberman's account, written in 1941, after O'Shea had become a dissident and government informer, left O'Shea out. Gustav Faber's account, written in 1950, when all of those at the meeting except Quill had been forced out of the TWU leadership, cites no specific attendees

and falsely implies that Faber had been active in the TWU in 1934. The 25th and 30th anniversary editions of the TWU newspaper listed no names, but implied that all present had been transit workers. Another mythology of the union's early history was constructed in 1947, when the government was trying to deport Santo. His defense committee issued a pamphlet, *John Santo, American* (New York, n.d.), which said that Santo had become involved in the TWU when he met a group of IRT ticket agents, including Quill, who convinced him to help them form a union. No mention of the CP appears.

59. *Dies Committee*, vol. 13, pp. 7905–06; interview with Maurice Forge, Jan. 7, 1979.

60. Faber, p. 22; *TWB*, Apr. 1934, pp. 1, 3.

61. *TWB*, Apr. 1934, pp. 1, 3.

62. *TWB*, May 1934, p. 2.

63. Santo was quite secularized; probably most TWU members did not realize that he was Jewish. *John Santo, American*; interview with Maurice Forge, Nov. 29, 1983. See also Report of Chicago Office, Nov. 28, 1942 (file #100-7319-115), pp. 5, 7–9, FBI-FOIA for a slightly different version of Santo's background.

64. U.S. House of Representatives, *A Communist in a "Workers' Paradise": John Santo's Own Story* (Consultation with John Santo, March 1, 4, 5, 1963), published in booklet form with Preface by Francis E. Walter (Washington, D.C., 1963), 5, 63; *Dies Committee*, vol. 2, p. 1073; "Report of Convention Section 15," Earl Browder Papers, microfilm edition, series 2–44, reel 3. Bebrits was part of a rather remarkable group of Hungarian-born Communists who became active in the CPUSA in the 1920s. Included were Louis Sass, Louis Weinstock, James Lustig, Abe Markoff, John Lautner, John Cyetvai, and Santo. They were to go on to assume important posts in several American unions, the CPUSA, and, in the cases of Santo, Cyetvai, and Bebrits, the postwar Hungarian government. See Glazer, pp. 77–79; *A Communist in a "Workers' Paradise"*, 14, 62–63.

65. For example, see "District Two—Control Tasks Adopted at Enlarged District Committee Meeting, March 8, 1936," reprinted in *Dies Committee*, appendix V, pp. 1640–47.

66. Interview with Maurice Forge, Dec. 30, 1978; *A Communist in a "Workers' Paradise"*, 58.

67. Interviews with Maurice Forge, Jan. 7 and Jan. 27, 1979; Victor Bloswick, Jan. 23, 1979; John Gallagher, Apr. 20, 1979; *Dies Committee*, vol. 2, p. 1070; vol 13, pp. 7898–7901, 7905, 7909–10.

68. See, for example, *TWU 1941 Convention*, 196, 201–03.

69. *Dies Committee*, vol. 13, pp. 7919–20; appendix V, pp. 1623, 1636–37; DW, May 1, 1934, trade union supplement, p. 2; June 11, 1934, trade union supplement, p. 3.

70. Not until November 1934 did the TUUL organ, *Labor Unity*, even mention the existence of the TWU. DW, Feb. 3, 1934, p. 1; Feb. 9, 1934, p. 4; Feb. 10, 1934, p. 2; Mar. 10, 1934, p. 1; and Mar. 19–30, 1934, passim; *Labor Unity*, Dec. 1933, pp. 2, 8; Mar. 1934, pp. 3–5; June 1934, pp. 3–4.

71. DW, May 1, 1934, trade union supplement, p. 2.

72. Interview with Gerald O'Reilly, May 15, 1978; *Dies Committee*, vol. 2, pp. 1044–48.

73. The following biographical sketch of Austin Hogan is based on interviews with Gerald O'Reilly, July 11, 1979; and Sean Cronin, Apr. 9, 1979; Shirley Quill, *Mike Quill—Himself, A Memoir* (Greenwich, Conn., 1985), 60–61; *Dies Committee*, vol. 13, p. 7901; and *New York Post*, July 7, 1937, p. 11. Both Cronin and Quill interviewed Hogan shortly before his death.

74. On the RIC, see Paul O'Dwyer Memoir, OHCCU; Conrad Arensberg and Solon Kimball, *Family and Community in Ireland* (Cambridge, Mass., 1940), 274 (includes "cut above"); Bell, pp. 9, 13–14.

75. Interview with John Gallagher, Apr. 20, 1979.

76. *TWU 1937 Convention*, typed transcript of the proceedings, pp. 702–4 (quote on p. 702); interview with Sean Cronin, Apr. 9, 1979.

77. *DW*, Nov. 8, 1933, p. 4; June 1, 1934, p. 6.

78. Hogan ran in the 24th Congressional District and received 6,450 of the 118,980 votes cast. *Annual Report of the Board of Elections in the City of New York, 1934*, 118.

79. Interviews with Sean Cronin, Apr. 9, 1979; Gerald O'Reilly, July 11, 1979.

80. Interviews with James Sullivan, Aug. 16, 1979; Maurice Forge, Jan. 27 and Aug. 9, 1979; Patrick Reilly, Sept. 7, 1978.

81. Forge's younger brother was also involved with the Food Workers and later became a leading official of the AFL Hotel and Restaurant Workers Union. Interviews with Maurice Forge, Jan. 7. 1979 and Nov. 27, 1983; *TWU 1937 Convention*, typed transcript, pp. 658–60.

82. Forge, for example, arranged for his friend Leon "Bubbles" Lee to help out in the TWU office and for Walter Case, a Texas-born Party member, to work as an organizer. Case served in that capacity, and later as a member of the TWU International Executive Board, until 1948. Interviews with Patrick Walsh, June 1, 1978; Maurice Forge, Dec. 30, 1978, Jan. 7, 1979 (includes quote), and July 29, 1979; *Dies Committee*, vol. 2, p. 1044; Committee Established by the Executive Board of the Transport Workers Union of America to Inquire into and Investigate Certain Matters and Developments in the Union, *Hearings*, Nov. 11, 1948, p. 8; *DW*, July 30, 1934, p. 2; Aug. 13, 1934, p. 3; Aug. 20, 1934, p. 3; *TWB*, Aug. 1934, pp. 2, 8.

83. For a discussion of the role of such types in building the UAW, see Peter Friedlander, *The Emergence of a UAW Local, 1936–1939: A Study in Class and Culture* (Pittsburgh, 1975), 122. The ISS was the one part of the the NYC transit system where workers with such backgrounds were not unusual, but in 1934 the TWU had not yet made inroads there.

84. *TWB*, July 1938, p. 14; *New York Post*, Jan. 9, 1966, p. 24; *TWU 1943 Convention*, 189–90; L. H. Whittemore, *The Man Who Ran the Subways: The Story of Mike Quill* (New York, 1968), 42–43; interviews with Maurice Forge, Jan. 7, 1979; Gerald O'Reilly, July 11, 1979.

85. Interviews with Maurice Forge, Jan. 7. 1979 (includes all quotes); Martin Young, Nov. 15, 1978. Carl Mann (interview on Apr. 5, 1984) disclosed MacMahon's Socialist ties, which few TWU members knew about.

86. On their post-TWU careers, see Chapter 14.

87. Interview with Maurice Forge, Feb. 25, 1979.

88. *Dies Committee*, vol. 13, pp. 7879, 7892, 7911; U. S. Department of Justice, Immigration and Naturalization Service, "In the Matter of Charges against DESIDERIU HAMMER, alias JOHN SANTO" (typescript of 1947 hearings), 627–28.

89. Interviews with Gerald O'Reilly, Jan. 11, 1979; John Nolan, June 1, 1978 ("great talker"); *Dies Committee*, vol. 2, p. 1074; vol. 13, pp. 7893–7911.

90. *TE*, Feb. 1966, p. 2; Shirley Quill, pp. 7–8; Huberman, p. 156; *Dies Committee*, vol. 13, p. 8094; interviews with James Sullivan, July 27 and Aug. 16, 1979; Jerry O'Brien, Sept, 12, 1979. There are several variant spellings of Gourtloughera.

91. Interviews with James Sullivan, July 27 and Aug. 16, 1979; Jerry O'Brien, Sept. 12, 1979; draft of letter by John D. Quill in application for Irish pension, in possession of Jerry O'Brien; Huberman, p. 156.

92. Interview with Jerry O'Brien, Sept. 12, 1979; *Dies Committee*, vol. 13, p. 8099; Shirley Quill, pp. 16–32.

93. Interview with James Sullivan, July 17, 1979; John D. Quill pension letter; *TE*, May 1964, p. 59; McGinley, p. 315.

94. Raskin, "Quill," p. 67; Address by Michael J. Quill over radio Station WHAT [Philadelphia], Dec. 7 [1943]," p. 4, JBF; Shirley Quill, pp. 39–46; Michael J. Quill's passport, in possession of Jerry O'Brien.

95. Interviews with Gerald O'Reilly, Jan. 11, 1979; Maurice Forge, Jan. 7, 1979; James Sullivan, July 27, 1979; Jerry O'Brien, Sept. 12, 1979; Patrick Reilly, Sept. 7, 1978.

96. Interviews with Gerald O'Reilly, May 15, 1978; James Sullivan, July 27, 1979; Maurice Forge, Jan. 7, 1979. The question of Quill's CP membership was endlessly debated throughout his career. Several ex-Communist transit workers told the Dies Committee that in 1934 and 1935 they attended regular CP meetings with Quill and collected Party dues from him. In addition, Father Charles Owen Rice reported many years later that Quill had privately told him that he had once formally joined the CP. Quill, however, repeatedly denied, even under oath, that he had ever been a member of the Party. In an October 1948 interview he said "I was kind of careful where my signature went in certain matters." Furthermore, Earl Browder said that he doubted that Quill had been a Party member. Although there is no way to establish definitively if Quill ever actually enrolled in the CP, the sum of evidence seems to indicate that in the first years of the TWU Quill's relationship with the CP was the same as that of other TWU Communists, but after 1935 a certain distance was carefully maintained between Quill and the normal Party apparatus. See *Dies Committee*, vol 2, pp. 1044, 1069, 1071; vol. 13, pp. 7913–16, 8101–02; Transport Workers Union of Greater New York, "We Must, and Will Re-Elect Quill to the City Council" [1939], JBF; Levering interview with Mike Quill, Oct. 31, 1948, p. 3, and Daniel Bell interview of Earl Browder, June 26 or 27, 1955, pp. 44–45, boxes 7 and 9 respectively, Daniel Bell Collection, Tamiment Library, New York University, New York; Charles Owen Rice to the author, Sept. 15, 1979.

97. Len De Caux, *Labor Radical: From the Wobblies to CIO, A Personal History* (Boston, 1970), 425.

Chapter 4

1. The TWU's brief organizational predecessor, the Committee for the Organization of a Transport Workers' Union, apparently aimed only at organizing IRT and BMT workers. See Notes on Nov. 22, 1933 meeting of Committee for the Organization of a Transport Workers' Union, JBF; Minutes of TWU Delegates Council, May 28, 1934, SQ-T.

2. Interviews with Victor Bloswick, Jan. 23, 1979; John Plover, Feb. 20, 1979; *TWB*, Feb. 1936, p. 8; *The I.R.T. News*, Sept. 22, 1927, p. 3; *Interborough Bulletin*, Aug. 1938, p. 4.

3. Interviews with Victor Bloswick, Jan. 23, 1979; John Plover, Feb. 20, 1979; Maurice Forge, Jan. 7, 1979. Plover, himself Irish-born, estimated that the Irish and Irish-Americans together made up about a quarter of the shop work force.

4. Interviews with Victor Bloswick, Jan. 23, 1979 (includes "mish-mash"); John Plover, Feb. 20, 1979; *TWB*, Sept. 1934, p. 4.

5. For another example, see list of IRT Lighting, Paint, and Ventilation Department pay rates, JBF.

6. Interviews with Victor Bloswick, Jan. 23, 1979; John Plover, Feb. 20, 1979 (includes first papers story); *The I.R.T. News*, Dec. 23, 1931, pp. 1–2.

7. *TWB*, Apr. 1934, p. 4; *DW*, Apr. 2, 1934, p. 2; May 1, 1934, trade union section, p. 1. According to one account, the shorter work week also had been promised by the IRT at the time of the 10% pay cut, but was never implemented. See *TE*, Apr. 1954, p. 2A.

8. Louis Sass, "Harlem Concentration on Transport," *Party Organizer*, 7, no. 3 (Mar. 1933), pp. 23–24; interview with Maurice Forge, Jan. 7, 1979.

9. Interviews with Victor Bloswick, Jan. 23, 1979; Maurice Forge, Jan. 7 and Aug. 9, 1979; John Plover, Feb. 20, 1979; Jerry O'Brien, Sept. 12, 1979; *TWB*, Nov. 1, 1935, p. 5; Feb. 1936, p. 8; Apr. 1937, p. 8; Oct. 1937, p. 11; March 1945, p. 14; *TV*, June 30, 1948, p. 3.

10. Interview with Maurice Forge, Aug. 9, 1979.

11. Interviews with Victor Bloswick, Jan. 23, 1979; John Plover, Feb. 20, 1979.

12. Interview with Victor Bloswick, Jan. 23, 1979.

13. Interviews with John Plover, Feb. 20, 1979; Victor Bloswick, Jan. 23, 1979.

14. *TWB*, July 1934, p. 4; Aug. 1934, p. 2; *DW*, Oct. 19, 1934, p. 4; interview with Victor Bloswick, Jan. 23, 1979.

15. Interviews with Victor Bloswick, Jan. 23, 1979; John Plover, Feb. 20, 1979; *DW*, June 4, 1934, NY trade union section, p. 1; Minutes of TWU Delegates Council, July 18, 1934, SQ-T; *TWB*, June 1939, p. 6.

16. No precise figures are available on the size of this shop, but delegate representation at the 1937 TWU convention would indicate between 500 and 600 employees. Nor is a detailed ethnic breakdown available, but one account mentions a large number of Irish and Italian workers. See *TWU 1937 Convention*, Oct. 5 morning session, p. 13; Oct. 5 afternoon session, p. 1b; interview with Adrian E. Cabral, Apr. 12, 1979.

17. Interview with Maurice Force, Jan. 7, 1979; Minutes of TWU Delegates Council, May 28, 1934, SQ-T.

18. *DW*, July 6, 1934, p. 4; *TWB*, May-June, 1934, p. 6.

19. Interviews with Maurice Forge, Jan. 7 and Jan. 27, 1979; Gerald O'Reilly, July 11, 1979; Adrian E. Cabral, Apr. 12, 1979; "Meet Bill Grogan," campaign leaflet, JBF; *TWU 1941 Convention*, p. 22; *TWU 1943 Convention*, p. 184; *TWB*, Nov. 1936, p. 3; March–Apr. 1944, p. 4

20. Minutes of TWU Delegates Council, June 25, 1934, SQ-T.

21. The IRT and BMT operated on direct current, which the electric companies were normally incapable of supplying. In a 1909 pamphlet James Connolly used the failure of unionized powerhouse workers to support transit strikes as an argument for industrial forms of organization. (Excerpts reprinted in *TE*, Apr. 1954, p. 3A).

22. The plant, which was modernized and expanded during the 1950s, is still in use, although now operated by Consolidated Edison. For descriptions of the plant, see Interborough Rapid Transit Company, *The New York Subway: Its Construction and Equipment* (New York, 1904; reprinted in facsimile, New York: Arno Press, n.d.), 67. 116; *TWB*, Dec. 1938, p. 16.

23. Except where additional sources are cited, the following discussion of the 59th Street plant is based on an interview with Joseph Labash on Aug. 3, 1979.

24. In addition, about 35 men worked outside the plant on the coal dock, unloading barges. Operating personnel, after five years, received paid vacations; maintenance men did not, perhaps because they got Sundays off.

25. See also interview with Maurice Forge, Jan. 7, 1979.

26. A few younger, college-educated engineers were hired in the early 1930s from General Electric, which had constructed the plant's turbines.

27. In addition to Labash, see interviews with Maurice Forge, Jan. 7 and July 29, 1979.

28. The town Labash came from, Nanty Glo, was also the home of UMW and CIO leader John Brophy. All three of Labash's brothers eventually joined the TWU; his sister worked in the union headquarters.

29. *TWU 1937 Convention*, Oct. 7 afternoon session, pp. 10–11; interview with Maurice Forge, Jan. 7, 1979; *TWB*, Aug. 1945, p. 2.

30. See also *TWB*, Nov. 1936, p. 3.

31. According to some reports, Faber was a Reichstag delegate; more probable are the

reports that he was a member of the Hamburg Municipal Council. Interviews with Maurice Forge, Jan. 7, 1979; Joseph Labash, Aug. 3, 1979; Transport Workers Union, *5th Biennial Convention, Report of the Proceedings, Sept. 15–28th, 1946* (hereafter *TWU 1946 Convention*), 56; Transport Workers Union, *Report of the Proceedings, Sixth Biennial Convention, December 6–10, 1948* (hereafter *TWU 1948 Convention*), 52; *TE*, Apr. 1954, p. 12; *CIO News*, Dec. 13, 1948, p. 12; *TWU 1939 Convention*, 224; Shirley Quill, *Mike Quill— Himself, A Memoir* (Greenwich, Conn., 1985), 223.

32. On 74th Street, see interview with Joseph Labash, Aug. 3, 1979; *R&FTN*, Apr. 1950, p. 3; *TE*, Apr. 1954, p. 9A.

33. Interview with Patrick Reilly, Sept. 7, 1978.

34. And Brotherhood and company agents did try to intimidate such workers. See, for example, draft of "Report of Unusual Occurrence," by Michael C. Cupiola, JBF.

35. *TWB*, July 1934, p. 3; *DW*, Aug. 13, 1934, p. 3; Aug. 20, 1934, p. 3; interview with Maurice Forge, Jan. 7, 1979.

36. Gustav Faber, *And Then Came TWU!* (New York, 1950), 29; *TWB*, Feb. 1935, pp. 1, 3; Dec. 1935, p. 1; Nov. 1936, p. 3; Jan. 1937, pp. 5, 8; Feb. 1937, p. 2; interviews with Gerald O'Reilly, May 15, 1978; Maurice Forge, Jan. 7, 1979; "Minutes of Joint Executive Committees Meeting Held Monday, Sept. 15 [1936]," JBF.

37. Interviews with Gerald O'Reilly, May 15, 1978; Maurice Forge, Jan. 7, 1979; *TWB*, Nov. 1936, p. 3; *TE*, May 1959, p. 5. After playing a brief but important role in the TWU, Mike Lynch returned to Ireland.

38. Interviews with John Nolan, June 1, 1978; Gerald O'Reilly, July 11, 1979.

39. Interviews with Maurice Forge, Jan. 7, 1979; John Nolan, June 1, 1978; Patrick Reilly, Sept. 7, 1978. It should be reiterated that the ex-IRA men were not among the most youthful Irish IRT workers, but rather were usually in their thirties and had been working on the line for a number of years. It was *their* age group, not the very youngest Irish, who were generally the first to join the TWU.

40. Interviews with Gerald O'Reilly, May 15, 1978, and July 11, 1979.

41. *TWB*, May 1934, p. 3; Sept. 1934, p. 8; Oct. 1934, p. 2; May 1940, p. 8; *DW*, Oct. 19, 1934; Faber, pp. 24–26; NLRB, "Stenographic Report of Hearing In the Matter of the Transport Workers Union vs. Interborough Rapid Transit Company, Oct. 31, 1934," pp. 32, 36, "Interborough Rapid Transit Co. 805," Regional Records, Region II, N.Y., National Labor Board, 1933–34, and National Labor Relations Board, 1934–35, RG 25, National Archives, Washington National Records Center, Suitland, Maryland (hereafter NLB and NLRB records, 1933–35, WNRC); U.S. House of Representatives, *Hearings Before Special Committee to Investigate Un-American Activities*, 75th Congress, 2nd Session, vol. 2 (Washington, D.C., 1938), 1074 (hereafter *Dies Committee*, vol. 2), pp. 1905–6; interviews with Maurice Forge, Jan. 7, 1979; Gerald O'Reilly, May 15, 1978; John Nolan, June 1, 1978; Minutes of TWU Delegates Council, June 25 and July 18, 1934, SQ-T.

42. *TWB*, July 1934, p. 3 (includes quotes); interview with John Nolan, June 1, 1978.

43. Interview with Gerald O'Reilly, May 15, 1978; J. Bowyer Bell, *The Secret Army: A History of the IRA* (Cambridge, Mass., 1970), 53–54, 69fn.

44. Thomas A. Brooks, "Lindsay, Quill, & the Transit Strike," *Commentary*, March 1966, p. 54. Men inquiring of one another if they were in the TWU would ask "did you see the light?" (Interview with Patrick Reilly, Sept. 7, 1978.)

45. See, for example, *DW*, Mar. 26, 1934, p. 6, for a description of a similar organizational structure used by Party members working in Ford plants.

46. Interview with Maurice Forge, Jan. 7, 1979.

47. *TWU 1943 Convention*, 114–15; interviews with John Nolan, June 1, 1978; Patrick Reilly, Sept. 7, 1978.

48. *DW*, Apr. 16, 1934, p. 4; interview with Maurice Forge, Jan. 7, 1979.

49. Sass, pp. 24–26; *DW*, Feb. 1, 1935, p. 6; Mar. 9, 1935, p. 8; "REPORT OF CONVENTION SECTION 15, DISTRICT 2, CPUSA./MIDDLE BRONX./," series 2–44, reel 3, Earl Browder Papers, Syracuse University (microfilm edition); *Dies Committee*, vol. 2, p. 1055; U.S. House of Representatives, *Hearings Before a Special Committee on Un-American Activities*, 76th Congress, 3rd Session, vol. 13 (Washington, D.C., 1940), pp. 7914–15 (hereafter *Dies Committee*, vol. 13), p. 7913; interview with Maurice Forge, Jan. 13, 1979; Rose Wortis, "Organization Brings Results," *Party Organizer*, Aug. 1937, p. 40.

50. Sass, pp. 24–26; *Dies Committee*, vol. 2, pp. 1044–55; vol. 13, pp. 7913–15; U.S. House of Representatives, *Hearings before a Special Committee on Un-American Activities*, 77th Congress, 1st Session, appendix V (Washington, D.C., 1941), pp. 1650–51 (hereafter *Dies Committee*, appendix V), pp. 1634–47; U. S. Department of Justice, Immigration and Naturalization Service, "In the Matter of Charges against DESIDERIU HAMMER, alias JOHN SANTO" (hereafter *Santo Deportation Hearings*), 602; Mark D. Naison, "The Communist Party in Harlem: 1928–1936" (Ph.D. dissertation, Columbia University, 1975), 289–90; interviews with Abner Berry, Dec. 5, 1978; Gerald O'Reilly, May 15, 1978.

51. *The Communist*, Sept. 1938, p. 833; *Red Signal*, n.d., in "Mayor's Commission on Conditions in Harlem—Periodicals" folder, box 677, LaGP; *DW*, Feb. 1, 1935, p. 6; *Party Organizer*, Mar. 1936, p. 35; Apr. 1936, p. 36.

52. *DW*, Feb. 2, 1934, p. 4; Nov. 5, 1934, p. 3; Feb. 1, 1935, p. 6; *Party Organizer*, Dec. 1937, p. 13.

53. *Dies Committee*, vol. 2, pp. 1045, 1051–53; vol. 13, pp. 7913–16, 7920–23; *Santo Deportation Hearings*, pp. 537–40, 602; interview with Maurice Forge, Jan. 27, 1979; New York Report, Sept. 10, 1943 (file #100-7319-210), pp. 2–4; New York Report, Aug. 13, 1947 (#100-7319-359), p. 9, FBI-FOIA.

54. *Dies Committee*, vol. 2, p. 1040.

55. *Motorman, Conductor and Motor Coach Operator*, June 1940, p. 8.

56. Interview with Gerald O'Reilly, May 15, 1978.

57. See, for example, interviews with Phil Bray, Aug. 13, 1979; John Gallagher, Apr. 20, 1979.

58. O'Reilly and his friends, for example, were taken aback to discover that Santo and Forge disliked and distrusted one another. Until then they had seen the outside Party men as above normal jealousies and disagreements. Interviews with Gerald O'Reilly, Jan 11, 1979; Maurice Forge, Jan. 27, 1979; *TWU 1941 Convention*, 202–3.

59. Wortis, "Organization," 40; Max Steinberg, "Rooting the Party Among the Masses in New York," *The Communist*, Sept. 1939, p. 833; interview with Patrick Walsh, June 1, 1978.

60. *Santo Deportation Hearings*, 590–91; New York Reports, Feb. 17, 1941 (#100-7319-2), and Oct. 8, 1942 (#100-7319-98in), FBI-FOIA; interviews with Gerald O'Reilly, May 15, 1978; John Nolan, June 1, 1978; Maurice Forge, Aug. 9, 1979; Martin Young, Nov. 11, 1978; *Dies Committee*, vol. 13, pp. 7950–52.

61. *Dies Committee*, vol. 2, p. 1070.

62. It is difficult to say precisely how large this group was and who was in it, since some of the available evidence is of questionable veracity. However, it apparently included, among others, Quill, O'Reilly, John Nolan, Jimmy Hughes, Patrick Reilly, Michael Lynch, Michael Clune, John Cassidy, and John Allen. See *Dies Committee*, vol. 2, pp. 1068–69; vol. 13, 7913; *TWU 1941 Convention*, pp. 84–85; interview with Gerald O'Reilly, May 15, 1978.

63. Thomas E. Murray, "To All Employees of Interborough Rapid Transit Company," May 25, 1935, in "IRT Election Petition #1516" folder, NLB and NLRB records, WNRC,

("agitators"); Brotherhood of IRT Employees, "Spilling the Beans" [pamphlet], (New York, 1935); Municipal Transportation Workers Industrial Union No. 540 of the IWW, "Join The Union!," copy in SQ-T; Sass, p. 24; *DW*, Aug. 17, 1934, p. 4; Nov. 30, 1934, p. 6 (includes "antagonism" quote); Feb. 1, 1935, p. 6; Mar. 9, 1935, p. 8; Sept. 13, 1935, p. 4; *TWB*, Nov. 1934, p. 2; Mar. 1937, p. 8; interviews with Gerald O'Reilly, May 15, 1978; Patrick Reilly, Sept. 7, 1978.

64. *DW*, Apr. 16, 1934, p. 4.

65. *DW*, Nov. 11, 1934, p. 6; Sass, p. 24.

66. See, for example, DW, June 22, 1934, p. 3; *TWB*, Sept. 1934, p. 5; Nov. 1934, p. 11; Oct. 1935, p. 5; Apr. 1, 1936, p. 3.

67. *New York World-Telegram*, June 18, 1941; *New York Post*, July 2, 1937. This was also the time when Quill began distancing himself from the regular CP apparatus.

68. Interviews with Gerald O'Reilly, May 15, 1978; Peter MacLachlan, Feb. 25, 1979; Lewis Fraad, June 30, 1980; Joseph Labash, Aug. 3, 1979; John Plover, Feb. 20, 1979. The FBI, for example, ended up with a mixture of quite accurate and wildly inaccurate information. See FBI-FOIA, passim.

69. *DW*, Nov. 5, 1934, p. 3; *TWB*, Apr.–May, 1935, p. 6.

70. *New York World-Telegram*, June 10, 1941; New York Report, Dec. 12, 1945 (#100-7319-319), pp. 3, 8, FBI-FOIA; Joe Leslie, "Shop Papers in New York District from November 1935 to February 1936," *Party Organizer*, Mar. 1936, p. 35; "Report on Shop Papers Issued from May 1935 to Jan. 1936," *Party Organizer*, Apr. 1936, p. 36; P. Cacchione, "A Foundation for Recruiting," *Party Organizer*, Dec. 1937, pp. 12–15; J., "The Daily Worker Gave Me the First Break," *Party Organizer*, Apr. 1938, pp. 43–44; William Z. Foster, *History of the Communist Party of the United States* (New York, 1952), 348–49.

71. *TWB*, May 1934, p. 6; Oct. 1937, 7; *TWU, Constitution* (New York, 1937), 1.

72. *Labor Unity*, Nov. 1934, p. 13.

73. Irving Howe and Lewis Coser, *The American Communist Party: A Critical History* (New York, 1962), 230, 233–34, 329–30 (quote on p. 230); interview with Maurice Forge, Jan. 27, 1979.

74. Interview with Maurice Forge, Jan. 27, 1979.

75. *DW*, Feb. 1, 1935, p. 6; Mar. 9, 1935, p. 8.

76. *DW*, Feb. 1, 1935, p. 6; Sass, p. 25 (includes second quote); interviews with Patrick Reilly, Sept. 7, 1978; Maurice Forge, Jan. 13, 1979 (includes first quote). The CP's approach to the Brotherhood was a direct application of its national policy on company unionism. See *Report of the Central Committee to the 8th Convention of the Communist Party of the U.S.A. Held in Cleveland, Ohio, April 2–8, 1934* (New York, 1934), 33.

77. Minutes of TWU Delegates Council, July 18, 1934, SQ-T; Faber, p. 24; interview with Gerald O'Reilly, May 15, 1978; *DW*, Apr. 3, 1934, p. 4; *TWB*, May 1934, p. 3; Sept. 1934, p. 1.

78. *TWB*, Dec. 1934–Jan. 1935, p. 2.

79. The new pension plan covered high-salary executives as well as hourly workers. However, the executives paid in a smaller percentage of their earnings. James J. McGinley, *Labor Relations in the New York Rapid Transit Systems, 1904–1944* (New York, 1949), 213–15; "Interborough Rapid Transit Company, Pension Agreement, Effective July 1, 1934," in "Interborough Rapid Transit Company, 805," NLB and NLRB records, 1933–35, WNRC; *TWB*, May 1934, p. 2; July 1934, p. 1; Sept. 1934, p. 1; Oct. 1934, p. 4; Dec. 1934–Jan. 1935, p. 2; *DW*, July 22, 1934, trade union supplement, p. 4.

80. Other TWU demands included shorter hours; minimum weekly pay of $30; two weeks' paid vacation; an end to speed-up, lay-offs, and company spying; and safe and sanitary

working conditions. *TWB*, July 1, 1934, p. 1; Aug. 1934, p. 8; Sept. 1934, p. 1; *DW*, July 30, 1934, p. 2.

81. Sass, p. 25; *DW*, Aug. 20, 1934, p. 3; *Santo Deportation Hearings*, 693–703; interviews: Maurice Forge, Jan. 27, 1979; James Sullivan, July 27, 1979; Victor Bloswick, Jan. 23, 1979; John Gallagher, Apr. 20, 1979; Patrick Walsh, June 1, 1978.

82. *DW*, Aug. 6, 1934, p. 2; interview with John Plover, Feb. 20, 1979.

83. Faber, pp. 26–27; interviews with Maurice Forge, Jan. 7, 1979; Patrick Reilly, Sept. 7, 1978.

84. "Interborough Rapid Transit Co. 805" file, NLB and NLRB records, 1933–35, WNRC; *New York World-Telegram*, Sept. 5, 1934; *TWB*, July 1934, pp. 2, 7; *Dies Committee*, vol. 2, pp. 1039–49.

85. John Santo to Ben Golden, Aug. 8 and 23, 1934; Golden to Santo, Aug. 10, 1934; Elinore Morehouse Herrick to Thomas E. Murray, Jr., Sept. 27, 1934; Herrick to Sidney Cohen, Sept. 29, 1934, in "Interborough Rapid Transit Co. 805," NLB and NLRB records, 1933–35, WNRC.

86. NLRB, "Stenographic Report of Hearing in the Matter of TWU vs. IRT Co., Oct. 31, 1934," in "Interborough Rapid Transit Company, 805" file; and "Interborough Rapid Transit Company, #1100" file, NLB and NLRB records, 1933–35, WNRC; "Reports to Washington-Weekly-Cases Pending-1934," and "Cases Closed-1935," New York ADM. File, Records of the National Labor Board, RG 25, National Archives; *TWB*, Nov. 1934, p. 4; Dec. 1934–Jan. 1935, p. 1; *DW*, Nov. 3, 1934, p. 2; interview with Maurice Forge, Jan. 7, 1979.

87. *TWB*, Sept. 1934, p. 3; Mar. 1935, p. 1; interview with Maurice Forge, Jan. 7, 1979; *Dies Committee*, vol. 13, pp. 7909, 7916.

88. Sass, p. 25; interview with Maurice Forge, Jan. 13, 1979; *Dies Committee*, vol. 13, pp. 7913–14.

89. Interview with Philip J. Carey, Oct. 13, 1977; Paul O'Dwyer Memoir, OHCCU; Bell, pp. 8, 16–19, 31–32, 154–55.

90. Minutes of TWU Delegates Council, July 18, 1934, SQ-T; *TWB*, Oct. 1934, p. 7; Mar. 1935, p. 4; May 1, 1936, p. 6; Faber, pp. 26–27.

91. *NYT*, Dec. 10, 1934, p. 46; Dec. 15, 1934, p. 15; *New York Post*, May 25, 1935; Thomas E. Murray, Jr., "Letter to All IRT Employees," May 25, 1935, in "Interborough Rapid Transit Election Petition, 1516," records of the NLB and NLRB, 1933–35, WNRC; "Defeat the New Yellow Dog Plan," leaflet reproduced in *TE*, May 1964, p. 7; *DW*, Dec. 21, 1934, p. 4.

92. Some reports of the January meeting say that those present actually voted to affiliate with the TWU. *TWB*, Dec. 1934–Jan. 1935, pp. 1, 3; Feb. 1935, pp. 1, 8; "Defeat the New Yellow Dog Plan"; *DW*, Dec. 21, 1934, p. 4; Jan. 11, 1935, p. 4; Feb. 1, 1935, p. 6; Mar. 9, 1935, p. 8; Sass, p. 25.

93. *DW*, Mar. 9, 1935, p. 9; Sass, pp. 25–26.

94. *TWB*, Jan. 1935, p. 1; Jan. 1939, p. 6; Faber, p. 27.

95. Ben Golden, "Report on Interborough Rapid Transit Company," "Minutes of Executive Board Meeting, May 27, 1935," and Elinore M. Herrick to Harry Sacher, May 31, 1935, all in "Daily Correspondence" file; and "Report to Washington, Weekly Cases Pending-1935" file, both in New York ADM. Files, records of the NLB, RG 25, National Archives; Sacher to Golden, May 26, 1935; Herrick to Thomas E. Murray, Jr., and Herrick to TWU, June 6, 1935, in "Interborough Rapid Transit Election Petition, 1516," records of the NLB and NLRB, 1933–35, WNRC; *New York World-Telegram*, Feb. 20, 1935; *TWB*, Feb. 1935, p. 2; *DW*, Mar. 8, 1935, p. 4.

96. Interview with Maurice Forge, Jan. 7, 1979.

97. Equally significant, of course, was the fact that over half the employees did not vote.

Interviews with Joseph Labash, Aug. 3, 1979; Maurice Forge, Jan. 7, 1979; *TWB*, Mar.– Apr. 1935, p. 1; Apr. 1939, p. 6; *R&FTN*, Mar. 1950, p. 3; draft of letter from Brotherhood, TWU, and Independent Union of I.R.T. Employees [*sic*] to Thomas E. Murray, Jr., and Independent Union of I.R.T. Workers leaflet, JBF.

98. Interviews with Maurice Forge, Jan. 7 and July 29, 1979; Joseph Labash, Aug. 3, 1979. There was a complication that arose from the Faber deal, for the union already had a financial officer, Clan-member Michael Clune. Clune had worked tirelessly as a volunteer financial secretary and could not simply be pushed aside. As a result, for several years the union had both a financial secretary and a treasurer. The situation was finally resolved after the TWU affiliated with the CIO; Clune was given the job of assistant CIO director in Buffalo, N.Y. He remained there until the CIO's Cold War purge. For part of that time he also served on the TWU's International Executive Board. *TWU 1943 Convention*, 114–15.

99. Manning had been elected on the TWU platform, but had then gone along with the Connolly leadership. Manning was also a member of the AFL Plumbers and Steamfitters union, and TWU members lodged complaints with that group about his conduct. Faced with possible expulsion from the AFL, Manning gave up his Brotherhood post. *TWB*, Dec. 1, 1935, p. 5; Mar. 1, 1936, p. 5; May 1, 1936, p. 6; Oct. 1936, p. 7; Dec. 1936, p. 1; Oct. 1939, p. 10.

100. Interviews with Victor Bloswick, Jan. 23, 1979; Maurice Forge, Jan. 7, 1979 (includes quotes).

101. *TWB*, Mar. 1935, p. 8; May–June 1935, p. 6; Nov. 1, 1935, p. 7; interviews with Adrian Cabral, Apr. 12, 1979; Maurice Forge, Aug. 9, 1979.

102. *TWB*, Feb. 1936, p. 8; Jan. 1939, p. 6; list of members of the TWU Executive Board, JBF; interview with Adrian Cabral, Apr. 12, 1979.

103. *TWB*, Feb. 1935, p. 6; May–June 1935, p. 1; July 1935, p. 1; May 1940, p. 8; Car Cleaners of Jerome and Other Barns to Thomas E. Murray, Jr., July 18, 1935; Murray to All Employees of IRT, Aug. 8, 1935; and E. M. Herrick, "Memorandum on I.R.T. Strike of July 9, 1935," all in "Interborough Rapid Transit" file, records of NLB and NLRB, 1933–35, WNRC; *Daily News*, July 11, 1935; *Herald Tribune*, July 11, 1935; *NYT*, July 13, 1935, p. 15.

104. The scant available evidence suggests that at the Jerome barn the TWU was led by a largely Irish group with Coughlinite tendencies, while the anti-TWU men, at least in later years, included many Italians and Slavs. John D. Moore, "I.R.T. Transport Workers Union, July 31, 1935," in "Interborough Rapid Transit" file, records of NLB and NLRB, 1933–35, WNRC; *TWB*, Nov. 1936, p. 3; *NYWTB*, Feb. 15, 1941, pp. 1, 3; interview with Maurice Forge, Jan. 27, 1979.

105. The others on payroll were Josie Nolan, a secretary, and "Jack McCarthy"—probably P. J. McCarthy, a CP cadre sent in from Boston to work on the TWU drive. Faber, pp. 27–29; *TWB*, Aug. 1934, p. 1; July 1935, p. 8; Aug. 1939, p. 6; TWU payroll lists and receipts, Aug. and Sept. 1935, JBF; interview with Maurice Forge, Jan. 7, 1979; *TE*, Apr. 1954, p. 5A; *TWU 1939 Convention*, 205–6; *Dies Committee*, vol. 13, pp. 7919–19.

106. *TWB*, May–June 1935, p. 4; July 1935, pp. 1, 5; Nov. 1, 1935, pp. 1, 7; *DW*, July 19, 1935, p. 4; *NYT*, July 18, 1935, p. 3; Aug. 11, 1935, p. 12; Sept. 5, 1935, p. 8; Car Cleaners of Jerome and Other Barns to Thomas E. Murray, Jr., July 18, 1935, and Herbert C. Holmstrom to Murray, Aug. 8, 1935, "Interborough Rapid Transit," records of the NLB and NLRB, 1933–35, WNRC; "Financial Standing of T.W.U. as of December 31, 1935," JBF; interview with Maurice Forge, Jan. 7, 1979. On shaming, see interviews with Philip J. Carey, Oct. 13, 1977, and Maurice Forge, Jan. 27, 1979.

107. Samuel Estreicher, "Collective Bargaining in the New York City Transit System, 1937–1950: A Case Study in the Politics of Municipal Unionism" M.S. thesis, Cornell University, 1974, p. 55; *TWB*, July 1935, p. 1; Oct. 1, 1935, pp. 1, 3; Jan. 1936, p. 1; "What

Happened at Grand Central Saturday?," TWU leaflet, JBF; *NYT*, Aug. 11, 1935, p. 12; Aug. 13, 1935, p. 13; transcript of testimony of William Flanagan at O'Shea-Quill-Machado trial, box 18, Vito Marcantonio Papers, NYPL; interview with Maurice Forge, Jan. 7, 1979.

108. *DW*, Aug. 29, 1935, pp. 1–2; Sept. 13, 1935, p. 4; *NYT*, Aug. 29, 1935, p. 13; interviews with John Nolan, June 1, 1978; Maurice Forge, Jan. 27, 1979. Quill was receiving tips on beakie activity from a union sympathizer in the IRT timekeeping office. See Mike Tierney to John Nolan, n.d., in possession of Nolan.

109   Murray owned an electrical engineering and manufacturing company, was a director of Chrysler Corp., and a trustee of two New York banks. Later, he served on the Atomic Energy Commission. *National Cyclopedia of American Biography* 49 (New York, 1966), pp. 464–65; interview with Maurice Forge, Feb. 25, 1979.

110. Mack was considered a specialist in politically sensitive cases; he had earlier presided over the trials of Marcus Garvey and Attorney General Harry M. Dougherty. Estreicher, p. 74; *NYT*, June 3, 1939, p. 9; John Gunther, *Inside U.S.A.* (New York, 1947), 530; *Dictionary of American Biography*, Supplement 3 (New York, 1973), 487–90; Harry Bernard, *The Forging of an American Jew: The Life and Times of Judge Julian W. Mack* (New York, 1974), 154, 307–10, 312–13; Bruce Allen Murphy, *The Brandeis/Frankfurter Connection* (New York, 1982), 44, 55, 60, 62, 64, 67–69, 79, 81, 146–49.

111. Dues-paying membership calculated from "Financial standing of TWU." Overall membership estimates for this period range from 1,200 to 5,100. See *New York Post*, July 2, 1937, p. 4; *TWB*, Feb. 1938, p. 12; *Dies Committee*, vol. 13, pp. 8102–3; appendix V, pp. 1640, 1657; Charles Lionel Franklin, *The Negro Unionist of New York* (1936; reprinted, New York, 1968), 336; interview with Maurice Forge, Jan. 7, 1979.

112. W. Z. Foster, *History of the Communist Party*, 303–4.

113. A CP official lent the TWU leaders money for their trip to Detroit, which they repaid after fund-raising stops at two upstate Communist camps. The TWU also explored affiliating with other unions, including the Brotherhood of Railway Trainmen. *TWB*, Mar.-Apr. 1935, p. 4; Oct. 1935, p. 4; *Motorman, Conductor and Motor Coach Operator*, Feb. 1937, p. 23; June 1937, pp. 5–6; *Herald Tribune*, Nov. 10, 1934; Dec. 21, 1936; *NYT*, Sept. 21, 1933, pp. 1, 6; Oct. 24, 1934, p. 15; *Dies Committee*, vol. 13, pp. 7920–25; TWU, Minutes of Meeting of Executive Board, Feb. 4, 1936, TWU of A.

114. *TWB*, Feb. 1936, pp. 3, 5, 8; Jan. 1939, p. 6.

115. The account of O'Shea's replacement by Quill is based on interviews with Gerald O'Reilly, May 15, 1978; John Nolan, June 1, 1978; Patrick Reilly, Sept. 7, 1978; Maurice Forge, Jan. 7, 1979; and John Plover, Feb. 20, 1979; and *Dies Committee*, vol. 13, p. 7910.

116. Homer Martin was the ineffective and unpredictable first president of the United Automobile Workers Union. His ouster led to a split in the union.

117. O'Shea later denied that he had advocated blowing up the subways, and his views may well have been exaggerated to discredit him. But the evidence is strong and consistent that at least on occasion he advocated terrorist tactics. For his denial, see *Santo Deportation Hearings*, 627–28.

118. For simplicity's sake, I use the name TWU, though formally incorrect, for the IAM period. Walter Galenson, *The CIO Challenge to the AFL: A History of the American Labor Movement, 1935–1941* (Cambridge, Mass., 1960), 495–97; James J. Matles and James Higgins, *Them and Us: Struggles of a Rank-and-File Union* (Englewood Cliffs, N.J., 1974), 37–47; Ronald L. Filippelli, "UE: The Formative Years," *Labor History* 17, no. 3 (Summer 1976): 357–59, 368–69; IAM, *Ritual of the International Association of Machinists* (revised and adopted by the eighteenth convention, Sept. 17–27, 1928), 7; *TWB*, Feb. 1936, p. 3; Mar. 1, 1936, pp. 1–3; Apr. 1, 1936, p. 3; "Transport Workers Lodge No. 1547 to All Transit Employees," JBF; IRT Brotherhood, "Spilling the Beans."

119. The source of this information asked to remain anonymous. Officially it was announced that Santo received 70% of the vote, but no absolute totals were released. TWU, Minutes of Joint Executive Committee, Dec. 8, 1936, TWU of A.

Chapter 5

1. Through 1936 the TWU executive board included only one non-IRT worker. See TWU, "Meeting Agenda," n.d., JBF; *TWB*, Feb. 1937, p. 5.

2. *TWU 1937 Convention*, Oct. 5 morning session, p. 11; *TWB*, Jan. 1936, p. 7; Apr. 1, 1936, p. 1; May 1, 1936, p. 6; *NYT*, Apr. 13, 1936, p. 19.

3. *TWB*, Nov. 1, 1935, pp. 1–2; May 1, 1936. p. 1; *NYT*, Nov. 24, 1935, p. 19; June 26, 1936, p. 2; *TWU 1939 Convention*, 160–61.

4. *TWB*, July 1, 1936, p. 1; Aug. 1936, p. 1; Oct. 1936, p. 1

5. Ironically, the meeting of the AFL council that endorsed the TWU's industrial jurisdiction ended in commotion over a resolution asking the AFL to rescind its suspension of CIO affiliates. *TWB*, Oct. 1936, p. 8; *NYT*, Aug. 21, 1936, p. 5.

6. *NYT*, Sept. 20, 1936, III:10; *TWB*, Oct. 1936, p. 2.

7. *NYT*, Oct. 8, 1936, p. 15; Oct. 17, 1936, p. 8; *TWB*, Oct. 13, 1936, pp. 1–3; Nov. 1936, pp. 1, 3–4, 6, 8; Dec. 1936, pp. 1, 5–6; Feb. 1937, p. 1; Michael J. Quill to Power Sub-station Workers," JBF; City Industrial Relations Board, "Minutes of Conference in Re Interborough Rapid Transit Company versus Unions and Brotherhoods, May 6, 1937," "City Industrial Relations Board: IRT" folder, box 677, LaGP (hereafter CIRB-IRT Conference).

8. *TWB*, Oct. 1936, p. 2; Nov. 1936, pp. 1, 3; Dec. 1936, p. 1; Feb. 1937, p. 5; Feb. 1937, p. 2; interviews with Joseph Labash, Aug. 3, 1979; Maurice Forge, Jan. 7, 1979; "Minutes of Joint Executive Committees Meeting, Sept. 15 [1936]," and collection of TWU leaflets, JBF.

9. *TWB*, Mar. 1935, p. 3; May 1, 1936, p. 6; Dec. 1936, p. 1; Jan. 1937, p. 5; *NYT*, Mar. 5, 1936, VII:8, 23; interviews with Maurice Forge, Jan. 7 and July 29, 1979; Phil Bray, Aug. 13, 1979; Mark Balinger (pseudonym), July 29, 1979; and John Nolan, June 1, 1978.

10. Michael Gillen, one of the first motormen to join the TWU and an early member of the delegates council, probably had ties to the left pre-dating the TWU. However, he was not a very effective organizer. *TWB*, Nov. 1936, p. 3; Jan. 1937, p. 5; Feb. 1937, p. 2; interview with Maurice Forge, July 29, 1979.

11. Interviews with Phil Bray, Aug. 13, 1979; Gerald O"Reilly, July 11, 1979; Maurice Forge, Jan. 13, 1979; Leo Huberman, *The Great Bus Strike* (New York, 1941), 18; *TWU 1946 Convention*, 176; *R&FTN*, Nov. 1949, p. 3; and Philadelphia Report, May 5, 1945 (#100-7319-296), p. 4, FBI-FOIA.

12. TWU leaflets: "Keegan's Answer to the Motormen," SQ-T, and "To ALL I.R.T. Motormen and Switchmen," and "Know the Truth," JBF; interview with Phil Bray, Aug. 13, 1979; *TWB*, Apr. 1937, p. 4; Feb. 1939, pp. 1, 14.

13. *TWB*, Feb. 1937, p. 2; Mar. 1937, p. 4; Apr. 1937, p. 6; interview with Joseph Labash, Aug. 3, 1979; TWU leaflets: "To ALL I.R.T. Towermen," and "Michael J. Quill to Power Substation Workers," JBF; *TWU 1937 Convention*, Oct. 6 morning session, p. 24.

14. IAM records indicated that in January 1937 the TWU had a membership of only 2,031. However, this was probably the result of deliberate misrepresentation by the TWU designed to minimize per capita payments to its parent body. *New York Post*, July 2, 1937, p. 4; U.S. House of Representatives, *Hearings Before a Special Committee on Un-American Activities*, 76th Congress, 3rd Session, vol. 13 (Washington, D.C., 1940), pp. 7914–15 (hereafter *Dies Committee*, vol. 13), p. 7934; *TWU 1937 Convention*, Oct. 6 morning session, p. 6; E. C. Davison to Michael Clune, Apr. 8, 1937, TWU-T.

15. Interviews with Peter MacLachlan and Maurice Forge, Feb. 25, 1979; Carl Mann, Apr. 5, 1984; Gerald O'Reilly, July 11, 1979; *TWU 1937 Convention*, Oct. 7 morning session, pp. 51–57.

16. When Quill went to give literature to one Brooklyn CP concentration unit, he was dismayed to discover that only the youngest member of the group was fluent in English; the others were older, Yiddish-speaking workers. Interviews with Nat Cohen, Dec. 7, 1978; Maurice Forge, Jan. 7, 1979; Peter MacLachlan, Feb. 25, 1979; and Carl Mann, Apr. 5, 1984; U.S. Department of Justice, Immigration and Naturalization Service, "In the Matter of Charges against DESIDERIU HAMMER, alias JOHN SANTO" (typescript of 1947 hearings, hereafter *Santo Deportation Hearings*), 779–81; U.S. House of Representatives, *Hearings Before Special Committee to Investigate Un-American Activities*, 75th Congress, 2nd Session, vol. 2 (Washington, D.C., 1938), p. 1074 (hereafter *Dies Committee*, vol. 2), pp. 1066–68; *TWB*, Dec. 1933, p. 3; Apr. 1934, p. 2; Aug. 1934, p. 5; Jan. 1936, p. 4; June 1, 1936, 3; July 1, 1936, p. 3; Dec. 1936; p. 7; Nov. 1939, p. 10.

17. Interview with Maurice Forge, Jan. 7, 1979; *TWB*, Dec. 1934–Jan. 1935, p. 3; *TWU 1937 Convention*, Oct. 8 afternoon session, p. 19; Gustav Faber, *And Then Came TWU!* (New York, 1950), 27, 30.

18. Interviews with Carl Mann, Apr. 5, 1984; Peter MacLachlan, Feb. 25, 1979; Nat Cohen, Dec. 7, 1978; Minutes of Delegates Council Meetings, May–July 1934, SQ-T. On the Amalgamated activities, see Joshua B. Freeman, "The Transport Workers Union in New York City, 1933–1948," Ph.D. dissertation, Rutgers University, 1983, pp. 233–35 (hereafter Freeman, "TWU").

19. Interviews with Peter MacLachlan, Feb. 25, 1979; Carl Mann, Apr. 5, 1984.

20. *TE*, Apr. 1954, pp. 6A, 9A; interviews with Peter MacLachlan, Feb. 25, 1979; Carl Mann, Apr. 5, 1984.

21. On the BMT bus men, see Freeman, "TWU," 237–39.

22. Minutes of Delegates Council, May 28, 1934, SQ-T; *DW*, July 16, 1934, trade union supplement, p. 2; *TWB*, Sept. 1934, pp. 1, 6; Mar. 1935, pp. 1, 4; Dec. 1, 1935, pp. 1, 2; June 1, 1936, p. 3; Nov. 1936, p. 8; *Santo Deportation Hearings*, 541–47.

23. Interviews with Peter MacLachlan, Feb. 25, 1979; Carl Mann, Apr. 5, 1984; *TWU 1937 Convention*, Oct. 8 afternoon session, p. 19; Faber, p. 30; *TWB*, June 1937, p. 4.

24. MacMahon was aided by two veterans of the CP's BMT concentration work, Carl Mann and Michael Butler. Both eventually became paid union organizers. Interview with Carl Mann, Apr. 5, 1984.

25. Contemporary newspaper stories describe the plant as having 300 to 350 workers; later union accounts mention 500. Because of their supervisory responsibilities, the engineers were not members of the BMT company union nor included in the intitial TWU bargaining unit. They were added to the latter in January 1939. Interviews with Carl Mann, Apr. 5, 1984; Maurice Forge, Jan. 13, 1979; James J. McGinley, *Labor Relations in the New York Rapid Transit Systems, 1904–1944* (New York, 1949), 176; *Party Organizer*, Aug. 1937, p. 40; *The Communist*, Sept. 1939, p. 833.

26. The following account of events at Kent Avenue is based on *NYT*, Jan. 26, 1937, pp. 1, 4, 5; Jan. 27, 1937, pp. 1, 3; Jan. 28, 1937, p. 2; *TWB*, Feb. 1937, pp. 1, 3, 7; Faber, pp. 11–12; *TE*, May 1959, p. 6; interviews with Maurice Forge, Jan. 13, 1979; Joseph Labash, Aug. 3, 1979; New York Report, Aug. 13, 1947 (#100-7319-357), FBI-FOIA.

27. The short time allowed for Menden to respond suggests that TWU leaders were actually seeking a confrontation as an organizing tactic.

28. *NYT*, Jan. 27, 1937, pp. 1, 3; Jan. 28, 1937, p. 2; *TWB*, Mar. 1937, pp. 1, 3; June 1937, p. 4. Fody and Pollack had both been with the BMT for nine years. Later that spring they became TWU staff organizers.

29. Santo's statement appears in *TWU 1937 Convention*, Oct. 6 morning session, p. 6; MacLachlan's in my interview with him on Feb. 25, 1979. See also *TWB*, Mar. 1937, p. 1; interview with Carl Mann, Apr. 5, 1984.

30. Rose Wortis, "Organization Brings Results," *Party Organizer*, Aug. 1937, p. 40: *Dies Committee*, vol. 2, pp. 1050–55; U.S. House of Representatives, *Hearings before a Special Committee on Un-American Activities*, 77th Congress, 1st Session, appendix V (Washington, D.C., 1941), pp. 1650–51 (hereafter *Dies Committee*, appendix V), pp. 1640–47.

31. Interview with Maurice Forge, Jan. 13, 1979.

32. The Fifth Avenue Coach situation can be followed in: "MF:Amalgamated Association of Street, Electric Railway and Motor Coach Employees" folder, Tamiment Library; *NYT*, Sept. 21, 1933, pp. 1, 6; Oct. 2, 1933, p. 4; Jan. 16, 1934, p. 15; Feb. 6, 1934, p. 1; Feb. 27, 1934, p. 9; Feb. 28, 1934, p. 14; Mar. 1, 1934, p. 15; Mar. 2, 1934, p. 21; Mar. 3, 1934, pp. 1, 7; Mar. 22, 1934, p. 23; Apr. 19, 1934, p. 5; Nov. 29, 1934, p. 3; *Herald Tribune*, Apr. 30, 1934; *TWB*, Sept. 1934, p. 5; and Brotherhood of IRT Employees, "Spilling the Beans" [pamphlet], (New York, 1935)." On Treanor (whose name was alternately spelled Traynor), see interview with John Gallagher, Apr. 20, 1979; and Curt Gentry, *Frame-up: The Incredible Case of Tom Mooney and Warren Billings* (New York, 1967) 67–75, 80, 86.

33. In spite of these failures, the Amalgamated kept trying to organize New York-area surface workers. Eventually it signed contracts with a number of small companies. In several cases this was the outgrowth of Mayor La Guardia's policy of issuing new bus franchises only to companies agreeing to engage in collective bargaining. To meet this criterion, some companies sought out the Amalgamated and signed what amounted to sweetheart contracts. Although this provided the union with an organizational base, it also resulted in considerable rank-and-file unrest. In the late 1930s and early 40s some such Amalgamated units, after long, bitter struggles, transferred their affiliation to the TWU. See interviews with John Gallagher, Apr. 20, 1979: Patrick Walsh, June 1, 1978; *Motorman, Conductor, and Motor Coach Operator*, Feb. 1937, p. 23; *TWU 1937 Convention*, Oct. 7 afternoon session, p. 45; Memo on Transit Unions in NYC [1937], "Transport Workers Union of America" file (hereafter TWU file), box A7-34, CIO Papers, Catholic University; "City Industrial Relations Board [hereafter CIRB]: Buses-Zone D" file, and "CIRB: Children's Bus Service" file, box 683, LaGP; *NYT*, Nov. 20, 1936, p. 20; Nov. 22, 1936, p. 26; *Herald Tribune*, Apr. 29, 1935; *TWB*, Apr. 1938, p. 4; May 1939, p. 5; Oct. 1939, p. 4; Feb. 1940, p. 4; Sept. 1940, p. 1; Sept. 1941, p. 10; *NYWTB*, July 20, 1940, p. 1.

34. *DW*, June 7, 1935, p. 4.

35. "To The Employees of the Fifth Avenue Coach Co.," and Minutes of Delegates Council meetings of June 25 and July 18, 1934, SQ-T; interview with Maurice Forge, Jan. 7, 1979.

36. *TWB*, Sept. 1934, p. 6; Dec. 1934–Jan. 1935, p. 4; Jan. 1937, p. 5; James Flatley, "To All Omnibus Brothers," JBF; Faber, p. 27; *TE*, Apr. 1954, p. 9A; interviews with John Nolan, June 1, 1978; John Gallagher, Apr. 20, 1979; *Dies Committee*, vol. 2, pp. 1078–81; Huberman, p. 18; *TWU 1937 Convention*, Oct. 8, afternoon session, p. 24.

37. Interviews with Maurice Forge, Jan. 7, 1979 ("wildfire"); John Gallagher, Apr. 20, 1979; Patrick Walsh, June 1, 1979; Faber, p. 30; *TE*, May 1959, p. 9.

38. Interviews with John Gallagher, Apr. 20, 1979; Maurice Forge, Jan. 13, 1979.

39. *American Labor*, June 1971, pp. 20, 24 (includes quote); interviews with John Gallagher, Apr. 20, 1979; Patrick Walsh, June 1, 1978; *TE*, Apr. 1954, p. 9A.

40. Interviews with John Gallagher, Apr. 20, 1979; Gerald O'Reilly, July 11, 1979; James Sullivan, July 17, 1979; and Patrick Walsh, June 1, 1978; *TE*, Apr. 1954, p. 9A ("leaps and bounds"); May 1959, p. 9; *TWU 1943 Convention*, p. 91; *TWB*, Oct. 1937, p. 11; *NYT*,

June 5, 1937, p. 1; *TWU 1939 Convention*, p. 20; William Martin and Richard Mason depositions, SQ-T.

41. At least three IRA veterans—two of whom had been in Quill's brigade—were active in the Third Avenue drive. The Clan na Gael as an organization, however, apparently did not play a major role. Interviews with John Gallagher, Apr. 20, 1979; James Sullivan, July 17, 1979; Patrick Walsh, June 1, 1978.

42. *TE*, Apr. 1954, pp. 9A–10A; May 1959, p. 6; *TWU 1946 Convention*, 210–11; *TWB*, Aug. 1941, p. 7; Huberman, p. 103.

43. David Montgomery, "To Study the People: The American Working Class," *Labor History* 21, no. 4 (Fall 1980), p. 504.

44. On internal union politics, see chapter 7. The ISS, which does not fit neatly into the above schema, is discussed in Chapter 8.

45. *TWB*, Mar. 1937, pp. 1, 4; Apr. 1937, p. 3.

46. *TWB*, Apr. 1937, pp. 1–2; Samuel Estreicher, "Collective Bargaining in the New York City Transit System, 1937–1950: A Case Study in the Politics of Municipal Unionism," M.S. thesis, Carnell University, 1974, p. 56; Telegram from Michael J. Quill to Fiorello H. La Guardia, Mar. 19, 1937, "Transportation, 1934–1939" folder, box 2642, LaGP.

47. CIRB-IRT Conference, pp. 22–23, 25, 41, 43–45, 50, box 677, LaGP; *New York Post*, May 5, 1937.

48. *TWB*, Mar. 1937, p. 4; Feb. 1939, p. 6; unlabeled newspaper clipping in "Clippings-IRT," Regional Records, Region II, N.Y., National Labor Board, 1933–34 and National Labor Relations Board, 1934–35, RG 25, National Archives, Washington National Records Center, Suitland, Md.; *Herald Tribune*, May 16, 1937; CIRB-IRT Conference, pp. 31–42, 51–52.

49. *NYT*, May, 1, 1937, pp. 1, 4; *New York Post*, May 5, 1937 (includes Sullivan quote).

50. *NYT*, May 1, 1937, pp. 1, 4; S. W. Huff to CIRB, May 12, 1937, "CIRB-Third Avenue Railway System" folder, box 677, LaGP.

51. CIRB-IRT Conference, pp. 1–22; *New York Post*, May 5, 1937.

52. *NYT*, May 1, 1937, pp. 1, 4; May 3, 1937, p. 10; May 4, 1937, p. 16; May 17, 1937, pp. 1, 13; CIRB-IRT Conference, passim; John J. Sullivan to Burton A. Zorn, May 12, 1937 (includes quote) and other miscellaneous material in "CIRB-Third Avenue Railway System," box 677, LaGP.

53. *Motorman, Conductor and Motor Coach Operator*, June 1937, pp. 5–6; *TE*, Apr. 1954, p. 7A; interview with Maurice Forge, Jan. 13, 1979; A. O. Wharton to Michael J. Quill, May 1, 1937, TWU-T; *NYT*, May 1, 1937, pp. 1, 4; *TWB*, June 1937, p. 9.

54. Interviews with Maurice Forge, Jan. 13, 1979; Gerald O'Reilly, May 15, 1978; Bert Cochran, *Labor and Communism, the Conflict that Shaped American Unions* (Princeton, 1977), 345; *Dies Committee*, vol. 13, pp. 7931–34; appendix V, pp. 1650–51 (Quill quote on p. 1651); *NYT*, May 8, 1937, pp. 1, 9; May 10, 1938, p. 9; May 11, 1937, p. 4; Memo on Transit Unions in NYC, TWU file, box A7-34, CIO Papers, Catholic University; "Resolution Adopted at Special Membership Meeting of the Transport Workers Union, May 7, 1937," and TWU, "March Under the Banner of the C.I.O.," JBF.

55. *Herald Tribune*, May 16, 1937; TWU, "Ten to One—Make It Unanimous," JBF.

56. Michael J. Quill to John L. Lewis, May 19, 1937, TWU file, box A7-34, CIO Papers, Catholic University; *NYT*, May 19, 1937, p. 14; May 28, 1937, pp. 1, 12; July 28, 1937, p. 9; Sept. 1, 1937, p. 29. The IRT contract is more fully discussed in Chapter 6; the full text is in Board of Transportation of the City of New York, *Proceedings*, vol. 36 (1940), pp. 1–4.

57. *NYT*, June 5, 1937, p. 1; June 23, 1937, p. 5; July 3, 1937, p. 11; July 22, 1937, p. 9; July 29, 1937, p. 13; Aug. 19, 1937, p. 20.

58. After June 30 the CIRB acted as an agent of the newly created State Labor Relations Board. *NYT,* 1937: May 10, p. 9; May 29, p. 1; June 3, p. 18; June 4, p. 1; June 5, p. 3; June 9, pp. 1–2; June 12, p. 3; June 17, p. 4; June 18, p. 5; June 23, p. 5; June 24, p. 4; June 26, p. 3; July 12, p. 4; July 20, pp. 1, 6; July 21, p. 5; July 30, p. 9; McGinley, pp. 274–76; *TWB,* Apr. 1937, p. 1; June 1937, p. 4; May 1938, pp. 1, 12. Fifth Avenue Coach also granted one-week paid vacations shortly before the TWU won recognition. Fifth Avenue Coach, *Annual Report, 1937,* p. 4.

59. Interviews with Gerald O'Reilly, May 15, 1978; Peter MacLachlan, Feb. 25, 1979; David E. Schmidt, "Catholicism and Democratic Political Developments in Ireland," *Eire-Ireland* 9, no. 1 (1974), pp. 64–65.

60. Joshua B. Freeman, "Review of *Catholic Activism and the Industrial Worker* by Neil Betten (Gainesville, Fla., 1976)," *Ohio History* 87, no. 3 (Summer 1978), pp. 349–50. The best introduction to Social Catholicism is David J. O'Brien, *American Catholics and Social Reform: The New Deal Years* (New York, 1968). See also Betten, *op. cit.* Douglas P. Seaton stresses the conservatism of Catholic labor doctrine in *Catholics and Radicals: The Association of Catholic Trade Unionists and the American Labor Movement, from Depression to Cold War* (Lewisburg, Penn., 1981).

61. Interview with Gerald O'Reilly, May 15, 1978.

62. Some transit workers and their supporters believed that there were close ties between the BMT and the Brooklyn diocese and that the two coordinated their attacks on the TWU. There is, however, no solid evidence confirming this. Interview with Carl Mann, Apr. 5, 1984; *TWU 1937 Convention,* Oct. 7 afternoon session, pp. 57–58; P. Cacchione, "A Foundation for Recruiting," *Party Organizer,* Dec. 1937, pp. 13–14.

63. *LL,* July 25, 1938, pp. 1, 3; Aug. 1, 1938, p. 1; *TWB,* Jan. 1938, p. 8; Statement of Michael Regan, Sept. 3, 1937, JBF; Ronald H. Bayor, *Neighbors in Conflict: The Irish, Germans, Jews and Italians of New York City, 1929–1941* (Baltimore, 1978), 196; Sheldon Marcus, *Father Coughlin: The Tumultuous Life of the Priest of the Little Flower* (Boston, 1973), 293; J., "The Daily Worker Gave Me the First Break," *Party Organizer,* Apr. 1938, pp. 43–44; Cacchione, "A Foundation for Recruiting," 13–14; *TWU 1937 Convention,* Oct. 7 afternoon session, pp. 57–58; interviews with John Nolan, June 1, 1978; John Plover, Feb. 20, 1979; Peter MacLachlan, Feb. 25, 1979.

64. The *Tablet* letter in turn was the basis for an anti-Communist attack on the TWU in the journal of the Amalgamated Association. *Tablet,* July 10, 1937; *Motorman, Conductor and Motor Coach Operator,* Aug. 1937, pp. 3–6.

65. Interview with Peter MacLachlan, Feb. 25, 1979; Cacchione, "A Foundation for Recruiting," 13–14; *TWU 1937 Convention,* Oct. 7 afternoon session, pp. 51–53.

66. *TWB,* Nov. 1, 1935, p. 6; Dec. 1, 1935, p. 4; Feb. 1936, p. 6 (includes Day quote).

67. ACTU members also distributed copies of the *Catholic Worker* to transit workers. *LL,* Jan. 3, 1838, p. 2; Feb. 28, 1938, pp. 1, 4; Aug. 1, 1938, p. 1; Mar. 11, 1940, pp. 1, 4, 8; Seaton, pp. 57–58, 65–72.

68. Interviews with Philip J. Carey, Oct. 13, 1977; Gerald O'Reilly, May 15, 1978; J. Bowyer Bell, *The Secret Army: A History of the IRA* (Cambridge, Mass., 1970), 88; Philip E. Dobson, "The Xavier Labor School, 1938–1939," 271–74 (quote on p. 271) [clipping of unidentified article in "History of Labor School" file, XA].

69. Andrew M. Greeley, *That Most Distressful Nation: The Taming of the American Irish* (Chicago, 1972), 84–85; interviews with Philip Bray, Aug. 13, 1979; John Nolan, June 1, 1978; Cacchione, "A Foundation for Recruiting," 13–14; Philip Dobson to Philip Carey, July, 8, 1941, in "41–42" file, XA; Dobson, "Xavier Labor School," 271–72.

70. Quill was quoted in *New York Post,* July 2, 1937, p. 4. See also interview with Gerald

O'Reilly, May 15, 1978; *TWB*, Apr. 1938, p. 12; May 1943, p. 10; Dobson, "Xavier Labor School," pp. 271–72; *Dies Committee*, vol. 2, p. 1054.

71. Interviews with John Plover, Feb. 20, 1979; Maurice Forge, Jan. 13, 1979.

72. Interview with Peter MacLachlan, Feb. 25, 1979; *TWB*, June 1937, p. 4.

73. *NYT*, Aug. 1, 1937, p. 12; *TWB*, Aug. 1937, pp. 1, 5, 15.

74. The Independent also had significant support among the trolley motormen, winning 39% of their votes. *Santo Deportation Hearings*, 848–50; interviews with Peter MacLachlan, Feb. 25, 1979; Carl Mann, Apr. 5, 1984; Maurice Forge, Jan. 27, 1979; *TWB*, May 1938, p. 1; Jan. 1939, p. 5; *NYT*, June 24, 1937, p. 4.

75. *NYT*, Nov. 4, 1937, p. 12; *TWB*, May 1938, p. 1; Jan. 1939, p. 4; Feb. 1939, p. 4; interview with Peter MacLachlan, Feb. 25, 1979; Michael J. Quill to Father C[harles] O. Rice, Jan. 12, 1939, Charles O. Rice Papers, Pennsylvania State University. The BMT-TWU agreement following the second agent election did not extend the $25 minimum wage to the agents; it took several years of struggle for the TWU to bring the BMT agents' pay up to the higher IRT level. See Board of Transportation, *Proceedings*, vol. 36 (1940), pp. 177–78, and Chapter 6.

76. *NYT*, July 21, 1937, p. 5; Nov. 4, 1937, p. 9; Nov. 27, 1937, p. 3; Jan. 1, 1938; interview with Phil Bray, Aug. 13, 1979; *TWU 1937 Convention*, Oct. 7 morning session, pp. 51–57; *Santo Deportation Hearings*, 541–42, 547; Peter F. Freund, "Labor Relations in the New York City Transit Industry, 1945–1960" (Ph.D. dissertation, New York University, 1964), 77–78. In 1954, when the TWU supplanted the BLE, the entire situation was quite different. See Chapter 14.

77. W. S. Menden to John L. Lewis, Aug. 5, 1937, Michael J. Quill to Lewis, Aug. 6, 1937, and Lewis to Menden, Aug. 9, 1937, TWU file, box A7-34, CIO Papers, Catholic University; *NYT*, 1937: Sept. 14, p. 7; Sept. 15, p. 10; Sept. 16, pp. 1, 16; Sept. 17, pp. 1, 11; Sept. 19, p. 40; Sept. 27, p. 2; "Wall Street versus the People," clipping of TWU newspaper ad, JBF.

78. *NYT*, 1937: Sept. 6, p. 30; Sept. 16, pp. 1, 16; Sept. 17, pp. 1, 11; Sept. 18, pp. 1, 36; Sept. 27, p. 2; Oct. 12, p. 1; "CIRB-BMT" folder, box 676, and "Strikes: BMT Strike" file, box 826, LaGP. The TWU-BMT pact differed from the IRT agreement in that half the 10% wage increase was deferred to the year's end, the time it took operating employees to reach top rates was shortened to five years, and there was a no-strike clause.

79. On taxi and out-of-town workers, see Chapter 11; on the ISS, see Chapter 8.

80. *TWU 1937 Convention*, passim. The record of the preliminary Madison Square Garden rally appears only in the original typed transcript of the convention proceedings, which Maurice Forge kindly lent me. Lewis's statement is on p. 60. See also *TWB*, Dec. 1937, p. 1; Jan. 1938, p. 5.

Chapter 6

1. Board of Transportation, *Proceedings*, 36 (1940), pp. 1–4, 165–68; *NYT*, July 28, 1937, p. 9.

2. *NYT*, July 3, 1937, p. 11; July 27, 1937, p. 13; Aug. 19, 1937, p. 20; *TWB*, Aug. 1937, pp. 1, 5; Oct, 1937, pp. 1, 2; Board of Transportation, *Proceedings*, 36 (1940), p. 167; "New York City Omnibus Corporation Pay Rates," in Michael J. Quill file, Charles O. Rice Papers, Pennsylvania State University.

3. *TWB*, Nov. 1938, pp. 1, 2; Board of Transportation, *Proceedings*, 36 (1940), pp. 4–13, 109–59, 173–87, 200–219; James J. McGinley, *Labor Relations in the New York Rapid*

Transit Systems, 1904–1944 (New York, 1949), 167–77; interviews with Maurice Forge, July 15, 1980; Carl Mann, Apr. 5, 1984.

4. *TWB*, Jan. 1939, p. 1; Feb. 1939, p. 3; June 1939, p. 1; July 1939, pp. 1, 2, 14; Oct. 1939, p. 6; New York Omnibus Corporation, *Annual Report for Year Ended December 31, 1949*, 9; TWU, "Factual Material and Background, TWU-3rd Ave. Controversy, September 9, 1941," JBF.

5. Board of Transportation, *Proceedings*, 36 (1940), pp. 1–2, 5, 7–9, 167, 176–77, 192–95; *TWB*, July 1937, pp. 1, 6; Aug. 1937, pp. 1, 5; Oct. 1937, pp. 1, 2; Jan. 1939, p. 1; June 1939, p. 1; Oct. 1939, p. 6; *NYT*, July 3, 1937, p. 11; July 29, 1937, p. 13; Aug. 19, 1937, p. 20; Gustav Faber, *And Then Came TWU!* (New York, 1950), 41–42.

6. *TWB*, Aug. 1937, p. 1, 5; July 1938, p. 13; *NYT*, July 28, 1937, p. 9; Sept. 1, 1937, p. 29; McGinley, pp. 216–17; *TV*, Sept. 20, 1947, p. 2.

7. *TWB*, May 1934, p. 2; July, 1934, 1; Oct. 1936, 2; *TWU 1937 Convention*, typed transcript, pp. 580–81, 612–15; 620, 630–31; *TWU 1939 Convention*, 54; interview with Gerald O'Reilly, May 15, 1978. On Steward, see David Montgomery, *Beyond Equality: Labor and the Radical Republicans* (New York, 1972), 249–60.

8. Board of Transportation, *Proceedings*, 36 (1940): 1–2, 14–16, 19, 25, 29, 32, 37, 42, 47, 54, 64, 67, 71, 74–75, 84, 136–37, 223, 239, 241, 249–50, 254, 259, 263, 265, 279, 283, 290–91, 319, 322, 325, 328; *TWB*, Feb. 1939, p. 3.

9. *TWB*, Aug. 1939, p. 6; *TWU 1937 Convention*, typed transcript, p. 615; *TWU 1939 Convention*, 54.

10. Board of Transportation, *Proceedings*, 36 (1940), pp. 259–60; Leo Huberman, *The Great Bus Strike* (New York, 1941), 21, 26; McGinley, p. 480; Peter F. Freund, "Labor Relations in the New York City Transit Industry, 1945–1960" (Ph.D. dissertation, New York University, 1964), 137, 142–49; *Agreement by and between the Third Avenue Railway and Subsidiary Companies and the Transport Workers Union of America, CIO, Effective to June 30, 1943* (hereafter *1941 Third Avenue contract*), 3, 9; New York City Omnibus Corporation, *Annual Report for Year Ended December 31, 1952*, 4–5; *TWB*, Jan. 1942, New York City supplement, p. 4; Dec. 1945, p. 4.

11. Board of Transportation, *Proceedings*, 36 (1940): 16, 20, 24, 32–33, 38, 40, 55–56, 59–60, 67–68, 224–27, 230–33, 244–47, 255, 261, 290, 298, 312–13; U.S. Department of Labor, Bureau of Labor Statistics, "Collective Bargaining on the New York Transit Lines," *Monthly Labor Review*, 46, no. 3 (March 1938), p. 691; *TWB*, Feb. 1939, p. 3; Oct. 1939, p. 6.

12. Board of Transportation, *Proceedings*, 36 (1940): 10–108, 188–98, 220–328; *TWB*, Feb. 1939, p. 3; Oct. 1939, p. 6.

13. Board of Transportation, *Proceedings*, 36 (1940): 169–72, 221, 295; *1941 Third Avenue contract*, 25–29; *TWB*, Sept. 1937, p. 3; Jan. 1939, p. 1.

14. *TWB*, May 1934, p. 2; Dec. 1938, p. 11 (includes quote).

15. Board of Transportation, *Proceedings*, 36 (1940): 305–10; *NYCTB*, Sept. 1944, p. 1.

16. *NYWTB*, Feb. 1, 1941, p. 1; Mar. 19, 1941, p. 1.

17. *TWU 1937 Convention*, Oct. 8 morning session, pp. 20–21; *TWB*, Mar. 1940, p. 17.

18. *TWB*, Feb. 1939, pp. 1, 14; May 1939, p. 2; Oct. 1941, p. 2; July 1942, pp. 1, 4.

19. McGinley, p. 290; Board of Transportation, *Proceedings*, 36 (1940): 10, 220; interviews with Victor Bloswick, Jan. 23, 1979; Patrick Walsh, June 1, 1978; Maurice Forge, Jan. 1, 1979; Patrick Reilly, Sept. 9, 1978.

20. Interviews with Philip Bray, Aug. 13, 1979; Peter MacLachlan, Feb. 25, 1979; Victor Bloswick, Jan. 23, 1979; and John Plover, Feb. 20, 1979; *TWB*, Apr. 1939, p. 11; Mar. 1940, p. 22.

21. Interviews with Joseph Labash, Aug. 3, 1979; Adrian Cabral, Apr. 12, 1979. Some 45

years later the TWU charged that supervisors at the NYCTS 207th Street shop, where the work once done at 98th Street is now performed, imposed a ban on coffee pots at work stations. In retaliation the union held a slowdown. *New York Post*, May 3, 1984, p. 3.

22. Interviews with Philip Bray, Aug. 13, 1979; Peter MacLachlan, Feb. 25, 1979; Victor Bloswick, Jan. 23, 1979; Adrian Cabral, Apr. 12, 1979; Patrick Walsh, June 1, 1978; and John Plover, Feb. 20, 1979; *TWB*, Dec. 1945, p. 4.

23. Interviews with Maurice Forge, Sept. 15, 1980; Victor Bloswick, Jan. 23, 1979; Fifth Avenue Coach Company, *Annual Report for the Year Ended December 31, 1938*, 14–16 (quoted passages on p. 15); *NYWTB*, June 15, 1940, p. 2; June 29, 1940, p. 1.

24. See, for example, *TWB*, Sept. 1941, p. 6; *TWU 1939 Convention*, 238. On the individual and collective nature of union rights, see Ronald W. Schatz, *The Electrical Workers: A History of Labor at General Electric and Westinghouse* (Urbana, Ill., 1983), 105–36; Chuck F. Sabel, *Work and Politics: The Division of Labor in Industry* (Cambridge, England, 1982); and Chapter 7.

25. The first TWU credit union was started by Local 100's newly established taxi division, where loan-sharking was an even more serious problem, but the idea quickly spread to the transit branches. *TWB*, Nov. 1, 1935, p. 3; Sept. 1938, p. 14; May 1939, p. 5; Oct. 1939, p. 4; interview with Victor Bloswick, Jan. 23, 1979; *TWU 1937 Convention*, Oct. 8 morning session, pp. 17–24.

26. Contractual provisions requiring doctors' certificates to qualify for sick leave undoubtedly encouraged medical plan utilization. Just before the plan was suspended, the TWU began moving toward mandatory payroll deductions to finance it. Interviews with Lewis Fraad, June 30, 1980; Maurice Forge, Jan. 7, 1979; *TWU 1939 Convention*, 56; *TWU 1941 Convention*, 158–61; L. H. Whittemore, *The Man Who Ran the Subways: The Story of Mike Quill* (New York, 1968), 79; *TWB*, Apr. 1939, p. 1, 2; Mar. 1940, p. 8; June 1940, p. 2; Aug. 1940, p. 5; Oct. 1942, p. 3; *NYWTB*, Jan. 11, 1941, p. 1; Board of Transportation, *Proceedings* 36 (1940): 195; New York City Omnibus Corporation, *Annual Report for the Year Ended December 31, 1942*, 20.

27. See, for example, Henry J. Browne, *One Stop Above Hell's Kitchen: Sacred Heart Parish in Clinton* (So. Hackensack, N.J., n.d.), 55–56.

28. Interviews with Peter MacLachlan, Feb. 25, 1979; Maurice Forge, Nov. 29, 1983.

29. Later on, leadership training courses were occasionally given by top International officers. *TWU 1939 Convention*, 102–3; *TWB*, Sept. 1937, p. 5; Feb. 1939, p. 4; *NYT*, Oct. 17, 1937, II:7; Apr. 10, 1938, X:7; *DW*, June 12, 1939, p. 7; *NYWTB*, Feb. 1, 1941, p. 1; *TV*, May, 3, 1947, p. 8.

30. *TWU 1939 Convention*, 154–56 (quote on p. 155); *TWB*, Dec. 1937, p. 11; Jan. 1939, p. 10.

31. *TWB*, Mar. 1935, p. 4; Apr.–May, 1935, p. 5; Mar. 1, 1936, pp. 5, 7; June 1, 1936, p. 1; Apr. 1937, pp. 5, 8; Dec. 1937, p. 11; Mar. 1938, p. 1; May 1939, p. 2; Sept. 1939, p. 2; Nov. 1939, p. 21; Mar. 1940, p. 17; *NYWTB*, Nov. 23, 1940, p. 3; interviews with Maurice Forge, Jan. 7, 1979; Patrick Reilly, Sept. 7, 1978; Gerald O'Reilly, May 15, 1978.

32. *TWB*, July 1939, p. 13; Aug. 1939, p. 10; Nov. 1939, p. 21; May 1940, p. 18; June 1940, p. 12; *NYWTB*, Nov. 23, 1940, p. 3; U.S. Department of Justice, Immigration and Naturalization Service, "In the Matter of Charges against DESIDERIU HAMMER, alias JOHN SANTO" (typescript of 1947 hearings, hereafter *Santo Deportation Hearings*), p. 850; Charles Thelen to Philip A. Carey, Mar. 29, 1947, "Correspondence-Approbations," and James Flatley to Carey, Sept. 29, 1946, "Correspondence-F," XA.

33. Interviews with Victor Bloswick, Jan. 23, 1979; Gerald O'Reilly, May 15, 1978; and Maurice Forge, Jan. 27, 1979; *TWU 1937 Convention*, Oct. 6 morning session, pp. 34–39.

34. Interviews with Gerald O'Reilly, May 15, 1978; Peter MacLachlan, Feb. 25, 1979;

James Sullivan, Aug. 16, 1979; *TWU 1937 Convention*, Oct. 6 afternoon session, pp. 34–39; *TWU 1941 Convention*, 234; *TWB*, Jan. 1, 1935, p. 5; Feb. 1935, p. 7; Oct. 1936, p. 4; Dec. 1937, p. 3; Jan. 1939, p. 1; Dec. 1939, p. 18; May 1940, p. 4; Nov. 1940, p. 8.

35. Huberman, p. 125; *TWB*, Feb. 1939, p. 12; Apr. 1940, p. 14; June 1940, p. 14.

36. *TWU 1937 Convention*, Oct. 6 afternoon session, pp. 34–39; *TWB*, Apr.–May 1935, p. 8; Sept. 1935, p. 3; Feb. 1937, p. 7; *DW*, June 25, 1938, p. 5.

37. *TWB*, Mar. 1935, p. 3 (includes quotes); Nov. 1, 1935, p. 5; Dec. 1, 1935, p. 5; July 1938, p. 12; May 1939, p. 12; Dec. 1940, p. 18; *NYWTB*, June 22, 1940, p. 4; *DW*, June 28, 1935, p. 5.

38. *TWU 1937 Convention*, Oct. 6 afternoon session, pp. 34–39 (includes quote); *DW*, June 25, 1938, p. 5; *TWB*, Mar. 1935, p. 2; Nov. 1, 1935, p. 5; Dec. 1937, pp. 3–4; *NYT*, Oct. 17, 1937, II:7.

39. Interviews with Maurice Forge, Jan. 27, 1979; Patrick Reilly, Sept. 7, 1978; *TWU 1937 Convention*, Oct. 7 morning session, p. 3; *TWU 1939 Convention*, 112, 211; *TWU 1941 Convention*, 233–34; *TWU 1943 Convention*, 230–31.

40. David Montgomery, *Workers' Control in America* (Cambridge, Eng., 1979), 13–14; Peter Friedlander, *The Emergence of a UAW Local, 1936–1939: A Study in Class and Culture* (Pittsburgh, 1975), 22–23; *DW*, June 15, 1934, p. 4; Studs Terkel, *Hard Times: An Oral History of the Great Depression* (New York, 1978), 156; Schatz, p. 117.

41. Sidney Fine, *Sit-Down; The General Motors Strike of 1936–1937* (Ann Arbor, 1969), 156; Claude Hoffman, *Sit-Down in Anderson: UAW Local 663* (Detroit, 1968), 33.

42. *TWB*, June 1939, p. 12; March 1940, p. 16; June 1940, p. 16; Dec. 1940, p. 8; interview with Martin Young, Nov. 15, 1978.

43. *TWB*, Dec. 1937, p. 4.

44. *TWU 1939 Convention*, 212; *TWU 1941 Convention*, 235–36; *TWU 1943 Convention*, 213; *TWU 1946 Convention*, 215–16; *NYWTB*, Jan. 11, 1941, p. 1; TWU Educational Department, "Union Training Pamphlet No. 1" (New York, 1937); interview with Maurice Forge, Jan. 27, 1979.

45. *TWU 1943 Convention*, 230; *TWU 1946 Convention*, 84–85, 215–18 (quote on p. 216); *TWB*, Feb. 1945, p. 1; interviews with James Sullivan (Aug. 16, 1979) and Maurice Forge (Jan. 27, 1979).

46. *TWB*, Sept. 1937, pp. 8–9; Oct. 1937, p. 3; Mar. 1940, p. 8; Aug. 1940, p. 5; *DW*, June 18, 1938, p. 3.

47. The quoted passages come respectively from *Santo Deportation Hearings*, 863; *TWU 1939 Convention*, 71; and *TWB*, Sept, 1941, p. 6.

48. Quotes from *TWU 1939 Convention*, 71, 69; and *TWU 1941 Convention*, 200 (see also p. 95).

Chapter 7

1. Nathan Glazer, *The Social Basis of American Communism* (New York, 1961), 119.

2. Interviews with Gerald O'Reilly, May 5, 1978; John Nolan, June 1, 1978; Maurice Forge, Dec. 30, 1978, and Jan. 7, 1979; and Martin Young, Nov. 15, 1978; Comparative Absolute Figures of Basic Industries, Chart VI, p. 6, Earl Browder Papers, Syracuse University (microfilm edition), series 2–47, reel 3; New York Report, July 11, 1950 (#100-7319-505), p. 13, FBI-FOIA.

3. Interview with Maurice Forge, Aug. 9, 1979.

4. Glazer, pp. 157–60; interviews with Gerald O'Reilly, May 15, 1978; Maurice Forge, Jan. 13 and Aug. 9, 1979; Martin Young, Nov. 15, 1978; Rose Wortis, "Organization Brings Results," *Party Organizer*, Aug. 1937, p. 41.

5. P. Cacchione, "A Foundation for Recruiting," *Party Organizer*, Dec. 1937, p. 12; Max Steinberg, "Rooting the Party Among the Masses in New York," *The Communist*, Sept. 1939, p. 833; "District Two—Control Tasks Adopted at Enlarged District Committee Meeting, March 5, 1936," reprinted in U.S. House of Representatives, *Hearings Before a Special Committee on Un-American Activities*, 77th Congress, 1st Session, appendix V (Washington, D.C., 1941), 1640–47; Wortis, "Organization," pp. 40–41.

6. Interviews with Maurice Forge, Aug. 9, 1979; Leon Strauss, Oct. 26, 1978; Daniel Bell interview of Earl Browder, June 26 or 27, 1955, pp. 44–45, 49–53, in box 9, Daniel Bell Collection, Tamiment Library.

7. Foster's views are summarized and quoted in Peggy Dennis, *The Autobiography of an American Communist: A Personal View of a Political Life, 1925–1975* (Westport, Conn., 1977), 129. See also William Z. Foster, *History of the Communist Party of the United States* (New York, 1952), 348–49; Joseph R. Starobin, *American Communism in Crisis, 1943–1957* (Cambridge, 1972), 38–41; interviews of Earl Browder by William Goldsmith, Aug. 1955, pp. 3–4, and by Daniel Bell, June 26 or 27, 1955, pp. 49–53, box 9, Daniel Bell Collection, Tamiment Library.

8. TWU, *Constitution* (adopted at First National Convention, Oct. 4–8, 1937); *TWU 1937 Convention*, Oct. 5 afternoon session, pp. 1a–1n, 5–36; Oct. 6 morning session, pp. 1–6, 25–35; Oct. 6 afternoon session, pp. 19–28; Oct. 6 evening session, pp. 3, 16–30; Oct. 8 morning session, pp. 17–28; interview with Maurice Forge, Jan. 13, 1979.

9. The primary motive for adopting the TWU's structure was apparently not to stifle opposition. Although there had been some discussion among TWU leaders of establishing smaller locals and a New York joint council, they settled on one large local because they believed that it would facilitate new organizing and the equalization of wage rates, ensure unity and strike support, and aid workers from the smaller companies. TWU leaders probably were influenced by the CP's predilection at the time for large locals. Also, CIO leaders encouraged the TWU to set up a strong, centralized structure. Nonetheless, TWU leaders soon realized that the structure they had established inhibited challenges to their power, which undoubtedly stiffened their resolve to resist restructuring proposals. See interviews with Maurice Forge, Jan. 13, 1979; Philip Carey, Oct. 13, 1977; *TWU 1937 Convention*, Oct. 5 morning session, pp. 2–10, Oct. 5 afternoon session, pp. 5–36; Oct. 6 morning session, pp. 1–6, 25–35; *TWU 1939 Convention*, 167–73.

10. Interview with Maurice Forge, Jan. 13, 1979.

11. TWU, *Constitution* (1937); interviews with Maurice Forge, Jan. 13, 1979; Patrick Reilly, Sept. 7, 1978 ("the business"); TWU, "Minutes of Joint Executive Committees Meeting Held Monday, Sept. 15 [1936]," JBF.

12. Interviews with Maurice Forge, Jan. 13 and 27, 1979.

13. Interviews with Maurice Forge, Jan. 27, 1979; Patrick J. Reilly, Sept. 7, 1978; James Sullivan, July 27, 1979; Simon Gerson, Dec. 18, 1979; Maurice Forge, "Autobiographical Manuscript," pp. 169–70, 176–77, John Santo to Forge, Jan. 11, 1940, Santo to Forge, Jan. 20, 1940, and Forge, "Memorandum on Bulletin, April 13, 1940," all in possession of Maurice Forge; *TWB*, July 1937, p. 2; Len De Caux, *Labor Radical: From the Wobblies to CIO, A Personal History* (Boston, 1970), 426.

14. Interviews with Maurice Forge, Jan. 27 and Aug. 9, 1979; Leon Strauss, Oct. 26, 1978; telephone interview with Hal Simon, Oct. 18, 1978; interview of Earl Browder by Daniel Bell, June 26 or 27, 1955, pp. 44–46.

15. Six BMT workers did challenge the TWU's closed shop, but their motion for an injunction against its enforcement was denied. See *NYT*, Jan. 19, 1938, pp. 2, 8; *TWB*, May 1938, p. 2.

16. Michael Regan affidavit, JBF; *TWB*, Jan. 1938, p. 8; Dec. 1938, p. 2.

17. Interviews with John Gallagher, April 20, 1979; Joseph Labash, Aug. 3, 1979; *TWU 1937 Convention*, Oct. 6 morning session, pp. 49–50; James Flatley, "TO ALL OMNIBUS BROTHERS" [1939], JBF.

18. *TWU 1937 Convention*, Oct. 5 afternoon session, pp. 24–36; Oct. 6 morning session, pp. 1–2; Oct. 7 afternoon session, pp. 7, 26, 28–41, 49–61; Oct. 8 afternoon session, pp. 18–29; *TWB*, Feb. 1938, p. 9.

19. TWU Executive Board, "Union Building vs. Union Busting" [1937], JBF; *TWB*, Jan. 1938, p. 5; Feb. 1938, pp. 1, 4; interviews with with Patrick Walsh, June 1, 1978; Patrick Reilly, Sept. 7, 1978.

20. Typewritten copy of AAAC leaflet "Locked Out," JBF; *LL*, July 25, 1938, p. 1, 3; Aug. 1, 1938, p. 1. The Fifth Avenue Coach men, of course had never been TWU members, although the TWU had taken up their fight. The TWU had unsuccessfully pursued the Murphy and Cashman cases with the RLB (see Chapter 4).

21.. *TWB*, Feb. 1938, p. 12; Apr. 1938, p. 12; Sept. 1938, p. 7.

22. *TWB*, Oct. 1938, p. 11; U.S. House of Representatives, *Hearings Before a Special Committee on Un-American Activities*, 76th Congress, 3rd Session, vol. 13 (Washington, D.C., 1940), 7914–15 (hereafter *Dies Committee, vol. 13*), 7892.

23. James J. Matles and James Higgins, *Them and Us: Struggles of a Rank-and-File Union* (Englewood Cliffs, N.J., 1974), 103–5; *NYT*, Aug. 21, 1938, p. 2; *TWB*, Sept. 1938, p. 3.

24. U.S. House of Representatives, *Hearings Before Special Committee to Investigate Un-American Activities*, 75th Congress, 2nd Session, vol. 2 (Washington, D.C., 1938), 1039–81 (hereafter *Dies Committee, vol. 2*). On Harmon's ties to Curran, see Philip Dobson to Philip Carey, July 7, 1941, "41–42" file, XA.

25. *NYT*, Sept. 17, 1938, p. 1, 18. The AFL Amalgamated Association also gave extensive publicity to the Dies hearing. See *Motorman, Conductor and Motor Coach Operator*, Sept. 1938, p. 11; Oct. 1938, pp. 2–4, 38.

26. *NYT*, Sept. 18, 1938, p. 42; *TWB*, Oct. 1938, pp. 1, 11, 13; Austin Hogan to Hon. William B. Bankhead, Sept. 22, 1938, Box 2, Labor Non-Partisan League Collection, Wisconsin State Historical Society, Madison, Wisc.

27. *NYT*, Sept. 23, 1938, p. 56.

28. Philip A. Carey, "History of Xavier," and Philip Dobson to Carey, July 8, 1941 (includes quote), "41–42" file, XA; Father Joseph P. Fitzpatrick, S.J., "Father Philip A. Carey and the Labor Movement," remarks at the Testimonial Dinner Honoring Father Philip A. Carey, S.J., Roosevelt Hotel, N.Y.C., November 15, 1977; interviews with Philip Dobson, Aug. 2, 1978; Joseph Fitzpatrick, Aug. 1, 1978; and Philip Carey, Oct. 13, 1977.

29. Interview with Joseph Fitzpatrick, Aug. 1, 1979; *LL*, Jan. 10, 1938, p. 2; Richard J. Ward, "The Role of the Association of Catholic Trade Unionists in the Labor Movement," *Review of Social Economy*, 14, no. 2 (Sept. 1956), p. 2; Carey, "History of Xavier"; Philip E. Dobson, "The Xavier Labor School, 1938–1939" [clipping of unidentified article in "History of Labor School" file, XA], 266–75.

30. Like many others, Dobson overestimated the percentage of TWU members who were Irish Catholic, mistakenly believing that they constituted about 75% of the union. Dobson, "Xavier Labor School," 268–70; Philip Dobson to Philip Carey, July 8, 1941, "41–42" file, XA.

31. Philip Dobson to Philip Carey, July 8, 1941, "41–42" file; and "Lists of former students, 1937–43," XA; interview with Philip Dobson, Aug. 2, 1978. Harmon, who had been born in Gastonia, North Carolina, and had worked in the New York transit industry since 1922, was not a Catholic, although his wife and children were. Nor was he still a TWU member, since the BLE had a closed-shop contract covering the BMT motormen. However,

he was deeply devoted to rooting out Communism from the labor movement, doing extensive research on CP activities, some of which he eventually gave or sold to sympathetic journalists. See Dobson to Carey, Nov. 23, 1940, "42–43" file, and various correspondence in "41–42" files, XA; interview with Philip Carey, Oct. 13, 1977; *Dies Committee*, vol. 2, pp. 1049–50.

32. TWU members probably constituted about half the students in Xavier's labor-oriented classes. Philip Dobson to Philip Carey, July 8, 1941, "41–42" file; unidentified newspaper clipping in "40–41" file; and "Lists of former students, 1937–43," XA; Dobson, "Xavier Labor School," p. 270; Xavier leaflets from 1938, JBF.

33. Dobson, "Xavier Labor School," 270–71.

34. "Rank and File Bulletin," Nov. 9, 1938, JBF.

35. Philip Dobson to Philip Carey, July 8, 1941, "41–42" file, XA; *TWU 1939 Convention*, 76.

36. Student list labeled "1938–1939" in "Lists of former students, 1937–43," XA.

37. Gary T. Marx, *The Social Basis of the Support of a Depression Era Extremist: Father Coughlin*, Monograph 7, Survey Research Center, University of California (Berkeley, 1962), 11, 13–16, 23–24, 55–56, 123; Sheldon Marcus, *Father Coughlin: The Tumultuous Life of the Priest of the Little Flower* (Boston, 1973), 182; Charles J. Tull, *Father Coughlin and the New Deal* (Syracuse, 1965), 227.

38. G. Marx, pp. 76, 79–80, 83, 93; Tull, pp. 171, 174, 177–180, 186–87; Neil Betten, *Catholic Activism and the Industrial Worker* (Gainesville, Fla., 1976), 104, 176fn; interviews with Joseph Fitzpatrick, Aug. 1, 1978; Philip Dobson, Aug. 2, 1978; John Plover, Feb. 20, 1979; John Gallagher, Apr. 20, 1979; and Maurice Forge, Jan. 13, 1979; *TWU 1939 Convention*, 189; "An Appeal to the President of the Transport Workers Union of N.Y.C." [Jan. 1938], in "M. J. Quill TWU-Organization 1934–38," TWU-T.

39. Interviews with Joseph Fitzpatrick, Aug. 1, 1978; Philip Dobson, Aug. 2, 1978; Federal Communications Commission to Joseph P. Fitzpatrick, Dec. 13, 1938, in "Letters: Oct. 1935 to June 1939 (to P.E. Dobson, S.J.)," XA; *TWU 1937 Convention*, Oct. 7 afternoon session, p. 49; *TWU 1939 Convention*, 71.

40. Dobson, "Xavier Labor School," 271; John Manning to Philip Dobson, Jan. 24, 1939; Dobson to Manning, Feb. 2, 1939; Dobson to Michael J. Bowler, Feb. 2, 1939; and Dobson to Michael J. Considine, Mar. 3, 1939, all in "Letters, Oct. 1938–June 1939 (to P.E. Dobson, S.J.)," XA; interviews with Philip Dobson, Aug. 2, 1978; Joseph Fitzpatrick, Aug. 1, 1978; TWU, *Constitution* (1937), 23. There is a hint that TWU leaders may not have been totally off the mark when they charged that Xavier was receiving money from pro-company forces in a letter from Fitzpatrick to Dobson dated Sept. 19, 1939, in "Letters-Term 1939–1940," XA.

41. Dobson, "Xavier Labor School," 271. See also New York Report, Dec. 12, 1945 (#100-7319-319), 7, FBI-FOIA, which apparently alludes to the same case.

42. Charles Garrett, *The La Guardia Years* (New Brunswick, N.J., 1961), 215–16, *NYT*, Sept. 7, 1938, p. 8; Dec. 3, 1938, pp. 1, 3; Dec. 4, 1938, pp. 1, 59.

43. *TWB*, Nov. 1936, p. 6; interview with Maurice Forge, Jan. 13, 1979.

44. *NYT*, Sept. 7, 1938, p. 8; Nov. 20, 1938, p. 4; Dec. 4, 1938, p. 59; *TWB*, Sept. 1938, p. 6; Dec. 1938, pp. 1, 2; Jan. 1939, p. 3.

45. *NYT*, Dec. 3, 1938, p. 3.

46. *TWB*, Dec. 1938, pp. 1, 2; Jan. 1939, p. 3; *NYT*, Dec. 5, 1938, pp. 1, 2; Dec. 8, 1938, p. 29; Dec. 9, 1938, pp. 1, 36; Dec. 13, 1938, p. 36.

47. *NYT*, Dec. 4, 1938, p. 59, Feb. 4, 1939, p. 2; "Transport Workers Protest," unidentified wire service clipping [Jan. 1939], JBF.

48. Gilbert Weisberger, John Donovan, and Thomas Gallagher, "Give Us Back Our

Seniority: An Appeal to the Seventh Biennial Convention of the Transport Workers Union of America" (New York, 1950); "Transport Workers Protest"; *TWU 1939 Convention*, 237–38. The TWU had separate working agreements with each of the three IRT divisions. See Board of Transportation, *Proceedings*, 36 (1940), pp. 14–74.

49. Ronald William Schatz, "American Electrical Workers: Work, Struggle, Aspirations, 1930–1950" (Ph.D. dissertation, University of Pittsburgh, 1977), 165; *TWU 1939 Convention*, 126–27, 191, 236–38.

50. *DW*, Feb. 5, 1939, p. 5; *TWB*, Apr. 1939, p. 2; *NYT*, Feb. 4, 1939, p. 2; "Transport Workers Protest"; Rank and File Committee, "Truth to Your Eyes" [1939], in "Anti-Union" folder, Santo Files, TWU-T.

51. *NYT*, Feb. 4, 1939, p. 2; Feb. 7, 1939, p. 21; "Transport Workers Protest" (includes quote).

52. Rank and File of the I.R.T. Co., "Save Your Seniority," JBF; "Transport Workers Protest"; Philip Dobson to Philip Carey, July 8, 1941, in "41–42" file, XA.

53. *NYT*, Feb. 4, 1939, p. 2; Feb. 7, 1939, p. 21; Feb. 8, 1939, pp. 1, 9; June 2, 1939, p. 9; *DW*, Feb. 8, 1939, pp. 1, 4; Feb. 9, 1939, pp. 1, 4; June 2, 1939, p. 4; *TWB*, Apr. 1939, p. 2; *TWU 1939 Convention*, 76.

54. *NYT*, Feb. 8, 1939, pp. 1, 9; Feb. 10, 1939, p. 19; *DW*, Feb. 8, 1939, pp. 1, 4.

55. *DW*, Feb. 9, 1939, pp. 1, 4; Feb. 10, 1939, p. 4; *TWB*, Apr. 1939, p. 2. During this period anti-Semitism among transit workers, especially those who followed Coughlin, was far from unknown. However, with relatively few Jews in the work force or union positions and virtually none in management, it mostly took the form of grumbling about Jewish bankers, lawyers, and the like. See Betten, p. 176fn; interviews with Maurice Forge, July 15, 1980; Lewis Fraad, June 30, 1980.

56. *DW*, June 2, 1939, p. 4; *TWB*, June 1939, p. 1; *NYT*, June 2, 1939, p. 9.

57. Interview with Maurice Forge, Jan. 13, 1979. See also Philip Dobson to Philip Carey, July 8, 1941, "41–42" file, XA.

58. See, for example, *TWB*, May 1939, p. 7; Oct. 1939, p. 15; *LL*, Sept. 18, 1939, p. 2; *NYWTB*, Oct. 5, 1940. p. 1; interview with Maurice Forge, Jan. 13, 1979.

59. *TWB*, July 1939, pp. 1–3; Nov. 1939, p. 1; Dec. 1939, pp. 1, 3, 5; *NYT*, Dec. 8, 1939, p. 12; Dec. 10, 1939, p. 34; Dec. 13, 1939, p. 22; *NYWTB*, July 30, 1940, p. 1; Nov. 2, 1940, p. 1. Most of the men laid off as a result of the 6th Avenue el demolition were eventually rehired. However, as of 1940 TWU efforts to restore transferred 6th Avenue workers to their former pay rates had not succeeded.

60. Anticipating the motorization of the BMT trolleys, the TWU also initiated a consolidation of the BMT surface seniority lists. However, the union moved very slowly; not until 1946 was there one system-wide list. *DW*, Aug. 22, 1939, p. 5; *TWB*, Sept. 1939, p. 3; May 1940, p. 1; Nov.–Dec. 1946, p. 11; *NYWTB*, May 15, 1940, p. 1; Mar. 22, 1941, pp. 1–5. The most important test of the TWU's ability to protect its members' jobs came with unification. See Chapters 8 and 9.

61. "Xavier Labor School," 274; Philip Dobson to Michael J. Considine, Mar. 9, 1939, and Patrick J. O'Shea to Dobson, May 1, 1939, "Letters, Oct. 1938–June 1939 (to P.E. Dobson, S.J.)," and Dobson to Philip J. Carey, July 8, 1941, "41–42," XA; interviews with Dobson, Aug. 2, 1978; Joseph Fitzpatrick, Aug. 1, 1978; *TWB*, Apr. 1939, p. 2; *DW*, June 1, 1939, p. 4; *TWU 1939 Convention*, 76.

62. Marcus, pp. 145, 155–58; Tull p. 193; Alfred McClung Lee and Elizabeth Briat Lee, eds., *The Fine Art of Propaganda: A Study of Father Coughlin's Speeches* (New York, 1939), 81–91; James Wechsler, "The Coughlin Terror," *The Nation*, July 22, 1939; Harold Lavine, *Fifth Column in America* (New York, 1940), 88; "Confidential Report on Outdoor Anti-

Semitic Meetings Submitted by the Anti-Defamation League," and Mayor's Press Release of Feb. 5, 1940, both in "Christian Front-Against, 1939–40" folder, box 728, LaGP.

63. "Christian Front-Against, 1939–40" folder, box 728, and boxes 794 and 795, LaGP; Lavine, pp. 88, 90–92; Marcus, pp. 157–58.

64. G. Marx, p. 123; Alden V. Brown, *The Tablet: The First Seventy-five Years* (New York, 1983), 36; Marcus, pp. 173–74; Wechsler, "Coughlin Terror"; Lavine, pp. 84–85, 92–94; and folders 26 and 28, box 794, LaGP.

65. The relevant police reports are in boxes 794 and 795, LaGP.

66. "[Police] Memo: May 8th, 1939," "Christian Front Meetings, 1939–1940," box 794, LaPG; *Let the Record Speak! The Truth About Michael J. Quill's Betrayal of Transit Workers in the T.W.U.* (New York, 1948), 21–22.

67. *TWB*, July 1939, p. 16; "[Police] Memo: Saturday, June 17th, 1939," and Report by Detective Mario J. Fochi, Alien Squad, June 17th, 1939, both in "Christian Front Meetings, 1939–1940," box 794, LaPG; Wechsler, "Coughlin Terror."

68. Lavine, p. 29; Wechsler, "Coughlin Terror"; Betten, p. 104.

69. Collection of anti-TWU leaflets, JBF.

70. Police memos on Christian Mobilizer meetings, dated Sept. 11, 12, 18, and 30, 1939, file 28, box 794, LaPG.

71. Patrick J. O'Shea to Philip J. Dobson, May 1, 1939, "Letters, Oct. 1938–June 1939 (to P.E. Dobson, S.J.)", and William Harmon to Joseph Fitzpatrick, Sept. 6, 1939, "Letters-Term 1939–1940," XA; *TWU 1939 Convention*, 189; interview with Maurice Forge, Jan. 13, 1979; undated *NYT* clipping in "Christian Front-Against 1939–40" folder, box 728, LaPG.

72. *LL*, Jan. 3, 1938, p. 2; Jan. 17, 1938, p. 2; July 2, 1938, p. 2; July 18, 1938, p. 4; Aug. 8, 1938, p. 2 (includes quotes).

73. Douglas P. Seaton, *Catholics and Radicals: The Association of Catholic Trade Unionists and the American Labor Movement, from Depression to Cold War* (Lewisburg, Penn., 1981), 75–99; *LL*, Sept. 18, 1939, pp. 1, 2.

74. *LL*, Sept. 18, 1939, p. 1, 4; Sept. 9, 1940, pp. 1, 3; *TWB*, Oct. 1939, p. 15; Seaton, p. 143–44; interview with Philip Dobson, Aug. 2, 1978.

75. There were sharp differences in political practice as well as ideology between ACTU and Xavier. ACTU sought a mass membership, admitted some non-Catholic associates and launched open, well-publicized campaigns. Xavier concentrated on developing a small cadre of politically and spiritually well-trained Catholics, who could operate behind the scenes. At one point Xavier leaders even bandied about the idea of infiltrating and taking over New York ACTU. William Harmon to Joseph Fitzpatrick, Sept. 6, 1939; Fitzpatrick to Harmon, Sept. 7, 1939; Fitzpatrick to Philip Dobson, Sept. 19, 1939, in "Letters-Term 1939–1940," and Fitzpatrick to Philip Carey, July 10, 1941, and Dobson to Carey, July 8, 1941, in "41–42" file, XA; interviews with Fitzpatrick, Aug. 1, 1978; Dobson, Aug. 2, 1978; and Carey, Oct. 13, 1977; *TWU 1939 Convention*, 20–21, 70, 76, 78, 137–38, 202; David J. O'Brien, *American Catholics and Social Reform: The New Deal Years* (New York, 1968), 206; Leo Huberman, *The Great Bus Strike* (New York, 1941), 110; John C. Cort to author, Sept. 8, 1980; and Seaton, pp. 56, 63–64, 154. Seaton (p. 162), like Betten (p. 140), erroneously identifies Xavier as an ACTU-affiliate.

76. *TWU 1939 Convention*, 6–9, 64–65, 69–75, 78, 114, 137–38, 200–202, 241.

77. Betten, pp. 77–83; *LL*, Mar. 14, 1938, p. 3.

78. *TWU 1939 Convention*, 81–86.

79. Charles Owen Rice to the author, July 24 and Aug. 2, 1979 (includes quotes); Samuel Estreicher, "Collective Bargaining in the New York City Transit System, 1937–1950: A Case Study in the Politics of Municipal Unionism," M.S. thesis, Cornell University, 1974, pp.

179, 181; Michael J. Quill to Charles Owen Rice, Dec. 21, 1938, Jan. 12, 1939, and March 3, 1939, and Rice to Quill, March 10, 1939, Charles O. Rice Papers, Pennsylvania State University; interview with James Sullivan, Aug. 16, 1979.

80. *TWU 1939 Convention*, passim, but esp. pp. 64–81, 111–16, 122–23, 167–73, 180, 183, 200–206, and 239–57.

81. Interview with John Gallagher, Apr. 20, 1979; Maurice Forge, Jan. 13, 1979; *LL*, Oct. 16, 1939, p. 1. For an account of a similar section rebuff of the top leadership, see *LL*, Nov. 13, 1939, p. 4.

82. *LL*, Oct, 16, 1939, p. 1; Nov. 13, 1939, pp. 1, 4; Nov. 27, 1939, p. 2; Nov. 29, 1947, p. 1; James Flatley, "To All Omnibus Brothers"; All-Union Campaign Committee, "The Rank & File Speaks"; T.W. Eldridge, et al., "To IRT Transportation Members"; and Michael Lyons, "A Message to the Members of 98 St. Shop Section No. 11," all JBF; Minutes of ACTU meetings of Nov. 10, 17, 20, and 26, 1939, "Anti-Union" folder, Santo File, TWU-T; New York Report, Dec. 12, 1945 (#100-7319-319), p. 4, FBI-FOIA.

83. *TWB*, Dec. 1939, pp. 1, 7; "Comparative Figures—N.Y. Local Elections—1937 and 1939," in "Local Elections, 1939" folder, and "Minutes of Meeting of A.C.T.U., Dec. 6, 1939," in "Anti-Union" folder, both in Santo File, TWU-T; interviews with John Gallagher, Apr. 20, 1979; James Sullivan, July 27, 1979.

84. *TWB*, May 1934, p. 6; Charles Lionel Franklin, *The Negro Unionist of New York* (1936; reprinted, New York, 1968), 336–37. The IAM convention debate took place in executive session and was not reported in the convention minutes. Nor did Quill or Santo mention it in their report on the convention in the TWU newspaper. However, see Matles and Higgins, pp. 46–45; John [Santo] and [Michael J.] Quill to Austin [Hogan] and [Maurice] Forge, Sept. 27, 1936, JBF.

85. *TWB*, Apr.–May, 1935, p. 5; July 1937, p. 11; Dec. 1937, pp. 3, 11; Jan. 1938, p. 5; Apr. 1939, p. 11; Dec. 1939, p. 7; August Meier and Elliot Rudwick, "Communist Unions and the Black Community: The Case of the Transport Workers Union, 1934–1944," *Labor History* 23 (Spring 1982), 169.

86. Meier and Rudwick, pp. 168–69; "Memorandum for Ben Davis, Jr." [March 1938], Michael J. Quill alphabetical file, TWU-T; *TWB*, Nov. 1934, p. 5; Mar. 1938, p. 7; May 1938, p. 16; July 1939, p. 13; Nov. 1939, p. 21; *NYWTB*, Nov. 23, 1940, p. 3; *TWU 1937 Convention*, Oct. 7 afternoon session, pp. 28–30, 61–62; *TWU 1939 Convention*, 131–32.

87. *TWB*, Sept. 1934, p. 8.

88. *TWB*, Nov. 1934, p. 5; Oct. 1, 1935, p. 4; Apr. 1937, p. 1; Mark Naison, "Harlem Communists & The Politics of Black Protest," *Marxist Perspectives* 3 (Fall 1978), p. 36; Meier and Rudwick, pp. 168–75.

89. James J. McGinley, *Labor Relations in the New York Rapid Transit Systems, 1904–1944* (New York, 1949), pp. 235–55; *DW*, May 10, 1935, p. 5; Milton Nixon to Fiorello La Guardia, Jan. 22, 1934, and Mayor's Secretary to La Guardia, Apr. 26, 1934, in "Transportation, Bd. of" file, box 644, LaPG; Meier and Rudwick, p. 168; *TWB*, Mar. 1940, p. 7; June 1940, p. 4; James J. Comerford, "Adjustment of Labor Unions to Civil Service Status: The Transportation Workers Union and the New York City Government" (M.A. thesis, Columbia University, 1941), 47–48, 98–99; Estreicher, pp. 195–97.

90. Meier and Rudwick, 169–71; Gustav Faber, *And Then Came TWU!* (New York, 1950), 43–44.

91. Mark Naison, *Communists in Harlem During the Depression* (Urbana, 1983), 262–67 (Powell quote on p. 266); Report on AAAC Meeting of July 26 [1938], in "M.J. Quill TWU—Organization 1934–1938 Correspondence" file, TWU-T; New York Report, Sept. 10, 1943 (#100-7319-212), FBI-FOIA, p. 4.

92. Meier and Rudwick, pp. 172–73; Estreicher, pp. 199–200; Report on AAAC Meeting

of July 26 [1938]; interviews with Patrick J. Reilly, Sept. 7, 1978; James Sullivan, Aug. 16, 1979; John Nolan, June 1, 1979.

93. McGinley, p. 253; Estreicher, p. 200; Meier and Rudwick, p. 175.

94. Interviews with Maurice Forge, Feb. 10, 1979; Gerald O-Reilly, May 15, 1978; Meier and Rudwick, pp. 175–81; Herbert R. Northrup, Howard W. Rusher, Jr., Richard D. Leone, and Philip W. Jeffress, *Negro Employment in Land and Air Transport* (Philadelphia, 1971), 26–27.

95. Interview with Maurice Forge, Feb. 10, 1979.

96. Interviews with Maurice Forge, Feb. 10, 1979, Nov. 29, 1983; Carl Mann, Apr. 5, 1984; Report on AAAC Meeting of July 26 [1938]; black employment figures calculated from *The Complete Record of Mayor La Guardia's Commission on the Harlem Riot of March 19, 1935* (New York, 1962), 32, and Northrup, et al., pp. 26–27.

97. LL, Apr. 11, 1938, p. 3; Apr. 30, 1938, p. 1; Aug. 8, 1938, pp. 1, 2, 4; Report on AAAC Meeting of July 26 [1938]; interview with Carl Mann, Apr. 5, 1984; *TWB*, Sept. 1938, p. 7.

98. Interviews with Maurice Forge, Feb. 10, 1979; John Nolan, June 1, 1978; Abner Berry, Dec. 5, 1978; Naison, *Communists in Harlem*, 318fn.

99. "Memorandum for Ben Davis, Jr. [March 1938], M. J. Quill alphabetical file, TWU-T.

100. Interview with Maurice Forge, Nov. 29, 1983; Estreicher, p. 196; New York Report, Sept. 10, 1943 (#100-7319-212), FBI-FOIA, p. 3.

101. All-Union Campaign Committee, "The Record and Your Future," JBF; TWU, "Welcome" (New York, 1941); *TWB*, Oct. 1937, pp. 5, 12; interview with Maurice Forge, Aug. 9, 1979.

102. The dispute over reducing hours, for example, was not part of the union's factional struggles. In fact, at the 1941 TWU convention both Flatley and Gallagher praised the leadership's negotiating record. See *TWU 1941 Convention*, 80–84.

103. Interviews with Philip Carey, Oct. 13, 1977; Jerry O'Brien, Sept. 12, 1979; Maurice Forge, Dec. 30, 1978. As Nathan Glazer and Daniel Patrick Moynihan pointed out in *Beyond the Melting Pot: The Negroes, Puerto Ricans, Jews, Italians, and Irish of New York City*, 2nd ed. (Cambridge, Mass., 1970), Irish political culture in the United States was characterized by "an indifference to Yankee proprieties. To the Irish, stealing an election was rascally, not to be approved, but neither quite to be abhorred" (p. 224).

104. Interviews with Maurice Forge, Aug. 9, 1979; Leon Strauss, Oct. 26, 1978.

105. The unedited versions of Quill's remarks appear in the typed transcript of the 1937 Convention, pp. 647 and 650 respectively; the edited versions in *TWU 1937 Convention*, Oct. 8 session, pp. 16–17.

106. NYT, Mar. 13, 1938, p. 35; *New York World-Telegram*, June 16, 1941; Detective Stanley Gwozdo, "Committee for the Defense of Public Education Meeting, December 18th, 1940," in "Coughlin Against, 1940, La Guardia," box 794, LaPG; Chicago Report, Oct. 28, 1942 (#100-7319-115), pp. 11–12, FBI-FOIA.

107. See, for example, *TWB*, Jan. 1939, p. 6; Feb. 1939, p. 6; Apr. 1939, p. 12; July 1939, p. 6; July 1940, p. 12; DW, Aug. 11, 1939, p. 3.

108. Interview with Maurice Forge, Aug. 9, 1979; *TWB*, Dec. 1940, pp. 1, 3, 5, 12; NYWTB, Nov. 2, 1940, p. 1; Nov. 23, 1940, pp. 2, 4. The 1939 switch of line did cause the TWU enormous *external* problems. On this, see Chapter 9.

109. *TWU 1941 Convention*, 64–67, 79–136. According to an FBI source of unknown reliability, Quill himself only reluctantly agreed to support Roosevelt's foreign policy—especially aid to Britain—under pressure from both Phil Murray and the CP. Quill certainly moved cautiously; he did not openly back the CP's new line until three months after the

invasion of the Soviet Union. See "Transport Workers Union Convention, New York City," Sept. 26, 1941 (#100-7319-25), FBI-FOIA.

110. As a result of his expulsion Reilly lost his job, but after prolonged court proceedings he won reinstatement and back pay from the union. William E. Leuchtenburg, *Franklin Roosevelt and the New Deal, 1932–1940* (New York, 1963), 223–24; interviews with Gerald O'Reilly, May 15, 1978 and Jan. 11, 1979; Lewis Fraad, June 30, 1980; Philip Carey, Oct. 13, 1977; *DW*, June 4, 1938, p. 2; June 27, 1938, p. 2; *LL*, Sept. 9, 1940, pp. 1, 3; Sept. 23, 1940, p. 1; Jan. 31, 1942, pp. 1, 3; June 30, 1942, p. 1; Dec. 16, 1942, pp. 1, 4.

111. Interviews with Gerald O'Reilly, July 11, 1979; Patrick Walsh, June 1, 1978; and James Sullivan, Aug. 16, 1979; telephone interview with Sean Cronin, Apr. 9, 1979; N.Y.C. Police Department report on Austin Hogan, in folder 485, box 2591, LaPG; *New York World-Telegram*, June 13, 1941; "Transport Workers Union Convention, New York City," Sept. 26, 1941 (#100-7319-25), FBI-FOIA; *TWU 1941 Convention*, 9–10.

112. Interviews with John Plover, Feb. 20, 1979; Philip Bray, Aug. 13, 1979; Patrick Walsh, June 1, 1978; and John Nolan, June 1, 1978; *Dies Committee*, vol. 13, pp. 7879–7952, 8093–8111 (Quill quote on p. 8104).

113. Estreicher, pp. 190–91.

114. Interviews with John Plover, Feb. 20, 1979; Maurice Forge, Feb. 25, 1979; Joseph Labash, Aug. 3, 1979; and Peter MacLachlan, Feb. 25, 1979.

115. Interview with Maurice Forge, Jan. 13, 1979.

116. Dobson, "Xavier Labor School," pp. 271–71; Philip Dobson to Philip Carey, July 8, 1941, "41–42" file, XA.

117. Interview with Peter MacLachlan, Feb. 25, 1979.

118. Interviews with John Plover, Feb. 20, 1979; John Gallagher, Apr. 20, 1979.

119. See, for example, Philip Dobson to Philip Carey, July 8, 1941, and Joseph Fitzpatrick to Carey, Aug. 10, 1941, "41–42" file, XA.

120. Interview with Maurice Forge, Jan. 7, 1979; Huberman, pp. 78, 97.

121. Union leaders, for example, made continual attempts to get more members to attend section meetings, including by imposing fines on those absent. See *TWB*, Oct. 1937, p. 7; July 1938, p. 5; *TWU 1937 Convention*, Oct. 6 morning session, pp. 27–31.

122. Interview with John Gallagher, Apr. 20, 1979.

Chapter 8

1. U.S. Works Progress Administration, *New York Panorama: The American Guide Series* (New York, 1938), 350; James J. Comerford, "Adjustment of Labor Unions to Civil Service Status: The Transportation Workers Union and the New York City Government" (M.A. thesis, Columbia University, 1941), 35; James J. McGinley, *Labor Relations in the New York Rapid Transit Systems, 1904–1944* (New York, 1949), 81–91, 104–5, 442; *NYT*, Dec. 12, 1936, p. 11; Samuel Estreicher, "Collective Bargaining in the New York City Transit System, 1937–1950: A Case Study in the Politics of Municipal Unionism" (M.S. thesis, Cornell University, 1974), 32; CCOHP, drawer 4, tapes 4 and 5, Mar. 26, 1974 (interview with a former ISS worker who was a Civil Service Forum and TWU leader).

2. Comerford, pp. 37–38, 43; interviews with Phil Bray, Aug. 13, 1979; Maurice Forge, Jan. 27, 1979; *TWU 1937 Convention*, Oct. 8 morning session, p. 19; McGinley, p. 268; John H. Delaney to Fiorello H. LaGuardia, Feb. 28, 1935, and LaGuardia to Harry Van Arsdale, Jr., Mar. 18, 1935, in "Transportation, 1934–1939," box 2642, and CIRB-IRT Conference, pp. 51–52, box 677, LaGP; *NYWTB*, Mar. 1, 1941, p. 2.

3. Estreicher, pp. 32–33, 64; John H. Delaney to Fiorello H. LaGuardia, Mar. 12, 1934, Thomas Rogers to Delaney, Mar. 13, 1937, in "Transportation, 1934–1939," box

2642, and Milton Nixon to La Guardia, Jan. 22, 1934, in "Transportation, Bd. of," box 644, LaGP; McGinley, pp. 276–78; *TWU 1941 Convention*, 59.

4. Wallace S. Sayre and Herbert Kaufman, *Governing New York City: Politics in the Metropolis* (New York, 1960), 408, 416, 432–35; Ralph T. Jones, "City Employee Unions: Labor and Politics in New York and Chicago," unpublished manuscript, 1975, pp. 83–88, 152–153; Charles Garrett, *The La Guardia Years* (New Brunswick, N.J., 1961), 105.

5. McGinley, pp. 278–85; *TWB*, Nov. 1934, p. 1; June 1, 1936, p. 8; *NYT*, Aug. 23, 1936, II:1, 5; Comerford, pp. 36, 59; interview with Maurice Forge, Jan. 27, 1979.

6. *TWB*, Apr. 1934, p. 1; July 1934, p. 4; Aug. 1934, p. 4; Sept. 1934, p. 4; Nov. 1934, pp. 1, 6; Apr.–May 1935, p. 2; *DW*, June 22, 1934, p. 4; May 10, 1935, p. 4; May 17, 1935, p. 5; May 24, 1935, p. 4; interviews with Patrick J. Reilly, Sept. 7, 1978; Phil Bray, Aug. 13, 1979; *TWU 1937 Convention*, Oct. 8 morning session, p. 19; Estricher, pp. 64–66; Comerford, pp. 94–95; *TE*, Apr. 1953, p. 6A; Peter F. Freund, "Labor Relations in the New York City Transit Industry, 1945–1960" (Ph.D. dissertation, New York University, 1964), 50.

7. *DW*, May 10, 1935, p. 4; *TWU 1937 Convention*, Oct. 8 morning session, p. 19; *TWU 1941 Convention*, p. 59; Estreicher, pp. 63–65; Comerford, pp. 48, 94; *TWB*, Oct. 1937, p. 11; Joe Flaherty, *Tin Wife* (New York, 1983), 61; McGinley, p. 125.

8. *TWB*, Aug. 1934, p. 4; Sept. 1934, p. 4; Mar. 1935, pp. 2–3; *DW*, May 24, 1935, p. 4.

9. *DW*, May 10, 1935, p. 4; *TWB*, Aug. 1934, p. 3; McGinley, pp. 104–5, 231; Estreicher, pp. 64–65; *TWU 1941 Convention*, 59.

10. *NYT*, Dec. 12, 1936, p. 11.

11. *TWB*, Nov. 1934, p. 1; Mar. 1935, p. 8; Apr.–May 1935, p. 2; May–June 1935, p. 2; *DW*, May 17, 1935, p. 4; May 24, 1935, p. 4; CCOHP, drawer 4, tapes 4 and 5; "An Appeal for Support for Bob Franklin" [1949], JBF; James C. Goulding, *Meany* (New York, 1972), 47; McGinley, pp. 234–36.

12. CCOHP, drawer 4, tapes 4 and 5; *TWB*, Jan. 1936, p. 1.

13. *New York Post*, July 7, 1937, p. 11; *NYT*, Oct. 17, 1937, II:7; interview with Maurice Forge, Jan. 7, 1979; McGinley, pp. 280–83. Jon Bloom kindly provided me with information about English's stay at Brookwood.

14. *TWB*, Jan. 1936, p. 1; Apr. 1, 1936, p. 1; May 1, 1936, p. 2; June 1, 1936, p. 1; July 1, 1936, p. 4; *NYT*, Apr. 1, 1936, p. 4; Apr. 2, 1936, p. 10.

15. Civil service rules allowed an agency making a promotion to choose any one of the top three candidates on the relevant civil service list. *TWB*, July 1, 1936, p. 8; Arthur W. MacMahon, "The New York Transit System: Public Ownership, Civil Service, and Collective Bargaining," *Political Science Quarterly* 56, no. 2 (June 1941): 180; Comerford, pp. 36–37; John H. Delaney to Fiorello H. La Guardia, Dec. 19, 1936; La Guardia to Paul J. Kern, Dec. 23, 1936; and Kern to La Guardia, Dec. 28, 1936, in "Transportation, 1934–1939," box 2642, LaGP.

16. Estreicher, pp. 32, 66–67; John H. Delaney to Fiorello H. La Guardia, Mar. 12, 1934, "Transportation, 1934–1939," box 2642, LaGP; Comerford, pp. 44–45; *NYT*, Aug. 23, 1936, II:1, 5; *TWB*, July 1938, p. 14.

17. A. MacMahon, pp. 170–71; *NYT*, June 26, 1936, p. 2; Jan. 14, 1937, p. 15; Allan Nevins, *Herbert H. Lehman and His Era* (New York, 1963), 98; "Jerry" Daly, "Delaney, 'The Subway Builder'," *Little Old New York*, Feb. 1930; interview with Warren Moscow, Jan. 8, 1987; Fiorello H. La Guardia to Paul J. Kern, Dec. 23, 1936, "Transportation, 1934–1939," box 2642, LaGP; Garrett, pp. 212–13, 216.

18. A. MacMahon, p. 171; *NYT*, Aug. 23, 1936, II:1, 5; *DW*, May 17, 1935, p. 4; *NYWTB*, Oct. 12, 1940, p. 2; Goulding, pp. 41–42.

19. NYT, Aug. 23, 1936, II:1, 5, 8; Aug. 27, 1936, p. 13; Estreicher, pp. 44–45; Goulding, p. 50; William Green to Fiorello H. La Guardia, Feb. 28, 1935, and La Guardia to Harry Van Arsdale, Jr., Mar. 18, 1935, "Transportation, 1934–1939," box 2642, LaGP.

20. TWB, May 1, 1936, p. 6; Oct. 1937, p. 11; "An Appeal for Support for Bob Franklin"; TE, Apr. 1954, p. 9A; CCOHP, drawer 4, tapes 4 and 5; interview with Maurice Forge, Jan. 27, 1979.

21. TWB, June 1, 1936, p. 8; July 1, 1936, p. 8; Aug. 1936, p. 5; Dec. 1936, p. 1; TWU, "Minutes of Regular Meeting of the Executive Board Held on Monday, June 1, 1936," TWU of A; McGinley, pp. 280–83.

22. TWB, Aug. 1936, p. 2; Oct. 1936, p. 5; Dec. 1936, p. 1; Jan 1937, p. 1; Apr. 1938, p. 16; NYT, Aug. 21, 1936, p. 5; TE, Apr. 1954, p. 6A; McGinley, pp. 281–83.

23. TWB, June 1937, p. 5; Oct. 1937, pp. 8, 11; TWU 1937 Convention, Oct. 5 afternoon session, p. 1e; NYT, June 14, 1937, p. 4; CCOHP, drawer 4, tapes 4 and 5.

24. Among the unions that grew out of Forum councils are Teamsters Local 237, the Uniformed Sanitationmen's Association, and the Civil Service Technical Guild (AFSCME Local 375). What remains of the Forum is now Local 300 of the Service Employees International Union. Jewel Bellush and Bernard Bellush, Union Power and New York: Victor Gotbaum and District Council 37 (New York, 1984), 7, 20; The Guild Newsletter [Civil Service Technical Guild], Nov.–Dec. 1986, p. 5; Jones, pp. 152–53, 158–59, 212; The Chief-Leader, Nov. 28, 1986, p. 8; A. Lawrence Chickering, ed., Public Employee Unions: A Study of the Crisis in Public Sector Labor Relations (San Francisco, 1976), 174–76; Foster Rhea Dulles and Melvyn Dubofsky, Labor in America: A History, Fourth Edition (Arlington, Heights, Ill., 1984), 389–91.

25. NYT, Jan. 14, 1937, p. 15; Jan. 23, 1937, p. 6; TWB, Feb. 1937, pp. 1, 2; Estreicher, pp. 67–69; McGinley, pp. 296; Comerford, pp. 38–40.

26. TWU 1937 Convention, Oct. 8 afternoon session, p. 2; TWB, Feb. 1937, pp. 1, 2; NYT, Feb. 1, 1937, p. 2; U.S. Department of Justice, Immigration and Naturalization Service, "In the Matter of Charges against DESIDERIU HAMMER, alias JOHN SANTO" (typescript of 1947 hearings, hereafter Santo Deportation Hearings), p. 728; interview with James Sullivan, July 27, 1979.

27. TWB, Mar. 1937, p. 1; NYT, Feb. 15, 1937, p. 4; Feb. 16, 1937, p. 19; TWU 1937 Convention, Oct. 6 afternoon session, pp. 2–3; Comerford, p. 40.

28. Michael J. Quill to Fiorello H. La Guardia, Mar. 16, 1937, "Transportation, 1934–1939," box 2642, LaGP; Comerford, pp. 41–46; Estreicher, pp. 67–69; McGinley, pp. 296–98.

29. TWU 1937 Convention, Oct. 6 afternoon session, pp. 2–3; CCOHP, drawer 4, tapes 4 and 5; James C. Jefferson to Fiorello H. La Guardia, June 30, 1938, and Jefferson to Herbert H. Lehman, June 30, 1938, "City Industrial Relations Board: Civil Service Employees," box 676, LaGP; Comerford, pp. 48–50; TWB, Nov. 1939, p. 20.

30. Michael J. Quill to Fiorello H. La Guardia, Mar. 23, 1937; Quill, "Memorandum on Bill Int. 879 Print 913," "Transportation, 1934–1939," box 2642, LaGP.

31. A. F. Whitney to Fiorello H. La Guardia, Mar. 24, 1937; La Guardia to Whitney, Mar. 25, 1937; Whitney to La Guardia, Mar. 25, 1937; La Guardia to Whitney, Mar. 27, 1937; A. A. Berle, Jr., "MEMORANDUM to Mayor La Guardia re Union Organization of Independent Subways," Mar. 26, 1937, "Transportation, 1934–1939," box 2642, LaGP; Comerford, pp. 45–48; NYT, May 17, 1937, p. 13.

32. McGinley, pp. 276–78; Bernard G. Brophy to Rev. John P. Boland, "City Industrial Relations Board: Independent Subway" (hereafter CIRB:ISS), box 677, LaGP; TWB, Feb. 1946, p. 15.

33. *TWB*, Feb. 1937, p. 8; Mar. 1937, pp. 1, 3; Apr. 1937, pp. 1, 12; Oct. 1937, p. 11; *TWU 1937 Convention*, Oct. 6 morning session, p. 6; Comerford, pp. 53–54.

34. Comerford, pp. 59–60, 63, 95, 98–99; interview with Maurice Forge, Jan. 27, 1979; *TWU 1937 Convention*, Report of the Executive Board, p. 3; McGinley, pp. 281–83, 442.

35. Comerford, pp. 53–54; *NYT*, July 9, 1937, p. 1; July 15, 1937, p. 9; Sept. 6, 1937, p. 30.

36. *DW*, Nov. 5, 1934, p. 3; *TWB*, Oct. 1934, p. 2; July 1935, p. 8; Dec. 1, 1935, p. 4; June 1, 1936, p. 6; Oct. 1936, p. 6; TWU, "Minutes of Joint Executive Committee Meeting Held Monday, Sept. 15 [1936], JBF; Kenneth Waltzer, "The American Labor Party: Third Party Politics in New Deal-Cold War New York, 1936–1954" (Ph.D. dissertation, Harvard University, 1977), 81–82 (hereafter "ALP").

37. Kenneth Waltzer, "The Party and the Polling Place: American Communism and an American Labor Party in the 1930s," *Radical History Review* 23 (Spring 1980): 106–18; Waltzer, "ALP," pp. 73–94; Garrett, p. 259; interview with Simon Gerson, Dec. 18, 1979.

38. Interview with Maurice Forge, July 17, 1981; Waltzer, "ALP," pp. 103, 107–8, 112–14, 123–23, 138–39; Waltzer, "The Party and the Polling Place," 116–17; Garrett, pp. 259–60.

39. *TWB*, July 1937, p. 2; Waltzer, "The Party and the Polling Place," pp. 116–17, 127–28fn; interviews with Simon Gersen, Dec. 18, 1979, Maurice Forge, Jan. 7, 1979; *New York Post*, July 2, 1937.

40. There was also discussion of running MacMahon for a Brooklyn Council seat, but nothing came of it. "Meeting of the Administrative Committee of the American Labor Party, March 4, 1938," folder 52, Elinore M. Herrick Papers, Schlesinger Library, Radcliffe College; *TWB*, Aug. 1937, p. 2; interviews with Simon Gerson, Dec. 18, 1979, Maurice Forge, Jan. 13, 1979, and James Sullivan, July 27, 1979; Shirley Quill, *Mike Quill—Himself*, A *Memoir* (Greenwich, Conn., 1985), 99–100.

41. PR eliminated primaries, and nominating petitions required only 2,000 signatures. Garrett, pp. 80–90, 220–40.

42. Interview with Maurice Forge, Jan. 13, 1979; Waltzer, "ALP," pp. 99–100; Estreicher, pp. 103–4; L. H. Whittemore, *The Man Who Ran the Subways: The Story of Mike Quill* (New York, 1968), 54; Ronald H. Bayor, *Neighbors in Conflict: The Irish, Germans, Jews and Italians of New York City, 1929–1941* (Baltimore, 1978), 41, 130.

43. Like the SP, the CP withdrew its own candidate from the mayoralty race to aid La Guardia. Waltzer, "The Party and the Polling Place," p. 118; Waltzer, "ALP," p. 116; interview with Patrick Walsh, June 1, 1978; CCOHP, drawer 4, tapes 4 and 5; *TWU 1937 Convention*, Oct. 6 afternoon session, pp. 5–6, Oct. 8 afternoon session, p. 46; Goulding, p. 65; Garrett, pp. 263–64.

44. The TWU also may have delayed its appeal to the SLRB in hopes of first resolving the situation on the BMT, where it did not sign its first contract until October 11. *NYT*, July 15, 1937, p. 9; Sept. 6, 1937, p. 30; Jan. 21, 1938, p. 38; Estreicher, p. 56.

45. Interviews with Simon Gerson, Dec. 18, 1979; James Sullivan, Jan. 27 and Aug. 16, 1979; Maurice Forge, Jan. 13, 1979; Gerald O'Reilly, May 15, 1978; Joseph Labash, Aug. 3, 1979; Adrian Cabral, Apr. 12, 1979; Martin Young, Nov. 15, 1978; and Lewis Fraad, June 30, 1980; *TWB*, Sept, 1937, p. 2; Oct. 1937, p. 2; Nov. 1937, p. 1; July 1938, p. 14; Nov. 1938, p. 4; Oct. 1939, pp. 1, 10; Nov. 1941, pp. 4–5; Estreicher, pp. 101–2; Gerald O'Reilly to Vito Marcantonio, June 2, 1947, in "ALP Campaigns-Misc. Corresp., 1939–53," and "ALP Campaigns, 1942–45," box 25, Vito Marcantonio Papers, NYPL. The Committee of One Thousand was apparently named after an earlier anti-Tammany, pro-Fusion group. Garrett, pp. 82–84, 96.

46. A Tammany effort to win labor and Catholic votes by setting up separate "Anti-Communist Party" and "Trades Union Party" lines failed miserably. The Bronx ALP vote was so strong that the party's candidate for Borough President was nearly elected. Simon W. Gerson, *Pete: The Story of Peter V. Cacchione, New York's First Communist Councilman* (New York, 1976), 79, 84–85; Waltzer, "ALP," p. 117; Bayor, pp.47, 137; Whittemore, p. 62; Garrett, pp. 265–67; "Comparative Tabulation of Vote Cast in Column of American Labor Party for President, 1936 and for Mayor, 1937," folder 52, Elinore M. Herrick Papers; Charles Krumbein, "Lessons of the New York Elections, *"The Communist* 42, no. 1 (Jan. 1938): 30–32.

47. Quill met his future wife, Mary (Mollie) Theresa O'Neill, in New York; though Irish-born, she had come to the United States as a young woman. After losing her job Mollie returned to her family's farm in County Kerry, where she remained until her marriage. Quill's trip set the stage for the inauspicious start of his career as a Councilman. First, his ship back to New York was delayed, causing him to miss the opening session of the Council. This was not a trivial matter, since the body was evenly divided between Tammany-backers and a coalition of dissident Democrats, Republicans, ALPers, and City Fusionists. Quill's absence allowed the regular Democrats to win organizational control of the Council. Then the Democrats challenged Quill's election on the grounds that he was not a Bronx resident. After lengthy hearings a Council committee recommended against seating him. Only a deal with Tammany, one of whose supporters was in a similar situation, saved Quill's seat. Thereafter things went more smoothly. *TE*, Sept. 1959, p. 20; Shirley Quill, pp. 49, 72, 150–51; Whittemore, pp. 64–68; Garrett, p. 233; Newbold Morris, in collaboration with Dana Lee Thomas, *Let the Chips Fall: My Battles Against Corruption* (New York, 1955), 124; interview with Maurice Forge, Jan. 13, 1979.

48. *TWU 1937 Convention*, Oct. 6 afternoon session, pp. 3–4; *NYT*, 1937: Oct. 23, p. 10; Nov. 13, pp. 1, 3; Nov. 14, p. 41; Nov. 18, p. 13; Dec. 5, p. 39; Dec. 6, p. 16; Dec. 11, p. 8; 1938: Jan. 2, p. 2; Jan. 8, p. 2; Jan. 18, p. 4; Jan. 21, p. 3; Jan. 23, p. 20; *TWB*, Nov. 1937, p. 3; Dec. 1937, p. 7; Jan. 1938, p. 10; Bernard G. Brophy to John P. Boland, and attached memo from Fiorello H. LaGuardia, Nov. 22, 1937, "CIRB:ISS," box 677, LaGP.

49. A copy of the SLRB ruling on the first TWU petition, Case No. SE398, is in "CIRB:ISS," box 677, LaGP. See also *NYT*, Jan. 17, 1938, p. 4; Jan. 23, 1938, pp. 1, 20; Jan. 25, 1938, p. 2; Comerford pp. 62–63.

50. *NYT*, Jan. 17, 1938, p. 3; Jan. 23, 1938, p. 1; Feb. 26, 1938, p. 16; Comerford, p. 60; *DW*, Mar. 2, 1938, p. 4; *TWB*, Dec. 1937, p. 13; Mar. 1938, p. 3.

51. *NYT*, Jan. 17, 1938, p. 4; Feb. 2, 1938, p. 11; Feb. 7, 1938, p. 4; Mar. 2, 1938, p. 27; *DW*, Mar. 2, 1938, pp. 1, 4; "Meeting of Administrative Committee of the American Labor Party, Feb. 25, 1938," in "M. J. Quill: American Labor Party—Administrative Committee Meetings—July 1937–June 1938," TWU-T.

52. *NYT*, 1938: Mar. 4, p. 8; Mar. 6, p. 2; Mar. 7, p. 4; Mar. 8, p. 5; Mar. 9, p. 8; Mar. 12, p. 12; Mar. 13, p. 13; Mar. 14, p. 9; Mar. 17, p. 11; Mar. 18, p. 2; Mar. 19, p. 2; *DW*, Mar. 15, 1938, p. 4.

53. *TWB*, Mar. 1938, p. 2; *NYT*, Mar. 17, 1938, p. 11; May 10, 1938, p. 1; Aug. 26, 1938, p. 3; Waltzer, "ALP," p. 129.

54. Freund, p. 52; McGinley, p. 269; Estreicher, pp. 72–73, 195–96; Comerford, p. 94; *TWB*, Apr. 1938, pp. 1–3, 12; May 1938, pp. 1–2; Sept. 1939, p. 16; Dec. 1939, p. 20; Mar. 1940, p. 7; All-Union Campaign Committee (TWU), "The Rank & File Speaks" (New York, 1939), p. 6; *NYT*, Apr. 14, 1938, p. 3; *TWU 1939 Convention*, 20, 187–89; *TWU 1941 Convention*, 59, 117–18; John B. Delaney to Fiorello H. LaGuardia, Sept. 6, 1938, "Transportation, 1934–1939," box 2642, LaGP; New York Report, Sept. 10, 1943 (#100-7319-

210), FBI-FOIA; *Santo Deportation Hearings*, pp. 772–74; interview with James Sullivan, Aug. 16, 1979.

55. Comerford, pp. 26–30, 60; *Santo Deportation Hearings*, 782–83; *The Survey Mid-monthly* 73, no. 7 (July 1937): 254; *NYT*, July 15, 1937, p. 9; interview with Maurice Forge, Jan. 13, 1979.

56. The following account of unification is based primarily on Garrett, pp. 210–19; Board of Transportation of the City of New York, *Report including Analysis of the Operations of the New York City Transit System for Five Years Ended June 30, 1945* (New York, 1945), 6–9; McGinley, pp. 66–68, 95–110; Morris, pp. 132–33; and Abraham Dollinger, "Father Knickerbocker, Transit Magnate: A Short History of Unification," May 31, 1940, in IRT files, Scudder Collection, Thomas Watson Library, Columbia University.

57. On La Guardia's early support for unification, see Arthur Mann, *La Guardia: A Fighter Against His Times, 1882–1932* (Philadelphia, 1959), 128–30.

58. See, for example, Committee for Interborough Rapid Transit Ten-Year Secured Convertible 7% Gold Notes, letter of May 25, 1937, and Whitehouse & Co. Bond Letter, May 24, 1938, both in IRT files, Scudder Collection.

59. *TWB*, Mar. 1935, p. 2; Oct. 15, 1935, p. 4; Jan. 1936, p. 1; *DW*, Oct. 7, 1935, p. 6.

60. *TWB*, Nov. 15, 1935, pp. 1–2. The appearance of CP and SP speakers at a TWU meeting was extremely unusual. In this case it probably reflected the format and issue involved, the CP's policy at the time of seeking a united front with the SP, and the union's paucity of potential allies in the upcoming fight over unification.

61. *TWB*, Dec. 1934–Jan. 1935, p. 8; May–June 1935, p. 6; Oct. 15, 1935, pp. 1–2; Jan. 1936, p. 1; Apr. 1, 1936, p. 4; May 1, 1936, p. 2; June 1, 1936, p. 1; July 1, 1936, p. 4; Oct. 1936, p. 8; Mar. 1938, p. 2; Sept. 1938, p. 6; Michael J. Quill to Fiorello H. La Guardia, Mar. 23, 1937, "Transportation, 1934–1939," box 2642, LaGP.

62. Garrett, pp. 214–25; Clifton Hood, "Underground Politics: A History of Mass Transit in New York City Since 1904" (Ph.D. dissertation, Columbia University, 1986), 347–52.

63. McGinley, p. 100; *NYT*, Sept. 18, 1938, p. 42; Oct. 1, 1938, p. 19; Oct. 23, 1938, p. 6; Nov. 28, 1938, p. 17; Dec. 8, 1938, p. 29; *TWB*, Sept. 1938, p. 6; U.S. House of Representatives, *Hearings Before a Special Committee on Un-American Activities*, 77th Congress, 1st Session, appendix V (Washington, D.C., 1941), 1719–20.

64. *NYT*, Jan. 16, 1939, pp. 1–2; Jan. 17, 1939, p. 13; Jan. 19, 1939, p. 8; Jan. 23, 1939, p. 15; Mar. 5, 1939, pp. 1, 15; *TWB*, Mar. 1939, p. 1.

65. *NYT*, Jan. 16, 1939, p. 2; *DW*, June 21, 1939, p. 2; interview with Warren Moscow, Jan. 8, 1987.

66. *TWB*, Feb. 1939, p. 6.

67. *NYT*, Jan. 16, 1939, pp. 1–2; Jan. 19, 1939, p. 8; Mar. 5, 1939, pp. 1, 15; Apr. 23, 1939, p. 2; Robert P. Ingalls, *Herbert H. Lehman and New York's Little New Deal* (New York, 1975), 17, 231.

68. *NYT*, Jan. 23, 1939, p. 3; Jan. 27, 1939, p. 3; Feb. 2, 1939, p. 3; Feb. 3, 1939, p. 8; Feb. 5, 1939, p. 13; *TWB*, Feb. 1939, p. 1; Mar. 1939, pp. 5–7, p. 12; John L. Lewis to Fiorello H. La Guardia, Feb. 2, 1939, TWU file, fox A7-34, CIO Papers, Catholic University. Although the proposed La Guardia-TWU-CIO meeting never took place, the Mayor did meet with Lewis to discuss unification. *NYT*, Mar. 5, 1939, p. 15.

69. *DW*, Feb. 15, 1939, p. 3; Feb. 22, 1939, p. 3; Feb. 24, 1939, p. 5; Feb. 27, 1939, p. 3; *NYT*, Mar. 12, 1939, p. 2; *TWB*, Mar. 1939, pp. 5–7, 12.

70. *NYT*, Feb. 17, 1939, p. 4; Mar. 5, 1939, pp. 1, 15.

71. *NYT*, Mar. 5, 1939, p. 15; *TWB*, Mar. 1939, pp. 5–7, 12; *DW*, Feb. 24, 1939, p. 5; Feb. 27, 1939, p. 3.

72. *NYT*, Mar. 31, 1939, p. 11; Apr. 1, 1939, p. 21; Apr. 24, 1939, p. 3.

73. *NYT*, Apr. 25, 1939, p. 5; Edward Sussna, "Collective Bargaining on the New York City Transit System, 1940–1957," *Industrial and Labor Relations Review* 11 (1958): 520; Comerford, p. 65; A. MacMahon, p. 176; McGinley, pp. 100–106.

74. *NYT*, May 2, 1939, p. 20; May 11, 1939, p. 1; May 14, 1939, p. 2 (includes quote); May 17, 1939, p. 3; June 16, 1939, p. 23; *TWB*, June 1939, pp. 1–2.

75. *NYT*, June 5, 1939, p. 36; June 16, 1939, p. 23; June 20, 1939, pp. 1, 22; June 21, 1939, p. 48; Draft of Telegram from Herbert H. Lehman to Fiorello H. La Guardia, June 15, 1939, and La Guardia to Lehman (n.d.), Herbert H. Lehman Governorship Papers, Reel 104, Lehman Library, Columbia University; *DW*, June 21, 1939, p. 3; Executive Board, Local 100, TWU, "Our Message Upon the Signing of the Wicks Bill," JBF.

Chapter 9

1. Interview with John Plover, Feb. 20, 1979.

2. Executive Board, Local 100, TWU, "Our Message Upon the Signing of the Wicks Bill," JFB; *DW*, June 21, 1939, p. 3.

3. *DW*, July 1, 1939, pp. 1, 4; *NYT*, Sept. 1, 1939, p. 38; Charles Garrett, *The La Guardia Years* (New Brunswick, N.J., 1961), 216–17.

4. *DW*, July 1, 1939, pp. 1, 4; July 8, 1939, p. 3; July 11, 1939, p. 5; July 13, 1939, p. 1; *NYT*, July 13, 1939, pp. 1, 5; *TWB*, July 1939, pp. 1, 14; Board of Transportation, *Proceedings* 36 (1940): 4–5, 7–13, 173–89. The improvements in wages, benefits, and conditions resulting from the 1939 contract extensions are discussed in Chapter 6.

5. *DW*, June 21, 1939, p. 3; June 29, 1939, p. 4; July 1, 1939, p. 4. In a similar vein, Quill, in a letter to La Guardia commenting on the Mayor's failure to respond to various TWU communications, chided, "How differently you treated the Morgans and Rockefellers! You did not seem to be able to give them enough of your time and the people's money." Michael J. Quill to Fiorello H. La Guardia, Mar. 4, 1940, folder 486, box 2591, LaGP.

6. The city incurred a debt of $310 million as a result of unification, which it did not finish paying off until June 1, 1980. *TWB*, July 1939, pp. 3, 14; *NYT*, June 2, 1939, p. 25; Mar. 30, 1980, V:6E; *NYWTB*, Dec. 14, 1940, p. 4.

7. *TWU 1939 Convention*, p. 248. For example, both James J. McGinley, in *Labor Relations in the New York Rapid Transit Systems, 1904–1944* (New York, 1949), 106–7, and Samuel Estreicher, in "Collective Bargaining in the New York City Transit System, 1937–1950: A Case Study in the Politics of Municipal Unionism" (M.S. thesis, Cornell University, 1974), 119, state that the TWU opposed unification.

8. Interviews with Simon Gerson, Dec. 18, 1979; Leon Strauss, Oct. 26, 1978; and Maurice Forge, Jan. 13, 1979. The *Daily Worker*, for example, gave little coverage to unification, and usually without editorial comment.

9. Except where otherwise noted, the following discussion is based primarily on the interviews cited above.

10. This point was suggested to me by Simon Gerson (interview of Dec. 18, 1979). As Kenneth Waltzer noted, once the CP committed itself to the ALP, unlike the SP or the Social Democrats, "the Communists . . . made an objective of unity itself." ("The Party and the Polling Place: American Communism and an American Labor Party in the 1930s," *Radical History Review* 23 (Spring 1980): 118). See also Daniel Bell interview with Earl Browder, June 26 or 27, 1955, p. 46, box 9, Daniel Bell Collection, Tamiment Library, New York University; Bella Dodd, *School of Darkness* (1954; reprint ed., New York, 1963), 115, 118–19; and Cynthia Horan, "Agreeing with the Bankers: New York City's Depression Financial

Crisis," in Paul Zarembka and Thomas Ferguson, *Research in Political Economy*, Vol. 8 (Greenwich, Conn., 1985).

11. Interview with Peter MacLachlan, Feb. 25, 1979; *NYWTB*, Mar. 8, 1941, p. 4; *TWB*, Jan. 1941, p. 10.

12. Estreicher, p. 107.

13. *TWU 1937 Convention*, Oct. 8 afternoon session, pp. 16–17; *New York World-Telegram*, June 16, 1941; Memorandum to L.M.C. Smith, Apr. 20, 1942 (#100-7319-36), pp. 21–22, 34, FBI-FOIA.

14. Prior to this the ALP had taken no stands on foreign policy. Kenneth Waltzer, "The American Labor Party: Third Party Politics in New Deal-Cold War New York, 1936–1954" (Ph.D. dissertation, Harvard University, 1977), 217–31 (hereafter "ALP"); *DW*, Oct. 6, 1939, p. 4; Louis Waldman, *Labor Lawyer* (New York, 1944), 289–95; Irving Howe and Lewis Coser, *The American Communist Party: A Critical History* (New York, 1962), 403–4.

15. Waltzer, "ALP," 231–32, 560 fn; *TWB*, Sept. 1939, pp. 1, 2; *DW*, Oct. 6, 1939, p. 4; Oct. 9, 1939, pp. 1–2; Oct. 11, 1939, p. 4.

16. Transport Workers Union of Greater New York, "We Must, and Will Re-Elect Quill to the City Council" [1939], JBF; *TWB*, Oct. 1939, pp. 1, 10; *DW*, Oct. 7, 1939, pp. 1, 4; Oct. 8, 1939, pp. 2, 4; Oct. 10, 1939, p. 4; Oct. 11, 1939, pp. 1, 4; Oct. 17, 1939, pp. 1, 4.

17. *DW*, Oct. 8, 1939, pp. 2, 3; Oct. 10, 1939, p. 4; Oct. 18, 1939, pp. 4, 5; Oct. 21, 1939, p. 2; Oct. 22, 1939, p. 2; Oct. 24, 1939, p. 1; Oct. 30, 1939, p. 1; Oct. 31, 1939, p. 3; *TWB*, Sept. 1939, p. 1; Nov. 1939, pp. 1–3, 6; Dec. 1939, p. 1, 20; Simon W. Gerson, *Pete: The Story of Peter V. Cacchione, New York's First Communist Councilman* (New York, 1976), 99–100; Estreicher, p. 108; *New York World-Telegram*, Oct. 6, 1939; copies of pro- and anti-Quill leaflets, JBF; interview with James Sullivan, July 27, 1979.

18. Quill's view of the relationship between politics and other union activities clearly emerges in his wartime letters to John Santo, in which he makes virtually no distinction between the two. The letters are in MF-T. See also *TWB*, Sept. 1939, p. 2; Nov. 1939, p. 2; Dec. 1939, pp. 1, 20; *DW*, Oct. 24, 1939, p. 4.

19. Len De Caux, *Labor Radical: From the Wobblies to CIO, A Personal History* (Boston, 1970), 361–62; *NYT*, Mar. 10, 1940, VI:10; interviews with Maurice Forge, Jan. 13 and 27, 1979.

20. "Greater New York IUC Z-235—New York" folder, box A7-14, CIO Papers, Catholic University; *NYWTB*, July 27, 1940, p. 1; Aug. 17, 1940, p. 2; Sept. 28, 1940, pp. 1, 3, 4; interview with Leon Strauss, Oct. 26, 1978; De Caux, p. 361; Howe and Coser, p. 396.

21. In issuing no endorsement in 1940, the TWU reversed the position taken by its 1939 Convention, which voted to back New Deal candidates in the next year's election. *TWU 1939 Convention*, 191; *NYWTB*, Nov. 2, 1940, p. 1; Nov. 23, 1940, pp. 1, 2, 4; *TWB*, Nov. 1940, pp. 1, 4, 12; Dec. 1940, pp. 1, 5, 12; interview with Abner Berry, Dec. 5, 1978; Report from Detective Stanley Gwozdo, Dec. 19, 1940, in "Coughlin Against, 1940, La Guardia," box 794, LaGP; Harvey A. Levenstein, *Communism, Anticommunism, and the CIO* (Westport, Conn., 1981), 92.

22. *NYT*, Feb. 18, 1940, p. 5; Feb. 23, 1940, p. 2; Mar. 3, 1940, p. 15; *TWB*, Mar. 1940, pp. 1, 3; Michael J. Quill to Fiorello H. LaGuardia, Mar. 4, 1940, folder 486, box 2591, LaGP.

23. Fiorello H. LaGuardia to Michael J. Quill and John J. Donnelly, Mar. 2, 1940, folder 486, box 2591, LaGP.

24. Michael J. Quill to Fiorello H. LaGuardia, Mar. 4, 1940, folder 486, box 2591, LaGP.

25. *NYT*, Mar. 6, 1940, pp. 1, 4; Mar. 7, 1940, p. 25; Mar. 8, 1940, p. 10; Mar. 10,

1940, p. 6; Mar. 11, 1940, p. 10; Mar. 12, 1940, p. 46; Mar. 14, 1940, p. 1; *TWB*, Apr. 1940, p. 14.

26. *NYT*, Mar. 14, 1940, pp. 1, 34.

27. *NYT*, Mar. 12, 1940, p. 46; Mar. 14, 1940, p. 1; Mar. 16, 1940, pp. 1, 7; Mar. 18, 1940, p. 19; Mar. 19, 1940, p. 27; Mar. 23, 1940, p. 15; N. Y. C. Police Department Report on TWU Joint Executive Committees Meeting on Mar. 25, 1940, folder 485, box 2591, LaGP.

28. *NYT*, Mar. 28, 1940, pp. 1, 15; Mar. 31, 1940, pp. 1, 42.

29. *NYT*, Mar. 29, 1940, p. 12; Mar. 30, 1940, p. 1; Mar. 31, 1940, pp. 1, 42; Apr. 1, 1940, pp. 1, 4; Apr. 2, 1940, pp. 1, 2; Apr. 3, 1940, pp. 1, 20; Apr. 4, 1940, p. 18; TWU, Strike Notice for April 3 [1940], box A7-34, CIO Papers, Catholic University.

30. Simultaneous with unification, operations on the 9th Avenue el, part of the 2nd Avenue el, and on the Fulton Street and Fifth Avenue els in Brooklyn were ended. Keeping to La Guardia's promise, workers from those lines were given other positions with the NYCTS. John H. Delany, "Board of Transportation," in Rebecca B. Rankin, ed., *New York Advancing: Victory Edition* (New York, 1945), 32–35; McGinley, pp. 5, 13, 15, 18–19; TWB, July 1940, p. 2; Board of Transportation of the City of New York, *Report including Analysis of the Operations of the New York City Transit System for Five Years Ended June 30, 1945* (New York, 1945), 25, 51, 100–101 (hereafter Board of Transportation, *Five Year Report*).

31. *TWB*, Feb. 1939, p. 4; Apr. 1939, p. 2; Aug. 1939, p. 2; June 1940, p. 4; July 1941, p. 3; Apr. 1942, p. 1; *NYT*, Nov. 2, 1940, p. 17; Nov. 7, 1940, p. 27; interviews with Maurice Forge, Jan. 1, 1979, and Peter MacLachlan, Feb. 25, 1979; Arthur W. MacMahon, "The New York Transit System: Public Ownership, Civil Service, and Collective Bargaining," *Political Science Quarterly* 56, no. 2 (June 1941): 176–77.

32. *NYT*, Feb. 5, 1940, p. 19; Apr. 7, 1940, p. 1; July 8, 1940, p. 17; *TWB*, Mar. 1940, p. 2; June 1940, p. 4; interviews with Maurice Forge, Jan. 1, 1979; Peter MacLachlan, Feb. 25, 1979.

33. *TWB*, June 1940, p. 4; July 1940, p. 2; *NYWTB*, June 15, 1940, p. 2; June 22, 1940, pp. 1–3; interview with Maurice Forge, Jan. 1, 1979; John Santo to Maurice Forge, Jan. 11, 1940, and Forge, "Memorandum on Bulletin," Apr. 13, 1940, in possession of Maurice Forge.

34. Board of Transportation, *Five Year Report*, 100–101; A. MacMahon, pp. 178–79; McGinley, pp. 183–85, 454–55, 480; James J. Comerford, "Adjustment of Labor Unions to Civil Service Status: The Transportation Workers Union and the New York City Government" (M.A. thesis, Columbia University, 1941), 86–89; *NYT*, Feb. 5, 1940, p. 19.

35. The problem of unequal wage scales became accentuated as workers began being transferred from one division to another, bringing their pay rates with them. *NYWTB*, June 15, 1940, pp. 1, 3; July 20, 1940, p. 3; Nov. 9, 1940, p. 4; Nov. 23, 1940, p. 1; Dec. 14, 1940, pp. 1, 3; Dec. 28, 1940, p. 1; Jan. 4, 1941, p. 1; Jan. 25, 1941, p. 1; Feb. 1, 1941, p. 1; Mar. 8, 1941, p. 4; Mar. 29, 1941, p. 1; *TWB*, June 1940, p. 4; *NYT*, Nov. 7, 1940, p. 1; Nov. 16, 1940, p. 19; Nov. 23, 1940, p. 8; Apr. 19, 1940, p. 8; Comerford, pp. 86–89; Board of Transportation, *Five Year Report*, 100–101; A. MacMahon, pp. 177–79; interview with Victor Bloswick, Jan. 23, 1979; and CCOHP, drawer 4, tape 5.

36. *TWU 1941 Convention*, p. 46; *NYWTB*, Aug. 10, 1940, p. 4; Aug. 24, 1940, p. 4; Dec. 28, 1940, p. 1; Apr. 3, 1941, p. 2; *TWB*, Jan. 1941, p. 10; *NYT*, Nov. 15, 1940, p. 1; Nov. 16, 1940, p. 19; Nov. 17, 1940, p. 2; Nov. 23, 1940, p. 8; Nov. 25, 1940, p. 19; *LL*, Mar. 10, 1941, p. 2; Chief Engineers Queens, TWU, "What Price Civil Service," in "M. J. Quill—Local 100—Negotiations, Proposals," TWU-T.

37. The following discussion of the impact of unification on workers' attitudes toward the

TWU is based on a report of 39 interviews with NYCTS workers conducted in late 1940 and early 1941, in Comerford, pp. 90–115; interviews with Patrick J. Reilly, Sept. 7, 1978; John Plover, Feb. 20, 1979; Philip Bray, Aug. 13, 1979; James Sullivan, Aug. 16, 1979; Patrick Walsh, June 1, 1978; Victor Bloswick, Jan. 23, 1979; Carl Mann, Apr. 4, 1984; and Peter MacLachlan, Feb. 25, 1979; NYWTB, Mar. 8, 1941, p. 4; TWB, Jan. 1941, p. 10; and L. H. Whittemore, *The Man Who Ran the Subways: The Story of Mike Quill* (New York, 1968), 93.

38. McCarthy, a onetime member of ACTU's executive board, had a history of changing positions under pressure from TWU leaders. However, his decision to recant may have been influenced by ACTU's reaction to the resignations; while condemning the TWU leadership, ACTU urged workers not to resign "leaving a once great union in the hands of the Communists." NYT, Aug. 1, 1940, p. 18; Aug. 12, 1940, p. 15; NYWTB, Aug. 17, 1940, p. 3; McGinley, pp. 325–26; LL, July 29, 1940, p. 1, 2.

39. NYWTB, Aug. 3, 1940, p. 1; Aug. 10, 1940, pp. 1, 3; NYT, Sept. 18, 1940, p. 25; Sept. 30, 1940, p. 19; Apr. 9, 1941, pp. 1, 19; Apr. 10, 1941, pp. 1, 42; A. MacMahon, pp. 183–84; Estreicher, pp. 125–26.

40. *Daily News*, June 26, 1941, pp. 2, 18; *Daily Mirror*, June 27, 1941, p. 2; NYWTB, Oct. 26, 1940, p. 4; Estreicher, pp. 124–25; Whittemore, pp. 93, 102; interviews with Patrick J. Reilly, Sept. 7, 1978; John Plover, Feb. 20, 1979; James Sullivan, Aug. 17, 1979; Victor Bloswick, Jan. 23, 1979; Carl Mann, Apr. 4, 1984; *TWU 1941 Convention*, 47; *TWU 1943 Convention*, 199, 205–6; *TWU 1948 Convention*, 12; "B.M.T. Dues Payments by Sections, March–April 1943," and "IRT Dues Payments by Sections, March and April 1943," TWU-T.

41. NYWTB, Aug. 10, 1940, pp. 1, 3; Aug. 17, 1940, p. 2; Aug. 31, 1940, p. 1.

42. NYWTB, Aug. 10, 1940, p. 1; Sept. 14, 1940, p. 2; Nov. 8, 1940, p. 1; NYT, Nov. 16, 1940, p. 16.

43. Comerford, pp. 71–72.

44. NYWTB, Dec. 7, 1940, p. 1; Apr. 12, 1941, pp. 2, 3; John Santo to Philip Murray, Dec. 9, 1940, box A7-34, CIO Papers, Catholic University.

45. NYWTB, Dec. 14, 1940, p. 1; Dec. 21, 1940; p. 1; Jan. 4, 1941, p. 1; Feb. 1, 1941, p. 1; Feb. 8, 1941, pp. 1, 3; Feb. 15, 1941, pp. 1, 3; Mar. 8, 1941, p. 4; Mar. 29, 1941, pp. 1, 4; Apr. 12, 1941, pp. 2, 3; TWB, Mar. 1941, p. 8; NYT, Feb. 3, 1941, p. 19; Mar. 3, 1941, p. 17; Apr. 15, 1941, p. 16.

46. NYWTB, Sept. 14, 1940, p. 2; NYT, Nov. 2, 1940, p. 17; Whittemore, pp. 94–95; Estreicher, p. 126; New York Report, Feb. 17, 1941 (#100-7319-2), pp. 4–5, FBI-FOIA.

47. Interview with Maurice Forge, Jan. 27, 1979; NYWTB, Dec. 14, 1940, p. 1; NYT, Mar. 3, 1941, p. 17; William Harmon to Philip Carey, Feb. 23, 1941, "41–42" file, XA.

48. NYWTB, Dec. 14, 1940, p. 1; Dec. 21, 1940, p. 1; Jan. 4, 1941, p. 1; Feb. 1, 1941, p. 1; Feb. 8, 1941, pp. 1, 3; Feb. 15, 1941, pp. 1, 2; Mar. 8, 1941, p. 4; NYT, Mar. 3, 1941, p. 17.

49. NYWTB, Dec. 7, 1940, p. 1; Feb. 15, 1941, pp. 1, 3; Apr. 12 1941, pp. 2–3; John Santo to Philip Murray, Dec. 9, 1940, box A7-34, CIO Papers, Catholic University; William Harmon to Philip Carey, Feb. 23, 1941, "41–42" file, XA; NYT, Feb. 3, 1941, p. 19; Feb. 22, 1941, p. 17; Fiorello H. La Guardia to Murray, Jan. 17, 1941, quoted in Estreicher, p. 126.

50. NYWTB, Dec. 21, 1940, p. 1; Feb. 15, 1941, pp. 1, 3; Apr. 12, 1941, pp. 2–3; interview with Maurice Forge, Jan. 27, 1979; NYT, Apr. 15, 1941, p. 16.

51. NYWTB, Aug. 31, 1940, p. 2; Oct. 26, 1940, pp. 1, 4; Feb. 15, 1941, p. 1; TWB, Apr. 1941, p. 6; interviews with John Plover, Feb. 20, 1979; Victor Bloswick, Jan. 23, 1979; and Patrick Reilly, Sept. 7, 1978.

52. In 1941 the IND had 6,622 workers, compared with 11,661 on the BMT and 13,573 on the IRT. Board of Transportation, *Five Year Report*, 51.

53. *TWB*, Nov. 1939, p. 20; Jan. 1940, p. 7; Mar. 1940, p. 7; Apr. 1940, p. 3; *NYWTB*, July 20, 1940, p. 3; Aug. 31, 1940, p. 2; Sept. 21, 1940, p. 2; Oct. 10, 1940, p. 2; *TWU 1941 Convention*, 59.

54. *TWB*, Apr. 1940, p. 3; May 1940, pp. 2, 3; Sept. 1940, p. 3; May 1941, p. 3; *NYWTB*, July 20, 1940, p. 3; July 27, 1940, p. 2; Aug. 31, 1940, p. 2; Feb. 15, 1941, pp. 1, 3; Feb. 22, 1941, p. 4; Mar. 8, 1941, p. 2; *NYT*, Apr. 25, 1941, p. 21; Comerford, p. 95.

55. McGinley, pp. 276–78, 283; *TWB*, May 1940, pp. 2, 3; *NYWTB*, Dec. 21, 1940, p. 4; Jan. 4, 1941, p. 2; Mar. 1, 1941, p. 2; Mar. 8, 1941, p. 3; John Santo to Philip Murray, Dec. 9, 1940, and attached flyer, box A7-34, CIO Papers, Catholic University.

56. Some of the non-TWU organizations represented engineering, supervisory, administrative, or clerical personnel. John Santo to Philip Murray, Dec. 9, 1940, box A7-34, CIO Papers, Catholic University; *TWB*, Apr. 1941, p. 10; McGinley, pp. 276–78, 325; *NYT*, June 19, 1941, p. 4; *LL*, Mar. 10, 1941, p. 3; Transportation Employees Industrial Union flyer, "Anti-union" folder, Santo Files, TWU-T; *Daily News*, June 19, 1941, p. 48; Fiorello H. LaGuardia to John H. Delaney, Apr. 4, 1941, "Transit-T.W.U.," box 788, LaGP.

57. *Daily News*, June 26, 1941, pp. 2, 18; McGinley, p. 283; Comerford, p. 78; N.Y.C. Police Department, memo from Patrolmen Joseph H. Hartley and Edward F. Fitzpatrick to Commanding Officer, Criminal Alien Squad, on meeting of TWU Joint Executive Committee and Delegates from the Greater New York Industrial Council, June 29, 1941 (hereafter Police Report on TWU meeting of June 29, 1941), folder 486, box 2591, LaGP.

58. *NYWTB*, Aug. 10, 1940, p. 4; Aug. 24, 1940, p. 2; Dec. 7, 1940, p. 1; Feb. 22, 1941, p. 1.

59. *NYWTB*, Feb. 8, 1941, pp. 1, 3; Feb. 15, 1941, p. 1; *NYT*, Mar. 3, 1941, p. 17.

60. Interview with Maurice Forge, Jan. 13, 1979. See also Leo Huberman, *The Great Bus Strike* (New York, 1941), 19–25.

61. A few Queens bus routes were also affected. *NYWTB*, Feb. 8, 1941, p. 2; Mar. 15, 1941, pp. 1–5; Huberman, pp. 26–31.

62. Estreicher, pp. 127–28; *LL*, July 28, 1941, p. 4; interviews with Maurice Forge, Jan. 7 and 13, 1979; Huberman, pp. 34–41. Quill later charged that "leaders of the Communist Party did everything possible to prevent the calling of the very justified 1941 bus strike—on the grounds that it would interfere with their so-called friendly relationship with LaGuardia." See *TWB*, July 24, 1948, p. 8.

63. Huberman, pp. 39–151; Estreicher, p. 128; *NYWTB*, Mar. 15, 1941, pp. 1–5; Mar. 22, 1941, pp. 3, 4.

64. *NYWTB*, Mar. 22, 1941, pp. 4–5; Huberman, pp. 103–4.

65. Huberman, pp. 128–33, 136–41; *LL*, Mar. 24, 1941, p. 1; interview with Maurice Forge, Jan. 13, 1979. Davis's ruling, issued on June 15, called for increases in pay, new overtime provisions, and limits on unpaid swing time. See *TWB*, Aug. 1941, p. 2.

66. Huberman, pp. 140–42; A MacMahon, p. 185.

67. Estreicher, pp. 127–28.

68. Arthur Wicks, who sponsored the bill, told *New York Times* reporter Warren Moscow that it was designed to "cut the balls" off Quill. Gustave Strebel of the ACW, who headed the State CIO, told LaGuardia that he did not agree with the TWU's view of the bill, but that if he failed to oppose it the State CIO "will split wide open immediately." Interview with Warren Moscow, Jan. 8, 1987; Ethel S. Epstein, "Memo to the Mayor," Apr. 11, 1941, folder 236, box 2555, LaGP; Comerford, pp. 81–83, 85; *NYT*, Apr. 15, 1941, p. 16; *NYWTB*, Apr. 12, 1941, pp. 1, 4; *TWB*, June 1941, p. 3.

69. *NYWTB*, Apr. 3, 1941, p. 2; *TWB*, June 1941, p. 3; TWU, "Declaration of Policy in Respect to Labor Relations on N.Y.C. Transit System," "Transit—T.W.U. 1941" file, box 778, LaGP.

70. *NYT*, Apr. 9, 1941, pp. 1, 19; Apr. 10, 1941, pp. 1, 42; Apr. 18, 1941, pp. 1, 17; Comerford, pp. 73–78; interviews with John Plover, Feb. 20, 1979; James Sullivan, July 27, 1979.

71. *NYT*, Apr. 10, 1941, pp. 1, 42; *NYWTB*, Jan. 1, 1941, p. 2; TWU, "Philip A. Murray answers F. H. La Guardia," "Transit—T.W.U. 1941" file, box 778, LaGP; *TWB*, June 1941, p. 3.

72. *NYT*, Apr. 20, 1941, pp. 1, 37; Apr. 23, 1941, p. 18; Apr. 25, 1941, p. 21; May 11, 1941, p. 29; *TWB*, May 1941, pp. 1, 2; June 1941, p. 3; interview with Maurice Forge, Jan. 13, 1979; *Daily News*, May 11, 1941, p. M6; June 2, 1941, p. 13; *Daily Mirror*, May 11, 1941, p. 4; June 21, 1941, p. 5; Huberman, pp. 152–55.

73. *Daily Mirror*, May 22, 1941, p. 12; *TWB*, June 1941, p. 3; "Press Information #1, Public Rally in Support of Collective Bargaining Rights for Transit Labor" and "Transit Tunes for 1941," "Transit—T.W.U. 1941" file, box 778, LaGP; Summary Report on TWU, Apr. 20, 1941, pp. 13–14, 41–42 (#100-7319-36), FBI-FOIA. On the preliminary maneuvering for the 1941 mayoral election, see Waltzer, "ALP," p. 251; *Daily Mirror*, May 24, 1941, p. 2; Gerson, p. 106; Paul O'Dwyer, *Counsel for the Defense: The Autobiography of Paul O'Dwyer* (New York, 1979), 102–3.

74. Murray put forward his views in two addresses on April 21, one at the Garden rally and the other over radio station WOR. The texts are in "Transit—T.W.U. 1941," box 778, LaGP. See also *Daily News*, June 6, 1941, p. 22; *TWU 1941 Convention*, pp. 29–36; interview with Maurice Forge, Jan. 13, 1979; and Levenstein, pp. 139–55.

75. *NYT*, Apr. 19, 1941, p. 8; Apr. 20, 1941, p. 37; *Daily News*, May 10, 1941, p. 2; *TWB*, June 1941, p. 3; *Daily Mirror*, May 24, 1941, p. 2.

76. *NYT*, Apr. 21, 1941, p. 21; Huberman, p. 149; Joshua B. Freeman, "The Transport Workers Union in New York City, 1933–1948" (Ph.D. dissertation, Rutgers University, 1983), 585fn; August Heckscher, with Phyllis Robinson, *When La Guardia Was Mayor: New York's Legendary Years* (New York 1978), 267.

77. Authur Mann, *La Guardia: A Fighter Against His Times, 1882–1932* (Philadelphia, 1959), 257–58, 311–12; Garrett, p. 264; Jewel Bellush and Bernard Bellush, *Union Power and New York: Victor Gotbaum and District Council 37* (New York, 1984), 17.

78. Garrett, pp. 132–36.

79. Garrett, pp. 142–44; Rachel Bernstein, with Steve Beck and Molly Charboneau, *Building a City, Building a Union: A History of the Civil Service Technical Guild* (New York, 1987), 1–4, 10–11.

80. F. H. La Guardia to John H. Delaney, April 7, 1941, "Transit-T.W.U.," box 788, LaGP; *NYT*, Mar. 14, 1940, p. 34.

81. Ralph T. Jones, "City Employees Unions: Labor and Politics in New York and Chicago," unpublished manuscript, 1975, p. 156; Bellush and Bellush, pp. 9, 17; *NYT*, Feb. 28, 1946, p. 5.

82. Heckscher, pp. 267–69; Beatrice Bishop Berle and Travis Beal Jacobs, *Navigating the Rapids, 1918–1971: From the Papers of Adolph A. Berle* (New York, 1973), 144; Robert Caro, *The Power Broker: Robert Moses and the Fall of New York* (New York, 1974), 471–4; Frances Perkins, "Memorandum for the President, Re: Subway Transportation Problem, New York City, June 24, 1941," President's Secretaries File, Box 185, "Strikes," Franklin Delano Roosevelt Papers, Hyde Park, N.Y.

83. *NYT*, Apr. 22, 1941, p. 24; *LL*, Apr. 7, 1941, p. 2; Apr. 21, 1941, p. 1; May 5, 1941, pp. 1, 2; June 7, 1941, pp. 2, 4; June 30, 1941, p. 4.

84. *NYT*, May 14, 1941, p. 23; June 7, 1941, pp. 1, 9; *TWB*, June 1941, p. 3.

85. *NYT*, June 19, 1941, p. 14.

86. *Daily News*, June 21, 1941, pp. 1, 5; June 25, 1941, p. 4; *Daily Mirror*, June 21, 1941, p. 5; *NYT*, June 19, 1941, p. 14; June 24, 1941, p. 21.

87. Edward Sussna, "Collective Bargaining on the New York City Transit System, 1940–1957," *Industrial and Labor Relations Review* 11 (1958): 530–31; *Daily News*, June 25, 1941, p. 4; June 26, 1941, pp. 2, 18; *Daily Mirror*, June 26, 1941, pp. 5, 6.

88. Interviews with Maurice Forge, Jan. 13 and 27, 1979; John Nolan, June 1, 1978; U.S. Department of Justice, Immigration and Naturalization Service, "In the Matter of Charges against DESIDERIU HAMMER, alias JOHN SANTO" (typescript of 1947 hearings, hereafter *Santo Deportation Hearings*), 715, 735–36; *Daily News*, June 27, 1941, pp. 2, 24.

89. Interviews with Maurice Forge, Jan. 13 and 27, 1979; Leo Woltman, "Quill and the Subway Crisis," *New York World-Telegram*, June 9–25, 1941; *Daily Mirror*, June 27, 1941, p. 25; *NYT*, June 25, 1941, p. 20. Xavier activist William Harmon was a paid consultant in the preparation of the *World-Telegram* series. According to Harmon, La Guardia cooperated with the paper, ordering the police department to make available its relevant files. Xavier director Philip Carey also secretly contributed to the press campaign against the TWU, publishing articles in the *Tablet* under the name Philip Bowen and funneling information from Harmon to *Tablet* editor Patrick Scanlon. William Harmon to Philip Carey, July 6, 1941; Carey to Patrick Scanlon, Feb. 17, 1941; and Carey to Rev. William J. Smith, S.J., Mar. 6, 1941, "41–42" file, XA.

90. Interviews with Maurice Forge, Jan. 27, 1979; Martin Young, Nov. 15, 1978.

91. Although some observers believed that the German invasion of the Soviet Union was the main reason for the TWU's ultimate decision not to strike, it appears that it was only one of many. The initial assessments by labor leaders close to the CP of the domestic implications of the invasion were varied and tentative. See Levenstein, pp. 156–58; interview with Maurice Forge, Jan. 27, 1979.

92. According to some reports, a significant number of non-NYCTS members of the TWU attended and voted at the strike meetings. Even discounting for this, the turnouts were an impressive testament to the union's following on the municipal transit system. *Daily Mirror*, June 27, 1941, p. 2; *Daily News*, June 27, 1941, pp. 1, 14; June 29, 1941, p. 2; *NYT*, June 28, 1941, pp. 1, 8; *TWB*, July 1941, pp. 1, 2.

93. Police report on TWU meeting of June 29, 1941, folder 486, box 2591, LaGP; Frances Perkins, "Memorandum for the President, June 24, 1941," President's Secretaries File, box 185, "Strikes," Franklin Delano Roosevelt Papers.

94. *NYT*, June 28, 1941, p. 8; Frances Perkins to Fiorello H. La Guardia, June 25, 1941, folder 486, box 2591, LaGP.

95. Police report on TWU meeting of June 29, 1941, folder 486, box 2591, LaGP; Frances Perkins to Edwin M. Watson, June 24, 1941; Perkins, "Memorandum for the President, June 24, 1941," and Franklin D. Roosevelt, Memorandum for General Watson, June 25, 1941, all in President's Secretaries File, box 185, "Strikes," Franklin Delano Roosevelt Papers.

96. Frances Perkins to Fiorello H. La Guardia, June 25, 1941, folder 486, box 2591, LaGP; Philip Carey to William Harmon, July 4, 1941, "41–42" file, XA; *NYT*, June 28, 1941, p. 8.

97. Police report on TWU meeting of June 29, 1941, and Fiorello H. La Guardia to Frances Perkins, June 26, 1941, folder 486, box 2591, LaGP; *Daily News*, June 27, 1941, p. 24; June 29, 1941, p. 2; *NYT*, June 28, 1941, pp. 1, 8. The full texts of the telegrams appear in Transport Workers Union of America, "Brief before the National War Labor Board in re:

Board of Transportation of the City of New York and Transport Workers Union of America" [1942], 10–15.

98. *Daily News*, June 29, 1941, p. 2; *Daily Mirror*, June 30, 1941, p. 6; Police report on TWU meeting of June 29, 1941, folder 486, box 2591, LaGP; *NYT*, June 1941, p. 1.

99. *Daily News*, June 30, 1941, p. 8; *Daily Mirror*, June 30, 1941, p. 6; Police report on TWU meeting of June 29, 1941, and Report by "24–80" on same meeting, folder 486, box 2591, LaGP.

100. *Santo Deportation Hearings*, 715, 735–36, 879; interview with James Sullivan, July 27, 1979; Report by "24–80," folder 486, box 2591, LaGP.

101. See, for example, William Harmon to Philip Carey, July 6, 1941, "41–42" file, XA.

Chapter 10

1. Joshua Freeman, "Delivering the Goods: Industrial Unionism During World War II," *Labor History*, Fall 1978, pp. 570–93, esp. 589; John Morton Blum, *V Was for Victory: Politics and American Culture During World War II* (New York, 1976), 90–100, 141; Katherine Archibald, *Wartime Shipyard: A Study of Social Disunity* (Berkeley and Los Angeles, 1947), 188.

2. Maintenance-of-membership allowed workers to decline to join a union during the first fifteen days after they were hired or after a new contract was signed. If they did not take advantage of these "escape periods," they had to maintain union membership to retain their jobs. On wartime labor relations, see Nelson Lichtenstein, *Labor's War at Home: The CIO in World War II* (Cambridge, Eng., 1982); Freeman, "Delivering the Goods"; Joel Seidman, *American Labor from Defense to Reconstruction* (Chicago, 1953); and Colston E. Warne et al., *Yearbook of American Labor*, Vol. I, *War Labor Policies* (Brooklyn, 1945).

3. Freeman, "Delivering the Goods," 574, 581–85, 590–92.

4. Boris Pushkarev and Jeffrey M. Zupan, *Public Transportation and Local Land Use Policy* (Bloomington, 1977), 2; Board of Transportation of the City of New York, *Report including Analysis of the Operations of the New York City Transit System for Five Years Ended June 30, 1945* (New York, 1945), 51, 99 (hereafter Board of Transportation, *Five-Year Report*).

5. *TWB*, Jan. 1941, pp. 2, 4; Aug. 1941, pp. 4, 8; Nov. 1941, pp. 1, 8; TWU Local 100, "Stand United in this Hour of Peril," and TWU, "Do Your Patriotic Duty NOW!", JBF. See Chapter 7 for a discussion of the debate at the TWU's 1941 convention.

6. Freeman, "Delivering the Goods," 590–91; *TWB*, Aug. 1942, p. 1; Merle Curti, *The Roots of American Loyalty* (New York, 1946), 243; interviews with Maurice Forge, Jan. 27, 1979; Gerald O'Reilly, May 15, 1978; and Philip Bray, Aug. 13, 1979.

7. *TWB*, Sept. 1943, p. 11; May 1944, p. 11; Jan. 1945, p. 1; June 1945, p. 9; interviews with Joseph Labash, Aug. 3, 1979; Victor Bloswick, Jan. 23, 1979; John Gallagher, Apr. 20, 1979; and Patrick J. Reilly, Sept. 7, 1978.

8. TWU leaflets, 1941–43, JBF; Shirley Quill, *Mike Quill—Himself, A Memoir* (Greenwich, Conn., 1985), 156; interviews with Maurice Forge, Jan. 27, 1979; Gerald O'Reilly, May 15, 1978; Adrian Cabral, Apr. 12, 1979; *TWB*, May 1942, pp. 6–7; July 1942, pp. 8–9; Nov. 1942, pp. 7–9; Apr. 1943, p. 1; *NYWTB*, Dec. 28, 1940, p. 2; *NYCTB*, Feb. 1945, p. 4; Mar. 1945, p. 4.

9. Between June 1940 and May 1945 the NYCTS had an annual average turnover of about 20%, including a quit rate of about 10%. Though low by war industry standards, these rates were very high in comparison with the equivalent rates before 1940. As of September 1943 the Board of Transportation had hired 1,200 women. Once World War II ended, it was not until 1973 that the NYCTS again began hiring female bus drivers. Board of Transporta-

tion, *Five-Year Report*, 25, 51, 99, 101; Rebecca B. Rankin, ed., *New York Advancing: Victory Edition* (New York, 1945), 33–35; *NYT*, June 21, 1941, p. 21; Dec. 16, 1942, p. 12; Jan. 11, 1943, p. 21; Apr. 13, 1943, p. 22; Sept. 29, 1943, p. 23; Jan. 9, 1944, p. 44; June 2, 1944, p. 17, Jan. 28, 1945, p. 1; Jan. 31, 1945, p. 12; Oct. 8, 1981, p. B3.

10. Interview with Gerald O'Reilly, May 15, 1978; *TWB*, July 1942, p. 16; July 1945, pp. 12, 16; Dec. 1945, p. 3.

11. Kenneth Waltzer, "The American Labor Party: Third Party Politics in New Deal-Cold War New York, 1936–1954" (Ph.D. dissertation, Harvard University, 1977), 251–55 (hereafter "ALP").

12. *TWB*, July 1941, pp. 1–3; Sept. 1941, pp. 1, 3; Oct. 1941, NYC supplement, p. 1; Board of Transportation, *Five-Year Report*, pp. 101–6; TWU Local 100, "TWU and B. of T. Meet on Working Conditions," JBF.

13. Paul O'Dwyer Memoir, OHCCU; Paul O'Dwyer, *Counsel for the Defense: The Autobiography of Paul O'Dwyer* (New York, 1979), 102–3; interview with Simon Gerson, Dec. 18, 1979.

14. The TWU delegates abstained in the NYC CIO Council vote endorsing La Guardia. *NYT*, Oct. 9, 1941, p. 46; Oct. 16, 1941, p. 14; Oct. 19, 1941, p. 39; Oct. 20, 1941, p. 19; Nov. 21, 1941, p. 19, Nov. 23, 1941, pp. 1, 45; interview with Patrick J. Reilly, Sept. 7, 1978; Simon W. Gerson, *Pete: The Story of Peter V. Cacchione, New York's First Communist Councilman* (New York, 1976), 106; Paul O'Dwyer Memoir, OHCCU; TWU Local 100, "Your 'Bread & Butter'," JBF.

15. *TWB*, Nov. 1941, pp. 4, 5; interview with Maurice Forge, July 17, 1981.

16. Waltzer, "ALP," pp. 256–57, 261–62; Ronald H. Bayor, *Neighbors in Conflict: The Irish, Germans, Jews and Italians of New York City, 1929–1941* (Baltimore, 1978), 130, 137, 143; Gerson, pp. 108–9, 115.

17. Transport Workers Union of Greater New York (Local 100), *10th Anniversary Celebration, 1934–44* (New York, 1944); interview with Maurice Forge, Jan. 27, 1979; *TWB*, Mar. 1941, p. 11.

18. Several left-wing unionists, including West Coast longshoremen's leader Harry Bridges, fought deportation while retaining their union posts. Santo's decision to leave the TWU was apparently an effort to protect the union from possible right-wing attacks. *TWU 1941 Convention*, 192–93; John Santo, *American* (New York, n.d.); L. H. Whittemore, *The Man Who Ran the Subways: The Story of Mike Quill* (New York, 1968), 108–10; *NYT*, Oct. 9, 1941, p. 4; Memorandum for the Director, Dec. 17, 1940 (#100-7319-), FBI-FOIA; interview with James Sullivan, Jan. 27, 1979; Harvey A. Levenstein, *Communism, Anticommunism, and the CIO* (Westport, Conn., 1981), 124–38.

19. *TWU 1941 Convention*, pp. 196–206, 243; *NYT*, Oct. 9, 1941, p. 4; *TWB*, Nov. 1941, p. 16; Dec. 1941, p. 7.

20. *TWB*, July 1942, p. 3; Sept. 1942, pp. 1, 3; Oct. 1942, p. 1; John Santo, *American*; U.S. Department of Justice, Immigration and Naturalization Service, "In the Matter of Charges against DESIDERIU HAMMER, alias JOHN SANTO" (typescript, 1947 hearings), 813–45; *TWU 1943 Convention*, 194.

21. *TWB*, Aug. 1942, p. 1; interview with Gerald O'Reilly, July 11, 1979.

22. *TWU 1941 Convention*, 196, 208; *TWB*, Oct. 1942, p. 6; interviews with Maurice Forge, Jan. 27, 1979 and July 15, 1980; Peter MacLachlan, Feb. 25, 1979.

23. It is possible that Young's assignment was not directly linked to Santo's departure. As Santo increasingly saw his primary role as trade union leadership, he became less reliable as a Party representative. Interviews with Abner Berry, Dec. 5, 1978; Maurice Forge, Jan. 27, 1979 and July 17, 1981; Max Gordon, Oct. 24, 1978; Martin Young, Nov. 15, 1978; and

James Sullivan, July 27 and Aug. 16, 1979; John Lopez to Douglas MacMahon, Aug. 28, 1945, JBF.

24. *TWB*, July 1942, p. 5; Dec. 1943, pp. 6–7; Sept. 1945, p. 11; *TWU 1943 Convention*, passim; interviews with Maurice Forge, Jan. 27, 1979, Gerald O'Reilly, May 15, 1978.

25. Maurice Forge, "Autobiographical Manuscript," in possession of Forge, p. 185; interviews with Maurice Forge, Jan. 27, 1979; James Sullivan, Aug. 16, 1979. Quill's growing mastery of every aspect of the TWU's affairs can be seen in his wartime letters to Santo, MF-T.

26. Interviews with Martin Young, Nov. 15, 1978; Gerald O'Reilly, May 15, 1978; Michael J. Quill, *Justice . . . for Ireland* (New York, 1944); Quill to Dan Breen, Nov. 22, 1944, and Quill to John Santo, Nov. 24, 1943 and undated [around Dec. 15, 1943], MF-T; *TWB*, May 1945, p. 16; *The Gaelic American*, May 26, 1945, pp. 1, 2.

27. Quill's victory was even more impressive when seen in the context of the city-wide results. Because of the low turnout, the new Council had only 17 members: 10 Democrats, 3 Republicans, 2 Communists (Cacchione and Manhattan's Ben Davis), Quill, and only one ALPer, Gertrude Klein, a Clothing Workers official from the Bronx whom the TWU had supported. *TWB*, Sept. 1943, p. 1; Oct. 1943, pp. 2–4; Nov. 1943, p. 2; Dec. 1943, p. 16; Gilbert Green, "The New York City Elections," *The Communist*, Dec. 1943, p. 1104; Waltzer, "ALP," 287; Michael J. Quill to John Santo, Nov. 12, 1943, MF-T; and Samuel Estreicher, "Collective Bargaining in the New York City Transit System, 1937–1950: A Case Study in the Politics of Municipal Unionism" (M.S. thesis, Cornell University, 1974), 216.

28. Forge, "Autobiographical Manuscript," p. 18; interview with Philip Bray, Aug. 13, 1979; Waltzer, "ALP," p. 276; *DW*, July 29, 1944, p. 4; Michael J. Quill to John Santo, Aug. 15, 1944, MF-T.

29. Waltzer, "ALP," pp. 288–89; *TWB*, Mar.–Apr. 1944, p. 10; Michael J. Quill to John Santo, Jan. 13 and Apr. 3, 1944, MF-T.

30. *TWB*, June 1942, p. 4; Aug. 1942, pp. 6–7; Oct. 1942, p. 7; Nov. 1942, p. 7; Aug. 1943, p. 16; Feb. 1945, p. 16; TWU, "You Have a Date with Your Future" [leaflet, 1944], JBF; *TWU 1943 Convention*, 158–59, 161, 180; *DW*, July 29, 1944, p. 4.

31. *TWU 1943 Convention*, 6, 104–7, 180; *Let the Record Speak! The Truth About Michael J. Quill's Betrayal of Transit Workers in the T.W.U.* (New York, 1948), 30; *LL*, Aug. 18, 1942, p. 3; *TWB*, Nov. 1941, p. 8; Aug. 1942, p. 16; Feb. 1945, p. 7; interview with Nat Cohen, Dec. 7, 1978.

32. *TWB*, June 1942, p. 5; May 1943, p. 10; Aug. 1943, p. 16; Apr. 1945, p. 16; *TWU 1943 Convention*, 80; TWU Local 100, *10th Anniversary Celebration*; Michael J. Quill to John Santo, Jan. 13, 1944, MF-T. For William Grogan's similar effort to combine leftism and Catholicism, see Rose Wortis, "Trends in the A.F. of L.," *The Communist*, Jan. 1942, p. 936.

33. Levering interview with Mike Quill, Oct. 31, 1948, pp. 1–2, box 7, Daniel Bell Collection, Tamiment Library, New York University; *TWB*, July 24, 1948, p. 8; interview with Maurice Forge, Jan. 27, 1979; Warren Moscow, *Politics in the Empire State* (New York, 1948), 89–92, 115–16; Lichtenstein, p. 286fn; Michael J. Quill to John Santo, Oct. 5, 1942, MF-T; Log of telephone conversation between Quill and Irene and Earl Browder, Mar. 31, 1945, (#100-7319-292), FBI-FOIA.

34. Levenstein, pp. 139–52; interviews with Peter MacLachlan, Feb. 25, 1979; Maurice Forge, Jan. 27, 1979; and Gerald O'Reilly, May 15, 1978; *TWB*, Jan. 1942, pp. 1, 4–5; Dec. 1943, pp. 6–7.

35. Interviews with Gerald O'Reilly, May 15, 1978; Maurice Forge, Jan. 13 and 27, 1979; *TWB*, Aug. 1942, p. 1; *LL*, Aug. 29, 1944, pp. 1, 4.

36. Melvyn Dubofsky and Warren Van Tine, *John L. Lewis: A Biography* (Urbana and Chicago, 1986), 242–67, 281–322 ("private labor army" on p. 286); Lichtenstein, pp. 155–71; *TWU 1943 Convention*, p. 113; *TWB*, Mar.–Apr. 1944, p. 10; John Ryan to Aaron Spelling, July 21, 1943, TWU-T.

37. Interviews with Gerald O'Reilly, May 15, 1978; Maurice Forge, Jan. 13 and 27, 1979; *TWB*, Feb. 1942, p. 5; *LL*, Aug. 29, 1944, pp. 1, 4.

38. Gallagher believed that the Third Avenue Railway management had a cozy relationship with the TWU leadership and worked with it to undermine the opposition. Interview with John Gallagher, Apr. 20, 1979; *TWB*, May 1942, pp. 1,3; July 1942, p. 7; Nov. 1942, p. 5; *DW*, May 15, 1942, pp. 1, 4; *LL*, May 18, 1942, pp. 1, 4; July 30, 1942, pp. 1, 3.

39. Interviews with John Gallagher, Apr. 20, 1979, Jerry O'Brien, Sept. 12, 1979; Patrick Walsh, June 1, 1978; *American Labor*, June 1971, p. 25; *TWU 1943 Convention*, 215; *TWB*, Nov. 1943, p. 6–7.

40. Letters from Michael J. Quill to John Santo: July 13, 1943; Nov. 24, 1943; undated [around Dec. 15, 1943]; Apr. 3, 1944; and May 12, 1944, MF-T; *TWB*, Oct. 1937, p. 11; Feb. 1942, p. 4; Jan.–Feb. 1944, p. 3; *TWU 1943 Convention*, 91, 119, 169, 213–16, 238–40.

41. District 50 originally hoped to extend its raid beyond the Third Avenue, but even before the election it abandoned such designs. With the help of ACTU, Greaney, Davis, and Keane appealed their firings to the SLRB, which ruled in February 1946 that they had been unfairly dismissed for union activities. It also found that the Third Avenue management had discouraged its employees from joining District 50. The three men, however, were not reinstated because they themselves had threatened co-workers with future job loss if District 50 won the election. *TWB*, Aug. 1944, pp. 1–3; Sept. 1944, p. 2; Mar. 1945, p. 3; *NYCTB*, Aug. 1944, p. 1; Feb. 1945, pp. 1–3; *LL*, Aug. 29, 1944, pp. 1, 4; Sept. 18, 1944, p. 4; Feb. 28, 1946, pp. 1, 3; Michael J. Quill to John Santo, Aug. 15, Aug. 30, and Oct. 18, 1944, MF-T; Quill to Philip Murray, Aug. 30, 1944, box A7-34, CIO Papers, Catholic University; New York Reports of Sept. 6, 1944 (#100-7319-268); Oct. 4, 1944 (#100-7319-270); and Jan. 16, 1945, (#100-7319-285), FBI-FOIA; interview with John Gallagher, Apr. 20, 1979; *TWU 1946 Convention*, 184; *NYT*, Feb. 21, 1946, p. 21.

42. Michael Quill to Philip Murray, Aug. 30, 1944, box A7-34, CIO Papers, Catholic University.

43. *TWB*, Oct. 1941, p. 2; July 1942, pp. 1, 4; Nov. 1942, p. 5; Jan.–Feb. 1943, p. 1; Jan.–Feb. 1944, p. 3; Mar. 1945, pp. 1–3; Apr. 1945, p. 5; *NYCTB*, Feb. 1945, pp. 1–3; Mar. 1945, pp. 1, 3; Sept. 1945, p. 1; N.Y.C. Omnibus Corporation, *Annual Report, 1942*, 18–24; N.Y.C. Omnibus Corporation, *Annual Report, 1944*, 9–11, 20–33; U.S. Department of Commerce, *Historical Statistics of the United States, Part I* (Washington, D.C., 1975), 170.

44. *TWB*, Aug. 1941, p. 3; July 1942, pp. 1–2.

44. Arthur Wiesenberger & Company, "Third Avenue Transit Corporation," Sept. 21, 1942," Scudder Collection, Thomas Watson Library, Columbia University; *TWB*, Oct. 1942, p. 1; Jan.–Feb. 1943, p. 1; Oct. 1943, p. 8; *DW*, June 16, 1942, p. 12; Michael J. Quill to John Santo, Oct. 18, 1944, MF-T.

46. *TWB*, Sept. 1941, p. 2; Jan. 1942, NYC supplement, p. 4; Feb. 1942, NYC supplement, p. 1; *TWU 1943 Convention*, 47, 140; TWU Local 100, "TWU and B. of T. Meet on Working Conditions"; *NYT*, Nov. 23, 1941, pp. 1, 42; Dec. 16, 1941, p. 29; July 30, 1942, p. 11; Transport Workers Union of America, "Brief before the National War Labor Board in re: Board of Transportation of the City of New York and Transport Workers Union of America" [1942] (hereafter TWU, "WLB Brief"), pp. 16–17, 19–21; Estreicher, pp. 145–47 ("most favored union").

47. TWU, "WLB Brief," 15–26; TWU Local 100 Executive Board, "A Four-Point Program for Victory," JBF; *TWB*, July 1942, pp. 1, 5; *NYT*, June 26, 1942, p. 16; Lichtenstein, pp. 41, 84–85.

48. *NYT*, July 30, 1942, p. 11; Aug. 21, 1942, p. 14; Aug. 28, 1942, p. 21; *TWB*, Oct. 1942, p. 1; TWU, "WLB Brief," p. 26.

49. *TWB*, Nov. 1942, pp. 1, 5; TWU, "WLB Brief," pp. 26–27; Michael J. Quill to John Santo, Oct. 21, Oct. 23, and Nov. 2, 1942, MF-T; *NYT*, Oct. 21, 1942, p. 15; Oct. 29, 1942, p. 10; Estreicher, p. 137.

50. *TWB*, Dec. 1942, pp. 1, 5; *NYT*, Nov. 17, 1942, p. 1; Dec. 11, 1942, p. 17; Dec. 16, 1942, p. 12; Dec. 17, 1942, p. 34; *New York World-Telegram*, Nov. 16, 1942, pp. 1, 9; Fiorello H. La Guardia to John Delaney, Nov. 15, 1942, folder 487, box 2591, LaGP; Estreicher, pp. 137–38; TWU, "WLB Brief," pp. 27–28.

51. *NYT*, Dec. 16, 1942, pp. 1, 12; Dec. 25, 1942, pp. 1, 21; *PM*, Dec. 16, 1942, p. 16; Michael J. Quill to John Santo, Dec. 16, 1942, MF-T.

52. Michael J. Quill to John Santo, Dec. 18, 1942, MF-T; *NYT*, Dec. 24, 1942, p. 17.

53. *NYT*, Dec. 25, 1942, pp. 1, 21; Michael J. Quill to John Santo, Dec. 29, 1942, MF-T; interview of Earl Browder by Daniel Bell, June 26 or 27, 1955, Daniel Bell Collection.

54. *NYT*, Jan. 5, 1943, p. 21; Jan. 6, 1943, p. 12; Jan. 7, 1943, pp. 1, 15, 40; Jan. 10, 1943, p. 52; Philip Murray to Fiorello H. La Guardia, Jan. 5, 1943, folder 487, box 2591, LaGP; Michael J. Quill to John Santo, Dec. 29, 1942 and Jan. 11, 1943, MF-T; interview of Earl Browder by Daniel Bell, June 26 or 27, 1955; Confidential National Defense Informant Report on TWU Meeting of January 6, 1943 (#100-7319-152), FBI-FOIA.

55. Michael J. Quill to John Santo, Jan. 11, 1943, MF-T; *NYT*, Jan. 11, 1943, p. 17.

56. TWU, Local 100, "Save Your Transit System," and "Arbitration—The Fair and Patriotic Way to Settle the Transit Dispute" [leaflets], JBF; *TWB*, Jan.–Feb. 1943, pp. 1, 4; *NYT*, Feb. 12, 1943, p. 27; Teletype, NY Office to Director, Feb. 10, 1943 (#100-7319-165); and Confidential National Defense Informant Report on TWU Meeting of February 9, 1943 (#100-7319-169), FBI-FOIA.

57. *NYT*, Jan. 7 1932, pp. 15, 40; Jan. 28, 1943, p. 21; Jan. 29, 1943, p. 21; Jan. 30, 1943, p. 26; Jan. 31, 1943, p. 26; *TWB*, Jan.–Feb. 1943, pp. 4–5; New York Report, Apr. 10, 1943, pp. 2–3 (#100-7319-180), FBI-FOIA; John H. Delany to Fiorello H. La Guardia, Jan. 30, 1943, box 2591, folder 487, LaGP.

58. *NYT*, Feb. 2, 1943, p. 21; Feb. 3, 1943, p. 21; Apr. 30. 1943, p. 12; *TWB*, Mar. 1943, p. 2; TWU Local 100, "Another Step In TWU March to Victory," JBF.

59. *NYT*, Jan. 5, 1943, p. 21; Feb. 1, 1943, p. 17; Feb. 2, 1943, p. 21; Feb. 3, 1943, p. 21; Feb. 4, 1943, p. 25; Feb. 13, 1943, p. 19; Feb. 15, 1943, p. 13; Feb. 25, 1943, p. 17; Apr. 30, 1943, pp. 1, 12; TWU Local 100, "To Every Transit Worker in the Transit System Who Needs A Raise!" and "Add it Up!" [leaflets], JBF; Committee of Citizens Formed to Aid in the Settlement of the Labor Controversy in the Transit System, *Labor Relations in the New York City Transit System* (New York, 1943).

60. *NYT*, Apr. 30, 1943, pp. 1, 12; *TWB*, May 1943, pp. 2, 4–5; McGinley, p. 312; Estreicher, pp. 140–41.

61. The new wage rates finally brought the pay levels for the largely female BMT agents up to the IRT and IND level. Since the NWLB had decided it did not have jurisdiction over the NYCTS, its "Little Steel formula" did not apply. *NYT*, Apr. 10, 1943, pp. 1, 12; June 16, 1943, pp. 1, 10; Aug. 6, 1943, p. 26; *TWB*, July 1943, pp. 1, 8, 11; TWU Local 100, "This is the T.W.U. Victory," JBF; Estreicher, pp. 140–41. The new work rules, as revised in December 1943, were published in Board of Transportation of the City of New York, *Proceedings*, 53 Supplement (1943).

62. *NYT*, June 16, 1943, p. 10; *TWB*, July 1943, pp. 1, 11, 16; Aug. 1943, pp. 3, 12; interview with James Sullivan, July 27, 1979; Michael J. Quill to John Santo, Jan. 28, 1944, MF-T; McGinley, pp. 313, 422–46; *TWU 1943 Convention*, 51–52.

63. *TWB*, May 1944, pp. 8–9; *NYT*, June 6, 1944, p. 17; June 6, 1944, p. 1; interview with Lewis Fraad, June 30, 1980; Michael J. Quill to John Santo, undated [around Dec. 15, 1943], MF-T.

64. *TWB*, July 1944, p. 3; Oct. 1944, p. 13; *NYT*, June 28, 1944, p. 19; *NYCTB*, Sept. 1944, pp. 1–2.

65. *TWB*, July 1944, p. 3; Nov. 1944, pp. 1, 2; Jan. 1945, p. 3; Feb. 1945, pp. 1–2; *NYCTB*, Aug. 1944, p. 2; Oct. 1944, p. 1; Nov. 1944, pp. 1–4; Jan. 1945, pp. 1–2; *NYT*, Aug. 1, 1944, p. 25; Nov. 11, 1944, p. 14; Nov. 12, 1944, p. 44; Nov. 29, 1944, p. 16; Nov. 18, 1944, p. 21.

66. *TWB*, Jan. 1945, p. 1; Apr. 1945, p. 3; *NYCTB*, Apr. 1945, p. 1; June 1945, pp. 1, 4; *NYT*, Dec. 4, 1944, p. 25; McGinley, p. 402; E. E. Conroy to Director, FBI, April 5, 1945, and attached telephone logs (#100-7319-292), FBI-FOIA.

67. Michael J. Quill to John Santo, May 8, 1945, MF-T.

68. August Heckscher, with Phyllis Robinson, *When La Guardia Was Mayor: New York's Legendary Years* (New York, 1978), 374.

69. See Lichtenstein; Martin Glaberman, *Wartime Strikes: The Struggle Against the No-Strike Pledge in the UAW during World War II* (Detroit, 1980); James Green, "Fighting on Two Fronts: Working-Class Militancy in the 1940s," *Radical America*, July–Aug. 1975, pp. 7–47. For a somewhat different view, see Freeman, "Delivering the Goods."

Chapter 11

1. Joshua Freeman, "Delivering the Goods: Industrial Unionism During World War II," *Labor History*, Fall 1978, pp. 574, 591–92; Robert H. Zieger, *American Workers, American Unions, 1920–1985* (Baltimore, 1986), 84, 100–101.

2. Taxi developments can be followed in the *NYT* (esp. May–Aug. 1937); *DW* (esp. Feb.–Mar. 1934, Mar. 1937, Mar. 1938, and Feb. 1939); and *TWB* (1937–45). See also, Memo on Transit Unions in New York City, TWU file, box A7-34, CIO Papers, Catholic University; New York Report, Aug. 13, 1947 (#100-7319-359), FBI-FOIA; *TWU 1937 Convention*, Report of the Executive Board, p. 3; Oct. 7 morning session, 24a–24c, and Oct. 8 afternoon session, p. 35; *TWU 1939 Convention*, 58–59, 183–86, 196; *TWU 1941 Convention*, 14; Shirley Quill, *Mike Quill—Himself, A Memoir* (Greenwich, Conn., 1985), 111–14; interviews with James Sullivan, July 27, 1979; Maurice Forge, Jan. 7, 1979, and July 15, 1980. For additional details and sources, see Joshua B. Freeman, "The Transport Workers Union in New York City, 1933–1948" (Ph.D. dissertation, Rutgers University, 1983), 307–10 (hereafter Freeman, "TWU").

3. *NYT*, July 7, 1937, p. 8; July 8, 1937, p. 8; July 9, 1937, p. 2; *TWB*, July 1937, pp. 3, 15; Nov. 1937, p. 1; June 1938, pp. 1–3; July 1938, pp. 1–3; Aug. 1938, pp. 1–3; *Motorman, Conductor and Motor Coach Operator*, Mar. 1939, pp. 9–10; George H. Rooney to John L. Lewis, TWU file, box A7-34, CIO Papers, Catholic University; *TWU 1939 Convention*, 42; *TWU 1941 Convention*, 217–19.

4. *TWU 1939 Convention*, 21, 30, 34, 129–31, 177–79, 181–82; *TWU 1941 Convention*, 53–58, 207–9, 258, 260, 264–65; *TWB*, Aug. 1937, p. 4; Jan. 1938, p. 4; Mar. 1938, p. 7; July 1940, p. 1; Aug. 1940, p. 1; Sept. 1940, p. 1; Oct. 1940, p. 1; Mar. 1, 1941, p. 1; Apr. 1941, p. 1; Aug. 1941, p. 10; Sidney Fine, *Sit-Down, The General Motors Strike of 1936–1937* (Ann Arbor, 1969), 117, 161, 317; *NYWTB*, July 20, 1940, p. 2.

5. *TWB*, Nov. 1941, p. 1; *TWU 1941 Convention*, p. 84; *TWU 1946 Convention*, p. 20;

Omaha Reports of July 21, 1942 (#100-7319-62) and Oct. 14, 1942 (#100-7319-99), FBI-FOIA.

6. *TWB*, Aug. 1941, p. 10; Dec. 1941, p. 2; *TE*, Apr. 1954, p. 12.

7. The Los Angeles situation can be followed in case files 196/6076, 196/8420, and 196/8420A, Federal Mediation and Conciliation Service, Subject and Dispute Files, RF 280, National Archives, Washington, D.C.; Los Angeles Reports of Aug. 9, 1941 (#100-7319-16) and Sept. 28, 1942 (#100-7319-91), FBI-FOIA; and *TWB*, Sept. 1941–Mar. 1942, passim.

8. *TWB*, Mar. 1943, p. 3; *TWU 1943 Convention*, 76; FBI Chicago Reports, Apr. 1943–Aug. 1945, FBI-FOIA (see Freeman, "TWU," 673–74 for full citations); interview with Maurice Forge, Jan. 27, 1979; "Bell-Labor's Month," "CIO-I" folder, box 4, and Levering interview with Mike Quill, Mike Quill folder, box 7, Daniel Bell Collection, Tamiment Library, New York University.

9. *TWB*, Mar. 1943, p. 3; June 1943, p. 3; Jan.–Feb. 1944, p. 6; Jan. 1945, p. 4; Dennis J. Comey to Philip Carey, Oct. 12, 1943, "Labor School Correspondence—June–Dec 1943 (P. Carey)," XA; John Edgar Hoover, Memorandum for the Attorney General, Oct. 10, 1943 (#100-7319-218); J.F. Sears to Director, FBI, Nov. 6, 1943 (#100-7319-222); and Philadelphia Report, May 3, 1945 (#100-7319-296), FBI-FOIA; interviews with Maurice Forge, Jan. 27, 1979; James Sullivan, Aug. 16, 1979; *TWU 1946 Convention*, 126.

10. Interviews with Maurice Forge, Jan. 13, 1979: Martin Young, Nov. 15, 1978; *TWB*, June 1943, p. 3; Aug. 1943, p. 6; Aug. 1944, p. 12; Michael J. Quill to John Santo, July 15, 1943, MF-T; John Edgar Hoover, Memorandum for the Attorney General, Oct. 10, 1943 (#100-7319-218); J.F. Sears to Director, FBI, Nov. 10, 1943 (#100-7319-223); Philadelphia Reports of Nov. 20, 1943 (#100-7319-244) and May 3, 1945 (#100-7319-296), FBI-FOIA; Allan M. Winkler, "The Philadelphia Transit Strike of 1944," *Journal of American History* 59 (July 1972): 81.

11. *TWB*, Aug. 1943, p. 3; Dec. 1943, p. 3; Jan.–Feb. 1944, p. 6; Mar.–Apr. 1944, pp. 1, 16; TWU, "Somebody's Face Is Red!" [leaflet], JBF; Philadelphia Reports of June 13, 1944 (#100-7319-258) and May 3, 1945 (#100-7319-289), FBI-FOIA; Dennis J. Comey to Philip Carey, Oct. 12, 1943, "Labor School Correspondence—June–Dec 1943 (P. Carey)"; Comey to Carey, Jan. 24, and Feb. 4, 1944, and Robert Lasher to Carey, Mar. 23, 1944, "Labor School Correspondence—Jan–June 1944," XA.

12. Winkler, pp. 73–79; Philip S. Foner, *Organized Labor and the Black Worker, 1619–1973* (New York, 1976), 266; John Edgar Hoover, Memorandum for the Attorney General, Oct. 10, 1943 (#100-7319-218), and Philadelphia Reports of June 13, 1944 (#100-7319-258) and May 3, 1945 (#100-7319-296), FBI-FOIA; Michael J. Quill to John Santo, Jan. 13, 1944, MF-T; *TWB*, Jan.–Feb. 1944, p. 11; Mar.–Apr. 1944, p. 16; TWU, "The Victory Way for PTC Workers" [Jan. 1944]; Dennis J. Comey to Philip Carey, Dec. 24, 1944, "Labor School Correspondence—June–Dec. 1943 (P. Carey)," and Comey to Carey, Feb. 4, 1944, "Labor School Correspondence—Jan–June 1944," XA; Herbert Hill, *Black Labor and the American Legal System, I: Race, Work and the Law* (Washington, D.C., 1977), 285, 288; August Meier and Elliot Rudwick, "Communist Unions and the Black Community: The Case of the Transport Workers Union, 1934–1944," *Labor History* 23 (Spring 1982): 186.

13. Michael J. Quill to John Santo, Mar. 10, 1944, MF-T; Dennis J. Comey to Philip Carey, Mar. 13, 1944, and Robert Lasher to Carey, Mar. 23, 1944, "Labor School Correspondence—Jan–June 1944," XA; *TWB*, Mar.–Apr. 1944, pp. 1, 16; Philadelphia Reports of June 13, 1944 (#100-7319-258) and May 3, 1945 (#100-7319-296), FBI-FOIA.

14. *TWB*, Mar.–Apr. 1944, pp. 1, 9; May 1944, p. 3; July 1944, p. 9.

15. Mark D. Naison, "The Communist Party in Harlem: 1928–1936" (Ph.D. dissertation, Columbia University, 1975), 216, 219–23; *DW*, May 28, 1934, New York trade union section, pp. 1, 4; *NYT*, Dec. 16, 1937, p. 4; Feb. 3, 1943, p. 21; Meier and Rudwick, pp.

176–82; Mark Naison, "Harlem Communists & The Politics of Black Protest," *Marxist Perspectives* 3 (Fall 1978): 38–39; Adam Clayton Powell, Jr., *Adam by Adam: The Autobiography of Adam Clayton Powell, Jr.* (New York, 1971), 66–67; Mark Naison, *Communists in Harlem during the Depression* (Urbana, 1983), 267–69, 306–8; Leo Huberman, *The Great Bus Strike* (New York, 1941), 30; Samuel Estreicher, "Collective Bargaining in the New York City Transit System, 1937–1950: A Case Study in the Politics of Municipal Unionism" (M.S. thesis, Cornell University, 1974), pp. 200–201; *TWB*, July 1942, p. 3; *NYWTB*, Apr. 5, 1941, p. 2; Frank Crosswaith to Fiorello H. La Guardia, April 30, 1941, with attachment, folder 236, box 2555, LaGP; interviews with Abner Berry, Dec. 5, 1978; Maurice Forge, Feb. 10, 1979; and Martin Young, Dec. 15, 1978.

16. See Chapter 7. In Chicago, the Packinghouse Workers informally arranged a similar preferential hiring program at Swift during this same period. See David Brody, *Workers in Industrial America: Essays on the 20th Century Struggle* (New York, 1980), 98.

17. *TWB*, Jan. 1942, p. 11; June 1942, p. 4; July 1942, p. 4; Nov. 1942, p. 7; Aug. 1943, p. 16; July 1944, p. 5; Ben Davis, *Communist Councilman from Harlem: Autobiographical Notes Written in a Federal Penitentiary* (New York, 1969), 140–41; *TWU 1941 Convention*, 137–38, 154, 191; *TWU 1943 Convention*, 25–31, 158–59.

18. Philadelphia Reports of June 13, 1944 (#100-7319-258) and May 3, 1945 (#100-7319-296), FBI-FOIA; Winkler, pp. 79–83; Hill, p. 295; Foner, *Black Worker*, pp. 266–68; *TWB*, Aug. 1944, pp. 1, 12; Michael J. Quill to John Santo, Aug. 15, 1944, MF-T; *DW*, June 10, 1945, magazine section, p. 4.

19. Winkler, pp. 82–85, 89; interviews with Maurice Forge, Dec. 30, 1978; Martin Young, Nov. 15, 1978; Michael J. Quill to John Santo, Aug. 15, 1944, MF-T.

20. Michael J. Quill to John Santo, Aug. 15 and Oct. 18, 1944, MF-T; interview with Martin Young, Nov. 15, 1978; *TWB*, Sept. 1944, p. 9; Oct. 1944, p. 7; Winkler, pp. 85–86; SAC Philadelphia to Director, FBI (#100-7319-297); Philadelphia Report, Dec. 5, 1945 (#100-7319-315), FBI-FOIA.

21. *TWB*, Nov. 1944, p. 5; Oct. 1945, p. 5; *DW*, June 10, 1945, magazine section, p. 4; Philadelphia Reports of May 3, 1945 (#100-7319-296) and Nov. 5, 1945 (#100-7319-315), FBI-FOIA; Dennis J. Comey to Philip Carey, Feb. 12, 1945, "Labor School Correspondence—Jan–June 1945 (Carey)," XA; interviews with Maurice Forge, Jan. 27, 1979, and James Sullivan, Aug. 16, 1979.

22. *TWB*, Sept. 1945, p. 3; Apr. 1946, p. 11; June 1946, p. 12; July 1946, p. 4; July 1947, p. 10; Oct. 1947, pp. 3, 7; Dec. 6, 1948, p. 6; *TWU 1946 Convention*, 31, 124–26; John Daugherty to Douglas L. MacMahon, Jan. 30, 1946, JBF; Michael J. Quill to Philip Murray, Apr. 22, 1946, and Warren G. Horie to Allan S. Haywood, June 9, 1942, box A7-34, CIO Papers, Catholic University.

23. In 1944 the Amalgamated claimed a membership of 125,000 in 453 locals. After the war the AFL union was increasingly willing to call strikes, even in the public sector. James J. McGinley, *Labor Relations in the New York Rapid Transit Systems, 1904–1944* (New York, 1949), 258–60; Beulah Amidon, "Strikes in Public Employment," *Survey Graphic* 35 (May 1946): 154; *TWU 1946 Convention*, 36–37, 179–80; interview with Maurice Forge, Jan. 13, 1979.

24. Interview with Maurice Forge, Jan. 27, 1979.

25. Minutes of TWU International Executive Board, March 29 and 30, 1941, TWU of A.

26. New Orleans Report, June 2, 1943 (#100-7319-197), FBI-FOIA. The strong CP presence in Local 206 did not ensure internal harmony. Throughout the early war years the local was wracked by a struggle between two factions, each dominated by CPers. For a more complete discussion of Local 206, see Freeman, "TWU," 662–66.

27. Columbia turned out to be a remarkably recalcitrant employer, stalling contract talks and even defying a War Labor Board directive, but a two-day strike right after the war finally brought a contract. The maintenance staffs at Barnard College, Julliard School of Music, and the Jewish Theological Seminary were eventually organized by the TWU as well. Interview with Maurice Forge, Jan. 13, 1979; Michael J. Quill to John Santo, n.d. [around Dec. 15, 1943], MF-T; *TWB*, Mar. 1945, p. 3; *TE*, May 1959, p. 10.

28. Robert S. Wechsler, *Burning Bright: The Story of Local 101, Transport Workers Union of America, AFL-CIO* (New York, 1981), 5–11; Freeman, "TWU," 666–70.

29. Utility Workers Union of America file, box A7-34, CIO Papers, Catholic University; *LL*, Jan. 31, 1942, p. 1; Mar. 31, 1944, p. 1; Apr. 30, 1945, p. 1; June 18, 1945, pp. 1, 2; July 1945, p. 1; *NYT*, Jan. 7, 1943, p. 40; J. Edgar Hoover to SAC, NY, Sept. 16, 1942 (#100-7319-84), and New York Report, Sept. 28, 1942 (#100-7319-102), FBI-FOIA; Michael J. Quill to John Santo, Nov. 24, 1943, n.d. [around Dec. 15, 1943], Jan. 13, 1944, July 13, 1944, and Oct. 18, 1944, MF-T; *TWB*, Feb. 1945, p. 2; *TWU 1946 Convention*, 36–37.

30. *TWU 1943 Convention*, 9; *TWU 1946 Convention*, 179–99; interview with Maurice Forge, Jan. 27, 1979; Miami Report, Dec. 31, 1943 (#100-7319-241), FBI-FOIA; Minutes of TWU International Executive Board, Oct. 18–19, 1943, TWU of A.

31. *TWB*, Mar.–Apr. 1944, p. 12; Feb. 1945, p. 7; Apr. 1945, p. 6; June 1945, p. 5; Michael J. Quill to John Santo, Nov. 24, 1943, Mar. 10, 1944, Oct. 18, 1944, Apr. 14, 1945, and June 8, 1945, MF-T; *TWU 1946 Convention*, 195–97; Miami Reports of Dec. 31, 1943 (#100-7319-241), Apr. 4, 1944 (#100-7319-251), and May 16, 1945 (#100-7319-300), and SAC, San Francisco to Director, FBI (#100-7319-307), FBI-FOIA; interview with Maurice Forge, Jan. 27, 1979; and Airline Mechanics file, box A7-22, CIO Papers, Catholic University.

32. Mark L. Kahn, "Airlines," in Gerald G. Somers (ed.), *Collective Bargaining: Contemporary American Experience* (Madison, Wisc., 1980); interview with Maurice Forge, Jan. 27, 1979; Paul Crouch to M. L. Edwards, Jan. 22, 1947, JBF; and Miami Report, June 10, 1946 (#100-7319-339), FBI-FOIA.

33. Interviews with Maurice Forge, Jan. 27, 1979; James Sullivan, Aug. 16, 1979; *TWU 1946 Convention*, pp. 155–57; Forge to Michael J. Quill and Douglas L. MacMahon, Oct. 26, 1946, and Forge to Austin Hogan, Aug. 6, 1946, in possession of Forge.

34. Air Mechanics file, box A7-22, CIO Papers, Catholic University; Michael J. Quill to John Santo, Apr. 14 and June 8, 1945, and William Grogan to Noah Tauscher, June 18, 1947, MF-T; *NYT*, Oct. 1, 1945, p. 8; Oct. 11, 1945, p. 16; Oct. 12, 1945, p. 15; Oct. 14, 1945, p. 38; Oct. 20, 1945, p. 2; Oct. 24, 1945, pp. 1, 14; Oct. 25, 1945, pp. 1, 2; Oct. 26, 1945, pp. 1, 11; *TWB*, Apr. 1945, p. 6; June 1945, p. 5; Oct. 1945, p. 8; Nov. 1945, p. 10; July 1946, p. 10; Aug.–Sept. 1946, pp. 10, 12; Nov.–Dec. 1946, p. 6; Jan. 1947, p. 2; Dec. 1947, pp. 1, 5; Oct. 6, 1948, p. 6; TWU, *The Record* (New York, 1946); *TWU 1946 Convention*, 35–36, 79–80, 123–24; interview with Maurice Forge, Jan. 27, 1979; TWU, "Proceedings of the Airline Conference, Air Transport Division, TWU, December 5, 1948," MF-T, p. 23; TWU, *The Record Speaks—Facts for Airline Workers* (New York, 1947).

35. Accurate TWU membership figures were not generally published, especially for locals without union shops. The estimate of non-Local 100 TWU membership at the end of the war was calculated from various sources cited throughout this chapter. The 1948 figures were derived from an internal TWU working document used to determine representation at the 1948 TWU convention (copy in author's possession). All figures are for actual, dues-paying members; since many TWU locals, including all the airline units, did not have union shops, the number of workers covered by TWU contracts was somewhat higher.

Chapter 12

1. Michael J. Quill to John Santo, Nov. 11 and May 8, 1944, MF-T; Kenneth Waltzer, "The American Labor Party: Third Party Politics in New Deal-Cold War New York, 1936–1954" (Ph.D. dissertation, Harvard University, 1977), 308 (hereafter "ALP").

2. DW, May 13, 1945, p. 6; May 17, 1945, p. 3; Waltzer, "ALP," 309–11; NYCTB, July 1945, p. 1.

3. Paul O'Dwyer Memoir, OHCCU; Michael J. Quill to John Santo, May 8, 1945, MF-T.

4. TWB, July 1945, p. 1; Aug. 1945, pp. 1, 8–9; Sept. 1945, pp. 8–9; Samuel Estreicher, "Collective Bargaining in the New York City Transit System, 1937–1950: A Case Study in the Politics of Municipal Unionism" (M.S. thesis, Cornell University, 1974), 223, 225; DW, May 13, 1945, p. 6; Waltzer, "ALP," 301; Max Gordon, "Labor Moves Forward in New York Elections," Political Affairs, Dec. 1945, p. 1086.

5. NYCTB, Oct. 1945, p. 1; Transport Workers Union of Greater New York (Local 100), Union Security Means a Good Job; Our Case for Collective Bargaining in the New York City Transit System (New York, 1946), 6–8.

6. O'Dwyer received 1,125,355 votes, of which 257,929 were on the ALP line. His Republican-Liberal-Fusion opponent, Jonah Goldstein received 431,601 votes, while independent Newbold Morris, backed by La Guardia, got 408,408 votes. Unless all the non-Democratic parties had united, O'Dwyer could have been elected even without ALP support, a fact that he could not have failed to notice. Gordon, "New York Elections," pp. 1079, 1086; Charles Garrett, The La Guardia Years (New Brunswick, N.J., 1961), 300, 395fn.

7. DW, June 12, 1945, p. 6; June 16, 1945, p. 12; NYT, Aug. 1945, p. 14; Aug. 17, 1945, p. 16; Aug. 18, 1945, p. 11; Nov. 9, 1945, p. 13; Nov. 10, 1945, p. 26; Nov. 22, 1945, p. 10; Memo from SAC New York, Jan. 24, 1946 (file #100-7319-326), FBI-FOIA; LL, Feb. 16, 1946, p. 3; TWB, Nov. 1945, pp. 3, 16; Dec. 1945, pp. 3, 4; Jan. 1946, p. 5; Apr. 1946, p. 11; TE, May 1959, p. 10; NYCTB, Dec. 1945, p. 1.

8. NYWTB, Nov. 30, 1940, p. 2; NYT, Oct. 26, 1945, p. 21; Nov. 16, 1945, p. 34.

9. NYT, Nov. 16, 1945, p. 34; Dec. 14, 1945, p. 26; Jan. 14, 1946, p. 21; Feb. 22, 1946, p. 14; Garrett, p. 128.

10. NYT, Jan. 8, 1946, pp. 25, 36; Jan. 14, 1946, p. 21; Jan. 16, 1946, p. 3; Jan. 20, 1946, pp. 1, 4.

11. NYT, Jan. 3, 1946, pp. 1, 40; Jan. 21, 1946, p. 15; Estreicher, pp. 227–28.

12. NYT, Jan. 19, 1946, pp. 1, 3; Jan. 20, 1946, pp. 1, 4; Jan. 21, 1946, p. 1; TWB, Feb. 1946, p. 4.

13. NYT, Jan. 22, 1946, pp. 1, 10; NYCTB, Jan. 1946, pp. 1–3.

14. Paul Windels Memoir, p. 123, OHCCU; NYT, Jan. 27, 1946, p. 4; Feb. 22, 1946, p. 1; Estreicher, pp. 228–29.

15. TWB, Feb. 1946, p. 1; NYCTB, Feb. 1946, pp. 1–3; NYT, Jan. 30, 1946, p. 19; Feb. 20, 1946, p. 27; Feb. 21, 1946, pp. 1, 27.

16. TWB, Mar. 1946, pp. 2, 16; NYT, Feb. 20, 1946, p. 27; Feb. 21, 1946, pp. 1, 12; Feb. 22, 1946, pp. 1, 14; Feb. 23, 1946, pp. 1, 10; Feb. 24, 1946, pp. 1, 2; Feb. 25, 1946, pp. 1, 16; Feb. 26, 1946, pp. 1, 13, 14; Feb. 27, 1946, pp. 1–3; Paul Windels Memoir, p. 123, and William O'Dwyer Memoir, p. 210, OHCCU, Estreicher, pp. 229–30.

17. Estreicher, pp. 230–31; NYT, Feb. 27, 1946, pp. 1–3; May 5, 1946, pp. 1–2.

18. James J. McGinley, Labor Relations in the New York Rapid Transit Systems, 1904–1944 (New York, 1949), 403; LL, Jan. 31, 1946, p. 3; NYT, Feb. 20, 1946, p. 27; Feb. 25, 1946, p. 24.

19. McGinley, pp. 422–26; *NYT*, Jan. 24, 1946, pp. 1, 12; Feb. 24, 1946, p. 3; Feb. 27, 1946, p. 2; Feb. 28, 1946, p. 15.

20. Estreicher, pp. 159–60; *TWU 1946 Convention*, 66; interviews with James Sullivan, Aug. 16, 1979; Gerald O'Reilly, Jan. 11, 1979; John Plover, Feb. 20, 1979; Joseph Labash, Aug. 3, 1979; and Maurice Forge, July 29, 1979; Transport Workers Union of Greater New York (Local 100), *Our Case for Higher Wages* (New York, 1946), 14–19.

21. *TWB*, Feb. 1946, p. 15; Mar. 1946, p. 13; Apr. 1946, p. 15; *NYCTB*, Feb. 1946, p. 4; *LL*, Jan. 31, 1946, p. 3; *NYT*, Feb. 25, 1946, p. 1; Feb. 26, 1946, p. 1; Mar. 27, 1946, p. 20; May 16, 1946, p. 3; May 17, 1946, p. 9; Estreicher, p. 231.

22. *NYT*, Jan. 27, 1946, p. 1; *TWB*, Jan. 1946, p. 5; Feb. 1946, p. 1; Apr. 1946, p. 6; June 1946, p. 5; TWU Local 100, *Union Security*, 24–31; Local 100, *Our Case for Higher Wages*, 8.

23. Local 100, *Our Case for Higher Wages* and *Union Security*; *NYT*, Mar. 4, 1946, p. 25; Mar. 13, 1946, p. 31; Mar. 14, 1946, p. 31; Mar. 23, 1946, p. 28; Mar. 27, 1946, p. 20; Mar. 28, 1946, p. 29; May 16, 1946, p. 3; May 17, 1946, p. 9; May 21, 1946, p. 17; *TWB*, Apr. 1946, p. 3; May 1946, p. 3; Aug.–Sept. 1946, pp. 3–4; Estreicher, pp. 232–34.

24. Estreicher, pp. 235–38; *TWB*, June 1946, p. 3; Oct. 1946, p. 1; Nov.–Dec. 1946, pp. 2–3; *NYT*, Nov. 10, 1946, p. 1; Nov. 12, 1946, p. 1; Nov. 13, 1946, p. 1; May 17, 1947, p. 7; interview with James Sullivan, Aug. 16, 1979; McGinley, p. 422.

25. *NYT*, Mar. 27, 1947, pp. 1–2; Mar. 29, 1947, pp. 1, 9; May 5, 1947, pp. 1, 16; May 8, 1947, pp. 1, 16; May 17, 1947, p. 17.

26. *NYT*, Mar. 19, 1947, p. 27; Mar. 29, 1947, p. 1; May 8, 1947, pp. 1, 16.

27. TWU, "TWU on Mayor's Annual Message to the City Council," press release of Jan. 28, 1947, JBF; *NYT*, Feb. 20, 1946, p. 27; May 5, 1946, pp. 1, 2; Mar. 29, 1947, p. 9; Apr. 8, 1947, p. 29; May 5, 1947, pp. 1, 16; interview with Peter MacLachlan, Feb. 25, 1979 (includes quote); *TWB*, Oct. 1947, p. 6; Theodore W. Kheel and J.K. Turcott, *Transit and Arbitration: A Decade of Decisions and The Path to Transit Peace* (Englewood Cliffs, N.J., 1960), 42.

28. *NYT*, Apr. 8, 1947, p. 29; May 8, 1947, pp. 1, 16; June 7, 1947, pp. 1, 2; *TWB*, Aug.–Sept. 1946, p. 6; Oct. 1947, p. 7; *TV*, Aug. 23, 1947, p. 3; Edward Sussna, "Collective Bargaining on the New York City Transit System, 1940–1957," *Industrial and Labor Relations Review* 11 (1958): 527–29; Shirley Quill, *Mike Quill—Himself, A Memoir* (Greenwich, Conn., 1985), 119–21; interviews with Adrian Cabral, Apr. 12, 1979; Maurice Forge, Aug. 9, 1979; SAC, New York to Director, FBI, Mar. 9, 1948 (#100-7319-379), FBI-FOIA.

29. *NYT*, June 11, 1947, p. 1; Oct. 3, 1947, pp. 1, 2; *TWB*, Oct. 1947, p. 6; interview with Adrian Cabral, Apr. 12, 1979; *TV*, Aug. 23, 1947, p. 3; Sept. 3, 1947, pp. 3, 10; Oct. 25, 1947, pp. 1, 3; Board of Transportation of the City of New York, *Proceedings* 63 (1948): 148.

30. The best account of the CP's wartime policies is Maurice Isserman's *Which Side Were You On?: The American Communist Party During the Second World War* (Middletown, Conn., 1982). See also Joseph R. Starobin, *American Communism in Crisis, 1943–1957* (Cambridge, Mass., 1972), 20–120; *Political Affairs*, Sept. 1946, p. 770.

31. Isserman, pp. 194, 284fn; Michael J. Quill to John Santo, Jan. 13, 1944, MF-T.

32. Interviews with Martin Young, Nov. 15, 1978; Maurice Forge, Feb. 10, 1979; and Gerald O'Reilly, May 15, 1978; Isserman, p. 200.

33. Interview with Maurice Forge, Feb. 10, 1979; Starobin, pp. 96–98.

34. Waltzer, "ALP," 317, 335–38; Bella Dodd, *School of Darkness* (1954; reprint ed., New York, 1963), 191–92; John Gates, *The Story of an American Communist* (New York, 1958), 104–11; interview with Max Gordon, Oct. 24, 1978; Irving Howe and Lewis Coser,

The American Communist Party: A Critical History (New York, 1962), 444–46, 453–57; Robert Thompson, "Conclusion from the New York Elections," *Political Affairs*, Jan. 1947, p. 44.

35. *TWB*, Jan. 1946, p. 4; Michael J. Quill to John Santo, Jan. 11, 1943, MF-T; Simon W. Gerson, *Pete: The Story of Peter V. Cacchione, New York's First Communist Councilman* (New York, 1976), 178–80; David A. Shannon, *The Decline of American Communism: A History of the Communist Party of the United States Since 1945* (New York, 1959), 52–54; Dodd, p. 193; interviews with Martin Young, Nov. 15, 1978; and Simon Gerson, Dec. 18, 1979.

36. Quill repeated this charge several times, but there is no independent collaboration. Quill's explanation for the CP's position, "that the national unity was still on," does not make obvious sense. There is some evidence that the CP strongly supported the TWU in its early 1946 clashes with the Board of Transportation. See Levering interview with Mike Quill, Oct. 31, 1948, box 7, Daniel Bell Collection, and Michael J. Quill to Peter Cacchione, Mar. 6, 1946, box 1, Peter Cacchione Papers, both in Tamiment Library, New York University; Max Kampelman, *The Communist Party vs. the CIO* (New York, 1957), 151; and interview with Gerald O'Reilly, May 15, 1978.

37. McGinley, p. 427.

38. *TWB*, Sept. 1945, p. 1; Dec. 1945, p. 2; Apr. 1946, pp. 12–13, 16; May 1946, p. 8; July 1946, pp. 6–8; Oct. 1946, pp. 9, 12; *DW*, May 28, 1945, p. 5; Waltzer, "ALP," 335–36.

39. *TWB*, July 1946, p. 8; Jan. 1948, p. 8; interview with Maurice Forge, Jan. 27, 1979; Miami Report, July 10, 1946 (#100-7319-339), pp. 2–3, FBI-FOIA.

40. *TWU 1946 Convention*, pp. 4–9, 22–26, 67–73, 92, 101–11, 115–19, 133–40, 169.

41. Waltzer, "ALP," 338–39, 346–47; *TWB*, July 1946, p. 14; Aug.–Sept. 1946, p. 14; interviews with Gerald O'Reilly, Jan. 11, 1979; James Sullivan, Aug. 16, 1979; Thompson, "Conclusion from the New York Elections," 37–46.

42. Mary Sperling McAuliffe, *Crisis on the Left: Cold War Politics and American Liberals, 1947–1954* (Amherst, 1978), 14–16; Len De Caux, *Labor Radical: From the Wobblies to CIO, A Personal History* (Boston, 1970), 475–76; Harvey A. Levenstein, *Communism, Anticommunism, and the CIO* (Westport, Conn., 1981), 208–14.

43. Interviews with Raymond Westcott, Oct. 5, 1978; Philip Carey, Oct. 13, 1977; Jules Weinberg, "Priests, Workers, and Communists," *Harper's Magazine*, Dec. 1948, pp. 49–50; Philip A. Carey to Raymond A. McGowen, Nov. 7, 1949, "Correspondence—Info. Requests (Misc.) 1946–1950" file, XA.

44. Read taught courses at Xavier in 1946 and 1948 and served as a conduit between the two Careys. James Carey was the most open anti-Communist in the CIO's national leadership. Nevertheless, sometimes he was not conservative enough for Xavier. In 1945, after James Carey supported the CIO position for action against Franco, Philip Carey seized on an excuse to cancel his scheduled talk at Xavier. *Bronx Home News*, Jan. 2, 1947, p. 3; interviews with Philip Carey, Oct. 13, 1977; Joseph Fitzpatrick, Aug. 1, 1978; "Biography— Philip A. Carey" file; Philip A. Carey to William Collins, undated; Carey to James A. Carey, Jan. 4, 1945; and Carey to Father [John] La Farge, Jan. 3, 1945, all in "Labor School Correspondence—Jan.–June 1945 (Carey)" file; Joe Duffy to Carey, Nov. 20, 1946, "Correspondence-D" file; "Correspondence-C" file; "Correspondence-READ, HARRY C." file; and "Attendance: 1940–Feb. 16, 1950," in "I-Labor School Instructors" file, all in XA; David Caute, *The Great Fear: The Anti-Communist Purge Under Truman and Eisenhower* (New York, 1978), 521–23; *LL*, Sept. 18, 1939, p. 3; De Caux, p. 406.

45. Other than the Omnibus clericals, few if any New York transit workers attended Xavier during the war. Weinberg, pp. 53–54; *TWB*, Nov. 1945, p. 5.

46. Interview with Raymond Westcott, Oct. 5, 1978; *TWB*, Nov. 1945, p. 5; Dec. 1945, p. 14; Feb. 1946, p. 6; *TV*, June 14, 1947, p. 6.

47. Interviews with Raymond Westcott, Oct. 5, 1978 ("kiss of death"); Philip Carey, Oct. 13, 1977; Philip Carey to Thomas Chapman, updated but around June 1945, in "41–42" file, and Carey to Rev. Thomas L. O'Brien, S.J., Oct. 31, 1949, in "42–43" file, XA.

48. Interview with Raymond Westcott, Oct. 5, 1978; interview with Philip Carey by Debra Bernhardt, Feb. 19, 1981, Oral History Collection, Robert Wagner Archives, Tamiment Library.

49. *TWU 1946 Convention*, pp. 138–39, 183–202, 210–12, 219–21; interviews with Raymond Westcott, Oct. 5, 1978; Maurice Forge, Feb. 10, 1979; *TWB*, June 1946, p. 9; *Miami Daily News*, Feb. 24, 1948, p. 1; *NYT*, Sept. 16, 1981, D27; Congress of Industrial Organizations, "In Matter of: Hearing on Charges Preferred Against Greater New York CIO Council, October 14, and 15, 1948," pp. 311–12, copy in AFL-CIO Library, Washington, D.C.

50. Robert Franklin, by then a member of the IEB, apparently also cooperated with the Westcott group, but from when and to what extent is unclear. Unlike prewar Xavier leaders, Carey was a vocal opponent of racism and anti-Semitism. Interviews with Raymond Westcott, Oct. 5, 1978; Philip Carey, Oct. 13, 1977; and Maurice Forge, Feb. 10, 1979; Bernhardt interview of Carey, Feb. 19, 1981; Weinberg, p. 55 (includes quote from Westcott); James Flatley to Rev. Philip A. Carey, S.J., Sept 29, 1946, "Correspondence-F" file; Carey to Maurice A. Walsh, Jr., Jan. 29, 1948, "Correspondence-W" file; and Carey to Ruth Taylor, Mar. 4, 1948, "Correspondence-T" file, XA; Third Avenue TWU Men for Free Speech and Fair Play, "An Open Letter to the President of Local 100 TWU-CIO" [1947], "TF Transport Workers Union of America-undated" folder, Tamiment Library.

51. *TWB*, Dec. 1947, p. 16; *NYT*, Feb. 17, 1947, p. 4; Feb. 18, 1947, p. 4; Mar. 6, 1947, p. 5; Estreicher, p. 170; *LL*, May 31, 1942, p. 1; undated clipping from the *Tablet*, probably late January 1947, JBF; James Flatley to Rev. Philip A. Carey, Sept. 29, 1946, and Carey to Flatley, Mar. 10, 1947, "Correspondence-F" file; Charles Thelan to Carey, "Correspondence-Approbations" file, XA.

52. ACTU's backing of the IAM soon wavered after it was criticized for supporting dual unionism. Interview with Raymond Westcott, Oct. 5, 1978; *NYT*, Oct. 30, 1947, p. 15; Oct. 21, 1947, p. 2; Oct. 25, 1947, p. 21; June 22, 1948, p. 13; *LL*, Oct. 31, 1947, p. 1; Nov. 29, 1947, p. 3; *Let the Record Speak! The Truth About Michael J. Quill's Betrayal of Transit Workers in the T.W.U.* (New York, 1948), 22; Richard N. Billings and John Greenya, *Power to the Public Worker* (Washington, D.C., 1974), 50–51.

53. Wurf is quoted in Billings and Greenya, p. 50; Carey's statement comes from his letter to Rev. Mortimer Gavin, S.J., Nov. 17, 1947, in "Correspondence-C," XA.

54. *LL*, Nov. 29, 1947, p. 1; Dec. 15, 1947, p. 3; *TWB*, Feb. 8, 1947; *TV*, Dec. 20, 1947, pp. 2, 5.

55. Norman D. Markowitz, *The Rise and Fall of the People's Century: Henry A. Wallace and American Liberalism, 1941–1948* (New York, 1973), 200–265; Robert Griffith and Athan Theoharis (eds.), *The Specter: Original Essays on the Cold War and the Origins of McCarthyism* (New York, 1974); Levenstein, pp. 208–52; and Howe and Coser, pp. 464–66.

56. Waltzer, "ALP," pp. 354–55, 376–77; Estreicher, pp. 249–51.

57. In 1949, the first Council election without PR, the Democrats won 24 of the 25 seats; four years later they won 23 seats. Since 1949 the regular Democratic organization has maintained continuous, solid control of the City Council. Garrett, pp. 240–42; Gerson, pp. 159–60, 186–91; *DW*, Nov. 5, 1947, p. 1; Nov. 9, 1947, p. 2; Ben Davis, *Communist Councilman from Harlem: Autobiographical Notes Written in a Federal Penitentiary* (New

York, 1969), 136–38; Wallace S. Sayre and Herbert Kaufman, *Governing New York City: Politics in the Metropolis* (New York, 1960), 453–54.

58. Gerson, pp. 191–203; *DW*, Oct. 10, 1947, p. 2; Feb. 16, 1948, p. 16; Feb. 17, 1948, p. 16.

59. U.S. Department of Justice, Immigration and Naturalization Service, "In the Matter of Charges against DESIDERIU HAMMER, alias JOHN SANTO" (typescript, 1947 hearings) (Alberto quote on p. 862); *John Santo, American* (New York, n.d.); L. H. Whittemore, *The Man Who Ran the Subways: The Story of Mike Quill* (New York, 1968), 129–36; *TV*, Sept. 20, 1947, pp. 3–4; Oct. 25, 1947, p. 1; John Santo to Michael J. Quill, April 25, 1957, MF-T; *TWB*, Oct. 1947, pp. 1, 8; Jan. 1948, p. 6; *DW*, Dec. 10, 1947, p. 5; "Minutes of TWU International Executive Board Meeting, Sept. 18–19, 1947," 3, 5, JBF; Transcript of Proceedings of Meeting of Executive Board of the CIO, Boston, Mass., Oct. 8, 10, and 17, 1947, pp. 208–9 (microfilm copy in AFL-CIO Library, Washington, D.C.); New York Report, Feb. 18, 1948 (#100-7319-373), pp. 11–13, FBI-FOIA; Regular Meeting of Executive Board, Oct. 7, 1947, and Regular Meeting of Mechanics Section, Nov. 14, 1947 (folder 31), and Regular Meeting, July 13, 1948 (folder 32), Records of Local 208, TWU (MSS 717), box 2, Ohio Historical Society.

60. Ritchie proposed to the FBI that the President or Congress call on state, county, and municipal governments to request that all their employees take oaths of allegiance to the United States and denounce membership in "un-American organizations" such as the CP. Once that was done, Ritchie argued, private employers could request similar oaths from their workers. Ritchie's plan was duly considered by J. Edgar Hoover and Attorney General Tom Clark, but Clark eventually rejected it. *TV*, Sept. 20, 1947, p. 3; *TWB*, Mar. 4, 1948, p. 6; *Utility News* (Local 101, TWU), Mar.–Apr. 1948, p. 4; *Let the Record Speak*, 23; Caute, pp. 235–38; Edward Scheidt, SAC to Director, FBI, Sept. 22, 1947 (#100-7319-361); Scheidt to Director, FBI, Oct. 20, 1947 (#100-7319-361x); Director, FBI to Attorney General, Oct. 31, 1947 (#100-7319-362); T. Vincent Quinn to Raymond P Whearty, Dec. 3, 1947 (#100-7319-366); and TCC [Tom C. Clark] to [J.] Edgar [Hoover], Dec. 9, 1948 (#100-7319-367), FBI-FOIA.

61. One of the slogans the TWU used was "Santo Raised the Workers' Pay—Let's Keep Him in the USA." Even many conservative critics of Santo within the TWU, like John Gallagher, opposed his deportation. Mark Kavanaugh, far from a radical, was a leader of the Santo Defense Committee. Interviews with John Gallagher, Apr. 20, 1979; Maurice Forge, Aug. 9, 1979; *Utility News*, Mar.–Apr. 1948, p. 4; *TV*, Sept. 20, 1947, pp. 3–4. Starting in late 1947, Santo received a series of messages from friends who had returned to Hungary indicating that his own return would be welcomed, and in fact was desired. Santo later came to believe that the Hungarian government had sought his return in order to involve him in the trial of Hungarian CP-leader Laszlo Rajk, then being planned. Several Hungarian-American Communists were caught up in this particularly ugly Stalinist episode. See U.S. House of Representatives, *A Communist in a "Workers' Paradise": John Santo's Own Story* (Consultation with John Santo, March 1, 4, 5, 1963), published in a booklet form with Preface by Francis E. Walter (Washington, D.C., 1963), 8–9, 16, 19–20; and Starobin, pp. 218–19.

62. The changes in the *Bulletin* paralleled those in the *Daily Worker*. Before the war the *Daily Worker* seemed modeled on, if anything, *The New York Times*. After the war it became a tabloid, with bolder headlines, larger print, and many more light features. *TV*, May 3, 1947, p. 2; June 14, 1947, p. 4; Aug. 23, 1947, p. 6; *TWB*, Oct. 1947, pp. 4, 7; Nov. 1947, pp. 1, 2, 11; interview with Maurice Forge, Feb. 10, 1979.

63. *TV*, May 3, 1947, p. 3; July 27, 1947, p. 2; Aug. 9, 1947, pp. 1, 4, 7, 8; *TWB*, Oct. 1947, pp. 4, 11; Nov. 1947, pp. 6, 12; *Utility News*, May–June 1947, pp. 1, 4–5; July–Aug.

1947, pp. 2, 3. On Taft-Hartley, see Christopher L. Tomlins, *The State and the Unions: Labor Relations, Law, and the Organized Labor Movement in America, 1880–1960* (Cambridge, 1985), 282–316; Levenstein, 216–19.

64. Interviews with Max Gordon, Oct. 24, 1978; Leon Strauss, Oct. 26, 1978; Simon Gerson, Dec. 18, 1979; Maurice Forge, Feb. 10, 1979; and Nat Cohen, Dec. 7, 1978; Shirley Quill, p. 69; Dodd, pp. 192, 195, 199–202; Gates, p. 104; Isserman, pp. 291–92fn.

Chapter 13

1. James J. McGinley, *Labor Relations in the New York Rapid Transit Systems, 1904–1944* (New York, 1949), 68–70; Charles Garrett, *The La Guardia Years* (New Brunswick, N.J., 1961), 211–13, 217–18; Paul Windels Memoir, OHCCU, p. 136; *NYT*, Mar. 11, 1940, p. 10; Robert Caro, *The Power Broker: Robert Moses and the Fall of New York* (New York, 1974), 758.

2. Paul Windels Memoir, OHCCU, pp. 128–36; Clifton Hood, "Underground Politics: A History of Mass Transit in New York City Since 1904" (Ph.D. dissertation, Columbia University, 1986), 368–71, 418–19fn; *NYT*, Jan. 12, 1942, pp. 1, 12; Jan. 25, 1942, pp. 32, 33; Feb. 1, 1942, p. 37; Feb. 19, 1942, pp. 21, 38; Mar. 13, 1944, p. 17; Apr. 2, 1944, pp. 1, 38; Mar. 26, 1945, pp. 1, 13; Mar. 27, 1945, p. 2; Peter Cacchione, *How to Save the 5-Cent Fare: A Memorandum on the Facts* (New York, 1942); Henry Feinstein to Herbert Lehman, Feb. 17, 1942, box 6, Peter Cacchione Papers, Tamiment Library, New York University.

3. Board of Transportation of the City of New York, *Report including Analysis of the Operations of the New York City Transit System for Five Years Ended June 30, 1945* (New York, 1945), p. 32 (hereafter Board of Transportation, *Five-Year Report*); "Address of the Honorable William O'Dwyer before Chamber of Commerce of State of N.Y., March 1946," item 3, vol. 7, William O'Dwyer Memoir, OHCCU; *NYT*, Jan. 23, 1942, p. 10; July 3, 1944, p. 1; Mar. 26, 1945, pp. 1, 13; Nov. 20, 1945, p. 12; Jan. 3, 1946, pp. 1, 40; Jan. 7, 1946, pp. 1, 12; Jan. 8, 1946, pp. 25, 36; June 13, 1947, p. 12; July 1, 1948, p. 4.

4. Samuel Estreicher, "Collective Bargaining in the New York City Transit System, 1937–1950: A Case Study in the Politics of Municipal Unionism" (M.S. thesis, Cornell University, 1974), 235–37, 245–47; *NYT*, Feb. 6, 1947, pp. 1, 32; July 1, 1948, p. 4.

5. Caro, pp. 758, 900; Cacchione, *How to Save the 5-Cent Fare*; *NYT*, Jan. 7, 1947, p. 12.

6. *NYT*, Jan. 25, 1943, pp. 32, 33; Apr. 18, 1944, p. 15; Oct. 25, 1945, p. 21; Feb. 24, 1946, p. 14; Mar. 3, 1946, p. 38; Cacchione, *How to Save the 5-Cent Fare*.

7. The TWU's position on the NYC transit fare through 1946 can be followed in: *TWB*, Dec. 1938, p. 6; Feb. 1942, p. 2; *NYCTB*, Feb. 1945, p. 3; *NYT*, Jan. 11, 1943, p. 17; Feb. 27, 1943, p. 3; and "Michael J. Quill: Press Release, September 12, 1945," quoted in *Let the Record Speak! The Truth About Michael J. Quill's Betrayal of Transit Workers in the T.W.U.* (New York, 1948), 4.

8. *DW*, June 18, 1934, trade union supplement, 3; June 22, 1934, p. 3.

9. *TWB*, Dec. 1938, p. 6. Similar statements were repeatedly made from the late 1930s through the mid-40s.

10. On the 1941 bus strike, see Leo Huberman, *The Great Bus Strike* (New York, 1941), 22, 24, 40.

11. On this last point, see Earl Browder, "The Decline of the Left Wing of American Labor," 30–31, Earl Browder Papers, Syracuse University, microfilm edition, reel 12, series 6.

12. *NYT*, Feb. 26, 1946, p. 14; Feb. 27, 1946, p. 3; Feb. 6, 1947, pp. 1, 32; Feb. 12,

1947, p. 1; Feb. 13, 1947, p. 1; July 1, 1948, p. 4; Estreicher, pp. 236–37; *Let the Record Speak*, 4; *LL*, Nov. 17, 1944, p. 3.

13. *NYT*, June 13, 1947, pp. 1, 2; June 18, 1947, p. 27; Oct. 3, 1947, p. 1; Levering interview with Mike Quill, Oct. 31, 1948, "Mike Quill" folder, box 7, Daniel Bell Collection, Tamiment Library, New York University; Estreicher, pp. 247–48; Kenneth Waltzer, "The American Labor Party: Third Party Politics in New Deal-Cold War New York, 1936–1954" (Ph.D. dissertation, Harvard University, 1977), 618 (hereafter "ALP"); *Let the Record Speak*, 5; Congress of Industrial Organizations, "In Matter of: Hearing on Charges Preferred Against Greater New York CIO Council, October 14 and 15, 1948," p. 270, copy in AFL-CIO Library, Washington, D.C. (hereafter "NYC CIO Council Hearings").

14. *NYT*, Oct. 3, 1947, p. 1; Oct. 24, 1947, p. 13; Oct. 18, 1947, p. 3; Dec. 18, 1947, p. 36; July 1, 1948, p. 4; Levering interview with Mike Quill, Daniel Bell Collection; Browder, "The Decline of the Left Wing of American Labor," 31; *TWU 1948 Convention*, 62; interview with Maurice Forge, Feb. 10, 1979; Theodore W. Kheel and J.K. Turcott, *Transit and Arbitration: A Decade of Decisions and the Path to Transit Peace* (Englewood Cliffs, N.J., 1960), pp. 30–32.

15. Estreicher, p. 248; *DW*, Nov. 20, 1947, p. 5; Dec. 12, 1947, p. 2.

16. *DW*, Oct. 10, 1947, p. 5; Nov. 11, 1947, p. 9; Nov. 24, 1947, p. 1; Nov. 30, 1947, p. 5; Dec. 1, 1947, p. 5; Dec. 3, 1947, p. 4; Dec. 7, 1947, p. 8; Dec. 8, 1947, p. 9; Dec. 12, 1947, p. 2; Dec. 15, 1947, p. 5; Waltzer, "ALP," p. 618.

17. *NYT*, Dec. 18, 1948, p. 36; *DW*, Nov. 11, 1947, p. 9; Nov. 25, 1947, p. 16; Dec. 16, 1948, p. 3; Dec. 18, 1947, p. 9.

18. *LL*, Dec. 27, 1947, p. 4; "NYC CIO Council Hearings," 63–66, 274–76; *DW*, Dec. 21, 1947, p. 3.

19. *DW*, Dec. 21, 1947, p. 3; Dec. 22, 1947, pp. 4, 10.

20. *TWB*, Jan. 1948, pp. 1, 8; *TV*, Jan. 17, 1948, pp. 1, 6.

21. *TV*, Jan. 17, 1948, p. 6; Feb. 1948, p. 1; *DW*, Jan. 8, 1948, pp. 2, 5, 10; Jan. 11, 1948, p. 3; interview with Maurice Forge, Feb. 10, 1979.

22. Norman D. Markowitz, *The Rise and Fall of the People's Century: Henry A. Wallace and American Liberalism, 1941–1948* (New York, 1973), 200–265; *TV*, May 3, 1947, p. 3; New York Report, Sept. 14, 1949 (#100-7319-486), 15, FBI-FOIA (Quill quote); Curtis D. MacDougall, *Gideon's Army* (New York, 1965), vol. I, pp. 172–75; Bella Dodd, *School of Darkness* (1954; reprint ed., New York, 1963), pp. 202–3, Waltzer, "ALP," 377–79; Joseph R. Starobin, *American Communism in Crisis, 1943–1957* (Cambridge, Mass., 1972), 155–77; and interview with Maurice Forge, July 17, 1981.

23. *Daily News*, Oct. 17, 1947; Harvey A. Levenstein, *Communism, Anticommunism and the CIO* (Westport, Conn., 1981), 219–21; Markowitz, p. 253.

24. Quill was the source of most of the information that later came out about these sessions. Although he contradicted himself about some details, the essence of his story has not been seriously disputed. The CP's position on a third party made more sense to those left-wing labor leaders who agreed with Party officials that a strong campaign for Wallace was the only way to prevent a war with the Soviet Union. MacDougall, I, pp. 248–63; Bert Cochran, *Labor and Communism: The Conflict That Shaped American Unions* (Princeton, 1977), 301–2; David A. Shannon, *The Decline of American Communism: A History of the Communist Party of the United States Since 1945* (New York, 1959), 172–77; Starobin, p. 293fn; interview with Leon Strauss, Oct. 26, 1978.

25. Shannon, pp. 138, 155–56; Starobin, p. 293fn; interview with Maurice Forge, July 17, 1981.

26. The TWU delegates voted against the decision of the State CIO Executive Board to

oppose Wallace, as well as its decision to support the Marshall Plan. However, Quill was extremely cordial to the ACW representatives when they announced that they were leaving the ALP. "NYC CIO Council Hearings," 66–69; *DW*, Jan. 8, 1948, p. 10; Jan. 11, 1948, p. 2; *LL*, Jan. 17, 1948, p. 1; Waltzer, "ALP," 385–87; "Proceedings-State Executive Committee, American Labor Party, Jan. 7, 1948," pp. 1–4, in "ALP Compaigns-Misc. Corresp., 1939–53; NY State Exec. Comm." file, box 25, Vito Marcantonio Papers, NYPL.

27. "Proceedings of the International Executive Board of the Congress of Industrial Organizations, Washington, D.C., January 22–23, 1948," 39–46 (microfilm copy in AFL-CIO Library); MacDougall, I, p. 260; II, p. 398; III, p. 803; *TWB*, Dec. 1947, pp. 3, 7; Jan. 1948, pp. 2–5, 8; Mar. 5, 1948, pp. 1, 5; Apr. 3, 1948, pp. 4–6; *TV*, Jan. 17, 1948, p. 8; Feb. 1948, p. 2; Mar. 20, 1948, p. 6; Oct. 20, 1948, p. 9; *DW*, Mar. 1, 1948, p. 6; interview with Maurice Forge, July 17, 1981; *Let the Record Speak*, 34.

28. *TV*, Feb. 1948, p. 1; Mar. 20, 1948, p. 3; *TWB*, Jan. 1948, pp. 1, 8; Mar. 5, 1948, p. 2; *DW*, Jan. 7, 1948, p. 2; Jan. 12, 1948, pp. 4, 5; Jan. 13, 1948, p. 9; Feb. 25, 1948, p. 16; Feb. 27, 1948, p. 9; Mar. 1, 1948, p. 2; Mar. 2, 1948, p. 5; Mar. 3, 1948, p. 5; Mar. 4, 1948, p. 7; Mar. 8, 1948, p. 6; Mar. 9, 1948, p. 16; Mar. 10, 1948, p. 16; *NYT*, Mar. 20, 1948, p. 17; Mar. 5, 1948, p. 15; Mar. 7, 1948, p. 4; Mar. 8, 1948, pp. 1, 14; Teletype, Scheidt to Director [FBI], Mar. 11, 1948 (#100-7319-381), FBI-FOIA.

29. Levenstein, pp. 224–25, 244; *DW*, Feb. 6, 1948, pp. 2–3; Feb. 12, 1948, p. 16; Feb. 25, 1948, p. 16; *LL*, Mar. 15, 1948, pp. 1, 3; *CIO Reporter* [NYS], Mar. 20, 1948; Estreicher, p. 252; *NYT*, Mar. 21, 1948, p. 39.

30. *Miami Daily News*, Feb. 17–19, Feb. 22, Feb. 24, Mar. 6, and Mar. 11, 1948; *Miami Herald*, Mar. 11, 1948; *DW*, Mar. 3, 1948, p. 11; Apr. 4, 1948, pp. 5, 6; *TWB*, Apr. 3, 1948, p. 8; June 19, 1948, pp. 6–7; *NYT*, Mar. 21, 1948, p. 39; TWU Local 505, "How to Get Rid of Raiders"; Christy D. Waishes to Maurice Forge, Apr. 5, 1948; and campaign ad for J. Tom Watson, JBF; Michael J. Quill to Philip Murray, May 22, 1948, in file "T," box A4-51, Philip Murray Papers, Catholic University; Miami Report, Mar. 5, 1947, p. 3 (#100-7319-353), and New York Report, Nov. 18, 1948, p. 27 (#100-7319-441), FBI-FOIA.

31. *TV*, Oct. 8, 1948, pp. 3–4; "NYC CIO Council Hearings," 70.

32. The Republican bill, unlike O'Dwyer's, permitted fare increases to cover debt service as well as operating expenses. *NYT*, Mar. 10, 1948, pp. 1, 21; Mar. 13, 1948, pp. 1, 2; Mar. 14, 1948, p. 1; Mar. 25, 1948, pp. 1, 23; Mar. 30, 1948, pp. 1, 46; *DW*, Mar. 9, 1948, p. 16; Mar. 10, 1948, p. 16.

33. *NYT*, Mar. 13, 1948, p. 2; Mar. 15, 1948, p. 34; Mar. 17, 1948, p. 28; Mar. 22, 1948, p. 25; *DW*, Mar. 12, 1948, p. 6; Mar. 17, 1948, p. 2; *TV*, Mar. 20, 1948, p. 3.

34. *NYT*, Mar. 22, 1948, p. 15; *DW*, Mar. 12, 1948, p. 6; Mar. 24, 1948, p. 8; Levering interview with Mike Quill, Oct. 31, 1948, p. 2, box 7, Daniel Bell Collection; *TV*, Oct. 8, 1948, p. 3.

35. Levenstein, p. 225; "NYC CIO Council Hearings," pp. 68–72, 278–79; *NYT*, Mar. 28, 1948, p. 37; Mar. 29, 1948, pp. 1, 12; *TWB*, Apr. 3, 1948, p. 2; *LL*, Mar. 15, 1948, p. 1

36. It is unclear if Santo et al. switched their positions on the fare before or after this purported meeting. Probably they had already done so. In any case, by early April they were clearly against raising the fare. "NYC CIO Council Hearings," 74–75, 290; Levering interview with Mike Quill, p. 3, box 7, Daniel Bell Collection; *DW*, Apr. 4, 1948, p. 9.

37. *NYT*, Mar. 28, 1948, p. 37; Mar. 29, 1948, pp. 1, 12; *Let the Record Speak*, 35; New York Report, Nov. 18, 1948, p. 11 (Quill telegram to Murray) (#100-7319-441), FBI-FOIA.

38. *NYT*, Mar. 29, 1948, p. 1; *DW*, Mar. 29, 1948, p. 9; Mar. 30, 1948, p. 9; Apr. 4, 1948, p. 9.

39. Levenstein, pp. 208–9, 218–23, 233; Waltzer, "ALP," 359; *NYT*, Mar. 19, 1948, p.

1; "New York City Industrial Union Council," Mar. 15, 1948 [unsigned memorandum], "Greater New York IUC, Z-235—New York" file, box A7-14, CIO Papers, Catholic University.

40. Charles Owen Rice to the author, Sept. 15, 1979; Michael J. Quill, "Dear Friend" letter, Apr. 16, 1948, series I, file 75, reel 2, Earl Browder Papers (microfilm edition); TV, Nov. 12, 1948, p. 12; DW, Mar. 1, 1948, p. 5; "Proceedings of the International Executive Board of the Congress of Industrial Organizations, Aug. 30–Sept. 1, 1948," pp. 167–77, microfilm copy in AFL-CIO Library (hereafter CIO Executive Board, Aug. 30–Sep. 1, 1948); interview with Maurice Forge, July 17, 1981. Quill was always a bit nervous about his own immigration status. See Quill to Gustav Faber, May 14, 1957, MF-T.

41. Interviews with Maurice Forge, Feb. 10 and Aug. 9, 1979; Gerald O'Reilly, May 15, 1978; and Martin Young, Nov. 15, 1978; and Browder, "The Decline of the Left Wing of American Labor," 17–36.

42. TWB, Aug.–Sep. 1948, p. 13; DW, Dec. 12, 1947, p. 2; Dec. 22, 1947, pp. 4, 10; Apr. 22, 1948, pp. 2, 6; Apr. 27, 1948, p. 8.

43. Interviews with Maurice Forge, Aug. 9, 1979; Simon Gerson, Dec. 18, 1979; NYT, Mar. 13, 1948, pp. 1, 21; Apr. 9, 1948, pp. 1, 5; Apr. 18, 1948, IV:10.

44. TV, Feb. 1948, p. 1; NYT, Mar. 28, 1948, p. 31; "Free Transit Workers" leaflet [spring 1948], JBF; interviews with Philip Carey, Oct. 13, 1977; Gerald O'Reilly, May 15, 1978; Martin Young, Nov. 15, 1978; and Maurice Forge, Aug. 9, 1979.

45. Estreicher, pp. 273–74. The Isaacson election was something of a fluke, but few realized it at the time. The strong support the CP and the Soviet Union were then giving Israel was probably an important factor in the heavily Jewish district. Still, as late as 1949 the ALP drew 356,222 votes in New York City. Waltzer, "ALP," 392–93, 441–42; Nathan Glazer, The Social Basis of American Communism (New York, 1961), 155–56; DW, Feb. 15, 1948, p. 6.

46. Kheel and Turcott, pp. 30–32; William O'Dwyer Memoir, OHCCU, pp. 210–15; Browder, "The Decline of the Left Wing of American Labor," 31–33.

47. Ronald W. Schatz, The Electrical Workers: A History of Labor at General Electric and Westinghouse (Urbana, 1983), 150–53; Estreicher, p. 268; wage comparison calculated from U.S. Department of Commerce, Historical Statistics of the United States, Part I (Washington, D.C., 1975), 169–70; and NYC Omnibus Corporation, Annual Report, 1952, 5.

48. Len De Caux, Labor Radical: From the Wobblies to CIO, A Personal History (Boston, 1970), 426. Charles Owen Rice made a similar point in a letter to the author (Sept. 15, 1979): "It was the 5 cent fare that caused the break, or was it just [Quill's] excuse for a graceful exit?" So did Saul Mills in his interview with Debra E. Bernhardt, Apr. 3, 1981, Robert Wagner Archives, Tamiment Library.

49. Estreicher, pp. 256–57; Levering interview with Mike Quill, Oct. 31, 1948, box 7, Daniel Bell Collection; interviews with Simon Gerson, Dec. 18, 1979; and Leon Strauss, Oct. 26, 1978.

50. Quote is from Waltzer, "ALP," 409. See also Quill, "Dear Friend" letter, Apr. 16, 1948; Starobin, pp. 141–94.

51. Watt is quoted in Maurice Isserman, Which Side Were You On?: The American Communist Party During the Second World War (Middletown, Conn., 1982), 291–92fn. Max Gordon made a similar point to the author (interview of Oct. 24, 1978).

52. A left-wing TWU probably would have had a harder time than the West Coast Longshoremen since it was primarily a public-sector union. O'Dwyer easily crushed the other left-wing unions of New York City employees such as the United Public Workers, which had of course always been far weaker than the TWU.

53. Quill also believed that to the extent that the TWU was a progressive force it could remain so without the CP, an extension of the crypto-syndicalist views that Quill, like many other left CIO leaders, had long held. Interviews with Leon Strauss, Oct. 26, 1978; Maurice Forge, Feb. 10, 1979; Starobin, pp. 38–41; Levering interview with Mike Quill," Oct. 31, 1948, box 7, Daniel Bell Collection; and Quill, "Dear Friend" letter, Apr. 16, 1948.

54. Interview with Maurice Forge, July 15, 1980; Levering interview with Victor Reisel, Oct. 28, 1948, "Mike Quill" folder, box 7, Daniel Bell Collection; CIO Executive Board, Aug. 30–Sep. 1, 1948, p. 177.

55. Interviews with Maurice Forge, Feb. 10 and Aug. 9, 1979; Gerald O'Reilly, May 15, 1978; and James Sullivan, Aug. 16, 1979; TWB, May 15, 1948, p. 8; Charles Owen Rice to the author, Sep. 15, 1979.

56. NYT, Mar. 30, 1948, p. 46; Apr. 8, 1948, p. 22; DW, Mar. 30, 1948, pp. 1, 4; Apr. 8, 1948, p. 16; Scheidt to Director [FBI], Apr. 8, 1948 (#100-7319-401) (includes quotes from Apr. 7 meeting); New York Report, Nov. 18, 1948, p. 14 (#100-7319-441), FBI-FOIA; LL, Apr. 12, 1948, p. 1.

57. A copy of this letter, on TWU stationary, appears, as previously cited, in Browder's papers. Philip Jaffe reprints it and discusses its background in *The Rise and Fall of American Communism* (New York, 1975), 144–51.

58. Kheel and Turcott, pp. 30–32; NYT, Apr. 7, 1948, pp. 1, 27; Apr. 8, 1948, p. 22; Apr. 10, 1948, p. 1; DW, Apr. 7, 1948, p. 16; Apr. 18, 1948, p. 2.

59. NYT, Apr. 8, 1948, pp. 1, 22; Apr. 9, 1948, pp. 1, 5; Apr. 10, 1948, pp. 1, 11; Apr. 11, 1948, pp. 1, 46; Apr. 12, 1948, pp. 1, 2; Apr. 14, 1948, pp. 1, 54; Apr. 14, 1948, pp. 1, 21; DW, Apr. 9, 1948, p. 2; Apr. 13, 1948, p. 16; Apr. 14, 1948, p. 3; Apr. 15, 1948, pp. 3, 6; "NYC CIO Council Hearings," 72–73, 281–82, 286.

60. NYT, Apr. 15, 1948, p. 36; Apr. 16, 1948, pp. 1, 20; Apr. 20, 1948, p. 23; LL, Apr. 12, 1948, p. 1; Apr. 26, 1948, pp. 1, 4; DW, Apr. 20, 1948, p. 4; TWB, May 15, 1948, p. 2.

61. DW, Apr. 15, 1948, pp. 3, 6; Apr. 16, 1948, pp. 1, 3, 6; Apr.18, 1948, p. 2; NYT, Apr. 16, 1948, pp. 1, 20; Apr. 17, 1948, pp. 1, 2; LL, Apr. 26, 1948, p. 4; TWB, Aug.–Sep. 1948, p. 4.

62. O'Dwyer partially ameliorated the impact of the fare increase by eliminating surface line fare zones, increasing the number of free rapid transit transfer points, and introducing five-cent transfers between the rapid transit and surface lines. NYT, Apr. 20, 1948, pp. 1, 2; Apr. 21, 1948, pp. 1, 21; Apr. 22, 1948, p. 16; DW, Apr. 20, 1948, p. 4; Apr. 22, 1948, pp. 2, 6; Apr. 23, 1948, p. 9.

63. Estreicher, p. 274; TWB, May 15, 1948, pp. 1, 6; Nov. 12, 1948, p. 12; Kheel and Turcott, pp. 31–32; William O'Dwyer Memoir, pp. 210–15, OHCCU; NYT, Apr. 22, 1948, pp. 1, 16; Apr. 29, 1948, pp. 3, 11; Board of Transportation, *Proceedings* 65 (1948): 340–43.

64. TV, Apr. 29, 1948, p. 2; May 29, 1948, pp. 1–3; Jun. 30, 1948, p. 3; TWB, Nov. 12, 1948, p. 12; *Let the Record Speak*, 5–6; DW, Apr. 29, 1948, pp. 3, 11; Apr. 30, 1948, p. 9; NYT, July 3, 1948, p. 8; Sep. 27, 1948, p. 34; interview with Gerald O'Reilly, May 15, 1978.

65. TWB, May 15, 1948, pp. 6, 8; TV, Apr. 29, 1948, p. 2; May 29, 1948, p. 3; June 30, 1948, p. 3; Aug. 1948, p. 2; interviews with Gerald O'Reilly, May 15, 1978; Maurice Forge, Aug. 9, 1979; DW, Apr. 10, 1948, p. 2; NYT, July 1, 1948, pp. 1, 4; July 2, 1948, p. 12; July 30, 1948, p. 12; "Your 24-Cent Wage Increase Is in Danger" [leaflet], copy attached to Edward Scheidt to Director, FBI [date censored] (#100-7319-423), FBI-FOIA.

66. L. H. Whittemore describes Quill's offer and its rejections (*The Man Who Ran the Subways: The Story of Mike Quill* (New York, 1968), 141–42) but misdates it as taking place

before Quill resigned from his CIO Council post. The rest of his account was confirmed in interviews with Gerald O'Reilly, May 15, 1978, and Maurice Forge, Feb. 10, 1979. See also *LL*, Aug. 31, 1948, p. 1.

67. *TWB*, July 24, 1948, p. 2; Aug.–Sept. 1948, p. 7; Oct. 8, 1948, p. 8; Nov. 11, 1948, p. 12; *NYT*, July 30, 1948, p. 12; *TV*, Aug. 1948, p. 2; Sept. 24, 1948, p. 2; Nov. 12, 1948, p. 2; "Minutes of Special Meeting of the International Executive Board of the Transport Workers Union, September 4th, 5th, and 6th, 1948" (hereafter "IEB Minutes, Sept. 4–6, 1948"), JBF; Committee Established by the Executive Board of the Transport Workers Union of America to Inquire into and Investigate Certain Matters and Developments in the Union, "Stenographic Minutes of Hearings of November 11th and 12th, 1948," 35–36, 119 (hereafter "International Investigation Hearings"), copy in possession of Maurice Forge.

68. Interviews with Martin Young, Nov. 15, 1978; James Sullivan, July 27 and Aug. 16, 1979; Maurice Forge, Feb. 10, 1979, Aug. 9, 1979, and July 17, 1981; Jerry O'Brien, Sept. 17, 1979; Lewis Fraad, June 30, 1980; and *TWU 1948 Convention*, 61–62.

69. Interviews with Jerry O'Brien, Sept. 17, 1979; James Sullivan, July 27 and Aug. 16, 1979; Maurice Forge, Feb. 10, 1979; and Gerald O'Reilly, May 15, 1978. Shirley Garry had had considerable experience in the left-wing of the CIO before meeting Quill; she was a onetime member of the Young Communist League and a former UE employee. She and Quill began a long affair during World War II. After Mollie Quill died in 1959, they married. The difference between Quill's two wives, the first a retiring Irish country girl, the second an outspoken New York Jew, was a measure of the cultural distance he traveled. See Shirley Quill, *Mike Quill—Himself, A Memoir* (Greenwich, Conn., 1985), 118–53, 218, 263.

70. *LL*, Apr. 12, 1948, p. 1; June 14, 1948, p. 4; Philip Carey to Jim [James J. Mc-Ginley], May 7, 1948, in "41–42" file; Carey to Rev. Charles Owen Rice, May 11, 1948, in "Correspondence-R" file; and Carey to Harry Read July 21, 1948, in "Correspondence-READ, HARRY C." file, XA; interviews with Philip Carey, Oct. 12, 1977; Raymond Westcott, Oct. 5, 1978; and John Gallagher, Apr. 20, 1979; Michael J. Quill, "For Immediate Release (Tuesday, June 8, 1948)," in "TF-Transport Workers of America—undated" folder, Tamiment Library; Levering interview with Mike Quill, pp. 2–3, box 7, Daniel Bell Collection; *NYT*, June 9, 1948, p. 20; Levenstein, pp. 262, 268n.

71. Cassidy was the key figure in the Nebraska Wallace campaign. Partially as a result of his resignation, Nebraska was one of only three states where Wallace did not appear on the ballot. Quite a few TWU leftists, including MacMahon and Forge, attended the late June Progressive party convention. MacDougall, II, p. 398; III, p. 803; Michael J. Quill, "A Letter to all Members of Local 223, Omaha," "Mike Quill" folder, box 7, Daniel Bell Collection; *NYT*, June 23, 1948, p. 1; interview with Maurice Forge, July 17, 1981.

72. Edward Scheidt, SAC to Director, FBI, Aug. 25, 1948 (#100-7319-420), p. 1, FBI-FOIA; Philip A. Carey to Harry Read, July 21, 1948, in "Correspondence-READ, HARRY C." file, XA; "International Investigation Hearings," pp. 112–14; *Utility News* [TWU Local 101], Aug. 1948, p. 1; *TWB*, July 24, 1948, p. 2.

73. *TWB*, July 24, 1948, p. 8; *TV*, Aug. 1948, p. 2; *NYT*, July 30, 1948, p. 12; Aug. 9, 1948, p. 32; Aug. 12, 1948, p. 16.

74. On August 20 O'Dwyer said that the O'Dwyer-Davis plan would not go into effect until after the TWU eliminated the Communists in its top leadership. Edward Scheidt, SAC to Director, FBI, Aug. 25, 1948 (#100-7319-420) and leaflets in file #100-7319-424, FBI-FOIA; *NYT*, Aug. 18, 1948, p. 50; *LL*, Aug. 31, 1948, p. 1; *TWB*, Aug.–Sept. 1948, pp. 4, 6; "International Investigation Hearings," 115.

75. Interviews with Patrick J. Reilly, Sept. 7, 1978; Maurice Forge, Feb. 10 and Aug. 9, 1979; *New York World-Telegram*, Dec. 7, 1948; New York Report, Nov. 18, 1948 (#100-

7319-441), p. 9, FBI-FOIA. To Quill's credit, even during the most heated phase of the faction fight he continued to oppose Santo's deportation. See "Statement of Michael J. Quill on the Order to Deport John Santo," Oct. 12, 1948, JBF.

76. *TWB*, Aug.–Sept. 1948, p. 6; interviews with Patrick J. Reilly, Sept. 7, 1978; Joseph Labash, Aug. 3, 1979; John Plover, Feb. 20, 1979; and Lewis Fraad, June 30, 1980.

77. SAC, New York to Director, FBI, Oct. 14, 1948 (#100-7319-431), p. 1; New York Report, Nov. 18, 1948 (#100-7319-441), pp. 21, 24, 37–38, FBI-FOIA; *TWB*, Oct. 8, 1948, pp. 4, 5; Nov. 11, 1948, p. 12; *TV*, Oct. 20, 1948, p. 2; *Utility News*, Oct. 1948, p. 2.

78. "International Investigation Hearings," pp. 6–9; "Meeting of the International Executive Board of the Transport Workers Union of America, November 15, 1948" (hereafter "IEB Meeting, Nov. 15, 1948"), pp. 156, 164 (copy in possession of Gerald O'Reilly); *TV*, Sept. 24, 1948, p. 9; Oct. 20, 1948, p. 12; Nov. 12, 1948, p. 3.

79. Interviews with Martin Young, Nov. 15, 1948; Patrick J. Reilly, Sept. 7, 1978; and Maurice Forge, Aug. 9, 1979; *TV*, Oct. 20, 1948, pp. 3, 4; *TWU 1948 Convention*, 44–47; *TWB*, Aug.–Sept. 1948, p. 6; "International Investigation Hearings," 115–17; *NYT*, Sept. 3, 1948, p. 13; Sept. 10, 1948, p. 14; Sept. 25, 1948, p. 10.

80. *TWB*, July 24, 1948, p. 2; Aug.–Sept. 1948, pp. 3, 9–11; Oct. 8, 1948, pp. 1, 3–8; Nov. 11, 1948, pp. 2, 8, 12; *TV*, Oct. 8, 1948, pp. 1–4; Oct. 20, 1948, pp. 2, 5–7, 9; Nov. 12, 1948, p. 5; *Labor's Voice* [TWU Local 176], Sept. 1948 (special edition); *Utility News*, July 1948, p. 1; Aug. 1948, p. 1; Oct. 1948, pp. 1, 3; Nov. 1948, pp. 2, 6; *NYT*, June 7, 1948, p. 38; July 29, 1948, p. 15; Sept. 12, 1948, p. 31; Sept. 18, 1948, p. 9; Angelo De Iulis, "An Open Letter to Mike Quill," Sept. 28, 1948, copy in possession of Gerald O'Reilly; "International Investigation Hearings," 10–16, 24–29, 33, 35–36, 53–55, 60–61, 69–74, 118; Records of TWU Local 208, May 6, 1947–Aug. 14, 1948, folders 31 and 32, box 2, MSS 717, Ohio Historical Society, Columbus, Ohio; interviews with Philip Carey, Oct. 13, 1977; and Gerald O'Reilly, July 11, 1979; Philip Carey to Harry Read, July 21, 1948, in "Correspondence-READ, HARRY C.," file, XA; Sorrell Hillman to Donald Bermingham, Dec. 8, 1948, p. 7, "Michael J. Quill Answers the Rantings of the Edwards-Smolnikoff Open Letter", and Michael J. Quill, "A Letter to all Members of Local 223, Omaha," all in "Mike Quill" folder, box 7, Daniel Bell Collection; E. R. Burns to William G. Lindner, Aug. 3, 1948, "A Modest Proposal for a *Quill Psychiatric Fund*" [Sept. 1948], Edna M. Van Benthuysen to Douglas MacMahon, Sept. 22, 1948, Maurice Forge to ALL ATD Locals, Sept. 18, 1948, and Air Transport Local 514 "For Immediate Release" (Aug. 1948), JBF.

81. MacDougall, III, p. 620; "CIO Executive Board, Aug. 30–Sept. 1, 1948," pp. 167–78; "IEB Minutes, Sept. 4–6, 1948"; *NYT*, Sept. 6, 1948, pp. 1, 2; Sept. 7, 1948, pp. 1, 16; *TWB*, Aug.–Sept. 1948, pp. 1–3, 10, 12–16; Oct. 8, 1948, p. 7.

82. *NYT*, Sept. 5, 1948, pp. 1, 9; Sept. 8, 1948, pp. 1, 34; Sept. 12, 1948, p. 31; "International Investigation Hearings," 116–19; *TWB*, Aug.–Sept. 1948, p. 7; Nov. 11, 1948, p. 10; *TV*, Sept. 24, 1948, p. 2.

83. *TWB*, Aug.–Sept. 1948, p. 16; Oct. 8, 1948, pp. 1, 4; Nov. 11, 1948, pp. 1, 4–6; Nov. 24, 1948, p. 8; *TV*, Oct. 20, 1948, pp. 1, 2; *NYT*, Sept. 23, 1948, p. 20; TWU, "Hearings of Committee to Investigate Fraud in Connection with Referendum Held by Local 100," and Supreme Court of the State of New York, New York County, "Austin Hogan Plaintiff against Gustav Faber," copies of both in possession of Gerald O'Reilly; "IEB Meeting, Nov. 15, 1948," pp. 2–96; TWU Local 100, "Save the TWU Treasury!" [leaflet], JBF.

84. Interview with Patrick J. Reilly, Sept. 7, 1978; Scheidt to Director [FBI], Sept. 10, 1948 (#100-7319-425), FBI-FOIA.

85. "International Investigation Hearings," 119, 134–38; Minutes of Local 100 Executive

Board meeting of Oct. 7, 1948, JBF; *TWB*, Nov. 11, 1948, p. 10; *TV*, Sept. 10, 1948, pp. 1, 4.

86. *TV*, Oct. 1948, p. 1; Sept. 24, 1948, p. 4; *NYT*, Sept. 4, 1948, pp. 1, 3; Sept. 5, 1948, pp. 1, 9; Sept. 10, 1948, pp. 1, 14.

87. *NYT*, Sept. 22, 1948, pp. 1, 35; *TWB*, Oct. 29, 1948, pp. 1–4; "International Investigation Hearings," 119–32; *TV*, Nov. 12, 1948, p. 9; Scheidt to Director [FBI], Oct. 27, 1948 (#100-7319-433), Oct. 27, 1948 (#100-7319-435), and Oct. 26, 1948 (#100-7319-437), and New York Report, Nov. 18, 1948 (#100-7319-441), pp. 22–24, FBI-FOIA.

88. *TV*, Nov. 12, 1948, pp. 1, 2, 6, 9; NYC Omnibus Corporation, *Annual Report, 1949*, 3–4.

89. Scheidt to Director [FBI], Oct. 27, 1948 (#100-7319-435), FBI-FOIA; *LL*, Nov. 16, 1948; p. 3; *TV*, Oct. 20, 1948, p. 4; Nov. 12, 1948, p. 2; *Let the Record Speak*, 25.

90. *TV*, Nov. 12, 1948, pp. 1, 2, 6, 12; *TWB*, Nov. 11, 1948, p. 4; "International Investigation Hearings," 132–33; New York Report, Nov. 18, 1948 (#100-7319-441), 24–26, FBI-FOIA; *LL*, Nov. 16, 1948, p. 3; Supreme Court of New York, "Hogan against Faber."

91. "International Investigation Hearings" (including appended draft report); *TWB*, Nov. 11, 1948, pp. 1, 4; *TV*, Nov. 12, 1948, pp. 3, 11; interview with Maurice Forge, Feb. 10, 1979.

92. "IEB Meeting, Nov. 15, 1948," 11–227; *TWB*, Nov. 24, 1948, p. 2.

93. *TWB*, Nov. 24, 1948, pp. 1, 3; Serrell Hillman to Donald Bermingham, Dec. 8, 1948, p. 5, box 7, Daniel Bell Collection.

94. Interview with Maurice Forge, Feb. 10, 1979.

95. Interview with Maurice Forge, Feb. 10, 1979; Maurice Forge et al., "To All Delegates to Air Transport Conference," Nov. 16, 1948, copy in possession of Forge; *TWU 1948 Convention*, 56, 58; "Proceedings of the Airline Conference, Air Transport Division, TWU, December 5, 1948," MF-T.

96. Forge insisted on the ATD-approved plan for the airline delegates alone to elect a vice president who would serve as ATD director. Levering interview with Mike Quill, Oct. 31, 1948, p. 4, and Serrell Hillman to Donald Bermingham, Dec. 8, 1948, pp. 5, 7, both in "Mike Quill" folder, box 7, Daniel Bell Collection; Estreicher, p. 280; *DW*, Dec. 8, 1948, p. 2; *New York World-Telegram*, Dec. 7, 1948; interview with Maurice Forge, Feb. 10, 1979.

97. *TWU 1948 Convention*, pp. 12, 16–31; "Statement of Austin Hogan, President, Local 100, TWU" (press release, Dec. 6, 1948), JBF; Serrell Hillman to Donald Bermingham, Dec. 8, 1948, pp. 3–4, "Mike Quill" folder, box 7, Daniel Bell Collection.

98. *New York World-Telegram*, Dec. 7, 1948; interview with Maurice Forge, Feb. 10, 1979.

99. There is an unexplained discrepancy between the vote for Quill in the printed roll call (466½) and the total announced on the convention floor (473). *TWU 1948 Convention*, 39–56.

100. *TWU 1948 Convention*, 39–43, 58–70.

101. *TWU 1948 Convention*, 71–168; *DW*, Dec. 8, 1948, p. 11; Serrell Hillman to Donald Bermingham, Dec. 8, 1948, pp. 5–8, "Mike Quill" folder, box 7, Daniel Bell Collection; interview with Maurice Forge, Feb. 10, 1979; National Committee for TWU Democracy, "FOR IMMEDIATE RELEASE, December 9, 1948," JBF.

102. *TWU 1948 Convention*, 168–75; Bernard Murphy and Benjamin Bailly, "Report to Members of Air Transport Local 501 on Sixth Biennial TWU Convention in Chicago," and Committee for Air Transport Autonomy, Local 500, TWU-CIO, "The New TWU Constitution," copies of both in possession of Maurice Forge; *New York Star*, Dec. 10, 1948, pp. 1, 18.

103. *NYT*, Dec. 11, 1948, pp. 1, 3; *DW*, Dec. 8, 1948, p. 11; *TE*, Dec. 20, 1948, pp. 2, 5, 17; Jan. 20, 1949, pp. 1, 5, 7; Mar. 7, 1949, p. 16; John A. Cassidy to Michael J. Quill, Dec. 13, 1948, JBF.

Chapter 14

1. James Bacon, *How Sweet It Is: The Jackie Gleason Story* (New York, 1985), pp. 6–9, 20–23, 146; interview with Peter MacLachlan, Feb. 25, 1979.

2. U.S. Department of Labor, Bureau of Labor Statistics, *Union Wages and Hours: Local Transit Operating Employees, Oct. 1, 1950*, Bulletin No. 1019 (Washington, D.C., 1950), 7; and *Occupational Wage Survey: New York, New York, January 1952*, Bulletin, No. 1101, (Washington, D.C., 1952), 23, 30; "New York City Omnibus Corporation Pay Rates," in Michael J. Quill file, Charles Owen Rice Papers, Pennsylvania State University; U.S. Department of Commerce, *Statistical Abstract of the United States, 1972* (Washington, D.C., 1972), 348.

3. Martin Segal, *Wages in the Metropolis: Their Influence on the Location of Industries in the New York Region* (Cambridge, Mass., 1966), 177–79; U.S. Department of Labor, Bureau of Labor Statistics, *Union Wages and Hours: Local Transit Operating Employees, July 1, 1958*, Bulletin No. 1244 (Washington, D.C., 1958), 6; Leon H. Keyserling, "Higher Pay for N.Y.C. Transport Workers: The Workers Deserve It, the City Can Afford It," December 1965, Part II, pp. 4, 10–11, copy in "L-100 Negot 1965 Demand" file, Box 150, TWU-T; interview with Maurice Forge, Nov. 29, 1983; Thomas R. Brooks, "Lindsay, Quill & the Transit Strike," *Commentary*, March 1966, pp. 53–54.

4. Samuel Estreicher, "Collective Bargaining in the New York City Transit System, 1937–1950: A Case Study in the Politics of Municipal Unionism" (M.S. thesis, Cornell University, 1974), 285; New York City Omnibus, *Annual Report, 1952*, 4–5; Shirley Quill, *Mike Quill—Himself, A Memoir* (Greenwich, Conn., 1985), 222–28, 279; *TE*, Jan. 1954, p. 21; Michael J. Quill to Herbert H. Lehman, May 26 and June 2, 1950, Special Files, Herbert H. Lehman Papers, Lehman Library, Columbia University.

5. "Meeting of the International Executive Board of the Transport Workers Union of America, May 5–7, 1949," JBF, passim (hereafter "IEB Meeting, May 5–7, 1949"); *TE*, Mar. 7, 1949, pp. 16, 22; *R&FTN*, July 1949, p. 4; Philip Carey to John O'Connell, Jan. 6, 1949, "Correspondence-O," XA; interview with James Sullivan, Aug. 16, 1979.

6. Interviews with Maurice Forge, Feb. 10, 1979; Peter MacLachlan, Feb. 25, 1979; Gerald O'Reilly, May 15, 1978; L. H. Whittemore *The Man Who Ran the Subways: The Story of Mike Quill* (New York, 1968), 166; U.S. House of Representatives, *A Communist in a "Workers' Paradise": John Santo's Own Story* (Consultation with John Santo, March 1, 4, 5, 1963), published in booklet form with Preface by Francis E. Walter (Washington, D.C., 1963), 12.

7. "An Appeal for Support from Bob Franklin" [1949], JBF; IEB Meeting, May 5–7, 1949, p. 8; Intelligence Division, Office of Chief of Naval Operations, New Orleans Report, Dec. 28, 1948, copy in file #100-7319-454, FBI-FOIA; New Orleans Report, Apr. 20, 1950, (#100-7319-503), FBI-FOIA; *TE*, Mar. 7, 1949, p. 22; "Bell-Labor's Month," in "CIO-I" folder, box 4, Daniel Bell Collection, Tamiment Library, New York University.

8. Lopez and Sheehan continued to lead Local 101 until the mid-1950s, when Sheehan went to work for the International and Lopez went to work for Brooklyn Union Gas as the company's safety director. *Utility News*, Dec. 1948, p. 2; Jan. 1949, p. 1; *TE*, Mar. 7, 1949, p. 16; IEB Meeting, May 5–7, 1949, p. 1; interviews with Gerald O'Reilly, Jan. 11, 1979; James Sullivan, Aug. 16, 1979; Robert S. Wechsler, *Burning Bright: The Story of Local 101, Transport Workers Union of America, AFL-CIO* (New York, 1981), 15–30.

9. IEB Meeting, May 5–7, 1949, pp. 6, 10–11; *TE*, Mar. 7, 1949, pp. 6, 21–22; *R&FTN*, Feb. 1949, p. 4; Mar. 1949, p. 3; Mar. 1950, p. 4; Boardman to Director and SAC New York, Feb. 23, 1949 (#100-7319-475); SAC, Louisville to Director, FBI, Dec. 27, 1949 (#100-7319-496); and Philadelphia Report, Feb. 2, 1950 (#100-7319-498), FBI-FOIA; Denis J. Comey to Philip Carey, Feb. 9, 1953, "Correspondence-C," XA.

10. The following discussion of ATD developments is based on extensive materials in MF-T; interviews with Maurice Forge, Aug. 9, 1979, and James Sullivan, Aug. 16, 1979; IEB Meeting, May 5–7, 1949, pp. 15–25; Levenstein, p. 292; Miami Report (#100-7319-491) and New York Report (#100-7319-505), pp. 16–17, FBI-FOIA; and *R&FTN*, Sept. 1950, p. 3.

11. There was an important aftermath to Crouch's accusations against the ATD leaders. Scala, who lost his job as a result of Crouch's charges, sued the Hearst Corporation, which had distributed Crouch's article, for libel. In October 1953 Scala won his case and was awarded $5,000. Since by then Crouch had become a key government witness in various judicial and administrative proceedings—in writer David Caute's view "one of the most brazen and colorful liars in the business"—the verdict was a serious blow to the credibility of the federal anti-Communist crusade. To recoup its losses the Justice Department had M. L. Edwards indicted for perjury for his testimony in the Scala suit. Edwards was acquitted by a New York jury, a significant incident in the unraveling of the domestic Cold War. On the extraordinary career of Paul Crouch and his involvement in the TWU, see David Caute, *The Great Fear: The Anti-Communist Purge Under Truman and Eisenhower* (New York, 1978), 126–28, 131–32, 138, 171, 200–201, 238, 242; Victor S. Navasky, *Naming Names* (New York, 1981), 14, 62; U.S. Senate, Subcommittee on Immigration and Naturalization, Committee on the Judiciary, 81st Cong., 1st sess., *Communist Activities Among Aliens and National Groups* (Washington, D.C., 1950), 138–58; Paul [Crouch] to [M. L.] Edwards, Jan. 22, 1947, JBF; C. H. Carson to Director, FBI, Apr. 1, 1948 (#100-7319-387), FBI-FOIA; interview with Maurice Forge, Aug. 9, 1979; and *New York Post*, Oct. 14, 1953, p. 50.

12. *R&FTN*, Feb. 1949 to Oct. 1949, passim; interviews with James Sullivan, July 27 and Aug 16, 1979 (includes quote); Maurice Forge, Feb. 10 and Aug. 9, 1979; Peter MacLachlan, Feb. 25, 1979; and Gerald O'Reilly, May 15, 1978; Philip Carey to Harry [Read], Sept. 20, 1949 [unsent letter], "Correspondence-READ, HARRY C.," XA; Estreicher, pp. 284–85.

13. *R&FTN*, Oct. 1949, pp. 1, 3; Nov. 1949 (no. 17), pp. 1, 3; Nov. 1949 (no. 18), pp. 1–3; Dec. 1949 (no. 19), pp. 1–4; Dec. 1949 (no. 20), pp. 1–3; Jan. 1950 (no. 22), p. 3; Feb. 1950, pp. 2–3; Apr. 1950, p. 2; "Support for Bob Franklin—Independent Slate," "The Unity Slate—For Executive Board—IND Branch," and "Local Election—December 2, 1949—Transport Workers Union of Greater New York" [vote tally], JBF; Whittemore, pp. 169–70; interviews with Phil Bray, Aug. 13, 1979; Patrick Walsh, June 1, 1978; Gerald O'Reilly, Jan 11, 1979; Jerry O'Brien, Sept. 12, 1979; Maurice Forge, Aug. 9 and Sept. 15, 1979.

14. Local 252 ignored Forge's expulsion from the International and Forge continued to advise the local's leadership on contract negotiations and other matters. In retaliation, in 1954 Quill put the local under an administrator and ousted its leaders. Gustav Faber to Alexander Coleman, Mar. 29, 1950, Faber to Maurice Forge, Mar. 29, 1950, and Forge, "A Letter to Quill," March 14, 1950, copies in possession of Maurice Forge; *Newsday*, May 7, 1954, June 22, 1954; *TE*, Apr. 1954, p. 11.

15. Gerald O'Reilly, "To All IRT Motormen—Conductors—Towerman," JBF; *R&FTN*, May 1950, p. 2; July 1950, p. 3; Sept. 1950, p. 3; Dec. 1950, p. 2; Apr. 1951, p. 2.

16. Interview with Maurice Forge, Feb. 10, 1979; Max Kampelman, *The Communist Party vs. the CIO* (New York, 1957), 155; Whittemore, p. 235.

17. *Long Island Press*, Dec. 9, 1950, p. 1; *TWU 1950 Convention*, 98–99.

18. *R&FTN*, Feb. 1951, p. 1, 3; Apr. 1951, pp. 1–4; Dec. 1954, pp. 1–4; interviews with Gerald O'Reilly, May 15, 1978; Peter MacLachlan, Feb. 25, 1979; and Maurice Forge, Aug. 9, 1979.

19. Caute, pp. 235, 344; Richard O. Boyer and Herbert M. Morais, *Labor's Untold Story* (New York, 1955), 368–69fn; interviews with John Nolan, June 1, 1978; Phil Bray, Aug. 13, 1979; and Gerald O'Reilly, May 15, 1978.

20. Estreicher, pp. 284–87; *TWU 1950 Convention*, 60–63; Peter F. Freund, "Labor Relations in the New York City Transit Industry, 1945–1960" (Ph.D. dissertation, New York University, 1964), 74–75; Mark H. Maier, "The City and the Unions: Collective Bargaining in New York City 1954–1973" (Ph.D. dissertation, New School for Social Research, June 1980), 115–16.

21. Estreicher, pp. 283–84; *Political Profiles: The Johnson Years* (New York, 1976), 331–32; Maier, "The City and the Unions," pp. 143, 150. Many of Kheel's rulings can be found in Theodore W. Kheel and J.K. Turcott, *Transit and Arbitration: A Decade of Decisions and the Path to Transit Peace* (Englewood Cliffs, N.J., 1960). On the outlook of NWLB and postwar labor relations specialists, see Howell John Harris, *The Right to Manage: Industrial Relations Policies of American Business in the 1940s* (Madison, 1982), 47–58; and Katherine Van Wezel Stone, "The Post-War Paradigm in American Labor Law," *The Yale Law Journal*, June 1981, pp. 1509–80.

22. The Mayor and the Governor appointed an equal number of TA members. Those appointees picked an additional member. Clifton Hood, "Underground Politics: A History of Mass Transit in New York City Since 1904" (Ph.D. dissertation, Columbia University, 1986), 405–14; Edward Sussna, "Collective Bargaining on the New York City Transit System, 1940–1957," *Industrial and Labor Relations Review* 11 (1958): 523–24.

23. In contrast to the TWU and the NYC CIO Council (which by then had been purged and reorganized, with Quill again as its head), the AFL remained neutral in the primary and endorsed Wagner less than a week before the general election. *TWU 1950 Convention*, 11; Raymond D. Horton, *Municipal Labor Relations in New York City: Lessons of the Lindsay-Wagner Years* (New York, 1973), 21–24.

24. A. H. Raskin, "Politics Up-Ends the Bargaining Table," in Sam Zagoria, ed., *Public Workers and Public Unions* (Englewood Cliffs, N.J., 1972), 126–28; Horton, pp. 23–28; Maier, "The City and the Unions," 70–75, 79.

25. Maier, "The City and the Unions," 79–82.

26. Deborah E. Bell, "Unionized Women in State and Local Government," in Ruth Milkman (ed.), *Women, Work and Protest: A Century of U.S. Women's Labor History* (Boston, 1985), 283–87; Ralph T. Jones, "City Employee Unions: Labor and Politics in New York and Chicago," unpublished manuscript, 1975, p. 235; Lee C. Shaw, "The Development of State and Federal Laws," in Zagoria (ed.), *Public Workers and Public Unions*, 23–24; Mike Davis, *Prisoners of the American Dream: Politics and Economy in the History of the US Working Class* (London, 1986), 147.

27. Warren Moscow, who helped run Wagner's 1953 campaign, believes that the support Wagner received from Parent-Teacher Associations was far more important than his endorsement by the TWU. Interview with Warren Moscow, Jan. 8, 1987. See also, Horton, pp. 23–24.

28. Mark H. Maier, *City Unions: Managing Discontent in New York City* (New Brunswick, 1987), 47–50; *TE*, Feb. 1954, p. 16; Jewel Bellush and Bernard Bellush, *Union Power*

and New York: Victor Gotbaum and District Council 37 (New York, 1984), 47–62, 69; Horton, pp. 35–44.

29. *TE*, Jan. 1954, p. 2; Feb. 1954, p. 2; May 1954, p. 2–3; June 1954, pp. 2, 23; Sept. 1954, pp. 2–3; Freund, pp. 76–78; Maier, "The City and the Unions," p. 118.

30. Raskin, "Politics Up-Ends the Bargaining Table," 126–28; Maier, "The City and the Unions," 120–21, 132–33, 136–39, 143–45; Joe Flaherty, *Tin Wife* (New York, 1983), 244–45; *NYT*, Dec. 30. 1950, p. 1; interview of Philip Carey by Debra Bernhardt, Feb. 19, 1981, Tamiment Library, pp. 32–35.

31. Hood, pp. 405, 411–15; *TE*, Jan. 1954, pp. 2–3; Feb. 1954, p. 2.

32. Raskin, "Politics Up-Ends the Bargaining Table," 126–27; "Transit Employees, The New York City Transit Authority, 1953–1964," "L-100 Negot 1965 Demand" file, Box 150, TWU-T; Peter Derrick, "Catalyst for Develpment: Rapid Transit in New York," *New York Affairs*, Fall 1986, p. 40; Maier, "The City and the Unions," 118–20, 122, 130; interviews with Joseph Labash, Aug. 3, 1979; Victor Bloswick, Jan. 23, 1979; *TE*, Sept. 1954, pp. 2–3; Mar. 1955, pp. 2, 23; Keyserling, Part II, p. 4.

33. Freund, p. 84; *NYT*, July, 17, 1954, p. 15; *TE*, May 1954, pp. 2–3; Oct. 1954, p. 18; Maier, "The City and the Unions," 121.

34. Freund, p. 85; Maier, "The City and the Unions," 120–22, 125.

35. *TE*, Sept. 1954, p. 20; Freund, p. 80.

36. Freund, pp. 84–91, 103–5, 111, 127; Maier, "The City and the Unions," pp. 126–131, 137–38; Motormen's Benevolent Association, "Now It Can Be Told," "MBA 1956" file, box 63, TWU-T.

37. Freund, pp. 114, 149–56; Maier, "The City and the Unions," 137–38; *TWU 1946 Convention*, 66; *TE*, Jan. 1954, p. 2; June 1954, p. 24 ("babble"); interview with John Plover, Feb. 20, 1979; Motormen's Benevolent Association, "Now It Can Be Told," and Conductors Benevolent Association, "Introducing . . . Conductors Benevolent Association, Inc." [1956], "MBA 1956" file, box 63, TWU-T.

38. Interview with Phil Bray, Aug. 13, 1979; Maier, "The City and the Unions," 126–31.

39. David Brody, "The CIO After 50 Years: A Historical Reckoning," *Dissent*, Fall 1985, pp. 457–72 (quote on p. 458).

40. Davis, pp. 121–24; David Brody, *Workers in Industrial America: Essays on the 20th Century Struggle* (New York, 1980), 204–6; Michael Musuraca, "Lonely Voices: Discontent and Dissent in the UAW, 1950–72" (M.A. thesis, University of Massachusetts, Boston, Sept. 1982), 63–75.

41. *TE*, May 1954, p. 3; Maier, "The City and the Unions," 125–27; Freund, pp. 80–84; Josephine Lynch, "Memo on MBA," and MBA and ATU leaflets, in "MBA 1956" file, box 63, TWU-T; interviews with John Plover, Feb. 20, 1979; Phil Bray, Aug. 13, 1979.

42. On the continually shifting relationships among workers in the same industry, see Chuck F. Sabel, *Work and Politics: The Division of Labor in Industry* (Cambridge, Eng., 1982), esp. 127–93.

43. Freund, p. 85–91, 97; Maier, "The City and the Unions," 122, 128–31; Maier, *City Unions*, 37–39, 142–43.

44. Maier, "The City and the Unions," 132–35; Sussna, pp. 524–25, 532; Freund, p. 121.

45. Maier, "The City and the Unions," 136–42; Freund, pp. 128–31.

46. Freund, pp. 127–28, 132–33.

47. Maier, "The City and the Unions," 147–49; *TE*, May 1954, p. 3; interview with Gerald O'Reilly, May 15, 1978; Philip S. Foner, *Organized Labor and the Black Worker, 1619–1973* (New York, 1976), 404.

48. Quill was quick to see the potential of television, and the TWU pioneered in its use,

sponsoring its own shows, buying blocks of time during strikes to present its case, televising a convention session, and even filming short news segments that were sent to local TV stations. *TWU 1950 Convention*, 54–55;*NYT*, July 15, 1954, p. 10; *TE*, May 1964, pp. 26–27; "Summary, Convention Representation, October 2, 1957," in "Convention, TWU of A October 1957," box 150, TWU-T; Shirley Quill, pp. 233–35, 259.

49. James J. Matles and James Higgins, *Them and Us: Struggles of a Rank-and-File Union* (Englewood Cliffs, N.J., 1974), 202; *TE*, Dec. 1954, p. 12; "MJQ Stand Against AFL-CIO Merger, Feb.–Dec. 1955" folder, TWU-T; Whittemore, pp. 201–6, 243–44, 254, 261; Michael J. Quill, "America's Survival Kit—Gov't Ownership of All Industry," *M.E.S.A. Educator*, June 1963, p. 5; Shirley Quill, pp. 244–48, 277–80, 296–99.

50. Whittemore, pp. 182–83, 235, 259; *TE*, Apr. 1954, p. 24; Feb. 1955, p. 2; *AFL-CIO News*, June 4, 1966; interviews with Gerald O'Reilly, June 15, 1978; Phil Bray, Aug. 13, 1979; and Jerry O'Brien, Sept. 12, 1979.

51. Interviews with Gerald O'Reilly, July 11, 1979; Maurice Forge, Aug. 9, 1979; William G. Lindner to Maurice Forge, July 24, 1984, in possession of Forge.

52. *A Communist in a "Workers' Paradise"*, passim; file of letters from 1957 between John Santo, Michael J. Quill, and Gustav Faber, MF-T; *New York Herald Tribune*, Nov. 24, 1956, pp. 1, 10; Nov. 27, 1956, p. 26; Feb. 11, 1957, pp. 1, 4 ; May 7, 1957, pp. 1, 6; Aug. 7, 1957, p. 6; Oct. 13, 1957, p. 7; *NYT*, Jan. 5, 1957, p. 2; William Rusher, *Special Counsel: An Inside Report on the Senate Investigations into Communism* (New Rochelle, N.Y., 1968), 159–82; Caute, p. 571.

53. Much to President Johnson's annoyance, the 1966 TWU contract far exceeded anti-inflationary federal wage guidelines then in effect. The 1966 transit strike also destroyed the Condon-Wadlin Act. The strike clearly violated the law, but the state legislature retroactively forgave the strikers. It then replaced Condon-Wadlin with the Taylor Act, which also outlawed strikes but had less Draconian penalties. Brooks, pp. 50–57; Whittemore, pp. 259, 265, 293–94; Maier, "The City and the Unions," 149–53; Raskin, "Politics Up-Ends the Bargaining Table, 129–32; Shirley Quill, pp. 308–21; Horton, pp. 85–86, 100; Hood, pp. 456–57.

54. *TE*, Feb. 1966, pp. 2–3; *NYT*, Jan. 29, 1966, pp. 1, 30; Feb. 2, 1966, p. 42; Whittemore, p. 260 (Rice quote).

INDEX

Page numbers followed by *f* and *n* indicate illustrations and notes, respectively.